PREFACE

Many Programming Environment (PE) conferences have been arranged over the last years, and more will come. Why this one?

We feel that several of these have failed to bring industry and academia together in a fruitful dialogue, partly because of the topics covered. A traditional conference also leaves too little time for plenary discussions. Since IFIP's Working Group 2.4 on Systems Programming Languages (with 29 members) had planned a meeting on June 10-13 1986 in Trondheim, Norway, some Norwegians conceived the idea to arrange a conjunctive workshop. Trondheim hosts the largest university and research center in computers and electronics in Northern Europe, totalling over 500 scientists. Trondheim in mid-June also represents an attractive site for a combined arrangement.

IFIP WG 2.4 accepted this idea by mid-October 1985, but did not have the time or resources to arrange a traditional conference with invited and refereed papers. A true workshop cannot have a too large attendance, either. We therefore decided on 6-7 major subjects, 30-35 invited speakers, and an additional open, but screened audience of 70-75 persons. Members of the working group were given first priority to attend, in case of space shortage.

By November 15 1985 we had acquired sufficient external support for travel grants and had received indications from ACM SIGPLAN/SIGSOFT about "cooperation". A formal workshop committee was then established and we invited 50 selected persons to submit papers. By January 15th 1986, a preliminary workshop program was set up, based on 35 submitted abstracts - whereof 3 from WG 2.4 members. The authors were instructed to submit a draft paper by April 1st, and a full paper by May 25th. The draft versions have been commented by colleagues in Trondheim and Karlsruhe, at SEI/CMU and Genrad. Final versions of the papers were received by Aug. 1st.

We sent out invitations to about 2000 persons, based on mailing lists from previous ACM conferences and other available lists. The workshop was advertised in ACM SIGPLAN Notices, in ACM Operating Systems Review, and on electronic bulletin boards (SW-ENG). We received 150 sign-ups by mid-April, twice as many as we could accomodate. See the enclosed attendance list.

The workshop committee would like to thank the people who made this arrangement possible: speakers, participants, referees, sponsors, WG 2.4 members and observers, local staff, and NTH's conference secretariat. The editors would also like to thank Sharon Berg and Øystein Valle for proofreading and typing of the discussion transcripts.

Trondheim, November 1986

The editors:

Reidar Conradi   Tor M. Didriksen   Dag H. Wanvik

Workshop committee

William Waite	Univ. Colo., Boulder	workshop chair, WG 2.4 chair
Mary Shaw	CMU, Pittsburgh	program chair
John Nestor	SEI, Pittsburgh	ass. program chair
Lynn R. Carter	Genrad, Phoenix	WG 2.4 secr.
Reidar Conradi	DCS/NTH, T.heim	organizing chair, editor
Tor M. Didriksen	DCS/NTH, T.heim	ass. organizing chair, co-editor
Dag H. Wanvik	RUNIT, T.heim	ass. organizing chair, co-editor
Else J. Svorkås	DCS/NTH, T.heim	treasurer
Mari Sæterbakk	NTH, T.heim	local arrangements

TABLE OF CONTENTS

An asterisk (*) marks 10 min. panel papers, otherwise 25 min.

PROGRAMMING-IN-THE-SMALL

PROGRAMMING-IN-THE-LARGE

CONFIGURATION/VERSION CONTROL

TOOL INTEGRATION

SOFTWARE ENGINEERING DATABASES

PROGRAM REUSE AND TRANSFORMATIONS

KNOWLEDGE-BASED AND FUTURE PROGRAMMING ENVIRONMENTS

SOURCE LEVEL DEBUGGERS:
EXPERIENCE FROM THE DESIGN AND IMPLEMENTATION OF CHILLSCOPE

Svein O. Hallsteinsen

RUNIT

The Computing Center of the University of Trondheim

N-7034   Trondheim-NTH   Norway

Abstract

This paper is based on experience from the design and implementation
of an interactive source level debugger as part of a programming
enviroment for CHILL. The debugger is based on a variant of the event
action breakpoint. By combining the ability to detect a rich
repertoire of events, including events concerned with the interaction
between concurrent processes, and a command language including the
source language, a very powerful tool has been obtained. The paper
describes the main features of the debugger and discusses some design
decisions.

1 INTRODUCTION

1.1 Background

CHILL is the   programming language recommended by the   CCITT for
programming SPC telephone exchanges. It is a Systems Implementation
Language (SIL) in the Algol tradition and includes features like user
defined types, modules a la Modula 2, programmable exception handling
and concurrent processing. CHILL was developed in roughly the same
period as Ada and is a language of the same sort.

A programming support environment for CHILL, called CHIPSY, is being
developed at RUNIT. CHIPSY is currently hosted on VAX and ND-100
minicomputers and produces target code for the INTEL-86 family of

microprocessors. It is intended for the development of professional real time software. This paper is based on experience from the design and implementation of CHILLscope, which is CHIPSY tool for testing and debugging CHILL programs at the source level. Here testing means executing the program with the intent to demonstrate the absence of bugs, while debugging means finding the exact cause of a bug that has been revealed during testing, and designing a correction that will remove it. Both are concerned with observation and analysis of program execution. As this is exactly what debuggers supports, they are useful both for testing and debugging. Testing and debugging are also strongly interleaved, so in the sequel we shall use debugging loosely to denote this mixed activity.

1.2 Interactive Debugging Techniques

The basic technique employed by most debuggers is user controlled breakpoints. This technique consists of permitting the user to specify points in the program where he wants execution to be interrupted and control transferred to the debugger. Typically the debugger will allow the user to inspect the state of the computation, modify the state of the program, or even modify the program (patching), before continuing execution.

Source level debuggers for high level languages employ basically the same technique but supports access to the program being debugged in source level terms. Ideally a source level debugger should releave the programmer completely from having to know about the machine level details, but the degree of source levelness varies from the ability to use symbolic names instead of machine addresser to full transparency.

Since the technique was first introduced in the FLIT debugger /Stoc60/, it has been considerably refined. A conditional breakpoint has a condition attached and is only effective when the condition evaluates to true. An event - action breakpoint has a sequence of commands attached which will be executed when program execution hits the breakpoint. Also,rather than placing the breakpoint at a point in the program, it may be attaced to an event that may occur during program execution. These may be simple events, e.g. assignment of a particular location, or more complicated ones like the generalized path expressions described in /Brue83/ or the behavioural abstractions described in /Bate83/ which supports detection of patterns of events expressed in a formalism resembling grammars.

Also the debugger should support viewing the program in terms of the abstractions introduced by the programmer by means of the abstraction mechanisms of the source language.

1.3 Programming the Debugging Activity

The most interesting quantities for analysing program behaviour is not always directly available as attributes of the objects of the program, but have to be derived by complicated computations. Also they may depend on observations at different points in time. E.g. complicated data structures may require extensive extraction and formatting before a suitable view can be displayed. Likewise lots of tedious inspection may be required before the interesting case occurs. This calls for considerable expressive power in the debugger command language. One approach is to include the source language in the command language of the debugger. This has been done successfully for languages like LISP, PASCAL and C and is also the approach taken in CHILLscope.

2 CHILLSCOPE COMMAND LANGUAGE

2.1 Traps

CHILLscope is based on a variation of the event - action breakpoint which we call a trap . The event specifications are of the form operation performed on object; e.g. executing a particular action statement, calling a given procedure or delaying a given process.

For specifying particular objects, the full object access capabilities of CHILL is supported. Both for objects and operations "any" specifiers are available, such that events like "delaying any process" or "any operation performed on a given process" may be expressed.

The action part of the trap is a sequence of commands. The available commands are a subset of CHILL plus the following:

```
DISPLAY:  display given attributes of an object,
          e.g. contents of a location, type of a procedure

BREAK:    suspend execution of action part and
          execute commands entered interarctively from .
          the user terminal

RUN:      resume execution of suspended action
          part or resume execution of program from a
          given point

ENABLE/   enables/disables a given trap
DISABLE:
```

The CHILL subset includes assignment, procedure call, conditional statement, concurrent processing and declaration of variables. The delineation of the subset was mainly motivated by budget limitations of the current implementation and may easily be extended. The following examples show trap definitions that might be used for debugging the sample CHILL program included in appendix.

```
TRAP tracePolling =            !a trap tracing state
WHEN linePoller:poll           !changes on the
DO                             !subscriber lines
    DISPLAY lineTable(1);
OD;

TRAP checkLineTab =            !a trap detecting
WHEN linePoller:poll           !inconsistencies in
IF lineTable(1).curState /= hookOn  !the lineTable
AND lineTable(1).server = NULL
THEN
    DISPLAY lineTable(1),1;
    BREAK;
FI;
```

We believe that the ability to call precompiled procedures, paired with the ability for precompiled procedures to execute debugger commands, is a very powerful concept that will stimulate the growth of libraries of debug utilities, both general ones and application specific ones. E.g. a procedure for displaying a linked list may look as follows:

```
displayList:PROC(list REF listElem);
    DO WHILE list /= NULL;
        CHILLscope('DISPLAY list->.value');
        list := list->.next;
    OD;
    END displayList;
```

The expressive power of the event specifications is inherently good, although it suffers in the current implementation because detection of access to arbitrary variables is not supported. This is due to lack of hardware support on the ND100 and we expect to be able to remove this restriction when porting to the VAX.

In /Brue83/ and /Bate83/ the detection of patterns of events is emphasized, but this is not explicitly supported in CHILLscope. This may however be outweighed by the expressive power of the action language. This is illustrated in the example below where checking an event pattern is implemented by combining traps detecting the individual events and a set of precompiled procedures implementing pattern recognition. The patterns are specified in a formalism resembling EDL /Brue83/.

```
CALL defPat('call','e1`((e2`e4)/e3/e4)`(e5?e6)');
TRAP e0 = WHEN START aServer DO CALL startPat('call',a); OD;
TRAP e1 = WHEN START bServer IF inPat(a,'e1') NOT THEN BREAK; FI;
TRAP e2 = WHEN SEND accepted IF inPat(a,'e2') NOT THEN BREAK; FI;
TRAP e3 = WHEN SEND noAnswer IF inPat(a,'e3') NOT THEN BREAK; FI;
TRAP e4 = WHEN SEND quit     IF inPat(a,'e4') NOT THEN BREAK; FI;
TRAP e5 = WHEN STOP aServer   IF inPat(a,'e5') NOT THEN BREAK; FI;
TRAP e6 = WHEN STOP bServer   IF inPat(a,'e6') NOT THEN BREAK; FI;
```

2.2 Identifier Binding

Throughout a CHILL program, the same identifier may be used in different meanings. The visibility rules of CHILL ensures that at any point in the program, the visible identifiers have a unique meaning. The debugger uses the current focus of execution as the default context to bind identifiers.

However, the debugger must also support access to objects whose identifier is not visible in the current context or is visible with another meaning. To cater for this a notation for indicating the context explicitly has been adopted. The context indication has a static part and a dynamic part. The static part specifics the static scope while the dynamic part selects the process instance and procedure invocation.

E.g. if i is a location defined in a recursive procedure p defined in a module m, and q denotes a process having just called p, then [q]m:p#2:i denotes the i in the 2nd recursive incarnation of p evoked by q.

This notation makes it possible to specify non existing objects. If that occurs during the evaluation of an action, the offending command is ignored. Another possibility is that the event specification of a trap refers to an object that does not exist. In that case our approach is that an event does not occur while its specification refers to non existing objects.

3 DEBUGGING CONCURRENT PROGRAMS

The CHILL language supports programming of concurrent processes and the applications CHILL is intended for are highly concurrent systems. Therefore the design of CHILLscope has emphasized support for debugging such programs.

It is common to distinguish between the debugging of each process as a sequential program, and debugging of the cooperation between the processes. Supplied with the ability to detect relevant events, the trap mechanism proved to be an adequate tool also for the inter-process activities. These events are starting, stopping, delaying and continuing processes and operations on synchronisation objects. The DISPLAY command is capable of displaying the state of processes and synchronisation objects.

In /Smit85/ a debugger designed solely for debugging inter process activity is described. This debugger has a concept called a demon which is very similar to the trap.

The role of the debugger in the system of concurrent processes requires some comment. It is essential that it is well defined which process executes the action part of a trap, and also who executes the commands entered interactively after a break command. In our approach, the effect is as if the action attaced to the trap was inserted in the trapped process at the point were the event occurred. The other processes may or may not continue execution depending on the scheduling algoritm. In the current implementation they will not, but the trapped process may cause another process to continue while the first one is still trapped by executing a forced scheduling action.

An alternative approach used in several other debuggers is

implementing the debugger as a separate process. Our choise was motivated by the following:

- In order to have full control over the inter process communication and the state of the processes and the synchronization objects in the debugger, it is necessary to be able to execute syncronization actions appearing in the action parts of the traps as if they were executed by given processes. Another possibility would have been to provide special commands for manipulating the data structures of the execution support system, but this was discarded because it was felt to be in conflict with the source level orientation.

- Admittedly, it is also very useful to have special debugging processes that observe the processes being debugged. For example, this is a common technique to reduce the probe effect when debugging in real time. However this may be programmed explicitly in the command language.

4 PIECEWISE DEBUGGING

Independent program modules is a valuable programming paradigm that should be supported also at debug time. Finding bugs during early testing of individual modules may prove conciderably more efficient than finding the same bug in test runs involving the whole program. The basic facility needed is some mechanism for simulating the absent part of the program.

In CHIPSY the linker builds stubs representing the objects imported by the module being tested from the absent part of the program. In the stubs for procedures and processes the body has been replaced by a breakpoint, such that their behaviour can be simulated by debugger commands. Debugger commands are also used to stimulate the object being debugged.

5 IMPLEMENTATION ISSUES

There are essentially two ways to implement a debugger of the kind described above, by interpretive execution testing for the events to be trapped in the inner loop of the interpreter, or by executing the compiled code with break instructions inserted to allow detection of the events. The break instructions may be inserted permanently by the compiler at regular intervals, e.g. between each statement, or dynamically by the debugger as needed to detect the events introduced in trap definitions.

In CHILLscope the latter appproach was chosen, mainly because of its superior performance. It is typically one to two decades better than interpretive execution.

A drawback of this approach, is that it restricts the types of events that are supported, because the events has to be detectable by break instructions inserted at a limited set of locations. It may be claimed that it is only a matter of inserting enough break instructions, or resorting to single stepping, but then the performance advantage is sacrificed.

How serious this drawback is depends on what hardware support is available. E.g. in the current implementation of CHILLscope, detecting access to arbitrary locations is not supported, while on computers supporting guards on arbitrary storage areas, this would be no problem. The repertoire of detectable events for concurrent processing is fairly complete, because they can be detected by break instructions inserted in the runtime support system.

Another drawback of this approach is difficulties with maintaining the source level correspondence if the code has been optimized by the compiler. However, work has been published showing practical solutions to these problems for a number of common optimizations /Henn82/ /Zell83/. The problem has not yet been addressed in the CHILLscope project, because the current compiler does no optimization that causes problems for the debugger.

The debugger works on the ordinary generated code. I.e. no additional or special code is generated to support the debugger. Although convenient, this is not so important in the current implementation were only debugging in the host environment is supported. However, CHILLscope was designed to be adaptable for debugging in the target environment also, and there it is important that the operational code is identical to the code that has been debugged. One may even want to debug code in operation.

In real time systems, the probe effect is a problem. That is, the precence of the debugger disturbs the execution in such a way as to mask bugs /Gait84/. To minimize the disturbance we envisage an implementation of the debugger, where the program being debugged and the machine near parts of the debugger runs in the target computer, while the rest of the debugger runs in the host environment. This will have the intended effect only if detecting events and executing the associated actions is possible without communicating with the host computer. This is achieved by translating the traps at definition time to an intermediate form where all relevant information is available, which is stored in the target computer. The break and display commands will still necessitate communication with the host computer, so these should be avoided in the time critical processes. The DICE system /Frit83/ employs a similar approach, but there the traps are compiled into machine code and inserted into the program by an incremental compiler. This gives more efficient execution of the trap action and thus less disturbance.

6 FUTURE WORK

CHILLscope has just been released to CHIPSY users, so the only experience with using it is from acceptance testing.

From this limited experience we can conclude that a windowed user interface is badly needed. To debug a program with concurrent processes with only a single stream oriented user interface is hard.

More flexible access to program data is another important area for improvement. Program information is now mainly accessed by name. In many situations, however, there is a need to pose queries more in the form of database queries.

Such access is supported in a limited form for dynamic process data. E.g. 'DISPLAY ALL ACTIVE aServer INSTANCES SIGNAL' means display the signal queue of all active instances of the process definition

aServer . But improvements are definitely needed. The OMEGA debugger /Powe83/ takes this line of thought to an extreme by viewing the whole debugging process as querying a database where both static data and program execution data is represented, using a language based on the query language of the INGRES database system.

7 REFERENCES

/Bate83/ P.C.Bates and J.C.Wileden: High Level Debugging of Distributed Systems: The Behavioural Abstraction Approach. The Journal of Systems and Software 3, 255-264 (1983)

/Brue83/ B.Bruegge, P.Hibbard: Generalized Path Expressions: A High Level Debugging Mechanism. The Journal of Systems and Software 3, 265-276(1983)

/Frit83/ Peter Fritzson: Symbolic Debugging Through Incremental Compilation in an Integrated Environment. The Journal of Systems and Software 3, 285-294 (1983)

/Gait84/ Jason Gait: A Probe Effect in Concurrent Programs Software-Practice and Experience, Vol 16(3), March 86

/Henn82/ J.Hennessy: Symbolic Debugging of Optimized Code. ACM Transactions on Programming Languages and Systems, Vol. 4, No. 3, July 1982

/Powe83/ Michael L. Powell and Mark A. Linton: A Database Model of Debugging. The Journal of Systems and Software, 3, 295-300 (1983)

/Satt79/ Edwin H. Satterthwaite, Jr.: Source Language Debugging Tools. Garland Publishing, Inc. 1979

/Smit85/ Edward T. Smith: A Debugger for Message-based Processes. Software - Practice and Experience, Vol. 15 (Nov. 85)

/Stoc60/ T.G.Stockham and J.B.Dennis: FLIT - Flexowriter Interrogation Tape: A Symbolic Utility Program for TX-0. Memo 5001-23, Dept. of Elect. Eng'g., MIT (July 1960)

/URD86/ CHIPSY Reference Manual. URD Information Technology AS, Trondheim 1986

/Zell83/ Polle T.Zellweger: An Interactive High-Level Debugger for Control-Flow Optimized Programs. Xerox Parc CSL-83-1, Palo Alto Jan 83

8 APPENDIX: CHILL module sketching part of the control program of a telephone exchange

```
example: MODULE

    SIGNAL
        offHook, onHook, accepted, noAnswer, timeOut;
    NEWMODE
        lineNo    = INT(1:100),
        lineState = SET(hookOn,hookOff),
        lineDescr = STRUCT(prevState, curState lineState, server INSTANCE);
    DCL
        lineTable = ARRAY (lineNo) lineDescr;

        linePoller:PROCESS();
            DO FOR EVER;
                DO FOR l IN lineNo;
                    DO WITH lineTable(l);
poll:                   CASE prevState, curState OF
                            (hookOn),(hookOff): IF server = NULL
                                                THEN server := START aServer(l);
                                                ELSE SEND offHook TO server;
                                                FI;
                            (hookOff),(hookOn): SEND onHook TO server;
                        ELSE
                        ESAC;
                        prevState := curState;
                    OD;
                OD;
                wait(10);
            OD;
            END linePoller;

        aServer:PROCESS(a lineNo);
            DCL
                b lineNo, bSr INSTANCE;
            DO
                /* handle dialling and find route to B subscriber */

                lineTable(b).server,bSr:= START bServer(a,THIS);
                startRingTone(a);
                RECEIVE CASE
                    (accepted): stopRingTone(a);
                    (noAnswer): stopRingTone(a); STOP;
                    (onHook):   SEND quit TO bSr; stopRingTone(a); STOP;
                ESAC;

talking:        RECEIVE CASE
                    (onHook): SEND quit TO bSr; STOP;
                    (quit):   STOP;
                ESAC;
            OD;
            END aServer;
```

```
bServer:PROCESS(b lineNo, aSr INSTANCE);
    DO
            startRinging(b);
            startTimer(10);
            RECEIVE CASE
                (offHook): SEND accepted TO aSr;  stopRinging(); stopTimer();
                (quit)  :    stopRinging(b); stopTimer(); STOP;
                (timeOut): SEND noAnswer TO aSr; stopTimer(); STOP;
            ESAC;
talking:    RECEIVE CASE
                (onHook):  SEND quit TO aSr; STOP;
                (quit):  STOP;
            ESAC;
    OD;
    END bServer;

END example;
```

DATA-ORIENTED INCREMENTAL
PROGRAMMING ENVIRONMENTS

Peter B. Henderson

Department of Computer Science
SUNY at Stony Brook
Stony Brook, New York 11794

ABSTRACT

As programming environments begin to mature researchers recognize the need to improve both their user interface and performance. The traditional command and batch oriented systems represent a poor match for the human cognitive system, which is very visually oriented and "computes" incrementally. This paper explores these latter two important aspects in the context of programming environments. A data-oriented system is a system in which users interact directly with system data (view and manipulate), instead of using a complex set of commands. Incremental systems are designed to improve performance by limiting computation to a restricted set of system data in response to a small - incremental - modification to this data.

1. Introduction

An important aspect of any user oriented system, be it an automobile, a typewriter, a software system, or a programming environment is that it be easy to learn to use and understand, be visually oriented, and be responsive by providing immediate feedback. As might be expected these three attributes are generally very difficult to achieve in a system. However, with the introduction of powerful bit mapped workstations it is easier to develop software systems, and environments with these important characteristics.

In this paper we discuss two particular concepts, data-oriented systems and incrementality, both of which impact the development of environments with these essential features. By data-oriented, we mean a system in which data may be directly manipulated [1] rather than manipulated only through commands - a command oriented system. An incremental system employs incremental algorithms to avoid unnecessary recomputation when possible. For example, an incremental parser [2] does not have to completely reparse the source text, but only reparses the local context in which a change has occurred. Many current systems are primarily batch oriented as opposed to incrementally oriented, since an operation must be reinitiated to effect recomputation in response to changes in the input data.

The concepts of incrementality and data-oriented are orthogonal. However, in practice most incremental systems tend to be data-oriented. For example, screen oriented text editors are incremental since the screen display is continuously updated to remain consistent with input text and editing commands. They are also data-oriented at the lowest level of granularity possible - individual characters. A system may be data-oriented but not incremental. Most Visicalc[1] environments, and their clones [3] permit the direct manipulation of data, but do not update results incrementally - although with sufficiently fast processors they do have the appearance of instant updating.

---

[1]Visicalc, developed by Software Arts, is a trademark of Visicorp.

The paper explores the nature and general characteristics of programming environments which employ data-oriented and incremental approaches. Specific examples of some environments are examined in the context of these concepts, and we present interesting ways in which familiar environments (UNIX, etc.) might be extented to incorporate direct data manipulation and incrementality. These ideas may also be applied to more conventional block structured languages, like Ada and Pascal. For example, the VisiProg environment [4] makes effective use of both direct data manipulation and instant updating via incremental execution. Data-oriented systems are currently being studied and developed at SUNY at Stony Brook under a five year grant from the National Science Foundation [5]. Specific applications being studied include a relational operating system, office automation systems, expert systems, graphics systems, and programming environments.

This paper is primarily tutorial in nature. It defines concepts, provides a summary of relevant work, and specifies future directions in programming environments.

2. Data-oriented Operating System Environments

The easiest way to introduce the concept of a data-oriented environment is to examine these ideas in the context of a well known operating system like UNIX†. Consider a user's interactions with the UNIX operating system. It maintains information on data objects such as files, users, processes and jobs. User requests such as "List my files", "Change access rights in this file", "Who is on the system", "Suspend a process", are all *data-oriented* requests. The user can view these requests in two ways. First, which is typical of most operating systems the user is provided with a large set of commands with numerous complex options, and the way the user learns of the available data and the organization of this data is through these commands. Here the user cannot easily formulate a conceptual *model* of the underlying data. Second, the user may conceptualize the underlying system data as a relational database model [6, 7], and be provided with an appropriate user interface for directly manipulating this data. For example, by utilizing an editor for information stored in relational, or tabular format. Such a uniform conceptual model and user interface would make interactions with the operating system simpler and much more natural for the user. An example is provided in Appendix A.

In a data-oriented environment the visual presentation of data should closely approximate its most natural representation for us to understand and manipulate. In the relational operating system project [6] system data is visually displayed in a tabular format. For example, the current working directory is displayed as illustrated in Appendix A. Here direct data manipulation could be utilized to delete a file by either directly removing the corresponding row in the table or marking it for deletion, changing the name of a file by directly editing the name field, modifying protection rights directly, etc. Certain fields, like time of last modification, and file size are non-editable.

Data-oriented does not just refer to modifying data, but also to changing the visual presentation to best match our conceptual views and needs. Using the current working directory example, our data interface mechanism (e.g., a relation editor) could support modifying our view by eliding specified columns, re-ordering the columns, re-ordering the rows by sorting on a specified attribute like file name, size, creation date, or selecting certain files matching specified constraints (e.g., all files created after April 1, 1986). Many of these data-oriented operations can be achieved by appropriately integrating a simple relational data base system with a special tabular display oriented editor.

A second example of an application of the data-oriented methodology is a simple software configuration management system. The primary purpose of a software configuration management system is to specify how various pieces of software are to be combined to form a complete software system. For example, the UNIX Make facility [8] provides a convenient mechanism for defining both the dependencies between various software pieces (e.g., object module B requires

---

†UNIX is a Trademark of Bell Laboratories

source module A) and the mechanism for creating new pieces (e.g., Pascal or C compiler with appropriate compiler options). By "executing" Make all the required software pieces are approriately updated, when possible to maintain consistency between the source and the object/executable parts.

Appendix B presents a simple configuration management system which utilizes relations, or tables to store the dependencies and the compilation details. Here software is assumed to exist in four different forms: source component modules, source modules, object modules, and load modules. Source component modules are sub-pieces (similar to include files) of compilable source modules. The first relation, Component to Source specifies the dependencies between the source sub-pieces and compilable source modules. For example, source module S1 version 2 (S1.V2) includes three components C1.V1, C2.V2 and C3.V3 as illustrated by both the graphical view and the tabular form. The Source to Object relation shows dependencies and provides the actual mechanism, including compiler options for generating object modules. The last relation specifies how the object modules are combined to form a load module. A forth relation might specify data sets to be executed using a generated load module.

In a data-oriented system a relation editor could be used to directly create/modify any of these tables. Likewise, a graphical editor might edit the graph corresponding to these relationships. Changes to the underlying tables defining the dependencies between modules, to source components or source modules, or to data sets could automatically "trigger" the appropriate incremental actions (recompilation, linking, execution, etc.) necessary to maintain complete consistency of the system configuration, or provide the appropriate warning that consistency cannot be achieved (due to missing parts, compilation/linking error, etc.). The granularity of this automatic updating could be defined by the user. For example, any change - no matter how trivial - could force updating, or the user could initiated updating after making numerous changes, as in Make. Observe that with this data-oriented model commands, such as compilation, linking and execution simply become side effects of data manipulation, and are not invoked directly. One can easily see the conceptual similarities between this approach and that presented previously for a data-oriented operating system environment.

3. Other Data-Oriented Environments

Numerous existing environments are data-oriented. Screen oriented text editors are data-oriented, although most do not incorporate any constraints on the data (syntactic or semantic) [9]. Language knowledgeable editors impose constraints on both the syntax and static semantics of the data [10, 11]. Visicalc like environments are another example[2]. Here simple arithmetic computational relationships between numerical data objects are defined by the user. With the modification of data the system recomputes the results to maintain consistency with these defined relationships.

Emerging graphical software development environments are also data-oriented. Consider the systems for data flow software systems design which are available from numerous companies (e.g., CADRE Technologies Inc., Providence, RI). Here designers graphically develop a data flow diagram by creating and connecting "bubbles," which represent data transformations. Bubbles and edges may be semantically labeled, and the system can automatically check for semantic consistency. These data flow diagrams may be subsequently transformed into structure charts via appropriate user guided data-oriented manipulations. Similar graphically oriented software design systems have been developed [12] or are currently under development [13, 14].

Smalltalk [15, 16] is an object oriented programming language. It is object oriented because the underlying programming paradigm defines and manipulates objects. However, Smalltalk's user interface is more data-oriented since the underlying objects can be displayed

---

[2]Experts in software development and programming environments may not consider Visicalc to be a "true" programming environment, but it is indeed, and there is much we can learn from its success.

and manipulated as data by the user. Taken together, the language and the user interface constitute a programming environment. Note the careful distinction made between the programming paradigm - object oriented - and the characteristics of the user interface - data-oriented. Many people believe they represent the same concept. For example, some data base systems are really not data-oriented since they do not provide a convenient direct data manipulation user interface.

Several research projects are currently trying to extend the conceptual, data-oriented simplicity of visicalc like environments to more expressive and powerful programming languages [4, 17]. The VisiProg (Visible Programming Environment [4]) project involves the design and development of a dynamic programming environment which is highly data-oriented and provides significant visual feedback to the user regarding relationships between data objects, and between data objects and the visual representation of the program.

VisiProg is a unique environment in which the functionality (input/output relationships) of a network of programs (like an analog systems network), single programs, or selected program fragments can be viewed continuously while changing either the system data or the program semantics. The user interface is very data-oriented as illustrated by the figures in Appendix C. Data be updated directly, with the system responding "instantly" to maintain consistency between the functionality defined by the network of programs and the data. In addition, the environment can selectively trace dynamic data flow relationships between and in programs. To view or control data at any point in a program the user may open control or observation windows. Dynamic program slicing [18] permits the user to selectively narrow their focus attention to those parts of the program of immediate interest for understanding the program's behavior. Other parts of the program are elided, or hidden from view.

A data-oriented programming environment for Prolog is described in [17]. This environment is based upon the conceptual similarities between spread-sheet environments and logic programming paradigms. That is, spread-sheet systems are based on a simple, declarative language for specifying equalities among a set of numeric variables, and a two-dimensional user environment that allows visualization and direct manipulation of the data. Prolog is a declarative language for specifying complex relationships among structured data objects. Prolog systems, lack a comparable data-oriented environment.

The underlying declarative language of the spread-sheet is very simple and rather weak as a method for specifying complex relationships. A pure Horn clause language is a declarative language for specifying much more complex relationships among a much richer set of data objects. The underlying computational mechanism is an SLD resolution theorem-prover, a solver of constrained logic definitions. The goal of this project is to develop a two-dimensional interface to the objects of Prolog's specification, so that Prolog users can form a static visualization of a declarative Horn clause system and directly manipulate the objects. A sample such interface is illustrated in Appendix D. Like the spread-sheet and VisiProg environments both data and functionality (programs) may be manipulated directly, and the system strives to maintain view consistency (i.e., consistency between the data the user sees and the functionality defined by the "program").

4. Incremental Systems

One of the most noticeable changes in research directions for software systems is a concentration on the development of incremental algorithms. This includes not only programming environments, but algorithms for almost every conceivable application. This is primarily in response to the interactive mode of interfacing with computer systems, which is becoming more prevalant (i.e., interactive systems more closely approximate our inherent incremental cognitive model).

Clearly, text editors process data incrementally. However, most other operating system functions are batch oriented. Incremental parsers [2], and syntax directed editors represent one of the first significant applications of incremental algorithms to the programming environments arena [10, 11, 19, 20]. Subsequently, researchers have been investigating a wide range of incremental techniques for environment based applications. These include: incremental updating for attribute trees [21, 22], incremental compilation [23, 24], data flow analysis, [25-27].

When comparing incremental algorithms and batch algorithms for the same problem there are three primary considerations: (1) development and implementation (incremental algorithms tend to be intrinsically more complicated than batch algorithms), (2) the degree of data updating (for small updates incremental re-computation may be more efficient than batch), (3) the nature of the problem (there are problems for which the worst case complexity for all incremental algorithms is the same as that for all batch algorithms (e.g., traveling salesman)). Currently there is a large amount of on going research into incremental algorithms for a wide range of applications.

In the area of programming environments much of this research is directed towards developing efficient incremental editing/semantic analysis/code generation environments. For example, Make [8] is a simple incremental system for a software development environment. In contrast to current work on incremental environments, the Make system controls, at a relatively large level of granularity (compilation/linking units) the amount of "work" required to maintain consistency of a system. The efforts of current research work is directed primarily towards reducing this granularity to a comfortable level supporting more interactive interfaces which provide immediate useful feedback to the user. This latter point is very important for it demonstrates the nice interplay between data-oriented user interfaces and incremental algorithms.

All of the incremental algorithms for incremental parsing, syntax-directed editing, semantic analysis, and code generation tend to be relatively complicated with more intricate underlying data structures. Consider incremental parsing/syntax directed editing. Here the underlying data structure is a parse tree or abstract syntax tree which is incrementally modified to maintain consistency with the textual version which the user is editing. The simplest such algorithms utilize pure syntax directed editing. That is, the user directly edits the underlying abstract syntax tree. New syntactic structures are created using templates, and changes are constrained so as to maintain a syntactically pure abstract syntax tree at all times.

More sophisticated algorithms permit the user to edit the program as text, and the system automatically updates the underlying data structure. Here there are three different approaches: (1) to use top down parsing techniques [11, 19], (2) to use bottom up parsing techniques [2, 28], or (3) to directly manipulate the abstract syntax tree using incremental tree transformations [20, 29].

The maintenance of a complete parse, or abstract syntax tree led naturally to the study of incremental static semantic analysis. Here the nodes of the tree are attributed with additional semantic information. In addition, functional relationships between this semantic information are defined. As incremental changes are made, the system strives to maintain consistency in these functional relationships [21, 22]. Once the tree structure is available and attributed, other forms of incremental analysis are possible. These include, incremental code generation [23] and data flow analysis [25-27].

The VisiProg project [4] is investigating the feasibility of incremental execution using this abstract syntax tree model. Execution is achieved by an incremental interpreter which "walks" the abstract syntax tree. As the user directly modifies the input data the system will incrementally re-compute its output. There are several approaches being investigated. The first is checkpointing at key locations in the program execution history. When data changes are made, the system backs up to the closest checkpoint which is not effected by the change and commences re-execution from there. A second approach maintains dynamic def-use chains tied to the abstract syntax tree. As data changes occur the system can either follow or modify these dynamic def-use chains as appropriate.

5. Conclusions

This paper has provided an overview of two important concepts in modern programming environments - data oriented and incrementality. It has attempted to illustrate the importance of these two concepts in future environments. Of necessity, future environments will be data-oriented so they can be used more effectively. This data-oriented view will force these environments to become more incremental so that they closely match the human cognitive model of computation and to make them more efficient.

6. Acknowledgements

I would like to thank Dave Warren, Ed Sciore and Mark Weiser who have collaborated with me on several of the projects mentioned in this paper, and have helped me to formulate the ideas and concepts presented in this paper. This work was supported in part by National Science Foundation Coordinated Experimental Research Grant MCS-83-19966.

7. References

1. B. Shneiderman, "Direct Manipulation: A Step Beyond Programming Languages", *IEEE Computer*, August 1983.

2. C. Ghezzi and D. Mandrioli, "Augmenting Parsers to Support Incrementality", *J. ACM*, **27**, 3 (July 1980), .

3. A. R. Miller, "TK!Solver: A Tool for Scientists and Engineers", *BYTE*, **9**, 13 (December 1984), 263-272.

4. P. B. Henderson and M. Weiser, "Continuous Execution: The VisiProg Environment", *Eight International Conference on Software Engineering*, August 1985, 68-74.

5. A. Bernstein, J. Heller, P. B. Henderson, E. Sciore, D. Warren and L. Wittie, "A Data Oriented Network System", Technical Report, Department of Computer Science, SUNY at Stony Brook, August 1983.

6. P. B. Henderson, E. Sciore and D. Warren, "A Relational Model or Operating System Environments", Technical Report #83/060, Department of Computer Science, SUNY at Stony Brook, September 1983.

7. H. F. Korth, "Extending the Scope of Relational Languages", *IEEE Software*, **3**, 1 (January 1986), 19-28.

8. S. Feldman, "Make - A Computer Program for Maintaining Computer Programs", *Software Practice and Experience*, **9**, 3 (March 1979), 225-265.

9. N. Meyrowitz and A. van Dam, "Interactive Editing Systems: Parts I and II", *ACM Computing Surveys*, **14**, 3 (September 1982), .

10. T. Teitelbaum and T. Reps, "The Cornell Program Synthesizer: A Syntax-Directed Programming Environment", *Comm. ACM*, **24**, (September 1981), 563-573.

11. C. Fischer, G. Johnson and et. al., "The POE Language-Based Editor", in *Proceedings of the ACM Symposium on Practical Software Development Environments*, P. B. Henderson, (ed.), April 1984, 21-29.

12. S. P. Reiss, "Graphical Program Development with PECAN Program Development Systems", in *Proceedings of the ACM Symposium on Practical Software Development Environments*, P. B. Henderson, (ed.), April 1984, 30-41.

13. S. P. Reiss, "The GARDEN Environment", Technical Report, Department of Computer Science.

14. M. Moriconi and D. Hare, "Visualzing Program Designs", *IEEE Computer*, August 1985.

15. *Byte Magazine*, **6**, 8 (August 1981), .

16. A. Goldberg and D. Robson, *Smalltalk-80: The Language and its Implementation*, McGraw-Hill, 1983.

17. P. B. Henderson and D. Warren, "A Data Oriented Prolog Environment", Technical Report #8/014, Department of Computer Science, SUNY at Stony Brook, March 1986.

18. M. Weiser, "Program Slicing", *IEEE Transactions on Software Engineering*, **10**, 4 (July 1984), 352-357.

19. N. M. Delisle, D. E. Menicosy and M. D. Schwartz, "Viewing a Programming Environment as a Single Tool", .

20. G. E. Kaiser and E. Kant, "Incremental Parsing without a Parser", *Journal of Systems and Software*, **5**, 2 (May 1985), 121-144.

21. T. Reps, "Generating Language Based Environments", in *The MIT Press*, 1984.

22. A. Demers, A. Rogers and F. K. Zadeck, "Attribute Propagation by Message Passing", in *Proceedings of the SIGPLAN Notices '85 Symposium on Language Issues in Programming Environments*, June 1985, Seattle, Washington.

23. S. P. Reiss, "An Approach to Incremental Compilation", in *Proceedings of the SIGPLAN Notices '84 Symposium on Compiler Construction*, June 1984, Montreal, Canada.

24. R. Medina-Mora and P. Feiler, "An Incremental Programming Environment", *IEEE Transactions on Software Engineering*, **7**, 5 (September 1981), .

25. B. G. Ryder, "Incremental Data Flow Analysis", in *Proceedings of the Tenth Annual Symposium on Principles of Programming Languages*, January 1983, Austin, Texas.

26. F. K. Zadeck, "Incremental Dataflow Analysis in a Structure Program Editor", in *Proceedings of the SIGPLAN Notices '84 Symposium on Compiler Construction*, June 1984, Montreal, Canada.

27. B. G. Ryder, "Incremental Algorithms for Software Systems", Technical Report Dept. of Computer Science-Tech. Rep.-158, July 1985.

28. R. Campbell and P. Kirslis, "The SAGA Project: A System for Software Development", in *Proceedings of the ACM Symposium on Practical Software Development Environments*, P. B. Henderson, (ed.), April 1984, 73-80.

29. P. C. Willnauer, "Extensions to Incremental Tree Transformations for Syntax Directed Editing", Department of Computer Science, November 1985.

Appendix A

Illustrative Examples

The model is "data-oriented" in the sense that one attempts to understand the operating system by understanding a relational model of the data, and relational operations on this data model. This provides a more orthogonal view of the system data, and its inter-relationships. In the examples which follow we use the current underlying UNIX implementation model for file information (other, potentially better relational models are possible). *Note*: The relational commands presented here are for illustrative purposes only, and are not a proposed operational language.

Example 1.

Consider the following relation *cwd* for the current working directory. The information displayed is equivalent to performing the UNIX *ls -lg* command. Hence the view displayed might appear as shown below. We assume this relation may be edited by an appropriate relation editor to delete a file, or to modify any of the editable fields (e.g., protection settings, file name).

cwd

protection settings	number links	owner name	group name	file size	creation date	file name
-rw-rw-r--	1	pbh	pbh	5730	Mar 29 09:17	INDEX
-rw-r--r--	1	pbh	dws	4165	Mar 29 08:42	appendix-A
-rw-rw-r--	2	pbh	pbh	20421	Mar 28 22:01	body.paper
-rwx------	1	pbh	pbh	50	Mar 29 09:20	print-body
-rw-rw-r--	1	pbh	pbh	4469	Mar 28 22:06	refs
-rw-rw-r--	1	pbh	jones	3276	Dec 19 14:27	summary
-rw-rw-r--	1	pbh	pbh	0	Mar 29 09:24	ta
-rwx------	1	pbh	pbh	34	Mar 27 13:46	tmp

Example 2.

Consider the two relations *cwd*, the "current working directory," and *fi*, the "file information" relation. At the moment, our *cwd* is the relation *NSF.Proposal*. The relations are:

cwd			*fi*					
file name	file id		file id	owner name	group name	size	creation date	...
appendix	12434		.	.	.	.	.	$...$
budget	8759		12434	pbh	dbms	3959	8Jan	$...$
part1	17746		8759	pbh	dbms	1200	12Jan	$...$
part2	1032		.	.	.	.	.	$...$
part3	12675		.	.	.	.	.	$...$
refs	6737		17746	dsw	dbms	10169	16Dec	$...$
titlepg	11979		12675	es	dbms	6932	22Dec	$...$

Suppose that entering the name of a relation means to output ("display") that relation on the standard output device (your terminal). Then entering *"cwd"* has the same effect as the UNIX command *"ls -i"*. That is, list all files in the current working directory, with their associated file id. Entering *"fi"* would produce a listing of all files in the system, with their associated attributes. Thus, *"cwd* **join** *fi"* produces a "long" listing of the files in the current working directory, and is equivalent to the UNIX *"ls -il"* command. The following command sequence, using a temporary relation *"tr,"* lists the files in the current working directory ordered by size:

$tr = cwd$ **join** fi *{ls -il > temp}*
sort on *size: tr*   *{sort +4n < temp}*

or, emulating UNIX pipes:

    sort on *size: (cwd* **join** *fi)*   *{ls -il | sort +4n}*

To obtain a listing of only file names and their associated sizes, ordered in ascending order of size one would use the following relational command sequence:

    project on *file name, size:* (**sort on** *size: (cwd* **join** *fi))*

A corresponding UNIX command exists, but is quite difficult to express. If we wanted a listing of file names and their corresponding owners and groups, we could use the relational command:

    project on *file name, owner name, group name: (cwd* **join** *fi)*

In UNIX, one cannot obtain this listing using a single shell command!

Clearly, users of the system should not be required to enter such verbose commands. Accordingly, a *transaction* mechanism may be utilized to abbreviate commonly used commands. For example, the transaction command *"ls -il"* would be equivalent to the relational command *"cwd* **join** *fi* ". Although defined transactions can mimic UNIX commands, they potentially provide a more comprehensive, consistent and flexible approach to command languages in general.

Appendix B

Illustrates a simple data-oriented configuration management facility like Make. Editing any of the components which combine to form a compileable source would "trigger" the appropriate actions (recompilation, linking, etc.). Also, the tables defining the relationships can be edited, and likewise would "trigger" the appropriate actions to maintain consistency. A more visually oriented configuration management system would permit editing the graphical representation directly.

CONFIGURATION MANAGEMENT

Modules

Component   Source   Object   Load

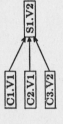

Component to Source Relation

Component	Source
C1.V1	S1.V2
C1.V2	....
C2.V1	S1.V2
C3.V1	....
C3.V2	S1.V2
....	....

CONFIGURATION MANAGEMENT

Modules

Component   Source   Object   Load

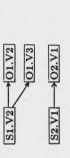

Source to Object Relation

Source	Compiler	Options	Object
S1.V2	Modula 2	debug	O1.V2
S1.V2	Modula 2	opt	O1.V3
...	...	...	...
S2.V1	C	-o -l	O2.V1

CONFIGURATION MANAGEMENT

Modules

Component   Source   Object   Load

O1.V2, O2.V1, O3.V2 → L1.V2

Object to Load Module Relation

Object	Load Module
O1.V2	L1.V2
O1.V2	L2.V3
O2.V1	L1.V2
....	....
O3.V2	L1.V2
....	....

Appendix C

The VisiProg Environment

VisiProg is a "data-oriented" environment which responds incrementally to all changes. Consider the fragment of a Pascal procedure for the bubble sort shown in below. Figures 1 illustrates three basic windows: one for input, one for the program, and one for output. Upon editing data in the input window (using appropriate mouse/keyboard actions) the environment "instantly" updates the output window to maintain consistency. For example, upon changing the value 37 in the input to 17 the output automatically updates (see Figure 2). Note the three dimensional display of iteration in the program window. Here execution time is viewed as the third dimension, into the window. Using appropriate actions a user may select any iteration for viewing and may examine the values of variables at any point in this iteration by opening a variable observation window. Figures 3 and 4 illustrate the selection of a data variable and the generated program dynamic data slice (Figure 4). This slice shows only those program statements which contribute to the determination of the values of the selected variable (NetPay) at the program location specified.

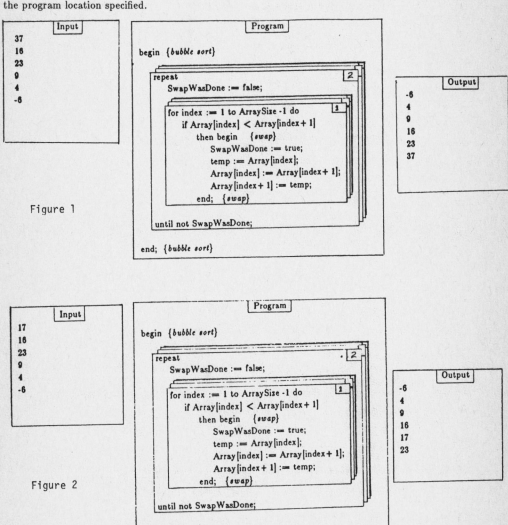

Figure 1

Figure 2

```
                    Program
begin {PayCheck}
    while not eof do                                    2
      begin
          readln (id, PayRate, HoursWorked, Dependents);
          writeln (id, PayRate, HoursWorked, Dependents);

          if (PayRate < MinimumWage) or (HoursWorked < 0.0) or
             (HoursWorked > 168.0) or (Dependents < 0)
          then
              writeln(' Illegal data for employee ', id,
                 ' no paycheck will be issued.')
          else begin
              if (HoursWorked > 40.0)
              then
                  GrossPay := (PayRate * 40.0) +
                      (PayRate * 1.5 * (HoursWorked - 40.0))
              else
                  GrossPay := PayRate * HoursWorked;

              FederalTax := 0.14 * GrossPay - (Dependents * 10);
              if FederalTax < 0.0 then FederalTax := 0.0;
              NetPay := GrossPay - FederalTax;

              writeln(' Net pay for employee ', id, ' is ', NetPay:10:2);
            end;
        end; {while}

end;  {PayCheck}
```

Input

```
4973 5.78 47   3
5792 6.37 37   2
6104 5.93 52   1
```

Output

```
4973 5.78 47   3
 Net pay for employee 4973 is 281.03
5792 6.37 37   2
 Net pay for employee 5792 is 222.69
6104 5.93 52   1
 Net pay for employee 6104 is 305.79
```

Paycheck program fragment displaying the second iteration of the while loop
Figure 3

```
                    Program
begin {PayCheck}
    while not eof do                                    2
          readln (id, PayRate, HoursWorked, Dependents);
          writeln (id, PayRate, HoursWorked, Dependents);

          if (PayRate < MinimumWage) or . . . .
          then
              . . . .
          else begin
              if (HoursWorked > 40.0)
              then
                  . . . .
              else
                  GrossPay := PayRate * HoursWorked;

              FederalTax := 0.14 * GrossPay - (Dependents * 10);
              if FederalTax < 0.0 then FederalTax := 0.0;
 *------>      NetPay := GrossPay - FederalTax;

              writeln(' Net pay for employee ', id, ' is ', NetPay:10:2);
            end;

end;  {PayCheck}
```

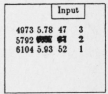

Input

```
4973 5.78 47   3
5792 ████ ██   2
6104 5.93 52   1
```

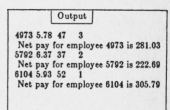

Output

```
4973 5.78 47   3
 Net pay for employee 4973 is 281.03
5792 6.37 37   2
 Net pay for employee 5792 is 222.69
6104 5.93 52   1
 Net pay for employee 6104 is 305.79
```

Paycheck program fragment showing dynamic backward slice on the program
variable NetPay after the statement indicated for the second iteration. ✶
Note highlighting of the appropriate input variables in the input window.
Figure 4

Appendix D

instructor (Instructor, Course)	
Instructor	*Course*
cs101	jones
mat210	smith
psy315	peters
cs221	smith

← Query

← Variable Names

← Extension

Tabular Display of a Simple Prolog Query
Figure 1

Prolog facts and the results of queries are displayed in tabular form. Using an appropriate relation editor, these facts may be modified (delete rows, update a row, or add a new row). The system would respond by recomputing the relations displayed in the dependent query windows.

:- enroll (Student, Course).	
Student	*Course*
mary	cs101
mary	mat210
john	cs221
john	mat210
bill	cs101
bill	psy315
< e n d >	

:- course (Course, Credits, Course_title).		
Course	*Credits*	*Course_title*
cs101	3	Introduction to Algorithms
cs221	4	Principles of Machine Organization
mat210	3	Modern Algebra
psy315	3	Personality
< e n d >		

:- enrolled_in (bill, Course_title).
Course_title
Introduction to Algorithms
Personality
< e n d >

: - enrolled_in (Students, 'Introduction to Algorithms').
Students
mary
bill
< e n d >

Four Query Windows Opened Simultaneously
Windows for enroll *and* course *show facts*
Windows for enroll_in *show results of two different queries*
Figure 2

Context-sensitive editing with PSG environments

Rolf Bahlke
Gregor Snelting

Institut für Systemarchitektur
Fachbereich Informatik
Technische Hochschule Darmstadt
Magdalenenstr. 11c
D-6100 Darmstadt, West Germany

Abstract.

The PSG-Programming System Generator developed at Darmstadt produces interactive language-specific programming environments from formal language definitions. From an entirely nonprocedural specification of the language's syntax, context conditions and denotational semantics, it produces a hybrid editor, an interpreter and a library system. In this paper, we give a detailed description of PSG-generated environments. The main features of PSG editors are discussed. In particular, we describe the interplay between text editing and structure editing, the PSG fragment concept, the interactive handling of syntax and context errors and the context-sensitive error prevention mechanisms. We include an example editing session demonstrating the user interface of the PSG implementation on PERQ workstations, utilizing graphical devices.

1. Introduction.

The PSG system /BaSn85a/ is a generator for interactive language specific programming environments. From a formal definition of a language's syntax, context conditions and denotational semantics, it produces a context-sensitive hybrid editor, an interpreter with interactive debugging facilities, and a library system. Recent papers on PSG concentrated on the language definition and generating aspects /BaSn85b/ and on the incremental semantic analysis algorithms /SnHe86/. A tutorial introduction to the language definition language can be found in /PSG85/. The aim of this paper is to give a detailed description of the PSG editors. We will discuss the user interface from a more practically motivated viewpoint, rather than describe the underlying technical concepts.

Until now, environments have been generated for Fortran77, Algol60, Pascal, Modula-2, Lisp, Prolog and the formal language definition language itself. PSG has originally been developed on SIEMENS BS2000 machines. The user interface was based on the usage of alphanumeric terminals. The first prototypes have been available since late 1983, and have been used intensively by students and the project team. It turned out, however, that the users, though appreciating the underlying concepts, did not accept the user interface. We therefore decided to port the system to UNIX-based personal workstations with high-resolution bit-map display and mouse, and to redesign the user interface completely. Early versions on a PERQ workstation have been available since late 1984. In early 1985, PSG has been chosen as the basic language interface for the so-called SUPRENUM machine. The

SUPRENUM project is a large-scale, nation-wide project with the aim to build a supercomputer for numerical applications. PSG will be used to generate programming environments for the SUPRENUM languages, namely MIMD-Fortran and Concurrent Modula-2. One of the most important design goals was to give the user maximum flexibility, while making the system as intelligent as possible in guiding the user and preventing errors. It is our opinion that it is a mistake to build systems which force users to do things which they do not want to do at the moment (e.g. to declare a variable or to correct errors on the spot). Therefore, the system must be able to handle incomplete and partially inconsistent programs. On the other hand, the system must of course be able to analyse the user's input and to use this information as good as possible in order to detect or even prevent errors. We therefore decided to build editors which obey the following general principles:

- They are *hybrid editors* and allow the user to construct and modify his program either as text or as a syntactic structure. Text and structure editing are fully integrated.

- They are *fault-tolerant* and allow the user to continue editing a syntactically or semantically incorrect program. Of course, all errors are detected immediately, but they need not be fixed until program execution.

- They guarantee, on the other hand, the *prevention* of *syntactic* and *static semantic* errors, if they are used as structure editors.

- They are able to handle *arbitrarily incomplete program fragments*. In particular, the semantic analysis guarantees the detection and/or prevention of semantic errors even in incomplete fragments.

- They utilize the modern developments of personal workstation hardware, in particular raster graphics and a mouse.

Thus, PSG editors are characterized by the interplay of flexibility and intelligence. The following sections describe our concepts in detail. All examples refer to the PASCAL environment, unless otherwise stated.

2. Abstract syntax trees and the fragment concept

Within a PSG environment, the basic units for editing and execution are not programs, but so-called *fragments*. A fragment is an arbitrary part of a program, for example a statement, a procedure declaration or a program. Fragments may be incomplete. That is, they may contain *placeholders* for still missing subcomponents. A procedure declaration fragment may contain, for example, placeholders for statements in the procedure body which have not been supplied by the programmer so far. Incomplete fragments may be edited and executed separately. All parts of an environment, the editor as well as the interpreter and the library system, are able to handle arbitrarily incomplete fragments. Each fragment is given a name by the user in order to select fragments from the library system for editing and execution.

Since fragments are named, they may refer to each other. For example, within a PASCAL environment, it is possible to have a program which calls a procedure, the declaration of which is not part of that fragment, but is a separate fragment and is refered to within the program by its fragment name. This feature, together with the possibilities to manipulate fragments (see below), allows a user to construct his program either bottom-up or top-down in a structured manner. The system will however not force a certain development strategy upon users.

Internally, fragments are represented by an abstract syntax tree together with its textual representation. During editing, the tree is built up or modified according to the user's input. The textual representation is obtained by pretty-printing the abstract tree using an unparsing scheme. For purposes of semantic analysis, the tree is furthermore decorated with semantic information. In order to make the system fault tolerant, syntactically incorrect parts of a fragment are not part of the abstract tree (they exist only in textual form), whereas semantically inconsistent parts of a fragment are represented by trees with empty semantic information attached. This allows users to edit arbitrary incomplete as well as incorrect fragments. Of course, if a user modifies a fragment, thereby making it correct, the corresponding actions of updating the tree and updating the semantic information, are performed at once.

During editing, there is always one node within a fragment's abstract tree corresponding to the part of a fragment which the user works on at the moment. This node is called the *node of interest* and its corresponding textual representation is called the *current selection*.

3. The context-free hybrid editor

During editing the display is divided into two windows. The top of the display contains the so-called *system window*. Below a descriptive title the window is split into two areas: The left part contains a picture indicating the current setting of the puck or mouse buttons (currently, three buttons are used). The right part contains the *system menu* and a textline of fixed size, which can be used either as a system message area or as a small input buffer. The system menu is used to select editing commands with the mouse. The menu items usually depend on the current selection: Editing commands like `Terminate Editing` are independent from the current text selection, whereas commands like

`Delete Statement, Insert Before,` or `Enter Fragment` depend on the current selection. A change of the current selection results in a change of the system menu items in such a way that only those items are displayed which are valid according to the current selection. Dynamically changing the system menu items gives the editor the possibility to create selection-specific menu item texts (e.g. `Modify Assignment` or `Delete Variable Declaration`) and prevents the user from unnecessary error messages (due to the selection of invalid commands).

The second window called the *text window* is spread over the main part of the screen and contains the text of the fragment to be edited. The current selection is underlined on the screen, additionally its descriptive title (as defined in the language definition) is displayed as part of the system menu's title line. Incomplete parts of a fragment, i.e. placeholders, are displayed in bold font as opposed to standard font. The current selection is changed either automatically by the editor resulting from an editor command or a refinement of a placeholder, or explicitly by the user pointing with the mouse (which's current screen position is shown on the screen by a cursor image) to the desired text position. If a text position is to be selected which is beyond that part of the fragment which is currently displayed on the screen, text scrolling is possible by means of a scroll bar.

For example, we are going to edit a new Procedure Declaration fragment. In the text window, only one line for its placeholder is displayed:

 <u>`{Procedure Declaration}`</u>

Attached to that placeholder is a pop-up menu, appearing to the right of the placeholder's text, which represents the *syntactic menu* of the placeholder. The items of a syntactic menu specify the syntactically allowed alternatives for refinement. In our example, their exists only one item, namely

`Refine Procedure Declaration.`

Now the user has two possibilities in order to edit the procedure declaration, either by structure editing using the syntactic menu or by text editing. Text editing starts by typing on the keyboard: If the first key is pressed the editor switches to text editing mode. Immediately, the syntactic menu disappears from the screen and the placeholder's title is replaced by the characters which have been typed by the user, e.g.

`procedure p; var i:`

Textual input is always displayed *in situ*, that is, in the correct position with respect to textual context. In text editing mode, the user has the usual possibilities to enter, modify, delete, search, copy etc. text. Of course, textual input is not restricted to one line. If the user presses a special function key, the textual input obtained so far will be analysed and the corresponding part of the abstract tree will be build up. It depends on the user's decision at what time he uses this function key: By simply ignoring its existence, PSG editors behave like pure state-of-the-art text editors. Note that in contrast to systems like GANDALF /No85/, the Synthesizer Generator /ReTe84/ or MENTOR /Ka83/, the system can handle incomplete textual input: any valid prefix conforming to the syntactic category of the current selection will be accepted. This feature (which we consider an important one) allows users to have their program text analysed in the granularity they prefer, thereby giving them more flexibility.

After analysis of the textual input and prettyprinting, the text window is redisplayed as follows:

```
PROCEDURE p;
  VAR
    i:
    {Type}
    ;
    {Variable Declarations}
  {Procedure Declaration}


  {Compound Statement}
  ;
```

The following pop-up menu is attached to the placeholder "{type}":

```
Simple Type      Array Type        Record Type      Set Type
  File Type      Pointer Type      Type Identifier
```

The user decides to continue editing the compound statement and points with the mouse to its placeholder. This placeholder is underlined and its attached syntactic menu is displayed, which consists of one item, namely to refine the compound statement. Selection of that item results in the following screen layout:

```
PROCEDURE p;
  VAR
    i:
    {Type}
    ;
    {Variable Declarations}
  {Procedure Declaration}

  BEGIN
    {List of Statements}
  END;
```

The user ignores the syntactic menu attached to the placeholder for statements and continues with typing:

```
i:=0; while i<100 then
```

thereby producing a syntax error. Now the text window is split in two windows, the upper one containing the original text of the fragment, and the lower one containing the following syntax error message:

```
Syntax Error in List of Statements
Correct Part of Input:
i:=0; while i<100
Incorrect Part of Input:
then
Symbols expected:
  DO AND OR DIV MOD + - * /
```

Note, that both the correct and the incorrect part of the user's input can be edited thus providing the user the opportunity to correct the error by simple text editing. Attached to the incorrect part of the input is a pop-up menu, which serves as an error-correction menu. In our example it consists of the following items:

```
Delete 'THEN'               Replace 'THEN' by 'DO'
Replace 'THEN' by 'AND'     Replace 'THEN' by 'OR'
Replace 'THEN' by 'DIV'     Replace 'THEN' by 'MOD'
Replace 'THEN' by '+'       Replace 'THEN' by '-'
Replace 'THEN' by '*'       Replace 'THEN' by '/'
```

Additionally, the system menu changes to the following items:

```
Accept correct Part of Input
Defer Error Correction           Reject Input
```

To correct the syntax error the user has either the possibility to edit the erroneous input text, to select one item from the error-correction menu (called *local recovery*), or to select one item of the system menu (called *global recovery*). Global recovery offers the possibilities to accept only the correct part of the input (in our example this results in the deletion of the 'then'), to defer the error correction, or to reject the complete input. If error correction is defered, the original input text will reappear on the screen and editing may continue, even with another current selection. Thus, it is possible to edit syntactically incorrect fragments.

Suppose the user's choice is to select the first item of the above error-correction menu, editing continues with the following screen layout:

```
PROCEDURE p;
  VAR
    i:
    {Type}
    ;
    {Variable Declarations}
  {Procedure Declaration}

  BEGIN
    i := 0;
    WHILE i < 100 DO
      {Statement}
    {List of Statements}
  END;
```

The pop-up menu associated with the "{Statement}" placeholder comprises the following items:

```
Assignment    Procedure Call   WHILE...DO   FOR...DO   REPEAT...UNTIL
CASE...OF        IF...THEN      Compound     GOTO     Labelled Statement
WITH...DO         Comment
```

After selection of the 'IF...THEN', the keywords IF, THEN and ELSE will be inserted by the system, together with the placeholders for the subcomponents of the conditional statement.

In order to modify a certain part of a fragment, this part must be made the current selection and the system menu item Modify must be selected. The selected program text will then be displayed in bold font and may be modified in textual mode or by selection among the corresponding syntactic menu. The user may modify a single identifier as well as a complete program. This feature makes it very simple to change e.g. a while-loop into a repeat-loop, which can be an unpleasant job if text editing is not possible.

Of course, it is possible to insert new placeholders within e.g. a parameter list or a list of statements. These placeholders may be moved freely within a syntactic list and may also be deleted again.

In order to delete e.g. a statement, the system menu item Delete Statement must be selected after selection of the statement. Since users sometimes modify or delete things which they afterwards would like to reappear, we have implemented a general undo mechanism: The last modification as well as the last deletion can always been undone simply by a selection from the system menu. As an ultimate rescue device, there is also an

'Undo Edit' option, which, if selected, terminates editing and leaves the fragment unchanged.

PSG editors have an internal save area, which can be used to copy parts of a fragment by writing them into the save area and inserting the contents of the save area for a placeholder. Of course, since a copy operation must obey syntactic restrictions, the corresponding menu items will not be displayed if the syntactic category of a placeholder does not conform with the syntactic category of the contents of the save area.

It has already been mentioned that fragments may refer to other fragments. This is done by writing the fragment's name into the program text:

```
"complicated-statement"
```

is a valid statement within the Pascal editor and refers to a statement with name 'complicated-statement' which is a separate library unit. It is possible to enter such a fragment directly by selecting its reference and selecting the menu item Enter Fragment. This fragment can then be edited; after the selection of Exit Fragment editing of the original fragment continues. It is also possible to replace the reference to another fragment by the fragment itself.

4. Context-sensitive facilities

In most programming languages, syntactically correct programs must meet additional requirements known as context conditions. For example, in PASCAL expressions must be correctly typed and variables must be declared before use. In order to detect or to prevent violations of context conditions, a semantic analysis subsystem which checks fragments for restrictions not captured by the syntax must be part of the editor. As another example, consider an editor for writing proofs in a logical calculus. Here, the semantic analysis must guarantee that proofs are correct according to the semantics of the calculus.

The semantic analysis within PSG has been of special interest, since the classical approaches do not work very well if arbitrarily incomplete fragments have to be analysed. Classical-style attribute grammars, for example, always follow the scheme: first inspect the declarations building up a symbol table, then use this symbol table to do semantic checking, e.g. check for type consistency in expressions. Therefore, a fragment which contains incomplete declarations or no declarations at all, cannot be checked for semantic errors. In order to overcome this difficulty, we have developed a novel incremental semantic analysis algorithm which is based on unification. The algorithm is generated from the language's context conditions, which are described by inference rules. It uses techniques which have been a contribution to artificial intelligence (although they have originally been designed in another context) in order to compute exactly the (incomplete) semantic information associated with an incomplete fragment. The technical details of the method are described in /BaSn85b/ and /SnHe86/.

After each modification of a fragment's abstract tree, the semantic analysis will analyse the changes in an incremental manner. The system guarantees that semantic errors are detected as soon as a fragment can no longer be embedded into a correct and complete program. First of all, the system checks for missing declarations and for double declarations. If, for example, a user types the fragment

```
PROGRAM p;
BEGIN
  READ(x)
END.
```

the system will complain in a second window that

```
"x" has not yet been declared
```

Missing declarations of identifiers are however accepted, if there is a possibility to declare them either within or outside the fragment. Thus,

```
PROGRAM p;
{Variable Declarations}
BEGIN
  READ(x);
  {Statements}
END;
```

and

```
PROCEDURE p;
BEGIN
  READ(x);
  {Statements}
END.;
```

are perfectly ok. In the first example, however, the system will not allow the user to delete the "{Variable Declarations}" placeholder (see below for dynamic context-sensitive menu filtering).

More interesting problems arise when type checking is taken into account. As an example, consider

```
PROCEDURE q(a:tl;r:t2);
BEGIN
  a[a[r.k-5]]:=3.14;
  {Statements}
END;
```

Here, the system deduces that there is a type conflict in the assignment and complains that

```
"3.14" has incompatible attributes
INTEGER  is not compatible with  REAL
```

Although the declarations of "t1" and "t2" are not part of the fragment, the system has infered that "a" must be a one-dimensional array with index and component type compatible with integer. This example demonstrates that the semantic analysis guarantees immediate detection of semantic errors even in incomplete fragments.

If a semantic error is detected, the symbol table will also be displayed (for a description of symbol tables, see below). The user can then decide what to do: He can fix the bug or he can do nothing, that is, simply ignore the error and continue editing. The system tolerates fragments containing semantic errors. Inconsistent parts of a fragment (the assignment in our example) are ignored for further semantic analysis, but semantic analysis of the fragment continues. In order to show the programmer that there are inconsistencies in his fragment, the inconsistent parts will be shaded on the screen. Thus, in our example, the constant "3.14" will be displayed on a grey background. In the fragment

```
BEGIN
   a:=b+c;
   IF a THEN
      {Statements}
END;
```

both occurences of "a" will be shaded. The general strategy for shading tree nodes is to shade all nodes which turned out to have incompatible attributes *after the last editing step*. Of course, shading of fragment parts must be done incrementally: If, in the last example, the assignment is deleted, the fragment is no longer incorrect; therefore, shading of the "a" within the "IF" is removed.

At any time, the user may have a look at the symbol table in order to see the semantic information derived so far. To do that, he has to select a position in his fragment and to select the system menu item Context Info. The symbol table of the scope enclosing the selected position is then displayed in a second window. For the fragment

```
PROCEDURE q(a:t1;r:t2);
VAR k: {Type};
BEGIN
   a[a[r.k-5]]:={Expression};
   {Statements}
END;
```

a selection of "k" within the assignment will result in the following symbol table:

```
CONTEXT INFORMATION

Current Scope:   Named Scope "r"

No locally declared names

Locally declarable:

  "k":  INTEGER
        FIELD SELECTOR
```

If the user then selects the system menu item Surrounding Scope, the system displays in the second window:

```
CONTEXT INFORMATION

Current Scope:  PROCEDURE q(a:tl;r:t2);

Locally declared names:

  "a":  ARRAY [INTEGER] OF INTEGER
        VARIABLE

  "r":  RECORD
        VARIABLE

  "k":  {Type}
        VARIABLE

Locally no longer declarable:

  "tl":  ARRAY [INTEGER] OF INTEGER
         TYPE

  "t2":  RECORD
         TYPE
```

Note that for identifiers which have inconsistent attributes (and are therefore shaded on the screen), no semantic information besides the fact that they exist will be displayed.
It is planned to allow the user to change variable names directly within the symbol table. Such a change will then be carried out by the system within the whole fragment for all occurences of that identifier (of course, scope rules will be taken into account).

One of the most remarkable features of PSG editors is the dynamic context-sensitive filtering of syntactic menus. If, in the above example fragment, the user selects the "{Expression}" placeholder, the menu for the syntactically admissible refinements will be filtered in such a way, that all items which would produce a semantic error after selection are filtered out. Thus, only the items

```
Variable   Constant   Function Call   Arithmetic Operator
```

are displayed, as compared to the unfiltered menu

```
Variable     Constant      Function Call      Arithmetic Operator
Relational Operator        Boolean Operator     Set Inclusion
```

After the selection of "Constant", only the item

```
Integer Constant
```

will be displayed, as opposed to the unfiltered

```
Integer Constant   Real Constant   Character   TRUE   FALSE   NIL
```

Since this kind of filtering is done for all syntactic menus with respect to the semantic information derived so far, the user can never introduce semantic errors by menu selection. Since even selection from an unfiltered menu guarantees syntactic correctness, and since the system menus are also filtered, a user can never introduce errors or try to do incorrect things by menu selection. Thus, as far as menu selection is concerned, PSG editors guarantee *prevention of both, syntactic _and_ semantic errors*. The errors discussed above can only be the result of textual input. Note that menus which belong to templates in inconsistent (and therefore shaded) fragment parts are not filtered because filtering would yield the empty menu, leaving the user in a deadlock situation.

5. Conclusion

PSG is in operation since late 1983 and has been used by many people; the system was also used to construct parts of itself.

We presented the user interface of PSG-generated editors as it has been developed in spring 1986. Since the implementation is very new, we do not have very much experience in using it. A critical evaluation of our design decisions is of course necessary and will take place in autumn 1986. It is our aim to build editors which satisfy the needs of professional programmers as well as beginners. We would ultimately like to achieve industrial acceptance, which cannot be seen for language-specific programming environments at the moment.

Work on the PSG System has been supported by the Deutsche Forschungsgemeinschaft, ICL England, Siemens Munich and the German Ministry of Research and Technology.

6. References

A detailed bibliography, as well as comparisons with related work, can be found in the second reference.

/BaSn85a/   Bahlke, R. and Snelting, G.: The PSG-Programming System
Generator. Proc. ACM Symposium on Language Issues in
Programming Environments, ACM SIGPLAN Notices 20, 7, pp.28-33,
July 1985.

/BaSn85b/   Bahlke, R. and Snelting, G. The PSG System: From formal language
definitions to interactive programming environments.
Report PU2R4/85, Fachbereich Informatik, Technische Hochschule
Darmstadt. Accepted for publication in ACM TOPLAS (October 1986).

/Ka83/   Kahn, G., Lang, B., Mélèse, B. and Morcos, E.: METAL: A formalism to specify
formalisms. Science of Computer Programming 3, pp. 151-188, 1983.

/No85/   Notkin, D.: The Gandalf Project. The Journal of Systems and Software,
5, 2, May 1985.

/PSG85/   Bahlke, R., Hunkel, M., Klug, M. and Snelting, G.: Language
definer's guide to PSG. Part one: Syntax and Static Semantics.
Report PU2R3/85, Fachbereich Informatik, Technische Hochschule
Darmstadt.

/SnHe86/   Snelting, G. and Henhapl, W.: Unification in many-sorted algebras
as a device for incremental semantic analysis. Proc. 13th ACM
Symposium on Principles of Programming Languages,
St. Petersburg, pp.229-235, Jan. 1986.

/ReTe84/   Reps, T. and Teitelbaum, T. : The Synthesizer Generator. Proc. ACM
Sigsoft/Sigplan Symposium on Practical Software Development
Environments. ACM Sigplan Notices 19, 5, pp. 42-48, May 1984.

Editing Large Programs
Using a
Structure-Oriented Text Editor

Ola Strömfors
Department of Computer and Information Science
Linköping University, S-581 83 Linköping, Sweden

Abstract

This paper will describe how a structure-oriented text editor, named ED3, is used as a practical and efficient tool for program development and maintenance. Unlike *syntax-directed editors* this editor does *not* use its tree structure to represent the parse tree of the program. Instead the user is free to build any tree structure of text nodes he wants. For a block structured language the tree can be built the same way procedures are defined inside procedures.

The tree structure helps the programmer handle big programs. Browsing is supported by menus automatically created from the first line of each node. To enter or modify a text node, a screen-oriented text editor is used. Syntax checking (currently for Pascal and Ada) is done by a fast combined parser/pretty-printer. A single-key command will parse and *pretty-print* the current text node.

1. INTRODUCTION

Most program editing is today done with the aid of text editors. A compiler is then used for both syntax checking and code generation. This means that detection and correction of syntax errors take long time, especially for large programs. Some text editors, e.g. EMACS [2], have modes for different programming languages. Commands to insert templates for different programming language constructs will save typing and avoid misspelled keywords. When the program text is modified only limited syntax checks, such as parentheses matching, are performed. For a language with simple syntax, e.g. Lisp, this can perhaps be enough. Many users also find it difficult to handle large programs (or documents) through the aid of a text editor. The reason is that most text editors only support a flat sequence of characters or lines, and not the subprogram structure of a program (or the paragraph and chapter structure of a document).

Today many program editors are based on a parse tree representation of the program, e.g. the Cornell Program Synthesizer [4]. The editing commands interact with the parse tree and

---

This work is supported by STU, the Swedish Board for Technical Development.

guarantees that no syntax errors are introduced in the program. In some *syntax-directed editors* template instantiation is the only way to enter a program. One problem with this approach is that expressions then must be entered in prefix notation. Other editors contain parsers that transform input text to the internal representation. Some editors even allow text editing to be done and include incremental parsers that update the parse tree after text editing.

The ED3 editor [3] is a bit different. The tree structure is *not* used to build parse trees. Instead the user is free to build any tree he wants. Often the structure follows the subprogram structure. But the user often wants to divide a long sequence of procedures on the same level into different groups. As *head* of each tree node he can put a comment describing this group of procedures. This is useful for programming languages without nested procedure declarations, such as *C* or even assembly languages. Different nodes could even be written in different programming languages.

The tree structure is also useful for documents. The need to handle structured documents was actually the motivation for the first version of ED3 (in 1980). The tree structure is then built like the structure of chapters and sections in the document. Programs and associated documents such as requirements specifications, program documentation, reference manuals, change logs, etc. can be handled with the same editor. They can even be on the screen at the same time as the program in different windows. This can help the programmer not to forget to update the documents when the program is modified.

The next section describes how a text editor and a *pretty-printer* can be combined into an efficient program editor, at least for small programs, and how a tree structure helps the user handle large programs. A more detailed description of the structure editor is found in section three. In section four there is a discussion on how this concept can be generalized.

2. HOW TO USE ED3 FOR PROGRAM DEVELOPMENT

The following example will show how ED3 can be used to enter a program and how syntax errors are removed interactively.

- The user enters program text as usual, but indentation and new lines are not important. The user then hits the *syntax check and pretty-print* key.

- When a syntax error is found, the cursor will be placed just before the first erroneous token. The error message will contain a list of correct tokens at this position. The user then perhaps enters one of the alternatives and hits the *syntax* key again. The text is parsed again from the beginning (of the current text node).

- If no syntax errors are found, the editor replaces the text with a *pretty-printed* copy. If the user does not like the result, he just has to hit the *undo* key. He can also redefine the *syntax* key to just check syntax and not *pretty-print*.

- If the entered text contains more than one procedure, the user normally will hit the *split* key, so that each text node contains only one procedure.

The user has complete freedom how to cut his program (or document) into text nodes and how to build a tree of them. ED3 just supplies a default. Dividing the program into text nodes, with for instance a procedure in each, gives the following advantages:

- It gives the user a good overview of his program. The tree structure is displayed like a table of contents, e.g. of procedures and modules or groups of procedures. The tree structure given by the author may also help other people to understand the program.

- The user will feel safer editing one procedure at a time. Replace and delete commands then just affect the current node. In Emacs a similar feature is called *narrowing*. In ED3 a copy is taken of the current node every time the text editor is entered. This makes it possible for the user to get back the old version or to compare them.

- The node structure also gives well defined starting points for syntax check and *pretty-printing*. I think that this is the main reason why syntax checking is not found in most text editors used for program development. The time needed to parse and pretty-print a node is of course proportional to the size of the node. For a small node the user will not notice any delay. But even if a node contains several hundred lines the delay will only be a few seconds.

```
program test(output);
var i:integer;
begin
 for i:= 1 □. 10 do writeln(i);
end.



*
?Expected "DOWNTO" or "TO"
ED3> e
```

Figure 1. A syntax error is found

```
PROGRAM test(Output);
VAR
   i: Integer;
BEGIN
   FOR i:= 1 TO 10 DO BEGIN
      Writeln(i);
   END;
END.

*
Pascal accepted
ED3> e
```

Figure 2. After the error is removed

3. STRUCTURE PRESENTATION AND EDITING

We call ED3 a structure-oriented text editor. The idea of such an editor is to superimpose a tree onto the text. Drawing analogies from books this tree will act as a table of contents. There are however differences. Changes in the tree structure will cause the text parts to be correspondingly reordered. Selection of text parts to be edited is made by traversing the tree structure (the table of contents) using menus automatically produced from the current structure, and then entering text editing mode when a leaf is reached.

3.1 Tree Structure

The present version of ED3 has two types of nodes, tree nodes and text nodes. Other node types have been added in the experimental version for interactive graphics. It is our intention that all structure editing commands shall be independent of the type of the objects in the tree.

A *text node* is a sequence of zero or more characters from the ASCII character set. If a single text node contains the whole program or document file, ED3 works like an ordinary display oriented text editor.

A *tree node* is represented as a list containing a *head*, currently a text node, and a sequence of zero or more references to other nodes, its *subnodes*. The subnodes can be of different types. Some can be text nodes and some can be tree nodes. If a subnode is a tree node it is the root of a *subtree*.

3.2 Structure Presentation

The terminal screen (or a window) is used to display the structure of a tree or the text in a node. If the current node is a tree node the first line of the head and the first line of each subnode is shown. The subnodes are numbered and these numbers can be used as commands or as arguments to a command.

If the current node is a text node the whole text is displayed. The screen is updated after every change in structure or text, or if another node is selected as new current node.

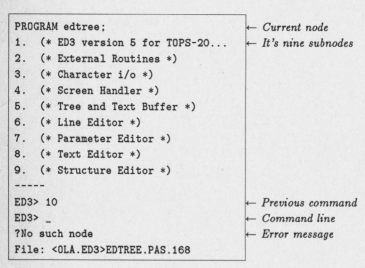

Figure 3. Example of screen layout.

All tree editor commands are relative to the current node and this is always the node that is shown on the screen. A command to visit another part of the tree is actually a command that changes the current node and thus changes the editor's attention to another part of the tree. Tree traversal is done by menu selection. An integer as a command selects the corresponding subnode as current node.

```
(* Screen Handler *)
1.   PROCEDURE xypos(x,y: Integer);...
2.   PROCEDURE clearscreen;...
3.   PROCEDURE keypad(on: Boolean);...
4.   PROCEDURE eraseeol;...
5.   FUNCTION nextx(ch: Char;x: Int...
6.   FUNCTION getx(VAR l: textline;...
7.   PROCEDURE appstr(y: Integer;s:...
8.   PROCEDURE appint(y: Integer;i:...
9.   PROCEDURE appchr(y: Integer;ch...
--MORE--_
ED3> 10
ED3> 4


File: <OLA.ED3>EDTREE.PAS.168
```

Figure 4. Subnode four is selected.

```
(* Screen Handler *)
1.   PROCEDURE xypos(x,y: Integer);...
     1.   PROCEDURE outnum(i: Intege...
     2.   BEGIN...
2.   PROCEDURE clearscreen;...
3.   PROCEDURE keypad(on: Boolean);...
4.   PROCEDURE eraseeol;...
5.   FUNCTION nextx(ch: Char;x: Int...
6.   FUNCTION getx(VAR l: textline;...
7.   PROCEDURE appstr(y: Integer;s:...
--MORE--_
ED3> 4
ED3> P


File: <OLA.ED3>EDTREE.PAS.168
```

Figure 5. The P Command.

Only a few commands are needed to make it easy for the user to walk around in a tree and get a general view of a program or a structured document. There are commands to select the n-th subnode (integer n>0), go up to the root node (∧), go one level up (0), go the next (NX) and the previous (BK) node on the same level in the tree.

In addition to the automatic display of one level of subnodes, there is a command to show several levels of the tree (P). This command normally displays three levels of the current subtree, but the *print level* is a parameter that can be changed. The indentation of node numbers is used to indicate how the tree nodes are connected.

3.3 Structure Editing

All structure editing commands are relative to the current node and therefore the commands — delete a subtree (D), — insert a node node after (IA) or before (IB) current node and — join current node with next (J), are commands without any parameter. The command to change order between nodes (SW) is one of two commands where more than one node have to be specified.

In order to move or copy a subtree *two* points in the tree must be specified. These points can be far from each other. This problem is solved by having two trees for a while. First the current subtree is moved or copied to the second tree (which actually is a stack of saved trees and text nodes). Any sequence of attention changing commands can then be used to reach the position where the saved tree is to be inserted. This means that two local operations are performed instead of one referencing two different points in the tree.

The creation of new tree nodes is done by grouping the nodes that shall be its subnodes. There is also a command to split a tree node into subnodes. The edit command (E) is used to change the information in a node. Depending on the type of current node the appropriate editor is used. For each node type in ED3 there must be an editor, like the text editor for the text nodes. The head is edited if current node is a tree node.

```
    PROGRAM edtree;                         ←Window 1 displays current path,
    4.  (* Screen handler *)                 i.e. the way from the root node
        1.  PROCEDURE xypos(x,y: I...
=>          1.  PROCEDURE outnum(i...
------------------------------------
PROCEDURE outnum(i: Integer);                ←Window 2 used by the text editor
BEGIN
  IF i>=10 THEN BEGIN
    outnum(i DIV 10);
  END;
  ttywrite(Chr((i MOD 10)+Ord('0')));
END;
ED3> E

File: <OLA.ED3>EDTREE.PAS.168
```

Figure 6. Path display and text editing in different windows

There are also commands to communicate with the file system. The whole tree or a subtree can be saved on files with or without the tree structure. For program files, the structure information is usually stored in comments. This means that the same file that stores the structure also can be read by compilers. Files with structure can later be loaded as a subtree at any position in tree. Files without the structure information can be loaded as text nodes. The user can then split the text and build a structure over it.

3.4 Implementation status

Since Pascal is available on many small computers it was selected as implementation language to obtain portability. Only a small number of low level input and output functions are written in machine language.

ED3 was first developed on a DECSYSTEM-20 computer and has been moved to all general purpose systems we have used, e.g. DECsystem-10, PDP-11/23 under RSX-11M, PDP-11/70 under UNIX (version 7 and 2.9BSD), VAX-11 under VMS, and the SUN-2 Workstation and other M68000-based UNIX systems (System III, System V and 4.2BSD).

Recently syntax checking and *pretty-printing* for full Ada and a simple Pascal to Ada syntax translator was completed. To test these tools (and to improve them) the whole ED3 editor (about 15 000 lines) where translated to Ada. The translation, including debugging, required about two man-weeks.

4. A GENERALIZED APPROACH TO EDITING

The structure editor in ED3 handles tree structures, which can be thought of as hierarchical directories of nodes of different types. The structure editor has commands to walk around in the tree, automatically displaying the current node and its subnodes, and commands to copy, delete and move subtrees or individual nodes.

ED3 must also contain an editor for each node type, like the text editor for the text nodes and the graphics editor for picture nodes.

A syntax-directed editor could also be integrated to handle program nodes, which can be parse trees for any thing from a small program fragment to a complete program. I think that a procedure would be the most common choice as it is today for text nodes.

The parser can transform a text node to a program node when the *syntax-directed* editor is entered, and the *pretty-printer* could transform a program node to a text node when the text editor is called (and when the program is sent to a traditional compiler). The user will then have a free choice between text editing and *syntax-directed* editing.

Both the text and parse tree representations could be kept until one of them are modified to reduce the need for reparsing or *pretty-printing*.

Since the parse tree representation is space intensive, see e.g. POE [1], scanning and parsing is time consuming and almost all compilers today only accepts program text as input, a large program could be stored as tree of text nodes and only one node at the time is parsed when the *syntax-directed* editor is entered.

5. SUMMARY

This paper does not say that *syntax-directed* editing is a bad idea. In an integrated programming environment, where the editor, interpreter, compiler, debugger can work on the same internal form a parse tree representation is natural.

A text oriented representation on the other hand, makes it easy to combine existing tools. The first version of the syntax check for Pascal only took about two hours to integrate into ED3. New tools, such as a parser and *pretty-printer* for Ada and a Pascal to Ada syntax translator, have then been added.

REFERENCES

[1] Fisher, C.N., *et al*, The Poe Language-Based Editor Project, *SIGPLAN Notices, vol 19*, no 5 (1984), pp 21-29.

[2] Stallman, R.M., EMACS the Extensible, Customizable Self-Documenting Display Editor, *Proc. of ACM SIGPLAN-SIGOA Symposium on Text Manipulation, SIGPLAN Notices, vol 19*, no 6 (1981), pp 147-156.

[3] Strömfors, O., and Jonesjö, L., The Implementation and Experiences of a Structure-Oriented Text Editor. *Proc. of ACM SIGPLAN-SIGOA Symposium on Text Manipulation, SIGPLAN Notices, vol 19*, no 6 (1981), pp 22-27.

[4] Teitelbaum, T., and Reps, T., The Cornell Program Synthesizer: A syntax-directed programming environment. *Commun. ACM vol 24, no 9* (1981), pp 563-573.

On the Usefulness of Syntax Directed Editors

Bernard Lang
INRIA
B.P. 105, 78153, Le Chesnay, France

Abstract

The intent of this position statement is to relate our experience with the actual use of a syntax directed editor (Mentor [5]) in different contexts: teaching, real software production, software maintenance and associated tasks, language design and development, development of programming tools and new programming structures.

1. Introduction

Originally the subject of this presentation was motivated by discussions to be found in the technical literature [1,2,3], and by the open questioning in less technical publications (as well as in private discussions) of the real usefulness of the syntax directed approach, its practicality and its high cost for allegedly low returns [4]. While the author does not dispute many of the points raised in the technical litterature, he believes they emphasize too much the role of syntax directed tools for program creation, and thus lead to a biased assessment of their real usefulness. This is currently resulting in the marketing of sophisticated syntax directed editors, restricted to program creation, whose cost effectiveness may indeed be questionable.

The ideas expressed here reflect only the point of view of this author, and are intended as a basis for discussion on the role of syntax directed editors. The personal judgements on various aspects of syntax directed environments are not meant as an assessment of the usefulness of research in those areas, but only as a tentative evaluation of the relative importance of these aspects for users, given the current state of the art and the author's own experience.

This experience is based almost solely on the use of the Mentor system [5]. Though comparison of several systems would be desirable, the youth of this technology makes it rather difficult to acquire extensive practical experience with more than one of them.

2. Functionality and Programmability

Our experience with syntax directed environments is based on the design, use and distribution (academic and industrial) of the Mentor system. Mentor is a syntax directed document manipulation system which we started developing at INRIA in 1974. The only previous experiment in this area had been Hansen's Emily system (ignoring Lisp environments that do not quite address the same problems). Mentor was written in Pascal and originally could manipulate only Pascal programs. In 1977 we began using Mentor for its own development. This bootstrap was an essential step in the evolution of the system, since it gave us first hand practical experience on the effectiveness of the approach for medium scale software production (about 50 000 lines of Pascal). Quickly Mentor became the main support tool for both program creation and maintenance. Indeed reference source programs were kept in tree form even on file storage (to prevent the loss of information on comments that is unavoidable when unparsing). Thus we had to use Mentor for all editing and maintenance activities, and we were barred from traditional text editors such as emacs.

The system was used in two ways:

- as an editor to enter or modify programs interactively, but in a syntax directed way,

- as a program analysis and transformation system.

This second use was possible because the command language of Mentor (for this implementation in Pascal) is a programming language called Mentol. This language has variables, control structures and recursive procedures, and it is designed with a very strong bias towards the manipulation of abstract syntax trees. Mentol was used to program a variety of program analysis, manipulation and transformation tools, that may be called interactively by the users of Mentor, or may be executed in batch mode.

The basic system provided elementary tree navigation and modification commands, quite independent from the actual semantics of the edited language (Pascal at first). The first use of Mentol is to program an environment of small functions that encapsulate some knowledge of the semantics of the edited language, and thus can better assist the programmer in his task. Examples of such tools are:

- search for the declaration of a procedure or of a variable,

- automatic declaration of labels,

- elimination of useless code,

- automatic commenting of loop or procedure ends, etc.

Heavier uses of Mentol include complex program analysis (e.g. alias analysis, software metrics) and mechanized program tranformations for optimization (e.g. recursion removal) or for porting programs on machines with different dialects. Mentor itself was ported mechanically on many very different dialects of Pascal, sometimes requiring complex syntactic or even semantic transformations (programmed in Mentol) because of the differences between these dialects. It has been developed successively on CII 10070 (Sigma7), CII IRIS-80, CII-HB DPS-8 under Multics, Vax with Unix (TM) and then VMS. It has been ported to the DEC-10, and is currently developed and maintained (by an industrial distributor) on many types of computers (VAX VMS or Unix, SUN, APOLLO, SM-90, RIDGE, HP-9000).

Actually the system is open and extensible, and new tools may be programmed in Pascal (by accessing directly the Pascal functions implementing the Mentol primitives) and called interactively as if programmed in Mentol.

There are several ways of using such a system (ignoring other features that will be discussed later).

a) simple use of elementary semantics-free editing commands: tree cut-and-paste, pattern matching and search, ... These commands act identically for syntactically similar structure such as, say, *assignment, sum* or *while* which are all tree binary operators. For such uses, it is not clear whether the little help provided by the structured view and manipulation of program warrants the conceptual and implementation costs. Also the author does not feel that the fast response of incremental tools usually integrated at this level, either syntactic (e.g. pretty-printing, syntax checking) or even semantic (e.g. type checking), brings an essential productivity improvement over an off-line use of the same tools.

b) use of pre-packaged environments of semantics dependent functions (supplied by another party) such as those described above. Such environments are in our case usually programmed in Mentol, but may also be programmed in Pascal or produced by any other means, though this is not relevant for the user. These language dependent tools have proved to be a substantial improvement over direct use of the raw syntactic system (i.e. semantics-free commands). Experience seems to show that, for a given edited language, each user makes a heavy usage of a small numbers of the available tools, but that these are not quite the same for all users. *Programmability of the system is essential* in order to select and tailor the environment to fit the standards, methods, style and abilities of teams and users.

c)   use of the Mentol language itself for programming special purpose editing and maintenance tools, either for personal use or for use by other members of a project. This requires the user to be fairly expert and to fully understand the system.

It is to be stressed that easy programmability of a syntax directed editor is a substantial qualitative improvement for maintenance activities, allowing the *reliable* mechanization of repetitive and error-prone analysis and/or modifications of the maintained program. An example is the systematic transformation in the edited program of expression using a given set of primitive functions into equivalent expression using a different set of primitives. An other example, evoked above, is the transport of programs between dialects.

We feel so strongly about the importance of syntax directed editing for maintenance, that we have undertaken the definition of a non-trivial syntax for Lisp in order to be able to maintain our Lisp programs with Mentor (cf. section 4).

3. The User Interface

The user interface of the older versions of Mentor was poor, rather similar to that of a line oriented editor with a glass or paper teletype. The user had a tree cursor, and could type in commands that applied to this cursor: cursor motion, tree modification, tree visualization, i/o commands, etc. From the very beginning the standard mode of input was through a parser rather than by syntax directed menus.

In 1981 we developed a full screen interface (analogous to that of Emacs) and in 1984 we started using a bit-map and mouse interface with direct pointing in the trees. Input of new programs by syntax directed menus was introduced only at this time, more as a help to beginners than for experienced users.

The originally weak interface was imposed both by the technology of the available terminals (the system was quickly distributed and had to use standard technology) and by the low bandwith of the computer connections (1200 baud at best in most cases) preventing fast full screen refresh.

At some point in this history, glass-teletype Mentor was competing with full-screen Emacs. It appeared that neither of the two systems could really replace the other. Emacs was most convenient for typing in new programs but could not compete with Mentor for the maintenance activities described in the previous section. Problems related to the correct placement of comments in the abstract tree representation prevented switching between Emacs and Mentor via the parser and pretty-printer.

Thus Emacs was commonly used to enter in a file a new sizable (more than 5 or 10 lines) fragment of program, which was then parsed into Mentor, and was henceforth edited within it. Syntactically incorrect fragments were refused by the Mentor parser and had to be first corrected with Emacs. A major improvement was the implementation of a link between Mentor and Emacs allowing a user to call Emacs from Mentor to input a new program fragment or to edit in a non-structured way an existing fragment (i.e. a subtree) unparsed for the purpose. This was especially useful for editing expressions, long literals, and textual parts (comments). It permitted the use of Mentor for languages with important textual components, such as the language Rapport for the production of technical reports.

The menu system was rarely used (if at all) by experts. Started as an experiment (all other syntax directed editors had menus) it turned out to be a good device (together with its associated help system) to introduce novice users to Mentor, or to assist an experienced Mentor user when learning a new language.

The conclusion of our experience is that for maintenance activities the advantages of syntax directed tools outweigh the friendliness of full screen editing. This conclusion is further supported by the fact that the better man-machine interface could have been developed somewhat earlier. However, as experts users of the system, we felt a greater need for better functionality than for a nicer user interface. What forced our hand was that the system became too difficult to learn for novice users (especially without local assistance), though those who made the effort to learn it where henceforth quite happy to use it. The better user interface was to a large extent a way to make our tool more acceptable by assisting the user, by bridging the conceptual gap of the syntax directed paradigm, and by simply looking nicer. The use of a pointing device (mouse) to move in trees is particularly effective in bringing the novice user gently to a tree-structured perception of textual objects.

We must however note that, even with a good user interface, the syntax directed paradigm is too complex and bothersome for inputting programs or for performing simple editing tasks. As might be expected, it is particularly inconvenient for editing text/program fragments that are non-structured (strings, comments) or poorly structured (expressions).

4. Language Independence

In 1981 Mentor became language independent. New languages can be specified to Mentor by means of the specification language Metal. In addition, different languages may be mixed in the same document through the commenting mechanism. Metal specifications are currently limited to syntactic aspects, while specification and generation of semantic tools (with a meta-language called Typol) is still at the prototype stage.

Language independence is essential for the adaptability of the environment to different dialects or to the evolution of a language. It is also a factor of uniformity between environments for differents languages.

Language independence allowed us to define environments for a large number of languages. But the important and unexpected effect was that a good part of our user community started using Mentor as a tool to assist the design of new languages. This is probably an important step towards the effective support of application specific languages, defined within a general purpose one, by easy generation of the corresponding environments.

However, even with a good language specification language, we believe that the definition of abstract syntaxes and finely tuned pretty-printers are non-trivial tasks that require much care and experience, especially if the language has been originally defined in terms of a concrete syntax, as is too often the case. Typically, independently of Mentor, the abstract syntax of Ada took several weeks and was revised several times.

Languages with a poor syntax (Lisp, Fortran) or with non-syntactic features (Lisp, C) such as string macros and arbitrary file inclusion fit with difficulty the syntax directed paradigm. The case of Lisp is interesting because though this language has a well defined syntax with parenthesis (ignoring the problem of macro-characters), this syntax is too trivial to be more useful than the structuring of a text as a string of characters, and it does not reflect the semantics of the language. Lisp does have a better structured syntax, but it is hidden under the parenthesis. Experiments to generate a Mentor environment for Lisp on the basis of its hidden syntax have not been too successful so far, both because there is a bad fit between concrete and abstract representation, and because Mentor cannot easily be used within an interactive Lisp environment.

We have only begun to explore the potential of mixing languages with different syntaxes, but we expect it to have impact on the organization of environment tools, and probably also on the structure of (programming) languages themselves.

5. Teaching and Learning

Mentor has been used to teach Pascal in several universities since 1977, apparently with some success. Younger people adapt very easily to syntax directed editing quite independently of their prior training. This has been confirmed by our own experience with young engineers from companies that collaborated with our research group. However, some older professionals have had difficulty fully adapting to the syntax directed approach.

Menu oriented user interfaces are of considerable help in learning the system, or learning a new language, and tend to be abandonned as the user gains experience. This has been observed consistently with students, who were however using alphanumeric terminals without a mouse.

6. Conclusion

The use of a syntax directed environment for trivial tasks is expensive. It is not clear that the advantages gained are sufficient to outweigh the cost of this technology, both in terms of the complexity of processors and computing power required, and in terms of the added difficulty for users learning more complex tools. There is however some benefit for novice users since syntax directed environments may be considered a good medium to help learn a new language and its structure. At this level, the quality of the man-machine interface plays an essential role.

For advanced users, a syntax directed environment is irreplaceable for program maintenance, especially when used to the full capacity of this technology, with the ability to use all tools and program new ones in terms of the syntax directed paradigm, i.e. on the basis of the abstract syntax of the manipulated languages. However, this implies playing the game without reservations and essentially accepting abstract trees as the standard representation of documents in place of text. Of course this may (and must) be mitigated by occasionally allowing the editing in textual form of small fragments of documents.

The author believes that the effective power and programmability of tools is more important than incrementality (which does not mean that incrementality is not worthwhile), especially when one considers the cost of incrementality within the current state of the art. In particular, high quality user interfaces are essential to lure and/or assist new users, but are probably less important than functionality for experienced people.

Finally, and unexpectedly, syntax directed environment generators are a privileged tool for language designers. In the long run, we expect that the new organizational facilities offered by these environments will foster the development of new linguistic structures in programming languages.

Acknowledgements: Though the points of view expressed here are the author's, the Mentor system and much of the experience that came with it is the result of the work of a great many people, developers and/or users of the system.

References:

[1] R.C. Waters, *Program editors should not abandon text oriented commands,* SIGPLAN Notices, vol. 17, n. 7, July 1982.

[2] U. Shani, *Should program editors not abandon text oriented commands?,* SIGPLAN Notices, vol. 18, n. 1, January 1983.

[3] R.J. Zavodnic, and M.D. Middleton, *YALE: The Design of Yet Another Language-based Editor,* SIGPLAN Notices, vol 21, n. 6, June 1986.

[4] B. Daniel-Jausine, Review of a meeting on software engineering, *O1 Hebdo,* n. 883, p. 61, December 1985.

[5] Donzeau-Gouge, V., Kahn, G., Lang, B., Mélèse, B., and Morcos, E., *Outline of a tool for document manipulation,* Proc. of IFIP '83 conf., Paris, R.E.A. Mason (ed.), North Holland, September 1983.

Space limitations prevent the inclusion of other references in this position paper. If need be, the reader will find expository papers and references in:

Proceedings of the ACM SIGSOFT/SIGPLAN Software Engineering Symposium on Practical Software Development Environments, P.B. Henderson Edit., Pittsburgh, April 1984.

PegaSys and the Role of Logic in Programming Environments

Mark Moriconi

Computer Science Laboratory
SRI International*

June 10, 1986

Abstract

The benefits of formal approaches to program development are widely recognized. However, most programming environments have taken little advantage of them. The problem of incorporating formalism into programming environments is discussed in light of two often-competing concerns: maintaining mathematical rigor and alleviating complication in the programming of large systems. The PegaSys system [1,2] represents a practical balance between the two. It deals with an interesting class of program properties that are easy to describe formally and to reason about mechanically. Systems such as PegaSys offer the possibility of increased use of formal methods in programming environments.

1   Introduction

For more than a decade, advances in programming environments have made programming increasingly easier. The advances include individual tools, such as sophisticated editors, automated software-management systems, and source-level debuggers, as well as integrated collections of tools of all kinds. The effectiveness of many of these tools is enhanced through the use of high resolution displays and personal workstations.

During the same period, a number of techniques have been developed to provide assurance that a program has a desired property. The techniques include desk-checking, testing, symbolic execution, proof, and even disciplined construction. From each of these techniques, we can obtain varying amounts of confidence and certainty.

The greatest amount of assurance comes from a rigorous proof of consistency between a program and a property stated in a precise and unambiguous specification language. Considerable progress has been made in this regard. In fact, it is changing the way we think about programs. Programs are not seen as just a sequence of instructions for a computer but as mathematical objects demonstrated to have desired properties.

---

*This research was supported by the Office of Naval Research under Contract N00014-83-C-0300.

The fields of programming environments and rigorous programming techniques have evolved in relative isolation. This insularity has accelerated progress in both fields. Research on formal methods has been able to focus on mathematical rigor at the expense of productivity (at least in the initial development of a program), while programming environments have had just the opposite tendency. Consequently, programming environments have had a much greater influence on programming in the large, while formal methods have provided much greater insight into small, complex programs.

In this paper, I consider the problems associated with the use of rigorous techniques in general programming environments. I discuss these problems and how they have been dealt with in the past. Lastly, I propose a different perspective that can lead to integration of the two fields.

2 Two Sources of Complication

The value of knowing with mathematical certainty that a program has a desired property can be offset by its high cost. In particular, start-up costs can be so high as to discourage the use of formalism entirely, even if it reduces the *overall* lifecycle cost of a program. (Researchers have conjectured, but have not proven, that formal approaches to program development will reduce overall cost.)

Significant start-up costs can be attributed to two factors:

1. Formal specifications can be difficult to write and to understand, especially for large programs.

2. Proofs of consistency most often cannot be mechanized and are too tedious and cumbersome to carry out by hand.

For formal techniques to receive widespread use in programming environments, these two sources of complexity must be minimized. It must be possible to specify properties in a formalism that is relatively easy to write and to understand, as well as to prove theorems both mechanically and with minimal user assistance.

The amount of complexity depends on the property to be proved. As explained below, programming environments prove very syntactic properties of programs for which both sources of complexity can be addressed. At the other extreme are traditional program verification systems, which prove functional properties of programs and address neither source of complexity. The PegaSys system [1,2] represents a point between these extremes.

3 Logic in Existing Programming Environments

According to *Webster's New Collegiate Dictionary*, a proof is "the cogency of evidence that compels acceptance by the mind of a truth or a fact." This implies that a proof must be a convincing argument, not necessarily one in classical logic.

In this sense, programming environments prove properties of programs. For example, compilers and syntax-directed editors prove that programs satisfy the specification of the syntax of the programming language, i.e., its grammar. The cost associated with such proofs is small. A grammar is specified by the language developer, not the programmer, and the consistency check is mechanical. Further, most programmers are familiar with grammars. A similar observation can be made about the other kinds of reasoning that occur in programming environments.

4 Logic in Existing Program Verifiers

In contrast, traditional program verification systems exhibit both sources of complexity and, therefore, have a very high start-up cost. This may explain why they have been used successfully in the proof of only small (albeit complex) programs, consisting of a few hundred lines at most.

With few exceptions, program verification systems reason solely about what a program is intended to do. The expectations for such systems have changed considerably over the years. The original goal of minimal user intervention in proofs has been replaced by a recognition that a user must supply crucial proof information, such as lemmas, definitions, and search strategies. In fact, most program verification systems attempt to mechanize only the uncreative parts of a proof, the work that is too tedious and detailed to carry out by hand. While this has been largely successful, the user is still required to provide detailed assistance, which is often quite difficult even for experts. Something approaching journal-level proofs is beyond the state-of-the-art.

To further complicate matters, the specifications input to program verification systems tend to be difficult to understand. This is attributable in part to their size, which generally increases with the size of the program. (The size of a grammar is independent of the size of the program.) As an illustration, suppose that the specification for a message system says that all sent messages are delivered to the intended destination in the proper order. This specification must be elaborated to specify the various transmission protocols used by the message system, including their operations, data objects (such as messages, packets, and acknowledgements), and error handling mechanisms. In the end, the specification will be quite large, perhaps as large as the program.

Although the size of a specification can be managed to a large extent through structuring techniques, it can still be difficult to understand because of notational conventions. Most general specification languages derive their syntax from classical logic. This syntax has definite advantages, but a large specification written in a logical notation can be difficult to write and to understand.

5 Logic in PegaSys

The PegaSys system deals with a class of properties that lies somewhere between the syntactic class dealt with by programming environments and the very general class dealt with by program verification systems. In particular, PegaSys supports the specification and analysis of data and control dependencies among the components of large programs. A formal description of dependencies is useful both as an aid to software engineers and as machine-readable input for automated software management systems.

PegaSys addresses both sources of complexity:

1. Formal specifications in PegaSys are pictures called *formal dependency diagrams* (FDDs), which are much more perspicuous than equivalent logical expressions.

2. The consistency between an FDD and a program is proved or disproved efficiently and without user assistance.

Consequently, PegaSys gives the illusion that logical formulas do not exist, even though it reasons about them internally.

PegaSys is harder to use than existing programming environments, but much easier to use than program verification systems. I believe that the start-up cost is low enough to make it a practical compromise between these two extremes. An overview of those aspects of PegaSys that address the two sources of complexity is given below.

5.1 Graphical Formalism

Figure 1 provides an example of an FDD taken from a PegaSys display.[1] The FDD contains several icons: four ellipses, a rectangle, several arrows, and several character strings.[2] These icons denote several concepts about the example network. Each of the four hosts in the network is modeled as a process (indicated by an ellipse); the communication line by a module (indicated by a dashed rectangle); and a packet of data by a type (indicated by a label on arcs). Dependencies among hosts, packets, and the line are described by the "write" relation (denoted by the letter W on arrows) and the "read" relation (denoted by R).

At first approximation, this FDD says that the broadcast network consists of four hosts that communicate by means of a line. More precisely, processes named $Host1, \ldots, Host4$ write values of type *pkt* into a module called *Line* and read values of the same type from the *Line* module.

An FDD is easy to construct in PegaSys through graphical editing operations. Icons in an FDD denote predefined or user-defined concepts about dependencies in programs. The predefined primitives denote objects (such as subprograms, modules, processes, and data structures), data dependencies (involving the declaration, manipulation, and sharing of data objects), and control dependencies (dealing with asynchronous and synchronous activities). A PegaSys user can define new concepts in terms of the primitives. It is easy to define, for example, a "dataflow" dependency between processes, a "calls" dependency

---

[1] PegaSys is implemented in Interlisp-D and runs on Xerox 1100-series personal computers.

[2] Note that type *pkt* is represented by text (in the lower left of the picture). If PegaSys does not have an icon for a concept, the convention is to display the actual predicate.

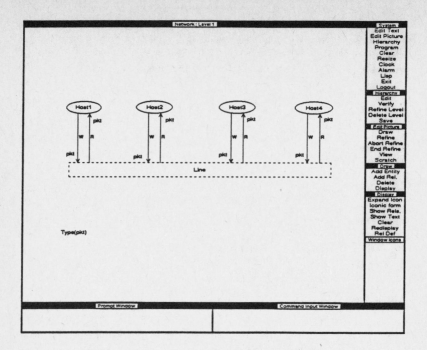

Figure 1: Formal dependency diagram for a network.

between subprograms (with and without side effects), and a "uses" dependency between modules.

5.2 Hierarchical Decomposition

Dependencies in a program are described by a hierarchy of FDDs, which can be constructed in a manner that greatly reduces the complexity of the specification. In general, complexity of a hierarchy as well as individual FDDs is managed by (1) the coarse grain of atomic objects, (2) object decomposition, and (3) dependency decomposition. Pictures often are less perspicuous than text if objects are finer grained than processes, subprograms, and modules.

To illustrate object decomposition, consider the hosts, the packets, and the line in Figure 1. Each can be replaced by a collection of interrelated objects at lower levels in the hierarchy. This sort of object decomposition has appeared in a variety of contexts, such as in graphical dataflow programming.

Dependency decomposition, however, is not supported by existing systems. These systems deal with a fixed set of dependencies, requiring each level in a hierarchy to be seen as a number of superimposed structures, such as control flow graphs, data flow graphs, and calling graphs.

These different structures can make it difficult to get an understanding of dependencies in the overall program. They can all be related in PegaSys by means of user-defined abstractions and multiple levels of description. For example, if the user-defined concept of a subprogram x calling a subprogram y by value occurs in an FDD, it can be decomposed at a lower level in the hierarchy into a call from x to y and an access (but not a modification) of a shared variable by y. At an even lower level, the notion of a call can be decomposed into a bidirectional transfer of control initiated by x.

5.3 Decision Procedures

Logical questions in PegaSys are answered by means of decision procedures. A *decision procedure* for a given class of logical questions answers "yes" or "no" to any question in the class. In practice, the application of a decision procedure may require more space and time than we have available to carry out the finitely many steps that lead to the decision. Ideally, a programming environment should use a decision procedure that gives an immediate response to the most commonly asked questions. A parser is such a decision procedure.

Formulas are proved in PegaSys for a number of reasons, such as to validate dependency decomposition and to establish the consistency between an FDD and a program. The formulas are decidable due to restrictions on the range of quantifiers. As an illustration, consider the following definition:

$$\text{ParameterlessCall}(x, y) \stackrel{\text{def}}{=} \text{Calls}(x, y) \wedge (\not\exists d : dataobject) \, \text{ReadOrWrite}(y, x, d)$$

This definition says that a parameterless call is a two-way transfer of control that does *not* involve the reading or writing of any data object d. The point of interest concerns the range of d.

In general, quantifiers range over known and finite domains that vary according to the FDD in which they occur. In the example above, variable d ranges over the values of type *dataobject* that occur in the FDD in which the *ParameterLessCall* relation occurs. This is consistent with our intuition, since an FDD describes dependencies among objects in a particular program, not the set of all possible program objects.

More specifically, the logic that underlies PegaSys is a multi-sorted, first-order logic where variables range over known, finite domains. Formulas in this logic can be decided using truth tables. In practice, PegaSys decides most formulas very quickly.

The decidability of whether an FDD and a program are consistent depends on more than the decidability of the logic. Additionally, it depends on certain simplifying assumptions, such as that the program has no "dead" control paths and that the aliasing of names results in shared storage for the entire object. These assumptions lead to a worst-case analysis of the sort common in most program manipulation systems, including compilers and cross-reference programs. Further, most of them coincide with our intuition. As a result of these assumptions, consistency does *not* depend on undecidable properties of the program.

6 Implications for Future Programming Environments

The continued isolation of the fields of programming environments and formal methods can be attributed to two factors. Existing systems prove properties of *every* program irrespective of cost, and these properties are either inexpensive or very costly to specify and prove. As a result, only the former are considered in programming environments.

This can be changed if two things are taken into account. First, we must recognize that an entire spectrum of properties can be proved with varying costs. They range from simple syntactic properties to functional properties. In between these extremes lie properties that deal with dependencies, security, safety, performance, and fault-tolerance, among other things.

We have seen that the incremental cost is very low for proofs of syntactic properties, somewhat higher for dependencies, and much higher for functional properties. The cost depends on the degree to which the two sources of complexity are addressed. In the short term, systems such as PegaSys that deal effectively with properties in the middle ground have the best chance of increased use.

The second point is that all properties are not of equal interest for every program. Further, if a property is of interest, it may not be cost effective to reason about every part of the program. The start-up cost may be too high for an entire program, but low enough for part of it. Even proofs of functional properties can be justified for crucial parts of programs in areas such as medicine and space.

These two observations imply that future programming environments can prove properties of programs in a cost-effective manner if they provide a spectrum of specialized proof components, one for each kind of property. Different proof components may be used for different applications. Some will be used all of the time (e.g., parsers and type checkers), some will be used most of the time (e.g., systems like PegaSys), and others very seldom (e.g., program verification systems).

This perspective on the role of logic in programming environments has a number of advantages. In the short term, it can lead to rapid but not abrupt changes in programming style, since formal methods can be used only when appropriate and in conjunction with informal program development. Eventually, it could lead to a mutually benficial symbiosis between the two fields. Finally and most important, any incremental cost associated with formal proofs can be carefully targeted and justified.

References

[1] M. Moriconi and D.F. Hare. The PegaSys system: Pictures as formal documentation of large programs. To appear in *ACM Transactions on Programming Languages and Systems*.

[2] M. Moriconi and D.F. Hare. Visualizing program designs through PegaSys. *IEEE Computer*, 18(8):72–85, August 1985.

GARDEN Tools:
Support for Graphical Programming

Steven P. Reiss
Brown University
Department of Computer Science
Providence, RI 02912/USA
(401)-863-1835, spr@brown

ABSTRACT

This paper describes the programming tools provided by the GARDEN system developed at Brown University. GARDEN is an environment for graphical programming. It is built around an object-oriented programming system in which the objects are directly executable. It uses an object-oriented database system to provide permanent storage for programs, data and pictures. It provides library packages that make effective graphical programming possible. It offers tools for accessing and editing objects and their types, for system control and interaction, for browsing, and for compiling and storing objects.

1. Graphical Programming

One way of simplifying programming is to allow the programmer to work with his conceptualizations. Rather than forcing the programmer to make his concepts of how a system should work conform to a given programming language and environment, the environment and language should conform to the programmer's concepts. Currently the programmer must translate his conceptualizations into a prevailing computer language. Moreover, he must translate back and forth between this language and his conceptualizations during the coding, debugging and maintenance phases of development.

Programming with conceptualizations has three important implications. A conceptual programming environment has to support a variety of views in a unified manner since people use a combination of interrelated concepts to describe a system. Secondly, the environment has to be flexible enough to allow new conceptualizations to be introduced. Conceptualizations are redefined slightly each time they are used. Moreover, new problems often require different methods of attack resulting in new conceptualizations. Finally, the environment has to be graphical. People often think in terms of pictures. Many of the conceptual views of programming are two-dimensional, graphical ones. The programmer must be able to work using the pictures that compose his conceptualizations and to assign meanings to these pictures.

A multiple-view approach to a graphical or conceptual programming system differs considerably from the extensive body of work aimed at developing single graphical representations.[1] This work extends from flowchart programming,[2, 3, 4] to simulating finite state automata,[5, 6] to graphical data flow representations, to design languages such as SADT, SREM or the Yourdon method,[7] to graphical data structure representations,[8] to graphical programming-by-demonstration,[9, 10] to functional programming.[11, 12] All these efforts are single view systems. They do not support the wide range of views necessary to have graphical programming be a practical approach to large-scale programming.

This approach also differs from the multiple-view program development systems for workstations developed over the past eight years. These include the CEDAR Mesa environment from Xerox PARC,[13] the Magpie system from Tektronics,[14] and the PECAN program development system at Brown.[15] These systems are based on a single textual programming language. The PECAN system and PV[16] attempt to provide alternative graphical representations to the textual programming language. The experience we have had with PECAN where the editable views are derived from abstract syntax trees has shown that such graphical views are limited in their power and usefulness when they are tied to syntax. The syntactic basis forces the user to treat these two-dimensional representations in a one-dimensional way, and the graphics do not provide any significant advantage over text. Because the wide range of graphical views that people use do not conveniently fall within the confines of a single language, it seems unlikely that a system based on a single programming language can effectively support them all.

2. The GARDEN Approach

The GARDEN system is a programming environment designed for conceptual programming. It provides a framework supporting a wide variety of different graphical program views in a consistent manner. It does this with an object-oriented programming environment where objects are used as programs as well as data. Using a sophisticated display package, GARDEN offers editable graphical views of these objects. Moreover, it allows objects to be directly evaluated, with the meaning of evaluating an object defined by the programmer. At the same time, GARDEN is a full programming environment, offering a range of tools, permanent storage, and a variety of programming facilities.

GARDEN uses objects as the medium for providing a consistent framework to a variety of graphical views. Pictures of structured objects such as programs or data have been naturally viewed as objects since the early work on Sketchpad.[2] Smalltalk[17] and other environments have shown that an object-oriented approach to programming is both practical and flexible. GARDEN combines these two ideas to provide objects with natural pictures to support programming.

The basis of graphical programming is to have pictures be the program. In GARDEN the picture is generated directly from a set of objects. To make the picture into a program, GARDEN allows these objects to be executed directly. It defines what it means to evaluate an object, and it allows this definition to be done dynamically for new classes of objects.[18]

Having objects denote both programs and data seems to be the right approach for graphical programming. It provides much flexibility, allowing a wide variety of executable pictures. For example, a data flow diagram can be derived directly from a set of objects whose evaluation does data flow. A structured flow graph can be constructed from objects representing the various types of nodes that execute accordingly. Design diagrams can be built from objects whose evaluation is undefined.

Supporting a wide variety of executable objects and their pictures requires a complete programming environment. To store graphical programs there must be means for saving and restoring objects. There must be a variety of tools to view and manipulate the objects, both graphically and textually. There must be tools supporting debugging and evaluation of the objects. There must be support for parallelism, for message passing, for control flow, and for a variety of powerful data structures.

GARDEN provides such an environment for graphical programming. In particular it offers:

- An underlying database system for storing and retrieving objects. The interface to this system includes a complete transaction mechanism and garbage collection.

- Library packages to support lightweight processes, exceptions, dependencies, and graphics.

- A compiler and a dynamic loader that allow a graphical program to be translated into C and made part of the system rather than being interpreted.

- A user-interface based on windows, menus and a pointing device.

- A variety of editors for viewing and manipulating objects.

- A Lisp-like command interface that includes debugging facilities.

- Browsers and a documentation editor for finding objects and information about them.

These tools are described in more detail later in this paper.

To illustrate how we expect GARDEN will be used and to demonstrate the need for a wide range of tools to support graphical programming, we consider the example of a programmer wishing to work in terms of finite-state automata. This is a standard graphical method that will be provided as a library package. However, we will assume for now that no such package is available.

The programmer would begin by defining the types for the objects needed to describe his program structure. In the case of a finite-state automaton, three types are needed: a type containing the complete automaton, a type describing a state, and a type describing an arc. These types could either be defined interactively using the type-definition editor tool in GARDEN, or could be defined textually using the interactive interface. The types are defined by describing their fields and their pictures. The pictures are designed using an interactive tool in the display package.

After the types are defined, the programmer defines their semantics. This is done by defining a function to perform the appropriate actions for each type. These functions are composed of other objects written using other graphical or textual metaphors that have already been defined. They are written using one of the editing tools. In this case, since the functions are simple, the text editor would probably be used.

Now the programmer would be ready to write his program using a finite-state automaton. This is drawn using the graphical editor tool of GARDEN. The programmer is able to create states, connect them by drawing arcs, and assign match values and actions to the arcs, all graphically. While drawing the automaton, he can test it interactively using the provided debugging tools.

3. Database Tools

GARDEN is built on top of an object-oriented database system to provide convenient storage of objects and to support multiple-programmer projects and larger systems. The database implementation is in two parts. There is an in-core management system providing fast access to known objects and there is a file-based object-oriented database system providing permanent storage of objects shared among programmers. The file-based system is a general-purpose object-oriented database system being developed at Brown by Stan Zdonik.[19]

The in-core database facilities provide an efficient interface to the permanent database system. GARDEN uses many objects. Initialization currently creates over eight-thousand objects. Even a simple program can be composed of several hundred objects. Since evaluation is generally done by interpreting these objects, it is essential that access to objects be efficient. Moreover, since objects represent data and variables, a typical user interaction with GARDEN will create large numbers of objects whose lifetime is short. The in-core facilities keep track of those objects known to the external database and treat these objects differently from objects that are purely internal. Moreover, the facility does garbage collection of the local objects either on demand or before storing objects using the external database system.

The database facilities include a transaction mechanism. This is used internally for synchronizing between lightweight processes, for supporting a general undo facility, and for triggering dependencies. It is used by the external database system for coordinating the use of objects between multiple programmers. This mechanism supports nested transactions, locking, two-phase commit, and marking. Marks are identified locations within a transaction used for undoing. The mechanism that supports backing out of a transaction also supports backing up to any of the marks within the current transaction.

Several types of nested transactions are supported by the in-core database system. Transactions can be either global or local. Global transactions are known to the external database; local transactions are only known within this invocation of GARDEN. Nested transactions are only supported locally since the external database system does not support nesting. Transactions can also be abortable or not. Long term transactions such as those representing the entire user session with GARDEN are typically not aborted. Similarly, there is little reason to abort a short term, local transaction used only to trigger a dependency.

The database facilities also include a garbage collector. This provides a programming environment where the user does not have to worry about explicitly freeing objects. It also insures that only essential objects are written out to the permanent database. Garbage collection is only done for objects created during the run of GARDEN. Objects read in from the database are assumed to be permanent. This avoids the need for traversing all objects in the database and insures objects that might be known to others are not removed.

4. Programming Tools

Effective conceptual programming requires the semantics of new graphical views be easy to specify. This requires that the underlying environment contain the programming facilities needed to support the different programming metaphors that can be modeled graphically. GARDEN was designed to provide such facilities.

Many of these facilities are provided by library-style packages that are either made a part of GARDEN or are loaded on demand. These include:

- The THREAD package supporting lightweight processes. This is being developed on top of UNIX at Brown by Tom Doeppner. It has been completely integrated into GARDEN so that GARDEN objects are used to represent threads and semaphores, and exception handling within GARDEN is done on a thread basis.

- The tools provided by the Brown Workstation Environment.[20] These are accessible as procedure calls or operations on a set of classes created to represent windows, input regions, menus, etc.

- Dynamic loading facilities. This have been written for UNIX at Brown by Joe Pato. It can be used for adding user-written C programs to the GARDEN system. It is used by the compiler to load in compiled code.

- Dependencies. GARDEN allows a program to establish dependencies between pairs of objects. At the end of a transaction in which the source object of the pair is changed, the target of the pair is notified by invoking a given object. These are used for maintaining the consistency of multiple views of the same object on the display, for automatic semantic updating between related views such as a symbol table and an expression, and for developing programming methods based on constraints as in Thinglab.[21]

- Lists, strings and tables. GARDEN provides dynamic lists and strings along with a full complement of operations for them. It also offers tables, indexed relations in the database sense, providing fast access based on arbitrary keys.

- A local buffer facility. This allows the user to pick and put objects anywhere on the display.

In addition, we are currently in the process of developing a library of graphical program views that would be available to the programmer as a basis for graphical programming. These include views for finite state automata, for data flow, for control flow, and for production systems of tree transformations.

GARDEN provides several facilities to simplify debugging. Evaluation dependencies can be set on any object. If such a dependency is set, an associated object will be evaluated in place of the given object. This facility is used to implement a trace package provided by GARDEN. GARDEN also allows the programmer to establish a debug handler and a trace handler for each thread. The trace handler is invoked before each object execution. It can be used for single stepping and similar debugging methods. The debug handler is invoked whenever an exception is raised on the thread. This places the user in a read-eval-print loop when an error occurs. Since this is invoked in the environment of the error, the user can interrogate his variables and do other debugging operations at the point of the error. Finally, the dependency mechanism can be used for debugging by providing notification whenever a targeted variable is changed.

GARDEN also includes a compiler. This package takes a set of objects describing functions or operations, translates them into a corresponding C program, uses the system compiler, and then uses the dynamic loader to bind them into the system. The current version of the compiler does a straight-forward mapping from object invocations into C calls. An object-based program translates into calls to the interpreter and appropriate run-time routines. Later versions of the compiler will handle object access and arithmetic in-line and will invoke message routines directly where possible.

5. Interface Tools

The user interface of GARDEN provides an array of tools to the user. Each tool runs in a separate window and uses a separate thread of control. The tools make extensive use of the Brown Workstation Environment. The interface is mouse-oriented, with pull-down, pop-up, or static menus providing most of the necessary commands, dialogue boxes requesting more complex input, and a consistent base editor providing transcripts and text editing facilities.

Most of the user's interactions with the system are done through editors. GARDEN provides both general-purpose and specialized editors for objects. It supports multiple views among editors using dependencies so that the user can view and change a set of objects in one editor and immediately see the changes in another.

The WEED editor allows the user to examine individual fields of an object. It displays all the fields of the object and allows the user to set or examine any of them. Since GARDEN uses fields to represent both the data associated with an object and the Smalltalk-style message handlers for the object, this editor can be used both to look at an individual object in detail and to examine and change the behavior of an object or a class of objects. WEED divides its window into two portions. The top contains a menu of all the available fields. The bottom is empty until the user selects a field. At this point, WEED runs the appropriate editor for the value of the field in this area.

The DAISY editor provides the user with a textual representation of an object and all its subobjects, allows the user to freely edit this, and then parses the result to build a new object to replace the original. It uses the mouse-oriented editor from the workstation environment.

The textual form developed for interacting with GARDEN is a Lisp-like syntax using the list-notation to describe both objects and object invocations. If the head of the list is an object type, then the remaining elements provide the values for the data fields of a new object of this type. This allows Lisp-like constructs of the form *(LAMBDA <x> statement)* to denote a *LAMBDA* object with an *arguments* field containing a list object consisting of the name object for *x*, and a *body* field containing the object that composes the statement. If the head of the list is not an object type, then the list-notation describes a *CALL* object where the head of the list is the object to be evaluated and the remainder of the list represent the parameters.

The VIOLET editor uses the GELO package for displaying a graphical version of an object.[22] It uses the PEAR package provided with GELO for editing this display. PEAR provides the user with a set of operations on the picture such as adding a node or connecting two nodes with an arc or replacing some picture component. VIOLET translates these operations into operations on the underlying structures.

The THYME editor is specialized for defining and changing type definitions. It allows the user to define the fields of a type, both those representing data and those representing messages. It also allows the user to define how objects of the type should be displayed by the GELO package in the VIOLET editor. This is done using the intuitive displays of the APPLE design editor that supplements GELO.

In addition to editors, GARDEN offers tools for finding out about the objects in the system. A general purpose browser, BALM, allows the user to scan over all the objects in the system. The object of interest can be selected based on its scope, its type, its name, its fields, or a user-designed criteria. Special instances of the browser where some of these selectors are predefined, some used, and some ignored, can be created by the user for his own applications. In addition, a specialized text editor is provided to let the user associate documentation with any object in the system. The documentation for an object can easily be found and read or modified.

Finally, GARDEN offers facilities for controlling the system. The LILY interface offers a read-eval-print loop using the textual language described above. This allows the user to interactively try out his programs. This interface is also used by the debugger to allow the user to examine the program at the point of an error. In addition, the COLEUS package provides a menu-oriented interface to the common high-level commands of GARDEN.

6. Example

As an example of the use of the GARDEN system, we consider a programmer wishing to build a finite-state automaton. This is illustrated in figures 1 through 4. The programmer would start off by creating a transcript window for interacting with the system. He clicks on

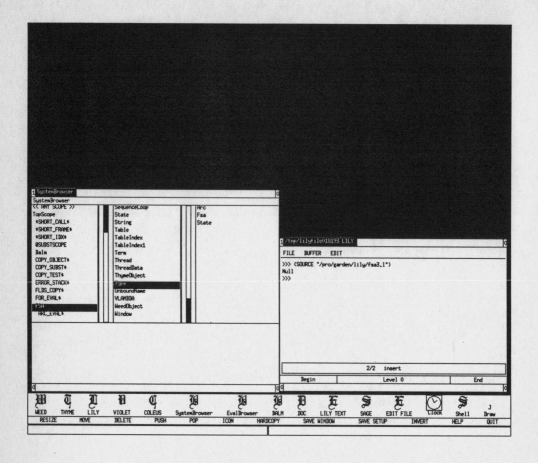

Figure 1: GARDEN view showing browser and transcript windows.

the *LILY* button in he lower-left of the display and then rubber-bands the area desired. Then he moves the cursor into the window and enters his first command. This command invokes the *SOURCE* function to load the definitions for finite-state automata. Next the programmer wants to see what types are defined for automata. He opens a system-browser by clicking over the *SystemBrowser* button at the bottom of the display and rubber-bands an appropriate window. Then in the browser he selects the proper scope, *FSA*, scrolls through the types using the scroll bar to the right of the center display of types in the browser window, to find *Type*, and selects this. The resultant display, shown in figure 1, names three types, *Arc*, *Fsa*, and *State.*

The programmer next wishes to examine these types and their graphical presentations. He first removes the browser with the *DELETE* button on the bottom of the display, clicking first on this button and then on the browser window. Next he puts up a window for each of the types. Each window is created by clicking on the *THYME* button at the lower-left and then rubber-banding to select the window's location and size. When each of these windows is created, a dialogue box appears in the middle asking the programmer to select the type to

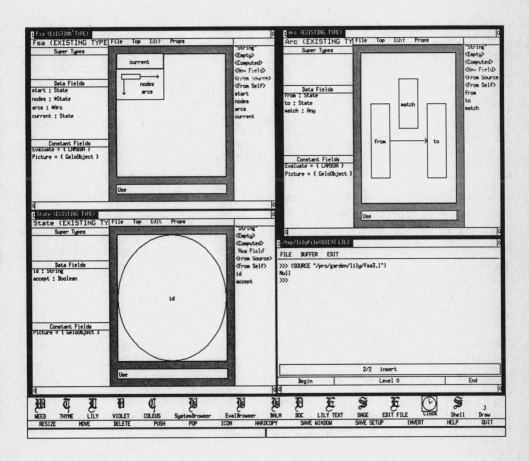

Figure 2: Types for finite-state automata and their pictures.

display. He types in the appropriate name for each window. The THYME editor displays the type in three parts. On the left it lists the fields, supertypes, and constant fields or message routines associated with the type. In the center it displays a stylized prototype of how an object of the type will be drawn. At the right is a menu of fields and values used for the drawing. This can be seen in figure 2.

The type display pictures shown in figure 2 illustrate a variety of the drawing techniques provided by the combination of GELO and APPLE. The type *Fsa*, displayed in the upper-left, is a tiled object consisting of two tiles. The top tile is a rectangular box containing the textual value of the field *current*. The bottom tile contains a layout object that is a graph containing the elements of the fields *nodes* and *arcs*. The type *State*, displayed in the lower-left, is drawn as a box object when it is part of a layout. The box object is drawn as a circle surrounding the textual contents of the *id* field. Finally, the type *Arc* in the upper-right, is drawn as an arc when it is part of a layout. The arc originates in the state identified by the *from* field, goes to the state determined by the *to* field, and is labeled with the contents of the *match* field.

The programmer next removes the THYME type editor windows for *State* and *Arc* using the *DELETE* command to prepare for creating the finite-state automaton. He creates a graphical editor window by clicking on the *VIOLET* button and rubber-banding a new window. He uses the PEAR editor associated with VIOLET and GELO to build the automaton. States are create by selecting the layout region and then the insert command. This causes a sequence of dialogue boxes to appear asking the programmer to define the state. Arcs are created by selecting the from and to states and then using the connect command. This causes a dialogue box to appear requesting the value of the *match* field. The result of the editing can be seen in the lower-left window of figure 3.

Figure 3 also shows the programmer experimenting with the newly created automatonm The programmer first assigns the automaton to a name. In the VIOLET view he clicks several times in the same location to select the whole object and then uses the make-current button to make it the current object. Then he moves to the LILY dialogue window and assigns to the name *f* the current object. The local buffer facility of GARDEN allows the selection of objects anywhere on the screen, makes them current, and then allows the current object to be used in any other view. After assigning the new automaton to *f*, he does sample evaluations. He first evaluates it with the special symbol *START*. This sets the current state to be the start state. The new current state is displayed. Next he tries it several times with different values. In each case the new current state is displayed. At the end, he chooses the update button on the VIOLET view and has the display redrawn to reflect the current state in the top tile.

Finally, the programmer wants to look at the definition of evaluation of an automaton. To do this he uses the WEED editor to display the newly created automaton. He clicks on the *WEED* button in the lower-left and rubber-bands a window at the upper-right of the display. GARDEN puts up a dialogue box in the new window asking for the object to display.

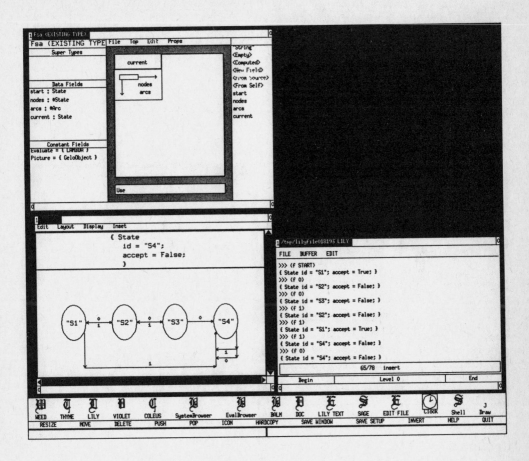

Figure 3: Graphical view of a finite-state automaton and its testing.

The programmer responds by typing the name, *f*, of his automaton. The resultant display identifies the object and lists the fields. An *Fsa* object has four data fields, *start*, *nodes*, *arcs*, and *current*. Two other fields are defined, *Evaluate* and *Picture*. These are constant fields and are associated with the type rather than with the particular instance. The *Picture* field contains the description of how to draw an object of this type. The *Evaluate* field contains the function defining evaluation of finite state automata. The programmer selects the *Evaluate* field by clicking on it and WEED uses the bottom portion of its display to provide an editor on the contents. Since the contents is a LAMBDA object, the DAISY text editor is chosen.

The resultant display is seen in figure 4. The textual display of DAISY utilizes the LILY language.

7. Experience

GARDEN has been under development at Brown since January of 1985. It is written in C and in the LILY language of GARDEN and runs on a variety of workstations including Suns, Apollos and Microvaxes.

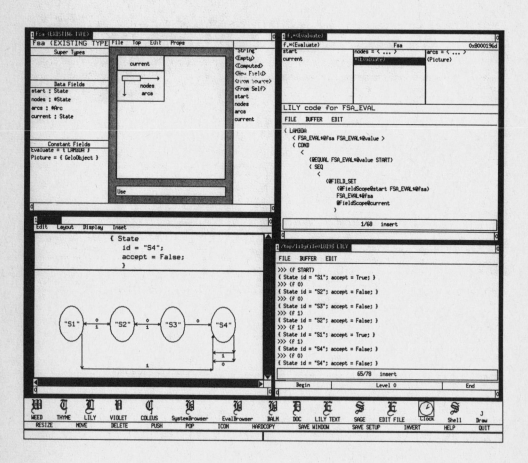

Figure 4: Object view of a finite-state automaton and its evaluation.

There has been a small group of users of GARDEN developing various applications. Most notable among these is a second version of the ThinkPad[10] programming-by-demonstration system that allows a user to illustrate his algorithms by manipulating graphical forms of his data structures. We are also developing a library of graphical views to show the power and flexibility of the system. Finally, we are using the system to build a moderate-sized example, a simple compiler, using mainly graphical techniques.

The experience we have had to date has shown that GARDEN offers a powerful programming environment that has the potential to provide the basis for a practical graphical programming system. The problems we have identified so far involve the need for a good free-hand graphical editor and the need for a more powerful compiler. A major task remaining with GARDEN is the development of and experimentation with a set of graphical programming views spanning a wide range of the conceptualizations that programmers use in developing new systems.

Acknowledgements

This research was supported in part by the Office of Naval Research and the Defense Advanced Research Projects Agency under contract N00014-83-K-0146 and ARPA Order No. 4786, by NSF Grant SER80-04974, by a contract with International Business Machines, by a grant from the AT&T Foundation, and by a grant from the Digital Equipment Corporation. Partial equipment support was provided by Apollo Computer, Inc.

References

1. Georg Raeder, "A survey of current graphical programming techniques," *IEEE Computer* **18**(8) pp. 11-25 (August 1985).

2. I Sutherland, "Sketchpad, A Man-Machine Graphical Communication System," PhD Thesis, MIT (January 1963).

3. H. P. Frei, D. L. Weller, and R. Williams, "A graphics-based programming support system," *Computer Graphics* **12**(3) pp. 43-49 (August 1978).

4. Steven L. Tanimoto and Ephraim P. Glinert, "Programs made of pictures: interactive graphics makes programming easy," U. Washington Dept of Computer Science FR-35 ().

5. Anthony I. Wasserman, "Extending state transition diagrams for the specification of human-computer interaction," Medical Information Science, U. California, San Francisco (1985).

6. Robert J. K. Jacob, "A state transition diagram language for visual programming," *IEEE Computer* **18**(8) pp. 51-59 (August 1985).

7. Mark Moriconi and Dwight F. Hare, "Visualizing program designs through PegaSys," *IEEE Computer* **18**(8) pp. 72-85 (August 1985).

8. Michael L. Powell and Mark A. Linton, "Visual abstraction in an interactive programming environment," *SIGPLAN Notices* **18**(6) pp. 14-21 (June 1983).

9. William Finzer and Laura Gould, "Programming by rehearsal," *Byte* **9**(6) pp. 187-210 (June 1984).

10. Robert V. Rubin, Eric J. Golin, and Steven P. Reiss, "ThinkPad: A graphical system for programming-by-demonstration," *IEEE Software* **2**(2) pp. 73-78 (March 1985).

11. G. Raeder, "Programming in Pictures," PhD Dissertation, University of Southern California (1984).

12. L. Cardelli, "A two-dimensional language for functional programming," in *Integrated Interactive Computing Systems*, ed. P. Degano and E. Sandewall,North-Holland (1982).

13. W. Teitelman, "A tour through Cedar," *IEEE Software*, (April, 1984).

14. Norman M Delisle, David E. Menicosy, and Mayer D. Schwartz, "Viewing a programming environment as a single tool," *SIGPLAN Notices* **19**(5) pp. 49-56 (May 1984).

15. Steven P. Reiss, "PECAN: Program development systems that support multiple views," *IEEE Trans. Soft. Eng.* SE-**11**(March 1985).

16. Gretchen P. Brown, Richard T. Carling, Christopher F. Herot, David A. Kramlich, and Paul Souza, "Program visualization: Graphical support for software development," *IEEE Computer* **18**(8) pp. 27-35 (August 1985).

17. Adele Goldberg and Dave Robson, *Smalltalk-80: The language and its implementation*, Addison-Wesley (1983).

18. Steven P. Reiss, "An object-oriented framework for graphical programming," Brown University (March 1986).

19. Stanley B. Zdonik and Peter Wegner, "A database approach to languages, libraries and environments," Proc. GTE Workshop on Software Engineering Environments for Programming-in-the-Large (June 1985).

20. Joseph N. Pato, Steven P. Reiss, and Marc H. Brown, "An environment for workstations," *Proc. of the IEEE Conf. on Software Tools*, pp. 112-117 (April 1985).

21. A. Borning, *Thinglab -- A constraint oriented simulation laboratory*, PhD Dissertation, Department of Computer Science, Stanford University (1979).

22. Steven P. Reiss and Joseph N. Pato, "Displaying program and data structures," Brown University (April 1986).

PROGRAMMING-IN-THE-SMALL

Chair   : Lynn Carter (GenRad, USA)
Assistant chair : Geir Green (RUNIT, NOR)

Questions after Reiss' presentation

Robert Schwanke (Siemens, USA):

Automatic layout, such as is done in VLSI, is a hard problem. What simplifications or insights have you used in your work?

Steven Reiss (Brown Univ., USA):

The difference between programming and VLSI is that a VLSI layout is quite flat, while a program is generally quite hierarchical. In doing a VLSI layout it is important that all details be present in the final presentation. In displaying a program graphically we can afford to show some portions of the program in detail and others as some sort of abstraction.

Robert Schwanke (Siemens, USA):

How do you automatically arrange boxes, connected by multicolored arcs, so that they make sense visually?

Steven Reiss (Brown Univ., USA):

The system is quite flexible. It allows several different layout heuristics that can be selected either by the program or by the user. Additional heuristics are relatively simple to add. However, doing a good job of laying out an arbityrary graph is very much a research problem, although some inroads have been made. One approach we will be taking is to allow the user to layout the graph and to have the system work from there.

Discussion

Lynn Carter (GenRad, USA):

The title of this session was programming-in-the-small, coined by DeRemer and Kron
in 1975. They discussed the issues of, and the differences between, programming-in-
the-small (PITS) and programming-in-the-large (PITL). We've heard several
discussions today about a spectrum of tools, from individual tools to a collection
of tools ("a gardener"), and we've touched on several issues of PITS. Many of these
tools are for beginners. I question whether many of these tools are appropriate for
both the more experienced and the more senior programmers. Moreover, as Mr. Cordy
commented to me, when one considers that 70-80% of the software life cycle cost
will be in maintenance, why are we spending so much time on program development and
program coding? I assert that many PITS issues should help understanding programs-
in-the-small, as a means of reusing and applying them toward improving further
problem solving. In raising this gauntlet, I would like to hear your comments.

Mary Shaw (Carnegie Mellon Univ., USA):

In George Polya's book called, "How To Solve It", he asked the question of
presentation which I'd like to raise in response to Carters'. Polya discusses the
difference between diagrams and proofs and points out that they both have a role in
problem solving. His particular domain is problem solving in mathematics. The
diagrams explain and explore intuitions. The proofs are used after the intuitions
are raised, both for convincing yourself and for convincing others. Polya argues
that proofs and diagrams have complementary roles in mathematics. The complementary
roles arise not from their applicability to different problems, but rather in their
ability to map different kinds of relations between human beings and relevant
aspects of mathematics.

I will pose a question to all those who spoke this morning. You presented a number
of different ways for programmers to interact with programs. Some are textual and
some are structural. The structures may be based on language syntax or programmer
input and some are pictorial. I'd like to hear how those systems can support
complementary views of the same program to be used at different points in program
development, or for different purposes in understanding the programs.

Reidar Conradi (Norw. Inst. of Tech., NOR):

I would like to add to Mary Shaw's comment because the way you develop a program is
not the way you describe it afterwards, e.g., mathematical theorems in textbooks
and articles are just a big hoax. They are reordered semantically after years of
work, but do not show the misunderstandings, blind alleys, etc., during the
original development. We should develop tools that map our continuous struggle with
a subject which may be represented as diagrams, English text, computer programs or
mathematical formulaes. What kind of tools do we need to assist our amorphous mass
of initial thought to become clear and sequential?

Lynn Carter (GenRad, USA):

There are text editing systems where you detect the differences between the initial
and final file as opposed to keeping track of every false start like in the VMS/VAX
editor. I question whether explaining a system to someone by showing all the blind
alleys, keystroke by keystroke, is really the most effective use of that person's
time. Furthermore, those blind alleys are often an issue of ego and personal
misunderstandings, and thus irrelevant to others.

Robert Schwanke (Siemens, USA):

Organizing design information _during_ design does indeed seem to be a desperate
task. However, I see hope of achieving it by combining three ingredients:

- Mark Moriconi's approach allows us to handle "light semantics" (analogous to
  light beer). We can say _some things_ about a program without having to say
  everything.

- Gregor Snelting's resolution techniques allow us to combine fragments of
  information and discover inconsistencies.

- Accepting inconsistency as a way of life, allows us to represent incomplete
  and inconsistent designs.

Our design tools should accept inconsistent designs routinely, then help us
identify and _analyze_ inconsistencies and present _alternative_ ways of eliminating
them.

Lynn Carter (GenRad, USA):

Excellent point. This is a frequent issue in the UNIX world, where someone asserts
that UNIX already represents the ultimate tool-box. I assert that UNIX is a long
way from being what I want, but it's at least a first step as compared to the more
simple machines and environments before UNIX came along. I'd like to point out that
we saw in Mr. Hallsteinsen's talk that programs execute, run, and have problems. I
find that particularly interesting because we spend more time in that portion of
the process. I'm curious if the more enhanced man-machine interfaces might aid our
debugging or reusability process. Do others wish to comment on this?

Kristen Rekdal (URD, NOR):

On maintenance costs: a very important aspect of the tools is how they can ensure
consistency after changes. Given one million lines of code and a change of one
little comma, the greatest gain is for the tool to assure that this modification
had the intended impact. In terms of total productivity the gain can not be
achieved because the original implementation process has some fundamental
limitations; our ability to create and organize ideas. It is very difficult to
automate this, but doing things over again is what computers are good for. I think
we can gain a lot by focusing more of the tool functions on this repetition process
rather than trying to automate original thinking.

Lynn Carter (GenRad, USA):

If we could start with a perfect tool environment to begin with, and then build the program given this environment, the world would be a lovely place. But the reality is that we have millions of lines of code that have been implemented without the aid of these tools. How do we address the maintenance of these systems and what kinds of tools can we build today to help us solve the problems of already <u>existing programs</u>?

Johannes Grande (MCC, USA):

Apparently, the speakers are not concerned about the problem they are trying to solve. That leads me to wonder if we are focusing too much on our favorite technology instead of understanding what PITS is. Is there a theory of PITS? What is good programming? What is good program design?

Lynn Carter (GenRad, USA):

The PITS phrase came out in contrast to PITL. The assertion is that there is some fundamental difference between how one programs-in-the-large vs. how one programs-in-the-small. A great deal of effort in the sixties and the early seventies was spent on structured programming: how to get rid of GOTO and similar small-scale issues. These techniques were developed as an answer to the "software crisis" (coined in 1968). The term PITS does not imply that we have nailed down all its theoretical ramifications, but rather that we have divided the problem of building systems into two parts. The first part is thinking of a well-defined problem and coming up with a solution that translates into an executable program. The second part is the more mind-boggling issue of a system which is much too large for anyone's mind to comprehend, and how one deals with such complexity. Is this a fair assessment of the distinction between the two phrases?

Johannes Grande (MCC, USA):

I don't think the perfect tool would help if you don't understand what programming is all about.

James Cordy (Queens Univ., CAN):

To me, the problem of PITL is, as Carter said, can we manage something that no single person can truly understand? For me, the distinction about PITS is that we assume that small things (algorithms, programs) can be understood by an individual programmer. The real problem about tools and maintenance is how to assist a single person to understand a given algorithm and program; how it works and how it can be modified.

Lynn Carter (GenRad, USA):

A piece of code may be ten, twenty, or thirty lines long. A formal specification of
that might be thirty or forty pages long if you fully specify all the
characteristics. Which would you rather read, the code or its specification? The
question is, what is it that you are looking for?

Mary Shaw (Carnegie Mellon Univ., USA):

I must rise in response to that comment. If indeed a full and complete
specification of a thirty line code segment is thirty pages then I believe the
specification must include additional information about many aspects of the
program. Just as it was necessary in the late sixties and early seventies to find
ways to impose structure on programs in order to understand them, we must impose
structure on specifications. The assumably thirty pages of specification must
surely break down into 30-40 sections of 10-20 line descriptions of particular
properties of the program; some lines about what the program computes, about how
fast it is, about its memory consumption, about its reliability, about the
assumptions it makes, and about its underlying environment, and sometimes to lock
all of these fragments together into a homogeneous and coherent document.

David Levine (Intermetrics, USA):

I think Mary's and Reidar's comments about proofs are very good. You know something
about the structure and even though you think about it one way you write it down
another, and it's not surprising to the reader. Somehow the reader can make that
leap back. I disagree with Carter, in that maintenance people desperately need
blind alleys, e.g., to explain why I'm adding 1 here instead of subtracting 1.

Something is different in the software discipline, and let me give an example. If
you look at this room, it's constructed in a fairly traditional architectural way.
If an architect were to make a modification, like to put in a modern window,
instead of the one with a crossbar, he could do that change with perfect security
because that beam across the three-meter level is not a structural member. Just
think about how many of our programs would collapse completely because it turned
out that the major electrical feed (laughter) had been brought through such a beam.
The difference is so striking that there must be something lurking.

Lynn Carter (GenRad, USA):

In response I don't assert that none of those false starts should be recorded. On
the other hand, there needs to be some way to hide the obvious embarrasing blunders
from those that are enlightening and educational. We want to tell people about our
program, not about our stupidity.

Bernard Lang (INRIA, FRA):

On the analogy between programs and proofs: Actually, a program is a proof, if you
think just of the functionality of the program, i.e., the specification of the
program is the theorem you are proving. So, my first comment is that when your
specification is longer than your program then your theorem is longer than the
proof. If I see that in a math book, I'm worried.

The second point concerns the use of drawings which can help us to understand and explain abstract entities (intuition). But drawings are not precise enough. It's very rare even in a math book, that drawings are completely accurate. Similarly you cannot reflect all the details of your program in the drawings that helped you program, though I fully agree that having good mechanisms for connections between drawings and the programs may be helpful. When I was a student 15 years ago people were told to use flow charts when writing programs in-the-small. Drawing flow charts, at least for Ph.D. students, is no longer required, because we have got good programming languages and other means to express programming details. So we don't need drawings for PITS any longer, but we do have them for PITL, e.g., with SADT and some of the tools presented this morning. I'm wondering whether the reason for this is simply that we lack the proper concepts for PITL. Maybe when we have proper concepts then we won't need drawings as much as we do now.

Lynn Carter (GenRad, USA):

I would like to comment about the size of program vs. the size of specification. Unlike mathematicians, most programmers (at least practitioners) tend not to develop their own notation. Therefore, they use other people's notation which is probably highly inappropriate for specifying algorithms and related things. Mathematicians invariably create specifications that are very short and totally incomprehensible if you jump into the middle of a mathematical paper. But your points are very well made.

Per Holager (ELAB-SINTEF, NOR):

I would like to emphasize what Lang said, that we do have lots of nice notations for PITL, but we usually call them design languages. Like SADT and other static descriptions, Structured Design Language (SDL) is one such supported by the CCITT. It supports data structure and interface notations of various sorts. So there are indeed languages for PITL.

Ian Thomas (BULL, FRA):

I would like to go back to the comment on debugging and try to integrate that with some other aspects of the discussion. One starts to debug because there is some mismatch between the actual and projected behavior of a program. The difficulty for the maintenance programmer is then to relate the mechanism used to establish the behavior against the actual behavior. That is, to determine the cause of the mismatch by looking at the mechanism. I suggest that there is a difference between PITS and PITL because the characteristics of the mapping between behavior and mechanism are different in PITS and in PITL, because a description of the mechanism in PITS is very different from the one in PITL. For instance, programming languages are used very differently, or used perhaps not at all in design langauges.

I suggest that Steven Reiss' comment about usefulness is that this permits the programmer to establish the precise mapping between behavior and mechanism. Graphics is a good way of describing such a mapping. I also agree with Taglia that given a hypothesis, one should first convince oneself that it is true before proving it. Graphical support can convince or support oneself that a given hypothesis is actually going to do the job. However, that's different from actually sitting down and proving it rigorously.

Steven Muchnick (SUN Microsystems, USA):

A couple of points. The first one is adressed to Lang and Carter. We do in fact invent our own notations for what we do. That's what subroutines are, that's what abstract data types are, etc.. Second, the question of not showing our false starts. I would suggest there are situations where it is very valuable to show our false starts, namely where we are trying to teach people how to do something. We learn as much from negative examples as from positive ones in almost everything we do.

Lynn Carter (GenRad, USA):

My comment is, yes, we're familiar with code abstraction, but when it comes to specifications, we don't have a similar notation and mechanism for modularization. This is why specifications tend to be bulky. Secondly, we tend to be constructive in our program developments, and when we're not sure what the important characteristics are, we tend to overspecify.

James Cordy (Queens Univ., CAN):

It's about tracking and documenting false starts and blind alleys during system development. I'm convinced that we _must_ do so. Just think of a new person who joins a project and has this brilliant idea about how it can be restructured to make it more efficient. He begins to work on it and then discovers that three years ago someone already had that idea, but it failed miserably. Such a waste of time is certainly worth documenting.

Mary Shaw (Carnegie Mellon Univ., USA):

I want to reply to James Cordy and those who raised the question. When there is significant false track on a piece of software development, the information about that false track needs to be reported. But I do not believe that the development history of the false track, and the retrenching and the recovering from it, is the appropriate way to report that information. I believe the documentation should include the _reasons_ for design decisions like analyses of cost rates which might explain why some other line of development had failed. That is, we must abstract from the experience of going down the wrong path and incorporate this into the design specification of the system.

Andy Rudmik (GTE Comm. Syst., USA):

I have a critical comment and then a question on different aspects of syntax-directed editors. The critical comment is that there seems to be a preoccupation or desire to build tools that allow one to edit and manipulate programs. There was a comment that a fundamental problem is that programs are in an inconsistent or incomplete state. My concern in pulling these two different plots together, is that maybe we should be more preoccupied with coming up with ways of representing and modelling the development process - whether it's program or engineering design. Maybe the syntax-directed editor is irrelevant. What is really important, including graphics and so on, is the underlying model and how we can reason about incomplete and inconsistent components. I am missing that aspect because we focus so much on the tool itself.

Reidar Conradi (Norw. Inst. of Tech., NOR):

Some discussion about tracking blind alleys and so on was due to a misinterpretation of my previous comment. My worry is that I have programs in different stages of development. The so-called waterfall model requires me to have everything specified in the beginning and then the rest comes more or less in a sequence. In contrast, I want a tool that allows me to have programs consisting of fragments in different stages of development. I'm usually working in different contexts at the same time, but this diversification is not reflected in any common programming tools.

On syntax-directed editors - they are wonderful devices if they can square out some of the pragmatical things that tend to strait jacket the advanced users. Indeed, most of these editors are not used by the authors themselves, maybe with the exception of Bernard Lang's Mentor. I like the connection to PITL because my problem in editing programs is not the placement of semicolons, but rather to see where a given symbol is defined or used. That is, I want to see different contexts at the same time and query at different levels. In short, I want more integration with other tools, and given this, I think a syntax-directed editor can be very useful.

Roy Campbell (Univ. Illinois, USA):

I think from various conversations that the discussion seems to be about design and questions of representing the design. Using graphics to represent design is obviously a very powerful idea. One could think of an executable sequence of abstract design steps or a set of declarations that generate a program. Design abstractions would include procedures that create specific designs. One might use an ACM published algorithm and use it to derive the specific algorithm in a favorite programming language. Such a design language would be very appropriate for PITS, allowing designs to be mapped, repeatably, into specific programming languages.

Stefan Jähnichen (GMD, FRG):

Ten years ago the problem was that productivity should be improved. Looking nowadays at the results in the programming environment, it seems to be as if we have asked: what was the problem? In my opinion it's still the productivity we should focus on and this means that we must be able to reuse development in order to avoid the elapsed time with doing program design. We should search for means to record and reuse developments.

Gerhard Goos (GMD, FRG):

I will continue Rudmik's remark on syntax- or semantic-directed editors being primarily concerned with, or should be concerned with, modelling problems instead of giving the syntax. I will emphasize that in creating models, we also create or take existing concepts and relate them to each other.

If we take concepts - we first must have some, and secondly, we should be able to communicate them to others. Communication between people could take place on the semantic or structural level. All syntax try to communicate concepts by writing down some structure which somebody else can recognize meaningfully. Syntax-directed editors are sometimes concerned too much with syntactic sugar. We should see that such editing means manipulating concepts, relating them to each other, and doing that in a structure-oriented way. A pertinent question is, to what extent do you feel your system supports this kind of modelling? Or rather, to what extent do you only handle syntactic sugar on the surface?

Robert Schwanke (Siemens, USA):

Structure editors are valuable because they manipulate structured information. Programs are one such type of structured information. Design information could be another. However, they must be fast to be useful. James Brady presented an excellent paper in the 1985 IEEE Workstations conference, describing the profound effect of system response time on productivity. In five separate experiments he observed that as the response time of a CAD tool dropped below 1 second, the user's productivity and quality increased much more rapidly than would be explained by the time savings alone. So, whatever we do, we must be sure that our structure editors are fast.

Brady's paper highlights another aspect of tool design: the kind of task being supported. His experiments all dealt with highly structured creative tasks, such as programming and circuit layout. His results did not apply to unstructured tasks, such as software system design. It's quite possible that good tools will not increase productivity on these tasks at all! And if they should slow the designer down, they simply won't be used.

Steven Reiss (Brown Univ., USA):

Many people want to use more graphics in their work. They may not need it as a design vehicle, but rather to express information along other dimensions than you normally get. In a graphical representation you don't get text, you get color and diagrams. Color can give you an extra dimension of positional information. Connectivity information is another dimension of information. Many people will do design in terms of pictures and think about the design this way.

Then on the difference between pictures and proofs, and how programs correspond to proofs. In that case the pictures are examples and are just as important as the programs themselves. We have underway at Brown - and there have been numerous other projects - programming by demonstration and with examples. That is, you use the examples as sort of a metaphore for showing what you want your program to do. Then you have to fill in the concrete details. We also use examples extensively during program testing.

Incompleteness and inconsistency in language editors is a challenging one. Most of my design pictures are just loose illustrations. I have pictures of various spots with lines between them. What those lines mean is very much up in the air; sort of informal. A current project at Brown is trying to derive a language that captures the informality in the design process.

On graphics for debugging - Interesting work has been done by several people, notably Brown and Sedgewick at Brown with the BALSA system, and Myers with INCENSE for XEROX's CEDAR. Moreover GARDEN is designed to provide dynamic graphics while debugging the program. In maintenance of programs we have to worry about all the existing versions. If we can develop a good way of constructing programs in the future, there will be much more code developed over the next ten years than over the past twenty years. However, we cannot wait for ultimate software technology; we must start using new tools today.

Bernard Lang mentioned he looked at drawings as an appropriate actual representation, but that the mechanism is different for PITS and PITL. I think that drawings can be used in PITS, it's just how you want to think about PITS. For data flow programming, or for programming for a data flow machine, most people do that graphically. Just because "textual" happens to be the right way for a Von Neumann machine, it may not be the only way for all programming, or the only mechanism you can use in PITS.

Lynn Carter (GenRad, USA):

In my opinion maybe too much code has already been written and we should be focusing on reuse as opposed to generating even more mountains of code!

Gregor Snelting (Tech. Univ. Darmstadt, FRG):

First, it's not true that Bernard Lang is the only one who uses his own system (general laughter), we actually do the same thing.

Then on Schwanke's remark on handling incomplete and inconsistent programs. PSG does exactly that. We can handle incomplete program fragments and, as I said this morning, we can also handle semantically inconsistent programs.

Then, the question by Carter about debugging. PSG also generates an interactive language to assist debugging based on a denotational semantics specification of the language, and this also uses the same user interface as the rest of the system.

Gerhard Goos asked: Does the system only support syntactic sugar or does it have more detailed knowledge of programs? We are especially proud of our semantic analysis with PSG, not of the syntactic sugar machinery. What we try to implement are inference systems which can make deductions about properties of programs.

Gerhard Goos (GMD,FRG):

Your semantics covers too primitive concepts.

Gregor Snelting (Tech. Univ. Darmstadt, FRG):

I'm not so sure about that. What we can do in PSG is static semantics, not more.

On Reiss' point on programming with pictures - Pictures can be a very helpful tool, but I must agree with Bernard Lang; often they are too imprecise. One should be careful to rely on pictures only.

Lynn Carter, (GenRad, USA):

You must be careful with pictures because their information content is informal and imprecise and they may rely heavily on the habits of the person drawing the picture.

Dag Wanvik (RUNIT, NOR):

I want to raise this issue of programmability touched upon both by Mr. Hallsteinsen and Mr. Lang. It seems to me that much of the reason for the success of the UNIX system is that it allows the programmers to invent proper tools by combining different ones and there's usually a programmable interface to the tools. In contrast, many tools that offer syntactic help and human interfaces have often failed to provide professional programmers with a programmable interface. I want a programmable interface so that I can have the tools, e.g., to do combinations of things in repetition. Therefore, I challenge you, do you have programmable interfaces, and what is their proper role?

Ralf Kneuper (Univ. Manchester, UK):

It was said earlier that productivity is the main problem in software development and I would not quite agree with that. I think <u>correctness</u> is much more important and we haven't really done much with that. Correctness has two sides: a) We want to know exactly what the program is supposed to do, i.e., we need to get the requirements right. b) we have to verify that the final system meets these requirements. For that reason, I think we should talk more about verification of programs and discuss Moriconi's talk.

Mark Moriconi (SRI International, USA):

On the use of graphics in programming environments: I mentioned that we use graphics just to denote various formal properties of programs. I wasn't arguing that it's good for everything. It turns out that many details of the program representation get more complicated than the overall picture itself.

Atomic objects in our world are on the procedural or design level. We want to prevent people from drawing flowcharts and data flow diagrams down to the statement level. The layout gets very complicated and I personally think in terms of text at that low level.

My third point regards Bernard Lang's comment on the size of a program vs. its specification. I don't see any reason to believe that the specification should be any smaller than the program. That would be nice, but a specification describes many different descriptions of a computation. The question is: Is one more perspicuous than the other? I think that's the real issue; not whether the specification is one line long and the program thirty lines, or whatever. So I think we're partly talking about the wrong issue.

Lynn Carter (GenRad, USA):

In some ways one can view certain aspects of the specification as being more comprehensive than the code. Given certain specifications you can deduce the code; given the code you can deduce some of the specifications. Maybe with a knowledge-based system we can assert specifications and let the code be generated for us?

Mark Moriconi (SRI International, USA):

That may be true, but if specifications are not small then they're not good specifications!

Steven Reiss (Brown Univ., USA):

I want to answer the comment by the people who said that pictures are too imprecise. There are two ways of looking at pictures; one is pictures as examples. The second way adopted by us, is pictures as languages with formal semantics: Petri nets, finite state automata, context-free grammar graphs as in the Pascal report, various data flow notations, tree transformation examples, flow charts, etc.. Moriconi's PegaSys is a formal graphical language in that sense, as well as the Boxer language and numerous other languages. These are real languages that also have a pictorial representation. So the pictures do have meaning; they are precise.

Bernard Lang (INRIA, FRA):

Specifications have two aspects: functionality and pragmatics. The pragmatics deals with implementational details, costs, etc., and their specification may be verbose. However, I insist that the ideal functional specification should be small if we knew how to write it. A large specification means that somehow you have not abstracted your program well. A large specification is likely to contain implementation decisions that should not be part of it.

Further, I do mean that specifications are theorems and that programs are proofs. Technically, it's not just an analogy. We talk about pictures and programmability. I've said that I'm for programmability and against drawings and I'll stick to that image. Pictures are useful, but very often the systems are so complex that pictures can no longer express all the interesting properties.

Another aspect concerns debugging. It's true that debugging with pictures is useful. I have had experience with a lot of programmers using a LISP debugger. It can print out any relevant data, but the output is unreadable because it prints out a list which is not the abstract object I had in mind. The problem is that the user is forced to supply the correct presentation. Most users don't do that, because it's a substantial overhead. So there is a "social" or educational problem to be solved.

Concerning programmability, are syntax-directed editors just syntactic sugar or do we want tools that address the semantic structure of both the data and the programs? My focus on programmability is precisely this: syntax is easy to define formally and to mechanize. Programmability is one way of being able to program in the system. Semantic tools work in semantic terms. This exists in Mentor's programming language, and as action routines in Gandalf. The ideal solution would be a specification language from which we can generate semantic tools. Only future research can give us such tools.

SunPro

Engineering a Practical Program Development Environment

Evan Adams, Wayne Gramlich, Steven S. Muchnick & Soren Tirfing

Sun Microsystems, Inc.
2550 Garcia Avenue
Mountain View, CA 94043 USA

20 May 1986

1. Introduction

At Sun Microsystems we are engaged in a long-term project called SunPro[1] which is intended to dramatically improve the programming environment available to software developers working in C, Fortran 77 and Pascal on Sun Workstations. The concerns we are addressing span the range of single- and multiple-programmer issues, from improved debugging, program browsing, and better integration of editing, compiling and debugging, to source code version control, configuration management, and release building. The project has both research and engineering components, in that some of the technologies being utilized have already been demonstrated to be effective, while others are significantly more speculative. This paper provides examples of the relatively short-term engineering efforts intended to provide a better integrated multi-language environment for the individual programmer and to improve version control and configuration management, while it also touches on the research efforts in both these areas.

The SunPro project started with a foundation of powerful tools available on Sun workstations: 4.2 BSD UNIX[2] with its standard utilities, Sun's C, Fortran 77, and Pascal compilers, the *vi* and EMACS editors, the *dbx* symbolic debugger, *make*, the Source Code Control System *sccs* and so on. While these tools provided a powerful programming environment in themselves, they lacked integration, provided no common interaction paradigm, took little advantage of the workstation's bit-mapped display and mouse, and were less capable and friendly overall than they ought to be. Succinctly, they did a reasonable job of meeting the needs of software developers of the early 1980's, but provided significantly less than is now possible. Our attack on quickly improving the programming environment, thus, has three major thrusts: (1) to increase the power and utility of existing tools, (2) to better integrate existing tools with each other, and (3) to create better user interfaces by making effective use of windows and the mouse. We discuss below some examples which illustrate each of these three areas.

In parallel with the short-term efforts to improve the programming environment, SunPro includes two other activities. One is exploring, for the long term, the construction of a highly integrated editing, incremental compilation and debugging system for C, Fortran and Pascal, based as much as possible on our existing tools. The other is pursuing long-term, order-of-magnitude improvements in the area of version control and configuration management.

---

[1] SunPro is a trademark of Sun Microsystems.
[2] UNIX is a trademark of AT&T Bell Laboratories.

2. Dbxtool

Dbxtool is a window- and mouse-based interactive source-level debugger for programs written in (a mixture of) C, Pascal and Fortran which increases programmer productivity by extending the facilities of the *dbx* debugger in 4.2 BSD UNIX and improving the user interface through the use of SunView[3], the Sun Microsystems user interface toolkit. By using the mouse in place of the keyboard as the primary input mechanism, *dbxtool* eliminates the need to type variables, line numbers, breakpoints, and most commands. *Dbxtool*'s windows provide a view of the source code of the program being debugged and detailed information about the state of the program, thus affording two qualitatively different and reinforcing perspectives on the problem of debugging. *Dbxtool* has also been extended to make it a much more powerful debugging tool. The new capabilities include the ability to debug multiple-process programs, processes which are already running when the debugger is invoked, and the Sun Operating System kernel (derived from 4.2 BSD UNIX).

An invocation of *dbxtool* consists of five subwindows called (from the top down): the *status* window, *source* window, panel of *command* buttons, *command* dialogue window, and variable values *display* window (see Figure 2). The status window displays the file and line number range of the code in the source window and information about the current state of the debugging process. The source window usually displays the current locus of execution, though it can be moved under user control by scrolling or regular-expression string searching to any part of a source file (or to any other file). The buttons panel contains a series of buttons representing commands that can be invoked with the mouse. The command window provides a command dialogue area where the user can type commands and where the commands invoked from the buttons window are echoed. The variable values display window (gen-

Figure 1

```
cmdtool - /usr/local/tcsh
int subr( );

main( )
{
        enum palette {RED,YELLOW,BLUE};
        struct ex {
                int             i;
                char            *cp;
                int             (*func)();
                struct ex       *next;
        } ex;
        int i;
        enum palette            color;
        extern int              printf( );
        extern enum palette     brush( );

        color = YELLOW;
        for (i = 0; i < 10; i++) {
                ex.i = subr(i);
                ex.cp = "This is a string";
                ex.func = printf;
                i++;
                ex.next = &ex;
        }
}

subr(n)
int n;
{       int m;

        m = (n * (n + 1)) / 2;
        return m;
}
garuda 2 %
```

erally called the "display window") displays the values of selected variables and expressions whenever execution of the debuggee is suspended. The source, command and display windows all have scroll bars, so the user can easily move his focus of attention within the displayed material.

Commands are constructed by making a selection with the mouse and clicking (with the mouse) on a command button, or by typing the command from the keyboard. Five different selection interpretations are provided and the user is given the capability to bind commands and selection interpretations to command buttons displayed on the screen. Thus, for example, the default **print** command button uses the *expand* selection interpretation, so that the value of a variable may be printed by selecting as little as one character of its name in the source window and clicking the **print** button. In contrast, the **stop at** button uses the *line number* selection interpretation, so a breakpoint may be set at a line by selecting a single character anywhere within the line and clicking the **stop at** button.

Figures 1 through 7 trace an example of using *dbxtool* on a toy C program. In Figure 1[4], we see the program example.c and, at the right, the "no bugs" icon which represents the debugger. In Figure 2, the programmer has used the mouse to open *dbxtool* and typed **debug example** to cause the program to be loaded from the file example into the debugger. The code appears in the source window, with the point at which execution will begin near the top of the window. In Figure 3, the user has, again using only the mouse, placed two breakpoints in the code (indicated by the stop signs in the source window) and initiated execution of the program. Note that each command constructed with the mouse is

Figure 2

```
Dbxtool
Awaiting Execution
File Displayed:   ./example.c                                    Lines: 15-29

            for (i = 0; i < 10; i++) {
                    ex.i = subr(i);
                    ex.cp = "This is a string";
                    ex.color = RED;
                    ex.func = printf;
                    ex.next = &ex;
            }
        }

        subr(n)
        int n;
        {       int m;

            m = (n * (n + 1)) / 2;
     print    next    step   stop at   cont   stop in   redo     run
(dbxtool) debug example
Reading symbolic information...
Read 207 symbols
(dbxtool)
```

---

[3]SunVIEW is a trademark of Sun Microsystems.
[4]The other icons are a clock, *mailtool*, *filemerge* (see Section 4 below), a *commandtool* (a scrollable, editable shell window), and a performance meter.

echoed in the command dialogue window, making it possible to save and replay a transcript of commands. Upon encountering the first breakpoint, the debugger places an arrow at the line the program is stopped on. In Figure 4, the user has typed the command **button expand display**, causing another button to appear in the buttons window for the **display** command and associating the expand selection interpretation with it, as for the **print** command. He has then used the mouse to cause the structure ex to be shown in the display window each time execution of the program is interrupted, and advanced two lines in the program using the **next** button. Note that the display of ex shows each field in a format appropriate to its type (see declarations in Figure 1). In Figure 5, the user has used the **cont** button to continue execution of the program to the next breakpoint. Note that the displayed value of ex has been appropriately updated. In Figure 6, the user has opened the pop-up menu for the source window and selected "Start Editing". In Figure 7, he has changed RED to YELLOW, brought up the menu again and selected "Stop Editing" (which now appears in place of "Start Editing") and typed the **make** command. In response, *dbxtool* has invoked *make* on the description file in the current directory, which rebuilds the object file example from its source. The user then types **debug example** to reinitialize the debugger and can continue debugging.

A more detailed description of *dbxtool* and the improvements we have made to *dbx*, along with insight into their design and our plans for future development can be found in [AdaM85].

3. Incremental Linking & the Edit-Compile-Link-Debug Cycle

The length of the edit-compile-link-debug cycle has long been recognized as a major determiner of the productivity of software developers and of how a computer system feels to a developer. Within limits, the more responsive the system is, the more responsive and efficient the human becomes, since he is

Figure 3

```
Dbxtool
Stopped in File:  ./example.c                    Func: main        Line:  19
File Displayed:   ./example.c                                       Lines: 15-29

                  for (i = 0; i < 10; i++) {
                          ex.i = subr(i);
                          ex.cp = "This is a string";
                      →  ex.color = RED;
                          ex.func = printf;
                          ex.next = &ex;
                  }
          }

          subr(n)
          int n;
          {       int m;

                  m = (n * (n + 1)) / 2;
```

```
    print    next    step   stop at   cont   stop in   redo   run
```

```
Read 207 symbols
(dbxtool) stop at "example.c":19
(1) stop at "example.c":19
(dbxtool) stop at "example.c":21
(2) stop at "example.c":21
(dbxtool) run
Running: example
(dbxtool) ◆
```

less likely to be distracted by extraneous thoughts or activities [Brad85]. It has thus been a major goal in building programming environments to eliminate mental context switches between finding a bug, fixing it and finding the next one. Building a fully integrated programming system for a language like C, Fortran or Pascal which preserves the semantics of an existing compiler is a very large undertaking.

We have measured the time taken in compilation, linking and debugger initialization for a series of medium-sized programs and found that if an entire program is rebuilt, linking typically accounts for a minimum of about 30% and *dbxtool* initialization for about another 30%. Further, for large programs, if only a single module needs to be recompiled, these percentages dominate much more strongly. Thus, another of our short-term efforts has been to develop an incremental linker which, upon being presented an executable object program and a relocatable module which is a recompiled version of one already linked into the object program, replaces that module with the new one in the object program. For large programs, if no additional library procedures are used by the new version of the recompiled module, this process is very much faster than relinking the entire program. Referencing additional library routines slows the process down, of course, but still nowhere near as much as rebuilding the entire object. Combined with the ability to edit the source code in *dbxtool*, invoke the compiler from there and reinitialize the debugger state quickly, this goes a long way in the direction of shortening the debug cycle.

The user interface to the incremental linker consists of adding one option to the existing linker interface, the -q flag. According to whether a suitable object file already exists or not, specifying this option either causes an object file suitable for incremental linking to be built *ab initio* or relocatable modules newer than the existing object file to be linked into it in place of previous versions.

Figure 4

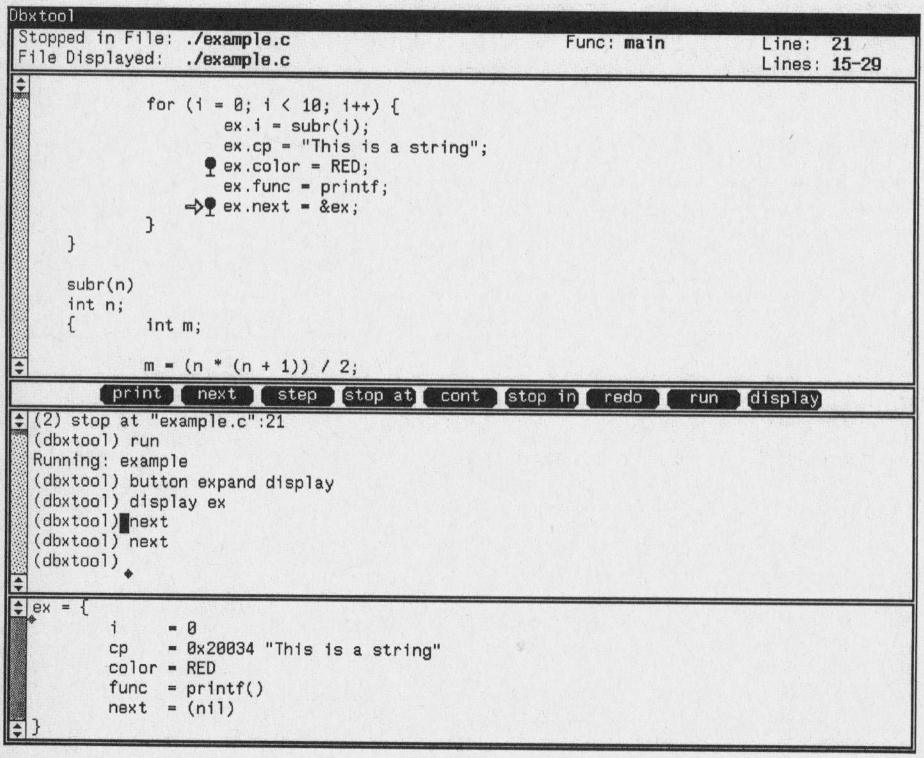

A prototype version of the incremental linker is currently available internally at Sun. While further work on it is expected to improve its performance, it is already a major improvement over the previous linker, as the following data show. The numbers in the table are for linking a large window-system program (20 relocatable object modules and five libraries searched, resulting in about 880K bytes of object code) and were collected on a Sun-3/75 with four Mbytes of main memory.

test case		time (sec.)
old linker		35
new linker	(used non-incrementally)	34
	(initial incremental link)	40
	(relink one module)	9
	(relink 13 modules)	15

Further tests using programs eight to ten times as large show performance in about the same ratios.

Previous efforts to speed up the edit-compile-link-debug cycle have included making our compilers faster and making *dbxtool* initialize itself significantly faster. Now the largest remaining component of the delay in getting back to debugging resulting from a simple change to a large program has been reduced by a factor of three by a relatively small engineering effort. Our next step in this direction will shift attention back to *dbxtool*, namely to lazy reading of the debugging symbol table. It has been observed that in most debugging sessions, especially on large programs, only a tiny fraction of the symbols are ever used [Brue85] and that reading all of them dominates the time necessary to load the program and initialize the debugger. Thus we are looking at reading only the global symbols during initial-

Figure 5

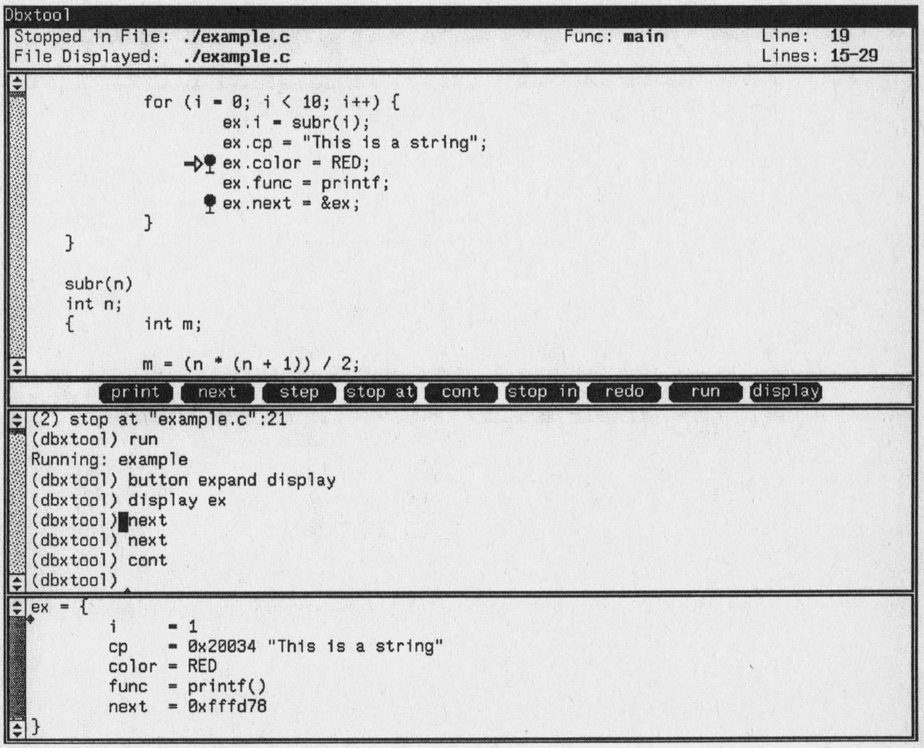

ization and others as needed during debugging. The measurements mentioned above also show that about 80% of the compilation time is typically spent in the C preprocessor (which we use as a macro and include processor for C, Fortran and Pascal) and the assembler, so they will be candidates for further performance improvement.

4. File Merging

It is frequently the case that several programmers are required to work on the same code at once, usually to maintain and enhance it. They generally will not all work on the same copy of the code, since chaos would result. Instead, they make separate copies, make their changes, and then must merge the results back together. Occasionally this is easy, when each developer's changes are to a different part of the code; generally, however, it is much harder. *Filemerge* is a tool which eases code merging by providing a combination of textual and graphical display of the parts of the code which have been changed. In actuality, it is a window interface to the UNIX user's traditional tool for finding differences in code, the *diff* utility, plus facilities which do some of the simpler merges automatically. The current version (see Figure 8) divides the window into six subwindows containing (across the top row in the figure) a control panel, a slider and two arrows, and instructions and other feedback from the tool to the user, and (across the bottom row) views of the two source files being compared, separated by a scrollbar and items which the user can invoke to control merging of individual differences. In the figure, the lower right window shows the program example.c used above in the discussion of *dbxtool* and the lower left one shows a slightly modified version. Each difference is highlighted with a combination of shading and lines across the code, and the items in the middle column can be used to merge changes (or exclude them) from either side to the other. In addition, the "Automerge" button can be used to cause differences in the two files which do not overlap other differences to be applied to both sides. If

Figure 6

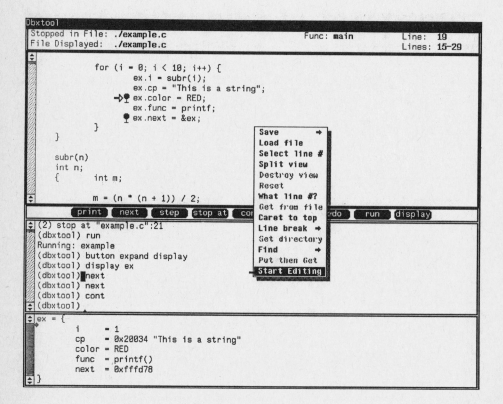

automerging has been selected, the button changes to "Unautomerge", which can be used to undo differences which were merged automatically. "Automerge" and "Unautomerge" ignore any differences which have been resolved by hand. The up and down arrows can be used to scroll to the next or previous difference and the slider to reallocate horizontal display space between the source text subwindows, so that one can view the ends of long lines without wasting space for them in general.

While *filemerge* does not attempt to deal with the semantic issues involved in code merging, experience with the prototype version suggests that the combination of simple graphical feedback, textual display of program versions, the ability to easily or automatically select desired changes to be merged, and editing of the versions are in themselves a powerful aid to code merging.

5. Program Browsing

The major problem faced by a programmer asked to modify or maintain a program with which he is unfamiliar is conceptualizing what the program does and how it does it. Cross-reference utilities have long provided significant help in this direction. However, they are generally run in batch mode and result in bulky listings which one must peruse by hand, or large files on which one must use an editor to navigate among the parts of the program and the cross reference. One can greatly increase their utility by providing a more effective user interface.

We are looking at creating a C program browser by developing such a user interface for an internally developed C cross referencer. It would provide multiple windows on the source code and such browsing activities as access to symbol declarations and uses via the mouse. Browsers for Fortran 77 and Pascal would follow, and later incorporation of data flow analysis information [MucJ81] collected by our global optimizer [Much86] into the browsing capabilities.

Figure 7

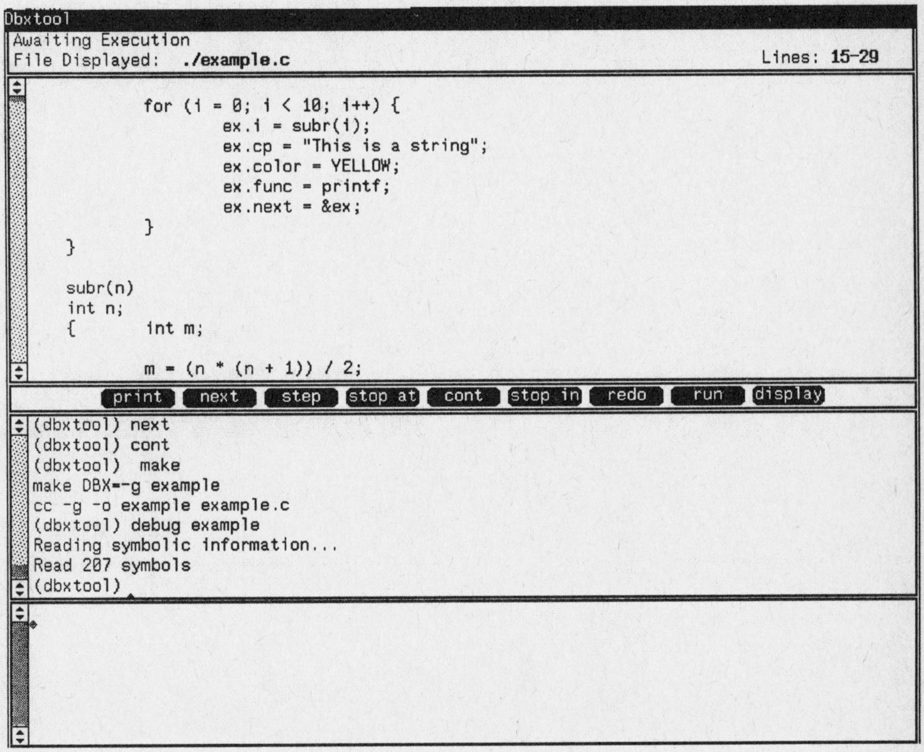

It is expected that one will be able to get answers to questions such as

- In what routine (in this Pascal program) is variable `Simulation_Type` declared?
- What places (in this Fortran program) branch to label 1305?
- What routines (in this C program) call `malloc`?
- Is the identifier `symtabrecord` ever used in this (mixed C and Fortran) program?

The browser's user interface would consist of several windows displaying source text, a control panel, a message window and so on. Highlighting would be used in the source windows to point out the items of current interest.

6. Enhanced Configuration Management

Our current configuration management tool is the UNIX system's *make* utility, which can be used to remake an object version of a program in response to changes in source files.[6] While *make* is very useful, it only goes halfway in solving the configuration management problem. It requires the programmer to build and maintain the description file, so that it can easily become out-of-date with no indication that it is. It relies entirely on file modification times to determine whether a component needs to be remade, so that changing the command sequence by which a file is built does not cause it to be remade unless

Figure 8

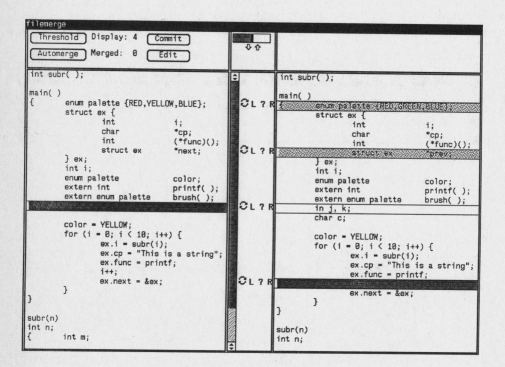

---

[6]Actually, *make* knows very little that is specific to compiling or linking, which is a source of both its strengths and its weaknesses. It is a weakness in that its criteria for remaking an object are not fine-grained enough, and a strength in that as a result of its ignorance it can be used for other purposes, such as rebuilding a document from changed text.

one of its source files is also touched, and inessential changes to source files (e.g. to comments) cause object files to be remade needlessly.

We have solved the first two of these problems by introducing the notions of *automatic dependency management* and *command consistency*. Automatic dependency management causes *make*'s header file dependency information for a project to be built and maintained automatically. Command consistency checks whether the command sequence used to build a file has changed since it was last used and, if so, causes it to be remade as if one of the sources has changed. This is achieved by cooperation between *make* and the C preprocessor *cpp* in maintaining a hidden file containing dependencies and commands in the format of a *make* description file.

Solving the problem of inessential rebuilding, unfortunately, awaits tools which are more knowledgeable of language syntax.

7. Flexible Compilation Environment and Cross Compilation

A problem frequently encountered by systems programmers is that they must build and test new versions of tools whose current versions are integral parts of their development environment. A similar problem for software developers in general is the need to deal with multiple versions of source code or source code from which multiple versions of the object program are built for different architectures. Cross compilation grows increasingly important as institutions build larger and larger networks of heterogeneous systems sharing information via protocols such as Sun's NFS (Network File System).

The flexible compilation environment provides a way for the developer to specify *virtual roots*, which are alternate directory paths to be used when searching for header files and libraries. Integrating this facility with utilities such as *make*, the C preprocessor and the linker makes it much easier to solve these problems. The version test problem is solved by specifying a virtual root that provides access to the system components to be used in building the new ones. Cross compilation can be done by providing access to the appropriate header files, libraries and executable programs for each target architecture via a distinct virtual root.

8. Conclusions

While each of the efforts described above significantly improves some aspect of the programming environment on Sun workstations, it is obvious that today's technology allows us to go further. Thus, in parallel with these short-term and comparatively easy but effective improvements, we continue to explore technologies which are expected to produce larger gains but which are much more expensive to achieve. These include fine-grained incremental compilation integrated with editing and debugging, as exemplified by Fritzson's DICE system [Frit84], and an effort to better integrate version control, configuration management, release building and bug tracking more tightly with each other and with an underlying database.

In general, our approach has followed two paths: 1) to identify areas where either major functionality was lacking or where a relatively small effort could result in large gains and to pursue hard-headed engineering solutions to such problems, and 2) to invest in research and follow others' research designed to provide longer-term solutions to larger needs. It is clear from our experience that the first path has paid off; whether the second will succeed as handsomely remains to be seen.

Acknowledgements

We thank Azad Bolour, Peter Fritzson, Richard Probst, and Warren Teitelman for their past and current efforts on the SunPro Project and for their helpful comments on this paper.

References

[AdaM85] Adams, E. & S.S. Muchnick. Dbxtool: A Window-Based Symbolic Debugger for Sun Workstations, *Proc. of the 1985 Summer USENIX Conf.*, Portland, OR, June 1985, pp. 213 - 227. A revised version will appear in **Software—Practice & Experience.**

[Brad85] Brady, J.T. A Theory of Productivity in the Creative Process, *Proc. of the First Intl. Conf. on Computer Workstations*, San Jose, CA, Nov. 1985, pp. 70 - 79.

[Brue85] Bruegge, B. *Adaptability and Portability of Symbolic Debuggers*, Ph.D. thesis, Tech. Rept. CMU-CS-85-174, Dept. of Comp. Sci., Carnegie-Mellon Univ., Sept. 1985.

[Frit84] Fritzson, P. *Towards a Distributed Programming Environment Based on Incremental Compilation*, Diss. No. 109, Dept. of Comp. Sci., Linkoping Univ., Linkoping, Sweden, 1984.

[Much86] Muchnick, S.S. Here Are (Some of) the Optimizing Compilers, *SIGPLAN Notices*, Vol. 21, No. 2, February 1986, pp. 1 - 15.

[MucJ81] Muchnick, S.S. & N.D. Jones (eds.) **Program Flow Analysis: Theory and Applications,** Prentice-Hall, Englewood Cliffs, NJ, 1981.

INFORMATION STRUCTURING FOR
SOFTWARE ENVIRONMENTS

Jeremy H. C. Kuo
Kevin J. Leslie
Michael D. Maggio
Barbara G. Moore
Hai-Chen Tu

Computer Science Laboratory
GTE Laboratories Incorporated
Waltham, Massachusetts 02254

Abstract

A major issue in the development of software engineering environments is the structuring of software information - both product and process information produced during the entire software life cycle. In existing environments, the database support for structuring such information is limited to the implementation phase; thus, tools in these environments are limited to supporting, at best, only 10 - 20% of the software development efforts.

This paper describes the research and prototyping activities of a software engineering environment project at the Computer Science Laboratory of GTE Laboratories Incorporated. The crux of our work is in the development of a software information base with a high degree of semantic expressiveness as the core of the environment. The project is developing a prototype software environment on state-of-the-art workstations.

1.0 INTRODUCTION

A major fundamental issue in the development of software engineering environments today is the structuring of enormous amounts of software information (both product and process information) to allow a variety of information processing activities during the entire software life cycle [Ridd86, DoD85]. It is fundamental because other issues (such as methodologies, tools integration and reusability) all rely on adequate support for information structuring. However, existing environments, based on file structures or on traditional database models (such as the relational model), offer only a limited solution.

Since software information tends to include many types of objects, and the relationships among these objects are also numerous and quite complex, the need arises for more sophisticated levels of data integration. More specifically, the following problems deserve immediate attention:

- Existing environments usually support only the implementation phase; therefore, information generated during the earlier phases of life cycle has to be manually processed.

- Existing environments usually do not structure and integrate the information produced in different phases of the life cycle; therefore, little support for traceability and accessibility is possible.

- Existing database models do not have sufficient expressive power to represent high level object types; therefore, information analysis can only be done at a very primitive level.

- Traditional database models lack support for capturing software process information; therefore, support for the software process after the first development cycle is only minimal.

To remedy these problems, it is necessary to develop a data model with sufficient expressive power to capture, structure, and integrate both the software product and process information. Furthermore, it is also necessary to develop schemas that allow us to access, analyze and process this information effectively. By capturing information structures with finer granularity and allowing the environment's other capabilities to interface with the database via higher level objects, it is possible to significantly improve the integration of the software environment.

This paper describes the system goals, design principles and prototyping activities of a software engineering environment project at GTE Laboratories. Initial investigations of this project started in 1984; the requirements analysis and high level design of the prototype software environment began in 1985. Presently, this project is in a prototype phase, and a prototype software environment is being implemented to run on Sun workstations under the Unix[TM][1] operating system. This paper focuses on the design and prototyping of the software information base (SIB) that is at the core of the environment.

1.1 RELATED WORK

During the last five years, a great deal of attention has been directed to the need for a comprehensive, reliable, and integrated software development environment to improve software productivity and quality. As a result, many organizations including DoD, MCC, SEI, Boeing, TRW, and others conducted

---

[1] Unix is a trademark of AT&T Bell Laboratories.

intensive efforts in researching and developing such a software environment. Although all of these efforts are still at the planning stage, the SEE [DoD85] of DoD, the Leonardo environment [Myer85] at MCC, and the Showcase environment [Barb85] at SEI have identified similar objectives for the information base issue. First level common objectives include data modeling, data capturing, and support for accessing the information base. A second level requires more integrated information base facilities to support distributed systems development, multiple languages, well-defined methodologies, reusability, and artificial intelligence assistance. Little technical information, however, is available in the literature on progress realized towards these longer term objectives.

A research project begun in 1984 at TRW [Pene85] investigated the requirements for a Project Master Database (PMDB). After conducting a domain analysis on their users, TRW researchers identified 31 objects, 220 attributes, and approximately 170 relationships. They concluded, however, that a data model of more expressive power than the Entity-Relationship-Attribute model was needed to enforce semantic constraints and data type consistency.

Some researchers who have adopted the term "knowledge base" to indicate the need for extensions to ERA technology also take a similar standpoint. Preferring the flexibility of expressing "constraints" in binary relations to the more rigid concept of "types," Meyer developed a "taxonomy of software relations and constraints" that is supported in his "knowledge base." [Meye85]

Horwitz and Teitelbaum [Horw85] showed three types of queries that could not be supported in a relational database. They also furnished several instances of such queries that are of high interest in software information retrieval. The solution they adopted combines the technologies of attribute grammars and relational databases. It has not, however, been applied to queries that address the higher levels of the software life cycle. We believe that the prototype software environment described here addresses, in a more comprehensive way, the issues that these researchers have identified.

1.2 SYSTEM GOALS

We are designing a prototype software environment to support multiple phases of the software life cycle. A fundamental goal is to enable the integration of tools appropriate to each phase of the life cycle, as well as to facilitate integration of information generated during different phases. The current stage of the prototype, however, focuses on support for the software design and implementation phases. We deem these two phases to be more critical for three reasons: they represent the phases that are most heavily involved with software development methods and their support tools; they offer the possibility of integrating tools to facilitate a higher degree of automatic support; and they constitute a central "hinge" at which issues of top-down and bottom-up system composition, traceability, and reusability converge.

1.3 SOFTWARE INFORMATION BASE GOALS

A primary objective of the software information base is to play a key role in the environment's integration framework, so that adding new tools will not affect existing tools and require only minimum modification to the tool interface.

The other two primary objectives of the software information base are to capture and structure "proper" software information, and to provide capabilities for a variety of tools to manipulate and process the information thus structured. In particular, the information base should be able to configure information in a variety of forms, such as flow diagrams, set relations, directed graphs, mappings, or even context-sensitive relationships. Some of this information can be easily captured in an entity-relationship model [Chen76]. The more complex forms, however, require a database model with more semantic expressiveness [Hamm81]. In the design of the prototype software environment, we enhance the entity-relationship model by borrowing some techniques from the attribute grammar model [Knut68] to handle semantic attributes.

2.0 OVERVIEW OF THE PROTOTYPE SOFTWARE ENVIRONMENT

The Prototype Software Environment (PSE) consists of the following four logical components:

1. User Interface - The PSE user interface is a highly interactive, graphical user interface that utilizes available packages like multi-window management, buttons, pop-up menus, and icons on workstations. This user interface also includes a general-purpose graphics display package. This display package is capable of displaying the following: icons, vertices, arcs, tables, graphs, flow-diagrams, trees, and index-charts.

2. Tool Set - This component consists of an open-ended software tool set. Each tool in this tool set either assists or automates software activities during the design or implementation phase. Since the objects in the information base have finer structures and richer semantics, the primary concern of each tool is how to "use" the information rather than how to define and maintain its own information structures. Also, the "piping" between tools can take place at higher level structures than files. Therefore, tools that introduce new "uses" of existing information structures can be easily integrated into PSE without affecting existing tools.

3. Software Information Base - The software information base provides capabilities for both tools and users to define, store, access, and process the software information. The SIB provides capabilities that allow the user to browse or query his/her project information.

4. Reusable Software Library - This library is designed to manage reusable software assets and sharable software modules. It is being designed as part of a related project (Software Reusability project) which is currently elaborating a classification scheme to identify domain-specific reusable components [Prie85].

In the rest of this paper, we focus our discussion on the software information base component. In section 3, we describe a data model for the SIB design, as well as the SIB's information structures and capabilities. A status report on the prototyping work of PSE is given in section 4, followed by the conclusions in section 5.

3.0 SOFTWARE INFORMATION BASE DESIGN

3.1 SIB DATA MODEL

In this section, we briefly specify the data model used for the SIB design. We first define the primitive data elements in the model, and then define a set of operations/mechanisms that allows us to construct more sophisticated information structures. Note that the term data element is loosely defined and used here to refer to anything representable in a computing system.

3.1.1 PRIMITIVE DATA ELEMENTS

Five primitives are defined in the data model: they are object, relationship, event, type, class, and attribute.

- Object: An object is a data element that contains a name and a value, and possibly a collection of attributes.

- Relationship: A relationship is a structural property that holds among a set of objects. This property can be specified as a structure among objects, or an assertion that all objects satisfy, or a combination of both. Examples of relationships will be given later.

- Event: An event is a happening that describes the behavior of a process (either manual or automatic) that affects some objects over a real or imagined time period. Examples of events will also be given later.

- Type: A type is an abstraction or template of a certain set of data elements (e.g., objects). Each element in the set, called an "instance," inherits the same structure from that abstraction, but may carry different values from the value domain that is also defined in the abstraction.

- Class: A class is a nameable collection of data elements (e.g., objects), where each element in the collection is called a member.

- Attribute: Like an object, an attribute has a name and a value. But, unlike an object, it has to be associated with another data element, and it is used to provide additional characteristics for the associated element.

Object is the most basic data element in the data model. The value of an object is so far unrestricted; that is why we chose to term it "object" instead of "entity" or "entity set" as in the entity-relationship model.

Relationship is a very important means to impose structures or associations over sets of objects. In this regard, more than one relationship can be defined over the same set of objects. For instance, two sorted employee lists, one ordered according to employee names and the other according to social security numbers, are two relationships over the same set of employees. From this example, one can see that we usually make use of the information stored in objects to define the structure (a sequence) and the property (ordering) of a relationship.

An event describes the behavior of certain operations on certain sets of objects. In general, the behavior is specified in terms of a set of primitive operations (e.g., reading and writing, comparing and updating the values of objects, etc.) that are connected with control constructs (e.g., sequence, branch, choice, iteration, etc.). The concept of event corresponds in a natural way to that of "procedure" or "subroutine" in any procedural design or programming language. Therefore, the mechanisms needed to specify events within a software product are already provided by the languages. The information needs to be captured in the SIB, however, including both the product information and the process information (such as development history and review process). Therefore, we found it desirable to include the concept of event in the data model.

Class is useful for managing or organizing a large number of data elements. The most important characteristic of a class is its membership property. The SIB also provides all needed operations such as insertion, deletion, union, difference, selection, and projection to manipulate classes.

A type is similar to a "user-defined type" or "abstract type" in some programming languages [Lisk77]. A type defines a value domain from which each instance assumes a value. In most cases, the value domain can be either a class of objects, previously-defined types, or enumeration of some constant values. A type resembles a class, insofar as it also denotes a collection of instances. It differs from a class, however, in the following ways: (1) all the instances of a type can only be created via a special operation called "instantiation" defined in that type; (2) no instance belongs to two different types, but a member can belong to several classes; (3) each type has a set of operations, including the instantiation operation, that is used to manipulate all instances.

By definition, an attribute cannot exist in isolation. Thus, it would be meaningless to reference an attribute without knowing with which data element it is associated. All the primitive data elements discussed above can have associated attributes, including attribute itself. In the case of attributed attributes, the chain of attributes can continue to indefinite length, but the leading attribute of the chain must be associated with a non-attribute element. Typical uses of attributes include (1) placing different interpretations (e.g., views) on a data element; (2) relating a data element to others (e.g., for defining a relationship); (3) adding application-dependent knowledge to a data element; and (4) miscellaneous, such as help information.

3.1.2 SEMANTIC RULES

In this section, we discuss briefly the "semantic rules" that enrich the semantic expressiveness of the SIB's data model.

A semantic rule consists of a condition-part and a rule-body. A set of semantic rules can be associated with an attribute type. When a reference is made to any instance of that attribute type, a "semantic evaluator" is triggered to evaluate the condition-part of the semantic rule and decide whether or not to activate the rule-body. The rule-body of a semantic rule is a predefined procedure that usually does not modify the data values but simply produces some useful results to inform the user about some facts (such as illegal usage of data, or inconsistency of semantic relationships).

The purpose of semantic rules in the SIB is two-fold. First, they can be used as constraints on the contents or uses of some information structures. For example, one can use a semantic rule to restrict the size of object names to 16 characters, or one can use another semantic rule to ensure that certain object types can only be accessed by a manager. Second, semantic rules and semantic evaluators facilitate dynamic semantics in the sense that the actual meaning of an attribute is not evaluated until it is referenced. For instance, consider the size-of attribute of a class C and each of its subclasses. When C's size-of attribute is referenced, the associated semantic rule references the size-of attributes of all the subclasses of C to synthesize the total size of C. Recursively, the actual size of C is dynamically updated even though the values of the size-of attributes might have been previously incorrect.

The price to be paid for the semantic evaluator appears to be high in terms of system performance. Therefore, we plan to use semantic rules only for useful but "less frequently" used semantic analyses such as interface control on design modules.

3.1.3 HIGHER LEVEL INFORMATION STRUCTURES

Given the primitive data elements discussed earlier, a software information base administrator would like to systematically construct higher level information structures suitable for his/her application environment. The SIB also provides capabilities for the administrator to define such structures.

In addition to low level types such as integer, real, character, string, etc., the SIB supports many pre-defined higher level object types and relationship types. Examples of object types are: project-description, document, software-product, program, module, etc.; examples of relationship types are: person-responsible-for, decomposed-into, versions-of, consists-of, etc. Higher level event types that comprise smaller events can also be defined in a similar way. Examples of event types are: progress-review, formal-design-review, development-history, etc. The information base administrator can also define useful attribute types such as size-of, instance-of, member-of, is-part-of, etc. in the SIB.

A higher level type can be defined in terms of primitive data elements and previously-defined types. The SIB's mechanism for defining higher level types is accessible, with necessary restrictions, to either the user, the information base administrator, or even the tool designer.

3.2 SIB LOGICAL ARCHITECTURE

The logical design of SIB can be perceived as a three-layered structure.

1. Internal Model Layer - This layer corresponds to a standard, portable DBMS that can be either a relational database or an entity-relationship database. This layer is the lowest level support for SIB to handle the internal storage of all information structures and other standard database management problems.

2. Conceptual Model Layer - This layer provides the definitions of all primitive data elements including objects, relationships, events, types, classes, attributes, attribute types, and semantic rules. Furthermore, useful types like integer, real, character, string, list, record, tree, and file are defined as primitive object types. Useful relationships like mapping, part-whole relationship, and is-a relationship are also defined as primitive relationship types at this layer. Note that all of the primitives defined at this layer are language- and application-independent; it offers a generic facility for the implementation of the external model described next. As methods evolve and new tools are added to the environment, project directors will be able to utilize this layer to make adjustments and additions to the external model layer.

3. External Model Layer - All information structures defined in an external model are oriented to the methods and languages of the application project. At this layer, multiple external models may coexist and interface with the same conceptual model. In PSE, we have designed an external model to support software design and implementation in GTEL-Pascal Design Language and GTEL-Pascal [Rudm82]. In the future, we may include other external models to support applications such as the development of information management systems.

3.3 SIB CAPABILITIES

The capabilities that SIB provides can be divided into (1) information structuring capabilities and (2) information processing capabilities. These two groups of capabilities complement each other and together provide overall SIB capabilities to the user and to the other tools in PSE.

3.3.1 INFORMATION STRUCTURING CAPABILITIES

From the user's point of view, the SIB (or, the external model of the SIB) provides capabilities for structuring the design information, the implementation information, the transformational information between design and implementation, the development history information, and the management information for a software project.

• Design Information

The SIB's external model supports very high level design objects like system, subsystem, abstract data module, abstract function module, abstract procedure module, and design document. All of these design objects can be easily tied to the design language constructs. Useful relationships among design objects such as data flow, decomposed-into, data-depends-on, document-of, and module-interface are also supported by the SIB. For each such design object or relationship, many associated attributes are also predefined and ready for tools to use to perform various design analyses.

• Implementation Information

In structuring the implementation information, the SIB supports information structures that can be easily tied to the constructs of a programming language. Most of the structuring capabilities needed at the implementation level are similar to those needed at the design level, and probably differ only in the granularity of the information structures. Some experience in dealing with implementation information was obtained from an earlier GTEL project, the CHILL Compiling System, which supports separate compilation, configuration management, and program documentation [Rudm82].

- Transformational Information

One of the main objectives of structuring the transformational information between design and implementation is to support traceability between design objects and implementation objects. Without the transformational information, the design and implementation information can not be truly integrated within the SIB. Though the current design of the PSE does not explicitly support a consistency checker, the transformational information can provide great help in maintaining the consistency between design and implementation (such as detecting effects of changes) in a semi-automatic way.

In the SIB, design objects and implementation objects are clearly distinguished by means of their object types (e.g., abstract data module vs. data structure declaration). A special relationship called refined-to is associated with each of the "implementable" design objects to keep track of the implementation objects that represent the implementation of that design object. In practice, the refined-to relationship is less straightforward. For example, an implementable design object can have several refined-to relationships that correspond to multiple implementations. Each refined-to relationship, however, contains its own attributes to identify its special characteristics (e.g., the implementation language used).

The SIB has semantic rules that utilize the refined-to relationship together with other relationships to further support the transformational consistency. A simple example of such semantic rules is given below.

Example: Consider the "uses" relationship between two design objects, say, D_1 "uses" D_2. Assume that D_1 and D_2 are both implementable objects and have been "refined-to" P_1 and P_2, respectively. Let "consistency-check" be an attribute associated with the "uses" relationship. A semantic rule associated with "consistency-check" states something like:

If D "uses" {X}, then refined-to(D) "uses" {refined-to(X)}.

In other words, the semantic rule checks if the semantic relationship "uses" between design objects is consistent with its counterpart between implementation objects. If in fact "P_1 uses P_2" is false, then the SIB warns the user about the inconsistency.

- Development History Information

In the current design of PSE, only the version control part of the development history will be supported. The SIB provides a generic attribute type to support version control of all objects that may bear different versions during the development and maintenance process. Certainly, not all the modifiable objects have versions. Whether an object should have versions or not is determined by the user's application environment.

- Project Management Information

  Both the technical and management information of a software project are structured in the SIB. For instance, project-description (problems, objectives, approaches, etc.), project-plan (budget, resources, milestones, deliverables, etc.), and progress-report, and reviewable-document, are defined as special object types in the SIB. Some of the management processes are also defined as events in the SIB. For instance, formal-design-review and progress-review are defined as two review events; each of them has different reviewable objects and different control flows.

3.3.2 INFORMATION PROCESSING CAPABILITIES

The SIB provides information processing capabilities for users and tools to effectively access and manipulate all of the information stored in the SIB. For predefined object types, all necessary operations such as create, delete, insert, update, move, traverse, and search are provided in the SIB. For predefined attribute types, some useful semantic rules are also provided.

Note that the "intelligence" of the SIB is really reflected in the tools rather than in the SIB's processing capabilities. In other words, these processing capabilities are only the "building blocks" to define more sophisticated processing capabilities in the tools. The SIB is responsible for capturing and maintaining the "knowledge" of software information, while the tools are responsible for the "optimal utilization" of such knowledge. Together, the SIB and the tools reflect the intelligence of the PSE.

However, the SIB provides two powerful processing capabilities on top of these building blocks. They are: the browsing capability, and the query capability.

1. Browsing Capability

    The browsing capability allows various users (such as managers, designers, programmers, design analysts, and librarians) to scan the relevant information in the SIB. The user can browse through the information base in either of the following two ways:

    - by project organization, development methods, and system structures as defined in the external model; or

    - by any relationship defined among information structures.

    The first method allows the designer to browse his/her system design according to, say, the module decomposition method, in a hierarchical manner. The second method allows the designer to browse the same system design in several other ways such as: browsing data modules based on the "data-depends-on" relationship, browsing all modules based on the "uses" relationship, or browsing all versions of a design object based on the "versions-of" relationship.

These browsing alternatives can be displayed in multiple windows so that the user has a better grasp of the information in terms of high level semantic relationships instead of low level database structures.

2. Query Capability

The SIB also provides the query capability that enables the user to access information by means of global use of information structures, relationships, and attributes. Some useful queries, for example, are given below in natural English:

> What other modules use module M?
> What other modules does module M use?
> What modules use type T?
> What are the design modules of subsystem A?
> Who are the responsible persons of module M?
> What are the design objects that are not yet completed?
> What are the design modules and programs owned by person P?
> What modules are used in both subsystem S1 and S2?
> What modules depend on module M?

These queries can be specified in a form similar to the following:

    FIND (<quantifier>, <object-list>), WHERE <predicate-list>

The quantifier specifies the number of occurrences of the <object-list> to be found (e.g., 1, n, or all); an object in <object-list> specifies the object type (required), its name, its attribute values, and its structural context; and a predicate in <predicate-list> specifies a relationship or constraint over the objects.

For example, to find a DESIGN-MODULE/PROGRAM-SEGMENT pair where PROGRAM-SEGMENT is the implementation of DESIGN-MODULE, and both are owned by John, the following query would be used:

    FIND (1, M: (type = DESIGN-MODULE, owner = John),
             P: (type = PROGRAM-SEGMENT, owner = John)),
    WHERE (refined-to(M) = P).

Note that the syntax presented above is only for the purpose of illustration. In the actual environment, the user issues a query by filling in the specifications in a tabular form via the window display. The query capability also allows the user to specify how the contents of the query's response are to be displayed in the window. For example, the user may choose to display only certain fields of the objects found, and may also want to sort these objects according to certain attributes.

4.0 PSE STATUS REPORT

The PSE project is currently at the detailed design and implementation stages. The prototype is being implemented in C on Sun workstations under the Unix (Sun Unix 4.2). Project members are currently implementing the SIB structures, browsing and query capabilities, an external model based on the GTEL Pascal Design Language, and the user interface. The detailed design and implementation of a sample tool-set including a template-driven editor, design analyzer, documentation generator, version controller, and multiple view constructor also began in 1986. It is expected that, at the end of 1986, a demonstrable prototype consisting of the user interface, sample tool-set, and the SIB will be completed.

5.0 CONCLUSIONS

In this paper, we have presented some preliminary results of our prototyping activities in an ongoing software engineering environments project at GTE Laboratories. We summarize below some of the problems in our prototyping work that we expect to be addressing in the near future.

- Human-engineering of the user interface is expected to be a time consuming and critical part of the research, probably requiring several cycles of experimentation.

- Abstract tool interface with the SIB is an important design issue in the PSE's evolvability. Selection of tools that support methods already in use, or already approved for use at GTE business sites is another concern. Although the intention is to develop a "generic" environment; i.e., one that can be adapted to a spectrum of languages and tools, much of the prototype effort will reflect relevance to current software engineering practice at GTE.

- The performance issue will be a challenge during the implementation phase. PSE is intended to be a prototype for studying, among other things, the applicability of the SIB as the core of a software environment. However, the complexity and generality of the SIB design may substantially affect the overall performance of the PSE.

Acknowledgment

The authors would like to acknowledge the department manager Dr. B. Dasarathy, and Dr. G. Jones, M. Feblowitz, and S. Sluizer for their comments on two earlier technical reports in this project, and E. Goldman for his editorial assistance in preparing this paper. We would also like to acknowledge the referees for their helpful comments.

References

[Barb85] Barbacci, M. R., A. N. Habermann, and M. Shaw, "The Software Engineering Institute: Bridging Practice and Potential," IEEE Software, Vol. 2, No. 6, IEEE, November 1985, pp 4-21.

[Chen76] Chen, P. P., "The Entity Relationship Model: Towards A Unified View of Data," ACM Transactions on Database Systems, Vol. 1, No. 1, March 1976.

[DoD 85] Department of Defense, Minutes of Operational Concept Document Workshop, Virginia Beach, Virginia, May 1985.

[GTEL82] GTE Laboratories, GTEL Pascal User's Manual, GTE Laboratories Incorporated, Waltham, Mass., 1982.

[Hamm81] Hammer, M., and D. McLeod, "Database Description with SDM: A Semantic Database Model," ACM Transactions on Database Systems, Vol. 6, No. 3, September 1981, pp 351-386.

[Horw85] Horowitz, S., and T. Teitelbaum, "Relations and Attributes: A Symbiotic Basis for Editing Environments," Proceedings of the ACM SIGPLAN 85 Symposium, June 1985, Seattle, Washington, pp 93-106.

[Knut68] Knuth, D. E., "Semantics of Context-Free Languages," Mathematical Systems Theory, Vol. 2, No. 2, 1968, pp 127-145.

[Lisk77] Liskov, B., et el., "Abstraction Mechanisms in CLU," CACM, Vol. 20, No. 8, August 1977, pp 564-576.

[Meye85] Meyer B., "The Software Knowledge Base," Proceedings of the 8th ICSE, August 1985, London, UK, pp 158-165.

[Myer85] Myers, W., "MCC: Planning the Revolution in Software," IEEE Software, Vol. 2, No. 6, IEEE, November 1985, pp 68-73.

[Pene85] Penedo, H. P., and E. D. Stuckle, "PMDB - A Project Master Database for Software Engineering Environments," Proceedings of the 8th ICSE, August 1985, London, UK, pp 150-157.

[Prie85] Prieto-Diaz, R., "A Software Classification Scheme," Ph. D. Dissertation, Department of Information and Computer Science, University of California, Irvine, 1985.

[Raed85] Raeder, G., "A Survey of Current Graphical Programming Techniques," IEEE Computer, Vol. 8, No. 8, August 1985, pp 11-26.

[Reis84] Reiss, S. P., "PECAN: Program Development Systems That Support Multiple Views," Proceedings of the 7th ICSE, March 1984, Orlando, Florida, pp 324-333.

[Ridd86]   Riddle, W. E., and L. G. Williams, "Software Environments Workshop Report," ACM Software Engineering Notes, Vol. 11, No. 1, January 1986, pp 73-102.

[Rudm82]   Rudmik, A., and B. Moore, "An Efficient Separate Compilation Strategy for Very Large Programs," Proceedings of the ACM SIGPLAN 82 Symposium, June 1982, Boston, Mass., pp 301-306.

An Architecture for Tool Integration[*]

Simon M. Kaplan   Roy H. Campbell   Mehdi T. Harandi
Ralph E. Johnson   Samuel N. Kamin   Jane W. S. Liu
James M. Purtilo[†]

Department of Computer Science
University of Illinois at Urbana-Champaign
1304 West Springfield Avenue
Urbana, Illinois 61801, USA

Abstract

The Illinois Software Engineering Program (ISEP) is an effort directed towards the design, development and exploration of software tools, techniques and environments. The primary objective of this program is to develop a set of interrelated and integrable software tools. These tools will facilitate the design, development and maintenance of more reliable and robust software systems and support their systematic reuse. To facilitate the integration of all tools, a general *open systems architecture* is under development.

1 Introduction

Future program development environments will provide to the user many tools designed to ease the program development process, including language-based editors, incremental compilers, dataflow analyzers and knowledge-based program design and development aids [1,4,5,6,11,15,16]. This list is open-ended, as new software technology will constantly be added to the programmer's software development arsenal. The Illinois Software Engineering Program (ISEP) is a project directed to the development of such a modern, fully integrated programming environment. This paper addresses a fundamental design issue associated with such an environment:

> *If we cannot fully enumerate all the tools which will eventually be included in such an environment (because this list is constantly changing), how do we lay the foundations for the environment in such a way as to be able easily to add (and delete) tools to (from) the environment at arbitrary points in time.*

To solve this problem we propose to use an *open systems architecture* (OSA) as the foundation for our environment.

The central concept of our OSA is that any tools should be capable of being added to a programming development system based on the OSA at any time. In order for this to work, the tools

---

[*]The authors are grateful for support received from the A. T. & T. Corporation
[†]Also supported in part by Department of Energy grant DEAC0276ERO2383.

have to be able to communicate with one another. Therefore we place great emphasis on using communications protocols (called sort morphisms) to achieve the openness of the architecture. A tool communicates with other tools by means of a predefined (for each tool) set of communications protocols. For any two tools to be able to communicate they must have a set of protocols in common, or have an "interpreter" that they use to provide translation services. Any tool can be added to the system by simply ensuring that it can communicate with the necessary tools already there, either directly or via an interpreter. Thus along with any new tool that is added to the architecture, it may be necessary also to add interpreters. From the viewpoint of communication between tools this achieves an open system. The system must also be open in terms of tools that were already there being able to use facilities provided by new tools. For this to be achieved a way of identifying what tools are in the system and what functions they provide is also needed.

Note that this sort of open system is much more complex than the layered open systems standard for communication. In that standard the communications protocol is fixed, and anything that can speak the protocol can communicate with other systems that can speak the protocol. In our OSA, however, we do not want to fix *anything*; thus, both the tools in the OSA and the communications between them are flexible, and this adds to the complexity of the system.

Section 2 describes informally our model of an OSA and concentrates on issues relating to inter-tool communication and how a general model of an OSA can be used to check designs of open systems of tools. The following section, Section 3, discusses testing and rapid prototyping of a particular OSA with fase and Polylith, two tools developed at Illinois. We then consider (section 4) the practical issues of how, if the architecture is open and tools can be added and deleted at any time, a tool can recognize if another tool is currently in the architecture. This is followed in section 5 with a discussion of a central cornerstone of many practical software development systems – a database tool. Many of the issues raised in the preceding sections can be incorporated into the database, thus simplifying and broadening the use of environments built on top of the OSA and simplifying the task of building new tools for use in environments.

2 Open Systems Architecture: An Informal Overview

By *open systems architecture* we mean an architecture which supports the integration of program development tools in such a way as to make the task of adding new tools to the environment as simple as possible. The architecture could be thought of as a *tool bus* or *software bus* or *software backplane* that provides the mechanisms for interconnection of, and intercommunication between, the diverse tools in a development environment. The architecture should be devised in such a way that the effort involved in grafting new tools into the environment is minimal compared to the effort of developing the new tools. Further, it should ideally be possible for tools which were not intended for use through the OSA also to be integrated into the environment via the OSA. This section discusses the model of the OSA, and some features that a generic OSA should possess, with particular reference to inter-tool communication.

In our model, a tool specification is considered to be a *signature* together with a set of *axioms*.

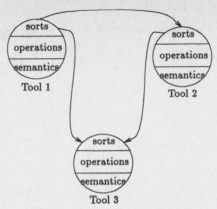

Figure 1: Graphical Representation of an OSA design

A signature is a collection of types (called sorts in discrete mathematical parlance) together with a set of operators. The operators fill the same role as function declarations in a programming language; they describe the types that the operator accepts as input and the type of the outputs, but do not describe the effect (the semantics) of the operation. The role of the axioms is to indicate the semantics of the operations provided by the tool.

Consider now the diagram in figure 1. In this diagram, the circles represent objects, and the arrows between them families of maps from the sorts of one object to the sorts of another. These objects are the tools in the architecture. Each tool presents a fixed interface to the universe containing all the other tools in the architecture. A tool can be thought of as being broken into three parts, viz. the sorts (types) on which the tool operates, the operation names and the semantics of the tool. In ADA[1] terms, a tool signature is a package specification; the addition of semantics makes it an ANNA package specification [10]. Specification languages such as IDL [13] can also be used to describe tools.

There are also arrows between the various objects in the architecture. These arrows represent families of morphisms (also called maps) between the sorts of the tools. There is one morphism per sort. Although these maps are all shown in one direction, there is no reason why they should not be bidirectional. These maps have two functions. First they indicate potential data transfers between tools. For example, figure 1 tells us that tool 1 can produce data that could be consumed by tools 2 and 3. Second they imply conversions between the sorts of the tools, for example, tool 1 may produce ASCII text, and tool 2 may require EBCEDIC text. The arrow represents a conversion function for each element of the family of maps. (Conversion functions are conceptually at a lower level of abstraction than the sort morphisms; whereas the sort morphisms take sorts to sorts, the conversion functions take elements of carriers (the concrete elements of the sorts) to elements of carriers. We will assume that the actual conversion algorithms are given *a priori* in some way. Because of this difference in levels of abstraction we will assume the actual conversion between carriers is subsumed by the discussion of sort morphisms).

---

[1]ADA is a trademark of the Government of the United States of America, ADA Joint Program Office.

Note that the arrows represent *potential* data transfers between tools. There is no indication that the communications will ever take place. Thus, these arrows represent design decisions concerning the tools in the architecture. Specifically they reflect the way the designer of the system has apportioned the functionality of the total system amongst the various tools. For example, if tool 1 is an editor and tool 2 a compiler, placing the arrow from tool 1 to tool 2 indicates that the designer expects users of the system to produce data with tool 1 (the editor) that will be consumed by tool 2 (the compiler). When designing a system decisions concerning which tools will go into an architecture and what data paths should exist between them must be made; because the system is open, these decisions cannot be absolute as the structure of the system must be capable of changing on the fly. However as we have discussed in the introduction, the key to a successful OSA is the ability to support inter-tool communication. By doing a careful design the chances of the correct communication protocols being in place are increased, thus decreasing the amount of work needed to add new tools.

What figure 1 does *not* tell us is the relative mutual visibility of the operations of the various tools; for example, tool 3 may call a 0-ary function in tool 1 and then operate on the results which are passed to back to it by the conversions implied by the arrow between tools 1 and 3. We will discuss this scoping issue further in Section 4 below.

Note that there are maps only between the sorts of the objects; in more traditional algebraic models, there would also be maps between the operations performed by the objects[3]. In this model, however, such maps would not in general be meaningful. Consider, for example, a simple architecture where there are two tools, an editor and a compiler. The editor would have operations like INSERT and DELETE, and the compiler would have a COMPILE operation. For there to be a meaningful map from the operations of the editor object to the operations of the compiler object there would need to be a meaningful analog to each editor operation in the compiler. INSERT, for example, would have no such analog in the compiler. For this reason, we do not map operators to operators, only sorts to sorts.

In fact, even mapping sorts to sorts is not good enough, as not all sorts will map meaningfully in exactly the same way that not all operators will map. We therefore allow only subsets of the sort sets of each object to map together. For this reason the morphisms are called *partial sort morphisms*. Note that while the *sort morphisms* are partial, the actual conversion functions between carriers are assumed to be total. The point here is that only some of the sorts will be mapped, but those sorts will have total conversion functions.

A model of a particular architecture can be created by building a diagram such as that of figure 1. This model shows the various tools and their interfaces (given by the sort morphisms). Once the model of a particular architecture is complete it can be used as a blueprint for the instantiation of an implementation. Figure 2 represents this process diagrammatically. The model of the design of the architecture (as per figure 1) consists of several objects (representing tools) connected together with arrows (representing partial sort morphisms). In figure 2, the objects and arrows of figure 1 have been employed as a blueprint for the implementation. The objects in the design have been taken to implementations (which can be shown to match the objects in the

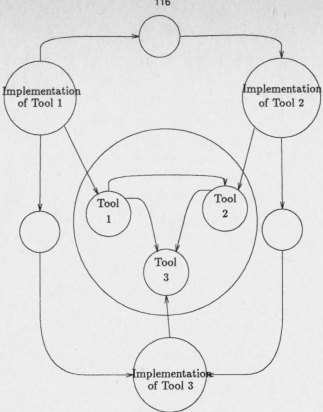

Figure 2: Design as a Blueprint for Implementation

design that they implement using techniques such as those described in [7]). The arrows in the design represented families of sort morphisms. These are taken to objects that encapsulate the conversion functions for each sort for which there is a morphism and identity morphisms that link these objects to the tools. We call these objects communication objects.

By making the morphisms into communication objects we increase the "openness" of the OSA. From the point of view of communication, a tool can be considered to be embedded in a set of communication objects. If any other tool wants to communicate with a particular tool it has to find a way to speak the input protocol of the communication objects and interpret their output. Thus any tool can be added to the OSA if it can communicate with the necessary communications objects. By making sort morphisms into independent objects we increase the potential for software reuse in our architecture, as the morphisms can be reused wherever a translation between the domain and codomain sorts of the morphisms are required. If no existing object can be used to bridge the gap between the two tools, an interpreter can be placed between two communications objects to provide the necessary translation facilities. This way we get truly open communication between tools. A practical disadvantage of this approach is that interpeters slow down the system. A good choice of morphisms in the initial design can help minimize this problem.

The model developed thus far, although not as yet instantiated to any particular architecture, can be employed to reason about the form that such an architecture can take. A traditional approach to building program development systems to to employ a *universal language* as the interface mechanism. All tools must be able to communicate in this universal language. Examples of this include UNIX[2], in which tools communicate using text streams, and the proposed DIANA [2] interface language for use with ADA.

UNIX assumes that tools can communicate among themselves using streams of text (typically via the UNIX *pipes* mechanism). Thus any tool that can communicate in this way can be connected into a program development system which is based on raw UNIX interfaces.

DIANA is an interface formalism based on the concept of *attributed abstract syntax trees, i.e.* a formalism where programs are represented as abstract syntax trees decorated with attribute information. A fundamental assumption behind DIANA (from the program development architecture viewpoint) is that many tools will be able to cooperate by passing amongst themselves abstract syntax representations of programs. This is more sophisticated than the UNIX text system in that a tool is always guaranteed to receive a syntactically correct program (or part thereof) to operate on.

There is a *temporal* distinction between these two systems; UNIX was developed just as terminals were becoming available and has an interface based on passing streams of data between programs. DIANA, developed approximately a decade later, realises that passing programs as text means that every tool must waste a considerable amount of processing resources reconstructing an internal representation of a program before it can begin processing. Passing trees guarantees correct structure and removes this pre-processing overhead. Further, the differences between UNIX text streams and DIANA abstract syntax trees reflects a shift from a program development paradigm based on text editing to one based on the editing of structures.

Just as the text stream paradigm of UNIX has been superceded by the abstract syntax tree based paradigm of DIANA, so we can expect that future program development technologies (knowledge-based program developments, semantically directed programming, visual programming languages) will have their own preferred intercommunications paradigms. We cannot know what these will be, so choosing a particular approach to tool interconnection and making that the standard which all tools must meet means that the OSA will be inherently limited (at best) to a mid-1980's view of program development.

We therefore propose a radical solution to this problem. We believe that there should be *no* universal interface language which *all* tools in a particular architecture use for intercommunication. Instead intercommunication between tools should be supported by using as many intercommunications protocols as required. Each of these corresponds to the partial sort morphisms of the model of the OSA.

Of course this is not to imply that there is no role for interface specifications such as DIANA. In any given system, a cluster of tools may communicate amongst themselves using a formalism such as DIANA, but *all* tools should not be constrained to use it as the only communications mechanism.

---

[2]UNIX is a trademark of AT&T Bell Laboratories.

Accepting, then, that there should be several communications mechanisms, the next task is to decide what these should be. In general it is impossible to enumerate them, but certain points seem obvious to us:

- There should be as few external sorts as possible. By *external* sorts we mean those that are visible in the interface of a tool. A tool may do whatever its implementors desire internally, of course, providing that the tool meets its specification. By sticking as far as possible with standard morphisms the ease of integrating new tools that use those morphisms is increased.

- The external sorts should be chosen to keep the conversions as simple as possible.

Thus, the partial sort morphism which takes text to text is in general preferable to the one that takes attributed abstract syntax trees to pictorial representations of LISP code in Sanskrit. Even simple morphisms like *text* → *text* may involve some conversions, such as swapping byte orders or changing from ASCII to EBCEDIC.

It may therefore trivially appear as if just using UNIX (text) interfaces throughout is preferable to using more complicated morphisms. This is not the case however. More sophisticated tools may require more complex morphisms and in such a case these should be provided. The following pithy moral[3] embodies our philosophy towards sort morphisms:

Keep the morphisms (and conversions) as simple as possible, but no simpler.

Obviously the strategy of sticking to a standard set of morphisms can only be carried so far; eventually tools that need new morphisms will be developed. We believe that our strategy of making the morphisms into objects in their own right will allow easy identification of the points where work must be done to integrate these new tools into the system using interpreters.

Having decided on what tools should go into an OSA, the following strategy should be adopted to complete the design:

- For each tool, decide on its interface: sorts and operators, and also on its semantics (so that other users of the OSA can decide what it is that the tool is meant to do.

- Decide on the partial sort morphisms between tools, and draw a blueprint as in figure 1 above. This involves identifying, for each tool:

  - What tools it may communicate with.
  - What sorts will be used for the data transfer. For example, our simple OSA discussed above could have had editors that can receive input of *text* and *syntaxtree* sorts, but where the compiler can only receive *text* sort. A morphism *syntaxtree* → *text* may be required if trees are to be passed to the compiler.

This process also supports the integration of existing tools into a new architecture. Any old tool can be added to an architecture provided only that its input and output sorts are clearly identified and morphisms provided where required. New tools can be integrated in the same way.

---

[3] Paraphrased from A. Einstein.

This architecture will be truly open in the sense that any tool can be added at any time simply by identifying the morphisms needed to make it communicate with other tools in the architecture. This is where there is considerable advantage to keeping morphisms simple and standard; other tools can then be added with minimum effort (and the minimum adding of new morphisms, one would hope!).

3 Testing and Prototyping Designs

Having built a design of a particular OSA, we can test the design using tools which can execute specifications. One such tool is the **fase** system [8].

In **fase** an abstract data type is specified by giving a final algebra for the data type. The **fase** system can then execute the specification of the data type, thus giving the ability to test data type specifications. One of the features of **fase** is that it recognizes that not all operations in all data types will in practice have executable specifications. To get around this problem **fase** allows the user to let the system determine the semantics for as many operations as it can, and then define semantics for the others as auxiliary functions. Any default (ie automatically determinable) semantics for an operation can be overridden by another implementation given by the user. This means that a user may define an abstract data type, and then test it. The default, automatically determined implementation can incrementally be replaced by an efficient, hand coded implementation, and the specification can be tested at each stage of the development process.

Now, in our model of an OSA each tool is specified as a signature together with axioms. Each tool can therefore be considered a data type, and can be tested using **fase**. Some of the operations will not have axioms that are directly executable; in this case implementations of the operations will have to be provided. **fase** can be used in this way to test tool specifications.

The individual implementations of the tools (implemented with **fase** or actual efficient implementations) are linked together using the Polylith system [14] developed at Illinois. Polylith is a tool (sometimes called a software bus) that supports the linking together, and intercommunication between, modules written in diverse programming languages. Initially intended to support communication between numerical analysis tools written in diverse languages such as LISP and Fortran, it has evolved into a software bus for the integration of modules for programming in the large. Polylith has an internal language for describing the effects of morphisms, and also a graphics based front end editor that can be used for visual interconnection of modules. The resulting visual programming language supports interconnections that look similar to the figures used above.

Polylith is used as the software bus in which the **fase** implementations are embedded. The resulting system can be used to build prototype implementations for testing purposes.

4 Recognizing one Tool from Another

The previous sections have discussed our model of tool interconnection, and how to quickly achieve working models of a particular architecture using two existing tools developed at Illinois – **fase** and

Polylith. This section of the paper addresses the issue of how one tool can access the operations provided by another.

As a running example we will consider a programming environment that contains the following tools:

- A compiler.

- A full screen editor such as vi, emacs or jim.

- A mailing system.

- A simple shell.

We will assume that the specific functions provided by each of these tools are the usual set found in UNIX. The external sorts required by the tools are:

- *Text*

- *TextFile*

- *MailFile*

- *BinaryFile*

All tools are of type *BinaryFile*. The tools (informally) provide these operations:

- The Compiler:

  - A COMPILE operation that takes *TextFile* to *BinaryFile*.

- The Editor:

  - A set of editing operations on *TextFile*, the details of which are not relevant here.

  - An EXEC operation that invokes the Shell.

- The Mailer

  - Operations to read and delete mail the details of which are not relevant here.

  - A MAIL operation that invokes the Editor to create a *TextFile* and then translates that *TextFile* into a *MailFile* and transmits it.

  - An EXEC command that invokes the Shell.

- The Shell

  - An EXEC command that takes *Text* as argument and attempts to invoke the argument as if it were a tool. (Naturally this may fail).

In this architecture, there are only simple morphisms required, as all tools communicate via *TextFile*. (We have not said as yet how these files are stored; see section 5 below). The morphisms provide communications channels only. They do not indicate how tools are aware of what other tools are available in the universe of tools. This is in general a fairly difficult problem.

One possible solution is to have a closed domain of tools, ie all tools are known *a priori* in some way to all other tools. Then the scope (visibility) of certain tools can be restricted by creating a net of visibilities that indicates what tools are visible to any given tool. This has advantages akin to those in programming languages which accrue from strong typechecking; any call on an operation of another tool can be verified in that the operation can be confirmed as existing and its input sorts can be typechecked against the sort used in the call. The disadvantage of this solution is its inflexibility; the addition of new tools is made difficult which contradicts the concept of an OSA.

Another possible solution (and the one adopted in systems such as UNIX) is to have an extremely loosely coupled system; If a tool wants to communicate with another tool it applies what it believes is the correct morphism and then calls the relevant operation of the target tool. This is a "wild swipe" approach; the calling tool expects the target tool to exist with the correct operation and input sorts, and will probably fail horribly if the target tool is incorrectly identified in some way. This provides absolute flexibility – the system as described above can be self maintaining and self extending as any new tool can be added by creating a *BinaryFile* with the correct program object code inside it (and *Binaryfiles* for the conversion functions where needed. Also, it is not possible to have any scoping; the domain of visible tools and operations is flat. This is also not desireable as in general one does not want any tool to be able to access operations of any other tool but instead some scoping structure is desireable. Nonetheless we are using this solution until the engineering database discussed in section 5 is available for more sophisticated experimentation.

A third solution would be a hybrid of the previous two; we maintain a database of tools, their operations and their sorts (effectively a database of signatures). When a new tool is added, its signature goes into the database. Then

- A net hierarchy of what tools are visible to what other tools can be constructed dynamically (ie modified each time the database is modified), thereby providing a scope structure.

- Calls on operations can be typechecked. The system can be made totally "strict" (all operations must be typechecked against the database) or can have any required degree of flexibility (some tools may be checked while others (such as the Shell, for example) can attempt to EXEC any tool) both in terms of scope and typechecking.

All this depends on some sort of database. The model we developed in section 2 was a *general model*. We introduced no constraints or limitations, such as requiring that a database exist in any OSA. But in practice such requirements are useful. We felt, however, that it would be better to develop a general model and constrain it later than to develop a specific model from first principles and (probably) get stuck when it came to generalizing it.

We believe that any viable program development environment will have in it a database tool. The following section discusses that database tool.

5 An Engineering Database

There are many practical issues concerning software development that the OSA model does not address, such as comprehensive support for the software life cycle. A way to provide this support is to include into a program development system an *engineering database system* that will provide such support. This database can also be used to help implement the hybrid approach to typechecking calls between tools that we discussed in the previous section.

Conceptually the engineering database should be thought of as a tightly coupled set of tools (hereafter referred to as the database system) providing multiple views of the information needed for successful computer-aided software development. The database system components must interact together to provide information on the designs and specifications of individual software systems, the software components within each system as well as information on relationships between these components, and codes and documentations associated with them. It must also provide a means for storing and interpreting the actual tools and their interfaces that make up the development system, thereby providing the form of support discussed in section 4.

By providing powerful interfaces for searching and retrieval of these information and view management to support different user views of these information, the database system can provide knowledge-bases for intelligent design and specification tools. To provide support for the development, testing and maintenance of software, the database system should also maintain information required for configuration management, version control, and change control. For this reason, the database system should contain the description of every version of every component, and information on relationships between the different versions generated throughout the software life cycle as well as the roles of these versions in different configurations. This information is vital if a development system wishes to support software reusability and retargetability.

A trouble reporting and maintenance facility should be an integral part of any configuration management and change control system. Problems, when they are reported, should be processed in an accountable manner so that information on the nature of the problems and subsequent correction and maintenance activities are recorded and made available on line and easily accessible to engineers and management. Hence, the database system should also maintain information required for automatic tracking and reporting of all changes, for updating documentation, and for maintaining consistency between implementation and documentation. By providing proper access and authorization control to the information stored in it, the engineering database system may also be used to enforce change authorization control. By providing facilities for collection and reporting management information related to all phases of software development, the engineering database system may provide support to the technical management decision making process. Thus, the engineering database system also serves as an effective communication channel between designers, engineers and managers.

The requirements of a software engineering database differ significantly from the requirements of traditional database system designed to support other applications. Instead of simple data items, an engineering database is required to handle complex objects, e.g., graphical elements, program substructures, and parse trees. The underlying database management support must be able to manage data of user-defined data types, and must incorporate support of data abstraction, i.e., be "object-oriented". The need to support knowledge based tools means that the database management system must deal with multiple views of data and "knowledge". To allow different programmers to work on different modules or different versions of the same modules requires innovative concurrency control mechanisms. These requirements are partially met by a number of object-oriented database systems which are the results of recent research on engineering databases [12]. These systems are similar to those already in existence in the artificial intelligence field. Designed using a top-down approach, they are typically small and cannot be easily extended to maintain large volumes of data. On the other hand, research on traditional database management systems and database machine architectures have provided the designers with powerful access methods and high-level logical data models to facilitate search and retrieval of massive amounts of data. Unfortunately, traditional data models and logical schemas, often based on rigid definitions of data items and simple relationships between data items, are frequently inadequate to model objects and concepts in engineering databases and knowledge bases.

As part of our tool integration project we are engaged in the design of an integrated engineering database and technical management decision support system capable of maintaining a massive amount of data and providing database and knowledge base support to a comprehensive set of intelligent design, development, and management tools. The major thrust of our current database research is the development of conceptual schema managers and view managers, and the investigation of solutions to problems related to the distribution of large quantities of data across large networks of heterogenous machines. We are using the Multiple Back-End Distributed Database system developed at the Naval Postgraduate School as our underlying implementation. This is a distributed system that supports multiple database organizational paradigms, eg relational and network. Although this work is in its formative stages, we believe that a sophisticated engineering database will be a necessity for any practical development environment.

6 Conclusions

We believe that integrated program development environments are going to play an increasingly important role in the software development process in future years. High-speed graphics workstations, high-speed networks and more powerful tools such as semantic editors and knowledge-based programming assistants will all be combined together to give the programmer more powerful assistance than ever before.

If this is to happen successfully then we must lay the foundations for the successful integration of all manner of program development tools. The problem with laying this foundation is that we have no real idea what these tools will be or when they will become available or how they will best integrate with existing tools.

We therefore propose the concept of a software *open systems architecture*. This architecture will form a "software backplane" or "software bus" through which tools will be able to communicate. This paper has discussed a general model of an OSA. The rationale behind such a model is that it is better to start from the formal and general where possible and instantiate to a specific implementation than to start from a specific implementation and try abstract a general model from there. We have had some experience with tool integration in the past, and feel that we have made sufficient mistakes to see the advantage of trying to get things correct this time around.

Along with the problems of tool integration come the problems of dealing effectively with very large sets of data for which there exist multiple views, from knowledge bases used by tools, to the actual storage and access control of the tools themselves. We believe that an *engineering database* – a large, distributed, object-oriented database – is needed in any practical development environment to provide support to program development tools. We are therefore designing and implementing a prototype engineering database system.

References

[1] Campbell, R. H. and P. A. Kirslis, "The SAGA Project: A System for Software Development", Proceedings of the ACM SIGPLAN/SIGSOFT Symposium on Practical Software Development Environments, ACM SIGPLAN Notices 19 (3), May 1984.

[2] Evans, A., K. J. Butler, G. Goos and W. A. Wulf, "Draft Revised DIANA Reference Manual", Tartan Laboratories, 1982.

[3] Goguen, J. A., and R. M. Burstall, "Introducing Institutions", Proceedings, Logics of Programming Workshop, Springer-Verlag LNCS 164, 1984.

[4] Green, C., D. Luckham, R. Balzer, T. Cheatham and C. Rich, "Report of a Knowledge-Based Software Assistant", Tech. Report KES.U.83.3, Palo Alto, California, 1983.

[5] Harandi, M. T., "A knowledge based programming support tool," Proceedings of IEEE Trends and Application Conference: Automating Intelligent Behavior, National Bureau of Standards, Gaithersburg, MD., (May 1983).

[6] Harandi, M. T., "Applying knowledge based techniques to software development," Perspectives in Computing, vol 6 (1), 1986.

[7] Kamin, S. N. and M. Archer, "Partial Implementations of Abstract Data Types: A Dissenting View on Errors", Proceedings of the International Symposium on Semantics of Data Types, Lecture Notes in Computer Science 173, Springer-Verlag, 1984.

[8] Kamin, S. N., S. Jefferson and M. Archer, "The Role of Executable Specifications: The fase System", Proceedings of the IEEE Symposium on Application and Assessment of Automated Tools for Software Development, November 1983.

[9] Kaplan, S. M., "The ISEP Open Systems Architecture: A Categorical Perspective", in preparation.

[10] Luckham. D. and F. von Hencke, "An Overview of ANNA, a Specification Language for ADA", IEEE Software, 2(2), March 1985.

[11] Medina-Mora, R. and P. Feiler, "An Incremental Programming Environment", IEEE Transactions on Software Engineering, 7 (5), September 1981.

[12] Lochovsky, F. (ed), IEEE Database Engineering Special Issues on Object-Oriented Systems, December 1985.

[13] Newcomer, J. "IDL: The Next Generation", Conference Record of the International Workshop on Advanced Software Development Environments, Trondheim, June 1986.

[14] Purtilo, J. M., "Polylith: An Environment to Support Management of Tool Interfaces", Proceedings of the ACM SIGPLAN Symposium on language Issues in Programming Environments, ACM SIGPLAN Notices, 20 (7), July 1985.

[15] Teitelbaum, T. and T. Reps, "The Cornell Program Synthesizer: A Syntax-Directed Programming Environment", Communications of the ACM, 24 (9), September 1981.

[16] Waters, R. C.," The Programmer's Apprentice: Knowledge Based Program Editing.", IEEE Transactions on Software Engineering SE-8 (1), January 1982.

Software Development in a Distributed Environment:

The XMS System

R.F. Kamel
BNR
P.O. Box 3511
Station C - Ottawa
Canada - K1Y 4H7

ABSTRACT

At BNR, a Software Development Environment (SDE) based on the XMS distributed architecture has been in use for 5 years.

This paper describes the XMS SDE. It shows how the SDE is built as a configuration of the XMS architecture and details some of the unique features of the system. These include the Helix file system and the support for third party software. The paper also presents some of the experience in developing software using a distributed SDE.

1. Introduction

In 1979, Bell-Northern Research (BNR) established a Computing Technology Group. The purpose of this group is:-

1. To create the base computing components for Northern Telecom's (BNR's parent company) products.

2. To build tools to be used in developing software for these products.

3. To explore new computing technology trends and to maintain a flow of relevant computing technology into BNR.

An early decision of the group was the choice of a distributed architecture as the product base. This architecture, named XMS (for eXtended Multicomputer System), is used in Northern Telecom's Meridian family of office products.

Another early decision of the group was that the architecture and software should be used extensively by its developers since this is the best way to come face to face with practical shortcomings. This reasoning led, naturally enough, to the use of XMS as the base for the software tools. Thus, one manifestation of XMS technology became the XMS distributed Software Development Environment (SDE).

The SDE hardware consists of LAN connected workstations built as a configuration of the XMS base hardware. Its base software consists of the XMS distributed operating system and file system. The applications are proprietary and third party software development tools.

The first SDE LAN was installed for the computing technology group in 1981. Today, there are in excess of 2000 SDE workstations distributed over 25 LANS in 15 geographic locations.

This paper describes the XMS architecture, shows how the SDE is built from it and presents the experience we have acquired. Two special topics which are dealt with are the Helix file system and the support for third party software in the SDE.

2. The XMS Architecture

XMS is a loosely coupled multicomputer system. The hardware consists of processing nodes, each with its private memory, connected by a high speed network. The network is used for inter-processor communication and there is no shared memory in the system.

The software consists of a distributed operating system which is replicated on each node. The operating system manages the node, allows process creation and supports inter-process communication both between processes on the same node and across the network. A detailed description of the XMS architecture may be found in [GC 85].

XMS Hardware Architecture

XMS hardware is organized as a set of processing *nodes* connected by a high speed network. This is illustrated in Figure 1.

A processing node minimally contains a processor, private memory and an interface to the network. In addition, it typically contains a Memory Management Unit (MMU) which supports multiple virtual address spaces. I/O devices are normally interfaced to a node but intelligent I/O devices may be connected directly to the network.

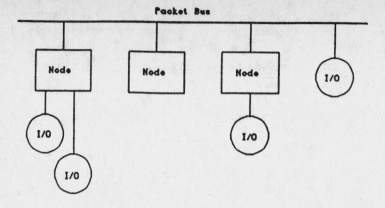

Figure 1:- XMS Hardware Organization

Today's XMS nodes use either a Motorola 68010 processor with a proprietary MMU or a Motorola 68020 with Motorola's Paging MMU (PMMU). However, it is a fundamental part of the XMS design that these specifics may be changed without impacting the overall XMS architecture.

Nodes communicate with each other over the network. The characteristics of the network change from product to product but the software is well insulated from this. Today, the XMS architecture has been configured for 5 different networks whose topologies include nets, rings and stars and whose media includes coax, fibre and twisted pair.

XMS Software Architecture

XMS software is organized as a number of independent but cooperating *programs*. A program is instantiated within a protected address space on a node and lives in that address space until it terminates. Several instances of the same program may exist in a system and programs may initiate other programs dynamically.

A program consists of one or more *tasks*. The main program is itself a task. It may initiate other tasks within the program. A task executes in parallel with other tasks in the system.

The standard XMS mechanism for inter-task synchronization and communication is the *Rendezvous*. An XMS rendezvous is similar to its Ada counterpart but, in XMS, rendezvous has been extended to allow communication between tasks in separate programs on potentially different nodes. This extension, called *Remote Rendezvous* is described in [GKC 86].

Applications may be divided into programs according to any structuring the user desires. XMS, however, encourages the use of the *client-server model*. This model divides an application into layers where each layer is a client of the services provided by a lower layer and, in turn, provides a service to the layers above. In an XMS structure, each layer is implemented by a program and its services are accessed by rendezvous.

A typical example of the structuring within a layer is a *Resource Manager* that manages hardware or software resources. Such managers are programs where the main program is a resource allocator and where each resource is managed by a task. A client rendezvous with the allocator to obtain a resource which is returned to him in the form of a task. He subsequently rendezvous with the task to access the resource.

XMS Software Components

Most XMS software is implemented in BNR Pascal, a proprietary language with extensive support for modularity, tasking and inter-process communication [GC 85, KG 85, Kam 86]. BNR Pascal presents a high level programming model to XMS applications and hides from them details of the processor and network used in a particular XMS configuration.

To implement the features required by BNR Pascal and to provide additional functionality, XMS includes a number of software components ranging from a kernel to an entity-relationship database system. In this section, we only describe three basic system components:- the Kernel, the Application Environment(AE) and the Operating System Program (OSP). Two additional important components, the file system and the support for Unix software, are described later in the paper.

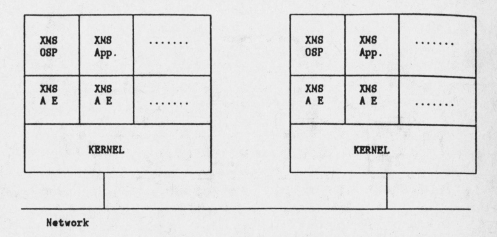

Figure 2:- XMS Software Components

The software organization on a node is shown in figure 2. The lowest layer of XMS is the *kernel*. The kernel deals with low level resource management for the node including memory management and real time. It also supports program and task initiation and termination as well as both local and remote rendezvous.

The kernel will, on request, allocate a new address space and initiate within it an *Application Environment (AE)*. The AE loads and starts an application program, monitors its execution and reports its termination to its parent program. The AE also supports the non-kernel features of BNR Pascal (e.g. heap management), implements shared libraries (e.g. string utilities) and offers interfaces to servers on the network (e.g. File System).

The first program that is loaded on each node is the *Operating System Program*. This program implements servers for local I/O devices as well as non-kernel distributed system functions (e.g. name Service). The OSP is also responsible for starting an initial set of application programs on the node.

3. The Software Development Environment

The XMS SDE is built as a configuration of the XMS architecture. It provides a network of personal workstations and shared servers which are used for software development. An SDE configuration is illustrated in Figure 3.

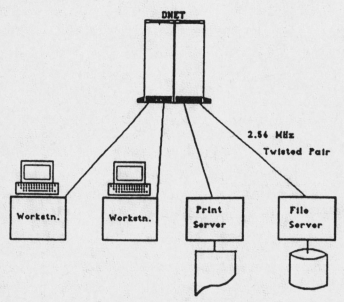

Figure 3:- XMS SDE Configuration

SDE Hardware

The basic node of the SDE is an XMS processing node packaged as a conventional engineering workstation such as a SUN, an Apollo or a VaxStation. Its local devices include a terminal (Ascii or graphics) and some local storage devices (floppy and winchester disks).

A server node is also packaged as a workstation but often has a special peripheral such as a laser printer attached. A server node provides a shared service for the workstations on the network. Examples of such services are shared file service, print service and external communications service.

The networking medium used in the SDE varies. Initially, the network was a 5 Megabit proprietary ethernet look-alike. Today, a twisted pair network (20 Megabits with 2.56 Megabit distribution) is becoming the SDE standard and a fibre network (at 80 Megabits) is also available.

SDE Software

The SDE base software consists of the XMS kernel, Application Environment, and Operating System Program. For the SDE, the OSP includes additional servers for the local terminal, floppy and winchester.

The first application initiated by the workstation OSP is a command interpreter (CI). The CI is used to synchronously (exec) or asynchronously (fork) initiate other programs on the node, including other instances of the CI. These programs may be user written or one of the over 100 proprietary applications written specifically for software development. A partial list of these applications is in figure 4.

An application interacts with the user through the terminal server. This server supports a number of full screen virtual windows. Applications may have their own window, may use several windows or may share a window with other applications (typically their parent).

Applications may also access shared servers on the network. Both local and remote server access is through rendezvous although, typically, the application is not aware of this as the rendezvous is packaged inside a procedure or a utility program.

Command Interpreter and exec language

Editors
　　　　text editor and graphics editors

Software development tools
　　　　compilers, assembler, dissassemblers, linkers, ...

Analysis Tools
　　　　debuggers, profilers, test tools, cross referencers, ...

Document Preparation Package
　　　　support for text and graphics, spelling checker, index generator

LAN communication
　　　　messaging and bulletin board

IBM communication
　　　　passthrough and file transfer

Project Management Tools
　　　　source management, problem database and project tracking

Figure 4: Partial list of SDE utilities

4.　　The Helix File System

A crucial component of computing systems is the file system. XMS is no different and provides the *Helix* distributed file system. Helix is used as part of products and also as a component of the SDE. Helix is described in detail in [FO 85].

Helix architecture

The primary goal of the Helix file system is to provide consistent access to the files on the network. These files may be private files on some local device or files on a file server.

The Helix architecture divides the software components that comprise the file system into two classes:- *Server Helix* and *Client Helix*. These components and their interactions are illustrated in figure 5.

Server Helix is a number of server programs, one for each device. The server program manages the files on the device and presents a rendezvous interface to its clients. This interface includes entries for directory manipulation, for opening and closing files and for reading and writing blocks within a file.

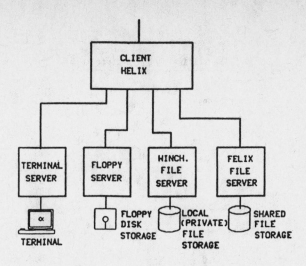

Figure 5: Helix File System Components

Client Helix consists of software that resides in the AE for the application. It contains procedures that implement the I/O facilities that the program expects and in turn implements these by rendezvous with the appropriate server. Examples of procedures provided in a BNR Pascal environment are the RESET, REWRITE, READLN and WRITELN.

Directory Structure

Helix servers maintain a hierarchical directory structure similar to that of Unix. The principal difference is that Helix allows multiple links to directories whereas Unix restricts multiple links to files only. As will be seen, this capability allows some desirable flexibility in the SDE environment.

Another difference from Unix is the way a user's rights to access a file are determined. Unlike Unix which maintains access rights for each file based on the user belonging to a group, Helix access rights are associated with links between directories. These rights include Read (R), Write (W), Link (L) and Unlink (U). A user's access rights to a file is determined by ANDing the access rights on all links he navigates on his way to the file.

To illustrate the use of these two features, consider the implementation of an SDE common object directory and postoffice as illustrated in figure 6.

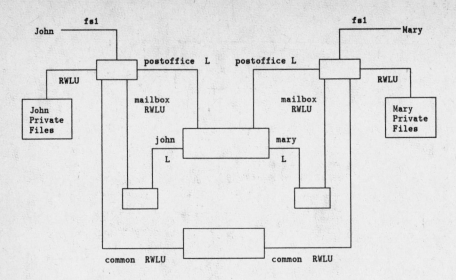

Figure 6: Example of Helix directory structure

In this structure, the directory *common* is used to share items of interest to all users, such as object code and online documentation. Typically each user has full access rights to this directory but only limited (i.e. Read) access to most of the directories below it. Thus designers can read and execute all the files they might need but are only allowed to change specific items that belong to them.

The other interesting directory is the *postoffice*. The postoffice contains a link to a directory for each user. This link is to the same directory that can be accessed as *mailbox* by the specific user. Users have only Link access through the postoffice, thus they can only create entries in other user's mailboxes. From the other direction, through the mailbox, the receiver has full access to the items in his mailbox.

An example of a typical use of the postoffice is as follows. John is managing a project and has a large directory, *project*, that contains his team's work. He has full rights to that structure. Mary is part of the test group and would like to access project but should not be able to modify it. John can give Mary read only access by executing the command

MAKEPATH :fs1:project :fs1:postoffice:mary:project +[R]

This would cause the directory project to appear in Mary's mailbox with read only access. Mary may move this directory to a more convenient place by executing the command

MOVEPATH :fs1:mailbox:project :fs1:dept.44:project

Network Helix

One feature of the Helix file system is transparent access to files situated at other geographic sites. This is achieved through *Network Helix* which is illustrated in Figure 7.

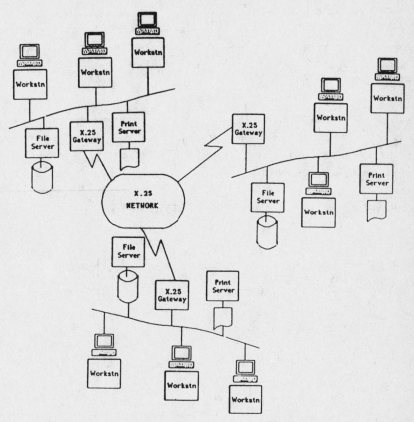

Figure 7: Network Helix

Network Helix consists of two parts: a *Near Side* and a *Far Side* The near side appears as a Helix server on the network. It offers the same rendezvous interface as a file server but implements its operations by going through an X.25 gateway over the public network to reach the Far Side of another network server. This Far Side then routes the operations to a file server on that network. Information is returned from that remote file server by the same sequence but in reverse.

Operations on a remote file server are transparent to applications.

Network Transparency

When an SDE user starts his workstation, he has the root of a file system that is initially empty. As he logs on to the servers he wishes to access, these servers appear directly underneath the root.

Logging on is done through a program that accepts a list of desired server names, the user id and password and submits them to the servers for validation. Logging onto a remote file server through network helix requires a slight variation that specifies the site at which the desired file server resides.

Applications may access any file within a user's visible directory structure on all logged on servers. The *Pathname* provided when opening a file is used to route requests to the appropriate server. In a pathname, the first components are used to determine the desired server. The remainder are passed to the server and used to navigate through directories on that server to reach the desired file. Thus, the distributed nature of the file system is hidden from applications and confined only to choice of pathnames. **Figure 8** shows examples of this transparency.

```
RESET(f,':Winch:A.File');
        Opens file on local Winchester

RESET(f,':FS1:A.File');
        Opens file on file server FS1

RESET(f,':California:FS1:A.file');
        Opens file on file server FS1 at the California site
```

Figure 8: Examples of network transparency

Commit Mechanism

The Helix file system has been designed with robustness as a primary concern. It supports robustness through the notions of *atomic actions* and *commit*.

When a user opens a file for writing, he is provided a logical copy of the file. As he writes to the file, he is updating this virtual copy. When he closes the file, or at other points at which he wishes his updates to be captured, he issues a commit operation. The commit operation is atomic. It results in either a fully updated version of the file or the return of a failure condition. It is never possible to have a partially updated version of a file and thus the file system is always consistent.

This feature is very useful in a distributed SDE environment where a power failure might bring several hundred (mainly local) servers down. On power up, the contents of all servers will be consistent although active user sessions would have been lost. Without commit, users might discover that their files are inconsistent or, worse, that the file system as a whole is corrupted.

5. Third Party Software

The SDE based on XMS with a set of proprietary tools is a powerful and flexible development environment. Nevertheless, it is desirable to have access to the large base of software that is available outside BNR.

From the SDE point of view, the single largest base of useful software is the Unix operating system. To support Unix applications, we have implemented a facility called DUX (Distributed UniX). Dux permits loading and running standard Unix applications on the XMS distributed system. Dux is illustrated in figure 9.

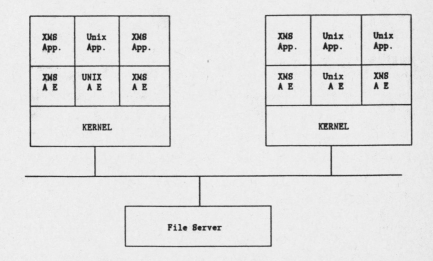

Figure 9: Unix support in XMS

From the point of view of the XMS architecture, Dux is another application environment:- It loads applications, monitors their execution and provides them with interfaces to the rest of the system. The difference from the XMS AE is that Dux loads Unix code files and provides them with the system call interface they expect. Internally, Dux implements Unix system operations in terms of the facilities of the XMS. For example, a Unix OPEN call is implemented using rendezvous to the appropriate server.

While it would have been possible to directly port a 'C' compiler and to provide the relevant Unix libraries in an XMS environment, this approach would require that software be recompiled. A Dux port consists of installing object code since the loader follows Unix code file conventions.

It is worth noting that, in our experience, source level porting between different Unix systems (e.g. System V, Xenix, BSD4.2) is not trivial since they tend to have small but cumbersome differences in such areas as the 'C' dialect supported, assembler conventions, library features, etc... Dux avoids these differences by porting at the object level and supporting simultaneously the object file format and system calls of several versions of Unix. Interestingly enough, at this level, not many differences actually exist between Unix systems and support of a new Unix dialect is not a major effort.

Unix applications running on Dux are immediately part of the XMS system and can transparently exploit many of its features. For example, a Unix editor under Dux can transparently access remote files through network helix.

6.   Discussion

Before presenting some statistics on SDE usage and comment on our experience, it is worthwhile to see how the features presented in the previous sections interwork to help solve day to day problems of software development. The scenario below is slightly exaggerated but provides an idea of SDE use.

An SDE scenario

-       Fred Ottawa arrives at work, sits at his personal workstation, logs on to servers and checks his mail.

-       One item of mail reports a class 1 problem from a product developer, Sam Francisco, at the California lab

        Since XMS is the base for both product and the SDE, Sam had encountered the problem while testing on the SDE. He has placed links to all relevant directories in :FS1:PostOffice:Ottawa:Fred.Ottawa on file server FS1 in California.

- Fred diagnoses and fixes the problem using Network Helix

Fred logs on :California:FS1 which gives him the California files as if they were on his own network. He examines the problem by loading the software remotely and executing it in a window on his workstation. In another window, he examines the remote source that uncovered the problem. In a third window, he examines his own software for interactions with the remote software. Fred quickly discovers that the cause of the problem is a boundary condition he did not handle and fixes it.

Throughout this phase, Fred is using a mixture of proprietary and Unix based tools. For example, he uses EMACS as his editor but works with the SDE software management tools.

- Power failure causes system to crash.

Just as he is about to finish, a power failure crashes the system. When power returns, 10 minutes later, Fred has lost nothing:- The file system and his files are intact. He merely need to log in again to resume where he was.

At this time, there are 50 other users on Fred's network performing a variety of activities. Fred is barely aware of their load on the system.

- Fred issues fix to California

Fred issues the fix to Sam by using network helix to place the new software in his mailbox on the California file server.

It is now 7:30 A.M. California time

SDE statistics

The SDE has been in extensive use at BNR, Nothern Telecom and some of their licensees for nearly 5 years. There are today over 2000 workstations configured in about 25 networks at 15 geographic locations ranging from California to Europe.

As an example of one of the larger SDE networks, the Computing Technology network has the following characteristics:-

1. 200 nodes totalling nearly 100 MIPS of computing power and 300 Megabytes of real memory.

2.   13 file servers totalling over 3 Gigabytes of storage.

3.   7 laser printer servers capable of a combined output of 100 pages per minute.

4.   3 communications servers that access to the public network for use by Network Helix and connectivity to IBM mainframes.

SDE advantages

Before the SDE, BNR software development was done mostly on large IBM mainframes. As the SDE became more and more popular, a number of advantages were noticed over the previous mode of computing:-

1.   The use of XMS as the base for both the product and the SDE allows much faster turnaround for testing and allows testing to commence well ahead of the availability of product hardware.

       In addition, designers now have only one system and runtime tools to become proficient in as opposed to learning different systems for their product and development environments.

2.   The personal workstations of the SDE offer better response time and more consistent performance than a mainframe. Both these stem from the fact that each user has his own dedicated CPU and is generally not affected by load created by other users.

3.   An SDE can start very small with only a few workstations and a couple of servers and can grow gracefully with the addition of new workstations and servers. This is to be contrasted with the upheaval that is typical of the large step upgrades with mainframes.

4.   The SDE has greater availability than mainframes. Maintenance, system software upgrades and hardware failures typicaly affect a single workstation or server and do not disable the entire user community.

5.   The SDE allows designers more choice of versions of software that run on workstations and servers. This allows both personal flexibility in selecting an environment and also testing on the network without affecting other users.

As an example, early testing of a new file server can happen on the SDE by installing the new file server on the network and upgrading the system software on some workstations. Later, more users may join in a beta test of this file server by also updating their system software and starting to use the file server. This is all transparent to other users on the same network who are not part of the test.

The only disadvantages we have found in the SDE approach are:-

1. Occasionally one needs the large centralized processing power available to the single user on a mainframe at 2 A.M.

2. Because of the increased personal freedom on the SDE, some extra time is spent by designers configuring their own environments. It also becomes necessary to be more careful with version numbers on such items as problem reports since each user may be running a different version of software in his personal environment.

However, we feel the advantages of the SDE significantly outweigh the disadvantages. While we have not conducted a controlled experiment to quantify the benefits of the SDE, one lab reported the following after switching to the SDE:-

1. A reduction by a third of the cost of computing per designer.

2. An increase by 25% in the number of debugged lines of code produced by designers.

3. An unquantified improvement in the quality of software and documentation.

Further Reading

[FO 85]   Marek Fridrich and William Older, "Helix: The Architecture of the XMS Distributed File System", IEEE Software, May 1985.

[GC 85]   Neil Gammage and Liam Casey, "XMS: A Rendezvous-Based Distributed System Software Architecture.", IEEE Software, May 1985.

[GCK 86]   Neil Gammage, Ragui Kamel and Liam casey, "Remote Rendezvous", submitted Software Practice and Experience.

[Kam 86]   Ragui Kamel, "The Impact of Modularity on System Evolution", to appear IEEE Software.

[KG 85]   Ragui Kamel and Neil Gammage, "Further Experience with Separate Compilation at BNR", IFIP Conference on System Implementation Languages: Experience and Assessment, North Holland 1985.

[Tel 84]   Telesis Vol. 11, no. 3, 1984. Issue on XMS.

Note: Any of the above papers may be obtained by contacting the author

The SAGA Approach to
Automated Project Management
(Supported by NASA grant NAG 1-138 and an AT&T Corporation research grant)

Roy H. Campbell
Robert B. Terwilliger

Department of Computer Science
University of Illinois at Urbana–Champaign
252 Digital Computer Laboratory
1304 West Springfield Avenue
Urbana, IL 61801–2987
(217) 333–4428

Abstract

ENCOMPASS, a prototype software development environment, is being constructed from components built by the SAGA project. Application of SAGA to the major phases of the lifecycle will be demonstrated through ENCOMPASS. The system will include configuration management; a software design paradigm based on the Vienna Development Method; executable specifications; languages which can be used to support modular programming, like Berkeley Pascal or ADA; verification and validation tools and methods; and basic management tools. EN-COMPASS is intended to examine many of the requirements for the design of complex software development environments such as might be used to construct the space station software. It is intended to be used as a prototype for examining many of the more advanced features that will be required in future generations of software development environments which support aerospace applications. In this paper, we describe the framework adopted within ENCOMPASS to provide automated management. We exemplify the approach using an example taken from problem tracking and change control during software maintenance.

1. Introduction.

Research into the software development process is required to reduce the cost of producing software and to improve software quality. Modern software systems, such as the embedded software required for NASA's space station initiative, stretch current software engineering techniques. Embedded software systems often are large, must be reliable, and must be maintainable over a period of decades. The software support environment for building such software systems must ensure a high–level of quality while enabling the embedded software and the hardware on which the software runs to change and the applications for which the embedded system is designed to evolve. Furthermore, such environments must be cost effective.

The SAGA project is investigating the design and construction of software engineering environments for developing and maintaining aerospace systems and applications software (5,7). The research includes the practical organization of the software lifecycle; configuration management; software requirements specification; executable specifications; design methodologies; programming; verification; validation and testing; version control; maintenance; the reuse of software; software libraries; documentation and automated management (5,11,15,17,18,19,23,24,27,28). An overview of the SAGA project components is shown in Figure 1. The tools and concepts resulting from SAGA are being used to develop a prototype software development system called ENCOMPASS (28). The ENCOMPASS

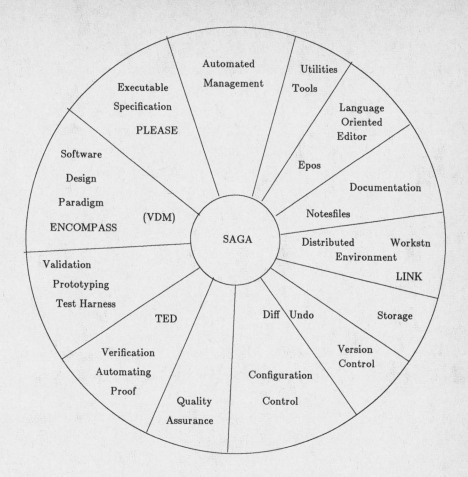

Figure 1: The SAGA workbench components

software development paradigm is shown in a diagrammatic form in Figure 2. Although the research has developed many general tools and concepts that are independent of the application language and domain, we hope to extend ENCOMPASS to support the development of large, embedded software systems written mainly in ADA.

In this paper, we study mechanisms to automate the management of ENCOMPASS using a simple example based on the maintenance activities of problem tracking and change control. We describe the prototype configuration management system underlying ENCOMPASS and discuss the interelationships between this system and the automated management mechanisms.

2. The Software Development Environment.

To be effective, a software development environment must actively support the software development process (5). It must be easier to use the software development tools and the environment than to use other tools and a general operating system.

The SAGA project is concerned with software development environments, not with the construction of a general operating system. We assume that SAGA will be used in conjunction with a general

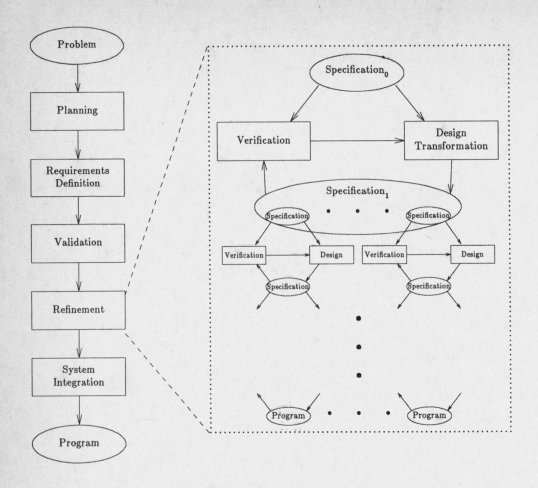

Figure 2: The ENCOMPASS software development paradigm.

operating system such as Berkeley UNIX 4.2BSD that provides a hierarchically structured file system, virtual memory, processing operations, and mail service. Further, we assume that SAGA will be used in conjunction with an extension of the operating system that supports a networked workstation environment, perhaps using LINK (25), a kernel based version of UNIX United (2), that supports transparent remote network file access, remote spooling and remote processing.

The SAGA environment consists of a configuration management system and a workbench of software development tools which are used in a set of development, management and maintenance activities.

The *configuration management system* stores and structures the software components developed by a project which may include programs, test data, documents, manuals, designs, proofs, specifications, and contracts.

The *development, management and maintenance activities* manipulate the software components being built. They include the actions of the software developers, managers, testers, quality assurance teams, and librarians, such as the editing, compilation, or testing of a program, formatting of a document, or delegation of a task.

The *workbench of software development tools* provides the means by which activities can manipulate the software components. In ENCOMPASS (28), this workbench is the set of SAGA tools. Development, management and maintenance activities interact with the configuration management system through the SAGA user interface, which includes the SAGA language–oriented editor Epos (5,18).

3. The Software Lifecycle.

The SAGA project has adopted a "management by objectives" (14) approach to the definition of the software lifecycle (1,12). Each phase in the lifecycle is oriented towards satisfying an objective by producing a milestone. For example, the requirements specification phase produces a set of properties that the software system to be constructed must satisfy. Validation consists of determining that the specification of the system satisfies the requirements of the system and provides an important milestone in the development process. Using PLEASE (27), an executable specification language, validation can take the form of "testing" or executing the system specification. In a large project such as the space station software development program, validation may take the form of prototyping using a mixture of tools including PLEASE, simulation, standardized library routines and walk–throughs.

The design phase consists of incrementally refining the requirements specification into algorithms and component specifications. It has been shown that neither testing nor formal verifications alone can guarantee correct software (9,10). ENCOMPASS can provide an effective verification process that utilizes both testing and formal methods. The execution of the PLEASE specification for a component provides a test oracle for later use in the verification of refinements. Formal specifications and design methods also aid software reuse (20,21,22).

In ENCOMPASS, we use the specifications not only for testing, but also as the basis for rigorous and formal proofs of correctness. Thus, we intend that the system specification can also be used to prove theorems concerning the requirements of the system and to prove that a design or refinement step correctly implements a specification.

PLEASE is based on specifying programs using pre– and post–conditions. PLEASE specifications are implemented as an extension of a programming language. Both ADA and Path Pascal (6) are being used as vehicles for ENCOMPASS. The predicates are transformed into logic programs which are executed in a Prolog environment (8) that is invoked from the principal programming language. Many of the transformations may be performed automatically. Research into automating these transformations continues.

Verification conditions for the refinement of an abstract program into a more concrete one can be generated during program design. These verification conditions may be inserted into a proof tree and TED (15), a proof tree editor, may be used to manipulate them. In particular, TED permits proofs to be decomposed into sequences of lemmas. Various theorem provers may be invoked to mechanically certify the verification condition.

The development methodology used for refining system specifications into programs is similar to the Vienna Development Method (16,26). A set of rules specifies the verification conditions that are required for a given form of refinement. These rules can be applied automatically, but in general proof of the verification conditions requires some manual labor. Figure 2 summarizes the ENCOMPASS approach.

The use of formal specifications in ENCOMPASS is encouraged not only to assist code and design reuse, to promote clarity, to aid testing, and to support verification, but also to provide acceptance criteria which may be used as management objectives for a design step. The objectives can range from a mechanical proof of the correctness of a design decision to a substantial set of test data for which the design is valid.

Many of the objectives of each software development phase can be made into a milestone by requiring the activities of the phase to generate a list of documented products. These products must be validated before the phase is complete to ensure that the phase has been successful. In SAGA and ENCOMPASS, we can use language–oriented tools such as the Epos editor to further enhance the documentation of milestones. These tools can, we believe, automate repetitive effort in preparing and validating the achievement of objectives (4).

Management for the software development lifecycle must identify, control, and record the development process. A management model can be based on a *trace* of the activities within the project. Such a trace can be used to understand the meaning of management in a similar manner to the use of traces in defining the meaning of a programming language (Campbell and Lauer (3)). In ENCOMPASS, we are implementing a limited set of management functions to record, monitor, initiate activities, and inhibit inappropriate activities. Instead of using a detailed model of management, we have adopted a simpler approach based on the larger granularity provided by milestones.

4. A Framework for Automated Management.

The use of a management by objectives approach (14) in the software lifecycle introduces clearly defined milestones that are agreed upon by the developer and manager. The management objectives for each activity must define the pre–conditions under which the activity may occur, acceptance criteria for the products produced by the activity, and a procedure for evaluating whether the acceptance criteria have been met. These objectives provide a framework around which the management of the software project can be automated.

A simple demonstration of how effective such a management scheme can be is given by the following simplified example of managing software maintenance. Figure 3 shows the organizational structure of a software maintenance group. Analysts and programmers are responsible to a change control board for their contributions to the maintenance activity. Bugs and requests for modifications to maintained software are received by the maintenance group. The change control board manages the manpower and resources of the maintenance group and decides which change requests should be satisfied and which change requests should be ignored.

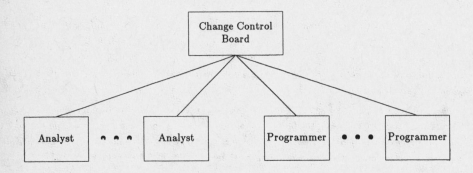

Figure 3: Organization structure

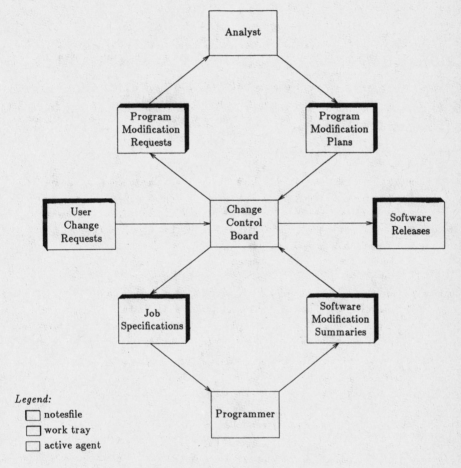

147

Figure 4 shows a simplified diagram of the flow of information that occurs within the maintenance group. Users submit change requests to the maintenance group. The change control board assigns program change requests to an analyst for further examination. A program change request may consist of a bug report or a proposal for enhancements to the software. The analyst reviews the requests and produces program modification plans for those that are valid. These plans are forwarded to the change control board for approval and scheduling. The change control board may either allocate a programmer to work on a job specification based on the plan, or it may reject the plan. A rejected plan will be reconsidered by the analyst.

Figure 4: Data flow for change requests

The programmer produces the appropriate software modifications and submits them to the change control board. The board examines the modifications and may either produce a new software release or generate a new job specification to reconsider the software modifications.

A more detailed flow diagram for the change requests would include additional feedback stages to allow analysts and programmers to negotiate their objectives with the change control board. For example, the programmer may wish to question the time allotted to accomplish the analyst's plan.

In ENCOMPASS, the management system for change control is implemented using SAGA tools. Activities within the change control system are coordinated using a combination of notesfiles, mail, makefiles, and work trays.

4.1. The Notesfile System

The *Notesfiles* system is a distributed project information base constructed for SAGA on the UNIX operating system (11). A file of notes can be maintained across a network of heterogeneous machines. Each file of notes has a topic; each note has a title. A sequence of responses is associated with each note. Notes and responses may be exchanged between separate notesfiles. Notes and responses are documented with their authors and times of creation. Updates to the notes and responses are transmitted among networked systems to maintain consistency. Notesfiles use the standard electronic mail facility to facilitate the updates. A library and standard interface permits any user program to submit a note or response to a notesfile. This library has been used in the construction of automatic logging and error reporting facilities in software and test harnesses. Within the SAGA project, we have used the Notesfile system to organize technical discussions, product reviews, problem tracking, agendas and minutes, grievances, design and specification documentation, lists of work to be done, appointments, news and mail.

4.2. Work Trays

A *work tray* is a new mechanism which has been introduced in order to manage and record the allocation, progress, and completion of work within a software development project. Each user may have a number of work trays, each of which may contain a number of *tasks* that contain software *products*. Products are stored as entities within the ENCOMPASS configuration management system. There are three types of trays: *input trays, in-progress trays,* and *file trays*. Each user receives tasks in one or more input trays. The user may then transfer these tasks to an in-progress tray where he will perform the actions required of him and produce new products. The user may then return the task via a conceptual *output* tray to an input tray for the originator of the task. A user may also create new tasks in in-progress trays that he owns. These tasks may then be transferred to another user's input tray. A task that has been transferred back into the in-progress tray of the user who created the task may be marked as complete and transferred to a file tray for long term storage.

Each task has a *home*, which is the tray where the task was created, a *location,* which is the tray where the task currently resides. and an attribute *time*, which is the time the last action involving that task took place. Status commands allow examination of the tasks in a tray and the products in a task.

4.3. Implementation of the Change Control Scheme

User change requests can be generated because of bug reports or user requests for enhanced functionality. These are sent to the change control system by electronic mail and are stored in a notesfile "User Change Requests".

A user change request is a form that can be filled in manually using an editor tailored for form filling or can be generated by software error reporting tools. It is entered into the notesfile mail system by standard mailing utilities. In this way, user change requests can be generated from a wide range of sources, some local and some remote.

The User Change Requests notesfile is the receiving station for all requests to change the software. The Change Control Board manager creates a particular "Program Modification" task in an in-progress tray. In addition to the details extracted from the notesfile, the manager may also add the amount of time within and the urgency with which a response to the request should be created. The manager transfers the task to the "Program Modification Request" input tray of an analyst, see Figure 4. The analyst will transfer the request to a in–progress tray in order to respond to the request. The analyst may create a product called an "Invalid Request" report as a result of his analysis if he believes that such a report is appropriate. Alternatively, the analyst may create a detailed description of the steps needed to implement the change or bug fix. The analyst transfers the task with the analysis of the request back to the manager's "Program Modification Plan" input tray. Should the analyst not respond to the request within a reasonable time, the periodic invocation of consistency checking programs can automatically detect the delay and enter a complaint in the "Problem Tracking Management" notesfile (which is not shown) and flag the Program Modification task with an item that documents the warning.

The manager may transfer the task back into his in–progress tray. Depending upon the products produced by the analyst, he may register the task as completed, transfer it to a file tray and write a response to the request in the notesfile that further action is unnecessary, convene the change control board, or reject the plan and reassign the task to the analyst with recommendations for a revised plan or to reject the request.

Should the manager wish to review the plan, the Change Control Board will be convened to discuss the Program Modification Plans. Alternatively, the Board may discuss the Plans electronically through the notesfile system. Given acceptance of a plan, the manager of the problem tracking system checks out the products that are needed to make the modification from the project library and enters them into the task. He then transfers the task to the "Job Specification" input tray of a programmer.

The programmer receives the task and transfers it into an in–progress tray. The programmer will add and modify code, documentation, test cases, and proofs of correctness to the products of the task. When complete, the programmer will transfer the task to the "Software Modification Summary" input tray of the manager.

When a Software Modification Summary is received, the manager will again convene the Change Control Board. If the review is satisfactory, he will check the new product into the project library as a new version of the software and announce the release of the software through the "Software Release" notesfile. If the review is unsatisfactory, he may create a new Job Specification.

At any time, the manager or programmers may query any of the tasks they have been assigned or have created. Acceptance criteria may be in the form of executable procedures which produce reports (for example, executable acceptance tests), records of compilations or examinations of the file activity of program files. These acceptance criteria may be automatically stored as products of the task. Status commands will summarize such records, report on who is currently working on the task, who is waiting for completion of the task, and what other tasks are needed to be completed before the current task can be completed.

Thus, very simple mechanisms can be used to automate management, provided that the objectives being managed are well–defined. In the example given, the problem and the resulting corrective maintenance need to be well–defined. In addition, the corrective maintenance must be validated. A feasibility study of the work tray concept has been completed and the concept is being extended. In the following section, we discuss the interaction between maintenance and the configuration management system.

5. Configuration Management System

The configuration management system is responsible for maintaining the consistency of, integrity of and relationships between the products of software development. In the SAGA project, Terwilliger and Campbell (28) model software configurations using a graph in which the nodes represent uniquely named entities or uniquely named collections of entities and the arcs represent relationships between entities. Layers within the graph represent different abstract properties of the software products. The graph also represents the organization of the software products into separate concerns.

In ENCOMPASS, software configurations can be decomposed by organizational relationships into vertical and horizontal structures. The vertical structures form a hierarchy and decompose the system into independent components. For example, within a software development *project*, the configuration may be structured into *subsystems*. These, in turn, are decomposed into *modules* which are decomposed into *compilation units*.

The horizontal structures represent dependencies between entities at the same hierarchical level. Thus, each project, subsystem, module, and unit may have a horizontal structure which includes dependencies between documents, version information, requirements and system specification, shared definitions, architectural design, detailed design, code, binaries, linked binaries, test cases, procedures for generating executable binaries, listings, reports, authors, managers, time and tool certification stamps, development histories, and concurrency control locks. Relationships may specify design, compilation and version dependencies. Depending upon the granularity of the entities, the graph can be represented by the UNIX directory structure, by symbolic links, or by databases. For example, in ENCOMPASS the vertical structure is stored using the UNIX directory structure. Shared definitions are represented by symbolic links. A database at each level in the vertical structure is being built to provide data dictionary capabilities and author manager relations.

Abstractions of the collection of software products are provided by *views*. A view represents a particular abstract property or concern and is implemented as a mapping from names into products. The "base view" is a complete collection of the software products. For example, a "functional test" view might represent the system as a collection of functional specifications, object code, test programs and test data. Other examples of views include a single version abstraction of a system that has many concurrent versions, documentation, and the work of a particular developer.

Continuing our discussion of change control within maintenance, we consider the problems arising in modifying an existing program. Figure 5 shows an example tree traversal program stored in an ENCOMPASS configuration management system (Kirslis et al (19)). Not all the dependencies and details

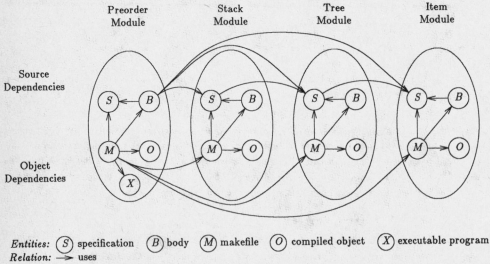

Figure 5: Base view for the *preorder* program

are shown. The program is presented as a subsystem containing four modules; preorder, stack, tree, and item. Each module contains entities including a makefile (Feldman (13)), specification, body or source code, compiled object code, and executable program. Only one type of relationship is shown, the *uses* relationship, which associates an entity with another entity if the former entity references the latter one. Each "uses" relationship should be accompanied by a "used by" relationship, not shown in the figure, which is simply the inverse of of the "uses" relationship, and which permits the references to a module/entity to be determined from that module/entity. Each body within a module references its own specification. The body of *preorder* references the specifications in the other modules. The makefile for each module references the specification and body to be compiled, and the compiled object which will be produced. In addition, the makefile in the preorder module also references the makefiles and objects in the other modules, since it needs these in order to produce an executable program.

A number of benefits are realized if this dependency graph is stored in machine accessible form and if the software tools in use are adapted to refer to the graph. A data retrieval tool can provide information about the hierarchical structure of the program. For a given module, the tool can show its dependencies with respect to other modules.

An editor, adapted to use this graph, can permit a programmer to specify a routine, module, or program to edit. If the programmer specifies a module, that module becomes the locus at the beginning of the editing session. The programmer edits within the context of that layer of abstraction. Only the local context of the module is important. The programmer can find and display other modules, routines, or programs which use this module. These references may be checked easily to determine how a change in the current module will affect them. Similarly, other modules that are referenced by the modules which reference the module under consideration may be located easily and displayed.

Compilation tools, which access the dependency graph, can support automatic, incremental recompilation on a module by module basis. For example since the body of *preorder* depends on the specification for *stack*, if the specification for *stack* has been changed since the time *preorder* was last compiled, then *preorder* will be recompiled. A compilation tool can use the dependency graph to resolve the dependencies at compile time and access all files needed to perform a compilation[1].

Versions of the preorder program are stored in a program library (28). Conceptually, these versions appear in the library as independent entities as depicted in Figure 6. The versions are, however, interdependent because of the history of their construction. The versions are constructed from revision control histories of preorder. Each preorder version is a collection of versions of the other modules. Each version of a module is stored using a history mechanism based on the Revision Control System (RCS) of Tichy (29). Similarly, the information describing a version of preorder is also stored under RCS. Library makefiles construct a specific version of preorder within the Library on a demand or check out basis. The specific version of preorder specifies the versions of each module that are needed to be extracted. The dependencies between modules and within modules are recorded in a format that can be stored within RCS. (In our prototype ENCOMPASS environment, these dependencies are recorded using the UNIX tape archiving facility *tar* and placed directly under RCS.)

To modify preorder, a read–only copy of the latest version of preorder is checked out. This version is still under configuration management and resides within the protection provided by the global library. Figure 7 shows how a view of preorder is constructed in a workspace. The workspace facilitates changing preorder. Each entity within preorder can be accessed read–only through this view. In the ENCOMPASS prototype, the view is implemented as a hierarchical directory structure which initially only con-

---

[1]In practice, by using UNIX we can do better than this. By an appropriate implementation of the source dependency information, we can make it appear as though all files needed for a compilation are resident in one place, permitting us to use an existing makefile interpreter program and compiler without modification (19).

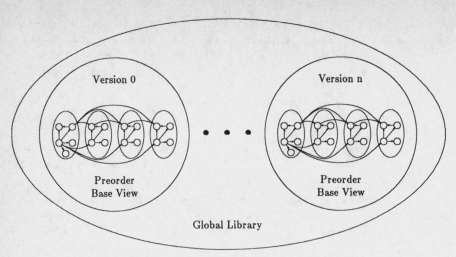

Figure 6: Global library containing versions of *preorder* base view

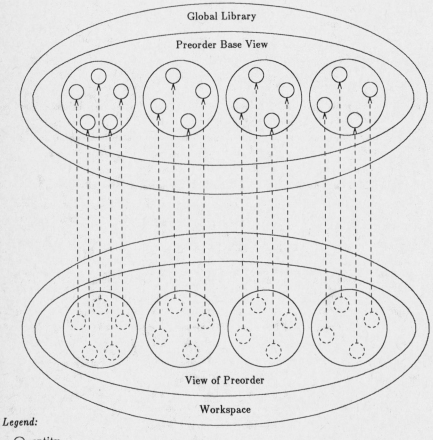

Legend:

◯ entity
◌ image
–> projects onto

Figure 7: Workspace containing view of *preorder*

tains symbolic links to the base view stored in the library.

In order to modify components of preorder, the entities concerned are checked into the workspace. In terms of implementation, the symbolic links are replaced by copies of the actual entities to which they correspond. Figure 8 shows a new version of preorder being developed in which two entities within module item are being modified. If the new version being developed is a sequential revision of preorder,

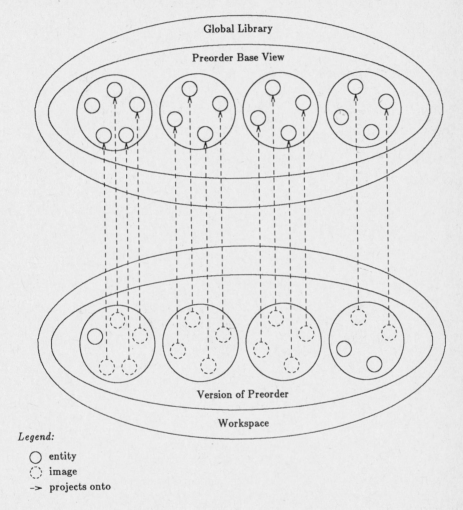

Legend:

○ entity
⊙ image
–> projects onto

Figure 8: Workspace containing new version of *preorder*

locks are placed within the library on those modules checked into the workspace. These locks prevent any parallel development of the same entities. The next version number of preorder and the modules concerned are assigned. If the new version is instead a parallel revision of preorder, locks are not imposed but parallel revision version numbers for preorder and the modules concerned are assigned.

Once the development and testing of a new version is complete, the programmer submits a summary of the modifications to the change control board. The change control board evaluates the modifications and makes a recommendation as to whether the work constitutes a valid version. (In a more complex change control system, the evaluation of the new software might be performed by a quality assurance group. Our management model and implementation are easy to extend to permit such a system.) Following a software release, the new version is integrated into the library system, as shown in Figure 9, and the RCS files of the individual modules that are altered are updated.

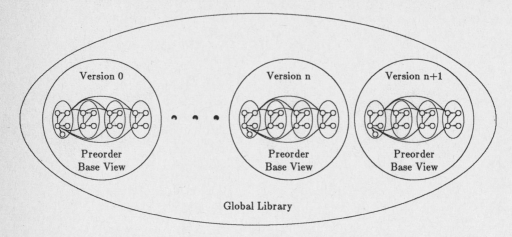

Figure 9: New version of *preorder* installed in global library

6. Summary

This paper describes a prototype management system that has been constructed on UNIX as part of the ENCOMPASS environment. The example change control system described has been built using the system. The prototype system demonstrates the feasibility of the approach, but further research and refinement are required to develop a practical management system.

The prototype implementation is not robust and offers no protection from misuse. A complete log of the actions performed on the tasks should be kept in a secure location to support auditing. Further, the implementation has limited goals and is not fully integrated into the SAGA set of tools and the configuration system. The system permits a task to be decomposed into subtasks but should maintain records of those relationships. Finally, the system ought to be coupled to management tools such as report generators, Pert chart analyzers and flow charting displays.

However, the approach is simple and provides a framework for building automated management. We believe our approach can be refined into a production quality system for managing software projects. We shall be exploring refinements of our approach to accomplish this end.

7. References.

1. Blum, B. I., 1982, *The Life–Cycle – A Debate Over Alternative Models*, **Software Engineering Notes**, vol. 7, pp. 18–20.

2. Brownbridge, D. R., L. F. Marshall and B. Randell, 1982, *The Newcastle Connection or UNIXes of the World Unite!*, **Software – Practice and Experience**, V. 12, pp. 1147–1162.

3. Campbell, R. H. and P. E. Lauer, 1984, *RECIPE: Requirements for an Evolutionary Computer–based Information Processing Environment*, **Proc. of the IEEE Software Process Workshop**, pp. 67–76.

4. Campbell, R. H. and Paul G. Richards, 1981, *SAGA: A system to automate the management of software production*, **Proc. of the National Computer Conference**, pp. 231–234.

5. Campbell, R. H. and P. A. Kirslis, 1984, *The SAGA Project: A System for Software Development*, **Proceedings of the ACM SIGSOFT/SIGPLAN Software Engineering Symposium on Practical Software**

Development Environments, pp. 73–80.

6. Campbell, R. H. and R. B. Kolstad, 1979, *Path Expressions in Pascal*, Proceedings of the Fourth International Conference on Software Engineering.

7. Campbell, R. H., C. S. Beckman, L. Benzinger, G. Beshers, D. Hammerslag, J. Kimball, P. A. Kirslis, H. Render, P. Richards, R. Terwilliger, 1985, *SAGA*, Mid–Year Report, Dept. of Comp. Sci., University of Illinois.

8. Clocksin, W. F. and C. S. Mellish, 1981, Programming in Prolog. Springer–Verlag, New York.

9. DeMillo, R. A., R. J. Lipton and A. J. Perlis, 1979, *Social Processes and Proofs of Theorems*. Communications of the ACM, vol. 22, no. 5, pp. 271–280.

10. Dijkstra, E. W., 1970, *Structured Programming*. In: Software Engineering Principles, J. N. Buxton and B. Randall, ed. NATO Science Committee, Brussels, Belgium.

11. Essick, Raymond B., IV., 1984, *Notesfiles: A Unix Communication Tool*, M.S. Thesis, Dept. Comp. Sci., University of Illinois at Urbana–Champaign.

12. Fairley, Richard, 1985, Software Engineering Concepts. McGraw–Hill, New York.

13. Feldman, S. I., 1979, *Make – A Program for Maintaining Computer Programs,* Software – Practice and Experience, Vol. 9, No. 4, pp. 255–265.

14. Gunther, R., 1978, Management Methodology for Software Product Engineering, Wiley Interscience, New York.

15. Hammerslag, D. H., S. N. Kamin and R. H. Campbell, 1985, *Tree–Oriented Interactive Processing with an Application to Theorem–Proving*. Proc. of the Second ACM/IEEE Conference on Software Development Tools, Techniques, and Alternatives.

16. Jones, C., 1980, Software Development: A Rigorous Approach, Prentice–Hall International, Inc., London.

17. Kimball, J., 1985, *PCG: A Prototype Incremental Compilation Facility for the SAGA Environment*, M.S. Thesis, Dept. Comp. Sci., University of Illinois at Urbana–Champaign.

18. Kirslis, P. A., 1986, *The SAGA Editor: A Language–Oriented Editor Based on an Incremental LR(1) Parser*, Ph. D. Dissertation, Dept. Comp. Sci., University of Illinois at Urbana–Champaign.

19. Kirslis, P. A., R. B. Terwilliger and R. H. Campbell, 1985, *The SAGA Approach to Large Program Development in an Integrated Modular Environment*, Proceedings of the GTE Workshop on Software Engineering Environments for Programming–in–the–Large.

20. Lanergan, R. G. and C. A. Grasso, 1984, *Software Engineering with Reusable Designs and Code,* IEEE Trans. on Software Engineering, Vol. 10, No. 5.

21. Matsumoto, Y., 1984, *Some Experiences in Promoting Reusable Software: Presentation in Higher Abstract Levels,* IEEE Trans. on Software Engineering, Vol. 10, No. 5.

22. Neighbors, J. M., 1984, *The Draco Approach to Constructing Software from Reusable Components,* IEEE Transactions on Software Engineering, vol. SE–10, no. 5, pp. 564–574.

23. Richards, P., 1984, *A Prototype Symbol Table Manager for the SAGA Environment*, Master's Thesis, Dept. Comp. Sci., University of Illinois at Urbana–Champaign.

24. Roberts, P. R. 1986, *Prolog Support Libraries for the PLEASE Language,* Master's Thesis, Dept. of Comp. Sci., University of Illinois at Urbana–Champaign.

25. Russo, V. F., 1985, *ILINK: Illinois Loadable InterUNIX Networked Kernel,* M.S. thesis, University of Illinois, Urbana, Il 61801.

26. Shaw, R. C., P. N. Hudson and N. W. Davis, 1984, *Introduction of A Formal Technique into a Software Development Environment (Early Observations)*, Software Engineering Notes, vol. 9, no. 2, pp. 54–79.

27. Terwilliger, R. B. and R. H. Campbell, 1986, *PLEASE: Predicate Logic based ExecutAble SpEcifications,* Proc. 1986 ACM Computer Science Conference.

28. Terwilliger, R. B. and R. H. Campbell, 1986, *ENCOMPASS: a SAGA Based Environment for the Composition of Programs and Specifications*, Proceedings of the 19th Hawaii International Conference on System Sciences.

29. Tichy, W., 1982, *Design, Implementation, and Evaluation of a Revision Control System,* Proceedings of the 6th IEEE International Conference on Software Engineering, pp. 58–67.

30. Wirth, N., 1971, *Program Development by Stepwise Refinement*, Communications of the ACM, vol. 14, no. 4, pp. 221–227.

A PROCESS-OBJECT CENTERED VIEW OF SOFTWARE ENVIRONMENT ARCHITECTURE

Leon Osterweil
University of Colorado
Boulder, CO 80309-0430

1. Introduction.

The essential purpose of a software environment is to provide strong, complete and readily accessible support for such key software processes as development and maintenance. The basis of such support must be a diverse and powerful set of functional capabilities supplied by what has previously been referred to as "software tools". Increasingly, however, it is becoming clear that the most challenging part of creating an effective software environment is not the creation of the software tools themselves, but rather the effective integration of those tools and presentation of their capabilities to the user.

Further, it is becoming quite clear that a software environment is very much like all other complex pieces of software in that it must be capable of growing, adapting and changing to meet the ever-changing needs of its users. Indeed, as software environments are a relatively new type of software product, it must be expected that our understanding of the requirements for this type of product is at a crude and primitive level. This makes it all the more important to be sure that the architectures which we develop for these systems be as flexible as possible. It also suggests that it behooves us to seek general--and probably new--paradigms and conceptual frameworks with which to organize and help understand the problems for which software environments are purported to be the solution.

In this paper we advance the notion that the key software processes of development and maintenance can be effectively modelled as an unexpectedly complex and intertwined collection of subprocesses supporting and communicating with each other through the exchange of software products. We further suggest that both these products and the processes themselves can profitably be viewed as software objects.

This leads to an architectural view of software development and maintenance which is elegantly uniform and encompassing, while also being quite amenable to extension and modification across a broad spectrum. Thus we believe that it a promising framework within which to study and understand the nature of software processes. We also believe that it suggests an architecture for a family of powerful, robust and flexible software environments which are good candidates for active partnership in experimental research which should be successful in leading to a fuller understanding and explication of software processes and the environment mechanisms capable of effectively supporting them.

2. Background and Related Work.

We believe that the more successful software environment efforts in the past have been most successful where they have attempted to convey to users the sense that the essence of their work was the creation of information in the form of software objects and products. In that such efforts have concealed the presence and actions of tools they have succeeded. In place of confronting users with the need to understand and manage tools, they have required users to understand and manage data objects and structures necessary to the creation of software end-products. Certainly in the process of managing software objects and products it has been necessary to manage their transformation as well. Here the need for tools arises, but here the most successful environment efforts have attempted to reduce the user view of the needed tools to the most simplified minimum--arriving at the view that tools are best thought of as functions or operators.

Some examples of environments which foster and support this view are Toolpack/IST [Osterweil 83, ClemOst 86], Smalltalk [Goldberg 84] and Interlisp [TeitMas 81]. In all cases the user of the environment is encouraged to think of his or her job as being the creation or alteration of software objects through functional transformations which either create new objects from scratch or transform older objects. These environments are viewed as being predominantly interactive, with user direction coming essentially one command at a time. In this we believe that these older environments have missed an opportunity to be more successful and to link up with another fruitful and active line of research.

We believe it is important to recognize that the user of a software environment does not issue random commands one at a time to an environment, but rather attempts to follow an orderly procedure for fashioning more highly developed products out of collections of software piece-parts. If one were to capture the stream of commands issued to a software environment such as Toolpack/IST or Smalltalk, one would presumably have the equivalent of an execution history trace taken through a procedure intended to create software product(s) in an orderly way. At present such procedures are kept informally in the minds of software practitioners. It is significant to observe, however, that increasingly researchers are attempting to realize and formalize these procedures. The most visible attack on this problem is work aimed at studying "The Software Process" [SPW1, SPW2]. But other research efforts [JeffTPA 81] have also been aimed at studying and formalizing such activities as software design.

Our hypothesis is that the best way of understanding how software is developed and maintained is to view these activities as coordinated sets of processes, rather than as a monolithic Process, and to think of these processes as being definable and expressible in actual well-defined procedural, algorithmic code. This view urges us strongly in the direction of viewing the processes used to effect software development and maintenance as pieces of software themselves. This suggests that software processes should be viewed as products which have to be developed and maintained in just the way that more classical software products also have to be developed and maintained.

This in turn suggests that there may be a great deal to be gained by extending the scope of what can be considered to be a software object to include software processes. Among the most important gains seems to be the possibility that the tools and procedures applicable to development and maintenance of classical software objects might also prove to be applicable and effective in developing and maintaining themselves.

Tempering this sanguine view of software processes as objects is the realization that software processes can also be activated and caused to operate on other software objects. Thus software processes seem to have a dual nature--passive objects upon which functional tools can operate and active operators capable of application to passive objects. This observation does not invalidate our view of environment architecture, but rather makes it clear that the architecture must recognize this dual nature of software processes and must, in fact, be a positive aid in effectively managing the duality.

The reward for doing this effectively is the widening of the scope of a software environment to encompass the processes which drive the application of tools to the development and management of software products. This widening should be a significant help to the user in carrying out the necessarily complex software processes. It should also enable precise visibility into the nature and functioning of software processes, thereby expediting the experimental evaluation and rapid evolution of software processes and the tools and aids by which they can most effectively be supported.

These ideas are more fully developed and more carefully presented in [Osterweil 86]. The interested reader is encouraged to explore the details and ramifications of these ideas in that paper. For the present paper, however, we proceed by indicating the implications that these ideas have for the architecture of a software environment predicated upon the desirability of supporting this view through the application of tools.

3. Process-Object Environment Architecture.

If we liken an environment's tool capabilities to the primitive capabilities furnished by a computer's underlying hardware, then the essential job of the environment can be likened to the job of a programming language, which must help users utilize these capabilities effectively and also encourage thinking and working at a higher, cleaner, and more concise level of abstraction. This analogy is well drawn and useful. Both environments and programming languages enable the composition and configuration of functional capabilities, and must store and tranfer information in order to do so. Both must exchange information with external media and with users as well. More recently it has become clear that both must also concern themselves with supporting the cooperative activities of many users.

Further, just as programming languages have been built to support the creation of processes for manipulating data (classical application programs), so we believe that the goal of an environment should likewise be to support the creation of processes for manipulating software. Examples of such processes are software development and software maintenance. Some very high level and very primitive examples of such processes can be found in [Osterweil 86].

Thus, a software environment must support the creation, assembly and manipulation of software objects and it must provide facilities for defining the way in which its tools operate upon these objects. In addition, however, the environment must also provide capabilities for orchestrating the application of these capabilities as processes.

Viewing an environment as a device for fashioning and executing precise descriptions of key software processes helps us to establish some basic architectural features. Consider, for example, software development--the most obvious software process. Development effects the creation of a software product, which should be viewed as a complex structure of such software objects as source text, executables, testcases, design criteria and documentation.

Hence development is the process of creating and aggregating software objects with tools. We believe that this and all other processes should be rigorously and precisely specified. Following the programming language metaphor we are led to consider the utility of typing. As shall be demonstrated, we have determined that superior process rigor and precision can be advanced by considering all software objects to be instances of types and all software tools to be operators whose operands are these type instances.

One important implication of this view is that software development can take place only after operand types have been carefully defined, tool functions have been rigorously expressed, and the development procedure itself has previously been considered, and defined. Clearly quite a bit of work must take place before the development process can begin. This work, moreover, must itself be precise and disciplined as its product is a precise and disciplined development process. In fact, it seems clear to us that this work should itself be defined as a process--namely a software process development process, or PDP.

Thus our belief that a software environment shares most of the goals and methods of a modern programming language and our belief that software processes can and should be expressed rigorously in algorithmic code have led us to conclude that in order to assure that a software development process (DP for short) produces highest quality products, the DP should first be thought of as itself the product of a PDP, the process aimed at the creation of the DP and the structures in terms of which it is defined. Shortly we shall see that this notion is useful in helping to conceptualize, control and organize the diverse activities supported by a software environment.

Consideration of the nature of software maintenance is also useful in this regard. The goal of software maintenance is to alter a software product. So far we have discussed two very different products--the DP and the more conventional software products which the DP produces. Maintenance may be aimed at altering either or both. Alteration of the convential software product is more straightforward, and we shall refer to it as product maintenance. It can be viewed as a simple case of a more difficult and significant type of maintenance, which we shall refer to as process maintenance. Process maintenance entails altering the DP, analyzing the software products which had been produced by the original DP, and altering these software products to make them consistent with the new DP.

An important example of process maintenance is the integration of a new tool into an environment. The new tool is presumably to be integrated because it is capable of creating objects of a new type or because it is more efficient in creating objects of existing types. Consequently, the development process description must also be changed to indicate where and how the new tool is to be used.

This example is particularly important because of our belief that environments must be extensible in order both to accomodate evolving tools and techniques, and to support experimentation and evaluation which must drive and direct such evolution. Thus software environments must be extensible, incorporating effective and orderly procedures for the insertion of new tools and types. The foregoing discussion indicates that procedures are not insignificant, suggesting the desirability of carefully defining them and carrying them out by means of still another type of process--namely a process maintenance process (PMP).

Thus we have introduced three separate but closely related types of processes which must be supported by an environment--development processes (DP's), process development processes (PDP's) and process maintenance processes (PMP's). In order to be sufficiently powerful and effective, a software environment must recognize the legitimacy and separate characteristics of all three, must support the careful definition of all three, and must offer tool and procedural support for all three. Indeed, we believe that effective software maintenance within a rigorous framework cannot be carried out without acknowledging and supporting all three.

We observe in passing that these three processes are by no means the only processes which a software environment must support. Some other processes, and considerable further discussion of the three we have already mentioned can be found in [Osterweil 86].

It is important not to leave the reader with a pessimistic view that software development cannot begin until a bewilderingly complex web of processes has been built from scratch. Instead, we must hasten to point out that it is likely that these different types of processes may share significant amounts of substructure and tool support and that, as all are objects, many might well be expected to have been developed by alteration or adaptation of other, preexisting processes.

3.1. Objects, Types, Tools and Processes.

We now proceed to more specific discussions of objects, types, tools and processes--the key architectural components of a software environment. We recall that an environment is best understood as a system for supporting the rigorous definition and subsequent interpretive execution of software process descriptions, where these descriptions are expressed by means of a language which supports the rigorous definition of objects, types and operators. Relatively little will be said about the flow of control facilities of the language. Preliminary work indicates, however, that the language will have to contain extensive flow of control and proceduring mechanisms and will also have to support structures for concurrency and task synchronization. This point is addressed in some detail in [Osterweil 86].

3.2. Object Management.

We have argued that tools should be viewed as functional tranformers acting upon objects in much the same way that machine language instructions act upon their operands. In both cases control and discipline result from allowing operands to be accessed only by a small selected set of accessing primitives and basic manipulative functions (which can, of course, be composed to produce higher level functionality).

This is how hardware systems implement primitive types, such as integer and real. Modern programming languages provide the user with additional types which are not implemented in hardware, but are offered to the user in a similarly restricted and disciplined fashion. Some languages also offer the user facilities for creating new types-- abstract data types--in which use and access are restricted and disciplined in the same way.

Data types in a process description language will be defined in this way also. Instances of a type will only be created, accessed and manipulated through a small set of previously defined functional primitives. Tools will be highly modular, generally being composed out of a number of smaller tool fragments. These tool fragments will all access a needed object only through an accessing primitive for the type of which the object is an instance. This will enable tool fragments to share, manipulate, and elaborate upon objects created by other tool fragments while also incorporating the sort of discipline in object access that will insure the integrity, modifiablility and extensibility of the environment.

Unfortunately current computer systems do not assure that persistent objects will always be accessed only in such a disciplined way. Such discipline can be assured within any single execution of a program written in a language such as Ada (TM). After termination of the execution of that program, however, persistent objects are generally made accessible and alterable with ordinary utility tools. Data base management systems often enforce such disciplined access control, but usually only for a very limited class of types (e.g., integers, reals, and character strings) and structures (e.g., relations). Moreover, they present a view of storage as one monolithic unit (e.g., the data base) with one set of general purpose operations.

Consequently, we have concluded that a software environment which implements the architectural view we are suggesting will have to incorporate its own object management subsystem for providing the sort of disciplined object access required to assure integrity, flexibility and extensibility.

3.2.1. Objects.

The objects which seem to require management in a software environment range widely in size and character. Small objects, such as tokens and graph edges, require management, but so do large objects such as entire programs or diagnostic output objects. Objects may be as diverse as text, object code, test data, symbol tables or bitmap display frames. One organizing premise which seems most helpful is to require that each object be considered to be an instance of a type. This by itself does not seem to provide enough structure and organization to support effective object management, however.

In addition, it seems important to recognize that each object is also generally related to a number of other objects in the store by a potentially large variety of types of relations. These interobject relations should be stored explicitly as objects in order to be of maximum utility. Some examples of types of interobject relations are: versioning, consistency, derivation and hierarchy.

Hierarchy relations enable users to, for example, model the inherent structure of systems being developed or maintained. Hierarchical structures should be implemented in such a way as to allow objects to be grouped, and to allow such groups to be objects which can then be included in other groups. It should be possible for these groups to overlap, making it possible for a user to include an object in several hierarchical structures. This inclusion should be logical rather than physical, however, to eliminate duplication of storage or difficulties in properly reflecting updates of shared objects. Our experience with a similar capability in the Toolpack project [Osterweil 83, ClemOst 86] indicates that this capability encourages users to think and operate at a higher level of abstraction.

The types, of which individual objects are instances, should also form a hierarchy. Types should be structured by a subtype relation similar to that in Smalltalk 80, in which subtypes inherit accessing primitives from their supertypes. Thus, for example, the type "flowgraph" might well have "set/use annotated flowgraph" as a subtype, in which case "set/use annotated flowgraph" objects will be manipulable by all of the accessing primitives applicable to objects of type "flowgraph." This should simplify the implementation, exploitation and conceptualization of both types and type instances (objects) in environments of the sort we are suggesting here.

It is worthwhile to point out that the objects of given type may also be organized hierarchically, and that their hierarchy may not bear any relation to the hierarchical structure which includes their types.

It is particularly important that the object store incorporate explicit consistency relations among its objects as consistency is the property whose establishment is the goal of testing and evaluation. Testing and evaluation seek to study the presence or absence of errors, and errors are essentially inconsistencies among software objects. Most often an error is an inconsistency between a specification of intent and a solution specification (eg. see [Osterweil 82, Osterweil 81]). Thus testing and evaluation tools can appropriately be viewed as operators aimed at either establishing or disproving consistency relations. It seems most logical and effective for these relations to be explicit.

The value of explicitly storing the derivation relation among objects will be addressed shortly.

It is important to point out that types and the type hierarchy itself should all be treated as objects. This observation is useful in further explaining our earlier comments on maintenance. As observed earlier, it is vital that an environment support the alteration or addition of new types to a DP. As types are to be defined as clusters of accessing primitives and are organized into a hierarchy, type alteration or addition entails potentially complex transformations to these clusters and hierarchy. That is why we believe that such alteration or addition is best thought of and carried out as a well-defined algorithmic procedure (a PMP). Certainly a PMP must be defined in terms of operations on objects, types and type structures are the objects.

This observation makes it clear that an environment cannot be viewed as a single process, but rather as an interconnected collection of processes. An environment must support a PDP by enabling the definition and manipulation of types and type structures as objects. These objects can then be frozen and perpetuated for use by the DP. Within a DP, however, it is generally desirable that these types not be considered objects, but rather collections of executable code procedures. Within a DP the integrity of a type definition can be maintained by stripping away any primitives capable of accessing the type definition primitives. This would imply that the type (ie. its collection of accessing primitives) could only be changed by a PMP within which the type is an object by virtue of the inclusion of primitives capable of accessing the type's accessing primitives. Such an approach offers the advantages of 1)control over the how a type is defined, 2) discipline in how type instances must be accessed and altered, but 3) a controlled and careful way in which type definitions can be altered.

3.2.2. Persistence.

An environment must also support persistence--the ability to save objects beyond the end of execution of any of the tool or processes that manipulate it. Nevertheless, the environment must assure that all accesses to that object are only through the object's accessing functions. Thus, an object should be allowed to persist only if its accessing primitives persist as well. Thus an instance of an object can not be separated from the defined operations on that object.

Returning to our previous discussion of types, we note that a type object does not persist from a PDP through to a DP, because it is no longer an object during the DP. The type object does persist from a defining PDP through to an altering PMP, because during the PMP it is possible to change the type definition. This necessitates the persistence of all of the type object's accessing primitives and the persistence of the type object as an object.

For the most part, tools should be unaware of the persistence of the objects that they manipulate. Thus tools should access objects without knowing how or when they were created. Objects produced by intermediate tool fragments, in response to user requests should be saved by the environment's object manager according to some algorithm for evaluating potential for future reuse. These persistent intermediate objects should then be available for reuse in responding to a subsequent user request, thereby expediting the environment's response. This notion was advanced and implemented in the Toolpack project through the Odin integration system [Clemm 86, ClemOst 86].

3.3. Tool Management.

Tool management capabilities complement object management capabilities. This is appropriate and logical because tools are viewed as functional tranducers defined on objects, and objects are instances of types defined in terms of functional primitives. Thus in this section we stress the relationships among tools and objects as a primary focal point of our discussion.

3.3.1. Tool Structure.

An environment must be a vehicle for providing extensive and growing tool capabilities. These capabilities should be furnished primarily by collections of small tools--tool fragments-- rather than by a few, large, monolithic tools. For example, the task of prettyprinting should be carried out by a collection of tool fragments including a lexical analyzer, a parser, and a formatter-- operating in concert. More sophisticated prettyprinting functions require the invocation of a static semantic analyzer. An instrumented test execution requires upwards of a dozen tool fragments, operating at times in sequence and at times in parallel.

One of the main advantages of composing larger tools out of smaller fragments is that, if the tool fragments are well chosen, they will prove to be usable as components of a variety of larger tools, thereby enabling the creation of these larger tools at lower cost. For example, both the prettyprinter and dynamic instrumentation tool just mentioned require lexical analysis and parsing in order to begin their work. Both tools incorporate these fragments, thereby saving the creators of these tools the effort of having to recreate these functional capabilities.

The tool fragment architecture also leads to the materialization of intermediate objects which, if made persistent, can, as noted above, lead to efficiency through reuse. We now see that an environment can support both reuse of tool fragments in the creation of tools during a PDP and reuse of intermediate software objects during a corresponding DP.

Another benefit of the tool fragment architecture is that it encourages toolmakers to think in terms of good modular decomposition for their tools and good organization for the objects which their tools use. Thus, we believe that the writer of a prettyprinter, for example, will create a better tool because correspondingly more time can be spent on the problem of prettyprinting, and no time need be wasted on creating a parser. In addition, because the writer of the prettyprinter accesses the output of a proven parser, the prettyprinter is likely to be better for its reliance on a more robust and thorough parser than would likely have been created from scratch. In short, we contend that the prettyprinter will be a better tool because it will be based conceptually upon such data and software constructs as lexical tokens, parse trees, and symbol tables and will be based physically upon major bodies of robust proven code.

3.3.2. Tool Structure and Relationships.

In previous sections we have described numerous benefits of treating tools as transformers of instances of types. We noted that this discipline makes it possible to prevent the application of tools to inappropriate objects; that it supports the definition of tool invocation sequences which rigorously stipulate potentially reusable intermediate products of such sequences. We shall also see shortly that it also contributes to version control, demand-driven (lazy) rederivation of modified objects, and a useful form of inferencing that can be exploited by planning tools.

In this section we see that it is also the basis for definition of a structure which relates tools-- the Type Dependency Graph (TDG). A TDG is a structure which contains as its nodes all of the types known to the environment's object manager, and has as its edges annotated designations of the various tools. Thus, a TDG summarizes the relationships between tools and objects. Specifically, a tool may only operate on objects that are instances of the types found at the origin of an edge in the TDG bearing that tool's designation. Similarly, the only tools that can produce objects of a given type are those whose designation appears on an edge that terminates in a TDG node corresponding to that type.

A TDG induces derivation relationships on the actual objects in the environment object store. This type of relation among objects was alluded to earlier. Objects, being instances of the types found in a TDG, are related by dependency relationships corresponding to those defined by (some subset of) the TDG edges. These relationships among objects then may be viewed as an Object Dependency Graph (ODG), created and maintained by interaction of the tool and object managers. In particular, newly created objects are said to depend for their creation upon the existence of their predecessors, in which case the object manager records this dependency relation by logically making the new objects descendants of their predecessors in the Object Dependency Graph (ODG).

Each object can be viewed as the root of a subtree of the ODG which we refer to as the object's own Dependency Tree. To be most useful and effective, this subtree should be doubly linked--upwards and downwards. The uplinks of the tree can be followed in order to determine all of the ancestor objects which were used, either directly or indirectly, to create the object; the downlinks of the Dependency Tree indicate which objects depend upon the object for their creation.

Dependency trees have already been exploited in certain version control systems such as RCS [Tichy 83]. In such systems, all descendants are created by the action of a single tool, generally a text editor. It is assumed that there is a single root version, and that this version has a tree of descendants, each of which can be built by successive applications of the tool. One value of this scheme that it helps make clear the potential range of the impact of changes to any one version.

We are suggesting the use of a similar dependency structure within the object store, but this structure is developed, not by successive applications of a single tool, but by applications of any legal sequence of tools. Thus, a user may use the environment to create a Dependency Tree for versions of source code as in RCS, or may create a complex tree in which objects of various types, the results of different sequences of tool applications, are all stored in a single Dependency Tree.

Such an environment must also incorporate algorithms for determining when objects at lower levels of a Dependency Tree have become obsolete because of alterations or deletions of objects higher up in the tree. Whenever an object at a higher level of the tree is changed, the object manager must recognize that all descendants of that object are to be viewed with suspicion. The environment need not take immediate steps to recreate these objects, however. Instead, it can employ a demand-driven reconstruction strategy such as that implemented in Odin [Clemm 86, ClemOst 86], under which new versions of an object are not created until they have been requested either directly or indirectly by the user. At that time, all the objects reachable by traversing uplinks from the object in the Dependency Tree are examined. If the object was, in fact, created from ancestor objects which have subsequently been altered, the object manager must begin the process of recomputing it from the current version of the ancestor objects. Objects between the altered ancestors and the desired object must be reconstructed. They must also be compared to their previous versions. If, at any point, the reconstructed objects match their previous versions, the reconstruction process can stop and the equivalence of old and new versions of objects lower in the tree relied upon.

3.3.3. Planning Tool Activations.

In general we have learned that the functional capabilities which users require and expect from tools tend to become so complex that it is difficult to determine in advance the order in which tool fragments will have to be invoked in order to derive a requested object from existing objects. For example, a data flow analyzer (eg. [FosdOst 76]) must analyze the compilation units of a program in two passes, where the order of analysis during the second pass is computed during the first pass. In this case it is impossible to predetermine the exact order of invocation of tool fragments on the separate software objects. An environment must support the synthesis of such tools. One way in which this can be done is by means of a planning tool fragment whose job is to dynamically create tool invocation sequences that are tailored and adjusted in accordance with the current state of the object store and preprogrammed conditions. Planner tools have been used in Odin to create tool invocation sequences in which tools are scheduled for future invocation and in which software objects are taken and produced in unexpected or changed orders. In addition, planners have been used to schedule the invocation of other planners at projected future critical points.

Finally it is important to point out that an environment must support the notion of active as well as passive tools. Active tools commence execution without direct invocation by users. They carry out their activities by acccessing objects according to plans designed in advance, probably by software engineers during the PDP. These active tools must be invokable by such control mechanisms as timers or daemons, whose job is to detect relevant changes in the object store.

This capability seems to be a particularly useful one to a PMP. Specifically, we expect that a maintenance process would have to incorporate a task consisting of or containing an active tool whose job would be to periodically, and on its own initiative, recompute certain prespecified consistency relations to see if changes had altered the value of the relations from true to false. If so, then the need for changes to other objects is indicated.

3.3.4. Tools as Objects.

In the environment architecture which we are proposing here tools and tool fragments are objects in precisely the same sense in which types are objects. Similarly, the Type Dependency Graph (TDG) is an object in the same sense in which a type structure is an object. Tools, tool fragments and TDG's are objects during a PDP, but are not objects during a DP. Thus, tools, tool fragments, and the TDG are key components and agents of any DP, but they have no accessing primitives associated with them and cannot be altered by or during a DP. On the other hand all are objects during a PDP and can therefore be altered. Of course, as with alterations to types, such alterations need to be communicated to, and their effects assimilated by, affected DP's. This is one of the jobs of a PMP.

The delineation of these three processes and identification of the objects upon which they operate has served to sharpen our appreciation of the functional roles of the various users of a software environment. For example, the internal composition of tools should be of limited interest to those using the tools as part of a DP, but must necessarily be a primary concern of tool developers as part of a PDP Thus tool developers are expected to develop and alter tools as part of a PDP. As part of that process they should be able to use tool and object managers to access tool specification objects, current tool fragment objects, and development object types to assist them in the creation (or modification) of new tool objects, and the alteration of TDG's to accomodate such additions and alterations.

Once tools or types have been changed, a PMP must evaluate the changes made and propagate their effects carefully and efficiently. For example, if an existing object type is modified in such a way that there are no changes in the set of accessing primitives that define the type, then a PMP should not need to make any consequent changes to a DP using that type and incorporating instances of that type.

On the other hand, if any of the accessing primitives defining that type are changed, then a new type is thereby created. This necessarily affects all tool fragments which either created or used objects of that type, and all DP's using the type and such tool fragments. Changes to tools, TDG's and impacted processes must be determined and made as part of a PMP. Clearly careful attention must be paid to this process and to the creation of new tools which might be of particular value in supporting the process. In particular, it may be desirable to create a tool that can transform objects of the old type to objects of the new, and incorporate a corresponding edge in the TDG.

4. Future Directions of This Research.

We are convinced that the foregoing ideas can form the core of the architecture of a very powerful, flexible and extensible software environment. Further we believe that these ideas bring a great deal of unity and focus to the efforts of software process researchers, software environment researchers and architects, and programming language researchers. We have already embarked upon a broad and vigorous program of research aimed at exploring the ramifications of these ideas, sharpening and refining them, and experimentally evaluating them. In this section we briefly present some of the key issues that we see as the prominent ones in this research.

We suggest that diverse areas of software engineering research can be significantly advanced by establishing a language in which software engineering processes can be effectively expressed, by expressing various key processes in that language, by creating compilation and runtime support systems for that language, and by then attempting to use these systems to provide effective automated support for the execution of these key software processes. Finally, we suggest that all of this is best pursued by creating and experimenting with an actual software environment predicated upon these ideas. Work on such a prototype environment is currently being begun. This environment is called Arcadia [Arcadia 86].

A central focus to this research is to to devise and study various algorithms for expressing software engineering processes. We have already begun to create algorithms for software development, software product maintenance, software process maintenance, software product evaluation and software process evaluation. As we have proceeded with the iterative refinement of these algorithms we have begun to learn much about the nature of these processes, their relations to each other and to other processes such as reuse. Thus we expect that continuation of this activity will lead to more important insights, and, eventually to sound process algorithms.

Our intention is to arrive at acceptable algorithms for describing development, maintenance, evaluation and testing, and reuse. Having devised these algorithms we propose to solidify our notions of superior language paradigms and constructs for expressing them, and to solidify our notions of tool and environment architecture by examining the runtime structures and procedures needed to effectively support execution of these algorithms.

4.1. Design of the Software Engineering Language Itself.

While exploratory development of process algorithms seems more central to the pursuit of this research, development of a language system in which such algorithms might be encoded also strikes us as important. As this area is somewhat better established, it seems, moreover, easier to categorize and organize the way in which this research might be pursued.

In this section we attempt to indicate how an orderly attack on the problem of creating a software engineering language might be organized.

4.1.1. The Language Paradigm.

The first task in defining this language will be to decide which linguistic paradigm is most suitable. Our early investigations have built upon a bias towards the use of an algorithmic language. This bias is at least largely based upon our belief that software engineers will be drawn from the ranks of software practitioners, and are most likely to be trained in programming in algorithmic, sequential (possibly parallel) programming languages. Thus it is most attractive to suggest that, as software engineers, they program in a language with a similar, and therefore comfortable, philosophy and paradigm. Making such an important decision based solely on the grounds of tradition and convenience is imprudent, however. Thus we have attempted to seek deeper justification for this prediliction.

Our second basis for believing that a parallel, sequential algorithmic language is best suited for programming software engineering is that software development and maintenance are to be carried out by human practitioners, and humans seem to us to be psychologically most self assured in thinking about their plans and actions in terms of discrete, sequential steps and activities. Thus, a programming language which will be use to describe, regulate and control their activities in building software should seem most natural and comfortable if it expresses their activities in similarly discrete and sequential steps.

Although our current predisposition is towards more traditional and comfortable algorithmic languages, we recognize the need to consider non-traditional languages as well. We have, accordingly, pondered a variety of non-algorithmic language paradigms. One interesting paradigm, for example, is that of a process control language. As previously described, software development and maintenance might well be viewed as a real-time processes involving the synchronization of the activities of people and mechanized aids. Borrowing from the idiom of process control software might thus be highly effective. From this perspective, activities such as code and design creation would correspond to synthesis (input) processes, and consistency checking activities would correspond to analysis processes. The software development program would then be a software system which incorporated a variety of such synthesis and analysis processes as asynchronous tasks, which, nevertheless communicated broadly among themselves, and paused at programmed intervals and events to synchronize and evaluate progress and consistency. Thus, control process software should be examined carefully as a model which might be worth emulating. Simulation languages capable of supporting the programming of such processes (eg. Simula and Simscript) are also worth examining.

Other potentially useful paradigms include object-oriented languages, functional or applicative languages and database language approaches. The appeal of an object oriented language approach is that it would clearly support and encourage the view of a software product as a collection of objects of diverse types. It seems clear that the designer of a language for software engineering should borrow heavily from object oriented language mechanisms for defining object types and operations on such types. In fact this strategy has been adopted by some KBSE researchers. Their work centers on the creation of a large and intricate knowledge structure which captures and correctly interrelates all information pertaining to the software being developed or maintained, and using that knowledge effectively in support of these processes. This is important to us, because, as observed earlier, our SPS can very reasonably be viewed as a knowledge structure, although it seems that the SPS and SP's we envision would probably be structures of much larger objects than are envisioned as the constituents of KBSE's.

We are still not persuaded that we should adopt an object-oriented language paradigm for our work, however, because of our relatively greater emphasis on the algorithms needed to develop and maintain the knowledge and information structures which we agree are central. We remain convinced that software engineers and practitioners do maintain a strongly algorithmic view of what they do, but that they have been thwarted in effectively exploiting it due to the lack of an adequate expressive device. Object oriented languages do not seem to us to sufficiently encourage the attention to algorithmic expression which seems urgently needed at this stage of exploration of the algorithmic nature of software engineering processes.

The appeal of a functional language is that it could support and encourage the view that software processes (eg. development and maintenance) are essentially the evaluation of large functions which are computed by the evaluation of a complex substructure of smaller functions. This view is appealing in that the software product which is the focus of these software processes is a complex composite of smaller objects and interrelations. Thus, it seems quite useful to describe processes on this product as the processes of creating its subcomponents and evaluating needed interrelations.

There appear to be significant problems in adopting a functional programming language approach, however. One is the need to at least partially linearize the order of evaluation of functions and subfunctions. The problem here is that some of the functions are to be carried out by humans who have difficulty carrying out unbounded parallel activities, and because the other functions must be carried out on a bounded number of computing devices. Functional programming systems assume the responsibility for such linearization, and take this process out of the hands of the software engineer. This strikes us as being awkward, at least for the present, when efficient compilation of efficient object code for large and complex functional programs is very much a research topic. Further, we continue to believe that some aspects of at least some software development processes are more straightforwardly describable in terms of sequential algorithmic steps rather than composition and nesting of functions. Testing and consistency determination would seem to be in this category. Thus, perhaps it is most reasonable to design the software engineering language in such a way as to combine both procedural and functional programming capabilities in such a way as to exploit the strengths of each in supporting software engineering process description and control.

Finally, it seems certain that at least some of the notational and descriptive devices used in database languages are useful as means for describing the software product in a software engineering language. Thus we would expect to borrow at least some of the descriptive mechanisms of such languages. We are not as sanguine about the prospect of exploiting such languages as vehicles for expressing software processes. We are particularly skeptical about how well such languages and associated support systems would be able to support software process maintenance. Earlier we observed that this sort of maintenance entails alteration of the software product structure (the database schema) while retaining and reassimilating most, if not all, of its contents. We believe that extensible algorithmic language compilation systems currently provide the most useful paradigms for how to approach this problem.

Whatever the language paradigms used or merged to form the basis for the software engineering language, there will have to be important further research in establishing an effective semantic base within that language for support of software activities. Thus another important aspect of this research will be the determination of the built-in primitive data types and operators which the language should provide, as well as the appropriate linguistic and conceptual treatment of the relations which bind software objects together to form software products.

4.1.2. A Compilation System for the Software Engineering Language.

As a primary reason for creating a software engineering language is to use it to coordinate the work of software tools and their integration into a cogent software environment, a prerequisite for such a language is that it be supported by an effective compiler for the language. This compiler will have to accept specifications of such objects as types, TDG's, and ODG's and transform them into object stores which will then be able to organize and structure software objects as they are created. The compiler will also have to accept development and maintenance process definitions and transform them into procedures which coordinate the work of human software workers with each other and with the activities of software tools which implement various automatically supported software operations.

Compilation issues can be divided broadly into three types--syntactic issues, semantic issues and code generation issues. The last two types of issues seem to be the most interesting.

4.1.2.1. Semantic Issues.

It is difficult to guess at which issues will pose the most difficulty in carrying out semantic analysis of the software engineering language, especially in view of the fact that not even the language paradigm has been selected. On the other hand, it does seem that a powerful and extensible type structure is essential, and this indicates that the semantic phase will have to be capable of potentially sophisticated type checking. In addition, the need for supporting extensions and alterations to the type structure of the language, while facilitating the large-scale retention of objects created under the previous type schema, indicate the need for a compilation system in which the type structure can be modified as an object and used to create a new semantic phase for the compiler. In addition, the compilation system must be capable of analyzing the differences between the old and new type structures to enable maximal reuse and retention of objects.

This last observation suggests a more precise interpretation of our earlier suggestion that the software environment which we are proposing might be useful in maintaining itself. We suggest that it is useful to consider the compiler for the software engineering language must be considered to be an object. Any single executable instance of the software engineering language compiler should be considered to be an operator in a PDP. The source text of the compiler, however, should be considered to be an object in a PMP, thereby enabling the PMP to alter the semantics of the language. Thus the semantics-alteration process we have described is a specific type of PMP.

4.1.2.2. Software Engineering Language Optimization Issues.

The task of the optimization phase of software engineering language compilation systems is to emit sequences of instructions to carry out and synchronize either human operations or computer based activities in such a way as to effect the algorithmic processes described by the coder. Language semantic definitions should assure that there is no doubt about how language operations are to be interpreted in terms of manual processes and mechanized tools. Further, control flow and synchronization operations will also require semantic definition in order to enable emission of effective object code.

Generation of efficient code is a more interesting problem. Two efficiency issues suggest themselves--one is the efficient storage of software objects and the second is effective reuse of intermediate software objects. The problem of achieving efficient storage of software

Thus, the desirability of optimizing the object code generated by the software engineering language compiler provides strong impetus for the implementation of functional tools as composites of smaller, lower level tools (called tool fragments in [Osterweil 83]). The strategy governing the way in which intermediate objects are selected for storage for potential reuse was a research issue in the context of [Osterweil 83]. Language statements were processed essentially interactively and there were no alternatives to statistical approaches to guide the strategy for saving intermediate objects. In this proposal, with our suggestion that software development and maintenance processes be captured in compilable code, it becomes clear that optimization algorithms and strategies much like those used in classical languages can and should be applied.

4.1.3. Runtime Support for the Software Engineering Language Processor.

It is clear that the software engineering language will require powerful runtime support subsystems in order to be the basis for effective execution of software engineering processes. Two key areas of support immediately suggest themselves for early consideration-- object management and input/output.

The need for a powerful object manager has been amply indicated by earlier sections of this paper. One of the central concepts in the approach we are suggesting here is that software development be thought of in terms of the need for creating, organizing and managing software objects. Clearly it is imperative to have effective ways in which to store them. The problems in doing so are badly compounded by our contention that objects are tightly interconnected to each other by such types of relations as hierarchy, derivation, and consistency. Clearly such simple organizational strategies as tree structures are woefully inadequate. We believe that relational database approaches have serious drawbacks as well. Some of these have been indicated earlier, and center on the dynamism of the structure of the object store.

We view the Odin system [ClemOst 86] as a prototype object management capability which incorporates a number of desirable features. From the perspective of this paper, we now understand that Odin actually incorporates some features of a software engineering language subset, a semantic analyzer modification and maintenance system subset, and an object manager. It seems clear that whatever object managment system is incorporated into the proposed software engineering language, it will have to have strong ties to the semantic analysis phase of the language compiler.

Input/output capabilities for the language are also quite interesting to ponder. Here we are inclined to view all processes which are carried out by humans as being input objects is an important one, which seems to fall more in the province of runtime support systems, and will be discussed shortly. The problem of achieving effective reuse of intermediate objects is a central issue in compilation and also affects the philosophy of tool implementation. Reuse of intermediate objects is only possible if the operations specified by the user can be seen as being composed of lower level operations which create such intermediate objects. Thus, if all of the operations in the software engineering language are implemented as monoliths, there would seem to be correspondingly little opportunity for reuse of intermediate objects. On the other hand, if operations are generally implemented as concatenations or structures of lower level operators, which produce intermediate software objects, these then become ideal candidates for reuse in subsequent computations.

processes, and therefore in need of language assistance. Such assistance would have to range from simple text I/O support, through interactive editor support, to support for interaction with graphical and pictorial images. It seems essential that all of these interactions be implemented and supported in terms of basic language I/O primitives to assure a reasonably uniform user view of the software processing capabilities offered. Thus, whether the user were creating source code, design elements, test data sets or functional specifications, there would be a strong sense of uniformity of interaction with the software engineering language's features.

Output would have to offer a similarly uniform feel. The purpose of output capabilities would be to enable the user to see objects and relations in the emerging software product. Thus, we expect that it will be important for the user to be able to view a variety of objects, perhaps from a variety of perspectives, and to interact with those objects. This suggests that the I/O package will have to incorporate such capabilities as windowing, and menus. The use of color might well also prove to be of value.

Finally, it should be noted that the software engineer is also likely to need to view the process-objects which are being created and to get some insight into the processes which have been constructed. This interaction is different from the interaction needed by software practitioners. It corresponds more to the needs of a debugger of a program than to the needs of a user of that program. Thus, it is expected that the runtime system will also have to incorporate tools and capabilities for enabling the software engineer to study the structure and contents of the software process-object itself, in addition to the structure and contents of its individual component objects and relations. Here too, we are struck by the fact that these needs do not differ signifcantly from the needs of the software practitioners. This again suggests that the software engineering language may be adequate for the development and maintenance of programs for the development and maintenance of software process-objects.

4.2. The Arcadia Protype Environment Project.

As indicated above, many of these ideas are to be experimentally evaluated through a collaborative effort to build a protoype environment implementing many of these ideas. This prototype environment is to be called Arcadia. The Arcadia project involves researchers from the University of California at Irvine, the University of Massachusetts at Amherst, the University of Colorado at Boulder, TRW, Inc., Aerospace Corporation, and Incremental Systems Corp. More details of the Arcadia approach and directions can be found in [Arcadia 86].

5. Acknowledgments.

The ideas described here have been developed over a period of a few years. The author has profited considerably from many useful conversations with a number of colleagues. Numerous conversations with John Buxton, Dick Taylor, Bob Balzer, Lori Clarke and Geoff Clemm have been particularly useful in shaping these ideas.

In addition, the author wishes to express his gratitude to the National Science Foundation, and the US Department of Energy for their support of this work through grants numbered, DCR-8403341 and DE-FG02-84ER13283 respectively.

6. REFERENCES.

[Arcadia 86]   R.Taylor, et.al., "Arcadia: A Software Development
Environment Research Project," Univ. of Calif.,
Irvine, Dept. of Info. and Comp. Sci, Tech. Rpt.,
April 1986.

[Clemm 86]   G.M. Clemm, "The Odin System: An Object Manager for
Extensible Software Environments,"
Univ. of Colo. Dept. of Comp. Sci. Ph.D. Thesis
Boulder, CO (1986).

[ClemmOst 86]   G.M. Clemm and L.J. Osterweil, "The Odin Environment
Integration Mechanism," Univ. of Colo. Dept. of
Comp. Sci. Tech. Rpt. #CU-CS-323-86 (May 1986).

[FosdOst 76]   L.D. Fosdick and L.J. Osterweil, "Data Flow Analysis
in Software Reliability," ACM Computing Surveys,
8 pp. 305-330 (Sept. 1976).

[Goldberg 84]   A. Goldberg, "Smalltalk-80: The Interactive
Programming Environment," Addison-Wesley, Reading,
Mass, 1984.

[JeffTPA 81]   R.Jeffries, A.Turner, P.Polson, M.Atwood, "The
Processes Involved in Designing Software," in
Cognitive Skills and Their Acquisition,"
(Anderson, ed.) Lawrence Erlbaum, Hillsdale, NJ, 1981.

[Osterweil 81]   L. J. Osterweil, "Using Data Flow Tools in Software
Engineering," in Program Flow Analysis: Theory and
Application (Muchnick and Jones, eds.) Prentice-Hall
Englewood Cliffs, N.J., 1981.

[Osterweil 82]   L.J. Osterweil, "A Strategy for Integrating Program
Program Testing and Analysis," in Program Testing,
(Chandrasekaran and Radicchi, eds.) North Holland,
pp. 187-229, (1982).

[Osterweil 83]   L.J. Osterweil, "Toolpack--An Experimental
Software Development Environment Research
Project," IEEE Trans. on Software Eng., SE-9,
pp. 673-685 (November 1983).

[Osterweil 86]   L.J. Osterweil, "Software Process Interpretation
and Software Environments," Univ. of Colo. Dept.
of Comp. Sci. Tech Rpt. #CU-CS-324 (May 1986).

[SPW1 84]   Proceedings of Software Process Workshop, Runnymede,
England, February 1984.

[SPW2 85]   Proceedings of Second Software Process Workshop,
Coto de Caza, CA, March 1985.

[TeitMas 81]   W.Teitelman and L.Masinter, "The Interlisp Programming
Environment," Computer, 14 pp. 25-33 (April 1981).

[Tichy 83]   W. Tichy, "Design, implementation and evaluation of a
revision control system," Proc. 6th Int. Conf. on
Software Engineering, Tokyo, (Sept. 1982) pp.58-67.

Software Development Environments: Research to Practice

Robert J. Ellison
Software Engineering Institute
Carnegie-Mellon University
Pittsburgh, Pa. 15213

1 Introduction

During the last few years, we have seen the appearance of a number of software development environments for support of programming-in-the-large [Boehm 84] [DeRemer 75]. The Software Engineering Institute at Carnegie-Mellon University has been tasked with speeding the transition of modern software engineering technology to practice [Barbacci 85]. Part of that effort has been devoted to examining large-scale software development environment efforts. This note represents the author's observations of that process as well as the comments expressed by the participants of the SEI workshop on the *Software Factory of the Future*, which was held in Morgantown, West Virginia in October, 1985. It also reflects the rationale that helps guide the definition of SEI projects on software development environments.

2 Transition of Environment Technology to Practice

While there has been significant research activity with respect to environment generation [Reps 84] [Habermann 82], very little of that work has yet to appear in practice. Current large-scale environments are primarily hand crafted and often reflect the organization's internal software methodology. There are a wide variety of implementation schemes. Some organizations integrate a large collection of internally developed tools, while others have adopted a strategy of using commercial tooling. There is little commonality of the underlying system support for networks, databases, tooling, tool interface conventions, or user interfaces. The potential for sharing among these environments appears to be rather limited.

The SEI's primary mission is the transition of modern software engineering methods to practice. Software engineering environments represent a good means to support that end. They provide the means both to integrate tools and to provide a uniform conceptual framework for the user. While from one point of view an environment can enforce unform practices, it also provides the means to maintain the rich information base that most likely will be required to support reusability of requirements and designs. The SEI's role with respect to environments is not to build a specific environment, but to help explore the validity of new concepts by building prototypes, to stimulate the research community to attack critical problems, and to refine the requirements for the next generation of large-scale environments.

This work was sponsored by the Department of Defense. The views and conclusions contained in this document are solely those of the author and should not be interpreted as representing official policies, either expressed or implied, of Carnegie-Mellon University, the U.S. Air Force, the Department of Defense, or the U.S. Government.

There are some pragmatic considerations that impact the design of industrial-grade environments that should be addressed if we want to see environments applied successfully to large-scale software development. The most critical issue may be the controlled evolution of the environment. Software development environments must adjust to new hardware such as workstations or graphical displays, and to software such as database technology or operating system support for distributing computing; they also must be able to reflect changes in the software process as the field of software engineering matures. In practice, an environment also must adjust over the life of a project to changes in project objectives or management policies. Within one organization, the demand will exist to tailor or extend the base-line environment to support needs specific to a project or application. This issue will be especially critical for an organization such as the SEI that has been charged with the task of speeding transition of research concepts to practice. While a specific environment might provide a good vehicle for the rapid introduction of Ada and associated software engineering practices, that same environment may be a significant impediment to the next wave of technological changes if it is not easy to modify or extend. Thus, while it may be hard to convince management to buy or build its first software development environment, it will probably be even harder to sell the second one given the initial investment. The state of the current practice and the relatively immature state of the theory for large-scale environments suggest that we would be naive to expect current environments to be long lived. On the other hand, it is not reasonable to continue to replace, rather than evolve, such expensive systems.

3 Scope: Environment Construction

A discussion of the construction of large-scale environments often turns to the management of scale. Such environments must not only manage a large amount of information, they also must coordinate the efforts of a large programming team. The issue is a natural one as many research prototypes have not demonstrated that they can manage a project even on the order of 100,000 lines of source code, and the existing industrial systems seem to stretch the capability of current database systems. Certainly scale will be one of the issues that the SEI will address, but several trends suggest that the scope of the environment should have higher priority in terms of increased functionality across the full life cycle as well as better integration between life-cycle phases.

Environment research in recent years has concentrated on the coding phase of software development and has been able to build on the theoretical foundations on language syntax and semantics. The design of full life-cycle environments does not yet have the equivalent underpinnings. The issue is not just the coverage of life-cycle phases, but the quality and type of tooling so that we can support the highly interactive and incremental style of processing demonstrated in [Habermann 82], [Reiss 84] or [Reps 84]. While work like [Kaiser 85] or [Taylor 86] is a first step, there is nothing of equivalent maturity for dealing with the semantics of a full life-cycle environment. Certainly work in artificial intelligence or formal methods will apply, but it is precisely because an environment must mix such a variety of approaches that the design of the foundation becomes so critical.

The construction of environment generators has primarily been a research topic, but the pragmatic considerations discussed above suggest that it will be critical to automate environment construction and that this topic should be given priority by the SEI. The size and complexity of modern environments demand resuable components. While first generation environment generators primarily concentrated on programming-in-the-small and the static semantics of ALGOL-class languages, they demonstrated the kind of reusability and extensibility that will be needed. Gandalf [Habermann 82] attempted to address some of the issues involved with programming-in-the-large, and experience with that system [Ellison 85] raised several issues that impact building large-scale environments.

The complexity of environments is driven by the desire to support the semantics of the software process in addition to the semantics of the implementation languages. A major goal of the Gandalf project was to address the semantic issues that arise with large-scale environments. The first environment prototypes constructed with the Gandalf system emphasized configuration management, version control, and project management, and the semantic issues raised by the effort is described in [Kaiser 85]. The Gandalf system is data driven. A procedure called an action routine is attached to each type of data and is responsible for maintaining consistency whenever that item is modified. Semantic information is effectively centralized in the action routine, and in most instances invisible to tool fragments. Whenever possible, tool activation is tied to the data rather than embedded in the tools themselves. This approach can make it easier to reuse tool fragments and to extend the system. This kind of separation will be more critical as we embed the semantics of the software process into environments. There are a variety of implementation schemes other than the Gandalf ones, such as a rule-based paradigm, that can obtain the same result. Kaiser [Kaiser 85] describes a more declarative approach.

Experience with environment generators, such as Gandalf, raises questions about the nature of tools in the next generation of environments. In most instances the user interface, the presentation of the data, and tool activation are separated from the tools themselves. That kind of architecture seems to be required if we are to manage effectively the change in environments as well as support tool fragments that are effectively reusable. That trend continues into new work such as Arcadia [Taylor 86] and was one area of agreement at the Morgantown workshop. Such a tool architecture raises difficult problems in terms of moving such a concept to practice. If the style of tool construction is too different, then importation of existing tools will be difficult. This is an issue that organizations such as the SEI must address.

4 Scope: The Environment User

The kind of general paradigms for environments range from an intelligent software assistant to an automated software factory driven by formal methods. While the complexity of the design and implementation of a large-scale environment often gets the most attention, the issue of the complexity of the user interactions may be more critical and suggests that we should address more carefully the user side of large-scale environments. The issue is not so much human factors but the underlying cognitive models that best support the various tasks. The classic life cycle demonstrates the variety of tasks that must be addressed during software development. The expectation is that the environment can provide integration across the full life cycle and better support users, particularly those in the maintenance or enhancement phase who must work across a variety of phases. While we seek common conventions with respect to the user interface across those tasks, it will be more important to have commonality with respect to the underlying cognitive models.

We should expect that the next generation of environments will support a variety of development paradigms. For example, the early phases of system design may be best attacked by an exploratory paradigm, while later development may be more closely controlled. In general, we should expect to see better support for incremental or evolutionary development and hence for tools that must work across life-cycle phases. Within a well-defined task such as design, there are a variety of paradigms. It may be appropriate to use both data-driven and process-driven methodologies for the same task. The limitations of our current technology or the shear effort of building an environment often lead us to support a single approach. The next generation of environments should support multiple paradigms.

5 SEI Projects

The SEI plans to address a number of the issues raised above. Environments are a continuing source of challenging research problems; but for a technology transition agent such as the SEI, the most difficult problem is to foster reasonable expectations for environments and to find a strategy for making productive use of a still maturing technology. It is not hard to draw the conclusion that the expectations are growing much more rapidly that our means to meet them. There appears to be an emerging consensus in the research community on the appropriate framework for the next generation of environments. Some pieces of that potential solution appear as prototypes, but certainly continued research is required for many topics.

One set of projects will address the infrastructure required of the advanced large-scale environments. The limited reusability that we now see among existing large-scale environments reflects the very limited commonality that we have with respect to user interfaces, database management systems, tool communication, and distributed computing that represent the infrastructure for environment construction. The SEI has set as one of its tasks the formation of a broader consensus on the infrastructure to make it easier to support reusability across environments and to establish a climate whereby the commercial marketplace can better contribute. The initial SEI efforts in this direction concentrate on support for distributed computing and on management of persistent data.

Distributed environments have been particularly difficult to design and build because of the limited support found in most operating systems. Production quality prototypes of distributed operating systems such as the Mach system at Carnegie-Mellon University [Accetta 86] are now available; the increased functionally of such systems will impact both the implementation and functionality of environment tooling. The SEI has two functions here. On one hand, we need to make sure that the operating system requirements for large-scale environments are reflected in the next generation of operating systems. While heterogeneity of hardware and software may be a fact of life, it will be important for a consensus, if not a standard, to be established for inter-process communication in distributed environments. The SEI will take an active role in that effort.

Management of persistent data will be an increasingly critical problem for environments that support extensive reusability or automation [Nestor 86]. The level of technology represented by classical file systems and database management systems may not be sufficient to deal with these information management problems [Nestor 86]. This is an area of on-going research and development where the SEI will be an active participant.

A second group of SEI projects will consider more domain-specific environments and concentrate more on user requirements. Real-time software is a major component of the Department of Defense software efforts. Such software usually must perform within severe constraints of efficiency, reliability, and resource utilization, and is generaly believed to be harder to specify and implement that other types of software. An environment for building real-time systems would appear to have high priority. On the other hand, there is no generally agreed on methodology for specifying, designing, implementing, and maintaining such software, and an environment construction project would be premature. The SEI effort in this area is twofold. One project will examine and evaluate existing methodologies for developing real-time software, perform a comparative critique of them, and recommend a methodology as the most suitable for use, both in general and specifically with Ada. A second project will examine some of the technical problems associated with real-time development environments such as support of debugging and testing.

Artificial intelligence has the potential for making major contributions to improving software development. AI can bring a different perspective to addressing complex problems, such as modeling intellectual processes, and contribute a fresh view on the software development process. It will be important for the SEI to follow those efforts that could impact the basic goals of environments. In addition, this project will address some of the issues we raised above with respect to providing support for multiple paradigms and to extending the notion of activity modeling to better reflect the semantics of the activity.

6 References

[Accetta 86]   Mike Accetta, Robert Baron, William Bolosky, David Golub,Richard Rasid, Avadis Tevanian, and Michael Young. Mach: A New Kernel Foundation for Unix Development. *Proceedings of USENIX Technical Conference.* Summer 1986.

[Barbacci 85]   Mario R. Barbacci, A. Nico Habermann, Mary Shaw. The Software Engineering Institute: Bridging Practice and Potential. *IEEE Software,* November 1985.

[Boehm 84]   Barry W. Boehm, Maria H. Penedo, E. Don Stuckle, Robert D. Williams, and Arthur B. Pyster. A Software Development Environment for Improved Productivity. *COMPUTER,* June 1984.

[DeRemer 75]   Frank DeRemer and Hans Kron. Programming-in-the-Large Versus Programming-in-the-Small. *SIGPLAN Notices,* June 1975.

[Ellison 85]   Robert. J. Ellison and Barbara J. Staudt. The Evolution of the Gandalf System. *The Journal of Systems and Software,* May 1985.

[Habermann 82]   A. N. Habermann and David S. Notkin. The Gandalf Software Development Environment. In *The Second Compendium of Gandalf Documentation.* Carnegie-Mellon University Computer Science Department, January 1982.

[Kaiser 85]   Gail E. Kaiser. *Semantics for Structure Editing Environments.* PhD thesis, Carnegie-Mellon University Computer Science Department, 1985.

[Nestor 86]   John R. Nestor. Toward a Persistent Object Base. May, 1986. This proceedings.

[Reiss 84]   Steven P. Reiss. Graphical Program Development with PECAN Program
                Development Systems. *Proceedings of the ACM SIGSOFT/SIGPLAN
                Software Engineering Symposium on Practical Software Development
                Environments.* ACM SIGSOFT/SIGPLAN, April 1984.

[Reps 84]   Thomas Reps and Tim Teitelbaum. The Synthesizer Generator.
                *Proceedings of the ACM SIGSOFT/SIGPLAN Software Engineering Sym-
                posium on Practical Software Development Environments.* April 1984.

[Riddle 86]   William E. Riddle and Lloyd G. Williams. Software Environments Workshop
                Report. *SIGSOFT Software Engineering Notes,* January 1986.

[Taylor 86]   Richard N. Taylor, Lori Clarke, Leon J. Osterweil, Jack C. Wileden, Alex Wolf
                and Michal Young. Arcadia: A Software Development Environment
                Research Project. January 1986. Carnegie-Mellon University.

Chair   : James Cordy,(Queens Univ., CAN)
Assistant chair : Dag Wanvik,(RUNIT, NOR)

Questions after Muchnick's, Kuo's and Campbell's presentations

Arve Meisingset (Norwegian Telecom., NOR):

I have two questions. The first is to Kuo's paper, which mentiones terms like external, conceptual and internal schemas. ANSI/SPARC produced the three-schema architecture in 1977. That architecture was refined by ISO and it was published in late 1985. Does your implementation intend to comply with these guidelines?

Jeremy Kuo (GTE Lab., USA):

The three layers - internal, conceptual and external - that I discussed are to assure that the higher layers can be supported by the lower layers. Actually, it does not follow any particular model. I'm not sure whether it should be called a schema either. Here, we simply provide data conversion among these three layers. We want to make sure this conceptual layer includes all the primitive concepts I mentioned earlier, and that whatever user-defined types at the external layer can be converted into these primitive concepts. These schemas simply ensure that this data conversion can be done systematically.

Arve Meisingset (Norwegian Telecom., NOR):

Second question: Is your software architecture a centralized architecture in the sense that many external or internal schemas map to a single conceptual one?

Jeremy Kuo (GTE Lab., USA):

The logical model of the database in our environment is very much centralized. As for distributed architectures, the data models are going to be basically the same. We haven't considered how the implementation would be if this environment is to be used in developing distributed software in a distributed computing system. But I would say the same conceptual model can be used in a distributed environment.

Mary Shaw (Carnegie Mellon Univ., USA):

We have heard about the appropriateness of many different ways of viewing program information, some formal, some informal, some pertaining to the functionality of the code, some pertaining to the abstract properties. We have also emphasized the maintenance process or the process of supporting the software after its initial release. Since maintenance is very costly, I have a question for all the three speakers: How does your system support both different views of software to enhance understanding, and also to maintain code that existed previously and was not developed within your system?

Jeremy Kuo (GTE Lab.,USA):

This point, which I mentioned as part of the discussion of the future issues that we would like to consider, is the extensibility of the database. What will happen to the database if we enhance the data model? How does the new information integrate with the existing information? This is one issue that we would like to look into. In one of our business units, some managers have proposed an approach to this problem: is it possible to come up with some technique or tool by which we can look at all existing programs - thousands of programs which are in use - abstract the design from those programs, apply whatever tools we have in the new environment, and then map those designs back down to implementation again? This means that programs that existed previously could be very randomly generated, but could still be useful if we could abstract the designs from them and then map them down again. We are looking into that possibility and it could be a possible approach to make sure that we can somehow use old programs.

Roy Campbell (Univ. Illinois, USA):

One of the advantages of our approach is that it is fairly easy to integrate old tools with new tools. The approach that we have adopted avoids the problem of going with one universal language that becomes difficult to interface to new tool technologies.

Steven Muchnick (SUN Microsystems, USA):

We don't yet provide a specific model of how to look at previous programs. Rather, we try to provide a set of tools to construct ways of looking at these programs. We have tools like a source code control system, a configuration manager to look at the history of the code, and a browser (under development) to inspect particular modules.

Questions after Campbell's 2nd presentation (Kaplan's paper)

David Wile (ISI, USA):

Did you say you specified the task in Pascal and implemented it in PROLOG?

Roy Campbell (Univ. Illinois, USA):

The scheme is to extend PASCAL (or ADA) with pre- and post-conditions. We map the pre- and post-conditions down to some function or data type. We use conventional predicates and transform them into PROLOG. (It can't always be done like that, but it usually works.) Then we execute that PROLOG program as a sort of a co-routine to verify these "specifications". We can also feed a modified version of these predicates into TED, our proof management system, and then use the theorem prover to prove the refutation conditions. We can feed these conditions back into TED and use TED to prove that the proof is applicable. There's a sort of link between the two schemes.

David Wile (ISI, USA):

Why don't you specify and verify in PROLOG, and then generate PASCAL programs - instead of the opposite way?

Roy Campbell (Univ. Illinois, USA):

We wanted to combine both aspects. What you could do is to feel fairly confident about the specification before you try to prove anything about the properties of the system. The execution gives you more confidence.

David Wile (ISI, USA):

That's the point! Why not say you have rapid prototyping in PROLOG and after getting confidence go off and build Pascal and verify?

Roy Campbell (Univ. Illinois, USA):

Ok, the specifications are the cornerstone of our work, a kind of VDM approach. The executable specifications are a tool for satisfying yourself that your activity makes sense. Similarly, the proof is a tool for satisfying yourself that you have actually done this VDM-method correctly.

Questions after Ellison's presentation
moving into general discussion

David Levine (Intermetrics, USA):

Do you have any rough statistics on current software production in terms of computer environment? Some are using rastergraphic SUN screens and UNIX, but many are still using conventional TSO-terminals and IBM/MVS. How can we develop common tools for all these people?

Robert Ellison (Carnegie Mellon Univ., USA):

It doesn't look good in some respects. For example, I recently visited one contractor. They were very proud that they finally made a commitment to buy every programmer a terminal, and a good many of them were actually going to have offices! (mumbling in the audience)

David Levine (Intermetrics, USA):

And these are TSO-type terminals?

Robert Ellison (Carnegie Mellon Univ., USA):

Yes. Their VAXes had 80-100 users. It's really an issue of capitalization - how much can you afford to pay for a programmer? That is, how to write off both the cost of new software and hardware against what the contractor really should be doing? Increased productivity can be counteracted by economical and contractual issues.

William Scherlis (Carnegie Mellon Univ., USA):

To follow the question, how many army contractors who are building software have adapted a workstation based system?

Robert Ellison (Carnegie Mellon Univ., USA):

The one who encourages it the most, would be Hughes Aircraft Co., which is using two different types of workstations. (questing sounds from public.....) They claim they have 2000 users. The majority are not truly workstations, but rather MacIntoshes and PCs.

David Levine (Intermetrics, USA):

Another worry - what shall we do with a contractor, typically a commercial company, that delivers an internally-developed software product to the government for further maintenance? To save maintenance costs, we must probably mandate use of the original development environment for this activity? This seems to be a tremendous problem, politically if not financially. You can't go to Boeing or Hughes and say that our shop uses VAX, when these contractors have a whole culture based on something else.

Robert Ellison (Carnegie Mellon Univ., USA):

NASA are going to mandate you to use an internal environment they are constructing now. But as a general rule, that's not the case. They certainly know the problem is there, they just don't know how to address it.

David Levine (Intermetrics, USA):

How can you make a dent in this major problem, if you have this fissure running down the middle of your integrated system world?

Robert Ellison (Carnegie Mellon Univ., USA):

It gets even more complicated. Even if the Defense Department could require those companies to provide them with maintenance tools, the legal issues on embedded software on weaponry complicates matters significantly.

Mary Shaw (Carnegie Mellon Univ., USA):

Robert Ellison mentioned that there is an active impediment to share maintenance tools in the current regulatory and fiscal climate in the U.S. The problem arises from rules about ownership. The encouraging side is that this problem is recognized and there are currently steps being taken to address it. But it is fundamentally an economic and regulatory question, not a technical one. This should remind us that in the area of getting new technology accepted by potential users, there are also problems of legal implications, property protection, economics, regulation, education, and training. These problems differ, but exist in all countries and one ignores them at one's own peril.

David Robinson (System Designers, GBR):

A comment on shortening the development time-span of, say, ten-fifteeen years. We could try to make visible the benefits to the responsible person from these new environments. One of our permanent problems is measuring the costs. Someone mentioned total productivity gains from the whole project, rather than individual tools within the project. What work do you see going on in that area?

Robert Ellison (Carnegie Mellon Univ., USA):

No one has worked too much on cost evaluation. The most well-known is Barry Boehm's measurements on his "productivity environment" at TRW. He predicts an increase by a factor of two in the early stages. Increasing to a factor of four with very simple changes. The most important factors are a common user interface on top of a UNIX environment, a fairly small set of common tools and ample terminals and workstations, etc.. The main problem is that there is no test case that you really control, and that you can easily manage.

Mary Shaw (Carnegie Mellon Univ., USA):

On productivity measurements - I've not heard today any proponent of a system supporting either PITL or PITS that mentions the facilities provided for the measurement or assessment of either the product that's being produced, or the process of producing that product. I'd like to hear from the proponents of those systems whether this was an omission of their presentation, and if so, what facilities are provided in those systems.

James Cordy (Queens Univ., CAN):

That's something I've been worried about too. It's seems that we've been talking a lot about various systems for programming. We have no solid evidence that we can measure any increase in productivity as a result, or that anyone even has attempted to measure such potential increases.

Johannes Grande (MCC, USA):

To follow up on Mary Shaw's comment about technology transfer: how do we get industry to use the technology? Past experiences with technology transfer show that typically 10-20% will accept and use new technology if proven economically viable, 10-20% will not use it at all, and 60-70% will not be committed one way or another. That may be one reason why it takes 10-20 years to get new technology into practical use. I don't think it is enough to develop some new technology and then sell it or give it away; you also need to go and develop a need for the technology.

James Cordy (Queens Univ., CAN):

Why should we expect industry to take on our new ideas, if we're not producing evidence that they actually do increase productivity? This may be a hint for our marketing strategies!

David Levine (Intermetrics, USA):

If I have a umpty-million dollar project with fifty people, I don't want to find out half-way through the project that I have exhausted the table size of the macro pre-processor and I still have fifty percent more to go. It's a kind of a CATCH-22 situation. You have a research project you would like to get into the world, and yet you need to convince somebody to put enough money in it to produce a product (which already has blown the budget by a hundred or two hundred percent). SUN is doing very well and I think it's one of the best hopes in that area. As an aside, I spent some time with people who felt that UNIX was not a production system, being totally unfit for production use. If I am trying to sell new ideas to those people, it doesn't give me a good feeling that the largest group in your company was six people. As an academic, it gives me a really good feeling that you've got high quality software. But if you told me that you had fifty people working on that thing, it would give me a better feeling about the ability of the system.

Roy Campbell (Univ. Illinois, USA):

I think it's a bit ambitious to think that facts or figures will influence existing managers. The key to the whole situation is education. We need to wait for 10-15 years until the next generation of students from universities reach middle management before there is any effect. One of the most dreadful things is to teach software engineering techniques when people that will be affecting decisions respond by simply doubling the size of their R&D departments! We introduced UNIX two or three years ago for our undergraduates, so there is hope in the long term . However, on the other hand, graduate students may not go into industry at all. Perhaps some of the university people could comment on the ripple effects of education?

David Robinson (System Designers, GBR):

An industry point of view is that we worked on research projects with universities, and some of the problems that we are addressing with these programming environments have to do with PITL. That is, large groups of people working and interacting together. My personal experience is that people within universities only know about PITS working in very small teams. Although I agree with your point that the education process will work through, I still think there is another generation to go through universities before we get there. They need to be taught the problems of management of big projects.

Roy Campbell (Univ. Illinois, USA):

Yes, it's difficult within universities to teach people about working in large development projects. What we can do right now is to show them in small proofs what these advantages of programming environments are.

Unknown speaker:

I think that good measurements increase the use of new technology to a large degree, but I'm not sure there is a sufficient financial incentive in the DoD contractors to improve productivity. If 70-80% of the cost is in maintenance and you get a contract to build the system and then get incremental contracts to maintain the system, a mediocre technology will increase your profit. I know of several examples where very large systems got built in assembly language and where the maintenance cost got so high that the government went out for another procurement. But the people that bid on it built the system in assembly language again. I can't think of any other justification except for maximization of profit.

Mary Shaw (Carnegie Mellon Univ., USA):

This is known to be a problem in the Department of Defense. This is part of the complex of software procurement problems that was mentioned earlier. It is being worked on.

Robert Schwanke (Siemens, USA):

One important way that a tool technology gets spread around is through "product champions": people who become excited about a tool or methodology and promote it within their organizations. Barry Boehm has described the spread of a new set of tools within TRW: The first project to use the new tools had grown to a staff of 50 before it was cancelled. When the programmers were reallgined to new projects, they insisted on bringing the tools with them!

Changing the subject: several discussants have claimed that structure editors can become strait jackets for experienced programmers. Is anyone aware of a valid experiment to test this hypothesis?

Lisa Neal (Harvard Univ., USA):

That's what my dissertation research is in. I did an experiment last summer on cognitive aspects of users, their underlying models, and how they used syntax-directed editors. My results were the identification of relevant user characteristics, such as learning strategy and levels of expertise. Instead of presenting one tool to all users, there should be an underlying user model which determines the functionality presented to that user.

Lynn Carter (GenRad, USA):

I have an interesting dual role in life (I'm both with Arizona State Univ. and with GenRad). I've been involved over the last twelve years in writing software for electronics applications. I have a rather large budget for procuring software tools, but they don't exist for something that I want to program. I have a Z-80 with a 22 bit address space and I use HP logic analyzers. I don't have a standard ASCII keyboard or a standard CRT. I'll pay 50-75,000 dollars for software which will allow my software engineers to use good tools like compilers, language-oriented editors, linkers, and debuggers. If I want to spend 2 or 3 million dollars I might be able to encourage a company to build the tools, however I would go ahead and do it for myself for that kind of money. The point is, if you're building stuff to run on a Unix machine you may find tools. But if you are building anything for something on the periphery, like embedded systems, there are no tools; we're back in the dark ages again. I'm using C much the same way as people are using assembly language; in fact, I assert there's very little difference. From my perspective, Program Development Environments may be a dream of the future, but for the common kinds of programming that I do, I look forward to the simple sorts of the things we had available at Textronix on the CDC-machines. If I could have those tools available to me today for my Z80 I would be in seventh heaven, but I don't.

Reidar Conradi (Norw. Inst of Tech., NOR):

I have a comment on the strait-jacketing effect of structure editors. Any software environment will enforce some model of the software development activity and will, of course, constrain you. Unless you have complete faith that this model is the universal truth and that the responsible company will remain liquid for the next 100 years, you will be reluctant to use it. As long as you stay with programs or other pieces of software, documentation, etc., which can be manipulated directly by conventional text editors, you know that you have an open-ended system. This may not be the case in a more "integrated" environment. Many such environments are more or less on the drawing table, or at best, used as prototypes in universities and introduced with big heralds. So we face a credibility question: Do we have faith or do we not? We cannot blame a company with thousands of programmers for not going into something which may look very interesting to the developers but is not mature. This was one of the reasons why I wanted to bring this workshop together, to get industry to talk to academia and vice versa. I feel we are starting to communicate, but it is a long way...

Terrence Miller (Hewlett Packard, USA):

My comment follows what Conradi was just mentioning. The tools that will be used in industry are the ones that someone is selling because then there's support and confidence. I think that the channel from which a lot of the development will come, is in fact the computer companies that have enough program development to produce and validate the tools internally, and then start selling them.

Steven Muchnick (SUN Microsystems, USA):

My first comment echoes what Robinson was saying a few minutes ago on organizing a programming team. Our model is to keep them as small as we can using the highest quality people. Look at our Network File System, which I think with 6 people is the largest team we've had on any project at SUN. We don't believe in the government model of putting fifty, or hundred, or two hundred people on the project. However, we do have some idea why it may be needed in some cases; and therefore, why there's a need for better tools for both large groups and small ones.

My other comment is to retell a story I heard by Mr. Glenn Self, of Electronic Data Systems, about his approach to improving productivity. It has nothing to do with tools; it's simply a matter of paying programmers on the basis of their productivity. It's a very simple formula, based on lines of code added and deleted, with a correction for comments. He claimed a 400% increase in productivity for paying his programmers based on their individual productivity!

Lynn Carter (GenRad, USA):

I'm not sure I want to pay programmers based on the lines of code they produce. I'd like to pay them on functionality with the minimum amount of lines of source code produced.

Steven Muchnick (SUN Microsystems, USA):

I am not suggesting in any way way that I would like to pay people this way; I'm just simply trying to be provocative.

James Cordy (Queens Univ., CAN):

It's evident that the best programmers are worth at least an order of magnitude more than the average programmer. But it is hard to say what we are measuring when we say that, and I think that we all agree that source lines is not the measure.

Joseph Newcomer (Carnegie Mellon Univ., USA):

You may be focusing on the wrong problem. If you look at the metric of "number of lines of code per day", there are systems that allow you to build lots of code quickly and build working prototypes that are absolutely unmaintainable. Then there are systems that allow you to spend forever getting your specifications right, and then the piece of code works the first day. We don't know what the right metric is because these systems are satisfying different needs. The amount of effort to do version maintenance - to support multiple instances of different versions of tools on different machines - all of these have different metrics. Too much of the tooling in PEs is concentrated on the smaller pieces of the problem and ignores the real needs. Unless we attack the real problems of industry, our PEs will not be accepted.

Bernard Lang (INRIA, FRA):

I'd like to come back to the remarks on syntax-directed editors. First there is a problem of education. I do believe what Campbell said about education. For most technologies it takes 15-20 years before they become accepted in industry. Now if you take the syntax-directed paradigm - how old is it? Maybe 12-15 years if you are generous. Here we have more than a problem of acceptance; we are hitting a social law.

Now on syntax-directed editors being strait jackets (I may now say the opposite of what I said this morning). You have to use a good interface with your system so that it won't feel like a strait jacket. You need the programmability to adapt it, because people won't use a bad interface. Maybe one of the reasons why we felt that the interface was not important in our system was that we had a parser in it from the very beginning. We would not force people into a template paradigm to create programs. We were able to bring all existing programs under the system just by parsing; so there were lots of problems we did not have. Certainly tools must not feel like strait jackets. Users must feel free to adopt a tool believing it will not change their ways. The change must come from themselves, when they understand through personal experience what the tool can give them.

Another point on syntax-directed editors is that, in our experience, those new concepts are hard to accept for managers. They are afraid: they don't want this new technology. With engineers we have found that younger engineers and students adapt truly well, but older people have trouble understanding. They will use the system but never think in terms of the system. It's like learning a foreign language.

James Cordy (Queens Univ., CAN):

Strait-jacketing involves more than the user interface. A PE often depends on a particular methodology, a way of thinking, a way of solving problems, and a way of programming. If that methodology does not exactly match with the user's practice then there is a problem, and it will feel like a strait jacket. Evidently, that will be more so for experienced people than for students, that have not yet learned a methodology that matches their thinking well.

William Scherlis (Carnegie Mellon Univ., USA):

Can you give an example of the kind of strait jacket you just described?

Reidar Conradi (Norw. Inst of Tech., NOR):

Let me respond: I'd like to repeat an example I heard from Robert Ellison about the Gandalf system. Gandalf maintains modules, but sometimes you want to split or merge them. Then you also want to have the entire pre-history (comments, specifications, etc.) split or merged, but the system wouldn't allow that. The system has a fixed concept of a module, which must be created from scratch. Modules can't be rebuilt from existing modules fragments, like you can with text.

Bernard Lang (INRIA, FRA):

You have given an example on Gandalf which may apply because Gandalf has covered a lot of ground in the software life cycle and there are areas where methodology is important. However, the strait jacket was applied specifically to syntax-directed editors and my belief is that in the advanced syntax-directed editors, there is no methodology implied. They are essentially similar to EMACS, with additional structural capabilities.

Mary Shaw (Carnegie Mellon Univ., USA):

On strait-jacketing - In some syntax-directed editors, the user is forced to use the syntactic structure of the language as the structure for the editing operations. This may be reasonable at the procedure or statement level, but it forces the user to create expressions in the form of a tree rather than typing them from left to right. For many users this model for creating arithmetic expressions is a strait jacket.

Juha Heinanen (Tampere Univ., FIN):

I have used several versions of structure editors and found that the only extra function you need (once you are an experienced programmer) is matching parentheses and automatic indentation when you press line-feed. I agree with Mary Shaw that in addition you might benefit from automatic procedure and statement generation. What increases productivity is a compiler _integrated_ with the editor. When you have written your program, you say 'compile', and will see the error messages in one window. Then by pressing one key you will get to the file and line where the next error occurred. Of course, the computer has to be fast. The worst thing is to have to wait for the compilation. The best thing is not to compile at all, which means that your language is user-friendly. That is, _interpretive_ languages like SMALLTALK, LISP, etc., and not like ADA, PASCAL, MODULA-2.

(Editor's comment: the compiler - editor integration in the UCSD PASCAL-system is almost 10 years old, but it is not based on a structure editor paradigm.)

James Cordy (Queens Univ., CAN):

I have a PE of the type you describe, based on a compiler that is so fast that you can't tell the difference. So it's the desired <u>functionality</u> you wish, not that the implementation is interpretive.

Juha Heinanen (Tampere Univ., FIN):

But that also requires that I can say from the command level 'call procedure with these arguments', without requiring any kind of stub programs to test my subroutines.

Robert Schwanke (Siemens, USA):

On the issue of strait-jacketing in editors - a language-oriented editor must provide substantial semantic help to overcome any clumsiness its users might perceive. Syntactic help is not worth the bother. In my departement our programmers favor EMACS as their "language-oriented editor". It gives them very little help with syntax, but allows them to create commands that perform semantic tasks, such as matching declarations and uses.

Andy Rudmik (GTE Comm. Syst., USA):

Some of the recent comments represent a rather academic position - looking at the neatness of new technologies and tools, etc.. From an industry perspective (where I'm now) we typically have several hundred people working on a single system where each programmer's task is actually very simple and sophisticated tools are not at all relevant to a single individual's task. We have database-driven, fairly highly integrated, configuration management change-tracking system tied into project management. We track status of software that's under development with many versions distributed all over the place. We can improve the productivity perhaps by a few percent by a syntax-directed editor. The fundamental problem is managing the engineering of large projects, which is a <u>social</u> activity involving people working in many different disciplines. We need to coordinate all that activity making information available so decisions can be made intelligently at various levels. I hear us talking about things that are at the noise level in terms of what really goes on in industry!

James Cordy (Queens Univ., CAN):

I must insert a comment on behalf of Ragui Kamel, of Bell-Northern Research in Ottawa, who was unable to attend. He always points out about technology transfer that not only is BNR (like GTE) using state-of-the-art programming environments, programming management and version control systems, but in many cases they are using the very forefront techniques. BNR is working on systems that are two million lines long and have incredible reliability requirements, and they work. They're used in telephone switching systems. I'm sure the same can be said about some of the CHILL efforts. I don't think it's justified for us as academics to claim that the problem is that industry doesn't use these tools. Of course they use them! They use them better than we (academics) do!

David Robinson (System Designers, GBR):

Two issues: You do have large project teams. You cannot limit your teams to six people because you have large, complex systems to build and maintain. But these teams are larger than they should be. The first reason is that a project doesn't reuse information and software previously generated; it starts from scratch. So you need a lot of people to perform a large number of related tasks. We're told about the quality of programmers, but I believe that so-called "superprogrammers" perform a number of tasks touching on design, implementation, specification and even on requirements. We should provide systems that will help us getting smaller teams, but we will still have large systems to develop.

The other point is on project support environments imposing particular methodologies. There are lots of efforts on PEs in Britain, trying to provide the generic base on which particular methodologies can be based. We must look for the general building blocks to give us customization, representation of information, abstraction at all levels, etc.. Further, managers want constraints at their level of abstraction. What building-blocks can we give to the PE to allow us to do that?

To conclude - we should try to identify the directions we want these development environments to go. At the end of the workshop we should see what building blocks we've got and what valuable advice we can give to people who go about these things.

Jeremy Kuo (GTE Lab., USA):

Mary Shaw said earlier that the success of new technology in improving productivity depends on many non-technical issues. Many of us have read articles about Japanese corporations. The Japanese took ideas which may not work in the U.S., and made them work. The reason lies in their social systems and corporate culture. I discussed this observation with Prof. Perlis at last year's ICSE conference in London. I asked him whether he thought the fundamental problem or bottleneck of software engineering was largely due to social problems of communication and management. The answer I got was, "Nonsense! It's a pure technical problem." Instead of trying to argue further, he made me start wondering again about this question.

Try to imagine what happened when the idea of banking was first introduced to the peasants. They simply found it difficult to accept the idea that they could trust the bank to keep their money. Using our terminology, how much is it the responsibility of the researchers to prove that a tool is useful, and how much is it the responsibility of the industry to accept new technology?

Jean-Pierre Keller (Thomson CSF/DSE, FRA):

First about strait-jacketing - Management is usually inclined to strait jacket people because it fits well with methodologies. Once management is happy, the rank and file has the power! I don't think that the problem of syntax-directed editors is a management problem at this point. The question is whether it is useful.

Also, what I have seen here so far represents a very limited school of thought. We haven't seen anything dealing with FORTRAN programs, not to mention COBOL. There are some very decent people working on programming environments for FORTRAN at Rice University, and they are applying very formal methods. I don't know whether they are much closer to the needs of industry because their ideas are concerned with some extremely difficult PITL issues. Nothing is mentioned about VLSI or CAD/CAM or other areas that also belong to programming environments. Also, we have had a similar effort to ADA and APSE going on in France on a language called LTR ("Le Temps Reel"). LTR has now reached its third version, LTR3. It is very similar to ADA and it's been imposed on all the defence contracts in France. In early 1986, France came out with a programming environment for this language on a workstation. This programming environment involves syntactic-directed functions, compilers, simulators, cross-compilers for host-target issues, and also software engineering database functions, etc.. French software houses have been trying to promote a model for something like APSE in the United States, and have had very poor reception. I suggest you get in touch with the French CELAR, a DoD-like standard organization, that gives information for free.

Now, about productivity and the abilities of the very advanced tools. I believe some people in my company have developed tools and claim that productivity arising from the integrated set of tools represents a factor of ten. Here the programmers, in terms of PITL, were involved with the requirements definition and each knew what they wanted. I have friends who are capable of producing from scratch a PROLOG interpreter over the weekend because they know what a PROLOG interpreter is, what it involves, and what they have to do. The programmers in the industry organization are basically in the same situation. Their tasks are never that hard and they really need to know what they are supposed to do. The programming tools only come into play upon configuration control or documentation. Basically, the problem is requirements engineering. I don't know whether anything's been mentioned about requirements engineering as part of a programming environment.

A reply to Mr. Robinson who asked what the problem of industry is. We all know that industry is comprised of individuals. My company view of the problem is that industry is facing 200,000 lines of C program and 20,000 lines of Z-80 assembly code which cost $2.5 million to create. I can't throw that away to take advantage of a new programming environment, even if that would make my programmers a hundred times more productive. What I need is an incremental set of tools which can move me from an un-integrated to an integrated environment. If the software maintenance process causes me to throw away old code and create new code, sometime in the future I'll end up with an integrated environment. This is what I think we need, and what I think would be very palatable to a large number of industry people.

James Cordy (Queens Univ., CAN):

We don't speak very often of the retrofit problem. That is, how do we serve those people who have huge existing pieces of software systems? How can we allow them to begin to use these new tools to maintain those systems and eventually to migrate toward a fully tool maintained system?

Roy Campbell (Univ. Illinois, USA):

We don't have the technology to take existing programs that are badly written, undocumented, and have no design guidelines, and do something with them! What we have to do is to proceed piece by piece, trying to develop theories and understand what we are doing.

Now, there were comments about syntax-directed editors as opposed to bigger system configuration managers. We should try to develop some ideas of how things behave. The nice thing about syntax-directed editors is that they allow people to think about editors as more than linear string editors. We can start talking about operations on _entities_ other than string text.

Indeed, when we look at the whole life cycle there are aspects about transformations, about manipulating life cycle processes, managing configurations, and manipulating management information, that we have no clue about. I think we are far too optimistic.

Joseph Newcomer (Carnegie Mellon Univ., USA):

I want to go back and sum up Mary Shaw's point in what I call Newcomer's Statement of the Three Problems of Technology Transition:

  1) The most serious problems are the legal problems.

  2) The next most serious problems are the managerial, social, and psychological problems.

  3) Oh, by the way, there are technical problems, and they are damned hard, but not nearly as hard as the first two.

The research labs at BNR and similar companies have eliminated the two first problems. They don't have legal problems because they are an internal product development division of a committed corporation that needs their products to develop other final end products. We now have a managerial commitment to develop and utilize tools. So we have eliminated the second problem, and we've got our minds set on training and everything else. This allows concentration on the technical problems. There is a message there.

Reidar Conradi (Norw. Inst. of Tech., NOR):

The legal problems are just embodiments of the social problems!

Joseph Newcomer (Carnegie Mellon Univ., USA):

There are social problems-in-the-small and social problems-in-the-large!!
(laughter, applause)

Mary Shaw (Carnegie Mellon Univ., USA):

We've heard a diverse collection of descriptions of work in production as distinguished from work in progress(!), and a diversity of complaints from people who wish they were happier. I think this is healthy. What we are seeking is people, proceeding individually, asking: "How can I improve that?" And I think we have an unusual opportunity here, with a mixture of research and development and industrial production people that we should not let pass by. Can the workshop come to terms with an issue by the time we wind up on Wednesday? We are a community of software engineers, not sociologists, or lawyers, and my question to the workshop is:

> **What three things could we the software engineering community do that would have the greatest chance of making an order of magnitude improvement in practical software development and maintenance?**

And I'm not speaking of the small things!

Question (anonymous):

Are those three technical things?

Mary Shaw (Carnegie Mellon Univ., USA):

Those are three things that we the software engineering community can do. Now our expertise is in software engineering, but if you could present an argument that says we should scrap all those things and go into law, well....

James Cordy (Queens Univ., CAN):

Maybe we should all study management. Why don't we think about that and try to come up with solid arguments for the final discussion session on Wednesday.

A Model of Software Manufacture

Ellen Borison
Department of Computer Science
Carnegie-Mellon University
Pittsburgh, PA 15213
USA

Abstract

Software manufacture is the process by which a software product is derived, through an often complex sequence of steps, from the primitive components of a system. This paper presents a model of software manufacture that addresses the amount of work that has to be done, after a given set of changes has been made, to consistently incorporate those changes in a given product.

Based on a formal definition of a software configuration that characterizes a software product in terms of how it was manufactured, the model uses *difference predicates* to discriminate between changes that are significant and those that are not. A difference predicate is an assertion about the relationship between two sets of components. Difference predicates determine when one set of components can be substituted for another. By predicting when existing components can be substituted for the output of a manufacturing step, difference predicates determine which steps in the manufacturing process can be omitted when incorporating a given set of changes.

1 Introduction

This paper considers what happens to the primitive components of a software system when they are combined and transformed, through an often complex sequence of derivation steps, into one or more software products. Since this derivation process is largely automatic, and since it increasingly involves tools other than just compilers and linkers, some call it *software manufacture*. Software manufacture establishes the relationships between the products that constitute a system and its primitive components, and it is by way of software manufacture that changes in the primitive components take effect in those products. If the manufacturing process is unreliable, then the relationship between primitive and product is compromised and so is the orderly introduction of changes.

This research was supported in part by a Xerox Special Opportunity Fellowship in Computer Science, and in part by the Defense Advanced Research Projects Agency (DOD), ARPA Order No. 4976, monitored by the Air Force Avionics Laboratory under Contract F33615-84-K-1520. The views and conclusions contained in this document are those of the author and should not be interpreted as representing the official policies, either expressed or implied, of the Defense Advanced Research Projects Agency or the US Government.

After elaborating on the problems of software manufacture and briefly surveying manufacturing technology in Section 2, this paper presents work in progress in developing a model of software manufacture that specifically addresses the question of how much work has to be done to incorporate a given set of changes consistently in a given software configuration.

The discussion of the model begins in Section 3. Section 4 presents a formal definition of a software configuration that characterizes a software product in terms of how it is manufactured. This definition provides a fixed base for identifying the sources of change in a configuration and delimiting their potential scope. Section 5 considers a number of alternative methods for incorporating changes in a configuration.

Section 6 introduces *difference predicates*, and herein lies the main results of the paper. Difference predicates are used to compare related components and to discriminate between changes that are substantial and those that are not. They model the criteria used to determine which steps in a manufacturing process must be performed to ensure that changes are incorporated consistently. Difference predicates generalize to arbitrary manufacturing steps the mechanisms used by some separate compilation systems to limit the amount of recompilation after a change to an interface [Tichy 85, Conradi 85].

2 Background

It has been said that the hardest decision a project manager has to make during the course of a software development project is when to remanufacture the entire system from scratch and how much regression testing to perform on the result [Cooper 84]. This decision has to be made because remanufacturing the system from scratch is seen as necessary to ensure that the product in hand does in fact consistently represent the components from which it was supposed to have been built. The decision is hard to make because manufacturing a system from scratch can be extremely expensive. The process can take days or weeks, and this time is often lost to the system's developers as they wait for a stable base to work from.

The culprit is change. The problem is knowing (1) what existing versions of what derived components were built from what versions of what primitives and (2) which of these derived components can be reused when a set of changes is introduced and which have to be remanufactured.

2.1 Change and the Manufacture of Consistent Configurations

Once a software system has been specified and its design roughcast, development begins in earnest with detailed design and implementation. Even if specification documents and the global design were to remain fixed, the state of the developing system as represented by its individual components starts to change and continues to change until the system is decommissioned.

Virtually all software systems are composed of a number of pieces, or components. Those components that are hand-crafted by the system's implementors are its primitive components. So are those (for example, an i/o library) that are imported ready-made from the outside. Those that are produced by the operations of tools on other components are derived. Components that are targeted for release or export to the outside are software products.

Whether planned, corrective or opportunistic, change is inevitable. Software systems are developed incrementally, by necessity converging toward completion, and if not correctness, at least adequacy. Some components will be completed before others. Some may be useful when only partially complete. Initial design decisions will be found wanting, and interfaces may be poorly specified, incomplete or misunderstood. Most components will not be implemented correctly the first time, and many will be mismatched. Thus the development process is characterized by the proliferation of primitive components and of versions of these components.

However, software developers are faced not only with the proliferation of primitive components and their versions, but also with the proliferation of versions of the derived components that are produced as the intermediate results or final products of the manufacturing process.

During its implementation and maintenance, a software system is repeatedly manufactured as each new set of changes is introduced. The result is then tested sufficiently to validate the changes and to discover additional problems. Individual programmers may independently manufacture subsystems or even pieces of subsystems to check their own work or to try out an idea. An integration team may manufacture designated versions of the entire system under carefully controlled conditions and may carry out extensive and demanding regression and progression tests. In either case, it is important for developers to be able to control which changes are to be included when a system is manufactured and which are to be excluded. This makes it possible to test portions of the system independently while other parts remain stable.

Whether casually manufactured by an individual programmer or officially by an integration team, it is imperative that the system undergoing testing accurately represent the components from which it was supposed to have been constructed; otherwise, any information gained from testing is worthless. If there is any doubt about which versions of which components were used to build a given version of a system, it is impossible to attribute any problems found in testing to specific components, or to know what to change in order to fix those problems.

2.2 A Closer Look at Software Manufacture

Unfortunately, it is difficult to maintain the correspondence between a manufactured system and the components from which it was built. Each time a system or part of it is manufactured, each step of the manufacturing process produces a new set of derived components. These components may be the same as others created in the past, or they may be different. There is little to distinguish one version of a derived component from another especially when the only identifying information bound to the component is a name and a date. When the immediate context of manufacture is lost, so too are the identities of the intermediate objects created in the process. If any of these objects are subsequently used in the manufacture of a new version of the system, any uncertainty about the identity of the object is simply transfered to the new system.

This problem is exacerbated by the size of a system, by its longevity (how old it is), and by the level of technology used. All these properties serve to increase the number and variety of versions of derived components.

In an idealized and stable minimal development environment where the software generation tools used are limited to a compiler, a linker and little else, the distinction between primitive and derived components is clear. All primitive components are source modules written in some programming language; all derived components are the relocatable object modules produced by the compiler or the executable programs produced by the linker. If one ignores any auxiliary components such as a "compool" of interface information or a set of include files, and if one does not change the way the compiler or linker is invoked, then there is a one-to-one correspondence between the versions of an object module and the versions of the source from which it was compiled.

However, realistic environments are neither stable nor minimal.

- "Auxiliary" components do change and can have profound effects on the derived components that depend on them. In fact, a failure to rebuild all dependent components after a change to an auxiliary component is a major source of inconsistency in manufactured systems.

- The ways tools are invoked may change. No responsible test team would release a version of a system built with optimization turned on if that system had only been tested with optimization off and debugging on.

- Tools themselves may change due to bug fixes or enhancements.

- The choice of tools or the order in which tools are invoked may change. Often this is one consequence of the reorganization of the logical structure of a system.

In advanced development environments, these problems are compounded by the greater variety of tools used and their increased interdependence. In such environments the derivation sequences between primitives and products are longer and more complex; each change has a potentially broader impact and there is more opportunity for instability.

One of the consequences of richer, more sophisticated technology is that the distinction between primitive and derived components can no longer be made on the basis of component type. While it is still the case that most primitive components happen to be "source" modules written in some programming language, not all "source" is primitive. Similarly, not all "object" is derived. With the increased use of tools such as program generators and other processors that produce program text from specifications, a "source" module may well be derived. And an "object" module which is produced by one programmer or organization as a product may be used by another programmer or organization as a primitive.

Even in simple development environments, derived components rarely depend on a single primitive. In advanced environments many derived components may depend on other derived components. The fan-out for a single change may be considerable, especially with interconnections such as those among modules written in separately compiled languages. In such cases, a single change to an interface not only affects the corresponding implementation and any direct clients, but can transitively affect clients of clients. The problems of maintaining consistency are accordingly complex and can be impossible to manage unless automated; the problem is compounded when changes are made independently to interdependent parts of a system. If the derivation steps necessary to reestablish consistency after a change are not performed in the correct order, some tools may detect version skew and refuse to process their input.

2.3 Tools for Software Manufacture, Their Capabilities and Limitations

There are a number of tools and techniques for dealing with change in the larger software development process. Many of these are relevant to software manufacture, and some do in fact obviate the need to rebuild some systems from scratch, sometimes. Still, there has been little systematic attack on the impact of change on software manufacture *per se*. For advanced environments especially, our tools are neither sufficiently general nor sufficiently reliable to provide software developers with an acceptable balance between the cost of incorporating changes in a system and the assurance that those changes have been consistently and reproducibly introduced. Despite our tools, the cost of incorporating changes in a system is still too often disproportionate to their scope.

A software manufacturing facility must provide two basic mechanisms in order to automate the manufacture of arbitrary and identifiable versions of a software system. The first is a means for selecting the versions of the primitive components that will be used in a given configuration, coupled with reliable persistent storage for those versions. The second is a means of describing the steps that must be performed by the manufacturing process. In addition to these mechanisms, it is incumbent on the manufacturing facility to provide a record of the system as built. This record serves to identify a given instantiation of the system and to distinguish it from all other instantiations.

These two mechanisms may be provided by a single tool such as an enhanced module interconnection language.[1] Examples of enhanced module interconnection languages include a series of languages developed at Carnegie-Mellon University as part of the Gandalf project and its antecedents [Cooprider 79, Tichy 80, Kaiser 83] as well as similar work done as part of the Adele environment [Estublier 84]. Because these languages are designed to enforce type consistency and information flow among modules, they are necessarily programming language dependent and do not accommodate tools other than compiler and linkers.

---

[1] A *classic* module interconnection language is used as a detailed design language for specifying the information flow among modules [DeRemer 76]; it may be used to enforce this information flow in an implementation, but it is not used to specify or to automate the manufacture of that implementation. *Enhanced* module interconnection languages are used to drive the manufacturing process and hence include version selection and other information used in manufacture.

As a byproduct of the manufacturing process, the Gandalf Software Version Control Environment (SVCE) [Kaiser 83] produces a *bound list* that enumerates the versions of the source components that appear in a particular configuration.

Alternatively, in some systems version selection and manufacturing process description are provided by separate tools such as SCCS [Rochkind 75] or RCS [Tichy 82] and MAKE [Feldman 79]. These tools operate with little support from the remainder of the environment and require careful usage conventions to be combined effectively. One such set of conventions is embedded in the Software Manufacturing System (SMS) [Cristofor 80]; others, based on enhanced versions of the tools, are used in the 3B20D Software Development System [Rowland 83, Erickson 84]. SCCS and MAKE do not place restrictions on the tools that can be used in the manufacturing process; SCCS will manage arbitrary text files and MAKE will describe arbitrary manufacturing steps. However, whether it is done by accident or by design, both tools can be easily subverted.

Like the Gandalf SVCE, SMS produces an enumeration of the components of a configuration as a consequence of manufacture.

Finally, and most effectively, version selection and automatic manufacturing may be provided by one or more tools that are integrated with and rely on support from other tools in the environment. These tools represent the most recent and sophisticated of the software manufacturing tools and include the Cedar System Modeler [Lampson 83] and the history and configuration managers of the Apollo Domain Software Engineering Environment (DSEE) [Leblang 84]. The System Modeler takes the view that a system model should be a complete and precise description of a manufactured system. In fact, the same description is both a record and a driver of the manufacturing process. The Apollo DSEE essentially uses the SCCS/MAKE paradigm, but provides adequate integration and control so that the tools are not so easily subverted. It also provides a full record of the manufacturing process that can be used subsequently to reinitialize the environment in order to recreate a version of a system or as a basis for creating a variant.

Although the above tools as a rule use existing derived components to avoid manufacturing an entire system from scratch, they do so conservatively. MAKE uses timestamp heuristics to determine what has to be rebuilt after a change; the System Modeler and DSEE use more precise version information. DSEE does have an escape that allows a user greater control over what gets rebuilt, but there is no guarantee that the information the user provides is accurate.

In addition to the basic mechanisms of version selection and manufacturing process description, a number of tools have been proposed or developed to limit the amount of manufacture necessary after a change. Most of these tools are associated with separate compilation systems. They range from relatively simple strategies such as "write-if-changed" that produce output only if that output differs from a previous version to the more elaborate recompilation predicates proposed by Tichy [Tichy 85] and Dausmann [Dausmann 84] that consider each change/client pair individually. Write-if-changed strategies are compatible with timestamp and version stamp methods, since both require a change to trigger a subsequent derivation step. Recompilation predicates replace timestamp or version stamp methods with explicit decisions about whether a derivation step is necessary.

The DSEE configuration manager provides two mechanisms to short-circuit the propagation of changes; neither mechanism is tool specific [Leblang 85]. The first mechanism requires that a user declare one version of a primitive component equivalent to another so that derived objects that depend on the latter can be used in place of objects that depend on the former. This mechanism makes it possible for already existing derived components to be used instead of manufacturing new ones. The second mechanism requires that the user describe a dependency as non-critical. A change to the non-critical component is not in itself sufficient to trigger the remanufacture of the client. Both of these mechanisms depend on the declaration of a user and neither is checked. Since their effect is project wide, they can be overridden upon command.

3 An Introduction to the Model

It is difficult to evaluate technology for software manufacture since there are a limited number of tools available and since these tools are sufficiently different from one another in conception and goals that there is little basis for comparison. Nevertheless, there are two quite general criticisms that apply. First, most existing tools represent expedient solutions to only some aspects of software manufacture, and none is based on an explicit and general model of the manufacturing process. Second, while the best of our tools can be used effectively to manufacture a snapshot of a changing system, none treats those snapshots as anything but independent points.

In the remainder of this paper, I describe a model of software manufacture that incorporates the best ideas from existing technology and generalizes and combines them in a single framework. The purpose of the model is to serve as a vehicle to better understand and explore the effect of change on software manufacture and to serve as a basis for evaluating current and designing new manufacturing tools. At issue is the reliability, efficiency and generality of these tools.

The model approaches the problem of software manufacture at quite a low level. It does not consider how one describes the implementation of a system or the interfaces among components, such is the province of the module interconnection languages. Nor does it consider what the system does, an issue for a specification language. Instead, the model concentrates on what a manufactured system is, on the derivation relationships among its components.

The model specifically addresses the question of how much work has to be done to incorporate a given set of changes consistently in a given configuration by substituting one set of components for another. To answer this question it is necessary, first, to recognize that the substitution has taken place, and then to delimit its potential scope of impact. Next, it is necessary to define what it means for the substituted components to be consistently incorporated. After having done these three things, it is possible to evaluate which derivation steps have to be performed to effect the change consistently. A manufacturing process is reliable if changes are incorporated consistently; it is efficient if it does not perform any steps other than those necessary to achieve this consistency.

The model is divided into two parts. The first part formally defines a configuration as a directed acyclic graph of components and manufacturing steps. This representation provides a basis for identifying change and delimiting its scope. The second part of the model uses difference predicates to define what it means for a change to be incorporated consistently and to identify the derivation steps to be performed in order to do so.

4 The Formal Definition of a Configuration

Although the term "software configuration" is widely used, its meaning is not very precise. In common usage, a software configuration is simply a collection of software artifacts that are identified as a unit for purposes of identification, coordination, or control. The criteria for grouping these artifacts may be functional, structural or even administrative. Sometimes the term is used generically to refer to any collection of artifacts that satisfies certain definitive criteria; individual members of such genera are distinguished as fully bound configurations.

In contrast to such generic usage, this paper takes the view that a configuration corresponds to a specific instantiation of a manufactured system and includes all information that might distinguish that instantiation from any other. All configurations are taken to be fully bound. Furthermore, the criteria for determining what constitutes a configuration are purely structural, being simply the derivation relationships between primitive components (including tools and their parameters) and the software products manufactured therefrom. A configuration includes not only primitive components but also products, and the intermediate results of the manufacturing process. Accordingly, a configuration not only identifies a version of a system, but also serves as a standard for reproducing or creating a known variation of that version.

4.1 Components and Manufacturing Steps

The formal definition of a configuration rests on definitions of components and manufacturing steps.

Components are software artifacts that are taken to be immutable objects[2]; each has a value (a concrete representation) and is labeled with a unique identifier. Components also may have attributes such as a name, a size, a date – time – created; while these attributes are important in classifying or managing components, they do not directly affect the outcome of the manufacturing process.

In principle, anything that can affect the manufacture of a software product may be

---

[2]Immutable objects are a fundamental concept in the Cedar System Modeler [Lampson 83]; such objects can be created and destroyed, but once created their values cannot be modified. For instance, editing an immutable file does not change that file; it simply causes a new file to be created that differs from the original according to the edits made.

represented as a component. This is a key concept in the model. Components are not limited to the objects conventionally considered as part of a configuration; that is, they are not limited to what might appear in a module interconnection description or system model as the actual arguments supplied to software generation tools. Since the tools themselves and the options supplied when they are invoked affect the outcome of manufacture, tools and options are components of configurations. So are artifacts like clock readings or processor identifiers which might be embedded in a product, for example, as the date – time – of – manufacture. A component is any software artifact that has a concrete representation and that can potentially affect the resulting configuration if replaced by another artifact with another value.

Unlike components, manufacturing steps have no concrete existence. A manufacturing step is a derivation relation between two sets of components; an input set and an output set. The manufacturing step is said to consume the input set and produce, or yield, the output set. Typically the input set consists of a tool, the files or other objects representing its actual arguments, and a string representing any invocation options. The output set consists of the outputs of the tool invocation.

In principle it is desirable to completely capture everything that might affect the outcome of a manufacturing step. Since this is impossible in practice, each separate invocation of a step, whether on different inputs or not, is considered distinct. This provides a hedge against transient hardware problems such as a faulty memory location or subversive tools that might behave differently according to the phase of the moon. Any such aberration might cause the output of one invocation of a tool to differ from another even if the inputs are the same. Hence the model does not make the *a priori* assumption that a manufacturing step is repeatable. Thus manufacturing steps as well as components are given unique labels. The second part of the model provides a mechanism for identifying steps that have equal-valued inputs and outputs.

```
yacc --------------->|   |
"-d" --------------->| m | -----> y.tab.c
grammar.y ---------->|   | -----> y.tab.h
/usr/lib/yaccpar --->|___|
```

Figure 1: A Manufacturing Step

As an example of a manufacturing step, consider the Unix tool YACC, a parser generator. When invoked with the "-d" option on an appropriately described grammar, YACC produces two outputs: a parser in a C source module named "y.tab.c", and a list of token numbers in a C include module named "y.tab.h". The file "y.tab.c" includes code taken verbatim from a parser skeleton named "/usr/lib/yaccpar". No other information is used in generating the output. The manufacturing step representing the invocation of YACC on the file "grammar.y":

```
yacc -d grammar.y
```

relates specific versions of inputs named "yacc", "grammar.y" and "/usr/lib/yaccpar" and an anonymous instance of the string "-d" to specific versions of outputs "y.tab.c" and "y.tab.h". This might be represented as in Figure 1, except that each named component and the manufacturing step itself would in fact tagged with a unique identifier.

Like components, manufacturing steps may also have attributes. One such attribute that is important in using the model to evaluate manufacturing cost is the cost, measured in processor time, of performing the step.

4.2 Manufacturing Graphs and Configurations

Formally, a configuration is a labeled directed acyclic graph (DAG) of components and manufacturing steps in which certain components are designated as software products, or exports. The graph is finite (a trivial property) and bipartite (manufacturing nodes alternate with component nodes).

A configuration C is a tuple $\langle G,E,L \rangle$ where

- $G = \langle C,M,I,O \rangle$ is a labeled finite bipartite DAG with nodes C and M and edges I and O.

  o The set of nodes C represents the set of components in the configuration.

  o The set of nodes M represents the manufacturing steps in the configuration.

  o The set of edges $I \subset (C \times M)$ represents the input relation between components and manufacturing steps.

  o The set of edges $O \subset (M \times C)$ represents the output relation between components and manufacturing steps.

  Since no component can be the product of more than one manufacturing step O is restricted so that
  $$\forall\, m_i, m_j \in M\, [\, \exists\, c \in C\, .\, ((m_i,c) \in O \,\wedge\, (m_j,c) \in O) \Rightarrow m_i = m_j\,].$$

- $E \subset C$ represents the components designated as exports of the configuration.

- L is a labeling function that assigns distinct labels to all components and all manufacturing steps (not just those in a single configuration). The domain of labels is arbitrary. L is simply a unique identifier generator for components and for manufacturing steps.

The structure of the manufacturing graph G captures the derivation relationships among the components of a system. If $D^* = (I \cup O)^*$ is the reflexive transitive closure of the union of the input and output relations I and O, then a component c_i depends on a component c_j if $(c_j,c_i) \in D^*$. Similarly, a manufacturing step m_i depends on a step m_j if $(m_j,m_i) \in D^*$, etc. Since the graph is acyclic, D^* is a partial order.

The designated exports of the configuration are those components that constitute the system represented by the configuration. So that extraneous information is not represented in a configuration, we require that each manufacturing step contribute to the production of some export.

- $\forall m \in M [\exists e \in E . (m,e) \in D^*]$

This requirement does not imply that G is connected. If a configuration has multiple exports, it is perfectly legitimate for each to be associated with a disjoint subgraph.

The status of a component as primitive or derived is not an independent property of the component, rather it depends on how that component is represented in a given configuration. What constitutes the set of primitive components of a given configuration is defined relative to that configuration. The set P of primitives of a configuration is simply that set of components that do not depend on other components in the configuration:

- $P = \{ c \in C \mid {\sim}\exists m \in M . (m,c) \in O \}$

These basic definitions make it straightforward to define the set of primitives that a given export e depends on:

- $P_e = \{ p \in P \mid (p,e) \in D^* \}$

or conversely, the set of exports that depend on some primitive p:

- $E_p = \{ e \in E \mid (p,e) \in D^* \}$

It is also straightforward to define the set of manufacturing steps that might be affected by a change to a given component c:

- $M_c = \{ m \in M \mid (c,m) \in D^* \}$

If manufacturing steps are attributed with costs, the cost of making the change is easily quantified in terms of the sum of the costs associated with each affected step. Similarly, one can determine the cost of producing a given component. Such cost information may be used to make remanufacturing decisions or to evaluate the tradeoffs between storing a component and regenerating it.

The most important property of the formal definition of a configuration is that it is explicit about the components that constitute a configuration and precise about their interdependence. The formal definition is also sufficiently general to admit arbitrary components and derivation processes. It includes no assumptions about what specific tools might be used, what information they might use as input or produce as output, or how they might be composed. Thus the model incorporates no special knowledge or requirements about the consistent use of tools or components.

The formal definition also makes no presumptions about what versions of a component may or may not appear in a configuration. In fact, the formal definition makes no distinction between two versions of one component and two otherwise unrelated components. It may be perfectly reasonable for two versions of some component to coexist in the same configuration, for instance certain generic code may be instantiated a number of times, or a tool may be used to bootstrap another version of itself.

4.3 Labels and The Universe of Configurations

Manufacturing steps are the basic entity in the formal definition of a configuration; they are the glue that holds components and configurations together. The same manufacturing step may be represented in more than one configuration; this is what gives structure to the universe of configurations.

The universe of configurations determined by the labeling function L is the set of all configurations $\langle G, E, L \rangle$ where:

- If two configurations each contain a manufacturing step with the same label then the *same* step is represented in both configurations. Each appearance of the step must have identically labeled input components and identically labeled output components.

- If two configurations each contain a component with the same label then the *same* component is represented in both configurations. Unless the component appears as primitive in one or both configurations, it must appear as the output of manufacturing steps that are identically labeled in both configurations.

The labeling function assigns labels to components and manufacturing steps independently of the configurations in which they appear. The same component or manufacturing step has the same label in all configurations in which it appears.

Given a labeling function, two configurations are equivalent if they designate the same set of exports, that is, if for each export in one configuration, there exists an identically labeled export in the second configuration and conversely. Equivalent configurations differ only in in how much information is represented about the manufacturing process; they differ in what is represented as primitive, or in how many manufacturing steps are included.

Control over the amount of information represented in a configuration allows one to represent a tool as primitive in one configuration knowing that there is an equivalent configuration that records more of its derivation history. This is particularly important in bootstrapped systems where one version of a tool is used as a component in the production of the next version.

Control over the amount of information represented in a configuration also provides the basis for modularity in the model. Even moderately sized systems are factored into subsystems that may be separately manufactured and tested prior to their integration. The labeling of components and manufacturing steps makes it possible to represent such subsystems as separate configurations which can be composed into larger configurations representing the whole system. The same subsystem can also be represented as part of more than one larger system.

The labeling function makes it possible for the exports of subsystems to be used as primitives in the larger system without loss of identity. In fact, what is considered primitive relative to one configuration might be an export of a second configuration and merely some intermediate derived object in a third.

4.4 Separately Manufactured Subsystems

In addition to representing subsystems as separate configurations, it is possible to represent a configuration at various levels of detail. When treating the manufacture of a large system, it may be desirable to hide the internal details of the manufacture of a subsystem so that a complex manufacturing sequence is encapsulated as a single step. This can be particularly desirable for manipulating subsystems that are used in multiple places.

A subgraph of a manufacturing graph that can be factored out and encapsulated within the larger configuration as a single manufacturing step is called a *separately manufactured subsystem*. Based on the formal definition, a separately manufactured subsystem is a subgraph $S = \langle C',M',I',O'\rangle$ of G where ($C' \subset C$), etc., such that

1. $\forall\, c_k \in C\, [\, \exists\, c_i, c_j \in C'.\, (\,(c_i,c_k) \in D^* \wedge (c_k,c_j) \in D^*\,) \Rightarrow c_k \in C'\,]$

   The subsystem includes all components that both depend on some other component within the subsystem and are depended on by another such component. In other words, if two components are in a subsystem then so are any components that come between them.

2. $\forall\, m \in M\, [\, \exists\, c_i, c_j \in C'.\, (\,(c_i,m) \in D^* \wedge (m,c_j) \in D^*\,) \Rightarrow m \in M'\,]$

   The subsystem includes all manufacturing steps that both depend on some component within the subsystem and are depended on by another such component. In other words, if two components are in a subsystem then so are any manufacturing steps that come between them.

3. $\forall\, c \in C\, [\, \exists\, m \in M'.\, (\,(m,c) \in O \vee (c,m) \in I\,) \Rightarrow c \in C'\,]$

   The subsystem includes all components that are produced by or consumed by manufacturing steps in the subsystem.

4. $\forall\, c \in C', m \in M'\, [\,(c,m) \in I \Rightarrow (c,m) \in I'\,]$

   The subsystem includes all input edges between components and manufacturing steps in the subsystem.

5. $\forall\, m \in M', c \in C'\, [\,(m,c) \in O \Rightarrow (m,c) \in O'\,]$

   The subsystem includes all output edges between manufacturing steps and components in the subsystem.

The primitives P' of the subsystem are simply those components that are not manufactured within the subsystem:

- $P' = \{\, c \in C' \mid \sim\!\exists\, m \in M'.\, (m,c) \in O'\,\}$

   Note that in general $\sim(P' \subset P)$; in fact, it may be the case that $P' \cap P = \emptyset$.

The exports E' of the subsystem are those components that are manufactured by the subsystem but are used in or exported by the parent configuration:

- $E' = \{ c \in C' \mid (c \in E) \vee \exists m \in (M - M') . ((c,m) \in I) \}$

A separately manufactured subsystem S can be represented within a parent configuration as a single manufacturing step s with inputs P' and outputs $(E' - P').$[3] This is the basis of abstraction in the model.

4.5 Properties of the Formal Definition

A configuration represents a record of a manufacturing process. However, configurations are manufactured in the real world and in practice it is impossible to quantify and represent everything that might affect the outcome of a manufacturing step. In the model, as a hedge against the missing dependencies or manufacturing steps that are not deterministic, we distinguish between separate invocations of the same manufacturing step. We also recognize that information represented in the model (such as an indication of the tool used to produce a given component) may not in fact be stored by an actual computer system. Although this information is not recorded, it does not mean that the dependency does not exist.

The formal definition places no constraints on what primitive components may be consistently combined with what others or whether some version of a tool can be invoked on some version of an input. These are semantic not structural properties of a configuration and are more appropriately treated by module interconnection or specification languages than by an underlying manufacturing facility.

In software manufacture, it is the correspondence between the manufactured system and the components from which it was built that is of concern. Since the formal definition is a record of a manufacturing process, a configuration is by definition consistent. That is, the exports of a configuration are by definition consistent with its primitives. Where consistency of manufacture becomes an issue is when incorporating changes in a configuration. In that case we want to produce a new configuration whose exports are consistent with the changes.

5 Change and the Relationships Between Configurations

The first part of the model, the formal definition, treats configurations in isolation. In so doing, it provides a fixed basis for considering the effect of change and the relationships between configurations. The second part of the model considers how changes are incorporated in a configuration, what it means for them to be incorporated consistently, and what it costs to do so. The first part of the model is designed to maximize the distinctions between configurations: if two configurations are equivalent it is because they represent the same set of exports. The second part relaxes those distinctions and takes steps towards developing a method for reasoning about the relationships between configurations.

---

[3] $(E' - P') \neq E'$ when some primitive of the subsystem is also an export.

Given the formal definition of a configuration, it is possible to pose the question raised earlier in this paper more precisely. That is, given a configuration C with primitives P, what steps have to be performed to manufacture the configuration C' in which primitives P' are substituted for P.[4]

There are many ways in which a set of changes might be incorporated in a configuration, and the model should be able to represent them all. For instance:

- A conservative project manager might decide to rebuild the entire configuration from scratch, regardless of what has changed. In this case the exports of the new configuration C' would be by definition consistent with the substituted primitives P'.

- Secondly, one might rebuild only those derived objects that depend on components that are in P' but not in P. The resulting configuration would not be identical to that manufactured from scratch (since it would share some components with the original configuration — unless of course, every step depended on at least one changed component), but its exports would still be by definition consistent with the primitives P'.

  This is the strategy that MAKE approximates using timestamps and that the Cedar System Modeler and the DSEE Configuration Manager perform more reliably using more precise version identification.

- Thirdly, there is a range of alternatives based on evaluating the differences between the components in P and P' (and their derivatives) and making a decision for each manufacturing step based on those differences whether to perform the step or not. This is what the smart recompilation mechanisms do for steps that involve compilers. It is also the subject of the remainder of this paper.

The third alternative is potentially the least expensive. However, if steps are omitted in producing the new configuration C', then the exports of C' will not be consistent, according to the formal definition, with the primitives P'. The exports of C' may actually depend on some components that are in P but not in P' and some of the components in P' may not have been used at all, except in comparison with corresponding components in P.

It is clearly desirable to be able to omit steps in the manufacturing process if the resulting configuration is guaranteed to be "as good as" one produced by manufacture from scratch or demonstrably "good enough". But how good is "good enough"? For the purposes of the individual implementor who wants to quickly check a small change, "good enough" is likely to mean something different than what is required by an integration test team, and that too will differ from what is required by the strictest release procedures. What is needed is a definition of consistency that will accommodate this range of possibilities, that will permit steps to be omitted from the manufacturing process in a controlled way while maintaining an explicit relationship between the exports of a configuration and its primitives. This is the role of difference predicates in the model.

---

[4]It is also possible to pose a similar question about the consequences of making a change to structure of a configuration; this question will not be treated directly in this paper.

6 Difference Predicates

A difference predicate is an assertion about the relationship between two sets of components. It is a boolean function on pairs of sets of components:

- $P: (K \times K) \rightarrow \{true, false\}$,
  where K is the set of all finite sets of components.

Depending on the predicate, the sets compared might be singleton sets (i.e. individual components), they might be the inputs or outputs of two manufacturing steps, or they might be the exports of two configurations.

Difference predicates determine when one set of components can be considered equivalent to another.[5] When the sets of components compared are the export sets of two configurations, difference predicates can be used to identify two configurations that would otherwise be considered different. When the sets are the inputs to two manufacturing steps, difference predicates can be used to determine whether the outputs of one step can be consistently substituted for the outputs of the other.[6] In either case, when we say that a set of components A is equivalent to another set B, it is always with respect to some difference predicate $P[A,B]$ that evaluates to *true*.

6.1 Difference Predicates on Individual Components

A difference predicate on individual components is a function

- $P: (C \times C) \rightarrow \{ true, false \}$
  where C is the set of all components.

that determines when a pair of components can be considered equivalent. If a predicate on two components evaluates to *true*, then those components differ only in ways that are "not interesting" with respect to the predicate.

Difference predicate may use any available information about a component including the component's label, its concrete representation, or the values of its attributes. For example, the following predicates might be defined for two components c_i and c_j.

1. The identity predicate uses a component's label to discriminate between any two different components.

   - $P_1[c_i, c_j] := (label(c_i) = label(c_j))$

---

[5] In the following discussion, difference predicates are formulated so that they map sets of components into equivalence classes. However, in practice, many predicates are not symmetric. For example, a predicate that admits upwardly compatible changes to source modules in some language might permit the addition of definitions but not their deletion. In this case, a module with an added definition is equivalent to the module lacking the definition in contexts where the definition is unused; however, the two modules are not equivalent in contexts where the added definition is used.

[6] In so doing, the predicate assumes the second step is repeatable. Were the second step executed, its outputs would be equivalent under some predicate to those of the first step.

2. A predicate that compares the concrete representation of two components classifies any two components with the same concrete representation as equivalent. (Here *value(c)* is the concrete representation of component *c*.)

$$\bullet\; P_v[c_i,c_j] := (\; value(c_i) = value(c_j)\;)$$

3. A smarter predicate might consider the syntactic structure of the components it compares. One such predicate might equate any two Pascal modules that differ only in their comments. While compatible with a Pascal compiler, this predicate would not be appropriate to use with a document generator that extracts commentary from Pascal modules.

4. An even more sophisticated predicate might consider the meaning of the components it compares. Such a component might equate any two components that display the same input-output behavior.

   A more rigorous predicate might require that the two components also have the same performance characteristics.

5. Another kind of predicate might classify together all components whose *name* and *type* attributes have the same values. For example, this predicate might equate all instances of a component named "binary – search" that also happen to be Pascal source modules.

Among the predicates described above, P_l is the strongest; P_v is weaker than P_l because it discriminates between fewer components. That is,

$$\bullet\; P_l[c_i,c_j] \Rightarrow P_v[c_i,c_j]$$

The third and fourth predicates are weaker still: P_v implies them both. Because components that are otherwise very different might have the same name and the same type, whereas similar components may have different names or types, the fifth predicate is incomparable with all the remaining predicates except the predicate on labels.

6.2 Using Difference Predicates to Compare Configurations and Other Sets of Components

The relationship between two configurations is determined by the relationship between the components in their export sets. Thus, in general, we use predicates on sets of exported components to compare configurations. Like the predicates used to compare individual components, those used to compare configurations are arbitrary in the sense that they may be chosen according to project needs. Again, when two configurations are said to be equivalent, they are equivalent with respect to some predicate. Any differences between such configurations are considered "not interesting".

Predicates on sets of components can be defined in terms of predicates on individual components. Given two sets of components A and B, a predicate $P_i[c_i,c_j]$ defined on individual components, and a one-to-one mapping from A onto B (*map*: $A \rightarrow B$), the corresponding predicate on sets of components would be defined as follows:

- $P_{i,map}[A,B] := \forall\, a \in A\, [\, P_i[a,map(a)]\,]$

Simple predicates defined on this basis can be quite useful. Consider for example, the predicates $P_{I,map}$ and $P_{v,map}$ formed from the predicates P_I and P_v. The former is simply the predicate used in Section 4.3 to equate two configurations that export the same components. The latter equates two configurations that export equal-valued components; among others, it will equate two configurations that were manufactured from the same primitives at different times, as long as all steps were repeatable.

Interesting predicates also arise when the mapping between component sets is one-to-one but not onto. Depending on how they are formulated, such predicates define partial orders between configurations rather than equivalence classes.

Nevertheless, defining predicates on sets as the conjunction of predicates on individuals is not always appropriate, particularly for weaker predicates. The problem is that components can interact. The extension of individual predicates to sets breaks down both by equating sets of components that might best be considered different and by failing to equate other sets of components that might best be considered equivalent. For example:

1. The use of pairwise comparisons might equate sets of components that otherwise might best be considered different.

   For instance, consider the predicate that allows the addition of definitions to a module interface. Consider next a configuration that exports a set of module interfaces. It is quite possible that the definitions added to two modules will conflict if used subsequently in the same compilation. In this case what was treated as an innocuous change in an individual module is no longer innocuous when combined with changes in other modules.

2. The use of pairwise comparisons might fail to equate two sets of components that might otherwise be considered the same.

   For instance, there may not be a one-to-one correspondence between the exported components of one configuration and those of another. Consider the case when one configuration exports a library of functions partitioned among some number of components. Depending on how that library is used, it might be desirable to equate any configuration that exports the same set of functions partitioned differently over some different set of components.

Predicates on sets of components can be used to compare arbitrary sets of components, not just the exports of configurations. Among the most interesting sets to compare are the input sets and output sets of two manufacturing steps.

6.3 Making Manufacturing Decisions Using Difference Predicates

Applied across pairs of manufacturing steps, difference predicates model the criteria used to determine which steps must be performed to consistently incorporate a given set of changes in a configuration. Unlike the predicates described in the previous two sections, when used to make manufacturing decisions, these difference predicates are not arbitrary.

Consider two manufacturing steps m and m' with input sets In and In', and output sets Out and Out'. A predicate $P_{out}[\,Out,Out'\,]$ has the following meaning:

- First, if the predicate is *true* then the outputs Out can be substituted for the outputs Out' in any configuration that contains step m'.

- In addition, if the predicate is *true* then the outputs Out are said to be consistent with the inputs In'.

In both cases, when the substitution is made and when we say that the set Out is logically (or weakly) consistent with the set In', it is with respect to the predicate P_{out}.

When applied to the input sets of two manufacturing steps, difference predicates predict the relationship between output sets based on the relationship between the input sets. If *step(In)* represents the predicted result of an invocation of a manufacturing step on the input set In, then a successful predicate on inputs implies a successful predicate on outputs:

- $P_{in}[\,In,In'\,] \Rightarrow P_{out}[\,step(In),step(In')\,]$

When the step m has already been performed, *step(In)* = Out. When P_{in} is *true*, the set Out can be used in place of the set *step(In')* so that the step m' need not be performed. As above, the set In' is said to be logically consistent with the set Out. Again, the substitution is made and consistency is claimed with respect to the predicate P_{in}.

As shown in the examples below, P_{out} is typically a stronger predicate than P_{in}.

Using the value of a component or its attributes or both as the basis of comparison, difference predicates across manufacturing steps model the full range of criteria used to make manufacturing decisions. In each case conclusions are made about the relationship between an existing output set Out and the set *step(In')* that would result if the step m' were performed based on the relationship between the input sets In and In'. For example:

- The constant predicate *false* applied to the inputs of manufacturing steps models the strategy of rebuilding an entire configuration from scratch. Whatever the relationship between the sets In and In', even if they represent the same components, *false* requires the manufacture of the output set Out'. The relationship between the existing set Out and the new set Out' is immaterial.

  Since it distinguishes between separate invocations of a manufacturing step on the same input, the predicate *false* is useful in modeling manufacturing steps that are not repeatable.

- Timestamp comparison uses only the date-time-created attribute of the sets In' and Out as a basis for making a manufacturing decision. Whatever the relationship between the sets In' and Out, a manufacturing step is not performed as long as the least date-time-created in Out is greater than the greatest date-time-created in In':

  $\circ\ \forall\, c_i' \in In'\, [\ {\sim}\exists\, c_o \in Out\ .\ date\text{-}time\text{-}created(c_i') \geq date\text{-}time\text{-}created(c_o)\,]$

  Timestamp comparison rests on the assumption that if the relation among timestamps is as given, then the input set *In* has not changed (i.e $P_{v,map}[In,In'] = true$); however this is simply an assumption and not justified by the formulation above. Based on this predicate, no conclusions can be drawn about the relationship between the output set *Out* and the set *step(In')*.

- Like most predicates, version comparison assumes that manufacturing steps are repeatable so that identical inputs produce equal-valued outputs. Since version stamps are approximations to unique identifiers, the following predicate is formulated in terms of unique component labels:

  ○ $P_{l,map}[In,In'] \Rightarrow P_{v,map}[Out,step(In')]$

  In fact, when the predicate

  ○ $P_{l,map}[In,In'] \wedge P_{v,map}[Out,Out']$

  is *true*, the step in question is repeatable.

While commonly used, the above predicates make no use of the value of the components in their comparison of input sets. They also take no account of the context in which the outputs are to be used. The invocation of additional steps can be suppressed by predicates that take into consideration the values of components or the contexts in which the outputs of a manufacturing step are used. For example:

- The predicate $P_{v,map}$ defined in the previous section is the basis of a simple strategy for avoiding obviously redundant steps. If a manufacturing step *m* is repeatable and uses only the values of its input components, then:

  ○ $P_{v,map}[In,In'] \Rightarrow P_{v,map}[Out,step(In')]$

  This strategy is comparable to but weaker than version stamp comparison based on unique identifiers since components with different unique identifiers may have the same value. Like version comparison, if the predicate

  ○ $P_{v,map}[In,In'] \wedge P_{v,map}[Out,Out']$

  is *true* then the step is repeatable.

  This predicate is the exactly the one that allows the model to identify derived components produced by different invocations of steps whose input sets are the same.

- Another manufacturing strategy is based on predicates that suppress a manufacturing step even if the values of the elements of *In* and *In'* differ. Using knowledge about the semantics of the manufacturing step, these predicates determine that the values of the components of *Out* and *step(In)'* would be identical whether *In* or *In'* were used as inputs:

  ○ $P_{sem}[In,In'] \Rightarrow P_{v,map}[Out,step(In')]$

Smart recompilation mechanisms use this strategy to admit changes that are upwardly compatible, allowing for example, the addition or deletion of definitions that are unused in a compilation step.[7]

- Write-if-changed mechanisms implement a variant of the semantic predicate strategy by executing the manufacturing step and comparing outputs instead of inputs. However, since the step is actually performed, not all pairs of members of the outputs sets need have the same value.

6.4 The Use of Context in Difference Predicates

In their full generality, difference predicates take into account the context in which a component or set of components is to be used. The context might be captured by a difference predicate itself, so that when the predicate is *true*, it is implicitly *true* only for the given context. A predicate that compares Pascal source files stripped of comments works implicitly only for steps that involve Pascal compilations; it fails in the case of a document generator.

Other predicates might take the context of comparison as an additional parameter.

- It is possible that a step need not be performed even if the values of the components of the set *step(In')* might differ from those in the set *Out*. In this case, a predicate on inputs still determines whether the existing outputs will serve in place of those that would have been produced using the new inputs *In'*. To do so, it is necessary to consider not only the step in question when making a manufacturing decision, but also the context in which the outputs of the steps are to be used.

  For example, consider a manufacturing step that produces a library of subroutines. Although routines might be added to the library, an existing version might be used anywhere that the added routines are not needed. A separate decision has to be made for each use site.

6.5 Practical Considerations on the Use of Difference Predicates

A very simple cost model is implicit in the discussion above. That is, each manufacturing step is equally costly and evaluating a difference predicate is free. Clearly a more refined cost model is not only possible but necessary.

When designing a manufacturing facility that uses difference predicates, the following must all be taken into consideration:

- the cost of invoking a particular difference predicate,

- the likelihood of its evaluating to *true*, and

- the amount of manufacturing that would be saved by such a positive response.

The variables in this equation are not only what predicate is evaluated, but where the predicate is applied and to what components.

---

[7]Note that changes admitted by this strategy in one manufacturing step may not be admitted in another step. For instance, a single change that does not affect a compilation may well affect a listing, and vice versa.

For example, there is a tradeoff between checking the inputs of a step for compatibility and checking its outputs: A weaker difference predicate allows a greater number of differences in the sets it compares before insisting that a manufacturing step be performed. The more changes a predicate allows, the more checking a predicate must do, the more costly the predicate evaluation.

- If the predicate costs more than the manufacturing step it is evaluating, it may be cheaper simply to perform the step and use simpler predicates on its outputs.

- However, if the step has considerable fan-out, it still may be cost effective to attempt to suppress it, rather than checking to see whether each subsequent step should be performed.

Additionally, although the use of difference predicates in software manufacture is formulated in terms of the input sets of manufacturing steps, using pairwise predicates on individual components can be effective when manufacturing decisions are based on the results of individual comparisons. In this way, the cost of a comparison can be amortized over all the steps that use a certain component as input. It thus becomes cost effective to spend more on the individual predicates. There are drawbacks to pairwise comparison, however, since it does not provide an opportunity to assess the interaction between changes. However, using simple pairwise comparison on the outputs of a manufacturing step may well be more effective than a lengthy comparison of input sets. It also may be reasonable to ignore some low probability interactions between changes when fast turnaround is more desirable than the increased confidence that comes with the use of more expensive predicates or predicates that suppress fewer manufacturing steps.

7 Summary

Software manufacture is a central part of the problem of dealing with change in the software development process, since it is through the manufacturing process that changes are incorporated in a system.

In the interest of taking steps toward the systematic treatment of software manufacture, this paper has outlined a model of software manufacture that addresses the question of how much work has to be done to consistently incorporate a given set of changes in a given configuration. The model is based on a formal definition of a configuration that allows us to precisely identify and delimit change. Difference predicates model the strategies used to determine what steps have to be performed in order to incorporate a set of changes. Their use weakens the very strict notion of consistency used in the formal definition, making it possible to omit steps from the manufacturing process and still produce a consistent configuration.

8 Acknowledgements

I have had the opportunity to discuss the issues raised in this paper with many people who have helped me refine my thinking, among them, David Garlan, John Nestor, Joe Newcomer, Ed Satterthwaite, and Mary Shaw.

I would like to thank David Garlan, David Lamb, Roberto Minio, Ed Satterthwaite and especially John Nestor for their comments on an earlier draft of this paper.

9 References

[Conradi 85]   Reidar Conradi and Dag Heieraas Wanvik.
                Mechanisms and Tools for Separate Compilation.
                Technical Report 25/85, The University of Trondheim, The Norweigian Institute of Technology, October, 1985.

[Cooper 84]   Jack Cooper.
                Software Development Management Planning.
                IEEE Transactions on Software Engineering 10(1):22-26, January, 1984.

[Cooprider 79] Lee W. Cooprider.
                The Representation of Families of Software Systems.
                PhD thesis, Carnegie-Mellon University, April, 1979.

[Cristofor 80] Eugene Cristofor, T. A. Wendt and B. C. Wonsiewicz.
                Source Control + Tools = Stable Systems.
                In *Proceedings of the 4th Computer Science and Applications
                Conference*, pages 527-532. IEEE Computer Society, October, 1980.

[Dausmann 84]   Manfred Dausmann.
                Reducing Recompilation Costs for Software Systems in Ada.
                March 30, 1984
                Draft of a Karlsruhe Technical Report presented at the IFIP WG 2.4 conference in Canterbury UK in September 1984.

[DeRemer 76]   Frank DeRemer and Hans H. Kron.
                Programming-in-the-Large Versus Programming-in-the-Small.
                IEEE Transactions on Software Engineering 2(2):80-86, June, 1976.

[Erickson 84]   V. B. Erickson and J. F. Pellegrin.
                Build - A Software Construction Tool.
                AT&T Bell Laboratories Technical Journal 63(6), July-August, 1984.

[Estublier 84] J. Estublier, S. Ghoul, S. Krakowiak.
                Preliminary Experience with a Configuration Control System for Modular
                Programs.
                SIGPLAN Notices 19(5), May, 1984.
                Proceedings of the ACM SIGSOFT/SIGPLAN Software Engineering Symposium on Practical Software Development Environments.

[Feldman 79]   Stuart I. Feldman.
                Make - A Program for Maintaining Computer Programs.
                Software-Practice and Experience 9(4):255-265, April, 1979.

[Kaiser 83]   Gail E. Kaiser and A. Nico Habermann.
                An Environment for System Version Control.
                In *Digest of Papers COMPCON Spring 83*, pages 415-420. IEEE Computer
                Society, San Francisco, California, February, 1983.

[Lampson 83]   Butler W. Lampson and Eric E. Schmidt.
                 Organizing Software in a Distributed Environment.
                 In *Proceedings of the SigPlan '83 Symposium on Programming Language Issues in Software Systems*, pages 1-13. ACM, San Francisco, California, June, 1983.

[Leblang 84]   David B. Leblang, Robert P. Chase, Jr.
                 Computer-Aided Software Engineering in a Distributed Workstation Environment.
                 SIGPLAN Notices 19(5), May, 1984.
                 Proceedings of the ACM SIGSOFT/SIGPLAN Software Engineering Symposium on Practical Software Development Environments.

[Leblang 85]   David B. Leblang, Robert P. Chase Jr., and Gordon D. McLean Jr.
                 The DOMAIN Software Engineering Environment for Large-Scale Software Development Efforts.
                 In *IEEE Conference on Workstations*. November, 1985.

[Rochkind 75]   Marc J. Rochkind.
                 The Source Code Control System.
                 IEEE Transactions on Software Engineering 1(4):364-370, December, 1975.

[Rowland 83]   B. R. Rowland and R. J. Welsch.
                 The 3B20D Processor & DMERT Operating System: Software Development System.
                 The Bell System Technical Journal 62(1):275-289, January, 1983.

[Tichy 80]   Walter F. Tichy.
                 Software Development Control Based on System Structure Description.
                 PhD thesis, Carnegie-Mellon University, January, 1980.

[Tichy 82]   Walter F. Tichy.
                 Design, Implementation, and Evaluation of a Revision Control System.
                 Technical Report CSD-TR-397, Department of Computer Science, Purdue University, March, 1982.
                 A version of this paper appeared in Proceedings of the 6th International Conference on Software Engineering, Tokoyo, September 1982.

[Tichy 85]   Walter F. Tichy and Mark C. Baker.
                 Smart Recompilation.
                 In *Principles of Programming Languages 1985*, pages 236-244. ACM SIGPLAN and SIGACT, January, 1985.

PROTECTION AND COOPERATION IN A

SOFTWARE ENGINEERING ENVIRONMENT

Belkhatir N. Estublier J.
L.G.I BP 68 38402 St Martin d'Heres
FRANCE

ABSTRACT

This paper describes the problems which arise when a team is developing or maintaining a software product. These problems are the sharing of objects, the side effect of modifications, the protection and structuring of teams and products. We discuss these problems and the solutions proposed by the Adele data base of programs

KEY WORDS: sharing, cooperation, protection, programming environment, side effects, rights.

1 INTRODUCTION

Software products, due to their growing size and life duration, need the long term collaboration of teams for their creation and evolution. Because of the complexity of the software products and of the different qualifications of the team members, a strict protection of software objects and a precise dispatching of the tasks is needed. Different persons can work on the same software; the interaction of the actions of these persons must be controlled.

To master the complexity of large software products and of their teams, we have to control various aspects.

Physical sharing of objects: control of concurrent access to physical objects.

Logical sharing of objects : control of the side effects of the different actions.

Access rights: control over actions allowed for each user.

Structuring of teams and products: control of the structure, visibility rules, characteristics and relationships between each subset of the software.

Of all these problems, only that of physical sharing is solved (concurrent access) and thus will not be discussed here. The problem of side effect detection is only partially solved while protection and control of the structure of software, after the initial phase of design, is an unsolved point. It is well known that these problems are the crux of maintenance and evolution costs. Thus control over the cost of software products needs better a solution to these problems.

In the Adele data base of programs we tried to propose and validate solutions of these problems. We will first give the basic notions of Adele. More details can be found in (Est 84, Est 85).

2 THE ADELE DATA BASE OF PROGRAMS

Adele can be seen as a data base of programs since it maintains software objects and their relationship, as a configuration manager since it maintains the versions of a software, build and manage configurations or as the kernel of a programming environment since it acts as a file system, control rights and users, detect inconsistencies... In Adele we began to redefine the notion of a module.

The notion of module was for a long time confused with that of compile unit, which is a very restrictive view. Actually, following notions found in Ada or Modula, a module is often seen as being the association of an interface which describes the resources of the module and a body which implements its resources. Resources are classicaly procedure headers, declaration of constant variables and types. In Adele we extend the notion of module and interface further.

2.1 Versions and revisions

Different algorithms are possible for implementing the resources of an interface. Each one of these interfaces is a body and constitutes a **version of realization.** Each version can in turn, follow minor modifications such as bug fixes and small improvements which constitute **revisions** of a version. This is now generaly accepted and can be found for example in SCCS (Christopher84), Gandalf (Haberman 82), ...

2.2 Interfaces

In Adele the interface of a module is a set of **interface versions.** The interface version notion is due to the fact that the interface of a module changes during the life of a project either for historical reasons or to cope with different requirements. Each one of these versions owns its versions of realization.

Each version of interface is in turn a set of **interface views**. An interface view defines in a given syntax a subset of the interface. Each view can be precisely protected. Thus a view, as in data base ,is a protection mechanism, and a multi-syntaxdeclaration. For instance, a view can be public or private; the private view being protected against foreign access and offers "dangerous" resources; the public interface is less protected and proposes immune resources. A view allows the definition of the same resources in different programming languages, thus modules written in different languages can access this interface (they can be compiled including this interface syntacticly). A view can also be a resource in itself: type and constant definition, macros, job control file, global variables, ...

2.3 Module and family

In its current meaning, a module is a compile unit, or a pair body/interface. An interface and its realizations is a set of versions of a module, apparently identical for its users. For Adele a module can have different interfaces (and views), and is the set of all the possible associations interface/bodies thus is the set of possible versions of the module. In order not to confuse wich the classical meaning of module (i.e a version of a module), we called it a **family** even if we sometimes use the word module in the
same meaning.

2.4 The dependency relation

The main relation in a software is the dependency relation between bodies and interfaces. A body or an interface can use the resources defined in an interface, they **depend** on this interface. A family F1 depends on a family F2 if at least one of its interface or realizations depends on an interface of F2. For a software product, we define the dependency graph where nodes are families and arrows are the dependency relations. We restrict this graph to be acyclic.

2.5 Names attributes and predicate

Objects in Adele (i.e family, interface and realization) can be referenced by their **name** or by a predicate using attributes. An **attribute** is a pair "*name = value*". Examples of attributes are "system = unix", "type = experimental", "date = 86_06_26". Some attributes such as date, author, state and language are created and maintained automatically by the system, the others are created explicitly by the users.

A **predicate** is a conjunction (and) of atomic predicates, "*attribute-name relation-operator value*". For instance , the expression (state = official, date > 85_09) refers to all objects with the atributes "state = official" **and** " date > 85_09".

3 COOPERATION

3.1 Concurrent modification of the same object

This is the case when two persons make changes in the same object (usually a module). These is a risk that the changes done by one of them overwrites the changes done by the other.

The usual solution is to store the objects in a separate file space, and to allow the modification of an object only through the commands "reserve" and "replace". The former being a lock on the object, the latter replaces the object and release the lock. This solution was used in Gandalf (Habermann82), Cedar (Swinehart85), Domain (Leblang84), Adele (Est84). Others systems as Make (Fieldman79) or RCS (Tichy82) does not manage a separate file but cannot solve this problem (which, however, is not their purpose).

Adele locks not only the reserved object but also all directly dependent objects. For instance, if a realization is reserved, its interface is also locked; preventing that somebody changes an interface while someone else changes the body, each one compiling with the old version and replacing an unconsistent pair body/interface.

3.2 Side effects of modifications

We say that a **side effect** is produced on the source element of a relation, when the target element of this relation is modified or deleted. A side effect: thus involves **the action** which modifies the **source object** and produces the side effect; the **relations** having this object as a source object, the **targeted objects** of the relation, and the **response actions**. This somewhat general definition must be detailed: which are the relations, when is the side effect to be detected and indicated, what kind of response actions are possible.

a) What relations are used

The relations used in the programming environment are usually implicit. For instance a Makefile is an indirect way of saying that there is a relation (undefined) between the files named therein. More often, the relation is the dependency relation. The related elements are provided by hand, or they can be extracted from the source code by a simple parser (Adele), or by the compiler itself (Gandalf, Cedar, Modula). Two systems Domain and Adele use the classical database technique and allow to define any kind of relation between any kind of objects. In Adele, the dependency relation ("depends_on") is predefined and can be automatically maintained. The other relations as "specify" between a document and a program, of "must_do" between a planning and a programmmer must be explicitly defined. These relations provide a way of handling semantic dependencies into account even if the granularity of the object is considerable (a file).

b) When the side effect is detected

The moment when the side effect is detected differs between systems. It can be before, during or after the side effect. It can also be on demand.

1) **Anticipated detection.** A detection before action confirmation allows shown its consequences and thus to prevent dramatic errors. It can also be used to compute (with a negative confirmation) what would be the consequences of the modification of an object thus providing, for instance, an element in the decision of how to make a modification with minimal impact. Adele always anticipates the detection of side effects for any action and asks for confirmation if a side effect is found. This detection allows more control over the possible incidence of dangerous actions.

2) **Immediate detection.** Most of the environments provide for detection of a side effect immediately after the action. In this class of systems we found most environments such as Gandalf, Modula, Cedar, Mesa, Fasp, ... Adele also is in this class since, when the action is validated, the information (action, author, relation, source object, date) is set in each impacted object.

3) **Postponed detection.** Side effects can also be pointed out when use is made of an object. Few environments provide this service because it needs the side effects on it be to recorded in each impacted object. In Adele, for any action on an impacted object, a

warning is issued describing the already ignored side effects on the object. The recorded side effects on an object are reset on its first modification. This mechanism avoids the unconscious use of a possibly inconsistent object. Also, in conjunction with the history mechanism of Adele, a backtracking of side effects can be undertaken.

4) **Detection on demand.** Ultimately, a user can ask for side effects on an object. Numerous environments provide this service using timestamps. Make is a well known representative of this class of products it is only on the activation of a Makefile that side effects are detected (and actions undertaken). Adele also provides this service, not on the basis of timestamps, but using the information encoded in the object itself (recorded in 2) which provides more information.

c) What action is to executed

Since only the dependency relation is usually known, environments can only recompile the modules using a modified interface and relink after modules have ben recompiled Cedar (Tetelman84), Mesa (Lauer82), FASP (Stuebing84). This approch is justified because the compilations order must be undertaken must be specified in detail, and because hundred of command lines can be involved.

Automatic recompilation is also a controversial topic: is it reasonable to produce a significant number of recompilations at each modification?. The problem is even more difficult if relations other than the dependency relation must be considered. We found that the response actions must be clearly dissociated from side effect detection. The former is in charge of the programming environment which knows the relations, whereas the latter is a policy decision and should be left to the user or a special tool. The environment must provide powerful mechanisms to define the relations, and to give the control to the user at the different moments when a side effect can be taken into account.

This approach is systematic in Adele. The data base is such that "Make policy", "Cedar policy", "Fasp policy", and any other policy can be easily defined. The data base allows general relations (between programs or anything else) and raises events at the 4 different moments indicated previously. These events, when caught, allow users to execute the response actions desired. In Adele, the desired policies can be set by the user, by a team or by parts of the data base, thus allowing different policies to be defined and executed inside a same data base.

To provide an illustration, let A and B be two teams each of which uses a different compiler but the same code generator. Suppose the A team changes the code generator. In Make, the B compiler is not impacted but at the next invocation of its Makefile the new generator will be used. In Cedar, the B team will ignore that a new generator is available. In Adele the A team will be warned about the side effect on the B compiler, and the B team will be warned that a new code generator is available at the next use of its compiler. The B team can thus rebuild its compiler with or without the new component.

4 PROTECTION AND ACCESS RIGHTS

The protection of objects in the software engineering environment is usually that provided by the operating system which classically defines the user concept (an active entity), and object concept (a passive entity). Different mechanisms have been defined to implement protection in operating systems:

1) **Access list** systems. Associated with each **object**, it specifies the possible rights by a user or user group (i.e the Unix system).

2) **Right list** (capability, view,) systems. For each (class of) **user** is defined a **domain** i.e the set of all accessible objects, and for each objects the allowed actions thereon (as in Hydra). For instance in an DBMS, each user can use views, a view beeing a domain.

More recently **access list and right list** systems (Minsky84) have been proposed. Objects are protected by an access list, and users are controlled by rights lists. This approch has two originalities: naming of objects and domains are done using attributes; and rights are controlled by privileges. A privilege is a tuple (operation, attribute, predicate) which signifies that the operation can be applied on any object defined by the attributes and satisfying the predicate. For instance, the right for the user U to drive the car V suppose that U has a driving licence (rights of U) **and** that V can be used by U (access list to V).

Objects in Adele can be referred to by attributes. It was then natural for us to choose such a policy which we will present briefly.

4.1 Access rights

Users play a double role in the system, they are active (the user at his terminal) or passive (an object on which an operation can be performed as creation, modification of its rights...). Users, as any other object, can be described by attributes, and rights can be uniformly expressed on objects as well as on users.

Privileges are expressed with pairs <operation, designation> where operation is a command and designation defines the objects on which the operation can be performed. We will write *object* informaly where an object designation must be found.

For instance, privileges for user U can be:
replace   *object* (**langage = pascal, state = experimental**)
creatuser *object* (**class = programmer, system = unix**)

These privileges expres that user U can execute the "replace" command on *object*s written in pascal and in the experimental state, and that it can apply "createusers" of the class programmer having competence on the unix system.

For instance, an acceslist for the realization R can be:
replace *object* (**class = programmer, system = unix**)
which means that R can be modified (by the replace command) by the users described by *object* of the class programmer and having the attribute system = unix.

4.2 User classes

We introduce the notion of a user class to express privilege patterns. Privileges expressed in a class can be partially instantiated. Non instantiated parts are prefixed by the key word "self_", as in the following example for the definition of the programmer class:

```
class programmer
     attributes
              F              = F1                    /* default attributes */
              system     = unix
              class        = programmer
     catal
              self_F (state = in_test, system = self_system)
end;
```

Programmers can execute the "catal" command only on objects with in_"test" state, in a domain F to be defined (F1 by default), and with a system attribute to be defined ("unix" by default). The setting of default values for a given user changes its corresponding attributes and can be used later to refer to this user. The creator must have the rights given to the new user. This check is simple in Adele: commands and constraints must be included in those of the creator and attributes must be at least those present in the corresponding privilege of the creator.

4.3 Conclusion

The main interest of this approch is its power and flexibility. Rights are not "frozen" for an object or a user, but evolve automatically with the evolution of the objects, and no hypothesis is predefined as to the user organization.

Thus we can express that programmers manage objects in the "in_test" state whereas integrators can do the same but only on "tested" objects, and customer engineers can read documents related to "distributed" objects. The last action a programmer can do on an object is to give it the "tested" state, which makes it accessible to integrators. This change of state also raises a signal which, when caught, can send a message to an integrator or modify a planning, or build a configuration.

5 PROTECTION AND STRUCTURING OF A SOFTWARE PRODUCT

We usually understand the structure of a software product as being the structure of the dependency relation between programs where a relative consensus seems to appear. For the most rigid approaches a pure tree is imposed. For most others any acyclic graph is sufficient. Efforts have been done to accept cyclical graphs, but theorical results show that there is risks of finding untractable link editions. Practice even shows that it produces badly structured products. Conception methodology (recursive refinement, abstract machine, abstraction levels, ..) use very similar ideas: an entity (conceptual, abstract) is broken down into more simple and elementary entities whose functionality and relationship with the other entities must be defined until only elementary entities (programs) are found. This strict methodology produces a tree... The structure need to be controlled in two ways: the control of the dependency relation, and the control and protection of the conceptual entities.

5.1 Control of the dependency relation

The control of the structure (for the dependency relation) is the control over the visibility of the module's interfaces. In Adele, each family maintains the access list of its interfaces. In some family F we could find:

usable_by
     * (standard)
     F2 (itforF2)
     object (i1, i2, i3)

Let F1 be a family defining a memory management module. We expressed in the previous example that the "itforF2" interface can be accessed only by the F2 family ("itforF2" could contain such dangerous procedures as init or reset), "standard" can be used by all modules (it can define the procedure getmem and freemem for instance), and "i1", "i2", "i3" are interfaces defining other kinds of memory management which can be used by *object* modules.

This protection can only be applied to the dependency relation and does not allow the structure of more general entities to be easily controlled. For that we need to give a real existence to the conceptual entities.

5.2 Conceptual entities and partitions

Using only the relation "is a decomposition of", all design methodologies of recursive refinement produce a tree, where nodes are the high level entities and leaves the elementary modules. It is often considered that only the leaves are real programs, and nodes are abstract conceptual entities. This "flat" view is wrong. Even at a high level, the conceptual entities define resources that can take the conventional form of procedures, functions, types and so on. This is especially obvious for a decomposition into abstract levels where each level provides a well defined interface for writing the next level.

A conceptual entity must be managed as an elementary entity, and behave in any case as any other object. Adele defines the notion of partition as being an extention of the notion of family in order to cope with the notion of conceptual entity. A **partition** is a set of families. These families are a sub-set of the dependency graph beginning at a family (called the root family). A partition is identical,to its users, to a leaf family (i.e. its internal structure and components are not directly visible and accessible).

For a family to become a partition, we must provide some extra protection and features:

1) **Protection.** In order to define the protection globally, a partition can be protected as a family. The name of a partition is the name of the root family followed by "*". In setting rights, a partition can be inserted anywhere the name of a family may be.

2) **Structural independence.** A configuration is an object similar to a realization (Est85). It is the list of the realizations (or configurations) that jointly really realizes the resources of an interface. No knowledge as of the components of a configuration is directly accessible. The only realisations accessible in a partition are the configurations of its root family.

3) **Logical independence.** A partition must be internally developped independently from characteristics and conventions defined outside the partition; and must be allowed to define its own internal characteristics and conventions.

We will see briefly the logical independence in Adel and especially the visibility heritage, the attribute control and the control of the evolution of the software products.

5.2.1 Visibility protection

This protection is provided by the visibility heritage. Partitions can define restrictions over the visibility of its interfaces, that will be automatically inherited by all its constituent families. For instance, if the F2 family define **"impose F2*"** then all families in the F2 partition will have **"imposed F2*"** which means that only families of F2* can see the families in F2*. In other words F2* enforces an abstract machine structure: only its root family is visible.

5.2.2 Attribute control

The partition plays the role of the block in a block structured language: the attributes used in a partition must be declared in this partition or in a higher level partition. Objects in a partition can be described by attributes known only therein. This feature allows the refinement of attributes i.e an attribute of the imbedding partition has an abstract meaning that can be refined by more precise attributes. This is logical since the notions managed in an abstraction level are different and more abstract than the one used in the next lower level. Configurations of the root family are external objects of the partition (they are the only visible objects of the partition) and at the same time are internal to the partition. Thus while they can be designated by attributes of the external partition they define their components using attributes which are valid inside the partition. In this way, these configurations define how a set of external attributes may be refined into a set of internal attributes. The notion of partition is similar to the notion of class and sub-classes as found in object oriented approches.

For instance, let "tdx24" be a configuration of the "disks" partition. This configuration is characterized by the attribute "disk_size = 120MO", and is internally defined by the constraints "disks* (driver = xyz, disk = tdx24)" meaning that the realization to be selected for the "tdx24" configuration must be able to manage the "tdx24" disk and the "xyz" driver. The "disk_size" attribute is the only characteristic accessible which differenciates the configurations of the disks's partition. This attribute is refined in the attribute driver and disk, but external users do not have to know that. This complexity level of the internal structure of the partition is hidden.

5.2.3 Control of the evolution of the structure

The correspondence between conceptual entities and programs, using the notion of partition, allows the user to see the structure of its software at the desired abstraction level and to refer to conceptual entities in an appropriate way. This view is static, whereas a software product is in constant evolution. This criticism is often made against design tools that forget the relation with the implementation after the definition of their entities, structure, functionality and organization. The evolution produced by maintenance, enhancements and parallel versions is not reflected in the conceptual structure, which is why the implementation slowly moves away from its original design.

When modifications are made, the ignorance of the design structure and decisions produce a "destructuration" and software becomes gradualy ossified until it is impossible to make any further change. Thus is very important because it is the reason for the limitation of the life duration of a software product and its high maintanance cost.

In Adele, the relation between conceptual entities and their implementation is maintained in both directions, therefore allowing for any version of a software product, at any moment of its life, to display its characteristics (conceptual structure, relation between entities, visibility, documents, attributes, ...). The side effect mechanism presented before, also works on partitions. When an action is undertaken in the data base, side effects are computed, structure modifications at all levels of abstraction are detected, recorded and reported. We are convinced that this mechanism allows for better maintenance without too much destructuration, provides better information, and contributes to lowering maintenance costs.

6 CONCLUSION

After four years of industrial and university experience, the notions developed in the Adele data base of programs are widely validated (except "rights" which are currently under implementation).

As indicated, the problems of side effect management have been very little studied, and the problems of structure control are unsolved, especially as for conceptual entities. We are convinced that these two aspect are of great importance in the control of maintenance costs and hope that the solutions proposed by the Adele data base are a step in this direction.

REFERENCES

Cristofor80   Cristofor E., Wendt T.A., Wonsiewicz B.C., Source Control + Tools = Stable systems, Proc. Compsac 80 (IEEE Computer Soc. Press). Oct 1980.

Estublier84   Estublier J., Ghoul S., Krakowiak S.
Preliminary experience with a configuration system for modular programs.
Proc. of the ACM Sifsoft/sigplan Software engineering Symposium on Practical Software Development Environment. April 1984.

Estublier85   Estublier J.
A Configuration Manager: the Adele data base of programs.
Workshop on software enginering environments for programming- in-the-large.
Harwichport, Massachusetts. June 1985.

Feldman79   Feldman S.I.
Make, a program for maintaining software;
Software Practice and Experience. Vol 9. 1979.

Habermann82   Habermann N., Flon L, Cooprider L.
"Modularization and hierarchy in a family of Operating Systems.
Comm. of the ACM, May 1976.

Lauer82   Lauer H., Satterthwaite E.
The impact of Mesa on Software Design.
Proc of the Fourth International Conference on Software Engineering, September 1982.

Leblang84   Leblang D, Chase R.
Computer-Aided Software Engineering in a distributed Workstation Environment. Proc. of the ACM Sigsoft/Sigplan Symposium on practical Software Development Environments. April 1984.

Minsky84   Minsky A., Borgida P.
The Darwin Software-Evolution Environment.
Proc. of the ACM Sigsoft/Sigplan Software Engineering Symposium on practical Software Development Environments. April 1984.

Stuebing84   Stuebing H.g.
A Software Engineering Environment for Weapon System Software.
IEEE Transactions on Software Engineering. July 1984.

Swinehart85
    Swineheart D., Zellweger P., Hagmann R.
The structure of Cedar.
Proc. of the ACM Sigsoft/Sigplan Symposium on practical Software on Programming Language and Programming Environments. June 1895.

Teitelman84   Teitelman W.
A Tour Through Cedar.
IEEE Software April 1984.

Tichy82   Tichy W.
Design Implementation and Evaluation of a Revision Control System. 6th International Conference on Software Engeneering.
Tokyo, September 1982.

The Integration of Version Control into Programming Languages

J F H Winkler

Siemens Corporate Laboratories
for Information Technology

D-8000 München 83 Fed.Rep.Germany

Industrial program products are often families of large and modular programs. Modern programming languages support the formulation of such program families only partially. At the time being it is usually not possible to describe different revisions, variants, and versions of single program building blocks and whole programs.

This paper presents a proposal for the formulation of such version information as part of the program text. In a newly introduced CONFIG part of a program building block the programmer can express: (1) to which versions the building block belongs, and (2) which versions of other building blocks it uses. In this new construct a version is defined as a pair (revision, variant), and a variant as a vector of attributes. With these language constructs the "knowledge" about the program versions can be expressed by facts and rules. The representation of this knowledge is adapted to the structure of the program, and the generation of specific program versions can be done automatically.

1 Introduction

The development of programming languages in the last 35 years is characterized by a steady increase of expressiveness. We understand expressiveness not in a purely theoretical sense, but rather in a more practical sense. The first languages before 1960 contained elements for the formulation of mathematical formulae, functions and procedures, and data of certain basic types [Bac 78a; PS 59]. Ten years later Algol 68 and Pascal added the user-defined type, enumeration, record and pointer types; and dynamic data structures [Wi 69a; Wir 71a]. Since then, concepts for modular programming, separate compilation, and concurrency have been added [CCI 85; MMS 79; Ref 83; Wir 80].

Industrial program products are often families of rather large programs. The features incorporated into programming languages during the last ten years support especially the construction of large and modular programs. But, contemporary programming languages do not yet provide constructs for the formulation of program families with revisions and variants, as they are mentioned in [Win 85]. Large and long-lived program products are typically such families. During a long period of usage, such programs usually evolve into a number of revisions [BL 76; Tic 85] (sometimes also called versions or releases [BL 76]). Large program systems are often used for and adapted to a range of functionally different purposes. Operating systems are often adapted to different machine configurations and/or different user requirements [SW 80], and programs for switching systems are used for different switches in different countries [Win 85; Win 86].

In this paper we propose language constructs to express the information that describes the configurations of program families with revisions and variants. By **revision** we mean different forms of a program that evolve in time during further development and maintenance. By **variants** we mean different forms of a program, that coexist in time and are rather functional alternatives. The distinction between revision and variant is somewhat fuzzy [Loc 83], but it is typically made in practice. The language constructs proposed in this paper describe

a) the revisions and variants a certain program building block belongs to, and

b) the revisions and variants of a building block B that is referenced by another building block A. The revisions and variants of B may depend on those of A.

We use the term "building block" to refer to those entities that are called "compilation unit" in Ada [Ref 83].
The information expressed by the descriptions mentioned above is sufficient for the automatic configuration of arbitrary program versions. In this paper we deal with the problem of program configuration at the building block level. [SW 80] reports about work on configuration at the statement level using program generation techniques.

The paper is organized as follows. Section 2 deals with families of large programs and section 3 with approaches to configuration control. In section 4 we propose a formal model of configuration descriptions. Section 5 deals with the incorporation of configuration descriptions in programming languages. Some examples are given in section 6, and section 7 offers some conclusions.

2 Families of Large Programs

As mentioned in the introduction, large program products are typically families of large programs where the members of such a family are characterized by revisions and variants.

A typical example for such a program family is the EWSD system (electronic digital switching system [Sie 81]). This is a family of CHILL programs for public telephone switches. Its main characteristics with respect to the topic of this paper are:

c1) it is quite large (several Mio Loc and several thousand modules) c2) it is expected to be in use for several decades. This will lead to a number of revisions.

c3) it is used for functionally different switches as eg local switches and long distance switches. This results in a number of functionally different variants.

c4) it will be installed in a number of different countries worldwide (21 up to now). This results also in a number of functionally different variants.

The process of developing and maintaining such families of large programs has the following three main characteristics:

p1) the programs are **multi-module** programs

p2) the development requires a **multi-library** system as the central database

p3) the projects for such developments are **multi-person** projects.

3 Configuration Control

Programming language facilities that support the realization of program families must take into account the properties and characteristics mentioned in the preceding section. We will generally assume that the programming languages used for the realization of program families allow the formulation of modular programs, like in Ada, CHILL, Mesa, and Modula-2. Since the term "module" is used in some languages for a specific kind of program unit, we will use the term "building block" for the textually self-contained program parts of a modular program.

The set of building blocks of a modular program, or a family of such programs, is a structured set in which certain relations between the elements hold. In the above languages some of these relations are already expressed directly in the source text of the building blocks. Examples of such relations are the relations expressed by the **with**-clauses in Ada, or the export and import clauses in Modula-2. More details are given in [Win 85].

As mentioned, we use the concepts revision and variant to describe the versions of building blocks and whole programs. A revision indication is usually a scalar entity, like a version number or a time stamp. As variant indications we take tuples of attribute values where such a tuple contains a value for some of the attributes that are used to span the space of program variants. In our model a version indication is therefore a pair *(revision indication, variant indication)* i.e. version = (revision,variant) . The formal details of this model are given in the next section.

Contemporary programming languages do not contain facilities to express the version information in a program family. Such facilities will be proposed in section 5.

From the point of programming languages we can distinguish between three different aspects of program configuration:

c1) **Syntactic configuration**: the programming language allows the description of the syntax of the interface of building blocks. This is the situation in programming languages like Ada, CHILL, and Modula-2.

c2) **Semantic configuration**: here the interface semantics is also described by the program text. This is not possible in contemporary programming languages [Win 82], but in the research area there are several approaches to this problem [GHW 85; HKL 84].

c3) **Pragmatic configuration**: the programming language allows additionally the description of the version information as already explained above.

Pragmatic configuration is the topic of this paper. We assume that a programming language allows syntactic configuration as in Ada, CHILL, and Mesa.

4 The Model of the Configuration Language

The configuration language, which will be introduced in section 5, is based on a simple model for the description of versions as pairs of revision and variant.

We assume a finite and nonempty set REV of **revision** indications:

$$REV := \{ r_1, r_2, ..., r_n \}$$

REV is often totally ordered, like for time stamps or version numbers . An example is: {1.1, 1.6, 1.8, 2.1, 2.12, 3.0}, where the order is that of the rational numbers.

REV may also be partially ordered as in [Tic 85], where some kind of hierarchically structured revision indications is used, eg: { 1.2, 1.2.1.1, 1.3 }. The ordering is given by: $1.2 <$ 1.2.1.1 and $1.2 < 1.3$ (1.2.1.1 and 1.3 are incomparable). The ordering relation in [Tic 85] expresses a true tree ordering. It is not possible to express the fact that a certain revision R combines different earlier revisions. With a general partial ordering such a recombination (merging [Apo 85: 2-12..2-15]) would also be possible.

A particular building block may belong to several revisions of a program. This is frequently the case if the different versions of a program should be homogeneous with respect to the revision indications [MTW 84]. Therefore, a revision description is defined as a subset of REV. The set of revision descriptions RevD is therefore defined as follows:

$$RevD := Pow(REV)$$

where $Pow(M)$ is the power set of a given set M.

The **variant** of a building block is characterized by the values of some of the attributes. We assume a finite and nonempty set of attributes ATT that are used to characterize the variants of a program family:

$$ATT := \{a_1, a_2, ..., a_m\}$$

Examples for attributes are "speed", "country", "kind", or "type-of-exchange".

For each attribute there is a finite and nonempty set of attribute values:

$$AV_1, AV_2, ..., AV_m$$

Examples for attribute values are "high", "low", "BRD", "USA", or "local".

A variant indication is a partial mapping that maps attributes into the corresponding sets of attribute values. The set of variants or variant indications VAR is therefore:

$$VAR := \{f \in ATT \rightsquigarrow AV \mid \forall a_i \in dom(f) : f(a_i) \in AV_i\}$$

where $\rightsquigarrow$ denotes the set of partial mappings, and $AV = \bigcup AV_i$.

An example for a variant indication is: {(country, BRD), (speed, high)}. A certain building block may belong to different variants and therefore the set of variant descriptions is

$$VarD := Pow(VAR)$$

A **version** is a combination of revision indication and variant indication and the set of versions is therefore:

$$VERS := REV \times VAR$$

An example of a version is: (2.12, {(country, BRD), (speed, high)}).
The set of version descriptions is:

$$VerD := Pow(VERS)$$

The building blocks of a program family reside in one or several libraries. If they reside in more than one library, references to external building blocks must also indicate the library the building block is supposed to reside in [Win 85]. In this paper we assume that the building blocks of a certain program family reside all in one library, ie we do not treat the problems that arise in a multi-library system. The library elements are identified in the library by a name and a version description. Therefore, the set of library elements LE is:

$$LE := N \times VerD$$

where N is the set of names. The names may be simple identifiers, (eg "QuickSort"), structured identifiers (eg "JFHW.QuickSort"), or may include the whole parameter and result type profile [Ref 83: 6.6]. In the rest of the paper we use only simple identifiers.

A library element $e = (n,v)$ determines a set of building block versions BBV(e), where a building block version is a triple (name,revision,variant). For $e = (n,v)$ BBV(e) is defined by:

$$BBV(e) := \{(n, r, a) \mid (r, a) \in v\}$$

A triple (n,r,a) must uniquely identify a library element in a library. This leads to the library consistency condition:

$$LCy(L) := (\forall a, b \in L : a \neq b \Rightarrow BBV(a) \cap BBV(b) = \varnothing)$$

where $L \subseteq LE$ is a library. In terms of data base technology this means that the triple (name, revision, variant) is a primary key [Cod 70a] in L. In the rest of the paper we assume that for all elements of libraries $BBV(e) \neq \varnothing$ holds.

A building block A may refer to (use) another building block B. These references define the use-relation $U \subseteq LE \times LE$. A library $L \subseteq LE$ is called closed if the following library closure condition holds:

$$LCl(L) := U \subseteq L \times L$$

The configuration of a certain program version can be done automatically. This process starts with the building block version that is the so-called main program (eg in the sense of Ada [Ref 83: 10.1]). The rest of the program is selected automatically by the external references. The set of building block versions belonging to the program to be configured is determined by the transitive hull of the external references beginning in the main program.

An external reference is a reference between separate building blocks. An example are the with-clauses in Ada [Ref 83]. Such references between building blocks exist also in programming languages in which single entities are exported and imported, as eg in CHILL and Modula-2. If entity E_A, that is contained in building block A, uses entity E_B, that is exported by building block B, then A refers to B. Thus, the uses relation between building blocks is obtained from the corresponding relation between entities by a factorization process.

The configuration process is based on external references in such a way that external references also indicate which version of the external building block is required. In this selection process the version of the referenced building block may depend on the version of the referencing one. Let A be a building block with version (r_s, a_s) (the selecting building block) and E be a building block with version (r_e, a_e), that is referenced by A. The external reference of A to E requires a certain version of E, which may depend on the actual version of A. The following list gives some possible dependencies between (r_s, a_s) and (r_e, a_e).

a) (r_e, a_e) = (r_s, a_s) E shall have the same version as A

b) (r_e, a_e) = (R, a_s) definite revision and same variant

c) (r_e, a_e) = (r_s, A) same revision and definite variant

d) (r_e, a_e) = (R, A) definite version required

e) (r_e, a_e) = $(f(r_s), a_s)$ revision depends on r_s and same variant

f) (r_e, a_e) = $(r_s, f(a_s))$ same revision and variant depends on a_s

g) (r_e, a_e) = $f((r_s, a_s))$ version is a function of (r_s, a_s)

5 Incorporation into Programming Languages

In order to integrate the configuration descriptions into programming languages, we must provide clauses to define

a) the versions a certain building block belongs to, and

b) the version that an externally referenced building block must have.

We will group this information in a new CONFIG part of a building block. This leads to the following structure:

```
[<name>]
CONFIG
    <configuration description>
<spec or block>
```

According to the points a) and b) above the <configuration description> consists of two parts:

> <configuration description> =
> > <version definition> [<definition of externals>]

The <version definition> describes the versions which the actual building block belongs to. The <definition of externals> describes other library elements that are used by the block.

From a theoretical point of view the formal configuration descriptions in sect. 4 would suffice. In order to achieve good usability more convenient and efficient descriptions must be added. If e.g. a certain building block A belongs to all but one of the revisions of REV, this can be expressed by listing explicitly all these revisions. If REV contains more than 10 - 20 elements, this enumeration will be tedious and error prone and the reader will not easily grasp the fact that A belongs to all but one of the revisions. From a practical point of view, it is therefore very useful to be able to express that a certain building block does **not** belong to certain revisions. The same holds for the descriptions of variants and versions.

5.1 Definition of the Versions of a Building Block

The <version definition> describes the versions a building block A belongs to. The following grammar defines the syntax of the <version definition>.

```
<version definition>     =
                VERS = <version description> [, <version description>]* ;
<version description> =  <revision list>: <variant indication>
<revision list>       = <list>
<list>                = <pos elems> | <neg elems>
<pos elems>           = <pos elem> [, <pos elem>]* | ALL
<pos elem>            = <value> [..<value>]
<neg elems>           = NOT <value> | NOT (<pos elems>)
<variant indication>  = <variant description> [,<variant description>]* | ALL
<variant description> = {<attr> = <set> [,<attr> = <set>]* }
<set>                 = <pos elem> | <neg elems> | {<list>} | ALL
```

Examples:
> > VERS = 1: {Speed = {High, Low}};
> > VERS = 1: {Kind = QuickSort};

The following remarks hold for constructs that contain no <neg elems>. Negation will be treated later.

With respect to the versions a building block B belongs to the <revision list> and the <variant description> are treated differently. B belongs exactly to those revisions mentioned in the <revision list>. If on the other hand a certain attribute a_j is not mentioned in a <variant description> this attribute is treated as a don't care, i.e. B belongs to all values of AV_j. This strategy is necessary for an efficient an convenient building process. During this process the version information is propagated from the building block, that is designated as the main program, to all building blocks belonging to the program to be build. If the information given in a build command mentions a certain attribute a_j that is not directly mentioned in the <version definition> of the main program but in that of any dependent building block D, the information about a_j must be propagated to D.

A <list> defines a set of values, ie the <list> "p_1, ..., p_l", where the p_i are all <pos elem>s of the form <value>, defines the set { p_1, ..., p_l }. The keyword ALL represents the set of all values that are possible at the resp. position. If ALL is a <revision list>, it represents the set REV. If ALL is a <variant indication>, it represents the set VAR, and if it is a <list> after <attr>, it represents the set $AV_{<attr>}$. The interval notation <value>..<value> can be used in case the corresponding set is totally ordered. The descriptions defined by the grammar depicted above are slightly more general than those in section 4. A <variant description> denotes a variant description in the following way. Let $v = \{attr_1 = l_1, ..., attr_q = l_q\}$ be a <variant description> and s_i the sets denoted by the <list>s l_i. For $i = 1(1)q$ $s_i \subseteq AV_{attr_i}$ must hold. Then v denotes the variant description VarSet(v):

$$VarSet(v) := \{ f \in VAR \mid dom(f) = \{ attr_1, ..., attr_q \} \wedge (\forall a_i \in dom(f): f(a_i) \in s_i) \}$$

If a <variant indication> vi contains several <variant description>s v_1, ..., v_p, the resulting variant description is :

$$VarSet(vi) := \bigcup_{j=1}^{p} VarSet(v_j)$$

A <version description> denotes a version description in an analogous way. Let vd = r : a be a <version description> and RevSet(r) be the set of revisions denoted by r and VarSet(a) be the set of variants denoted by a. Then the set of versions denoted by vd is:

$$VerSet(vd) := RevSet(r) \times VarSet(a)$$

If a <version definition> vd contains several <version description>s v_1, ..., v_p, the resulting version description is :

$$\mathrm{VerSet(vd)} := \bigcup_{j=1}^{p} \mathrm{VerSet(v_j)}$$

The incorporation of NOT into the descriptive framework above leaves us with two problems to be solved:

p1) what is the semantics of this construct, and

p2) in case we choose a semantics where inconsistencies are possible, to check a <version definition> for such inconsistencies.

There are at least three different semantics for NOT possible:

NOT-1

NOT is interpreted in a set theoretical sense as complement operator. In this case it is not guaranteed that a specific version is really excluded from the set of versions of a building block. This can be seen in the next example where a <variant indication> is given:

$$\{\,\mathrm{Country} = \{\mathrm{BRD, USA}\}, \mathrm{Speed} = \mathrm{High}\,\},$$
$$\{\,\mathrm{Country} = \mathrm{USA}, \mathrm{Speed} = \mathrm{NOT\,(High)}\,\};$$

If $AV_{Speed} = \{\,\mathrm{Low, Medium, High}\,\}$ the resulting variant description is:

$$\{\{(\mathrm{Country, BRD}), (\mathrm{Speed, High})\},$$
$$\{(\mathrm{Country, USA}), (\mathrm{Speed, High})\},$$
$$\{(\mathrm{Country, USA}), (\mathrm{Speed, Low})\},$$
$$\{(\mathrm{Country, USA}), (\mathrm{Speed, Medium})\}\}$$

because $\mathrm{NOT(High)} = \{\mathrm{Low, Medium}\}$.

This variant description contains that very variant that we intended to exclude: {(Country, USA), (Speed, High)}. We therefore call this interpretation of NOT a **weak negation**.

NOT-2

A second interpretation preserves the idea of complementary sets, which was originally the motivation for the incorporation of NOT, but avoids such inconsistencies as shown above. According to the grammar given above a <version description> has the following form: r:var$_1$, var$_2$, ... This is merely a shorthand for r: var$_1$, r: var$_2$, ... Therefore we may restrict the discussion to the simple normalized form where a <version description> is of the form

$$r : \{\mathrm{attr}_1 = v_1, ..., \mathrm{attr}_q = v_q\} \quad \text{for some } q \geq 1.$$

r is either r_s or NOT r_s for some set $r_s \subseteq REV$, and the v_i are either av_{j_s} or NOT av_{j_s} for some set $av_{j_s} \subseteq AV_{attr_j}$. We call an element negative if it begins with NOT and positive otherwise. A <version description> of this simple form, that contains positive elements only, is a positive version, and one containing at least one negative element is called a negative version. The version set VS of a simple <version description> vd is defined as follows:

$$VS(vd) := \quad \text{IF vd is positive} \Rightarrow VerSet(vd)$$
$$\square \quad \text{vd is negative} \Rightarrow Compl(vd) \quad FI$$

$$Compl(r : v) := \quad Comp(r) \times Comp(v)$$

$$Comp(r) := \quad \text{IF r is positive} \Rightarrow r$$
$$\square \quad \text{r is negative} \Rightarrow REV - r \quad FI$$

$$Comp(\{a_1 = v_1, ..., a_q = v_q\}) :=$$
$$\{f \in VAR \mid dom(f) = \{a_1, ..., a_q\} \wedge (\forall i \in \{1, ..., q\} :$$
$$\text{IF } v_i \text{ is positive THEN } f(a_i) \in v_i \text{ ELSE } f(a_i) \notin v_i \text{ FI})\}$$

(We assume that both v_i and $AV_i - v_i$ are nonempty.)
Note that Comp is overloaded on revisions and variants.

$$ExclSet(vd) := \quad \text{IF vd is positive} \Rightarrow \emptyset$$
$$\square \quad \text{vd is negative} \Rightarrow VS(Pos(vd)) \quad FI$$

Here is Pos(vd) = vd', where vd' is obtained from vd by eliminating all NOTs.

With these definitions we can define the consistency of a <version definition>. Let vd be a <version definition> and let $vd' = v_1, ..., v_s$ be its normalized form. Then vd is called consistent iff

$$(\forall i \in \{1, ..., s\} : v_i \text{ is negative} \Rightarrow \forall j \in \{1, ..., s\} : ExclSet(v_i) \cap VS(v_j) = \emptyset))$$

It is easy to see that any <version definition> containing the <variant indication> given in the paragraph NOT-1 would not be consistent.

If vd is consistent the version set determined by vd is given by $\bigcup_{i=1}^{s} VS(v_i)$.

An example for a consistent <version definition> is :

$$VERS = 1.2 : \{Country = \{BRD, USA\}, Speed = \text{High}\},$$
$$\{Country = USA, \quad Speed = \text{NOT (Medium)}\};$$

NOT-3

A third interpretation of NOT is a strong (strict) interpretation, in which a negative version is always excluded, even in such cases that are inconsistent in the sense of NOT-2. For such a strict NOT two different definitions are possible. Let vd be a $<$version definition$>$ and $vd' = v_1,...,v_s,v_{s+1},...,v_t$ be its normalized form, where $v_1,...,v_s$ are all positive and $v_{s+1},...,v_t$ are all negative. For the first definition of a strict NOT we obtain :

$$VS(vd) := \bigcup_{i=1}^{s} VerSet(v_i) - \bigcup_{i=s+1}^{t} ExclSet(v_i)$$

and for the second one

$$VS(vd) := \bigcup_{i=1}^{t} VS(v_i) - \bigcup_{i=s+1}^{t} ExclSet(v_i)$$

In the rest of the paper we will use the semantics of NOT-2 for NOT.

5.2 VERSIONS OF EXTERNAL BUILDING BLOCKS

The selection process starts at the building block that plays the role of the main program. The complete information about the required version of the program to be configured is given in the form of a single version. This information is transitively propagated along the external references in order to select the building block versions that belong to the program to be configured. The information in the variant part of the version description is usually split and distributed over the program. An example of the splitting of the variant part is given in the following Ada example.

```
        with A, B;
            -- A is selected by the attribute a1, and
            -- B is selected by the attribute a2 of the
            -- version of C
    procedure C  is
        -- the version of C is   (1.2, { (a1 = v1), (a2 = v2) })
```

In a specific situation a_1 may stand for "Device" and a_2 for "Speed".

The example above can be represented by the following program graph:

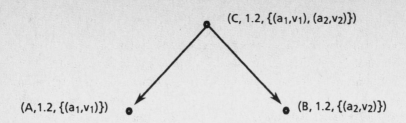

The variant part of the selecting building block need not be split into disjoint parts; in the general case an external building block may be selected by a subset of the attribute values of the selecting building block.

The splitting and selection strategies mentioned at the end of section 4 lead to the following structure of the <definition of externals>.

```
<definition of externals> = <use clause>*
<use clause>              = USE <id>
                            VERS = ( <revision selection> : <variant selection> |
                                     <version pair> [, <version pair>] *
         -- the list of <version pair>s must define a mapping VERS ↝ VERS
                                     [, ELSE ⇒ ( SAME | <version> ) ] ) ;
<version pair>            = <version> ⇒ <version>
<version>                = <revision value> : <variant>
<revision selection >    = SAME | <revision value> |
                           <revision pair> [ , <revision pair> ]*
         -- the list of <revision pair>s must define a mapping REV ↝ REV
                           [, ELSE ⇒ ( SAME |  <revision> ) ]
<revision pair>          = <revision value> ⇒ <revision value>
<variant selection>      = SAME
                           <variant> |
                           <variant pair> [, <variant pair>]*
         -- the list of <variant pair>s  must define a mapping VAR ↝ VAR
                           [, ELSE ⇒ ( SAME | <variant> ) ]
<variant pair>           = <variant> ⇒ <variant>
<variant>                = { <attr> = <value> [, <attr> = <value>]* [ , ELSE = SAME] }
```

Note that (,), [,] are characters of the metalanguage.

The <use clause> describes which version of an external building block E is required by the building block S containing the <use clause> in its <configuration description>. The <id> after USE is the name of the external building block that is being referenced by the <use clause>.

There are two ways to define the version of E that is required by S:

    (1) by a pair <revision selection> : <variant selection> where each of the elements
         may denote a specific revision resp. variant or a mapping in REV resp. VAR;
    (2) by a mapping in VERS.

The semantics of the constructs used in the <definition of externals> will be explained together with the building process in the next section.

The USE clause can also be used to select different bodies of packages. The package name used in the CONFIG part of the package specification refers automatically to the corresponding package bodies.

5.3 The building process

The building blocks in the program library are identified by triples (name, revision, variant). The building process starts with a build command of the following form:

$$\text{BUILD } <name> \text{ VERS} = <revision> : <variant>$$

The <name> is the name of the main program. <revision> and <variant> determine the exact version of the program to be built. After the exact version of the main program has been selected from the library the <use clause>s in the main program are used to select further building block versions of this program. This process works in a transitive manner until all <use clause>s in the program have been satisfied.

The basic step in the building process is that of the selection of the building block version of a building block E referred to by a <use clause> in building block S. For the following discussion we assume that the actual version of S is (r_a, v_a). This version is transformed in a version (r_s, v_s) by means of the <use clause>, and (r_s, v_s) is then used to select the actual version of E.

We describe the selection process for revisions first. Depending on the different forms of <revision selection> r_s is defined as follows:

(a) $<$revision selection$> =$ SAME: $r_s := r_a$

(b) $<$revision selection$> = r_u$: $r_s := r_u$

(c) $<$revision selection$>$ is a (partial) mapping $f \in$ REV $\leadsto$ REV :

$$\text{IF } r_a \in \text{dom}(f) \Rightarrow r_s := f(r_a)$$
$$\square\ r_a \notin \text{dom}(f) \Rightarrow undefined \text{ FI}$$

A library element with name E may belong to a set of revisions R_E. The building process selects that library element with name E for which $r_s \in R_E$ holds. If there is no such library element an error is reported.

In the case of REV being totally ordered we assume a special $<$revision value$>$ LAST. LAST denotes always the last value of any subset of REV under discussion. In a $<$use clause$>$ USE P VERS = LAST: {Country = Norway} ; it indicates that for P the latest (newest, most recent) revision of the variant for Norway is to be selected.

For variants the selection step is a little bit more complicated because a variant is a whole tuple of values. Depending on the different forms of $<$variant selection$>$ v_s is defined as follows:

(a) $<$variant selection$>$ = SAME: $v_s := v_a$

(b) $<$variant selection$>$ = $\{a_1 = x_1, a_2 = x_2, ..., a_q = x_q\} =: v_u$:

   if v_u does not contain SAME then $v_s := v_u$.

   if v_u contains SAME as attribute value the values for these attributes are taken from v_a. If v_a does not contain values for those attributes an error is reported. If no error is reported $v_s := v_u'$, where v_u' is obtained from v_u by replacing SAME.

   If ELSE is used in v_u it stands for all attributes mentioned in v_a but not mentioned in v_u.

(c) $<$variant selection$>$ is a (partial) mapping $f \in$ VAR $\leadsto$ VAR :

$$\text{IF } v_a \in \text{dom}(f) \Rightarrow v_s := f(v_a)$$
$$\square\ v_a \notin \text{dom}(f) \Rightarrow undefined \text{ FI}$$

Let $A_s = \text{dom}(v_s)$. The library elements with name E belong to certain variants v_{ei}. Let $Av_{ei} = \text{dom}(v_{ei})$. If there is one of these variants for which $|A_s \cap Av_{ei}|$ is maximal and v_{ei} is unique in this respect, and if the common attributes have the same values in v_s and v_{ei} , then the library element, to which v_{ei} belongs, is selected with the variant $v_e = v_s \cup v_{ei}$; otherwise an error is reported.

5.3 EXAMPLES

The first example shows a main program MainProgram that uses different variants of a subprogram Sort.

```
        MainProgram
CONFIG VERS =  1 : { Speed  = { High, Low }};
        USE Sort  VERS = SAME: {Speed = High} ⇒ {Kind = QuickSort},
                               {Speed = Low} ⇒ {Kind = BubbleSort};
PROC MainProgram IS
        ...
        Sort(A, B);
        ...
END  MainProgram;
```

```
        Sort
CONFIG VERS  = 1 : {Kind = QuickSort};
PROC  Sort(...) IS
        -- QuickSort algorithm
END Sort ;
```

```
        Sort
CONFIG VERS  = 1 : {Kind = BubbleSort};
PROC  Sort(...) IS
        -- BubbleSort algorithm
END  Sort;
```

We can also use the name of a building block as one of the attributes in the variant part of a version. This would be a predefined attribute whereas attributes like "Speed" or "Country" may be freely chosen by the user. The example depicted above then reads like this :

```
        MainProgram
CONFIG  VERS =  1 : { Speed  = { High, Low }};
        USE Sort  VERS = SAME : { Speed = High } ⇒ { Name = QuickSort },
                               { Speed = Low } ⇒ { Name = BubbleSort};
PROC  MainProgram IS
        ...
        Sort(A, B);
        ...
END  MainProgram;
```

```
     QuickSort                          BubbleSort
CONFIG VERS = 1 : {Speed = High}   CONFIG VERS = 1 : {Speed = Low}
PROC QuickSort(...) IS             PROC BubbleSort(...) IS
    -- QuickSort algorithm             -- BubbleSort algorithm
END QuickSort ;                    END BubbleSort;
```

In the next example we see that it is very easy to distinguish between a baseline and a maintenance variant.

```
         CONFIG VERS = 1 : ALL;
                 USE P VERS = SAME : SAME;
   PROC Main  ....

         CONFIG VERS = 1 : {Kind = BaseLine};
   PROC P ....

         CONFIG VERS = 1 : {Kind = Maintenance};
   PROC P ....
```

With the command

```
         BUILD Main VERS = 1 : {Kind = Maintenance}
```

we can build that version of Main that contains the maintenance variants of all building blocks for which such a variant exists.

The version information in a program can be used by other components of the programming environment, too. In order to achieve this some attributes must be predefined as already mentioned in the second example above for the attribute "Name". Another predefined attribute could be "Debug" which could be used to convey information to the compiler. It would then be possible to build a program variant for debugging purposes:

```
         BUILD Main VERS = 1 : {Kind = BaseLine, Debug = Yes};
```

6 Comparison with other Work

Program configuration has up to now been carried out by means outside the programming language. The means for program configuration are typically based on facilities provided by operating systems: files and commands for compilation and linking.

The use of files instead of building blocks has the drawback that there is usually no guaranteed correspondence between a file name and the name of the building block contained in that file [Win 85]. Furthermore the operating system based facilities are usually used for languages that do not contain constructs for programming-in-the-large. If those facilities are applied to languages like Ada or CHILL, that contain constructs for programming-in-the-large, this may lead to structural clashes.

The Make facility [Fel 79] is based on the Unix® operating system. A Makefile is a kind of command file and contains two different kinds of elements: (1) elements that describe dependencies between building blocks, and (2) commands that must be executed in order to make (build) the program system. Make is used for C and similar languages, that do not provide constructs for programming-in-the-large. The dependency descriptions allow the description of some aspects of programming-in-the-large, but there remains the problem of the consistency between the source text of the building blocks and the text of the Makefile, e.g. with respect to external references in the source text of the building blocks [Wal 84]. The question of different versions of a program is addressed in Build [EP 84], that is build on top of Make. Different versions of a program are realized in Build by different file directories. There is no facility to characterize the versions by attributes or version numbers. SCCS [Roc 75] and RCS [Tic 85] concentrate on the aspect of storing similar versions of texts efficiently using different kinds of deltas. RCS furthermore uses a state attribute to indicate different variants of a building block.

DSEE (Domain Software Engineering Environment) of Apollo [Apo 85] is one of the most sophisticated configuration tools based on Unix. It distinguishes between a system model and a configuration thread. The system model describes the structure of the program in the large as a block structure in the classical sense, and provides for this a quite elaborated syntax. The configuration thread describes the versions of the building blocks of a corresponding system model. The versions are characterized by version numbers and by version names that are similar to the elements of an enumeration type. These version indications do not provide attributes as they are used in this paper.

The GANDALF system [Hab 85; Not 85] also contains some facilities for version control. There successive versions and parallel versions are distinguished where the former correspond to our revisions and the latter to the variants. The parallel versions are characterized by simple values instead of the tuples used herein. The term "version" is also used with a somewhat different meaning: to distinguish between source, object, documentation etc. belonging to one program unit. Similar as in DSEE a syntax for programming-in-the-large has been developed which is based on boxes and modules [HP 80, 80a] and uses some sort of Module Interconnection Language similar to MIL76 [DK 76].

In the Cedar programming environment [HSZ 85] a system modeller has been built that allows for the description of program configurations [LS 83a]. A system model is a hierarchy of lists of system components, or to be more exact of lists of references to system components. The references refer to the files containing the source text of the building blocks. The file versions are identified by a pair consisting of a name and a time stamp. The models may be parameterized by interfaces as they are defined in Mesa [MMS 79]. There are no further facilities for the description of revisions or variants.

In the Adèle programming environment [Est 85, 86] building blocks are identified by a quadruple (family name, family id, version id, revision number), where the family name corresponds to the usual name, the family id selects a variant in the set of alternatives of the family, the version id identifies a version, and the revision number determines a revision of the version. Version and revision are very similar in this approach: a new version is established after a "major" modification, especially a modification of an interface, and a "small" modification yields a new revision.

The approaches taken in different systems use two different strategies for the organization of the version information: (1) a centralized approach e.g. in Make and DSEE, and (2) a decentralized approach as in Adèle and in our proposal. The main advantage of the decentralized approach is that the representation of the version information is adapted to the program structure. The main advantage of the centralized approach is that the coarse structure of the program can be recognized more easily when inspecting the (centralized) configuration description. But this can also be achieved by a decentralized organization. It is easy to provide a (zooming) function in the programming environment that only displays the CONFIG part of the building blocks.

The main disadvantages of the centralized approach are:
(1) it separates information that belongs together;
(2) it implies the duplication of some information. In the centralized approach the central configuration description must refer to the source modules of the program building blocks. Let B be a program building block that exists in several versions v_1, v_2,...,v_n. For reasons of identification the source modules representing the different versions must have different names. If the names are chosen arbitrarily and do not resemble B it is difficult to recognize that they all are versions of B. Thus the names should indicate in some form the identifier B. A similar argument holds for the versions: it would be very useful if the name also contained some hint to the version. The consequence of this is that the name of the source modules should contain some of the version information, i.e. it is quite inevitable that at least part of the version information is repeated in some decentralized representation.

7 Conclusions

The approach in this paper is source oriented. We want to describe different configurations of modular programs using constructs that are integrated into the programming language. We assume that the host language already provides constructs for programming-in-the-large like Ada or CHILL. This distinguishes our approach from most other approaches, that are usually oriented towards languages like C or Pascal. We add to a language with constructs for programming-in-the-large constructs to express versions as pairs of revisions and variants. For the description of variants we provide a very general concept based on tuples of attributes. The information for program configuration is given where it is used and needed: in the building blocks and the references between building blocks. The constructs described in this paper can be characterized as follows

- the language used to express the version information is a "natural" extension of the programming language;
- a version is a pair (revision,variant);
- the "knowledge" about the program configurations is represented explicitly by facts and rules;
- the representation of this knowledge is adapted to the structure of the program;
- the construction of program versions can be done automatically.

For practical applications it could be useful to define the sets REV, ATT, and AV_i in a central package VERSION.INFO in order to have some control over them. The definition of those sets could be done using appropriate data types like range types and enumeration types. A further enhancement would be the generalization of the information given in the Build command in order to express the fact that certain variants apply to certain building blocks only.

Acknowledgments

The author would like to thank R.Conradi, T. Mehner, and William G.Wood for their constructive comments that led to the improvement of this paper.

8 Literature

Apo 85   Apollo Computer Inc.: DOMAIN Software Engineering Environment (DSEE) Reference Manual. Order No. 003016, Rev. 03, July 85.

Bac 78a   Backus, John: The History of Fortran I, II, and III. SIGPLAN Notices 13,8(1978) 165..180.

BL 76   Belady, L.A.; Lehmann, M.M.: A model of large program development. IBM Syst. Journal 15,3 (1976) 225..252.

CCI 85   CCITT: CCITT High Level Language (CHILL), Recommendation Z.200, Geneva 1985.

Cod 70a   Codd, E.F.: A Relational Model of Data for Large Shared Data Banks. CACM 13,6(1970) 377..387.

DK 76   DeRemer, F.L.; Kron, H.H.: Programming-in-the-large versus Programming-in-the-small. = [NS 76: 80..89].

EP 84   Erickson, V.B.; Pellegrin, J.F. : Build - A Software Construction Tool. AT & T Bell Laboratories Technical Journal 63, 6(1984) 1049..1059.

Est 85   Estublier, J.: A Configuration Manager: The Adèle Database of Programs. Workshop on Software Engineering Environments for Programming-in-the-Large. Cape Cod, June 85, pp. 140..147.

Est 86   Estublier, Jacky: ADELE - A Data Base of Programs. Presentation Manual. Laboratoire Genie Informatique, 38402 St.Martin d'Heres, Juin 1986.

Fel 79   Feldman, Stuart I. : Make - A Program for Maintaining Computer Programs. Software - Practice and Experience 9 (1979) 255..265.

GHW 85   Guttag, John V.; Horning, James J.; Wing, Jeanette M. : The Larch Family of Specification Languages. IEEE Software 2,5 (1985) 24..36.

Hab 85   Habermann, A. N.: Automatic Deletion of Obsolete Information. The Journal of Systems and Software 5,2(1985) 145..154.

HKL 84   Luckham, David C.; Henke, Friedrich W. von ; Krieg-Brueckner, Bernd; Owe, Olaf: ANNA - A Language for Annotating Ada Programs. Stanford Univ. Comp. Syst. Lab. Tech. Rep 84-261.

HP 80   Habermann, A. Nico; Perry, Dewayne E.: System Composition and Version Control for Ada. Carnegie-Mellon Univ., Dept. of Computer Science, May 1980.

HP 80a   Habermann, A. Nico; Perry, Dewayne E.: Well-Formed System Compositions. Dept. of Computer Science, Carnegie-Mellon Univ., CMU-CS-80-117, Pittsburgh, March 1980.

HSZ 85   Swinehart, Daniel C.; Zellweger, Polle T.; Hagmann, Robert B.: The Structure of Cedar. SIGPLAN Notices 20,7(1985) 230..244.

Loc 83   Lockemann, Peter C. : Analysis of Version and Configuration Control in a Software Engineering Environment. = Davis, C.G.; Jajodia, S.; Ng, P.A.; Yeh, R.T. (eds) : Entity-Relationship Approach to Software-Engineering, North Holland, Amsterdam 1983.

LS 83 a   Lampson, Butler W.; Schmidt, Eric E.: Organizing Software in a Distributed Environment. SIGPLAN Notices 18,6(1983) 1..13.

MMS 79   Mitchell, James G.; Maybury, William; Sweet, Richard: Mesa Language Manual. Xerox, Palo Alto Research Center, Palo Alto 1979. Version 5.0, CSL-79-3.

MTW 84   Mehner, T.; Tobiasch, R.; Winkler , J.F.H. : A Proposal for an Integrated Programming Environment for CHILL. Third CHILL Conference, Cambridge, September 23-28, 1984, pp. 65..71.

Not 85   Notkin, David: The GANDALF Project. The Journal of Systems and Software 5,2(1985) 91..105.

NS 76   Schneider, H.-J.; Nagl, M. (eds.): Programmiersprachen - 4.Fachtagung der GI, Springer Berlin usw. 1976.

PS 59   Perlis, A.J.; Samelson, K. (eds) : Report on the Algorithmic Language ALGOL. Num. Math. 1 (1959) 41..60.

Ref 83   Reference Manual for the Ada Programming Language ANSI/MIL-STD 1815A. United States Dept. of Defense, Washington, January 1983.

Roc 75   Rochkind, Mark J.: The source code control system. IEEE Trans. on Softw. Eng. 1,4(1975) 364..370.

Sie 81   Siemens AG: EWSD Digital Switching System. telcom report Vol. 4(1981) Special Issue.

SW 80   Winkler, J.F.H.; Stoffel, C. : Methode zur Erzeugung angepaßter und übertragbarer Betriebssysteme.
= Schneider, H.J. (Hrsg.): Portable Software, B.G. Teubner Stuttgart, 1980, pp. 34..47.

Tic 85   Tichy, Walter F.: RCS - A System for Version Control. Software - Pract. & Exp. 15,7(1985) 637..654.

Wal 84   Walden, Kim: Automatic Generation of Make Dependencies. Software - Pract. & Exp. 14,6 (1984) 575..585.

Wi 69a   Wijngaarden, A. van: Report on the Algorithmic Language ALGOL 68. Num. Mathematik 14(1969) 79..218.

Win 82   Winkler, J.F.H.: Ada: die neuen Konzepte. Elektron. Rechenanlagen 24,4(1982) 175..186.

Win 85   Winkler, J.F.H.: Language Constructs and Library Support for Families of Large Ada Programs. Workshop on Software Engineering Environments for Programming-in-the-Large. Cape Cod, June 85, 17..28.

Win 86   Winkler, J.F.H.: Die Programmiersprache CHILL. Automatisierungstechnische Praxis 28,5(1986)252..258, 28,6(1986)290..294.

Wir 71   Wirth, Niklaus: The Programming Language PASCAL. acta informatica 1(1971) 35..63.

Wir 80   Wirth, Niklaus: MODULA-2. Eidgenössische Technische Hochschule Zürich, Institut für Informatik Bericht 36, March 1980.

CONFIGURATION/VERSION CONTROL

Chair   : Per Holager (ELAB-SINTEF, NOR)
Assistant chair : Arne Venstad/Ole Solberg (RUNIT, NOR)

Discussion

Arthur Evans (Tartan Labs, USA):

Mr. Winkler described how to keep the configuration information distributed throughout the source programs, which is an interesting approach. We have been using at Tartan Labs an approach in which we maintain a central database to control our building process. We found that once we got everything sorted out, it was moderately easy to keep things straight. Comments?

Jurgen Winkler (Siemens, FRG):

My approach parallels the one taken in programming languages that provide constructs for PITL, like ADA, CHILL, MESA and MODULA-2. In ADA, the with- and use-clauses are distributed in the program. With this strategy the information is where it belongs. If I inspect a program module, I also want to see its relationships to other modules. If the information is presented in this "object-oriented" manner at the user interface, it does not imply any specific internal structure. Indeed the question of internal structure is not addressed at all.

Jacky Estublier (L.G.I. C.N.R.S., FRA):

The reason why we chose a similar distribution of the configuration information, is that we got fast file access to the object because of good locality of information. The same locality also reduces network traffic and minimizes updating conflicts in a distributed environment.

Andy Rudmik (GTE Comm. Syst., USA):

A question for Ellen Borison on the model for software manufacture. I can see the benefit of coming up with models like this, and I think it is applicable to perhaps a significant part of the life cycle. When I look at the kind of software life cycles in our software development effort, I would characterize the functions as having a high degree of concurrency (needing mutual synchronization), and a lot of non-determinism (not repeatable because of non-recorded user input). I can certainly see that this model might apply to compilation and linking which have fairly straight-forward mapping functions. But a large percentage of the software development activities such as requirements and design involves a high degree of non-deterministic interaction between the various functions. Therefore, I'm suggesting that the model might be extended to incorporate some of these issues.

Ellen Borison (Carnegie Mellon Univ., USA):

The model is intended to apply to software manufacture only, not to the entire software life cycle. In particular, I am not interested in how primitive components of a system come into being or why they might need to be changed. I agree with you that task coordination and other aspects of software development that are not mechanized are considerably more complex than software manufacture. Perhaps once we get a better understanding of the latter, it might be fruitful to try to extend the model to treat the former.

Andy Rudmik (GTE Comm. Syst., USA):

What I'm sying is that the functions are not as simple as you've indicated. There is a lot of human interaction to be incorporated if you want to capture the software engineering process. This human interaction takes place in a non-deterministic and ad hoc fashion while we are performing these mapping functions. My observation is that software manufacturing is a very, very complex process. I do see the value of your work and think it does apply. I'm just thinking it needs to be extended over time.

Ian Thomas (BULL, FRA):

Can I just make a comment on that interchange? There is a confusion between derivation and reproducibility. Even if you have good information on the derivation process, that may not guarantee reproducibility. It may be that your compiler is putting timestamps into your object code to indicate date and time of production, and this may lead to non-reproducibility.

Ellen Borison (Carnegie Mellon Univ., USA):

You are correct. A record of the derivation process does not guarantee reproducibility. I have tried to capture this in the model.

Mary Shaw (Carnegie Mellon Univ., USA):

One of the ways that Borison's model can be extended to accommodate precisely this, is by allowing some of the primitives to be non-deterministic or non-reproducible. Although you can keep a trace of an interactive dialogue, it may be better to admit the possibility of primitives that did exist in the form of interactive dialogues, but are no longer reproducible. Then I think you capture exactly the distinction requested by Rudmik in which the human interaction of the derivation is absent or extremly difficult to reproduce.

Andrew Symonds (IBM, USA):

I don't think software manufacture is synonymous to software engineering. It's a piece of the process. Further, is the issue of quality control addressed by your model so that each derivation step can be controlled by some criteria about its possible successful completion? How do you recognize that, and what action can you then take?

Ellen Borison (Carnegie Mellon Univ., USA):

I haven't dealt with quality control issues in the model and haven't considered imposing any criteria to measure the success of a manufacturing step.

Terrence Miller (Hewlett Packard, USA):

A question on the distribution of configuration information: I'm envisioning an extension of the Sort program where a new programmer decides on a new implementation and wishes to bind the new version into the specified MainProgram. But because of access control or some other problem, he has no authorization to change the text of the embedding MainProgram. This example exposes a weakness in the incorporation of your configuration information in source programs.

Jurgen Winkler (Siemens, FRG):

If a third version of Sort (Sort-3) is included in the program library, and MainProgram is supposed to use the new one, the knowledge of this new version must also be communicated to MainProgram. How else could MainProgram know about Sort-3?

Reidar Conradi (Norw. Inst. of Tech., NOR):

To Estublier and Winkler: I haven't yet heard arguments for why the distribution of configuration information is better than, for instance, a separate configuration language, like C/MESA. Binding all this detailed information within the program introduces tremendous maintenance problems, like if you have selective exports of symbols - every time you want another module to use it, you have to go into the defining module and change it.

To Borison: If something goes wrong during the derivation process - cpu resources run out, file quotas get exceeded, or even trivial compilation errors due to library changes (name conflicts!) - how much regeneration work can be done without really destroying something? Also, how to use the derivation graph and associated relations for the purpose of program development? E.g., the programmer would like to know the cost estimates of regeneration because if a change really inflicts most of the universe, it probably requires a managerial approval anyhow.

Jurgen Winkler (Siemens, FRG):

With respect to maintenance, the effort to modify the configuration information does not depend on how this information is represented, centralized or decentralized. In a programming environment I would expect some assistance for doing such modifications, e.g., searches in the library should be done by the system and not manually.

Ellen Borison (Carnegie Mellon Univ., USA):

Reidar Conradi stressed detection of errors, but the kind of errors you mentioned can easily be detected. If I run out of file space, if I can't read a file, if there is an error in compilation, I can detect those. There is no reason why these can't be detected in the model. I thought Andrew Symonds' earlier question addressed tricky things like a bad bit in memory or some garbled object file.

Reidar Conradi (Norw. Inst. of Tech., NOR):

My point is only the pragmatics during regeneration. It's very important.

Ellen Borison (Carnegie Mellon Univ., USA):

Reidar Conradi also said that given cost estimates of the derivation process, one can decide whether or not one should proceed with the manufacturing process during, for example, prime time or not. My point is that even if one does proceed, given that one is able to distinguish between new and old objects, one can always restore the previous ones. At least one doesn't destroy any state.

Robert Schwanke (Siemens, USA):

Borison's model can be applied to quality assurance problems in the following way: Augment translation tools to produce quality measures, such as error severity levels. Then write difference predicates that compare quality measures to decide whether a step must be redone.

Where to record variant selection information must be decided both on the physical and logical levels. For performance, one should store the information on the same disk block. For logical integrity, one should store it with related information. However, variant selection relates both to PITS and to PITL, so we need tools that can present the same piece of information (not replicated!) in both programming contexts.

One example of PITS-related variant information: Suppose the performance specification of a particular module variant assumes it will use only certain variants of other modules. Then the particular module variant should specify which other module variants it can use.

Jurgen Winkler (Siemens, FRG):

As I already mentioned, the information about relations between program building blocks is represented in a decentralized manner in those languages that provide facilities for PITL. The idea behind the proposed notation is to expand these facilities by augmenting and refining the relations between program building blocks. The notation would not be compatible with those languages if the refinements were represented in a centralized manner.

John Nestor   (Carnegie Mellon Univ., USA):

First on the previous discussion about reproducibility - Absolute reproducibility need not be our goal. Someone mentioned that timestamp may lead to irreproducibility. The essence about Borison's model is that the predicates extract out the key properties. For example, a predicate could ignore the timestamps.

A question for Mr. Winkler: I got the implication that this was a step forward in terms of programming language features. To me it looks as though it's just another mechanism for conditional compilation which has been around for a long time. Could you respond to that?

Jurgen Winkler   (Siemens, FRG):

Neither ADA, nor CHILL, nor MESA, nor MODULA-2, have any facilities for conditional compilation. Apart from that most modern programming languages lacking conditional compilation, it is not clear to me that this mechanism can achieve the same as the configuration descriptions proposed in my paper.

John Nestor   (Carnegie Mellon Univ., USA):

Why not use the C pre-processor on your ADA programs? (!)

William Waite   (Univ. Colorado, USA):

About quality control - We have had a system running for the last couple of years, which is very similar to that described by Ellen Borison this morning. It uses some conditional information out of each tool and it has the concept of a sentinel; an arbitrary condition defined by the user. If anything changes that would affect the sentinel, it will be reevaluated. Any modification causing the sentinel to report an error is not allowed. I think that handles your question, Mr. Symonds.

Jacky Estublier   (L.G.I. C.N.R.S., FRA):

A comment on configuration information distributed in the source code. There are two independent aspects: to have distribution or not; and, to have information in the source code or not. What we do in the Adele environment is to distribute the information in other files than source files and put a copy of it into the source code as a comment. This is a "reliable" comment with the name, date, user and all relevant attributes. Thus the programmer can see in his source the file where the last attributes of the object are. Thus the information used by the database is in a separate file, and the comments in the source file are automatically derived from this.

David Robinson   (System Designers, GBR):

My first point is an observation. Ellen Borison talked about cost of predicates, and Reidar Conradi warned about automatically recompiling the entire universe at arbitrary times. Maybe raw computing power will be one of the things that can benefit us the most? We should not constrain ourselves to various models because the limiting cost happens to be computing power. Secondly, have the discussions on centralization of the versioning and configuration information been accompanied by experimental data? My question, particularly to Mr. Winkler, is: How many of the textual changes in modules involve their functionality, and how many reflect version changes (e.g., because it is using another version of some other module)?

Jurgen Winkler (Siemens, FRG):

There are no exact figures available at the time being.

Andy Rudmik (GTE Comm. Syst., USA):

I have a comment to the entire audience, and especially those that may be organizing future environment workshops or conferences. I would like to see a few papers and some discussion on software manufacturing models and project models. Many of us, including myself, tend to have our favorite hobbyhorse, whether it's a specific tool technology, a project database, or something else. We very seldom say what we are trying to support. That's why I appreciate the paper on modelling software manufacturing.

Mary Shaw (Carnegie Mellon Univ., USA):

The models from this morning are motivated primarily by the edit/compile/link-edit world. Tomorrow morning we're going to have some papers on program transformations. Here, you keep a relatively static base and collect transformations to be repeatedly applied to this base. How will that shift of modelling affect the systems from this morning? Is a shift toward the design domain discussed in this session, and will it stress our systems beyond their design limits?

IDL: Past Experience and New Ideas

Joseph M. Newcomer
Software Engineering Institute
Carnegie-Mellon University
Pittsburgh, Pa. 15213

Abstract

This paper is based on the author's experience in constructing an implementation of the Interface Description Langugage (IDL). The result of this experience was some insights into language design, human interfaces, and system structuring, as well as methodologies for the composition of complex tools. Certain complexities of the IDL implementation are discussed in this paper, showing that quite efficient implementaions are possible. Finally, a set of interesting directions for IDL and IDL-derived systems are suggested, including programming environment and database related work.

1 Introduction

IDL, the Interface Description Language, was developed at Carnegie-Mellon University as a second generation to the compiler research support system LG [15]. IDL has been used in the specification of Diana, the intermediate language for Ada compilers [10] [6], and was used as the core technology for the compiler automation tool set developed at Tartan Laboratories.

It is outside the scope of this paper to attempt to provide an in-depth discussion of IDL, either as a language or from a tutorial viewpoint. For these, the reader is referred to the IDL formal description [12] [13], the Diana description [10] [6] and the body of work from the University of North Carolina [19] [22]. This paper presents a brief introduction to the IDL notation, which should be sufficient for the topics discussed in this paper.

This paper consists of observations about and reflections on a particular implementation of IDL and, from this, speculations about the use and structure of IDL in the future. Some of these speculations are on the use of IDL in ways not thought about, or considered only vaguely, during its initial design. Most of these are extensions of the original IDL design goals, or implementation considerations which are in some way orthogonal to the high-level IDL design.

One of the interesting properties of IDL is that the semantic specification does not constrain the implementation strategies which may be used to achieve it. With the combination of the small

This work was sponsored by the Department of Defense. The views and conclusions in this document are those of the author and should not be interpreted as representing official policies, either expressed or implied, of the Software Engineering Institute, Carnegie-Mellon University, the Department of Defense, or the U.S. Government.

design, formal model, and flexibility of implementation choices, I[1] consider it an interesting set of exercises to see how far the ideas can be carried. This paper is intended to suggest what I consider some promising directions for research based on the IDL model.

2 IDL as a tool

The IDL language is a specification language. When used in the context of a tooling effort, there is an associated IDL translator, which takes a specification written in the IDL language and converts it to a collection of specification and implementation files for a target language in which programs will be written. The simplistic model of an IDL runtime environment is shown below in Figure 1.

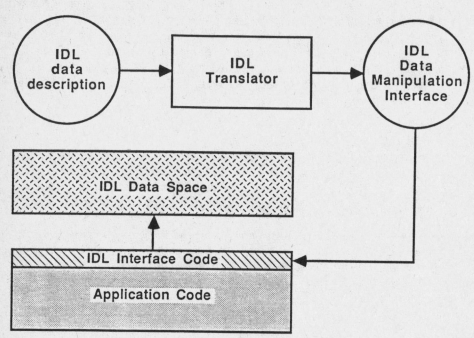

Figure 1: A simple model of IDL

The IDL data space consists of instances of data described by the IDL specification. It is created and manipulated by the user application code via an IDL interface. The task of an IDL translator and an associated IDL runtime support system is to provide the necessary interface between the user application code and the IDL data.

---

[1]In this paper, the first person singular and first person plural forms are not interchangeable. "I", "my", and similar forms refer to ideas of the author or more frequently opinions held by the author, and for which it would be unfair to distribute the blame. "We", "our", etc. refer to efforts which involved more people than the author, and for which it would be unfair to have the author apparently claim exclusive credit.

3 Philosophical Aside

IDL was one of the central tools chosen by Tartan Laboratories for its compiler construction tool set. One effect of using IDL at Tartan was that it formed the common domain of discourse for the Tartan tooling. The language was rich enough to support the basic data structuring required for applications tools such as symbol table generators, user interface generators, table packers, attribute grammar systems, and many other applications. Each application tool had an input language which used IDL as its core language and then included, in an extension language, application-specific specifications (for example, the symbol table generator allowed specification of the types of scope and nesting, whether overloading was present, etc.). The output from many of the tools was an enhanced IDL description which was fed to the IDL translator. Often such tools had associated runtime environment packages. For example, the symbol table generator system structure was as shown below in Figure 2.

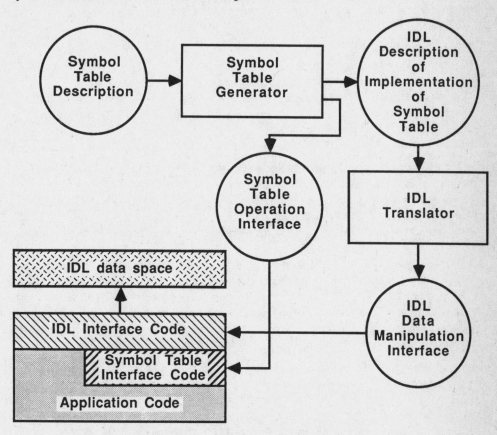

Figure 2: Symbol table generator structure

As shown, IDL was not only a component of the input specification language to the tools (such as the symbol table description), but was also the output from the tool. Extended IDL descriptions supported a symbol table generator, table packer, user interface generator, and an attribute grammar system.

A direct benefit of this was that insofar as training there was only one data definition language to learn. From the implementors' viewpoint, tools such as the IDL translator and the table packer provided a "common object format" for many application tools. Because these provided machine-independent specifications, many tooling efforts did not require any machine-dependent knowledge in the tool; at the worst, representation specifications in the IDL definitions handled the few cases where such control was required.

I have therefore developed a strong bias in favor of the use of machine-independent languages (even those as low-level as Ada, C, Modula-2, Pascal, etc.) as the *output* of machine-independent tool sets, and uniform high-level notations (such as IDL) as input to these tool sets. (I am certain my categorization of the preceding languages as "low level" may seem strange, but read on!) As a simplifying piece of notation, I shall use the phrase "conventional programming languages" to include languages comparable to Pascal, C or Modula-2.

4 IDL Type Model

The IDL type model is significantly more expressive than the type models of most programming languages. The notion of non-hierarchical classes also gives it power and generality beyond Simula-67. This section will discuss the impact this more powerful model has on the structure of programs, and will then discuss briefly how one can integrate an IDL type system into an existing programming language.

4.1 Target Language Considerations: Objects

The basic aggregate data object in IDL is the *node*, which implements a concept similar to that of *record* in most languages. A node possesses *attributes*, analogous to record fields. These attributes are typed, and are references to *objects*. An *object* may have a simple scalar type (e.g., integer), a node type, or an aggregate type (set of or sequence of objects of some type).

There are many models for implementing the concept of a node, but the most common implementation is heap-based. This choice is often dictated by a desire to avoid various pointer-into-the-stack anomalies, or to accommodate languages (such as Ada) which have strong mechanisms to avoid this type of problem. However, it is important to understand that this choice is not *required* by the IDL definition; it is an implementor's choice but may be constrained by requirements of the target language.

4.2 Specification Level: Classes

Sets of node types which conceptually share information may be combined as a *class* type. A class type may specify attributes which are common to all objects in the class. However, a class is significantly different than the Simula-67 class; a class is not an object, and cannot be created; it is a name for a set of nodes[2]. (In the expected way, a class definition may name other classes, but this ultimately names a set of nodes).

An attribute is associated with a node or class by a production of the form:

---

[2]The semantics are more complex than this; this will be discussed in more detail later in the paper.

```
node_or_class_name => attribute_name : type;
```

and a class is defined by productions of the form:

```
class_name ::= node_or_class_name | node_or_class_name | ... ;
```

where, as indicated, a class may be defined in terms of nodes or other classes. The attribute-defining productions make no syntactic distinction between assigning attributes to nodes or attributes to classes.

Taking a trivial example, and ignoring some of the subtleties of IDL, a description of the following form might be written:

```
N => truth: boolean;
N => count: integer;
N => subnodes: Seq Of N;
N => parent: N;
```

where a realization in some application language[3] might be

```
type N is record
        boolean truth;
        int count;
        array[0:?] of N subnodes;
        ref N parent;
end record;
```

A simple tree could be defined by the productions

```
tree ::= inner | leaf;
inner ::= unary | binary;

unary => operand: tree;
binary => left: tree,
            right: tree;

leaf => value: value;

value ::= integer | name;

integer => value: integer;
name => name: string;
```

In this example, the attributes are declared only at the level of the nodes, i.e. the left side of an attribute production ("=>") does not appear on the left hand side of any class production ("::="). Classes are used to specify the types of the attributes. This example also illustrates that the names for nodes and classes and the names for attributes are in separate name spaces, and there is no conflict in assigning the same attribute name to different nodes (note the use of the word "value" as an attribute name in two separate productions and as a class name).

Attributes can be associated with classes as well; for example,

```
tree => depth: integer;
```

declares all members of the class tree to have an attribute depth whose type is integer.

---

[3]Examples of application languages will attempt to convey intuitions of targets rather than reflect the precise syntax of any particular programming language, unless otherwise specified.

It is worth pointing out here that in the original IDL publications a class was seen as a purely syntactic device for abbreviation, e.g., instead of declaring attributes individually on each node type, they could be declared for a class containing those nodes. Under this previous interpretation, it would have been the case that the declaration

```
inner => depth: integer;
leaf  => depth: integer;
```

would be identical to the declaration

```
tree => depth: integer;
```

Use of IDL has demonstrated that in fact a class has semantic significance beyond the simple syntactic abbreviation mechanism, both in the IDL conceptual model and in the resulting implementation model. Existing IDL documents [12] [13] still refer to the class mechanism as an abbreviation mechanism; a proposed revision 3 design (which includes a new formal semantic definition) is intended to reformulate the class as a semantic entity. The impact of classes on the implementation model will be discussed in section 5. The implications on the target language model are that if the declaration is written

```
tree => depth: integer;
```

it is meaningful to have a program fragment of the form:

```
var T: tree;
...
   T.depth := T.depth + 1;
```

because the type tree possesses a depth attribute, whereas if the attributes had been declared as

```
inner => depth: integer;
leaf  => depth: integer;
```

then the fragment would not be valid since the type tree does not have a depth attribute, even though any particular instance of the type tree (inner or leaf) does.

4.3 Target Language Considerations: Classes

At the user's conceptual model level, the class can be used as a mechanism for effecting generic procedures, a particularly useful mechanism in languages which do not possess such a capability. A procedure which operates on a class may operate directly on any attributes defined in the class, regardless of the actual node which may be operated upon. Thus, many of the questions generated by the presence of true generic procedures in a language (such as optimizations, collapsing common code bodies, etc.) can be totally avoided.

As an example, consider the a language with generic procedures; one might wish to write a procedure to increment the depth attribute:

```
generic(T) procedure inc( N: T)
    N.depth := N.depth + 1;
end inc;
```

The same effect could be obtained in a language with overloading, but without generic procedures, by the following:

```
procedure inc(N:inner)
    N.depth := N.depth + 1;
end inc;

procedure inc(N:leaf)
    N.depth := N.depth + 1;
end inc;
```

The same effect can be can be obtained by declaring a non-overloaded, non-generic procedure of the form

```
procedure inc( N:tree)
    N.depth := N.depth + 1;
end inc;
```

Such procedures are obvious and natural in languages such as Simula-67 but not possible in conventional programming languages without extremely careful use of features such as union modes or variant records. The complexity of achieving this for complex class hierarchies, or the even more complex case of non-hierarchical classes, is frequently intimidating and often unmanageable and unmaintainable.

I refer to procedures which can accept class types as parameters but which require neither overload resolution nor generic mechanisms in order to be realized as "imitation generic" procedures. They are, in general, much less powerful than full language-supported generic mechanisms and suffer some limitations over full language-supported overload mechanisms, but are a substantial improvement over the simplistic mechanisms supported by conventional programming languages.

An interesting problem with respect to both overloading and generic procedures in languages which support them is the "documentation problem": for what types is this procedure name overloaded or for what types may this generic be instantiated? Some languages which support polymorphic procedures (such as Smalltalk, if one may loosely apply the term "procedures" to the operation invocation mechanism used in that system) provide extensive and comprehensive support for the user in the form of "browsers". Modern programming environments being constructed for Ada provide similar mechanisms.

When an IDL class is used as a parameter, the range of types which are valid parameter types to the procedure may be determined by knowing only the parameter type and the class definition. It is certainly clear that there are advantages to knowing the scope of the types for which an instantiation is valid, but this requires that the set of types can only be extended by adding new members to the IDL class definition. This severely limits the generality of such "generic" procedures, a feature which may or may not be desirable.

When IDL classes are used to make procedures polymorphic, a mechanism as complicated as generic instantiation is no longer required; the ordinary compilation process generates a single code body which is shared by all the members of the class (the "types" for which it is "instantiated"). This is quite similar to what the type mechanisms of Simula-67 or Smalltalk permit, where a procedure may operate on an object in a class but not know anything about the extensions to the class; but the non-hierarchical class model of IDL lends additional flexibility to how the procedures may specify the collection of object types on which they operate. Some of the questions of how to collapse multiple instantiations of generic procedures into a single procedure when the generated code bodies are identical also become moot; the ordinary compilation process creates but one body which is polymorphic on its input classes.

4.4 Information Hiding

In languages which support data abstraction, it is possible to specify a "visible" part of the implementation, which is exported to the clients of a package, and a "hidden" part of the implementation, which is private to the package providing the service. This simple dichotomy is not sufficient in many applications, and something akin to the view mechanism used in databases is more appropriate.

Consider the case of a multiphase compiler, consisting of phases P_1 through P_n. Information computed by a particular phase may, at the very least, be considered read-only by subsequent phases, or perhaps should be hidden entirely. If two phases, say P_1 and P_7, agree on a means of communicating information, it may well be desirable that P_7 be forbidden to modify the information and that P_2 through P_6 be forbidden even to examine it. Often this is done by a "handshake agreement" rather than a "contract agreement" between the initial coders involved, but over time and changes of personell the (undocumented) limitations are lost and unanticipated dependencies are introduced. Even if documented, the limitations cannot be enforced by the target language[4]. If P_1 and P_7 renegotiate their agreement, they may suddenly find that P_5 now modifies the information and P_3 depends upon it, making the whole system refractory to change.

In the original LG system, a capability was provided but never exploited: the ability to selectively hide information at each phase of the processing. There were many reasons this was not exploited, not the least of which was the fact that the view had to be specified on a per-field basis for each node. Furthermore, we were unable to specify read/write restrictions because of the target language model used; a field was either visible to the programmer and fully accessible (and thus modifiable), or hidden and completely inaccessible.

A new design has been proposed and is currently under consideration for a revision of the notion of an IDL "process" specification [14]. It is impossible in the space available to discuss in detail what earlier IDL documents termed an IDL "process"; for this the reader is directed to [12] [13] and [19].

Briefly, an IDL process was intended to represent some activity on an IDL structure, which may include starting by reading in an existing structure and/or concluding by writing out a structure; during the process a structure or structures may be created, modified, enhanced, or even deleted. A set of invariants specify the input requirements (if any input were to be performed), output requirements (if any output were to be performed), and static structural requirements of the structure. The new proposal includes these capabilities, as well as being able to restrict selectively such operations as assignment to fields, reading from fields, whether or not new instances of particular nodes may be created, and other operation specifications.

---

[4]And who reads or believes documentation?

A goal of this is that when properly used this mechanism enforces contractual agreements between phases on what operations may be performed on each node, class, attribute, or attribute value set. In our above example, phases P_2 through P_6 could not depend upon or modify the information agreed upon by phases P_1 and P_7, because such information would be both unknown (in principle) and inaccessible (in practice). An example of providing controlled views is shown below in Figure 3.

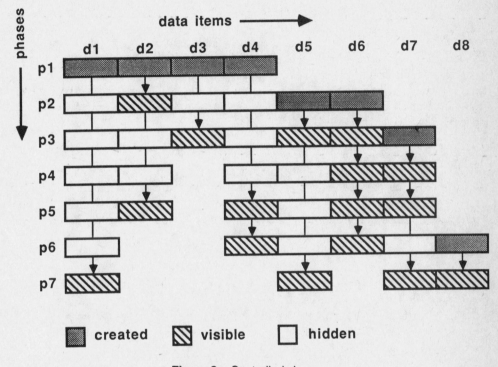

Figure 3: Controlled views

An interesting historical development is that initially IDL emphasized the data specification portion of the abstract type model; the new proposal is beginning to deal with the operation specification portion of the abstract type model.

4.5 Target Language Considerations
The typical IDL implementation involves taking the IDL description, running it through a translator program, and obtaining as output some definition files which when combined with source files from the target language allow the user to write code using IDL objects. Typically these definition files will include type declarations, define record types in particular, provide enumeration literals, and of course define various operations that can be done to the data objects.

A significant problem with the power of IDL, however, is the fact that it is much more powerful than conventional programming language type systems. The result is that the programming language type system, in effect, fights the type system used by IDL. This is compounded in some languages because the language designers still foster the illusion that programs are written by human beings, and make no provision for the case where programs are written by other programs. Mechanisms of type safety introduced for the necessary and desirable goal of preventing "stupid" errors when human programmers are involved are not only excess baggage but require immense overhead to circumvent when programs are constructing code. Global disabling mechanisms are not sufficient, since it is often the case (such as with IDL) that human-written code and machine-written code are intertwined; one must be checked carefully while the other must not be. Even low-level languages such as C encounter significant problems [17].

Part of this is caused by a desire to maintain a language interface consistent with the target language. For Ada or Modula one wishes to use dot-qualified field selectors; for C, dereferencing arrows ("->"); etc. Operations such as assignment should remain as ":=" or "=". Furthermore, a goal which often introduces significant complication to the target language model is a desire to exploit the compile-time type checking mechanism of the target language to provide type checking for IDL data types.

Because of the power of the IDL type model, it is extremely difficult to meet all of the above requirements. In Ada, for example, the best we could come up with was an assignment procedure (ideally to be compiled in-line) so that the left and right sides could be properly type-checked at compile time. The use of **inout** and **out** parameters was impossible to properly type-check, because of the extremely strong type model of Ada. Various restrictions had to be placed on what could be written by the user in order to preserve type checking for IDL types at compile time.

As an example, since Ada forbids procedures from returning reference (access) types as parameters and forbids procedures on the left-hand side of assignments, and in addition does not allow the selector operator (dot) to be user defined, a number of rather cumbersome circumlocutions are required. Without supplying excruciating detail, consider a simple program fragment in an idealized language:

```
var N1: node1;
var N2: node2;
...
    N1.a.b := N2.x.y;
```

IDL does not require that N1 or N2 be implemented as record types, or be heap-allocated, or that the attributes be necessarily stored as bit patterns in memory. A read-only attribute may well be computed dynamically (writing such dynamic attributes is an amazingly complicated topic, and outside the scope of this discussion). However, the only way one can support data abstraction in Ada is to use a procedural interface, since dot-selection reflects implementation decisions which should not be visible to the user. Thus, at the very least the code would have to be written as

```
    b(a(N1)) := y(x(N2));
```

as our expression. But since procedures cannot appear as left-hand-side values the code must be written as

```
    store(b(a(N1)), y(x(N2)));
```

which is fairly unnatural (the use of overloading to have functions that evaluate to left-hand-side and right-hand-side values is also necessary, but a subtlety too deep to discuss here). In addition, if there were a procedure which took an **in** parameter:

```
proc print_value(in i: integer)
```
then it could be written as
```
var T: tree;
...
print_value(depth(T));
```
but if the procedure took an **inout** or **out** parameter
```
proc increment(inout i: integer)
    i := i + 1;
end increment;
```
then an attribute access which involved a procedural interface could not be used:
```
var T: tree;
...
increment(depth(T));   -- illegal!
```
although it could be written as
```
var T: tree;
var i: integer;


...
i := depth(T);
increment(i);
store(depth(T),i);
```

In general, this set of limitations is not acceptable. Users do not wish to distort their thinking to accommodate incidental restrictions; remembering completely arbitrary limitations and circumlocutions is painful at best.

A major deficiency of most of conventional programming languages, including Ada, is that the abstract interface and the implementation are somewhat hopelessly intermixed. A typical example is the issue of how to represent an array of structured data: is it optimum to represent it as an array of records or as a record of arrays? In many cases the optimum representation for conceptualization is as an array of records, but the optimum representation for implementation (whether access speed or packing density) is as a record of arrays. Conceptually, the user wishes to write an access to some field in the ith array element as
```
Array[i].fieldname
```

but since the representation choice becomes explicit in the language it may be necessary (in order to achieve the desired space/time performance) to write:
```
Array.fieldname[i].
```

If it is discovered well after the implementation has begun that the second representational form is required, or during a port that because of the target architecture that the second representational form is significantly faster on the new architecture, potentially massive amounts of code must be changed. There is no easy way to indicate that the mapping of "Array[i].fieldname" is an abstract mapping because abstraction exists only at the procedural level, not at the subscript or selector level. The only solution is to use a procedural interface to effect the mapping, which has many other undesirable effects (see section 8.4). Since IDL allows high-level specification of the abstract interface but includes low-level representation control, a simple one-line change in an IDL specification (for example, changing an array-of-records representation to one of record-of-arrays) would necessitate massive changes in the target code. This violates a principle of parsimony: small changes should have small effects.

An additional constraint which introduces significant complexity to the IDL target language interface is a belief that compile-time type checking is a good idea. If you subscribe to this belief (as I do), then it is desirable to have the target language compiler insure that illegal programs are diagnosed (insofar as possible) at compile time. In the presence of non-hierarchical classes the design of an interface to adequately support the compile-time type checking mechanism, the attribute access mechanism, and the parameter passing mechanism, and still maintain a style consistent with the target language interface for simple nodes and attribute values produces significant tensions. Several proprietary designs for Ada interfaces to IDL have been done; all required (in my opinion) significant design compromises to achieve the necessary goals. In general the user interface has been compromised to meet the functional goals, particularly compile-time type checking. Alas, since these are all proprietary, no citations to these clever designs can currently be made.

One solution which has been proposed is to use a pre-processor: in effect, to write in a language which is a superset of the target language in which the IDL type model is fully supported. The source language is then compiled into the target language, with all necessary idioms, restrictions, and circumlocutions handled by the preprocessor. Ordinary user code which uses none of the extended type model may be freely interspersed with the extended type model code. For most languages, the complexity of such a preprocessor approximates the complexity of a semantic analyzer for the language. With languages such as C, Pascal and Modula-2 this is not particularly complex; for Ada, an interesting and important target, the complexity is intimidating. Consider the conceptually trivial problem of deciding that the parameter to a procedure is **inout** and using a rewrite rule to create a temporary variable into which to store an attribute; this requires that the overload and generic instantiation methods used by the Ada compiler be invoked to determine exactly which procedure is involved so that its parameters may be examined and the appropriate decision made, which requires, in essence, a complete Ada semantic analyzer.

One of the more promising approaches is to simply design a language whose native type model is consistent with IDL, but which is otherwise in the Pascal/Modula-2 class of language complexity.[5] Such a language could then be compiled into a variety of target languages, such as C, Pascal, Modula-2, and Ada, in the latter case using only a small subset of the total power and complexity of the language. This course is not without its pitfalls (as is any language design project); in addition to the usual language design issues, the goal of generating high-level language output introduces the additional problems of compiler incompatibilities and idiosyncracies, machine-dependent targeting problems, and of course the incompatibilities between the IDL type model and the limitations of the target language type model. The advantage of this is that the output language might contain idioms, phrases, and techniques which a user would consider horrible or which, if written by a user would result in unmaintainable code, but which are legitimate for an automated tool to write; in the same way a compiler is free to

---

[5]I realize this reflects a bias toward statically-type-checked procedural languages. This paper assumes that such languages are useful and desirable.

produce outrageously obtuse machine code, a translator from the IDL-oriented language to, say, C, is free to write outrageously obtuse C code.

5 IDL/Target Language Packing Considerations

The designers of IDL had an implementation model in mind during the design process. An important consideration was the use of classes. If a procedure is to operate on a class, and access attributes of the class, it is clearly desirable that this be no more expensive than accessing attributes of a simple node. If it were necessary to determine which member of the class was being accessed in order to determine the offset into the node where an attribute could be found the time performance would be unacceptable.

The intent was that all attributes in a class would be packed in the individual nodes in the class in such a way that they were all at the same offset within the class. Thus an IDL definition fragment of the form

```
A ::= B | C;
A => aval: integer;
B => bval: integer;
C => cval: integer;
```

where *integer* is represented by a 32-bit word might result in a packing of the form:

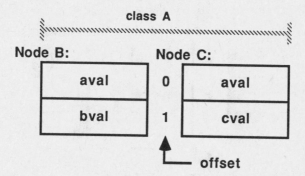

(It is worth observing that this is one of the many issues that emphasizes the fact that classes are more than simple syntactic abbreviations. Even in the early IDL implementations if aval had been declared separately in productions for B and C there was no constraint that it be of the same type in each or that it be packed to the same location).

The complications of the packing requirement in the presence of overlapping or non-hierarchical classes should now be obvious; consider adding the fragment

```
E ::= C | D;
E => eval: integer;
```

to the above example. Now *one* of the possible packings of information is

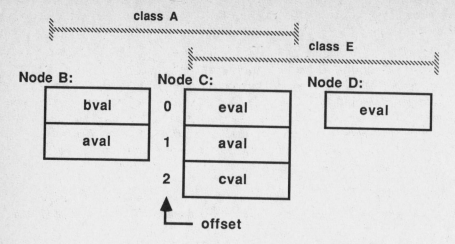

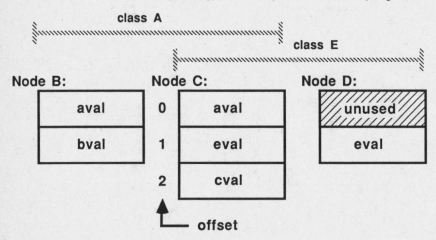

while another (using a different packing strategy, such as "pack classes first") might be:

In this latter example, in order to satisfy the constraints of identical offset, some of the space in the D node is unused. It turns out that this space is often used by attributes unique to the node (or some class containing the node) for which such a packing is valid; so in practice the packing density actually can be very high.

While in general this problem is NP-hard, in practice simple heuristics and costing functions give very good approximations to an optimal packing.

6 Separately Compiled IDL Specifications

In the original IDL model, IDL is seen as being a single description encompassing all of a system. This model is not practical, as it makes it difficult to support separately compiled libraries in the traditional ways. The Tartan implementation supported separately compiled IDL definitions, but the mechanism was essentially a type-defeat mechanism at the IDL level which was checked only during compilation of the target language. There is a need for additional work in this area.

This problem with the IDL model became apparent after we began to use it at Tartan Laboratories. The assumption of a single global data specification ran counter to basic engineering requirements that separately compiled subsystems be able to be linked together without recompilation. Information hiding and modularity considerations required that client users not be able to modify the structure of information managed by various application packages such as parse tree generators and symbol table managers. Realities of computer time dictated that massive recompilation of every component of a system were infeasible (more on this later!) We therefore had to consider how to achieve, using IDL, what other systems with more conventional type systems already had: completely separate compilation.

In practice, we had been doing this for some time with IDL; IDL was originally targeted to the LG support system [15] which was part of the Bliss language [5] environment developed at CMU for the Production Quality Compiler Compiler project (PQCC). Since Bliss was an untyped language we could, and did, use this untyped property to allow various separately compiled IDL structures to reference each other. However, if a typed language had been used we would have had significant type violations. As we built our proprietary implementation language, Gnal, a modern strongly-typed language, the difficulties became apparent.

The solution was to define a base IDL type which had a single definition point shared by all IDL clients. This type was a generic type whose instances were the separately compiled IDL specifications[6]. Thus a specification, for example a symbol table, which needed to reference another specification, for example a name table, would simply name that type as an instance of the generic IDL type definition. This was accomplished in IDL by using a representation specification clause (one might argue about whether or not this is a "representation specification" or something else; indeed, a different mechanism is being considered in the draft 3 IDL specification):

```
symbol => name: NTE;

type NTE;

for NTE use separate "name_table";
```

The use of separately compiled IDL descriptions also pointed out a serious limitation in many modern languages: the namespace problem. A node of type "A" in package "X" must be distinguished from a node of type "A" in package "Y". Unless the language itself provides unique-qualification mechanisms to disambiguate such names, the disambiguation must be done by a naming convention. While the desired goal might be illustrated as

```
use X;
use Y;

var A1: X.A;
var A2: Y.A;
```

it may be achieved in a language like C only by naming conventions, such as:

---

[6]In Ada, this might be handled by using the derived type mechanism to create new derived IDL types from the base IDL type.

```
#include <X.h>
#include <Y.h>

X_A A1;
Y_A A2;
```

The conventions required for such subterfuges may require additional "representation" specifications to the IDL translator.

The mechanism used was a type-defeat mechanism; the "separate" declaration essentially said to the IDL translator "there is an external specification of this; trust me, and use this name to refer to it". Ultimately this was checked by the target language compiler, but it would have been much better if the IDL translator had checked all of this at the time it ran. Such checking requires that the translator be able to read interface specification files from other IDL runs. The use of abstract IDL descriptions (or "IDL intermediate languages"), such as Candle [18], are an important component of such a design. Candle and its implications are discussed in section 7.

7 IDL-based tooling

The Tartan tooling suite encompassed many IDL-based tools. Each of these tools read an input language which included IDL as a subset. A uniform extension mechanism was added for supporting the appropriate tool-specific declarations.

In retrospect, I consider this to have been a good abstract decision which had significant implementation problems. For example, it meant that each tool had to parse and to some degree semantically analyze the IDL language, and in addition most had to reconstruct syntactically correct IDL source as its output. Even when these tools shared code for these purposes (as some did) it created unnecessary overhead in the tool development.

The Candle description [18] has been developed at the University of North Carolina. Candle is to IDL what Diana is to Ada: an intermediate representation of a source program. Candle, like Diana, provides both a syntactic structure and a semantic structure. Thus the burden of parsing and analyzing an IDL description is handled where it properly should be: in an IDL front end. Candle is a communication specification from an IDL front end to various application back ends, such as target language interface generators (thus forming what is now thought of as an IDL translator) and tooling generators.

IDL-based tools may now be written in a declarative style, but when an IDL description is required, the appropriate **with** clause naming an IDL compilation output of a Candle description would be given. For example, a symbol table generator input file might look something like

```
declare primary_symbol_table is
    with user_application.structure_name;
    symbols are ...;
    scopes are ...;
    ...
end primary_symbol_table;
```

where the output of this would be a new Candle structure which could be fed to an IDL target-language module.

In the same way that the designers of Diana imagined Diana representations of Ada source supporting code generators, flow analyzers, syntax-directed editors, cross-referencers, and dozens of other tools, the Candle designers expect this representation will support IDL-based tooling. It is being used for this purpose already in the University of North Carolina IDL Toolkit.

8 Programming Project Support

8.1 Recompilation Triggers

One major engineering problem in working with large systems is that small changes in central definition files of the system can result in truly major expenditures of computing time as the dependency ripples out through the system. This is particularly painful in any system in which the definition file includes more than simple procedure interface specifications. C header files which contain macro specifications are prime examples; however, any language in which an in-line procedure can be defined will trigger such events.

In order to rebuild a system after some specification file has changed, some number of modules must be recompiled. The worst-case scenario is that all modules of the system are recompiled, whether they need to be or not. The best-case scenario is that only the modules which are affected by the change are recompiled.

The recompilation process could be considered as an application of a predicate to a module and the specifications it references. If M is a module and $S_1..S_n$ are the specification files it references, then a recompilation predicate R could be defined

$$R(M, S_1, \ldots, S_n)$$

which returns "true" if the module M needs to be recompiled and "false" if it does not need to be recompiled.

The degenerate case which guarantees consistency is the predicate which always returns "true" no matter what its arguments. This predicate is trivial to implement but incurs a high cost when a change occurs. A predicate which is frequently used is one which returns "true" in almost every case where recompilation is required; it is implemented by the system builder looking at the list of modules and for each one saying "I think that one requires recompilation..."; unfortunately, this is a somewhat flaky predicate. If the system is large, if the dependencies are complex, and/or if the person making the decision is not totally familiar with the system structure (eidetic memory is a great help in this task), some module which requires recompilation will not be recompiled. This scenario is familiar.

The simplest program which, if used properly, guarantees consistency is the Unix[7] 'make' facility. This takes a specification of the dependencies and, if any specification module has changed, forces a recompilation of all modules which depend on it. It has the significant drawback that the user is responsible for guaranteeing the consistency of the dependency graph described to the 'make' program and the actual dependency graph of the system being constructed. The 'make' facility predicate requires knowing the output, O of a "compilation", and thus applies a predicate

---

[7]Unix is a trademark of AT&T Bell Laboratories

$$R(M, O, S_1, \ldots, S_n)$$

if the module M or any specification file S_i is newer (by date stamp comparison) than the output O, the recompilation is required.

Programs such as the Unix 'make' facility which rely on primitive date-comparison algorithms cannot detect changes in content as distinct from changes in form (e.g., adding a comment). Various distortions are required to circumvent major rebuilds, all of them requiring manual intervention and usually error-prone. Introducing auxiliary definition files (a frequent practice among C programmers), removing actual dependencies from the 'make' file, and utility programs which update file dates are all common work-arounds.

8.2 Recompilation Predicates

Work began at Tartan in 1980 to develop a more sophisticated predicate than a simple date comparison. In particular, adding upward-compatible specifications to a definition file should not trigger massive recompilations. (Independent work on this problem was done by Walter Tichy at Purdue [21] for the C language, and was reported by Evans *et al.* for Praxis [7]; many others have, or are now looking at this problem).

In modern languages with overloading, it is certainly true that adding a procedure could introduce an overload conflict, and failing to recompile all modules which use the definition would mean that the inconsistency would not become visible until the next major system build. However, in practice the probability of such an event is actually rather low, and a more liberal interpretation which significantly reduced recompilation costs was chosen for the Tartan implementation. Under the liberal interpretation, any specification file which had changed but which was identical to or upward compatible with a previous version of the same file would not trigger a recompilation event for the files which depended upon it.

Consider the issues of upward compatibility if a procedural interface is used. If the input and output specifications are held constant the body can change without affecting the interface; the new interface is identical (and thus compatible) with the old interface. In a package definition, the addition of a new operation on the data types described in the package is (in general) an upward compatible change; existing code using the existing interface is not rendered obsolete, and new code which requires the new operation would be recompiled simply because it has been changed to use the new operation. Changing the number or type or mode of the parameters to a procedure, or the result type, would not be an upward compatible change; however, only the modules which use that particular procedure need to be recompiled, *not* all the modules which use that interface specification file. The specification is upward compatible for all clients except those that use the changed procedure.

However, when code is compiled inline, a new dependency is introduced. The validity of the code in client modules now depends not only on the abstract specification but also upon the implementation. The modification of the body of a `#define` in a C header file is an example of modifying the implementation while holding the interface constant. All clients of that definition must be recompiled.

The impact of IDL on the smart recompilation system used a Tartan, and which would be true for any other system supporting inline expansion of the IDL structure accesses, was such that it was very unlikely that an IDL target language module was upward compatible with a previous version. This is because the most frequent change was adding or deleting attribute definitions, and this almost always resulted in a repacking of the data structure, so that all of the field offsets changed. This meant that the inline bodies of the accessing operations changed; even though the interfaces remained constant (requiring no code changes) the implementation changed, and recompilation of all clients was necessary. The upward-compatible predicate did not (and could not) ask on a per-module basis if the module used any bodies which changed; if any repacking was done, all client modules had to be recompiled. Thus, any change in an IDL definition file resulted in the complete recompilation of all files which depended upon it. (In addition, the predicate did not detect "upward compatible" changes of the structure, although this certainly could have been added). Because the compiler also supported in-line expansion of user-defined functions (which could access IDL data objects), the recompilation effects could frequently encompass the bulk of the system.

8.3 Minimizing Repacking

When using conventional hardware architectures, the use of inline expansion of IDL accesses meant that any change in the IDL definition which resulted in a repacking would invalidate existing code, and there is in general no good way to determine if such repacking has occurred. Recompilation can be minimized only if a *compatible* packing of information can be maintained between separate executions of the IDL tool.

An important implementation feature which any IDL system should possess, then, is what I have called "cached allocation", an idea I first encountered in a slightly different guise in the SIL circuit-drawing package developed at Xerox PARC [20]. The particular aspect of SIL which was interesting to me dealt with how SIL handled the gate-packing problem. In many integrated circuit packages there are multiple instances of the same logical component, e.g., four 2-input NAND gates in a type 7400 chip. SIL would "pack" unallocated NAND gates into uncommitted packages. The packing was then recorded. On a subsequent run, if this assignment of gates and pinouts to physical packages was satisfactory then no repacking was done; the result was that the existing wires on the board could be left in place. Any new NAND gates added to the drawing would be packed into remaining uncommitted chips.

As adapted to the IDL environment, the basic idea of cached allocation is that the structure packer is normally run only *once* on a definition file, and that packing is recorded in a "cache". In subsequent runs, the previous packing is read in and used, and any new fields are "tacked on the end" of the data structure. Thus, all previously compiled modules will still have the correct field offsets for the existing fields; any modules that reference the new fields have obviously been changed and will, as a matter of course, be recompiled. Only when space utilization degenerates below acceptable levels (caused by class fields being added or deletion of existing fields) is it necessary to repack the structure. For example, consider the effects of adding a new declaration to the example given in section 5:

```
A => nval: integer;
```

the optimum packing would be something like that shown below in Figure 4, but to use cached allocation and the packing shown earlier in section 5 which now must be preserved, it must be packed as shown in Figure 5 below, which artificially increases the size of the A node with some unused space. If the next run adds a new declaration

```
E => mval: integer;
```

the effect becomes more obvious. At some point the wasted space will necessitate a new packing, thus invalidating all existing code and requiring a complete recompilation of the system.

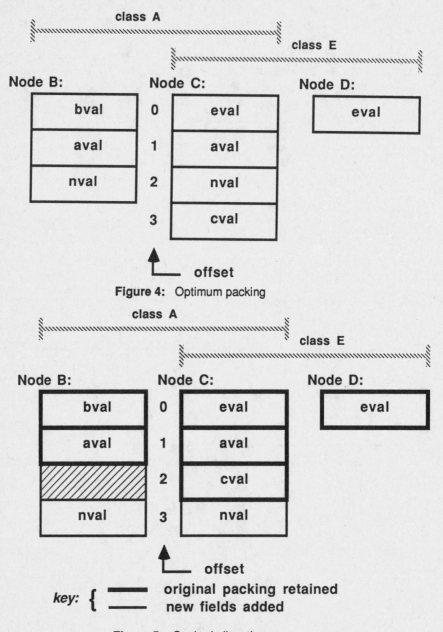

Figure 4: Optimum packing

Figure 5: Cached allocation

A direct implication of this is that the node size may not appear in-line in any generated code; for example, using the C "sizeof" operation would require that any module which created nodes would have to be recompiled, as would the use of "new" in Pascal or Modula-2, since these operations typically are implemented as requiring compile-time knowledge of the size of the data object to be created. Unless the recompilation tool knows which modules perform "new" operations, all clients of the IDL interface specification file would have to be recompiled if the node size changed.

However, if nodes are identified by unique numbers, and the sizes are obtained by a link-time binding of node ids to sizes, then there is no need to recompile any code which creates nodes; as the node size changes from run to run of the translator, existing code continues to run.

An important consideration in using this technique, however, is *monotonicity* of the alterations. A node may never be decreased in size. Since existing code is not recompiled, it can contain references to fixed offsets in the node which, if the node decreased in size, would now have undefined effects.

A very careful analysis of the effects of adding or deleting nodes, adding or deleting attributes, and adding or deleting nodes from class definitions is required to determine the effect of such changes on the validity of existing code. Careful engineering of the IDL target mapping and run-time environment in response to these changes is also required. Some of the simpler cases are discussed briefly here.

However, it is now possible to have the IDL tool interface to the target environment to support smart recompilation, even when the target environment cannot. By "lying" to the 'make' facility about the interface specification file date, the need to recompile modules can be avoided. Having a tool with complete knowledge effect the subterfuge is considerably more reliable than having a user with incomplete or possibly incorrect knowledge attempt the same trick.

When cached allocation is used, some careful analysis of the possible changes the user can make and their impact on compatibility must be made. In some cases, careful engineering decisions about the runtime environment can allow certain decisions to be bound sufficiently late in the process that changes can be upward compatible; the node-size example cited above is one such case.

Adding attributes is a simple problem when cached allocation is used. Such new attributes are, as shown above, appended to the end of the structure. If the attribute is an attribute of a class, all members of the class must be extended so that the attribute can be appended to the node of maximum size. This may create significant wasted space in the class members, and eventually a repacking will be required.

Deleting an attribute requires some consideration of the overall effect on the system development. One solution is to delete the attribute and the language interface to it, but otherwise assume the existing compiled code is valid. Such existing code (which may reference the attribute) will not be recompiled unless there has been some other triggering criterion (such as modification of the file), and any recompilation of such files would generate errors. Of course, existing uses of the attribute within the (un-recompiled) system may now find meaningless information in the (now unused) attribute, leading to erroneous program behavior. In the absence of more sophisticated smart recompilation strategies, such as those described by Tichy [21], the actual decision is more a managerial strategic decision than a technical decision; It is based upon considerations such as (alleged) knowledge of the usage and recompilation costs; the IDL translator should permit a high-risk option of minimum recompilation. Whether smart recompilation is used or not, the monotonicity must be preserved, the "unused" field may not be allocated for any other purpose because it is purportedly "free"; it is "undefined" but "unavailable" for future modifications.

Note that this above discussion suggests something which I said earlier was a bad idea: letting the user make the decision about whether to recompile a system or not. While I believe this as a principle, there are times when a simple cost/risk analysis shows that the risk is low and the cost is high, e.g., I just added an attribute, decided after a quick test that it was the wrong thing to do, and deleted it. If I must take risks, I would rather have a reasonably controlled expediency mechanism than a totally anarchic one.

Continuing on, nodes may be added to a class. Again, recompilation minimization depends upon the usage patterns and cost/risk analysis. Most procedures which operate on objects in the class will continue to operate even though a larger set of object types is permitted. Only those cases in which a complete discrimination of class members appears within the procedure body will there be any anomalies. Proper initial construction of the code (for example, not assuming a "case" discrimination on a class gives complete coverage and including appropriate "otherwise" clauses) will reduce the risk of such changes. Code used to check class membership of a type within a class must also be a link-time rather than a compile-time binding. The link-time binding of class membership checking was carefully engineered in the Tartan implementation, but it would take too long to describe here.

Obviously decisions which require human intervention are always subject to error. The high payoff of using cached allocation and high risk/low risk/no risk decision mechanisms are that it is possible to reduce the cost of change during the development/prototype cycle, particularly when rapid turnaround is required for productivity. Since all the decisions with risk involved have a no-risk fallback (to require the recompilation of all client modules), the no-risk fallback can be frequently handled by such strategies as off-time (usually overnight, or over-weekend) massive recompilations, while the higher risk strategies allow for rapid turnaround during the work-time (usually daytime) period.

8.4 Abstract Interfaces?

A typical argument against the complexity of the recompilation mechanisms and the careful engineering required to use them effectively is that the abstract interface "ought to" hide the implementation, so that accessing fields is done entirely through procedural interfaces which are insensitive to the actual "record" layout. Thus, the implementation can be readily changed without impacting the users at all.

This is certainly a laudable goal, but several realities interfere with it. First, procedural interfaces are rather clumsy to use; a separate "store" procedure must be used to modify each attribute and a "fetch" procedure to read one. This is somewhat unnatural, but given certain goals of the interface design and programming standards it might construably be an acceptable way to write programs. Obviously such linguistic features as user-definable selectors could eliminate this by providing the desired syntactic sugar.

The overwhelming argument against the procedural interface, however, is the access time argument. If the cost of a procedure call is nonzero (as it almost always is!), the performance of a system can be reduced by large factors, if not orders of magnitude, by having to use a procedure to read and write every attribute. Programmers, understanding such costs, then distort their code to fit it, caching attribute values in local variables and generally reducing the intelligibility of the code in an attempt to make it perform reasonably. Therefore, even if the procedural interface is a desirable programming paradigm, it is too expensive to use if implemented in a conventional language.

The next obvious step is to provide for in-line expansion of such a procedural interface. As soon as this is done, the generated object code now contains fixed offsets into the data structures, and is indistinguishable from code which used ordinary selectors (at least to someone reading the object code). The cached allocation model addresses the problems of generated target code, not the issues of abstract interfaces, and is, in fact, largely insensitive to the abstract interface (except for how to convince an environment that a new interface is "upward compatible" with the previous version).

Of course, all of this is an incidental property of our current computer architectures, in which the knowledge of how to access information resides in the code. If an architecture providing descriptor-based access to data structures were used, many of these problems simply disappear; knowledge of how to access the code would reside "with the data", or at the worst case in a single link-time or run-time bound definition. While I know of several sophisticated link-time-binding mechanisms for manipulating offsets, I know of very few, if any, linkers which can handle link-time data-size specification. In addition, the actual instruction (even if the size remains fixed) often changes depending upon the alignment of the data; bit-field extraction often requires multiple instructions so accessing an 8-bit byte-aligned field moved to a non-byte-aligned position is not something easily modified at link time unless one is willing to allow significant performance degradation.

Database systems responded to this problem years ago; most of them abstract the representation from the code ("representation independent code") but pay a high price in performance; certainly higher than would be acceptable for implementing data structures such as compiler data structures. In general, the only way sophisticated deferral of binding decisions can be implemented efficiently is if the compiler can be modified to support new kinds of inline access via strange implementation schemes (e.g., all data structure access via indirect descriptors). While sophisticated inline mechanisms sometimes help, they only succeed insofar as they can take advantage of existing code generation templates. If obscure instructions or strange addressing modes are required for maximum efficiency, and inline machine code insertions cannot be made, one is limited to what the compiler can support. The mechanisms described above could be implemented in most plain-vanilla-compiler environments.

All of the above complex mechanism is therefore in response to the reality of current architectures and how to cope with their all-too-real problems.

8.5 Implications on Target Language

To take full advantage of the packing techniques, both for ordinary IDL and for cached allocation, requires that the IDL system actually be able to control how a record is laid out in memory. The control may either be explicit (for example, the use of representation specification clauses in Ada) or implicit (the order of declaration of fields in C). For some languages it may be possible to subvert their type systems or use interesting substructuring to avoid the need for layout control for simple IDL, but it is not clear that such tricks can work across multiple compilers or when cached allocation is desired.

8.6 Implications on Target Environment

When interesting techniques such as cached allocation are used, the way in which the updated definition files produced by an IDL translator interact with the target *environment* must also be controlled by the IDL translator. As discussed earlier, in a simple C/'make' environment, to suppress unnecessary compilations it may only be necessary for the IDL translator to set the date of the new header file to the date of its previous version. For languages where the definition files are themselves compiled entities a more sophisticated mechanism will be required to defeat the environment's recompilation predicate. Ideally, a recompilation predicate should be general enough that the user could extend it; in practice, unified environments are typically "closed" to user extension and modification, being viewed as complete and sufficient. This is unfortunate, since the implementors of such environments cannot predict all possible uses, and even if they could would not have the resources to provide support for every conceivable use.

Implementors discovered that simple date-stamp comparisons can fail (either forcing unnecessary recompilations or failing to force a necessary recompilation), especially in distributed computing environments without centralized clocks, so in these environments more sophisticated mechanisms which include processor ids, compiler ids, and other information (such as checksums of the source files), some intrinsic and some incidental to the validity of the interface, are sometimes used. The increasing sophistication of such equality predicates is rarely based on the semantic content of the file, but is instead based on totally incidental and often unrelated properties, but which are "very fast" to compute. More sophisticated predicates based on actual semantic content are required [2] [21].

8.7 Lessons

There are some important issues here for language designers, compiler implementors, and environment implementors.

When programs are generating the record or structure definitions, bit-by-bit layout control may be required. If the language is sufficiently simple and the compiler is equally simple, the tool can take advantage of the compiler's data packing algorithm to indirectly effect control. Sophisticated compilers which give the user no layout control and which do "optimized" packing, however, are extremely difficult to interface to. While one may not wish to give layout control to a programmer, or document how it is done, such control and/or documentation is essential to program generating tools.

Mechanisms which are intended to prevent errors caused by failure to recompile dependent modules and which are based on anything other than actual semantic compatibility (e.g., changes in comments, names of formal parameters in interface specifications, indenting, and other incidentals must be ignored) at the interface level (and implementation compatibility when inline expansion is permitted) must have ways of being subverted by sophisticated tools which have precise knowledge of what constitutes compatible or incompatible changes. Better still, a well-defined notion of upward compatibility under both strict and liberal interpretations must be supported. If complex problems are ignored (such as upward compatibility of record structures under repacking minimization strategies in an IDL tool) the mechanisms will have to be subverted.

My basic complaint about programming languages and their environments was summed up rather succinctly by the statement "It is time we stopped designing languages in which people write code and started designing languages in which tools will write code" [8].

9 Data Base Interface

The nature of data is changing. Data now far outlives the programs which create it. The original goals of IDL were to specify a language- and machine-independent data description, to be able to communicate it in a language- and machine-independent fashion, and to be able to control its mapping to physical representations. This would allow programs written in a variety of languages on a variety of machines to communicate with each other, while still maintaining the efficiency required for internal manipulation.

To date, the realizations of this model have largely dealt with short-lived data, such as compiler interphase communication, representations of separately compiled module specifications, and similar applications. However, the descriptions of the data were encoded in the programs. In a database environment, the data description must live with the data.

In the Tartan IDL environment, there was long-lived data (such as the module interface or separate compilation files produced by the compilers) but the data descriptions lived in the producers and consumers, not in the files. This meant that any repacking of the information invalidated all of the existing interface files, because the formats were usually incompatible. Even the use of the proposed (but never implemented) cached allocation was not a sufficient solution, since the high-performance binary reader/writer modules would have to detect nodes stored in the files with one size but which had been extended to a new size.

To adequately use IDL in a database environment, the full IDL description of the data (often referred to in IDL documents as "the IDL symbol table", [18]) must be part of the information transmitted when a connection to an IDL information structure is "opened".

It is worth noting that the use of IDL to describe and interface to a database (in the sense of a hierarchical, network, or relational database) rather than the classical memory-resident data model usually used for IDL appears to be an issue of implementation engineering; the basic IDL specification mechanism appears to be quite suitable for expressing an interesting collection of database specifications. Several of us involved in IDL consider the use of an IDL model for databases, and comparison to existing data definition specifications [1], to be an interesting and promising area of research.

Another aspect of database system integration deals with separate IDL instances which must have cross-links. For example, consider the case where IDL is used by a compiler to represent interface specifications. There may be two modules of the following form:

```
module A
   use B;

   var bvar: BType;       -- type BType is defined in module B
end A;

module B
    type BType is ...
end B;
```

The implementation strategy chosen (not necessarily the optimum one, but one which illustrates this example well) is to separately compile module B and then module A, but not include any of the content of the module B interface file in module A's interface file. Thus the interface file for module A contains, in some form, a *reference* to information in module B's interface file (Figure 6).

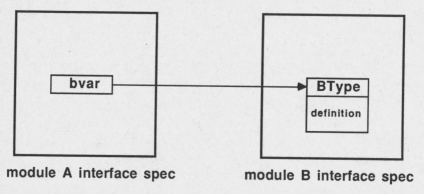

module A interface spec   module B interface spec

Figure 6: Reference between modules

After having participated in two efforts to implement this type of system, I have become convinced that the problem is exactly that of doing a classical relational "join" operation. This model, having a sound theoretical underpinning and suitable mathematical description, has clarified my understanding of the problem and promoted it from the domain of an "implementation hack" to something which can be reasoned about and communicated much more readily.

Consider a relational tableau presentation: it might show how the variable becomes associated with its type definition by a simplistic picture of the form shown in Figure 7.

This is obviously a great simplification; the actual tableux used would be far more complex: for example, encompassing multiple interface specification files and multiple associations (such as might be induced by overloaded function names). Several other liberties with the relational model have been taken to simplify the presentation here; a much more complex formal model is actually required to properly express this as relational operations. In addition, the complex data structures used in compilers do not lend themselves easily to the tableau representation com-

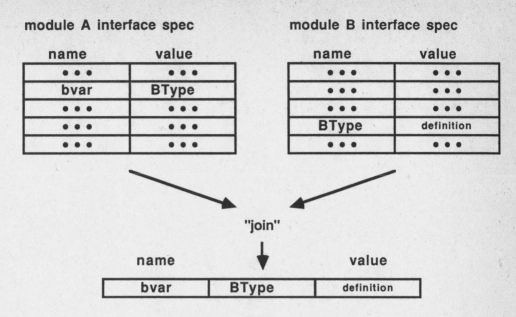

Figure 7: Simplistic relational tableau

mon in relational models; but the semantic problems are quite similar. By thinking of the problem in terms of "surrogate keys" [4] a model closer to the non-database world of "pointers" can be created. I now believe no extensions to the IDL language are required to support this mechanism; rather, a higher-level IDL-based "applications" tool would provide the necessary functionality, providing the mechanisms and support code by which such complex interfaces can be crafted by clever code rather than clever coders.

Another relationship to database work is in the use of various normalization methods. Normalization is a class of operations on database structure which have the property of reducing what are called "update anomalies" by guaranteeing that each object of interest has but a single definition point. Normalization tends to run counter to the need for redundancy for performance reasons; in fact, a nontrivial amount of database engineering seems (to an outsider such as myself) to center around how to achieve both a normalized database and one which performs adequately. This is complicated by the fact that the higher-order normal forms have no algorithms by which they may be achieved given a completely arbitrary database structure as a start.

Consider the case of how to distribute information in a tree or graph structure. Classically, implementors have expended a tremendous amount of design effort saying things like "the cost of recomputing this value is quite high, so I'll stuff a local copy of it here in this node..." and "these two pieces of data are the same, so I'll create one instance and share it by creating a new node type and a pointer from the other places...". Many of these problems have already been addressed in the database world. In particular, new work on distributed databases has to deal with the high cost of not caching certain computations on the local machine. Classical normalization deals with sharing common data and preventing update anomalies. Tremendous amounts of effort go into debugging problems in compilers and other classical system structures caused by update anomalies, errors in sharing, failures to share, dangling pointers, etc. and these appear to me to be the result of the same *ad hoc* engineering decisions that plagued the database world prior to the introduction of automatic and semi-automatic design aids and sound theoretical bases for describing data.

Many of the design tradeoffs made in classical data structure engineering (such as replication of data, additional pointers, etc.) deal with performance issues, and knowledge of the semantic domain which indicates which information is likely to or will remain constant. In the database world, it appears that everything can change, and because of the long-lived data, almost certainly *will* change given enough time. In system structures, the data at some point in the processing is frequently read-only (and in linear systems such as compilers is never modified once it has been created). Thus current techniques are not directly applicable. Nonetheless, some automated help on the design of data structures is certainly desirable. Having such automated tools work on IDL-level descriptions which are both language- and machine-independent strikes me as more valuable than tools which would work on Ada, Pascal, C, or other language-specific representations. Since the lower-level language specific representations can be derived from the IDL specifications, there is a significant gain in applicability by using the IDL level model.

The result is that by having high-level specifications of the data, and in particular by the use of specifications that allow an automated system to deduce usage (e.g., write-once vs. read/write, or read-only after a certain point in the lifetime) extensions of many of the normalization techniques used in the database domain will find applicability to IDL definitions. Some of the tasks currently performed by those writing IDL definition files, such as creation of classes (especially non-hierarchical classes), creation of views, and the choice of how attributes are assigned to various nodes and classes may well become automated. In addition, because of the richer information on lifetimes new kinds of "normalization" not applicable in the general database domain may become apparent. This is an interesting area for future research.

10 Object Based Systems

One issue raised at an SEI workshop session on future technology was the issue of active databases and object-based systems. As the balance shifts from long-lived programs and short-lived data to long-lived data and short-lived programs, problems such as semantic consistency are creeping in. If the database is extended to support program X, and program Y (which has been around for years) does not understand how to maintain the invariants required by program X, then any use of program Y on the database may destroy its integrity as far as program X's view. This is the classical "editing through views" problem [9].

The core of this problem is that the semantics are embodied not in the data but in the programs which manipulate it. Active databases, particularly those based on the object-based paradigm, appear to be a way of achieving the necessary consistency.

IDL includes an "assertion language" in which invariants about the data structure may be written. Using a transaction-based model for updating a database, such that the invariants are expected to hold after the completion of each transaction, it should be possible to validate the integrity of an IDL database after each transaction. Using specification systems such as attribute grammars based on IDL [11], it should be possible to create databases which maintain their consistency. These appear to be interesting areas for research.

11 Non-traditional Data Presentation

The use of graphical input languages has increased dramatically in the last few years. However, most of these languages deal with the high-level design aspects. Some create COBOL or PL/1 data definitions for the database design. However, in most of these systems there is no inverse operation; given an instance of a data object there is no way to graphically display the data during debugging. In most cases, graphic display of the data is based on sets of data objects and is restricted to pie charts, histograms, and other "business graphics". The simplifying assumption of "no pointers" also makes the display in some of these systems rather simple compared to what is needed to support an IDL based system.

While some of what is presented here seems obvious, in fact very few systems actually provide the necessary support for complex information output. Graphical output, discussed later in this section, is an old desideratum, but very few systems in everyday production use for systems programmers actually provide it (whereas in the database world it is becoming commonplace). Our experience at CMU and Tartan with a variety of graphical output systems resulted in the incorporation of several specialized graphical output systems as an integral component of the Tartan development environment, and which are in daily use by many users. Even the simple text forms for complex structures are beyond what most debuggers provide today, particularly if more than one level of structure is to be displayed.

A substantial piece of power and flexibility in the CMU LG system and the Tartan IDL implementation came from the fact that the a complete run-time symbol table was available during development. With a debugger interface this allowed the developers to display the internal data structures in the IDL external form.

A matter of considerable debate arose during the LG and IDL efforts. This dealt with the "human factors" issues of how information is presented to the user. The LG system would display its data in a "flat" form; for example, a simple addition tree for "17+22" might be displayed as

```
1: binary
   (op +)
   (left 2:)
   (right 3:)

2: const
   (value 17)

3: const
   (value 22)
```

However, for deeply nested structures the flat form made understanding of the actual structure very difficult, since the distance on the listing between nodes was often based on an NLR treewalk[8]. We spent a lot of time either rearranging the output with a text editor for easier examination or drawing lines on listings.

---

[8]Node, Left subtree, Right subtree. Notation due to W.A. Wulf.

It was obvious from this experience that the "right" representation was a nested tree representation. Consequently, when IDL was implemented, a nested form was used:

```
L1103: binary [op plus; left
    L1747: const [value 17];
    right
    L406: const [value 22]]
```

This turns out to be at least as bad to read; the labels are completely arbitrary values (they happened to be the machine addresses of the nodes, because that was convenient when debugging, but many other naming conventions could have been used). Since there is generally no
look-ahead, a label must be displayed because it *might* be referenced (in the above example,
L1747 and L406 are not referenced). When references did appear (as in a dag or cyclic graph),
locating the referenced node in a listing was nearly impossible. A slight improvement was made
on the debug output by numbering the lines of the output and encoding the line number in a
label, e.g., "L1747_201^" meant that the referenced label was defined on line 201. Also, it turns
out that people cannot read indentation well. Putting "ruler marks" on the listing helped some;
an example of such output (with a reference to a label given) is shown below.

```
200|  ....|....|....L1103: binary [op plus; left
201|     |    |    |    L1747: const [value 17];
202|     |    |    |    right
203|     |    |    |    L406: const [value 22]]
...
1507|    |    |    |    | L2347: unary [op unary_minus; operand
1508|    |    |    |    |           L1747_201^]
```

In spite of this, we ended up drawing a lot of lines on listings.

Some of the applications actually had built-in data structure printers which worked in a domain-
specific fashion. The code generator components had tree-printer utilities that displayed the internal tree structure as a tree structure on the screen (but not on a listing), in a form much like
this:

```
            L1103: plus
        _____/ _____
       /               \
    L1747: 17        L406: 22
```

The attribute-grammar system we built had an internal unparser so that internal structure could
be immediately related to the source; in addition various internal structures, such as symbol
tables, could be "unparsed" into a meaningful display. Important properties of both of these systems included depth-limited cutoff so only the relevant material was displayed.

Both of these systems were considered indispensable by their users.

What has become obvious to me is that many people, myself included, tend to *think* of data
structures graphically, reduce the thoughts to strings of ASCII text, convert from that to a
representation of bits, and at best we get back strings of ASCII text (unless we are so unfortunate as to be able to get back only the bits!); only in rare cases do we get anything ap-
proximating the model in which we first thought of the problem.

A project I hope to pursue, but which I also hope others will investigate, is the use of graphical input specifications for complex data structures which do not necessarily have a natural representation as relational tableaux. For my own goals, I hope to someday produce another highly integrated environment in which the normal form for data structure display on input or during debugging is graphical. Equally important, this should not be a passive output form but one with which the user may interact. A significant effort on the use of graphical output form has already produced a working system in the North Carolina SoftLab project [3] and a major system using graphical I/O is being done at Brown University by Steven Reiss [16].

12 Conclusion

This paper has presented, rather briefly, some experiences with IDL. These experiences suggest some possible future directions for IDL-based tooling and the IDL language itself. These include, as possible research, development, and/or engineering ideas:

- Design of target languages supporting the IDL type model,
- Providing support for separate compilation of IDL specifications for use as components in a system,
- Providing support for ameliorating some of the problems of large system construction, particularly those following from the use of IDL or other high-level descriptive languages,
- Providing graphical data presentation for both specification and debugging,
- Designing automated design support tools for the construction of complex IDL definitions.
- Designing support for persistent data objects ("database" support), or support for object-based models using IDL specifications.
- Using and adapting techniques from the database world to allow for more correct and robust data design without compromising the performance of a system.

13 Acknowledgements

The work described here actually began about 1977 with the PQCC project. It would be impossible to list the dozens of people who contributed to the LG and IDL work over that time. Primary and core contributors, however, include Paul N. Hilfinger and Steven O. Hobbs, major contributors to the LG design, and John R. Nestor, David Alex Lamb and William A. Wulf, designers of the IDL language. Valuable experience was gained at Tartan Laboratories on the use of IDL in a practical environment, and thanks are extended to all those from Tartan who provided valuable feedback on IDL, including those who made significant contributions to the IDL system implementation. This includes but certainly is not limited to Edward N. Dekker, David A. Syiek, Guy L. Steele, Jr., John Nestor, David Lamb, Steven B. Byrne, and Kenneth J. Butler. Continuing discussions with John Nestor, David Lamb, Richard Snodgrass, and Karen Shannon (among many others) have been quite valuable. I apologize to anyone I have inadvertently omitted. Thanks to the many reviewers of this paper, especially David Alex Lamb and David Garlan. Purvis Jackson of SEI provided both critical input and significant production support.

14 References

[1] American National Standards Institute, Draft Proposal, *Information Resource Dictionary System*, Technical Committee X3H4, April 1985.

[2] Borison, Ellen, A Model of Software Manufacture, *International Workshop on Advanced Programming Environments*, Trohdheim, Norway. June 1986.

[3] Butler, N., Curry, J., Konstant, S. and Rosenblum, D., *Treepr Users Manual*, SoftLab document No. 4 (copyright 1985), Computer Science Department, University of North Carolina at Chapel Hill, June 1985.

[4] Codd, E.F, Extending the Database Relational Model to Capture More Meaning, *ACM Transactions on Database Systems*, Volume 4, Number 4, December 1979.

[5] Digital Equipment Corporation, *Bliss Language Guide*, Digital Equipment Corporation, 1978.

[6] Evans, A., Jr. and Butler, K. J. (editors), *Diana - An Intermediate Language for Ada, Revised[6] Version*, Springer-Verlag, 1983.

[7] Evans, A., Jr., Morgan, C. R., Greenwood, J. R., Zarnstorff, M. C., Williams, G. J., Killian, E. A. and Walker, J. H., *Praxis Language Reference Manual*, Lawrence Livermore Laboratory, January, 1981.

[8] Firth, R., private communication.

[9] Garlan, D., Views for Tools in Integrated Environments. *International Workshop on Advanced Programming Environments*, Trohdheim, Norway. June 1986.

[10] Goos, G. and Wulf, W. A. (editors), *Diana Reference Manual*, Technical Report CS-81-101, Carnegie-Mellon University Computer Science Department, March 1981.

[11] Nestor, J. R., Mishra, B., Scherlis, W. L. and Wulf, W. A., *Extensions to Attribute Grammars*, Technical Report TL 83-36, Tartan Laboratories Incorporated, April 1983.

[12] Nestor, J. R., Wulf, W. A. and Lamb, D. A., *IDL - Interface Description Language - Formal Description*, Technical Report CS-81-139, Carnegie-Mellon University Computer Science Department, August 1981.

[13] Nestor, J. R., Wulf, W. A. and Lamb, D. A., *IDL - Interface Description Language - Formal Description (draft revision 2)*, reprinted with permission of the authors by the Software Engineering Institute, March 1986.

[14] Nestor, J. R., *Revised "Process" Model for IDL*, informal presentation, *IDL Implementors' Workshop*, Kiawah Island, May 1986.

[15] Newcomer, J. M., Cattell, R. G. G., Dill, D., Hilfinger, P. N., Hobbs, S. O., Leverett, B. W..

Reiner, A., Schatz, B. and Wulf, W. A., *PQCC Implementor's Handbook.* CMU Internal Technical Report, copyright 1978, 1979, 1980, October 1980.

[16] Reiss, Steven, GARDEN Tools: Support for Graphical Programming, *International Workshop on Advanced Programming Environments*, Trohdheim, Norway. June 1986.

[17] Shannon, K. and Snodgrass, R., *Mapping the Interface Description Language Type Model into C - Extended Summary*, Internal Document, Computer Science Department, University of North Carolina at Chapel Hill, 1985.

[18] Shannon, K. and Snodgrass, R. *Candle: A Common Attributed Notation for IDL*, SoftLab document No. 19 (draft version), copyright 1986, Computer Science Department, University of North Carolina at Chapel Hill, March 1986.

[19] Snodgrass, R., (editor) *IDL Manual Entries (Version 2.0)*, SoftLab document No. 15 (copyright 1985), Computer Science Department, University of North Carolina at Chapel Hill, December 1985.

[20] Thacker, C. P., Sproull, R. F. and Bates, R. D., *SIL, Analyze, Gobble, Build: Reference Manual*, Xerox Palo Alto Research Center, internal document (not for distribution), February, 1981.

[21] Tichy, W. F. and Baker, M. C. *Smart Recompilation*, published in *Principles of Programming Languages, 1985 Conference Proceedings*, ACM, January 1985, pp 236-244.

[22] Warren, W. B., Kickenson, J. and Snodgrass, R., *A Tutorial Introduction to Using IDL*, SoftLab document No. 1, Computer Science Department, University of North Carolina at Chapel Hill, November 1985.

Supporting Flexible and Efficient Tool Integration

Richard Snodgrass[†] and Karen Shannon

Department of Computer Science
University of North Carolina
Chapel Hill, NC 27514

We present a model of tool integration intermediate to the monolithic approach and the toolkit approach. Tools are developed separately, as in the toolkit approach, and then combined to form a new tool. The Interface Description Language (IDL), a notation for describing the characteristics of data structures passed among collections of cooperating processes, is extended to specify tight integration as exhibited in the monolithic approach. A composite tool can be formed by grouping a collection of existing tools linked through connections. Representations for connections that differ in flexibility and efficiency can be specified. Certain portions of the tool can be generated automatically from its specification.

1. Introduction

Previous work in programming environments (PE) can be characterized in terms of two rather different approaches of tool integration [Habermann 1979]. In one approach that may be termed the *monolithic* approach, the PE consists of one large program that does everything. Generally, this environment manipulates a database that usually contains an intermediate representation of the program being constructed and supports commands that edit, execute, debug, manage, and analyze the contents of the databases. Examples of this approach include Gandalf [Notkin 1985], the Cornell Program Synthesizer [Reps & Teitelbaum 1984, Teitelbaum et al. 1981], and PECAN [Reiss 1985]. The benefits of the monolithic approach include a uniform interface and ease of communicating between tools; the approach has the disadvantage that it is difficult to integrate new tools into the PE. At the other end of the spectrum is what may be called the *toolbox* approach in which the PE consists of a large collection of fairly small tools that can be coupled together in various ways to provide functions similar to those of the monolithic PE. Unix is an example of the toolkit approach [Kernighan & Mashey 1981]. The benefits of the toolkit approach are flexibility of combining tools together to perform a task and ease of using new tools. One disadvantage is that information interchange between tools is at a low level (e.g. a sequence of characters) complicating close interaction.

Lamb has suggested a model of tool integration intermediate to the two approaches [Lamb 1983]. Tools are developed separately as in the toolkit approach and then combined in a coherent, organized fashion. The program database consists of a collection of typed instances that may be read or written by tools. Lamb discusses how the Interface Description Language (IDL) [Nestor, et al. 1982, Warren, et al. 1985] may describe the characteristics of data structures passed among a collection of cooperating processes. We first review the structure and

---

[†]This author was supported in part by an IBM Faculty Development Award.

process specification components of IDL, indicating why it is appropriate for the specification of a single module and why it is deficient when several modules interact. In Section 3 we extend the model of tool integration and propose several new IDL constructs. In the fourth section, we discuss issues that arise when supporting this model. In the remaining sections, we compare our approach with that of others, and suggest areas of future work.

2. Review of IDL

The current definition of IDL may be found in the "Version 2 document" [Nestor, et al. 1982]. In IDL, structures are specified as directed graphs of attributed nodes. These structures encompass many of the data structures provided by procedural programming languages, and are especially useful in specifying those structures employed by compilers. IDL is a strongly-typed language; the types supported are the scalar types boolean, integer, rational, and string, the structured types set and sequence, attributed nodes, and user-defined private types. Classes, which are collections of node and class types representing common aspects of the nodes in the class, are also present in the language. The IDL type model can be used to place restrictions on the operations permitted on instances of IDL structures while they are being manipulated within a target language program. A structure specification may also contain constraints on these types. These constraints can be representational constraints or assertions. Representational constraints specify particular representations for types. For example, an integer could be represented with 4 bits. Assertions specify other interesting properties of the structure. An IDL structure specification can be considered as an abstract data type specification. A tool, the IDL translator, maps these descriptions into code fragments in one or more target programming languages. These code fragments contain declarations of data structures in the target programming language that are equivalent to those described in the IDL specification. The code fragments also define memory resident manipulation and input and output of instances of the data structures. The user writes programs in terms of the target language data declarations and utilities produced by the IDL translator. These programs process instances of the IDL-specified data structures.

Structures can be specified in one of three ways. The first is as a new structure. An example is the `ExpDefinition` structure.

```
Structure ExpDefinition Root expression Is
        expression ::= operation | constant;
        expression => exp_pos: sourceposition;
        operation ::= binary_operation | unary_operation;
        operation => op: operator;
        binary_operation => left: expression,
                            right: expression;
        unary_operation => argument: expression;
        operator ::= plus | minus;
            plus =>; minus =>;
        constant ::= integer_constant | real_constant;
        integer_constant => value: Integer;
        real_constant => value: Rational;

        Type sourceposition;
        For sourceposition Use Integer;
    End;
```

In this structure, `expression` is a class with direct members `operation` and `constant` and indirect members `binary_operation`, `unary_operation`, `integer_constant`, and `real_constant`. `binary_operation` is a node with direct attributes `left` and `right` and an inherited attribute `exp_pos`. The for clause states that the private type `sourceposition` is represented as an integer. The root of the structure, `expression`, is a class from which all other types in each instance of the structure can be reached.

A second way of specifying a structure is as a *derived structure*. Derived structures are modifications of other structures. Modifications include additions and deletions from the original structures. An example of a derived structure is the `TypedExpDefinition` structure.

```
Structure TypedExpDefinition Root Expression
                                   From ExpDefinition Is
        expression => exp_type: etype;
        etype ::= inttype | realtype;
              inttype =>; realtype =>;
End;
```

The `TypedExpDefinition` structure is derived from the `ExpDefinition` structure. Modifications include the addition of the new attribute `exp_type`.

Structures may also be *refined* from other structures. Refining a structure constrains the structure toward a concrete representation. As an example, in the refined structure `TypedExpDefConcrete`,

```
Structure TypedExpDefConcrete Refines TypedExpDefinition Is
    For etype Use Enumerated;
    For operator Use Enumerated;
End;
```

the node `etype` is represented as an enumerated type. Refinement, in constraining the structure, allows the IDL translator to, among other things, generate more efficient code, since the full generality need not be supported.

A *process specification* describes the flow of data in a program. Pre and post statements specify the input data structures read by the program and output data structures written by the program. They can also be thought of as preconditions and postconditions for the process [Nestor, et al. 1982]. An example is the specification for the lister process.

```
Structure ExpInv Is
    ...
End;

Process Typing Inv ExpInv Is
        Pre  INexp:      ExpDefinition;
        Post Outexp:     TypedExpDefinition;
End;
```

In this example, there is one input port and one output port. The Inv clause names the invariant structure of the process. This structure must include all the types defined in the port structures of the process. In addition, new types can be defined that are used internally in the program.

Using IDL simplifies the development of complex software systems. IDL permits a higher level of data abstraction than that provided by most programming languages. Abstract data types such as sets and sequences for any type, complete with all necessary data declarations and data manipulation routines, are supported by IDL. Consequently, the user has the opportunity to more naturally express the algorithm in terms of these abstractions without becoming mired in implementation detail. Since a large portion of the data manipulation routines are provided by the IDL system, the user must write and debug less code. Finally, the software system that has been developed using the IDL system is documented by its specification and thus is easier to maintain. IDL has been used in several compilers and programming environments [Butler 1983, Zorn 1985]; the Diana intermediate representation for Ada programs [Goos, et al. 1983] is expressed in IDL, as is the Ivan intermediate representation for VHDL programs [Gilman 1986].

A limitation in the current language is that it cannot describe the interaction between several modules. The deficiency lies in the process construct. This construct expresses the interaction of modules in a localized fashion by focusing on each module individually. There is no means of specifying how modules may be composed. Once such a means is provided, the module connectivity is known and the support environment can handle more of the details of integrating modules, including computing representations for data structures, generating code tailored to the module connectivity, and allowing the late binding of certain decisions. Automating these analytical and generative tasks is not possible without the environment having access to the connectivity structure.

3. The Model

In this section we extend Lamb's model for tool integration and introduce new IDL constructs for specifying the integration. This model is presented at a fairly high level; the details (and problems) of supporting the model are examined in the next section. We had several requirements in mind when we defined these constructs:

• *The conceptual integrity of IDL should be preserved.* IDL is a simple, declarative, strongly-typed specification language; additional constructs should also reflect these aspects.

• *Derivation and refinement should be supported for tools.* These quite powerful specification techniques should be applicable both to structures and to tools, in analogous ways.

• *Efficient implementations of tools should be supported.* For the language to be used, it must admit an efficient implementation, both of the IDL translator (less important) and of the code generated by the translator (very important).

The reader should note that the augmented IDL language described in the remainder of the paper differs from both the language described in the Version 2 document, and from the language implemented in the UNC IDL toolkit [Snodgrass 1985].

3.1. Tools

The basic entity is the *tool*. Each tool contains one or more *ports* that allow it to communicate with other tools and with the program database. Each tool also contains an *algorithm* that performs some function. Finally, associated with each tool is an *invariant structure*, which in some sense ties the ports and the algorithm together. At this level a tool is very similar to the Process concept in the original IDL. They differ in two respects. First, the term 'tool' was chosen to avoid any connotations carried by the term 'process', which is often confused with the term as used in the operating system sense of 'dispatchable unit' [Deitel 1984]. A tool may or may not be a process in this sense (more on this distinction later). Secondly, as we will see shortly, tools can contain other tools; such was not allowed with processes in the original IDL.

A tool in this model is somewhat smaller than that in the toolkit approach, where tools were compilers, editors, debuggers, cross references, etc. In this model, examples of tools are parsers, semantic analysis phases, an error listing generator, an include file expander, etc. Several of these tools may in concert form a more conventional tool. For example, the IDL translator of the UNC IDL system contains seven individual tools, as will be seen in Section 3.3.

A port within a tool is both a conceptual handle on the tool and an entity that can be called by the algorithm. A procedure may be automatically produced for each port from the description of the tool. Ports are typed; associated with each port is an IDL structure. *Input ports* read an instance of the structure into main memory and return the root of the instance to the algorithm; *output ports* write from main memory the instance referenced by the root object passed to it as a parameter. A tool may also perform additional input and output not specified in the model. Ports are one of the two sites where nodes are initialized and attributes given default values; the other is the node creation operation (see Section 4.4). Auxiliary structures such as hash tables, that are required by certain attribute representations, are also created by the ports. While instances may be transitory within a tool, they are well-defined at the ports. Hence it is possible to characterize (perhaps incompletely) the processing performed by a tool by specifying the instances read in and written out and the relationship between these instances. The assertion language [Nestor, et al. 1982] can be used to specify constraints on individual structures or relationships between structures. An assertion checker takes the instances read or written by the tool and indicates which assertions failed [Kickenson 1986]. There is no required ordering of calls to ports, and in fact the ordering can be data dependent and a port can be called more than once by a tool.

An example tool is the `lister` used within several compilers in the UNC IDL toolkit [Shannon & Snodgrass 1985]. This tool is specified as

```
Tool lister Is
        Input INerrorinfo: ErrorInfo;
        Input INfiletransitions: FileTransitions;
        Input INerrorinstances: ErrorInstanceStream;
        Input INfile: ASCIIStream;
        --- also produces listing files
    End;
```

and has four input and no output ports (we assume the structures associated with these ports have already been specified). The algorithm reads data providing relevant details on errors (e.g., their severity and textual message), data specifying the include file hierarchy (we assume that source files can include other source files), a sequence of error reports from various phases of the compiler, and an expanded source stream (where all necessary files have already been included). It produces zero or more listing files, not specified in IDL. This tool is illustrated graphically in Figure 1, with each port labeled.

The invariant structure specifies the data structures existing in main memory that are available to the algorithm and is computed automatically from the tool specification. In most cases it is the union of all the port structures. Should the algorithm require additional attributes, nodes, and/or classes temporarily, these can be added using the following syntax:

```
Tool Lister Is
    Invariant Is
        sourcefile => name: String,
                    errors: Seq Of ErrorInstance;
    End;
    Input ...
End
```

A port is a representation converter: it maps an instance of a structure in one representation into an instance of the same structure in another representation. For instance, an output port maps the instance residing in main memory into a sequence of characters written to a file. The information content is not altered, but the form may be, often dramatically.

Figure 1: The `lister` Tool

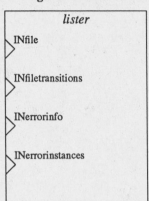

Finally, the algorithm is specified indirectly, by stating the implementation language and the location of the source code. This need not be specified initially. For example, these aspects were not specified for the `lister`.

Tools can be refined from other tools, much as structures can be refined from other structures. For example, the the implementation language for the `lister` is specified in the refined tool `ConcreteLister` (this is a new construct in IDL, as is the tool name following **End**):

```
Tool ConcreteLister Refines lister Is
    Target C;
End ConcreteLister;
```

3.2. Tool Integration

Tool integration is supported by permitting tools to be composed from other tools. A collection of tools can be grouped together, thereby forming a new tool, termed a *composite tool*. A tool not containing any tools is termed a *basic tool*, and tools contained within a composite tool are termed the *nested tools* of the composite tool. The composite tool will have its own input and output ports. It may or may not have an invariant structure (see Section 3.5), and its algorithm may be implicit or explicit (see Section 3.6). The composite tool's ports are termed the *external ports* of the tool; the *internal ports* are those of its nested tools.

Nested tools are linked together through *connections*. There are four kinds of connections, each coupling an input composite port or output nested port with an output composite port or an input nested port. Connections associate

> • an output port of one nested tool with the input port of another nested tool;
> • an input port of the composite tool with an input port of a nested tool;
> • an output port of a nested tool with an output port of the composite tool; or
> • an input port of the composite tool directly with an output port of the composite tool.

Figure 2 illustrates a tool consisting of two nested tools, the lister examined earlier and the gentransitions tool. The gentransitions tool is a basic tool, and the Lister-System, which contains gentransitions, is a composite tool. gentransitions scans an input stream, searching for include statements, which are replaced with the contents of the file named in the statement. At the same time, a data structure is built indicating the point each file was included. The composite tool, ListerSystem, has three input ports, the initial file, the error information data, and the sequence of error reports, and two output ports, the expanded source file and the include data (listing files, not specified in IDL, may also be written).

To specify connections, we use the connect construct:

Connect INfile **To** gentransitions.INfile;

In this construct, unqualified port names (e.g., INfile) refer to ports of the composite tool, while qualified port names (e.g., gentransitions.INfile) refer to ports of a nested tool. The port types and *parity* (i.e., input or output) are checked for consistency. For the ListerSystem tool, seven connections are necessary (see the appendix).

Figure 2: The ListerSystem Tool

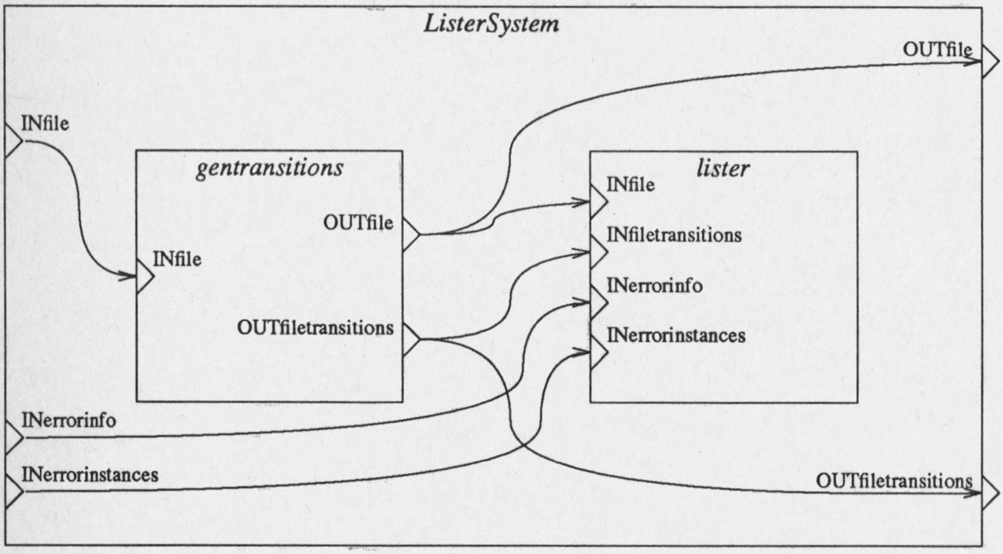

One possible representation of a nested tool is as a procedure. Each port of the nested tool would be associated with a (procedure) parameter to this procedure in this representation. The algorithm for the composite tool, if it is supplied, would call the nested tools in some order.

Composite tools can be derived from other composite tools, much as structures can be derived from other structures. The details of derivation are beyond the scope of this paper.

When the nested tools and the external ports are viewed as nodes, and the connections are viewed as directed arcs, the composite tool becomes a directed graph, termed the *structure flow graph*. This graph must be fully connected, with one or more arcs originating from each external input port, one or more arcs terminating at each external output port, and an appropriate number of arcs originating and terminating at each nested tool, corresponding to the input and output ports, respectively, of the tool. Cycles in the structure flow graph are permitted, as are arcs that originate and terminate at the same tool.

3.3. Separate Compilation

Specifications get more complex when several tools and structures are involved. To reduce compilation time, the structures and tools may be partitioned into files, each processed separately by the IDL translator. For example, the `lister`, `ConcreteLister`, and `ListerSystem` tools were all specified at once, in the source file "ListerSystem.idl". This file is processed by the IDL translator, and an intermediate representation of the structures and tools (in this case four explicit structures, three implicit structures, and four tools) is written to "ListerSystem.Cdl". This file contains an instances of the IDL structure Candle, which consists of the abstract syntax tree extensively decorated with semantic attributes [Shannon & Snodgrass 1986A]. Specific structures or tools can be extracted from this file:

Import Tool ListerSystem;

This is similar to importing Ada packages [Ada 1983] or Modula-2 modules [Wirth 1983], in that the inclusion is semantic, rather than textual as in C's "#include" [Kernighan & Ritchie 1978]. We assume that there is some mechanism, such as a configuration file, for mapping symbolic names such as "ListerSystem" into actual file names such as "/usr/softlab/src/idlc/specs/ListerSystem.Cdl". This mechanism is operating system specific and is not in the domain of IDL.

Only structures and tools defined in the outer scope of a file may be extracted by name; structures defined within a tool are extracted only when a tool referencing them is explicitly extracted. Hence, the structure `FileTransitions` and the tool `ListerSystem` may be extracted from "ListerSystem", but the tool `gentransitions` may not be extracted individually. If `ListerSystem` is in fact extracted, the following are also extracted with it. The indentation indicates the tool (or structure) that is extracted when processing another tool (or structure). For example when processing the `ConcreteLister` tool, the `lister` tool and the visible invariants for both tools must also be extracted. Visible invariants will be discussed in Section 3.5.

```
Tool ConcreteLister
        Visible Invariant for ConcreteLister
        Tool lister
                Visible Invariant for lister
Tool gentransitions
        Visible Invariant for gentransitions
Structure FileTransitions
Structure ErrorInfo
Structure ASCIIStream
Structure ErrorInstanceStream
```

As a more complex example of tool integration, consider the tool `IDLSystem`, as depicted graphically in Figure 3 and specified in the appendix. This tool is in fact a compiler implemented at UNC (for the original IDL, incidently). It is somewhat unusual in that the semantic analysis is divided into two phases, one for structures and processes, and one for assertions. `mergeErrors` is particularly simple, combining four input sequences into a single output sequence of error reports. The only explicit output of the `IDLSystem` is the `SymbolTable`; the other outputs of the compiler are not specified in IDL.

Figure 3: The `IDLSystem` Tool

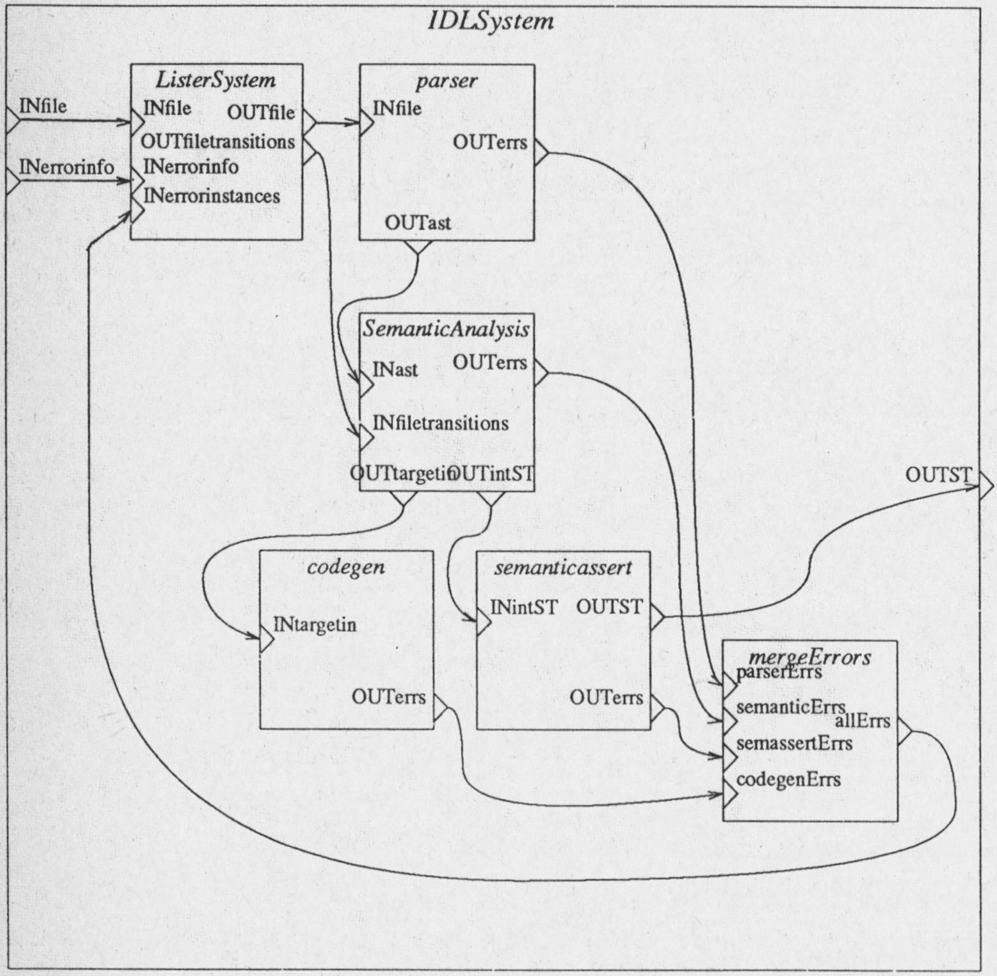

3.4. Specifying Representations

Little has been said about the form of IDL instances communicated between tools via the ports. Representations are associated with the invariants of the basic tools and with connections. An input port converts an instance in the representation associated with the connection into an instance in the representation associated with the tool invariant. Aspects of the representation of the invariant may be specified through a for clause associated with the affected structure; an example using an enumerated type representation was given in Section 2. A representation may also be associated with a connection in a for clause:

```
For parser.OUTast Use ASCIIExternalRep;
```

By naming one of the ports participating in the connection, we are indicating the connection without having to name it. Either port in a connection may be used in the for clause.

The for clause can be used in refinement. The declaration of the tool `IDLSystem2.0`, which is the program *idlc* included in release 2.0 of the UNC IDL toolkit, is as follows:

```
-- Release 2.0 of IDL System

Import Tool IDLSystem;

Tool IDLSystem2.0 Refines IDLSystem Is

    Target csh;

    For ListerSystem Use Target csh;

    --specify port modes
    For gentransitions.OUTfiletransitions Use ASCIIExternalRep;
    For parser.OUTast Use ASCIIExternalRep;
    For parser.OUTerrs Use ASCIIExternalRep;
    For semanticanalysis.OUTtargetin Use ASCIIExternalRep;
    For semanticanalysis.OUTintST Use ASCIIExternalRep;
    For semanticanalysis.OUTerrs Use ASCIIExternalRep;
    For semanticassert.OUTST Use ASCIIExternalRep;
    For semanticassert.OUTerrs Use ASCIIExternalRep;
    For codegenerator.OUTerrs Use ASCIIExternalRep;
    For lister.OUTerrs Use ASCIIExternalRep;

End IDLSystem2.0;
```

The algorithm for this tool is a cshell script [Joy 1980] that invokes each tool as a separate process. The `ASCIIExternalRep` representation is a machine, language, and structure independent format, termed the *ASCII external representation* [Nestor, et al. 1982]. As an example, a simple addition tree in this representation would be expressed as

```
L1103: binary [id plus;
               left const [value 17];
               right const [value 22]]
```

The node name (e.g., `binary`, `const`) is followed by attribute-value pairs enclosed in square brackets. The `binary` node has three attributes, `id`, `left`, and `right`; the `const` node has one attribute, `value`. This representation uses a subset of the ASCII character set, thereby ensuring that instances can be stored in files or transmitted through UNIX pipes. Such an arrangement, while somewhat inefficient, is very helpful for debugging. By using tools such as *treepr*, a graphical IDL instance printer [Butler, et al. 1985], and *treewalk*, an interactive alphanumeric instance display [Snodgrass 1985], a user can examine the instances read and written by a tool.

Higher efficiency is obtained by specifying other representations. The declaration of the tool `FasterIDLSystem`, which is another realization of the same *idlc* program, is

```
Import Tool IDLSystem;

Tool FasterIDLSystem Refines IDLSystem Is

    Target C;

    For ListerSystem Use Target C;

    --specify port modes
    For gentransitions.OUTfiletransitions Use InCore;
    For parser.OUTast Use InCore;
    For parser.OUTerrs Use InCore;
    For semanticanalysis.OUTtargetin Use InCore;
    For semanticanalysis.OUTintST Use InCore;
    For semanticanalysis.OUTerrs Use InCore;
    For semanticassert.OUTerrs Use InCore;
    For codegenerator.OUTerrs Use InCore;
    For lister.OUTerrs Use InCore;

End FasterIDLSystem;
```

This refined tool uses the InCore representation for most connections; the representation of connections that are not specified defaults to ASCIIExternalRep. The InCore representation specifies that the two linked tools transfer instances by passing node references, usually pointers to the roots of the instances, in memory. This representation requires that the tools share the same address space. Hence we are indirectly specifying that gentransitions, lister, parser, semanticanalysis, semanticassert, and codegenerator all execute in the same operating system process.

Let us compare the two refined versions of IDLSystem. Since the representations of the composite tool's ports (INfile, INErrorInfo, and OUTST) are unchanged, the observable behavior of IDLSystem2.0 and FasterIDLSystem are identical. However, FasterIDLSystem, while utilizing the same external interface and source code for the basic tools, is much more time efficient than IDLSystem2.0. It may or may not be more space efficient. Certainly there is less object code, because the complicated ASCII readers and writers have been replaced with pointer passing routines. On the other hand, since more ports have contributed to the process invariant, the number of nodes and classes in the invariant will be larger, and the node sizes may be larger, requiring more space at runtime. There is another price for time efficiency in FasterIDLSystem: debugging is now more difficult, although one can optionally link in a debug writer. However, we can instruct the IDL translator to first produce IDLSystem2.0. Once the code has been debugged, we can have FasterIDLSystem produced by the translator.

Choosing the representation for a connection involves trade-offs along several dimensions. We have already seen one aspect, that of debugging flexibility vs. runtime efficiency of the ports. Also involved are flexibility in changing the representation (i.e., early vs. late binding of the representation) and compile time efficiency. Recompilation requirements, aspects of the external representation, and many other concerns come into play. These trade-offs are related to the concept of *coupling* between representations associated with a basic tool's invariant, with connections, and with the external ports of a composite tool. Two representations are said to be *weakly coupled* if a change to one does not necessitate a change to the other (assuming that the structures themselves remain unchanged). We abuse the terminology by discussing the coupling of a port (meaning of the representation consumed by the port and of the representation produced by the port), of a basic tool and a connection (meaning of the representation of the invariant of the tool and of the representation of the connection), and even of two tools linked directly or indirectly via connections (by the transitivity of weak coupling). For example, in IDLSystem2.0, the parser tool is weakly coupled with the semanticanalysis tool, because the representation of the connection over which the AbstractSyntaxTree passes is specified as ASCIIExternalRep. The representation of an integer attribute in the parser's invariant could change, say, from 8 bits at offset 3 in the node record to 16 bits at offset 10, without affecting the representation written out by the OUTast port, which in either case is an IDL Integer.

The inverse of weak coupling is strong coupling. In FasterIDLSystem, the parser and the semanticanalysis tool are strongly coupled. These tools share the same address space and pass instances via pointer copying, so the representation must be identical, right down to the exact bit assignment of attributes in nodes. Strong coupling is also transitive.

Coupling is actually a spectrum, anchored at the extremes by weak and strong coupling. Note that coupling is *not* a unique aspect of a pair of tools: two tools can be both weakly and strongly coupled, if they are linked together over several paths.

Coupling and port object-time time efficiency are correlated: the stronger the coupling, the more efficient the port. The reason is that ports are effectively an 'impedance match' between representations. In IDLSystem2.0, the OUTast port of the parser must map the specific memory resident representation (as records, pointers, etc.) into the ASCII external language, incurring significant overhead. On the other side of the connection, the INast port of the semanticanalysis tool has to parse the instance in the ASCII external language, creating an memory resident representation that is potentially different from that of the parser. Both conversions are expensive because the representations are so different. For strongly coupled tools, there is no conversion at all to do. For moderately coupled tools, the ports have to perform some conversion, but less than for weakly coupled tools.

3.5. The Invariant Revisited

In Section 3.1, we discussed the invariant of a tool. In fact, two invariants are present. One, associated only with a basic tool, is the *visible invariant*. This is the data structure definition seen by the algorithm. Without the invariant clause, the visible invariant is by default the union of the port structures. The invariant clause allows nodes, attributes, and classes to be added to and removed from the visible invariant. Entities (i.e. nodes, classes, attributes) added to the visible invariant may be used by the algorithm, but not read in or written out by the ports. Entities removed from the visible invariant are still included in the data structure definition, but may not be accessed or modified by the algorithm. Adding and removing entities in the visible invariant allows the view of the data to be tailored to the algorithm, thereby utilizing the substantial machinery supporting the IDL model in a directed fashion. In effect, the user is describing some aspects of the algorithm to the system, which can then use this information for enhanced error checking, debugging aids, or greater efficiency.

The *process invariant* is associated with a collection of tools sharing an address space, rather than with a particular basic tool. This structure describes the layout of the IDL instances when residing in main memory. The process invariant is computed by taking the union of the port structures associated with these basic tools, and adding the entities added in the invariant clause of these tools, using the semantics of structure derivation. Hence, the visible invariant of each tool is a subset of the process invariant of that tool. In the IDLSystem tool, there are seven visible invariants, one per tool. In IDLSystem2.0, there are seven process invariants, also one per tool, since each tool is invoked as a separate process. In FasterIDLSystem, there is only one process invariant, since all share the same address space.

The interface presented to the algorithm of each tool concerns the visible invariant. The internal data structures of a process, as well as the behavior of the ports, concern the process invariant.

3.6. The Algorithm Revisited

The algorithm of a basic tool is responsible for invoking the ports, and for manipulating the IDL instances in memory described by the visible invariant. The algorithm of a composite tool has the additional responsibility of invoking the nested tools. While the algorithm of a basic tool must be supplied by the user, the algorithm of a composite tool is often quite simple. In such cases, all the processing is done within the basic tools, with the composite tool's algorithm serving only to get the right instances to the right ports. The algorithm then becomes a simple data-flow-oriented scheduler, executing each basic tool in turn until it becomes blocked on some input or output port. The IDL translator can generate such data-flow algorithms automatically.

4. Supporting the Model

The previous section explored a model of how tools can be combined in an organized fashion, and introduced several new constructs to specify the model in IDL. Once a tool has been specified in this way by the user, it must be *realized* by the IDL translator as an executable program. Realization involves several steps performed by the translator:

• syntactic and semantic checking of the specification;
• calculating representations for the structures associated with the tool;
• generating the port procedures; and
• generating the interface code the algorithms within the tools use to access the IDL instances resident in main memory.

We will first describe each step individually, and then examine some of the ways they can be ordered.

4.1. Analyzing the Specification

First, the specification is checked for syntactic correctness, using conventional parsing techniques. To fully analyze a tool, its components must be collected. If the inclusion construct discussed in Section 3.3 is used, potentially many files must be consulted. In the analysis of the file "release3.0.idl" (see Section 3.4), the following structures and tools are first gathered. Again, the indentation indicates the tool (or structure) that is extracted when processing another tool (or structure). Hence, in processing the gentransitions tool, the visible invariant structure must also be extracted.

```
Tool IDLSystem
        Structure AbstractSyntaxTree
        Structure IntSymbolTable
        Structure ErrorInstanceStream
                Structure ErrorInstance
        Structure TranslatorDataStream
                Structure TranslatorData
        Tool ListerSystem
                Tool ConcreteLister
                        Visible Invariant for ConcreteLister
                        Tool lister
```

            Visible Invariant for `lister`
      Tool `gentransitions`
          Visible Invariant for `gentransitions`
      Structure `FileTransitions`
      Structure `ErrorInfo`
      Structure `ASCIIStream`
   Structure `SymbolTable`
   Tool `parser`
      Visible Invariant for `parser`
   Tool `semanticanalysis`
      Visible Invariant for `semanticanalysis`
   Tool `semanticassert`
      Visible Invariant for `semanticassert`
   Tool `codegenerator`
      Visible Invariant for `codegenerator`
   Tool `mergeErrors`
      Visible Invariant for `mergeErrors`

a total of ten explicit structures, eight automatically computed structures (the visible invariants), and ten tools. Fortunately, these structures and tools have already been analyzed, so the post-analysis descriptions, each an instance of the IDL structure Candle [Shannon & Snodgrass 1986A], are already available.

In the next step of the analysis of the specification, algorithms for derivation and refinement are applied to compute the necessary structures, both explicit and automatically computed, and tools. In particular, the visible invariant for each newly analyzed tool and the process invariant for each identified process is computed. In this case, only one tool, `FasterIDLSystem`, and one process invariant need be computed. Most of the semantic checking occurs at this time.

4.2. Computing Representations

Representations must be computed for structures passed through external ports, for structures passed across connections, and for process invariants. The user may have already placed constraints through representation specifications (i.e., the for clause). In particular, there is little to be decided with structures specified as `ASCIIExternalRep`. InCore structures have much more latitude. The representation of an attribute may have been specified in some detail by the user (e.g., 6 bits encoding values from -20 to 40) or may have been left as an IDL basic type (e.g., Integer). Alternatively, the user may have constrained the operations permitted on an attribute (e.g., `appendrear` and `removefront` for sequences represented as streams), thereby suggesting an appropriate representation. In any case, the final representation must be determined at this time.

A related decision is the ordering of attributes within nodes, often termed *packing* [Newcomer 1986]. Several factors enter into choosing the position of an attribute:

• Attributes associated with classes must appear in the same place in every node of the class to permit efficient access.

• Non-hierarchical classes necessitate putting unused fields in some nodes. Attributes of different sizes complicate the ordering, although a graph coloring algorithm works well [Ambler & Trawick 1983, Shannon & Snodgrass 1986B].

• Lifetime analysis [Aho, et al. 1986] can be applied to attributes. If two attributes have non-overlapping lifetimes within a process invariant, they can occupy the same location within the node [Newcomer 1986]. The lifetime of an attribute is calculated by examining the structures of the input and output ports of each basic tool.

• Techniques to reduce recompilation of IDL specifications or algorithm source code may dictate where attributes are placed [Newcomer 1986].

4.3. Port Procedures

The procedure generated by the IDL translator for each port is affected primarily by the coupling of the representations and by the flexibility desired for the port (see Figure 4). For strong coupling, the port procedure is trivial. In Pascal, the OUTast output port of the parser tool in FasterIDLSystem is simply

```
procedure OUTast (this: AbstractSyntaxTree);
begin
        tempAbstractSyntaxTree := this;
end;
```

where tempAbstractSyntaxTree is a global variable of type AbstractSyntax-Tree. The input port INast of the semanticanalysis tool is

```
function INast : AbstractSyntaxTree;
begin
        INast := tempAbstractSyntaxTree;
end;
```

This is point (A) in Figure 4.

Figure 4: One Spectrum of Port Procedure Alternatives

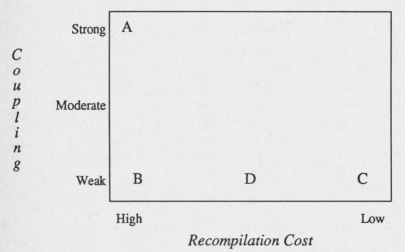

For weak coupling, there are a range of possibilities. The most expensive output port (in terms of recompilation cost) is a customized procedure (point (B)). For the OUTast port of the parser in IDLSystem2.0, a procedure is generated for each node and class type. At the other end of the spectrum (point (C)) is an interpretive writer that examines the Candle description of the structure as well as the instance residing in main memory, writing out each node as it is encountered. An intermediate position in the spectrum is a table-driven writer (point (D)); if the representation changes, the tables must be modified but the same writer is used.

In release 2.0 of the UNC IDL toolkit, ASCII external language writers are customized procedures (point (B)) while readers are table driven (point (D)) [Shannon, et al. 1985].

Coupling also affects execution efficiency of ports. Moderate coupling involves instances communicated between address spaces that are somewhat specialized to the structures that are being passed, making them more efficient to read and write. These *binary* representations [Lamb 1983] range from more efficient encodings of the ASCII external language (e.g., mapping node names to one-byte integers) to core images where all pointers have been normalized. As with recompilation cost, there is a continuum from strongly coupled fast ports to more weakly coupled slower ports.

4.4. Generating the Interface Code

The source referenced in the location construct (defined in Section 4.1) utilizes operations provided by the IDL support tools (e.g., [Shannon, et al. 1985]), including

• attribute accessing and modification;
• type conversion (e.g., *widening* a node to a class or *narrowing* a class to a subclass or node [Shannon & Snodgrass 1986B]);
• node creation and deletion; and
• sequence and set manipulation (e.g., `insertfront`, `length`).

One means of providing these operations is to define a package or module containing data structure and procedure declarations that can then be imported by the user's code. This option is available for languages such as Modula-2, Ada, and some variants of Pascal. A second means is to define a collection of macros, and is available in C and Bliss (of course, the efficiency benefits of macros are also available in some languages, such as Ada, through inline procedures). Finally, a third means is to use a special preprocessor that would use the Candle description of a tool to expand operations on IDL instances into operations in the target language. The benefits and costs of these alternatives is discussed elsewhere in the context of the C language [Shannon, et al. 1985]. As noted in Section 3.5, the interface code is generated from the visible invariant of the tool. As an example, the visible invariant of the semantic analysis tool does not include the `componentDepth` attribute of the `internal` node. This attribute would be hidden in the data structure definition if one of the first two options were used. or would generate an error from the preprocessor if accessed in the user's code, if the third option was used. Each basic tool requires its own data structure definitions (mapped into the same process invariant), because each visible invariant is unique.

4.5. Binding the Representation

Various aspects of the representation may be bound at different times. The following milestones of a tool's development may be identified:

• Basic tool specified by the user
• Basic tool specification processed
• Composite tool specified by the user
• Composite tool specification processed
• Port procedure generated
• Algorithm interface generated

- Algorithm compiled
- Tool linked
- Tool executed

A partial ordering on these milestones is imposed by the model. In particular, all the nested tool specifications must be processed before the composite tool specification is processed; a tool's specification must be processed before the algorithm interface for that tool is generated; and the port procedure and algorithm for a tool must be compiled before it is linked or executed. Other, more subtle, orderings that have significant ramifications in terms of compilation time, object-time space, and object-time time are also present. While a complete analysis is beyond the scope of this paper, we will identify a few of the more important interactions.

If two tools are weakly coupled, a change in the representation of one tool's invariant will not require regenerating and recompiling the second tool's port procedures and algorithm interface. On the other hand, if two tools are strongly coupled, a change in the representation of one tool's invariant may cause significant recompilation. If the port is table-driven, then generating the port procedure is less onerous. Node lengths may be bound at link time [Newcomer 1986]. A connection representation may be bound at object time, if the representation is specified as a parameter to the port (e.g., ASCIIExternalRep or Binary). In that case, recompilation is a function of the most strongly coupled alternative. Finally, if the port is driven from a Candle description of the structures, no recompilation at all is necessary.

5. Comparison with Other Work

This work draws on related research concerning more conventional languages. The most relevant is that on module interconnection. Generally work in this area has focussed on specifying the interconnections between separately or jointly compiled modules that reside in the same address space. Some investigators have proposed special languages for this task (e.g., MIL75 [DeRemer & Kron 1976], INTERCOL [Tichy 1979], C/Mesa [Mitchell, et al. 1979]); others have included it as part of the language (e.g., Modula-2 [Wirth 1983], Ada [Ada 1983]); and still others have defined language extensions (e.g., PIC/Ada [Wolf, et al. 1984], Anna [Luckham & von Henke 1984]). This paper proposes extensions to a language, IDL, in order to connect modules together. However, the granularity is much larger. Previous efforts specified the interaction in terms of shared variables, types, and procedures; our tools are fairly disjoint, interacting by passing usually large data structures. All these efforts utilize the concepts of encapsulation and import/export control (implicit or explicit) to describe how access to information is portioned out to interacting modules.

Polylith [Purtilo 1985] differs from these module interconnection languages in that, while the granularity of information is similar (e.g., instances of basic types, record types, and array types), the tools are much smaller, generally consisting of individual procedures. The tools described in this paper, as well as the data structures communicated between tools, are larger. The techniques described here and in Polylith both support tools in separate address spaces and utilize interface specifications that are separate from the algorithmic portion of the tool.

ToolPack [Osterweil & Clemm 1983] shares our emphasis on the structures passed among tools, rather than on the tools themselves: tools in both systems are described in terms of the objects they produce and the objects they consume. Our approach differs from ToolPack in the degree of specification of the data objects. By using IDL, structures can be described precisely, down to minute representational aspects. Such specifications allow the ports to be automatically tailored to the structures they read or write. On the other hand, ToolPack provides more management support, in terms of a file system and a command language interface.

The approach proposed in the Illinois Software Engineering Program (ISEP) for tool integration is similar to ours [Kaplan, et al. 1986]. In particular, their concept of "sort" is analogous to our "structure" and their "sort morphism conversion function" is analogous to our "port". In their model the algorithm of the tool may also be specified. Our model is more specific concerning what the ports actually do and how they can be specified and automatically generated.

6. Conclusion and Future Work

In this paper, we proposed a model of tool integration intermediate to the monolithic and toolkit approach. The IDL language was extended to specify this kind of integration. The new model allows tools to be composed from existing tools. A composite tool can be formed by grouping a collection of existing tools. The nested tools are linked through connections. Representations for connections can be specified with for clauses. Such a specification is an example of refinement of a tool.

Representation choices for connections involve flexibility-efficiency trade-offs. These trade-offs are related to the concept of coupling between representations associated with a basic tool's invariant. Weakly coupled representations are more flexible because a change to one representation does not necessitate a change to the other. Hence, the mapping performed by a weakly coupled port is less affected by changing a representation. However, the mapping is less efficient because the representations are less similar. Strongly coupled representations can be more efficiently mapped but are less flexible.

The model also allows the specification of the algorithm. In some cases, the algorithm can be generated automatically. This is possible for composite tools where the algorithm is a simple data-flow-oriented scheduler.

Our new model meets the requirements we set in Section 3. First, it preserves the conceptual integrity of IDL. It is simple and declarative. In addition, it is strongly typed. For example, port connections can be easily checked at compile-time for consistency. Secondly, the model supports derivation and refinement of tools analogously to derivation and refinement of structures. This powerful specification technique is quite useful in system descriptions. Finally, the model allows efficient implementation. Separate compilation is possible through inclusion constructs. Higher object-time efficiency is obtained by specifying strongly coupled representations for connections.

There are two fundamental directions that should be pursued next. The first is pragmatic: the proposal should be implemented and the engineering trade-offs hinted at throughout the paper should be addressed in a comprehensive manner. The UNC IDL Toolkit supports the full language as described in the Version 2 document. It utilizes the Candle intermediate representation. We plan to implement the extensions discussed in this paper over the next six months. Of particular concern is the *big inhale* [Conradi & Vanvik 1985], i.e., the reading of many files that occurs whenever a complex structure in analyzed. For example, Section 4.1 showed that, in analyzing `FasterIDLSystem`, 28 entities (structures or tools) from nine files had to be assimilated by the IDL translator. This component of the processing promises to be expensive in terms of compilation time and I/O requirements. A second problem is that changing a single structure can cause massive recompilation of refined and derived structures and tools using that structure. Fortunately, techniques developed for other languages appear to be applicable here [Borison 1986, Rudmik & Moore 1982, Tichy & Baker 1985].

The second direction is more conceptual: the model should be extended to incorporate those situations not adequately dealt with in the present model. As one possible area of extension, the model now assumes that tools execute sequentially, or in a coroutine fashion, even when they share an address space. There is no provision for one tool invoking a procedure of another tool. Nestor has made a proposal for extensions to IDL that addresses this situation and appears to be consistent with the extensions discussed here [Nestor 1986]. A similar topic concerns incremental ports. The model is organized around the concept of a tool interacting with its environment only through ports reading or writing complete structures. A less restrictive model may be desirable.

7. Acknowledgement

Discussions with John Nestor and Joseph Newcomer of the Software Engineering Institute were quite helpful in developing these concepts. In particular, John Nestor pointed out the usefulness of removing entities from the visible invariant, and showed how to support cycles in the structure flow graph. John and Joseph both showed us aspects of lifetime analysis, and helped us develop a precise definition of a port. David Lamb, Anund Lie, and John Nestor also provided useful comments on a previous draft of this paper.

References

[Ada 1983] *Reference Manual for the Ada Programming Language.* (ANSI/MIL-STD-1815A) ed. United States Department of Defense, Washington, D.C., 1983.

[Aho, et al. 1986] Aho, A.V., R. Sethi and J.D. Ullman. *Compilers: Principles, Techniques and Tools.* Reading, Massachusetts: Addison Wesley, 1986.

[Ambler & Trawick 1983] Ambler, A. and R. Trawick. *Chatin's Graph Coloring Algorithm as a Method for Assigning Positions to Diana Attributes. ACM SIGPlan Notices,* 18, No. 2, Feb. 1983, pp. 37-78.

[Borison 1986] Borison, E. *A Model of Software Manufacture.* in *Proceedings of the International Workshop on Advanced Programming Environments,* IFIP WG 2.4. Trondheim, Norway: June 1986.

[Butler 1983] Butler, K.J. *DIANA Past, Present, and Future.* in *Lecture Notes in Computer Science Ada Software Tools Interfaces,* Ed. G. Goos and J. Hartmanis. Workshop, Bath: Springer-Verlag, 1983, pp. 3-22.

[Butler, et al. 1985] Butler, N., J. Curry, S. Konstant and D. Rosenblum. *Treepr Users Manual.* SoftLab Document No. 4. Computer Science Department, University of North Carolina at Chapel Hill. May 1985.

[Conradi & Vanvik 1985] Conradi, R. and D.H. Wanvik. *Mechanisms and Tools for Separate Compilation.* Technical Report 25/85. The University of Trondheim, The Norwegian Institute of Technology. October 1985.

[DeRemer & Kron 1976] DeRemer, F. and H.H. Kron. *Programming-in-the-Large vs. Programming-in-the-Small. IEEE Transactions on Software Engineering,* SE-2, No. 2, June 1976, pp. 80-86.

[Deitel 1984] Deitel, H.M. *An Introduction to Operating Systems.* Reading, MA: Addison-

Wesley, 1984.

[Gilman 1986] Gilman, A.S. *VHDL--The Designer Environment. IEEE Design and Test,* , Apr. 1986, pp. 42-47.

[Goos, et al. 1983] Goos, G., W.A. Wulf, A. Evans and Butler. K.J. . *DIANA An Intermediate Language for Ada.* Vol. 161 of Lecture Notes in Computer Science. Springer-Verlag, 1983.

[Habermann 1979] Habermann, A.N. *Tools for Software System Construction*, in Software Development Tools. Pingree Park, Co: Springer-Verlag, 1979. pp. 10-21.

[Joy 1980] Joy, W. *An Introduction to the C Shell.* Dept. of EE and Computer Science, UCB, 1980.

[Kaplan, et al. 1986] Kaplan, S.M., R.H. Campbell, M.T. Harandi, R.E. Johnson, S.N. Kamin, J.W.S. Liu and J.M. Purtilo. *An Architecture for Tool Integration.* in *Proceedings of the International Workshop on Advanced Programming Environments*, IFIP WG 2.4. Trondheim, Norway: June 1986.

[Kernighan & Ritchie 1978] Kernighan, B.W. and D.M. Ritchie. *The C Programming Language.* Englewood Cliffs, NJ: Prentice-Hall, 1978.

[Kernighan & Mashey 1981] Kernighan, B.W. and J.R. Mashey. *The Unix Programming Environment. Computer,* 14, No. 4, Apr. 1981, pp. 12-24.

[Kickenson 1986] Kickenson, J.S. *An IDL Assertion Checker.* Computer Science Department, University of North Carolina at Chapel Hill, Aug. 1986. SoftLab Document No. 28.

[Lamb 1983] Lamb, D.A. *Sharing Intermediate Representations: The Interface Description Language.* PhD. Diss. Computer Science Department, Carnegie-Mellon University, May 1983.

[Luckham & von Henke 1984] Luckham, D.C. and F.W. von Henke. *An Overview of Anna, a Specification Language for Ada.* in *Proceedings of the IEEE Computer Society 1984 Conference on Ada Applications and Environments*, St. Paul, MN: Oct. 1984, pp. 116-127.

[Mitchell, et al. 1979] Mitchell, J.G., W. Maybury and R. Sweet. *Mesa Language Manual Version 5.0.* Technical Report CSL-79-3. Xerox PARC. Apr. 1979.

[Nestor, et al. 1982] Nestor, J.R., W.A. Wulf and D.A. Lamb. *IDL Formal Description, Draft Revision 2.0.* Technical Report. Computer Science Department, Carnegie-Mellon University. June 1982.

[Nestor 1986] Nestor, J.R. *Revised Process Model for IDL.* 1986. (Informal presentation, SEI-UNC Workshop on IDL, Kiawah Island, SC.)

[Newcomer 1986] Newcomer, J.M. *IDL: Future Directions.* in *Proceedings of the International Workshop on Advanced Programming Environments*, IFIP WG 2.4. Trondheim, Norway: June 1986.

[Notkin 1985] Notkin, D. *The GANDALF Project. Journal of Systems and Software*, 5, No. 2, May 1985, pp. 91-106.

[Osterweil & Clemm 1983] Osterweil, L. and G. Clemm. *The Toolpack/IST Approach To Extensibility In Software Environments*. in *Lecture Notes in Computer Science Ada Software Tools Interfaces*, Ed. G. Goos and J. Hartmanis. Workshop, Bath : Springer-Verlag, 1983, pp. 133-163.

[Purtilo 1985] Purtilo, J. *Polylith: An Environment to Support Management of Tool Interfaces*. in *Proceedings of the ACM SIGPlan '85 Symposium on Language Issues in Programming Environments*, Seattle, WA: July 1985, pp. 12-18.

[Reiss 1985] Reiss, S.P. *PECAN: Program Development Systems that Support Multiple Views. IEEE Transactions on Software Engineering*, SE-11, No. 3, Mar. 1985, pp. 276-285.

[Reps & Teitelbaum 1984] Reps, T. and T. Teitelbaum. *The Synthesizer Generator*. in *Proceedings of the ACM SIGSOFT/SIGPLAN Software Engineering Symposium on Practical Software Development Environments*, Ed. P. Henderson. Association for Computing Machinery. Pittsburgh, PA: ACM, May 1984, pp. 42-48.

[Rudmik & Moore 1982] Rudmik, A. and B.G. Moore. *An Efficient Separate Compilation Strategy for Very Large Programs*. in *Proceedings of the Symposium on Compiler Construction*, Boston, MA: June 1982, pp. 301-307.

[Shannon & Snodgrass 1985] Shannon, K. and R. Snodgrass. *Listers Users Manual*. SoftLab Document No. 11. Computer Science Department, University of North Carolina at Chapel Hill. Sep. 1985.

[Shannon, et al. 1985] Shannon, K., T. Maroney and R. Snodgrass. *Using IDL with C*. SoftLab Document No. 6. Computer Science Department, University of North Carolina at Chapel Hill. May 1985.

[Shannon & Snodgrass 1986A] Shannon, K. and R. Snodgrass. *Candle: Common Attributed Notation for Interface Description*. SoftLab Document No. 26. Computer Science Department, University of North Carolina at Chapel Hill. Jan. 1986.

[Shannon & Snodgrass 1986B] Shannon, K. and R. Snodgrass. *Mapping the Interface Description Language Type Model into C*. SoftLab Document No. 24. Computer Science Department, University of North Carolina at Chapel Hill. Mar. 1986.

[Snodgrass 1985] Snodgrass, R., editor *IDL Manual Entries (Version 2.0)*. SoftLab Document No. 15. Computer Science Department, University of North Carolina at Chapel Hill. Dec. 1985.

[Teitelbaum et al. 1981] Teitelbaum, T., T. Reps and S. Horwitz. *The Why and Wherefore of the Cornell Program Synthesizer*. in *Proceedings of the ACM SigPlan SigOA Symposium on Text Manipulation*, Association for Computing Machinery. Portland, OR: acm, june 1981, pp. 8-16.

[Tichy 1979] Tichy, W.F. *Software Development Control Based on Module Interconnection*. in *Proceedings of the Fourth International Conference on Software Engineering*,

Munich, West Germany: Sep. 1979, pp. 29-41.

[Tichy & Baker 1985] Tichy, W.F. and M.C. Baker. *Smart Recompilation.* in *Proceedings of the 1985 Conference on Principles of Programming Languages,* Association for Computing Machinery. Jan. 1985, pp. 236-244.

[Warren, et al. 1985] Warren, W.B., J. Kickenson and R. Snodgrass. *A Tutorial Introduction to Using IDL.* Softlab Document No. 1. Computer Science Department, University of North Carolina at Chapel Hill. Dec. 1985.

[Wirth 1983] Wirth, N. *Programming in Modula-2, 2nd Edition.* of Texts and Monographs in Computer Science. Springer-Verlag, 1983.

[Wolf, et al. 1984] Wolf, A.L., L.A. Clarke and J.C. Wileden. *An Ada Environment for Programming-In-The-Large.* in *Proceedings of the IEEE Computer Society 1984 Conference on Ada Applications and Environments,* St. Paul, MN: Oct. 1984.

[Zorn 1985] Zorn, B. *Experiences with Ada Code Generation.* Technical Report UCB/CSD 85/249. University of California, Berkeley. June 1985.

Listings

Several IDL specifications referenced in the text are collected in this appendix. For conciseness, specifications of most basic structures are omitted.

ListerSystem.idl

```
Import Structure FileTransitions;
Import Structure ErrorInfo;
Import Structure ASCIIStream;
Import Structure ErrorInstanceStream;

Tool lister Is
        Invariant Is
            sourcefile => name: String,
                         errors: Seq Of ErrorInstance;
        End;
        Input INerrorinfo: ErrorInfo;
        Input INfiletransitions: FileTransitions;
        Input INerrorinstances: ErrorInstanceStream;
        Input INfile: ASCIIStream;
        --- also produces listing files
End;

Tool ConcreteLister Refines lister Is
    Target C;
    Location "lister";
End ConcreteLister;

Tool ListerSystem Is

    Tool gentransitions Is
      Target C;
```

```
    Location "gentransitions";

    Input INfile: ASCIIStream;
    Output OUTfiletransitions: FileTransitions;
    Output OUTfile: ASCIIStream;
End gentransitions;

Tool ConcreteLister;

Input INfile: ASCIIStream;
Input INerrorinfo: ErrorInfo;
Input INerrorinstances: ErrorInstanceStream;
Output OUTfiletransitions: FileTransitions;
Output OUTfile: ASCIIStream;
-- also creates listing files

Connect   INfile To gentransitions.INfile,
          gentransitions.OUTfile To ConcreteLister.INfile,
          gentransitions.OUTfile TO OUTfile,
          gentransitions.OUTfiletransitions To OUTfiletransitions,
          gentransitions.OUTfiletransitions
                  To ConcreteLister.INfiletransitions,
          INerrorinfo To ConcreteLister.INerrorinfo,
          INerrorinstances To ConcreteLister.INerrorinstances;


End ListerSystem;
```

IdlSystem.idl


```
-- IDL declarations for the IDL System

Import Structure SymbolTable;
Import Structure ASCIIStream;
Import Structure ErrorInfo;

Tool IDLSystem Is

    -- structure declarations

    Import Structure AbstractSyntaxTree;
    Import Structure IntSymbolTable;
    Import Structure ErrorInstanceStream;
    Import Structure TranslatorDataStream;

    -- tool declarations

    Import Tool ListerSystem;

    Tool parser Is
       Target C;
       Location "frontend";

       Input INfile: ASCIIStream;
       Output OUTast: AbstractSyntaxTree;
       Output OUTerrs: ErrorInstanceStream;
    End;

    Tool semanticanalysis Is
       Invariant Is
           NT ::= UnknownNT;
           UnknownNT =>;
           Without internal => componentDepth;
       End;
       Target C;
       Location "semantic";

       Input INast: AbstractSyntaxTree;
       Input INfiletransitions: FileTransitions;
       Output OUTtargetin: TranslatorDataStream;
       Output OUTintST: IntSymbolTable;
```

```
      Output OUTerrs: ErrorInstanceStream;
   End;

   Tool semanticassert Is
      Target C;
      Location "semanticassert";
      Input INintST: IntSymbolTable;
      Output OUTST: SymbolTable;
      Output OUTerrs: ErrorInstanceStream;
   End;

   Tool codegenerator Is
      Invariant Is
         flags ::= GSELF | WSELF | MSELF;
         GSELF =>; WSELF =>; MSELF=>;
      End;
      Target C;
      Location "backend";

      Input INtargetin: TranslatorDataStream;
      Output OUTerrs: ErrorInstanceStream;
      -- also produces code
   End;

   Tool mergeErrors Is
      Target C;
      Location "mergeerrors";

      Input parserErrs: ErrorInstanceStream;
      Input semanticErrs: ErrorInstanceStream;
      Input semassertErrs: ErrorInstanceStream;
      Input codegenErrs: ErrorInstanceStream;
      Output allErrs: ErrorInstanceStream;
   End;

   -- input and output port declarations

   Input INfile: ASCIIStream;
   Input INErrorInfo: ErrorInfo;
   Output OUTST: SymbolTable;

   -- link declarations

   Connect   INfile To ListerSystem.INfile,
             ListerSystem.OUTfile To parser.INfile,
             OUTST To semanticassert.OUTST,
             parser.OUTast To semanticanalysis.INast,
             parser.OUTerrs To mergeErrors.parserErrs,
             ListerSystem.OUTfiletransitions
                     To semanticananalysis.INfiletransitions,
             semanticanalysis.OUTtargetin To codegenerator.INtargetin,
             semanticanalysis.OUTintST To semanticassert.INintST,
             semanticanalysis.OUTerrs To mergeErrors.semanticErrs,
             semanticassert.OUTerrs To mergeErrors.semassertErrs,
             codegenerator.OUTerrs To mergeErrors.codegenErrs,
             mergeErrors.AllErrs To ListerSystem.INerrorinstances;
End IDLSystem;
```

Views for Tools in Integrated Environments

David Garlan
Department of Computer Science
Carnegie-Mellon University
Pittsburgh, Pa. 15213 USA

Abstract

This paper addresses the problem of building tools for integrated programming environments. Integrated environments have the desirable property that the tools in it can
share a database of common structures. But they have the undesirable property that
these tools are hard to build because typically a single representation of the database
must serve all tools. The solution proposed in this work allows tools to maintain appropriate representations or "views" of the objects they manipulate while retaining the
benefits of shared access to common structures. We illustrate the approach with two
examples of tools for an environment for programming-in-the-large, and outline current
work in progress on efficient implementations of these ideas.

1 Introduction

This paper addresses the problem of building tools for integrated programming environments in which component tools can share a database of common structures [Notkin
86, Reps 84, Reiss 84, Donzeau-Gouge 84a]. In these environments the common database
allows close cooperation between tools; the effects of one tool on an object in the shared
database can immediately be seen and acted upon by the other tools in the environment.
But it has the undesirable effect that tools in the environment are hard to build because typically a single representation of the database must serve all tools. The representation that a
semantic analyzer requires, for example, may produce a poor interface for a structure editor,
and conversely. What is needed is a way to retain the benefits of tool cooperation through
sharing while at the same time allowing each tool to interact with a representation of the
database that suits its needs.

The solution proposed in this paper is to allow an implementor to associate with each tool a
collection of "views" of the objects it seeks to manipulate. A view is a virtual description of
the common database, defined in such a way that objects can be shared among a collection
of tools, each tool accessing objects through the views it defines. The common database
then becomes the *synthesis* of all of the views defined by the tools in the environment.

This research was supported in part by the United States Army, Software Technology Development Division
of CECOM COMM/ADP, Fort Monmouth, NJ. and in part by ZTI-SOF of Siemens Corporation, Munich
Germany.

In the following sections we describe view mechanisms that in combination lead to a substantial improvement in the ability to produce environments of integrated tools. We begin by characterizing the use of views as a synthesis of two common models of tool integration. Next we discuss the view mechanisms and show how views can be composed into working systems of integrated tools. Then we illustrate the potential of this approach by showing how views can be used to define tools for programming-in-the-large. We describe two implementations of views that are currently under development. Finally, we summarize by showing how these ideas unify and extend other related work in the area of tool integration.

2 The View-Oriented Model of Tool Integration

Current approaches to tool integration are frequently variations on two widely accepted models. One approach, illustrated in figure 1, might be characterized as the *sequential* model. Here tools communicate in stages through well-defined interfaces. The output of one tool becomes the input of another tool, perhaps with some transformation involved at each end. Examples of such systems are Unix™ pipes [Thompson 78], the Programmer's Work Bench [Dolotta 77], the common edit-compile-debug loop of traditional software environments, and systems based on IDL readers and writers [Nestor 86].

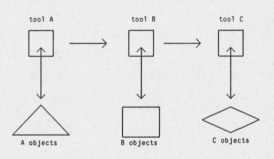

Figure 1: The Sequential Model of Tool Integration

For an implementor there are a number of advantages to this approach, including:

- Appropriate representation: Tools maintain representations of data that are appropriate for their individual needs.

- Encapsulation: The implementor of one tool need not be familiar with the implementation details of the other tools in the environment.

- Abstraction: Dependencies between tools are simplified since tools access other tools through well-defined interfaces.

- Protection: A tool can operate freely on private data representations without interference from other tools.

- Evolution: It is relatively easy to augment the functionality of existing tools or to encorporate new tools in a system.

- Reusability: If the input/output formats are simple enough then it may be possible to use a tool in a wide variety of contexts.

- Composability: Simple input/output formats make it relatively easy to compose a tool in sequence with other tools. (Consider, for example, the success of the tools under Unix that adopt a simple character stream as the primary form of tool communication.)

But there are also a number of disadvantages, including:

- Batch orientation: A tool may have to wait for the entire output of another tool before it can proceed. (This is, of course, not true for *all* sequentially-oriented tools, Unix pipes being an example to the contrary.)

- Redundancy: Tools may be forced to create and maintain duplicate representations of data. Tool functionality may also be duplicated.

- Expense: Communication may require expensive transformations between tools. Parsing textual input, for example, is a common aspect of many tools.

- Uni-directionality: Communication is primarily in only one direction.

A second approach, illustrated in figure 2, might be characterized as the *concurrent* model. Here tools communicate through shared access to a common database of programming objects. The results of an operation performed by one tool can immediately be "seen" by all other tools, which in turn can contribute to that operation. Frequently, although not necessarily, the form of the shared database is an attributed abstract syntax tree. Examples of this approach include virtually all structure editor-based environments [Notkin 86, Reps 84, Reiss 84, Donzeau-Gouge 84a], and some knowledge representation systems (such as Balzer's [Balzer 85]).

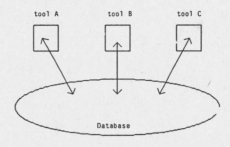

Figure 2: The Concurrent Model of Tool Integration

The advantages of this approach are:

- Cooperation: Tools can cooperate in providing functionality. For example, the creation of an object in the database might trigger a number of tools, each tool implementing some aspect of object initialization.

- Sharing: Neither data nor tool functionality need be replicated. Common data is shared through the database; common functionality need only be provided by one of the cooperating tools.

- Kernel support: A database manager can provide support for tool invocation, information retrieval, and a rich set of primitive datatypes (lists, tables, sets, etc.), as well as guaranteeing the structural integrity of the database. This makes the construction of tools simpler, since they need not provide these facilities themselves. It also benefits the user by supporting a common interface to all tools, and implicit, data-driven invocation of those tools [Notkin 86].

The disadvantages are the dual of the advantages in the sequential model:

- No support for abstraction: Since all tools have access to all data representations there is little that an implementor can do to provide protection, encapsulation and abstraction of data for individual tools.

- Inappropriate representations: It may be difficult, if not impossible, to find common representations that simultaneously satisfy all tools.

- Constraints on evolution: It may be difficult to add new tools to an environment once a particular set of representations is chosen. Moreover, it may be hard to change the functionality of an existing tool in isolation from other tools, since there is such tight coupling between the tools.

- Limited reusability: While the code associated with kernel support for the shared database may be reused in different environments, the tools themselves usually cannot. This is because the description of a tool is closely tied to the structure of a particular environment database and to the other tools in the environment.

In this paper we propose a third approach that we term the *view-oriented* model. It is illustrated in figure 3. In this model tools access a common object-oriented database through an interface called a *view*, which defines a virtual representation of the database. The system synthesizes all views of an object to produce a composite representation of that object in the shared database. Views allow a tool to define an appropriate structural interface to the database and to other tools, but at the same time allow concurrent access to a shared representation. This provides the advantages of both models. Adding a new tool to an environment is largely a matter of defining a new view. Tools can evolve by changing their views without necessarily affecting other tools. And yet each tool can immediately see the effects of other tools and can cooperate with those tools in providing functionality. The disadvantage of this approach is that in order for the system to merge the various views of an object, there may be restrictions on the freedom with which a tool can define its own views of shared objects. As we will try to show in the remaining sections, for many applications the benefits of using views far outweigh this disadvantage.

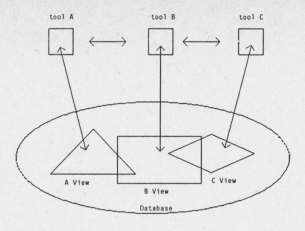

Figure 3: The View-oriented Model of Tool Integration

3 Static Views

We take as our starting point the well established fact that certain programming environments can be automatically generated from a formal description, or grammar of the language to be supported by the environment, together with a description of the actions that
should take place to support the various tools in the environment (semantic analysis, run-
time system, *etc.*). The grammar is typically an extended form of BNF, while the description
of actions consists of a collection of either attribute equations [Reps 83] or action routines
[Ambriola 84]. The formal description of a particular programming language and its associated tools is combined with a language-independent kernel to produce an environment
that supports the construction of programs in that language. The kernel provides such
facilities as a user interface (often in the form of a structure editor), maintenance of a shared
database of program objects (usually in the form of an abstract syntax tree), support for the
invocation of operations associated with objects in the database, and an interface to a file
system [Notkin 86].

Figure 4 illustrates a portion of such a formal description. With a few notable differences it
resembles the descriptions found in a typical grammar used for generating a programming
environment (such as [Medina-Mora 82] or [Reps 84]). The description contains a collection
of productions: non-terminals (*eg.*, PROC-DECL), terminals (*eg.*, PROC-NAME), and unions
(*eg.*, PROC-STATUS). Each non-terminal production has a list of components, where each
component is another production or a typed collection of productions such as "sequence".[1]

---

[1] The choice of "collection" types that can be used to define a component of a non-terminal production is
somewhat arbitrary; our system includes the types "sequence", "array", "table", "sorted-table", "set", and
"unary". The latter is the special case of a collection containing only one production.

A terminal production is one of a set of primitive terminal types.[2] Associated with each production is one or more "unparse" schemes to indicate how the structures should be displayed to a user [Garlan 85]. A complete description would also contain an operational component in the form of action routines and/or attribute equations (for example, to set the *status* component). The operational component will be considered in more detail later (Section 6). The primary notational differences between this formalism and more typical descriptions are (a) subcomponents of a non-terminal are named, (b) there is no notational distinction between the subcomponents of a non-terminal and its attributes (*eg.*, the *status* component of PROC-DECL would probably be represented as an attribute in most systems), and (c) the notation supports a rich collection of component types, in the style of IDL (*viz.*, sequence, set, *etc.*).

```
PROC-DECL    ::=   name: PROC-NAME
                   params: seq of PARAM
                   decls: seq of DECL
                   body: PROC-BODY
                   status: PROC-STATUS

       Equations: .....

       Unparse: "Procedure <name> (<params>) ....."

   PROC-NAME    ::= identifier

   PROC-STATUS ::= UNTOUCHED | DIRTY | COMPILED
   ....
```

Figure 4: A Portion of a Grammar

We diverge from existing approaches to environment generation in that we allow a system to be specified by not one, but by a collection of formal descriptions called *static views*.[3] As we will see, each static view implements a logical unit of functionality for a system. Collections of views may be bundled together and given an interface, which is another view. These bundled collections of views are called *features* and are discussed in the next section. Here we describe the way in which view descriptions produce "shared" descriptions of objects. As we will see, the novel aspect of views lies in the fact that the type of an object defined in one view can be combined with the types defined in other views to produce a composite type that simultaneously satisfies each view description. We call this *view sharing*.

---

[2]Again, the choice of terminal types is somewhat arbitrary; our system supports "integer", "text", "real", "identifier".

[3]Some systems such as ALOE [Gandalf 84] and Mentor [Donzeau-Gouge 84b] allow multiple grammars, but all but one of these grammars are strictly auxiliary grammars for describing attributes and are independent of the "primary" abstract syntax description. The one notable exception is the system proposed by Notkin [Notkin 84], which would support multiple grammars, although those grammars are combined in quite different ways from those described in this paper.

3.1 A Simple Example

An example should help illustrate view sharing. Figure 5 shows a specification of PROC-DECL in both the *Semantics* and the *Code* views.[4] The two views agree in the definition of certain components but not in others. Assuming that the two views are to share in the definition of PROC-DECL, the contents of the *name* component will be the same in both views. The *decls* component will also represent the same collection of objects in both views, but will be treated as a linked sequence in the *Code* view and as a hash table in the *Semantics* view.[5] When a new element is added, modified, or deleted in the *decl* sequence in the *Code* view, a corresponding addition, modification, or deletion will automatically take place in the *decl* table of the semantic view. Note that in current integrated environments a semantic tool would have to choose between sharing the representation used in the *Code* view or copying the information into a more appropriate form for its own use. In the first case we have sharing at the expense of inefficient access; in the second we have duplicated information together with the burden of maintaining consistency between the two representations.

```
View Code-View
        ....
        PROC-DECL ::=  name: PROC-NAME
                       params: seq of PARAM
                       decls: seq of DECL
                       ....

        .....

View Semantics-View
        ....
        PROC-DECL ::=  name: PROC-NAME
                       decls: table of DECL indexed by .decl-var
                       checked: CHECK-STATUS
                       ....

        .....
```

Figure 5: Two Views of the PROC-DECL Object

This example raises a number of questions. To what extent can different views specify different representations? What is the meaning of an operation performed through a view, given the existence other views? How does the system know which object definitions are meant to be different views of the same object? We answer the first two questions in the remainder of this section, and we return to the third question in the following section.

3.2 Compatibility

The ability of multiple views to define different but shared representations of objects is based on a notion of type *compatibility*. Roughly stated, two types are compatible if there exists a mapping between the operations of one type and the operations of the other. The formal details are described in [Garlan 86a]. Here we summarize the main ideas.

---

[4]In the examples used in this paper, view names are distinguished syntactically by the postfix "-View". This is simply a notational device to make the meanings clearer; any name can be used for a view.

[5]We are assuming, for simplicity, that a DECL has the form "DECL :: = decl-var: DECL-TYPE ...".

The primary motivation behind a definition of type compatibility is to provide the environment kernel with a way of inferring operational correspondences between two views of the same object. As we will see, this allows the system to *automatically* maintain consistency across views. It also allows an implementor to combine arbitrary views without having to know the details of the implementations of those views; since the system can statically determine view correspondences in an environment-independent way, no implementor-supplied mappings are needed. However, if desired, an implementor can also supply additional tool-specific mappings using the mechanisms of dynamic views, discussed in Section 5.

The definition of compatibility for views proceeds in three steps. First, we define compatibility for the base type constructors that are used in the description of the fields of a non-terminal production. Second, we extend this to a definition of compatibility between two productions. Third, we define compatibility for collections of productions, or views.

The collection of productions in a view can be seen as a system of types. The types are formed out of the primitive types (integer, real, string, *etc.*), the two basic type constructors *record* and *union*, and some number of *collection* type constructors (sequence, set, table, array, unary, *etc.*). Primitives, records, and unions correspond to the basic terminals, non-terminals, and unions, respectively. Collection type constructors define the types of the components of a non-terminal. By adopting the "types are values" approach of Donahue and Demers [Donahue 85] we can treat these types as collections of operators. The primitive types support the usual scalar type operators: integer addition, string concatenation, *etc.* The record type provides accessor operators for its fields. The collection types provide operators that depend on the nature of these types. For example, the type "sequence" might provide "append", "prepend", "nth", *etc.* The type "table" might provide "enter", "remove", "lookup", *etc.*

We begin by defining compatibility between the collection types (set, sequence, *etc.*) that define components of a non-terminal production (*viz.*, the fields of a record type). We say that two such types are *compatible* if there exists a pair of signature-preserving mappings between the operators of one type and the operators of the other. (If the types are T_1 and T_2, then one mapping associates operators of T_1 with operators of T_2; the other mapping associates operators of T_2 with those of T_1.) By *signature preserving*, we mean that under the mapping the new parameters are of the correct type for the new operator. For example, we might decide that the "enter" operation of type table is mapped to the "prepend" operation of the type sequence. We allow that an operator of one type can be mapped to a "do nothing" function, which is implicitly considered to be an operator of every type.

Several things should be noted about this definition of type compatibility. First, compatibility will depend on what we take to be the operations defining the types. Second, the pair of maps between two types need not be inverses. Third, the maps are not unique. For example, we could just as easily have mapped the "enter" operation of type "table" to the "append" operation of type "sequence". Fourth, their are no semantic constraints placed on the mapping. One could, for instance, map all of the operations of one type to the "do nothing" function of another. Fifth, these mappings are independent of the productions in which the base type occur. Thus they can be specified in advance by an implementor of a view compiler and later applied to a given environment description.

Once we have defined type compatibility between the types that determine the *components* of a non-terminal production we can define compatibility between any two *productions*. We say that two *non-terminal* productions are compatible if the types of each common component are compatible. A component is said to be *common* to two productions if it has the same name in each. In the previous example, the two definitions of PROC-DECL would be compatible if the *name* and the *decls* components were compatible. The former is trivially compatible (by the identity map); the compatibility between the "seq" and "table" collection types would have been determined in advance by the implementor of the view compiler. To complete the picture, we say that two *union* productions are compatible if they contain the same production names and two *terminal* productions are compatible if their primitive types are the same type.

Type compatibility extends to views - that is, collections of productions - as follows. If two views are designated as "shared" (in a way to be described in the next section), then any two productions with the same name in each are taken to be shared descriptions of the same object type. For instance, if the *Code* and *Semantics* views illustrated earlier are designated shared views then the PROC-DECL productions in each view are taken to be shared descriptions. Since the compatibility mappings are specified in advance, a view compiler can determine whether two shared views are compatible simply by checking for type compatibility between the productions common to each.[6]

Type compatibility also provides an operational interpretation of a shared view of an object. Any operation performed on an object in the system is invoked with respect to a particular view of the database. That is, every operation on an object is of the form <view, op>. Whenever an operation is performed through one view, the view kernel guarantees that the corresponding operation (as determined by the compatibility maps) is performed for each of the shared views of the object. It is as if the system maintains a separate representation for each view. In practice, of course, components of objects can in many cases be physically shared between views (*eg.*, the *name* component of PROC-DECL in Figure 5).

3.3 Consistency

The definition of type compatibility is weak in the sense that it imposes no semantic constraints on the definition of compatibility between types. Intuitively, however, we would very much like it to be the case that shared views actually refer to the same objects even though the ways in which those objects may be accessed or manipulated may differ across the views. We would expect, for example, that if a declaration is added to the *decls* component in the *Code* view of a PROC-DECL, it would also appear in the table representing the *Semantics* view of the *decls* component. To capture this notion we introduce the concept of view *consistency*. Loosely speaking, we say that a set of compatibility mappings together with an implementation for those types is consistent provided that the effect of performing an operation on one view of an object is the same has having performed the corresponding operation — where "correspondence" is determined by the compatibility mappings — in any

---

[6]Note that while the set of primitive and constructor types is open ended, for a given implementation of views it will be fixed set with a fixed set of compatibility mappings.

other view of the object. The reader is referred to [Garlan 86a] for a formal treatment of this idea.

Demonstrating that a particular system is consistent, in the sense just outlined, is a non-trivial matter. It involves, among other things, specifying a precise semantics for the primitive types and type constructors in the system. On the other hand, it need only be done once by the implementor of the view processor and view support kernel, and not for each new environment that is generated. Unless new types are added or compatibility mappings are changed, any environment generated by a demonstrably consistent view system will itself be consistent.

4 Features

Given the ability to define shared type representations of an object in different views, we need some way for a system to describe a collection of views and to indicate how those views are to be composed into an integrated environment. This is done by defining *features*. A feature implements a logical unit of functionality and corresponds roughly to a tool or component of a tool.[7] Whereas views provide the raw descriptive matter for the objects and corresponding operations of an environment, features package views into collective units, establish scoping for names and view sharing, and provide abstract interfaces for use by other features.

The basic structure of a feature is illustrated in figure 6. As shown there, a feature has an implementation and an interface. Through its interface a feature can import zero or more other features and can export zero or more views. A view that is exported by a feature must either be implemented by the feature itself, or be one of the views exported by a feature that it imports. However, we allow that an exported view be virtual in the sense that it may consist of a subset or a synthesis of the views in its implementation. In other words, the implementation of a feature may contain details that are hidden from users of the feature. In the example, the Pascal Environment feature imports three other features, Std-Definitions, Documentation Handler, and Incremental Compilation. It exports a single view, the *Code* view.

The implementation part of a feature consists primarily of a collection of "merged" views. These views can either be obtained via the importation of other features or directly specified within the feature itself. In the example, Pascal Environment directly provides the *Code* and *Semantics* views, but "merges" these views with the imported *Documentation* and *Compiler* views (respectively supplied by the "Documentation Handler" and "Incremental Compilation" features).[8] "Merging" causes a collection of views to be taken as shared views of some collection of objects. For example, since PROC-DECL appears in both the *Code* and *Semantics* views within the implementation of Pascal Environment, the view ker-

---

[7] We do not, however, define "tool" as a formal entity.

[8] Since the interface of a feature is one or more views, that feature can be treated by all of its users as simply representing those views.

```
Feature Pascal Environment

Interface:

    Exports Code-View

    Imports Std-Definitions, Documentation Handler, Incremental Compilation

Implementation:

    Uses Std-Defs-View

    Merges Documentation-View, Compiler-View

    View Code-View
        .....
        PROC-DECL ::= ....
        ......

    View Semantics-View
        .....
        PROC-DECL ::= ....
        ......
End Feature Pascal Environment

-----------

Feature Documentation Handler

Interface:

    Exports Documentation-View
    ....
End Feature Documentation Handler
```

Figure 6: A Feature Implementing a Pascal Environment

nel will automatically maintain both views of any instance of that production created by a tool in the feature. If, in addition, PROC-DECL also appears in the imported *Compiler* view, the definition given there would be added as a third view. In Section 6 we will discuss how the names used in an imported view can be redefined for merging with other internal views.

The definitions provided by a view in the exports list of an imported feature can also be used directly to enrich the name environment of the importing feature. The importer can use the names provided by the imported view, although it does not have access to the implementation of those names. This corresponds to the usual notion of "imports" in modules used in algebraic languages. The opening of a feature for such use within an implementation of another feature is indicated by the "Uses" clause. In the example above, Pascal Environment "uses" the *Std-Defs* view allowing reference to the names provided by feature Std-Definitions.

Thus features act like abstract datatypes [Shaw 84] with the important difference that in addition to supporting the usual forms of abstraction (for data and operations) and modularity they also support sharing of type descriptions (through view merging). Since they support both tool modularization and sharing they are an appropriate descriptive framework for synthesizing the benefits of the Sequential Model and the Concurrent Model. As the examples in Section 6 will illustrate, this makes it possible to describe systems as reusable, tailorable collections of integrated functional units.

5 Dynamic Views

A dynamic view allows a tool implementor to describe collections of database objects that have a certain set of properties. Dynamic views serve the purpose of associative retrievals commonly found in relational databases. They can also be used by an implementor to specify mappings between the objects that appear in one view and those that appear in another. To illustrate, consider the *Semantics* view of a PROC-DECL, shown below with a new *use-sites* component. An associated equation (to be described in more detail later) specifies a dynamic view that collects all instances of objects of type ID-USE in the *Code* view that have as the value of their *def-site* attribute[9] the PROC-DECL in question.

```
View Semantics-View
    .....
    PROC-DECL ::=  ....
                   use-sites: set of ID-USE
                   ....

    Equations:
    use-sites := Dynamic is-type("ID-USE") AND target.def-site = self
                 context Code-View
    .....
```

Figure 7: Example of a Dynamic View

The effect of this declaration is to produce a set of all use sites of the procedure declaration. This set has two important properties. First, it can be operated on exactly as if it had been constructed "in place". Second, the set will be dynamically updated (hence the term "dynamic view") as new use-sites are added.

Dynamic views are generated by specifying a pattern that, in principle, acts like a dynamic filter on the database. By default, the pattern is applied to all objects appearing within the static view for which it is defined. However, the pattern may also be used to select objects from other views. In the above example, use-sites are selected from the *Code* view for encorporation in the *Semantics* view. Patterns are written in a small, applicative language, powerful enough to express, for example, "the collection of all statements that assign a value to the variable 'x' and are contained in procedures whose documentation contains the word 'blah'".

A complete discussion of dynamic views and their implementation is beyond the scope of

---

[9]We are, of course, assuming that each instance of an ID-USE has a *def-site* attribute that points to its definition site.

this paper. (See this author's Ph.D dissertation [Garlan 86a].) Here we summarize the notation, called DVS,[10] used in describing patterns for dynamic views.

DVS assumes the existence of two kinds of functions:

- predicates: These are boolean functions supplied by the basic type constructors and the primitive operators on instances of productions. Examples: component-of, equal, element-of, in-table, *etc*.

- selectors: These take a single node as an argument and return another node as a result. The available selectors will depend on the type constructors of the view system. Examples: component selection, the next element in a list, the nth element of an array. When applied to a single node we often write the application of a selector in postfix notation, using '.' to represent application. Examples: "x.bool-cond", "x.value", "x.next", "x.statements.first".

A pattern is a function from collections of objects to collections of objects. Patterns are composed out of primitive predicates, primitive selectors, and other patterns. The resulting composition is either a new predicate or a new selector. The effect of applying a predicate pattern to a collection is to produce the subcollection of objects that satisfy that predicate. A predicate pattern thus acts like a filter. The effect of applying a selector pattern to a collection is to produce a *new* collection of objects that is obtained by selecting on each element and then eliminating "NULL" results. For example, ".bool-cond" applied to a collection will yield the *bool-cond* components of all those objects that have *bool-cond* components.

A pattern is constructed out of other predicates, selectors, and patterns with the following operators:

- The 'is' operator: This operator transforms a primitive predicate on n values to a predicate on 1 value. Examples: if "component(t_1, t_2)" is a predicate on two values "is-component(t_1)" is a predicate on a single value, returning true for any component of 't_1'. Similarly, "is-sibling(t)" - returns true for any sibling of 't'.

- Boolean operators (AND, OR, NOT): These join other predicates in the obvious way. Example: "is-son(t_1) AND is-sibling(t_2)".

- Composition: Selectors and predicates are composed using the symbol '|' and read from left to right.[11] For example, the pattern "is-son(t) | .bool-cond" applied to a collection would yield the boolean subcomponents of all sons of the object represented by 't'.

Finally, patterns can use the keywords, *self* and *target*. The first represents the object at which the pattern is defined. The second represents the object at which the pattern is being evaluated.

---

[10]DVS stands for Dynamic View Specification, and is pronounced "devious".

[11]The similarity to Unix pipes is not accidental.

The examples in figure 8 should help make this a bit clearer. (In these examples we assume that 'marked' is a predefined predicate.)

```
marked | .foo        -- the 'foo' component of all marked objects

.foo | marked        -- all 'foo' components that are marked

is-prod("ASSIGNMENT") AND target.LHS.value = "x"

                     -- places where variable "x" is assigned a value

is-prod("PROC") | .doc.value | is-superstring("foo")

                     -- procedure documentation containing the word "foo"
```

Figure 8: Some Examples of Dynamic Views

Dynamic views are specified by giving a pattern with which to select members of the view. Dynamic views may also be qualified along a number of dimensions that determine whether, for example, the view will persist across multiple user sessions with the environment, how frequently the view is updated, *etc.* As we have already illustrated (Figure 7), one of these qualifications allows an implementor to provide a view *context* from which to evaluate the dynamic view. By default a dynamic view is evaluated with respect to the static view in which it is defined, but any other view may be specified in its place.

6 Applications

In this section we present two examples from programming-in-the-large that further introduce some of the basic ideas of the view-oriented approach and demonstrate how tool integration takes place. The first example shows how we can use views to extend a simple module description environment with a module interface checker. The second example illustrates the use of views to construct reusable tools. We show how a memory manager can be specified using views in such a way that it can be tailored to the specific needs of an implementor over a variety of environments.

6.1 An Interface Checker

Consider the module description environment shown in figure 9. Here a project is defined as a collection of modules, where each module consists of a sequence of components. For simplicity, a module does not have nested modules, and we assume that IDENT, TEXT, and SIG-TYPE[12] are productions defined in the imported feature Std-Definitions. We also assume that each of the module's components can provide the list of the signatures that it

---

[12]Actually, in a real implementation the SIG-TYPE would be given as a view parameter to a *generic* feature similar to the one described. This would allow the module environment to be used with any number of programming languages, the interface between the language and the module environment being determined by the view that characterizes the signatures in the programming language. For ease of illustration we do not discuss generic features here. See [Garlan 86a].

requires from its surrounding environment. The operational component of the description is not pictured here.

```
Feature Module Description Environment

Interface:

    Exports MDE-View

    Imports Std-Definitions

Implementation:

    Uses Std-Definitions

    View MDE-View

    PROJECT          ::= proj-name: IDENT
                         modules: seq of MODULE

    MODULE           ::= mod-name: IDENT
                         imports: seq of IMPORT-ITEM
                         exports: seq of SIGNATURE
                         components: seq of COMPONENT

    IMPORT-ITEM      ::= mod-name: IDENT

    SIGNATURE        ::= sig-name: IDENT
                         sig-type: SIG-TYPE

    COMPONENT        ::= signature: SIGNATURE
                         body: TEXT
                         requires: seq of SIGNATURE

End Feature Module Description Environment
```

Figure 9: Specification of a Module Description Environment

Now suppose we would like to add interface checking to this environment. Using the old concurrent model (Section 2) we would probably add this capability by embedding it directly in the description of the module environment. Using the sequential model we would probably write a new tool to parse module interfaces into convenient structures with associated symbol tables for use-site information, and so on. Alternatively, we might use IDL readers and writers to avoid parsing, although the interface checker tool would still maintain separate symbol table structures. Using the view-oriented model, however, we can simply add a new feature to the system.

Before showing how to do this, we need to be clear about what we mean by interface checking. Following Habermann and others [Habermann 80, DeRemer 76] we can divide the functionality of an interface checker into these logical components:

1. **Consistency.** The same facility is not provided twice, either (a) by the module itself, or (b) through the module's imports.

2. **Completeness.** The module provides the promised export items. They can be provided as components or via an imported module's exports.

3. **Sufficiency**. The facilities required by the implementations in the module are either available as imports or are provided directly by the module.

4. **Necessity**. Modules are not imported unnecessarily. That is, some facility in each imported module is used somewhere in the importer.

The skeleton of a feature to implement this functionality is shown below in figure 10. Note that the "exports" of the feature consists of the view provided by the Module Description Environment plus the new operation "check" that can be applied to the objects of type MODULE and PROJECT. The implementation of the views that actually do the interface checking is hidden from users of the feature. Note also that the decomposition of the feature parallels the logical functional organization outlined above.

```
Feature Enhanced Module Description Environment

Interface:

    Imports Std-Definitions, Module Description Environment
    Exports MDE-View, check(MODULE), check(PROJECT)

Implementation:

    Uses Std-Defs-View

    Merges MDE-View

    View Self-Consistency-View .....

    View Import-Consistency-View .....

    View Completeness-View .....

    View Sufficiency-View .....

    View Necessity-View .....

End Feature Enhanced Module Description Environment
```

Figure 10: Module Description Environment enhanced with interface checking

First we describe the Self-Consistency view (figure 11). In order to check that no component of a module implements the same signature twice, the view need only bother with the productions for MODULE and COMPONENT. Each COMPONENT is given a new attribute, "redundant", which is a set of pointers to other components with the same signature. This is described as a dynamic view containing all siblings whose signatures are "equal", as defined by the operator "eq-sig" that we will assume is provided by the type SIGNATURE. Note that using views, the implementation of the check for self-consistency can be restricted to a universe consisting of just those structures that are relevant to this aspect of consistency checking.

While the use of views does not presuppose any particular formalism for describing the operational aspect of a view, the notation used here is an extended form of attribute equations developed by Kaiser [Kaiser 85]. The primary differences between this notation and the more familiar attribute equations (such as [Reps 83]) are the following:

- Attribute equations can be attached to *events*, meaning that those equations are only evaluated when an object receives a signal with that event name.

- Some events are system events. These include ACCESS, CREATE, and DELETE. They are automatically propagated by the system to the nodes that the corresponding system action affect. Other events can be defined by an implementor and propagated explicitly by an equation of the form; "Propagates ⟨event-name⟩ To ⟨node-expression⟩".

- There is an *assert* equation. This is of the form "Assert ⟨condition⟩ Error ⟨equations⟩", and has the meaning that if the condition is ever violated the associated "error" equations are activated.

- The value of a component can be specified by a dynamic view.

Referring to figure 11, we see that the "check" operation is implemented as an event of the same name. The module simply forwards the event to each of its components, which in turn collect the set of redundancies as dynamic views.

```
View Self-Consistency-View     -- check that a signature is not implemented twice

    MODULE     ::= components: seq of COMPONENT

        Equations:

            check --> Propagates check To components[all]

    COMPONENT ::= signature: SIGNATURE
                  redundant: set of COMPONENT

        Equations:

            check -->

            redundant := Dynamic brother(self)
                         AND target.signature = self.signature
```

Figure 11: The Self-Consistency View

A second view is illustrated in figure 12, showing the implementation of the *Import-Consistency* view of interface checking. The important thing to note here is that an IMPORT-ITEM of a module is no longer just the name of a module (as it was in figure 9), but now has as one of its components the 'def-site' attribute, which gives it direct access to the exports of the imported module. This is necessary because to check for import consistency the module has to "see" all of the exports of its imports, and not just the name of the imported module. Also, in this view PROJECT maintains an alternative view of its MODULE subcomponents as a table. This allows fast lookup of module locations, necessary for efficient resolution of module definition sites. Similarly, the exports of a MODULE are represented as a set, allowing the implementor to take unions and intersections of them efficiently.

The only complex aspect of this view specification is the pattern for specifying the *redundant* component of an IMPORT-ITEM. Like the component of that name in the *Self-Consistency* view, this component is to represent the set of items that have duplicate signatures. In this case we collect pointers to duplicate signatures in *other* imported modules.

```
View Import-Consistency-View

-- check that a signature is not imported twice

    PROJECT       ::= modules: table of MODULE key mod-name.value

    MODULE        ::= mod-name: IDENT
                      imports: seq of IMPORT-ITEM
                      exports: set of SIGNATURE key sig-name.value

Equations:

    check -->

        Propagates check To imports[all]

    IMPORT-ITEM ::= mod-name: IDENT
                    def-site: MODULE
                    redundant: set of SIGNATURE key sig-name.value

Equations:

    def-site := lookup(^PROJECT.modules, self.modname)

    check -->

        redundant := Dynamic is-element(def-site.exports) |
            lookup(target.sig-name, others) != NIL where
            others = Union(brother(self).def-site.exports)

    SIGNATURE     ::= sig-name: IDENT
                      sig-type: SIG-TYPE
```

Figure 12: The Import-Consistency View

The remaining views that define the interface checker are shown in figure 13. There are several general points to notice about these views. First, we gain considerable compactness of expression by treating various collections as sets. For example, we can define the collection of missing signatures in the *Completeness* view simply as "exports - (provides + gets)". Second, we explicitly use other views as the context in which we generate some of the dynamic views. For example, the *gets* component of the *Completeness* view of MODULE collects all the exports of all the imports as provided by the *Import-Consistency* view. Third, we can use the fact that other views have generated the appropriate components, as with the *provides* component of MODULE in view *Sufficiency*.

```
View Completeness-View   -- check that all of the exported signatures are provided

    MODULE        ::= exports: Sig-Set
                      provides: Sig-Set
                      gets: Sig-Set
                      lacks: Sig-Set

  Equations:

      check -->

          provides := Dynamic self.components.signature
                       context Self-Consistency-View
          gets      := Dynamic is-element(imports.def-site.exports)
                       context Import-Consistency-View
          lacks     := exports - (provides + gets) -- set union and difference

    SIGNATURE    ::= sig-name: IDENT
                     sig-type: SIG-TYPE

View Sufficiency-View    -- check that all required signatures are provided

    MODULE        ::= provides: Sig-Set
                      requires: Sig-Set
                      missing: Sig-Set

  Equations:

      check -->

          -- 'provides' is already done in View Completeness
          requires := Dynamic is-element(components.requires) context MDE
          missing  := requires - provides -- set difference

View Necessity-View    -- check that some signature is required from each import

    MODULE        ::= requires: Sig-Set    -- shared with Sufficiency-View
                      imports: seq of IMPORT-ITEM
                      exports: Sig-Set

  Equations:

      check --> Propagates check To imports[all]

    IMPORT-ITEM ::= def-site: MODULE
                    superfluous: BOOLEAN

  Equations:
      check -->

          superfluous := !empty(intersect(father.requires, def-site.exports))
```

Figure 13: Completeness, Sufficiency, and Necessity Views

6.2 A Memory Manager

In the previous example, the interface checker was tightly integrated with the Module Description Environment. That is, the definition of the views to implement interface checking depended in a fundamental (albeit implicit) way on the existence of the information provided in the Module Description Environment. In this section we illustrate how features can be written in a much more context-independent way. This allows them to be used across a variety of environments as reusable building blocks.

Let us suppose we would like to augment an environment, such as the one already described, with the ability to do memory management. For example, we might like that each of the components of a module exist as a separate object that could be loaded from and stored to disk as needed. We might also like the system to exhibit some form of working set behavior. Using features we take the approach illustrated in figures 14 and 15.

```
Feature Memory Manager

Interface:

    Exports MM-View: MM-ROOT[maxobjects], MM-OBJECT[]
    Imports TimeStamp, DiskIO

Implementation:

    View MM-View

    MM-ROOT     ::= curid: OBJ-ID
                    maxobjects: integer
                    inuse: integer
                    allobjects: set of MM-OBJECT
                    loaded: sorted-table of MM-OBJECT key uniqueid
                        ordered low by lastuse

    MM-OBJECT   ::= uniqueid: OBJ-ID
                    incore: boolean
                    lastuse: TIMESTAMP
                    diskid: DISK-ID

    OBJ-ID      ::= integer

End Feature Memory Manager
```

Figure 14: Feature Description for a Memory Manager

Figure 14 describes the world as seen from a simple memory manager's point of view. It consists of a collection of memory managed objects grouped together under a memory manager root. Each memory managed object has a unique identifier, a disk location, a designation of whether it is loaded in core or not, and a timestamp representing the most recent access to it. The root maintains a table of loaded objects sorted by this timestamp. We will assume (simplistically, for illustration) that the default memory management policy is to allow a maximum of, say, 100 memory managed objects in core at one time; as new objects are accessed the least recently accessed objects will be stored on disk to make room. Later we will see how this policy is tailored to meet the specific management policies of a system in which it is used. Note that the view exported by Memory Manager is *virtual* in the sense that it exports an abstraction of the view actually implemented within it. In particular, it exports the MM-ROOT as if it had single component, it exports MM-OBJECT without any components, and it does not export OBJ-ID at all. Not shown in these figures are the equations to implement the functionality just described. See [Garlan 86b] for the complete description.

We are now in a position to explain how a feature such as Memory Manager can be used to augment a programming environment. In this case, of course, we want to integrate the memory manager with the module description environment described earlier. We will do this by establishing a connection between the MM-ROOT and PROJECT productions, on the one hand, and between the MM-OBJECT and MODULE productions, on the other. Figure 15 illustrates how this is done.

```
Feature Memory Managed Module

Interface:

    Exports MDE-View
    Imports Module Description Environment, Memory Manager

Implementation:

    Merges

    View MDE-View        -- from Module Description Environment
    View MM-View         -- from Memory Manager
                 with MM-ROOT as PROJECT
                      MM-OBJECT as MODULE

    View Auxiliary

    PROJECT ::= maxobjects: integer

        Equations:

            maxobjects := 200

End Feature Memory Managed Module]
```

Figure 15: Merging Memory Manager and Module Description Environment

In the example above, the Memory Managed Module feature composes a new feature out of the views provided by the existing features, Memory Manager and Module Description Environment. It also adds its own view. In the merging process we rename MM-ROOT to PROJECT, and we rename MM-OBJECT to MODULE.[13] The process of renaming produces a correspondence between the external names provided by the view interface of a feature and the internal names used within the implementation of another feature. The internal view *Auxiliary* provides yet another view of the production PROJECT, allowing us to initialize its "maxobjects" field to 200 (overriding the default assignment of 100 specified in Memory Manager).

In a more realistic, larger system we would probably merge a large number of such features

---

[13]It is possible to rename a production more than once. Each such renaming results in a new copy of the renamed production.

as illustrated, for example, by figure 16.[14]

```
Feature A Larger System

Interface:

    Exports ....
    Imports ....

Implementation:

    Merges

        Feature Module Description Environment
            ...
        Feature Memory Manager
            ...
        Feature Compilation Unit
            ...
        Feature Documentation Facility
            ...
        Feature My Error Handler
            ...
End Feature A Larger System
```

Figure 16: Skeleton of a More Realistic, Larger System

6.3 Range of Applicability

We have illustrated the use of views and features in defining two tools for programming-in-the-large. The first example described the definition of tightly integrated views, and the second the definition and instantiation of reusable, view-oriented building blocks.

It is reasonable to ask how widely applicable these techniques are. While a definitive answer must wait until we have had more experience using the view-oriented approach, we believe that it can be successfully applied to virtually any system of integrated tools. Our confidence is supported by our prototype design of other components for programming-in-the-large, including a configuration manager with incremental recompilation, as well as components for programming-in-the-small, including support for incremental recompilation, interpretation, and language-oriented debugging (described in [Garlan 86b], [Kaiser 85] and [Kaiser 86]). Moreover, as Notkin has shown [Notkin 84], the environment generation paradigm applies not only to the generation of programming environments, but also to a wide variety of integrated systems including mail systems, document editors. Finally, as we outline later (Section 8), the use of views for describing tools has much in common with other approaches with well established track records.

---

[14]In the example, we merge features rather than views. This is simply shorthand for merging all of views exported by those features.

7 Implementation

Two implementation efforts are currently underway. The first of these is confined to the special case of static views for the user interface. It is part of a production version of a Pascal environment that runs on the Macintosh and will be marketed commercially within the next year. In this implementation there is a single "abstract" view (represented as an attributed abstract syntax tree) and numerous display views. The creation of views is driven dynamically by the user's interest in observing varying aspects of a program. The system supports several display views of the code, a documentation view, runtime views, and monitoring views for debugging [Gnome 85]. In addition it provides support for ellipsis and various kinds of context-dependent and space-dependent conditional formatting [Garlan 85]. In this system views are generated from a specialized notation developed for expressing the flexible display of syntax structures. They correspond in functionality to the multiple unparse schemes pioneered by ALOE editors [Medina-Mora 82] and more recently the "views" of Pecan [Reiss 84].

In this implementation, each view of a database is maintained as a separate (tree) structure, with links between alternative representations of an object in each of the views in which it appears. When changes are made to one view, the links are followed to make corresponding changes in other views. Given the need to drive the display of a production-quality programming environment, the primary consideration in this implementation has been efficiency and flexibility. The former is achieved through incrementality; small changes to a program result in correspondingly small changes to the views. The latter is achieved by supplying a powerful set of formatting tools and by giving the user considerable control over the appearance of the display (indentation style, ellipsis, font choice, display of keywords, *etc.*)

The second implementation, called MELD,[15] is an object-oriented prototype (written in CommonLoops [Bobrow 85]) of dynamic and static views in their full generality, although minimal attention has as yet been given to the user interface. This implementation is based on an object-oriented database in which the views play the part of super classes, events and the corresponding attribute equations play the part of methods, and components play the part of instance variables [Stefik 86]. The primary superclass of each object in the system is the type "node". It is provided automatically and determines the basic generic behavior of each database object (component access, maintenance of view consistency, *etc.*). Figure 17 illustrates this inheritance scheme. Methods are described in terms of attribute equations.

As an object-oriented system, MELD has a number of distinctive characteristics that are a consequence of type compatibility and consistency. The most significant of these are (a) MELD supports sharing of instance variables, which are typed, but allows them to have different (compatible) types, and (b) unless explicitly overridden, MELD guarantees that the constraints that implement methods are simultaneously satisfied in *all* views. The former is distinctive because in other object-oriented systems, instance variables are either typed and must have the same types, or are untyped and implicitly merged into a single representation.

---

[15] MELD stands for Multiple Elucidations of Language Descriptions and is also a concatenation of the words "melt" and "weld".

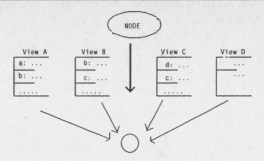

Each object in the system is a synthesis of the views that define it, each view contributing some fields and operations. The basic behavior of the composite object is determined by the "node" superclass. Multiple inheritance is performed implicitly by the system; the implementor can only access objects through particular views. Common fields in inherited views are "shared" in ways determined by view compatibility.

Figure 17: Views as Multiple Inheritance

The latter is distinctive because the order of "method" evaluation (*viz.*, constraint satisfaction) can be determined automatically by attribute analysis similar to [Reps 83], whereas other systems typically have to search to find a primary implementation of a method (*eg.*, [Stefik 86]), or they require the inheritor to fully understand the implementation of the inherited type in order to explicitly resolve method conflicts. (*eg.*, [Keene 85]).

8 Related Work

The use of the word "views" is quite common. The primary differences between the "views" proposed here and those in other systems can be summarized as follows:

- In other systems views act primarily as a filtering mechanism; they can only be used to *limit* the amount of information viewed, and there is no variation in the way in which that information can be viewed. In the view-oriented approach, the database is a *synthesis* of a collection of views defined by the tools in the environment. New information can be added by encorporating new views. Moreover, different tools can view the same information in quite different ways.

- In other systems views are often only available to the user, whereas the tools interact directly with the raw database. In the view-oriented approach, tools also interact through views. In fact, the process of defining a tool's interface to the environment is precisely that of defining its view of it. User views are a special case of the more general notion.

- Other systems have a problem with resolving view updates when a change to a view might have ambiguous effects on the actual database. In our system, the fact that objects are typed (and have an associated semantics) leads naturally to automatic techniques for equating operations in one view to corresponding operations in another view.

One way to categorize existing and proposed view designs is along a spectrum. At one end of the spectrum lie view mechanisms that allow little difference between two views of the same objects. For example, views might act as simple filters. The advantage of such mechanisms is that it is relatively easy for the kernel of the environment to automatically generate mappings between different views. The disadvantage is that tools have relatively little flexibility in defining those views when sharing is to take place. At the other end of the spectrum lie view mechanisms that allow arbitrary differences between two views. For example, one view of an object might be a program's source code, and another view might be its executable code. The transformation between the two views would have to be provided by an implementor-supplied compiler. The advantage of these mechanisms is that considerable flexibility is allowed. The disadvantage is that the implementor must shoulder a substantial burden for defining all view mappings. The views described in this paper can be seen as addressing an intermediate range of mechanisms. These mechanisms allow flexibility in defining overlapping views, but are constrained enough (through type compatibility) to allow the generation of automatic mappings between those views.

Additionally, this work is related to on-going research in a number of areas.

Structure Editing. The primary motivation for views grew out of the problems encountered in building large, practical structure editor-based environments for software development (eg., [Notkin 86]) . While solving many of the problems of tool integration for these environments, the use of views also turns out to simplify the basic architecture of structure editing since many aspects of structure editors that were developed as ad hoc enhancements to make it easier for tools to coexist are now subsumed in the more powerful and general mechanism of views. This work also extends Notkin's [Notkin 84] by providing new ways in which systems of multiple grammars can be combined.

IDL. A view can be seen as a collection of IDL-like structure descriptions [Nestor 86] that define the types of the objects to be manipulated by a particular tool. Thus the view-oriented approach extends recent work in IDL interfaces for tools by providing a way for certain kinds of IDL descriptions (namely, those that describe "compatible" types) to exist interactively. Rather than using IDL to describe interfaces between batch-oriented phases of a tool or environment, these interfaces can be used to describe integrated tools. Moreover, this work provides a natural way to extend the rather weak "view" mechanism available in IDL (through "derivation") to views that are not simply filters of other views.

Database Views. "Views" have been around a long time in the world of relational databases [Chamberlin 75], and to some extent the dynamic views proposed here can be seen as an application of those ideas to integrated environments. However, unlike other work in this area (such as [Horwitz 85]), dynamic views are based on an object-oriented database and they adopt the use of pattern-oriented queries within the framework of the specification of object structures, rather than attaching a separate database facility on the side. Moreover, as mentioned before, the views proposed here avoid the more problematic aspects of view updating [Keller 86].

Unparse Views. In the literature on programming environments, the word "views" is frequently taken to mean the user views of a program (eg., [Reiss 84, Goldberg 83]). In this work views that represent what the user sees as concrete text and graphics fall out as a special case of views for tools.

Data Abstraction. This work is related to data abstraction in several ways. First, it proposes a mechanism by which objects can be assigned multiple types. Second, through view interfaces, it makes it possible to encapsulate the tools of an environment while still allowing sharing. Third, it introduces a rather novel aspect to data typing, in which the client of a data type can contribute to the type definition of an object.

Object-Oriented Programming. As we described in Section 7, views can be treated as a system of multiple inheritance, in which events and attribute equations act like methods, and views act like multiple object superclasses. As we pointed out there are a number of important differences between existing object-oriented systems and the implementation of views, relating to method invocation and type compatibility. These are described more fully in [Garlan 86c].

Specification Languages. Views are similar to specifications languages such as Larch [Guttag 85] and Clear [Burstall 77] in that the motivation behind them is to provide reusable, tailorable system components. Moreover, like specification languages, view descriptions are not directly executable (in the sense of a traditional programming language). This work differs from specification languages in that views are more concerned with describing the behavior of system components and less with the relationships between them. Also, the current notation is not (yet) convenient for verification.

9 Summary

We introduced the view-oriented approach to tool integration as an attempt to merge the best of both the concurrent and sequential models. As we have tried to illustrate, views provide the benefits of modularization (abstraction, encapsulation, protection) with the benefits of sharing (integration, incrementality, and lack of duplication). In addition, the resulting system supports a high degree of reusability through renaming and merging, and naturally supports the evolution of tools in an environment. Moreover, as the examples show, the combination of static views, dynamic views, and extended attribute equations results in a compact, relatively transparent, and modifiable notation for describing and integrating tools. What used to require dozens of pages of code, which was inextricably tied to context, can now be expressed in two modularized, reusable pages of view description.

The use of views does, however, add a new form of constraint to the specification of cooperating tools — namely type compatibility. The examples in this paper have tried to show that this is not a serious problem. Our confidence in views is further supported by their successful application to other tools for programming-in-the-large [Garlan 86a], tools for programming-in-the-small [Kaiser 85, Kaiser 86, Gnome 85], and more general collections of integrated tools [Notkin 84, Garlan 86c]. Finally, work in progress on efficient implementations of these ideas suggests that they are practical as well as elegant.

10 Acknowledgements

The current version of this report has benefited greatly from suggestions made by numerous people. In particular, we thank Nico Habermann, Charles Krueger, Barbara Staudt, Reidar Conradi, Chuck Weinstock, and especially Ellen Borison and Benjamin Pierce for their critical reading of earlier versions. We would also like to acknowledge Gail Kaiser and Nico Habermann for their formative input on many of the basic ideas contained in this paper.

11 References

[Ambriola 84]   Vincenzo Ambriola, Gail E. Kaiser, and Robert J. Ellison.
                  An Action Routine Model for ALOE.
                  Technical Report CMU-CS-84-156, Carnegie-Mellon University, Computer
                      Science Department, August, 1984.

[Balzer 85]   Robert Balzer.
                  A 15 Year Perspective on Automatic Programming.
                  IEEE Transactions on Software Engineering SE-11(11), November, 1985.

[Bobrow 85]   D.G. Bobrow, K. Kahn, G. Kiczales, L. Masinter, M. Stefik, & F. Zdybel.
                  *CommonLoops: Merging Common Lisp and Object-oriented
                      programming*.
                  Technical Report ISL-85-8, Xerox PARC: Intelligent Systems Laboratory,
                      August, 1985.

[Burstall 77]   R.M. Burstall and J.A. Goguen.
                  Putting Theories Together To Make Specifications.
                  In *Fifth International Joint Conference on Artificial Intelligence*, pages
                      1045-1058. Cambridge, MA, 1977.

[Chamberlin 75]   D. D. Chamberlin, J. N. Gray, I. L. Traiger.
                  Views, authorization, and locking in a relational data base system.
                  In *AFIPS Conference Proceedings*, pages 425-430. AFIPS, 1975.
                  NCC 1975, Anaheim, CA.

[DeRemer 76]   Frank DeRemer and Hans H.Kron.
                  Programming-in-the-Large Versus Programming-in-the-Small.
                  IEEE Transactions on Software Engineering 2(2):80-86, June, 1976.

[Dolotta 77]   T.A. Dolotta and R.C. Haight.
                  PWB/UNIX -- Overview and Synopsis of Facilities.
                  Technical Report, Bell Laboratories, June 1977.

[Donahue 85]   James Donahue and Alan Demers.
                  Data Types Are Values.
                  ACM Transactions on Programming Languages and Systems
                      7(3):426-445, July, 1985.

[Donzeau-Gouge 84a]
Veronique Donzeau-Gouge, Gerard Huet, Gilles Kahn, and Bernard Lang.
Programming Environments Based on Structured Editors: The Mentor Experience.
Interactive Programming Environments.
McGraw-Hill Book Co., New York, NY, 1984.

[Donzeau-Gouge 84b]
Veronique Donzeau-Gouge, Gilles Kahn, Bernard Lang and B. Melese.
Documents Structure and Modularity in Mentor.
In *Proceedings of the SIGSOFT/SIGPLAN Software Engineering Symposium on Practical Software Development Environments.* April, 1984.

[Gandalf 84]   The Gandalf Project.
ALOE Users' and Implementors' Guide (Fourth Edition).
Technical Report, CMU Department of Computer Science, October 1984.

[Garlan 85]   David Garlan.
Flexible Unparsing in a Structure Editing Environment.
Technical Report CMU-CS-85-129, Carnegie-Mellon University, Department of Computer Science, April, 1985.

[Garlan 86a]   David Garlan.
Views for Tools in Software Development Environments.
PhD thesis, Carnegie-Mellon University, 1986.
In progress.

[Garlan 86b]   David Garlan and Gail E. Kaiser.
Features: An Approach to Reusable Software.
1986.
Submitted for publication.

[Garlan 86c]   David Garlan and Gail E. Kaiser.
MELD: An Object-Oriented Language for Describing Features.
1986.
Submitted for publication.

[Gnome 85]   Chandhok, Garlan, Goldenson, Tucker, and Miller.
Structure Editing-Based Programming Environments: The GNOME Approach.
In *Proceedings of NCC85.* AFIPS, July, 1985.

[Goldberg 83]   A. J. Goldberg and D. Robson.
Smalltalk-80: The Language and Its Implementation.
Addison-Wesley Publishing Co., 1983.

[Guttag 85]   John V. Guttag, James J. Horning and Jeannette M. Wing.
The Larch Family of Specification Languages.
IEEE Software 2(5):24-36, September, 1985.

[Habermann 80] A. N. Habermann and D. Perry.
                Well-Formed System Compositions.
                Technical Report CMU-CS-80-117, Carnegie-Mellon University, Computer
                    Science Department, March, 1980.

[Horwitz 85]   Susan Horwitz and Tim Teitelbaum.
                Relations and Attributes: A Symbiotic Basis for Editing Environments.
                In *ACM SIGPLAN 85 Symposium on Language Issues in Progrmming
                    Environments*, pages 93-106. ACM, June, 1985.

[Kaiser 85]   Gail E. Kaiser.
                Semantics for Structure Editing Environments.
                PhD thesis, Carnegie-Mellon University, June, 1985.

[Kaiser 86]   Gail E. Kaiser.
                Generation of Run-Time Environments.
                In *SIGPLAN '86 Symposium on Compiler Construction*. June, 1986.
                To appear.

[Keene 85]   Sonya E. Keene and David A. Moon.
                Flavors: Object-oriented Programming on Symbolics Computers.
                In *Common Lisp Conference*. December, 1985.

[Keller 86]   Arthur M. Keller.
                The Role of Semantics in Translating View Updates.
                IEEE Computer 19(1):63-73, January, 1986.

[Medina-Mora 82] Raul Medina-Mora.
                Syntax-Directed Editing: Towards Integrated Programming Environments.
                PhD thesis, Carnegie-Mellon University, March 1982.

[Nestor 86]   Nestor, J.R., Wulf, W.A., Lamb, D.A.
                IDL - Interface Description Language: Formal Description.
                Technical Report, Software Engineering Institute, Pittsburgh, PA,
                    February, 1986.
                Reprint of Technical Report CMU-CS-81-139.

[Notkin 84]   David S. Notkin.
                Interactive Structure-Oriented Computing.
                PhD thesis, Carnegie-Mellon University, February, 1984.

[Notkin 86]   D. S. Notkin and A. N. Habermann.
                Gandalf Software Development Environments.
                IEEE Transactions on Software Engineering , 1986.
                To appear.

[Reiss 84]   Steven P. Reiss.
                Graphical Program Development with PECAN Program Development Sys-
                    tems.
                In *Proceedings of the Software Engineering Symposium on Practical
                    Software Development Environments*. ACM-SIGSOFT/SIGPLAN,
                    April, 1984.

[Reps 83]   Thomas Reps, Tim Teitelbaum and Alan Demers.
                 Incremental Context-Dependent Analysis for Language-Based Editors.
                 ACM Transactions on Programming Languages and Systems (TOPLAS)
                      5(3), July, 1983.

[Reps 84]   Tom Reps and Tim Teitlebaum.
                 The Synthesizer Generator.
                 In *Proceedings of the Software Engineering Symposium on Practical
                      Software Development Environments*. ACM-SIGSOFT/SIGPLAN,
                      April, 1984.

[Shaw 84]   Mary Shaw.
                 Abstraction Techniques in Modern Programming Languages.
                 IEEE Software 1(4):10-26, October, 1984.

[Stefik 86]   Mark Stefik and Daniel G. Bobrow.
                 Object-Oriented Programming: Themes and Variations.
                 AI Magazine 6(4):40-62, Winter, 1986.

[Thompson 78]   K. Thompson.
                 UNIX Implementation.
                 The Bell System Technical Journal 57(6):1931-1946, July-August, 1978.

TOOL INTEGRATION

Chair   : Arthur Evans (Tartan Labs, USA)
Assistant chair : Anund Lie (Norw. Inst. of Tech., NOR)

Discussion

Arthur Evans (Tartan Labs, USA):

Summary: We've heard about putting together the data that the various components of the environment will deal with. We've heard about IDL, a data description language, and about a toolkit to exploit IDL for tool integration. We've also heard about a way for tools to share data from different viewpoints.

Andy Rudmik (GTE Comm. Syst., USA):

I wish I had something like IDL when I was developing tools. We've just built a prototype ADA environment where the data model was the entity model providing views on that database. We were able to integrate diverse tools such as an ADA compiler, linker, VAX-based editors, some configuration management tools, and various other tools using the view mechanism.

Unfortunately, we chose to publish some of our work at database - instead of environment conferences. However, our results were very positive. In our views we also included the data operations as part of the view definition. It wasn't clear to me from the presentations whether or not IDL can offer this. If not, why not?

Joseph Newcomer (Carnegie Mellon Univ., USA):

IDL does not specify the operations that you can associate with the data. There is however a process model undergoing revisions. We have an extension to the specification part, where you can somehow specify the operation set. I really think that IDL should be altered to include the operation set, but IDL was originally developed to formalize only the data structure part. Maybe John Nestor, one of the IDL architects, can respond to that?

John Nestor (Carnegie Mellon Univ. USA):

Indeed, merely dealing with the data issues seemed more than enough as an initial project! But it is correct that we also have to worry about the operation set.

David Garlan (Carnegie Mellon Univ., USA):

In the notation I introduced, the operational component is directly associated with the definitions. The preferred technique for specifying them is probably the use of "extended" attributes. Using established algorithms for attribute dependency evaluation, you can automatically resolve the various dependencies across the views. When various tools are accessing the same information in different views, you can make that all work together. A procedural approach fails.

Richard Snodgrass (Univ. North Carolina, USA):

There is the assertion language in IDL where you can declare or specify some aspects of the tools' behavior. You specify how the output of the tool relates to the input through assertions. However, it is not quite the same as specifying the operations.

William Waite (Univ. Colorado, USA):

IDL provides a mechanism for describing complex data interactions in a relatively simple way. This may lead directly to performance problems by allowing the designer to avoid thinking about how to simplify these interactions. Do you care to comment on that?

Joseph Newcomer (Carnegie Mellon Univ., USA):

It is certainly possible to build an inefficient IDL tool, based on an inefficient IDL implementation. Even in a good IDL implementation, we can build horribly inefficient tools by bad use of rep-specs. Our goal was to allow the user to tune the performance of the system without actually violating the high level specifications of the IDL formal model. Both the designers and the implementors were very conscious of these issues. One of the typical counter-arguments is: "Why do you have a complicated system like IDL when all you need is the 'malloc' of C? Give me a row of storage, and I'll do the rest!" I believe we can produce a system which is significantly faster than any existing 'malloc' or record-based implementation, and we actually do better on size and space than most people believe is a "quick, efficient way of doing it".

William Waite (Univ. Colorado, USA):

Suppose that I'm a compiler writer, and I decide to use IDL to describe my intermediate data structures. Am I going to design more complex intermediate data structures, simply because IDL makes it easy to do?

Arthur Evans (Tartan Labs, USA):

Any tool can be misused; and IDL, like any other powerful tool, permits you to hang yourself by a much more complicated rope than you would have had from a simpler tool! (Laughter)

Joseph Newcomer (Carnegie Mellon Univ., USA):

In any complex system, one can decide to use or misuse a particular feature. Based on costs or/and performance, I may choose to avoid a specific feature of the language, like procedures. If I ignore the reality of engineering decisions I will get poor performance. I don't see why you should expect a simple description of a complicated structure. A more fundamental question is why is the structure so complicated; but that is not the fault of the tool for making it easy to describe.

Gerhard Goos (GMD, FRG):

The first application of IDL was the original DIANA design; it illuminates exactly Bill Waite's problem. It shows that people will design an interface that has everything they believed could be useful at some time. So the interface became very complicated because it was too easy to describe in IDL.

Prof. Bauer's law says that if something is difficult to implement, it should also be difficult to express because otherwise people don't realize what they are doing. I certainly don't say that the use of IDL should be more difficult, but I would say, the guy who is using IDL should be able to develop some feeling of what he is doing in implementation terms.

Arthur Evans (Tartan Labs, USA):

That comment could be made about anyone who provides any tool whatsoever. In any tool we need measures of - "What will it cost me to do it, to use it?".

Joseph Newcomer (Carnegie Mellon Univ., USA):

In any piece of engineering you'd better be prepared to measure what you've built and identify your problems. We have built several probing tools and they were fairly easy to write in IDL. We have tools that did storage measurements to find out how people accessed the data structures. I also added one that dynamically counted what structures were created and deleted, and how often. Then, were the tools being used in less than optimal ways? Those instrumented tools were easy to build in the environment. We were able to easily identify the critical components in our system and make improvements. Many of those changes were implementation pragmatics rather than basic restructuring.

David Wile (ISI, USA):

One of the ways that IDL could force the user to specify more than he needs, is by not providing generic facilities, like sequences and sets of objects. Are sets and sequences part of IDL?

Joseph Newcomer (Carnegie Mellon Univ., USA):

Yes. IDL has structures called **set of** and **sequence of**. A **sequence of** has many alternate implementations, like an array, a singly or doubly linked list threaded through certain attributes, etc.. Similarly, **set of** can be represented as vectors, bitmasks, maps, association lists, or whatever. All these implementations (and new ones) can be put into the IDL translator and be activated upon request from the user.

Terrence Miller (HP, USA):

In the IDL approach every instance of a given "data type" has the <u>same</u>
representation and is accessed in the same way. This contrasts with some of the
object-oriented approaches, like FLAVOURS. Could any of the authors add to that
comparison?

David Garlan (Carnegie Mellon Univ., USA):

IDL and object-oriented languages have more or less the same data-oriented concepts
concerning productions, structures, sizes, etc.. What you don't see in IDL is
attaching operations to the data. But there is a close correspondence between
object-oriented approaches that you can map fairly directly, and the <u>views</u> that I
was talking about. In fact, the second implementation in my talk was for
CommonLoops.

Richard Snodgrass (Univ. North Carolina, USA):

There is also a difference in granularity. FLAVOURS and such support very small
objects, while IDL structures in general are quite large, like parse trees for
entire modules.

David Robinson (System Designers, GBR):

The published papers on the ICL's CADES system in 1975, had a "systems description
language" which had similar concepts to IDL and also supported packaging and
monitor organization.

Further, we did similar work in the British MID project, which was based on the
entity-relationship model. It had a public tool interface allowing integration of
tools, but the hard problem was the power of the manipulation. We wanted views and
wanted the capability of views, but we found that the E-R model constrained us
somewhat.

This work was continued into the ASPECT project under the ALVEY program in Britain.
It was Codd's extended relational model, giving us the entity modeling
capabilities. We now have the power of a formal relational algebra and we can
express constraints through first order predicate calculus. All the view mappings -
between views, using views, and views on the conceptual level - are expressed in a
common notation. The manipulation of the information and the mappings are all
stored and represented in one common representation and can be accessed using one
common manipulation language. So, it's nice to see related work all coming to the
same conclusions.

David Garlan (Carnegie Mellon Univ., USA):

There have been lots of view mechanisms scattered throughout the literature over
the years. The relational system has serious problems on view updating and this is
currently a hot research topic.

David Robinson (System Designers, GBR):

Indeed, you are mostly dealing with view updating. But this involves not only the
representation of data, but all the operations as well. So your view mappings must
include abstractions of both data and operations.

Joseph Newcomer (Carnegie Mellon Univ., USA):

At the WG 2.4 meeting last week, I talked about the application of database
technology and various mathematical models to describe data structures for IDL
compilers. We really need better formalization to instrument our tools.

David Robinson (System Designers, GBR):

We are now formally specifying all our concepts. We're using a notation which
originated in France, but is being reworked by somebody at Oxford University to "Z"
notation.

James Cordy (Queens Univ., CAN):

I have worked on a S/SL tool kit system which has an intriguing relationship to IDL
and similar systems. We observed that much time and space was devoted to
interfacing, views, and input/output. That part of the system required a lot of
hand tuning, so we did <u>not</u> try to automate that too much. On the other hand, we
observed that the critical component for achieving portability was not so much the
interface, but the algorithms inside the tool.

So we developed a tool algorithm specification language, S/SL. It allowed you to
specify the functionality of a tool independently of the data structures of
communicating tools. That is, you develop a specification of the given tool in S/SL
notation. Then you develop a description of the tool's interface (the view) to the
data, independent of the interfaces or views of other tools. We can then in a
separate base language, hand-build the viewer and the interface to the data. Later,
we can choose the data representation based on the total set of views. This
approach gives us portability and uniform handling of tool families, while allowing
flexible tuning of data representations and interfaces. For example, we are free to
change the host language, computing system, or whatever. That freedom has paid off
because the major inefficiency lies in the interfacing to the data representation,
rather than in the tool algorithms. (This relates to Bill Waite's earlier comments
on efficiency of data interfaces.)

Robert Schwanke (Siemens, USA):

If you are interested in IDL tools, you may be interested in the DOSE structure
editor <u>editor</u>. It was developed at Siemens Research in Princeton, by my colleagues
Peter Feiler and Gail Kaiser. DOSE structure difinitions are written in a language
very close to IDL. During a single editing session you can write such a definition
and immediately use it to interactivly create examples of that structure. You
provide display rules for presenting the structure on the screen, and you can add
incremental action routines and extended commands that examine and possibly modify
the structure. Unfortunately, the system does not currently support multiple views,
nor is it format-compatible with other IDL tools. DOSE should be available to

researchers, at distribution cost, some time this fall. It will be running on SUN workstations.

Now an IDL toolkit question: What kinds of implementation advice can the IDL author give the toolkit, to control representation (and thus performance)?

Richard Snodgrass (Univ. North Carolina, USA):

It is a major problem that you can always say, "let's also put this in the tool generator". IDL only supports a FOR clause with which you can assign representation aspects to attributes, types, nodes, and classes. You may, for example, also want to restrict operations on set types. The UNC tool currently supports only a moderate number of FOR clause specifications.

Joseph Newcomer (Carnegie Mellon Univ., USA):

As Rick Snodgrass pointed out, adding representation specifications to the tool takes resources, destabilizes the tool, and all sorts of other things. What we now can do in IDL is to control the number of bits in packed fields and to choose between arrays and linked lists for sequences.

Then on measurements - Time and space depends much more on the basic tool algorithms, rather than on representation choices.

John Nestor (Carnegie Mellon Univ., USA):

How many representation specifications are "enough" is a tough question. Even if Rick Snodgrass were to take all suggestions he has received to date for new representation specifications, the next person with a slightly different application domain would need yet one more representation. As long as the representations are added by the tool builder, a certain tyranny of latter prevails. But hopefully(?), we can offer a satisfactory repertoire of tuning primitives to refrain people from resorting to assembly language to get their interfaces working!

Arthur Evans (Tartan Labs, USA):

I represent an user of the IDL systems John Nestor and Joseph Newcomer implemented. IDL potentially offers a great deal of flexibility and power to the users, but the current implementation has a very limited number of representation specifications. Some of our users then claimed that IDL was not giving them the advertised benefits. (We were, on the other hand, giving them some benefits that they didn't understand were very valuable!)

A piece of advice for anyone who's providing any tool for anybody: You get judged on what you didn't think were the important matters!

James Cordy (Queens Univ., CAN):

I've heard Bill Wulf (now at Tartan Labs) argue at an IFIP/IFORS working conference in Canterbury in Sept. 1984, that eventually all tools constrain you. His suggestion was that therefore we should use tools as little as possible! Obviously he doesn't believe that and neither do any of us. But how can we keep saying they're helping when we all have this experience that "Oops, I can't do what I wanted to do!".

Richard Snodgrass (Univ. North Carolina, USA):

Regarding strait jackets - IDL also provides private types which are a way of putting your favorite representations in a controlled fashion into an IDL structure.

Joseph Newcomer (Carnegie Mellon Univ., USA):

I have a retrospect comment on what Bill Waite and Gerhard Goos said earlier about building complicated things. For years, there were arguments against high-level languages; that programs written in these were bigger and slower than assembly programs. There's two reasons for this: The compilers optimize poorly, and, you could more easily build bigger and more complicated programs that appeared to solve the same problem. Over the years this language debate disappeared, but it has just raised itself on high-level data description languages vs. other mechanisms. In a few years we'll have arguments of high-level X vs. low-level Y!

David Levine (Intermetrics, USA):

My company represents a large user of IDL, and it is heavily used in our ADA compiler system. Its main virtue is to serve as the next step in high-level language development. However, you chose not to do control structures in IDL at this time, and to implement it by piggybacking it on other languages which gives you both problems and advantages. From the user point of view, the disadvantages are enormous because I now have two sets of configuration management headaches (IDL and target language), instead of one.

My question is: can you clarify what aspects of IDL really need this separation? Are there features of IDL that are inherently valuable having separated from programming languages? Or, are we just seeing a transitory phase, so that if we come back in 5 years we'll be able to write programs in a high-level language which will make its choice of data representations, automatically provide readers and writers, supply us with memory allocators and garbage collectors, etc.?

Joseph Newcomer (Carnegie Mellon Univ., USA):

IDL's view mechanism (which is part of describing a configuration) is done by so-called derivations: One first writes a base description, then a derivation, and says that "this" is a new view of "that". Then one writes another derivation and says this is yet another view of "this-and-that". However, if you put all these derivations in one linear text file, and you think of your model as text files, this description becomes very hard to maintain. If I could have illustrated it in some graphic tool as a set of drawings and used those drawings as my configuration management, and had some tools to manipulate those drawings, it would have been very helpful. Maybe this is a challenge to Steven Reiss?

David Levine (Intermetrics, USA):

That's a good answer, but not to the question I thought that I was asking!

Joseph Newcomer (Carnegie Mellon Univ., USA):

You were asking me if IDL should have a mechanism outside the language that provides (configuration) control, and I thought I'd answered "yes", by giving a particular example.

Alfons Geser (Univ. Passau, FRG):

There is not a single reference to the Abstract DataType research which has been successful in the field of data representation models, views, information hiding, implementation relations, etc.. Any comments?

Joseph Newcomer (Carnegie Mellon Univ., USA):

Abstract DataTypes are too low-level to be interesting - IDL is the next step beyond them! (Wows from the audience)

Mary Shaw (Carnegie Mellon Univ., USA):

I am dissatisfied with the outcome of the overall exchange between Bill Waite/Gerhard Goos, and the IDL hold. The exchange went roughly: "Gee, isn't this tool too rich for your own good?"; answer: "Well, you can say that about every tool; and besides, this one's an easy to use."

With other languages and tools, we didn't stop at that point in the argument, but also provided some examples of how they ought to be used. The development of ALGOL-like languages was accompanied with an activity called structured programming, that emphasized how the structures in the language should be used. UNIX, for all of its faults, comes not only with a set of system calls, but with a set of attitudes about how to build new things and connect them all together.

In response to the Waite and Goos' question, the IDL folks should not say: "I'm trying to be everything to everybody, but I can't quite do it"; but rather say: "Here is a tool that's intended to be used in the following style to support the following kinds of things. If you use it in this way then you can use it to your advantage, and if you try to use it in another way, you're on your own". My question to the IDL people is: Are you doing this, and if so, when will Bill see it? (Laughter)

Joseph Newcomer (Carnegie Mellon Univ., USA):

I can respond to part of that question. John Nestor and I are working on a book describing IDL, part of which will be introductory tutorial material and complete with examples on the "right" way to use IDL. Richard Snodgrass will also, among others, be a contributor to this book.

Richard Snodgrass (Univ. North Carolina, USA):

I think we're still a long way from identifying an appropriate IDL style. However, recall that structured programming came out more than a decade after ALGOL came out. It's going to take a while before we really understand the limits of the application domain of IDL.

Arthur Evans (Tartan Labs, USA):

Structured programming couldn't happen until we had done a lot of programming and learned a lot about it. We haven't yet done enough data description with a language designed for that purpose to get some ideas about how it really ought to be done.

Gerhard Goos (GMD, FRG):

Newcomer remarked that we have to solve larger and larger problems and therefore IDL is good. Yes, that's true for programmers working in industry, but what about the scientists who still maintain that small and fast is beautiful?

I see the following descriptional methods, one beside the other. The relational algebra approach is underlying PROLOG, Lambda calculus and lists are the paradigms behind LISP; and, directed attributed graphs are the domain of IDL. My belief is that all those approaches are basically the same, and that we could learn a lot from comparing and synthesizing these methods. Presently, IDL's data types are a much better description of templates than PROLOG terms, and it certainly is much better than the templates you can develop on LISP-based systems. Other arguments can be made on predicate vs. Lambda calculus, etc..

Joseph Newcomer (Carnegie Mellon Univ., USA):

Final comment: small and beautiful is always preferable to big and complex!

DAMOKLES – A Database System for Software Engineering Environments

Klaus R. Dittrich   Willi Gotthard   Peter C. Lockemann

Forschungszentrum Informatik an der Universität Karlsruhe
Haid-und-Neu-Straße 10-14, D-7500 Karlsruhe 1

Abstract

Comprehensive software engineering environments consist of a large number of cooperating tools in order to support the various phases of some software life cycle. The cooperation depends largely on the availability of basic mechanisms that manage the large quantities of information involved in a consistent fashion. While database concepts are desirable for this purpose, current systems prove to be unsuitable.

This paper discusses some of the reasons, and lists the requirements that more appropriate solutions have to meet. One major requirement concerns a data model that should specifically be tailored to the software engineering world. The paper presents a new approach to data modelling currently under development. Some other system features as well as implementation aspects are also sketched. We conclude with some perspectives on how the construction of future software tools might be facilitated in the future by virtue of a common underlying database system.

1. Why database support for software engineering environments?

Comprehensive software engineering environments (SEEs) consist of a large number of programs (*software tools*), that together assist software engineers in producing and maintaining quality software. Usually, software development follows a *life cycle model*, and the tools support the work to be done in the various *phases* like requirements specification, coding, testing and so on.

From an information management viewpoint, tools generate, transform or analyse *documents*. Some of these documents are part of the product to be developed (e.g. source and object code, manuals), others represent intermediate results of the design process and may be used as starting points for eventual design iterations. A document is often called a *representation* of the software product being designed (the *design object*).

The management of a potentially large number of design objects in a software engineering enviroment has to fulfill numerous requirements. First, abstracting from the document contents itself, the following major problems have to be dealt with:

- Various interrelationships, like e.g. "depends on" or "has been constructed from", exist between the different representations of a design object and have to be managed consistently.

- In the design of software systems, engineers should try to reuse (parts of) existing systems and modules where appropriate. Thus, libraries of reusable software components and simple ways for accessing them and selecting from them have to be maintained.

- Software systems are complex systems that are always decomposed into manageable parts; their structure usually shows some sort of hierarchy, which should be reflected and exploited in the management of design objects.

- As a result of the development of alternative solutions for a given task, or of revisions due to changing requirements, error corrections and so on, the "same" document exists more than once, though in slight variations. Thus, we have to deal with *versions* of representation objects. Eventually, the designer has to choose a *configuration* of the (sub-) system by selecting a consistent set of versions, one for each representation needed.

- The production of large software systems usually is a team effort. Management of the design documents, therefore, has to provide for the controlled cooperation of a number of people, which entails proper synchronization, access control and the supervised exchange of both, completed and "in work" documents. Also, recovery capabilities in cases of user errors or system failures are needed.

A closer look at the documents themselves reveals a second set of requirements:

- Documents often have themselves an internal structure that may again be interpreted as a large number of objects and relationships among them. Consider, e.g., an attributed syntax tree. Moreover, relationships may exist between objects located in two or more different documents.

- Other documents do not show any sort of meaningful structure at all (e.g. the decomposition of a textual description usually is not relevant for tools of a software engineering environment).

- Complex consistency constraints have to be enforced for the objects and relationships of one document and across documents (e.g. entities imported by one module have to be exported by some other module).

Not surprisingly, this list of requirements does not look all that different from those for other design areas like CAD for VLSI-design or mechanical engineering [Lock85]. In all these cases, powerful yet efficient information management mechanisms are needed as basic components in order to relieve tools from trying to meet all mentioned requirements themselves.

Business and administration applications (e.g. banking, payroll processing, inventory control, airline reservation), over the years have come to appreciate the features of database management systems (DBMSs). The same features should be attractive for use in SEEs, too:

- data integration (single, standardized data mangement and retrieval interface for all tools)

- application-oriented (in contrast to machine-oriented) concepts for structuring and accessing data: the database thus captures more of the application semantics instead of hiding it within the application code

- consistency control

- multi-user operation (synchronization)

- recovery

- authorization and access control

- data independence (each tool has only the view of the database it needs, and thus remains immune against structure changes caused by others, changes in storage management techniques, changes in hardware devices, etc.)

Previous approaches to software engineering environments tended to use conventional file systems to store their documents. As file systems do not offer most of the features just mentioned, additional management components had to be developed. They usually concentrated on version and configuration control [Tich85] and are not built to deal with all the other requirements.

2. Difficulties in using traditional database technology

Summarizing and interpreting the requirements gathered in the previous section from a database system point of view, we obtain the following list:

- The data model should allow the declaration and manipulation of complex objects (accounting for their elaborate internal structure) and of arbitrary inter-object relationships; object versions should be supported and a special domain type for the representation of unstructured information should complement the usual standard types.

- Complex consistency constraints have to be supported that may be checked at arbitrary times; in addition the reactions to constraint violations should be explicitly definable.

- Long transactions to model meaningful units of work in the software development process should use non-suspending synchronization techniques; special recovery features should prevent the loss of results during such transactions even though the transaction may not yet have been committed.

- Authorization and access control techniques should be tailored to the objects supported by the data model.

- Libraries of predefined design objects, products currently under development and private data of the individual engineers should be accessible in a uniform way.

- A hardware architecture comprising a network of workstations and possibly a database server should be supported.

- Performance of the whole system should be high enough not to hamper the work of the software engineers.

Traditional database systems that are currently available in the marketplace have been constructed with the typical requirements of business and adminstration applications in mind. In these areas (often referred to as "record-keeping systems"), to mention only the most salient differences,

- data objects are usually simple, flat records composed of a number of attributes or homogeneous sets of such records (i.e. records within a set show identical structure),
- relationships are rather simple,
- consistency constraints show little complexity, have to be checked at predetermined times, and result in a rollback of work if violated,
- transactions are very short and involve only very few records.

Typical systems are built around the meanwhile classical data models (hierarchical, network, relational) [Date81] and offer rather standard mechanisms for the other features.

Several projects tried to solve the data management problems of software engineering environments and other design systems by using one or the other of these systems [Habe82, Nara85, Lint84]. Not surprisingly, they experienced major problems, mainly emanating from the data model [Sidl80]. In a nutshell,

- simple record-oriented data models have too little expressive power to conveniently deal with complex object-oriented application semantics; consequently, database descriptions and access programs tend to become very obscure and tedious to handle,
- system internals are tailored towards flat records or homogeneous sets of records; thus, performance of object-oriented operations becomes extremly poor (recent results in the area of geometric modelling by [Härd86] show that one object-oriented operation may cause around 70 record-oriented operations in a network database system).

Augmenting a conventional database system by putting an object-oriented interface on top ("frontend") will cure the first problem, but leaves the second one unchanged. Another popular solution, keeping documents in files and using a conventional database system as a manager of the administrative information associated with them [Nara85], addresses only part one of the requirements (namely management of interdocument relations) and even introduces new problems with regard to the controlled cooperation between the file system and the database system.

To sum up, the only meaningful way of providing extensive database support for software engineering environments is to develop new systems that offer the necessary features in an integral way in order to obtain acceptable performance. The *DAMOKLES*[1] system currently under development at our institution is one approach in this direction. The remainder of this paper presents its data model in some detail, shows its application to software production, and sketches some of the other systems features.

3.   The DAMOKLES approach

3.1   The data model

A *data model* defines the facilities for structuring and handling information from a DBMS point of view. It is thus the most decisive part of the user interface. Three parts of a data model have to distinguished:

- a framework of basic types and type constructors (represented by a DDL — data definition language) to build a database *schema* that includes the definition of database types,
- a set of (generic) operators to create, manipulate, retrieve and delete instances of the defined types (represented by one or more DMLs - data manipulation languages); at any point in time, all existing instances together form the current *database state*,
- model-inherent *consistency constraints* that impose further restrictions on the allowed database states and/or on transitions from one state to another.

The *DAMOKLES* data model (called *DODM — design object data model*) comprises concepts in all these areas, that allow to express the typical semantics of SEE documents in a natural way. Generally, a balanced approach to developing a data model should always keep in mind that the model

- be general enough to be useful for any arbitrary SEE, not just the specific one the designer currently has in mind (for economical reasons, one cannot afford a dedicated DBMS for each SEE),
- avoid to become overloaded with concepts and thus too complicated to apply,
- be pragmatic enough to allow an efficient implementation with today's hardware and techniques (which excludes some of the "semantic" data model concepts that can be found in the literature; cf. e. g. [Brod84] for an overview).

From a bird's eye's view, the DODM tries to achieve this balance by providing for

- *structured* (or *complex*) *objects* that may have *versions*,

- *relationships* between objects and/or their versions,

---

(1) Database Management System of Karlsruhe for Environments for Software Engineering

- object and relationship *attributes* that associate further information in a more or less structured way.

DODM may be characterized as to belong to the entity-relationship class of data models, but its expressive power goes far beyond the classical approaches of this class [Chen76, ISO82]. In the sequel, we discuss each of the above constructs in turn.

Structured objects

A *simple* DODM object, like in classical data models (then called a record or a tuple) is composed of a number of *attributes* much like a record in programming languages. One or more of these attributes may be designated to be the object *key* and is thus required to be unique within the set of current database objects of the respective type, at any point in time. In addition, *DAMOKLES* automatically assigns a unique object identifier (OID) to any object upon its creation. Attributes form the *descriptive part* of an object. *Structured objects* also consist of a *structural part*: it includes a set of *subobjects* (perhaps with relationships among them) that, in turn, are objects in their own right and thus may themselves be simple or structured.

In the database schema, the descriptive part of an object type is specified as usual by enumerating the desired attribute names and their associated value sets. For the structural part (if any), the type names of desired subobjects are listed. As there are no further restrictions,

- recursive objects may occur by (directly or indirectly) using their own object type within their structure,
- structured objects need not always be simple hierarchies of lesser objects but may overlap in arbitrary ways.

Instances of structured object types originate in two ways. First, an object of a subobject type may be created together with a given instance of (one of) its superobject types. Second, an existing subobject may dynamically be inserted into its superobject. Subobject removal, automatic subobject deletion upon superobject deletion are also supported.

Operators for objects further include

- locating in sequential order the objects of a given type,
- retrieval based on object identifiers or on attribute values (using a *cursor*, to be discussed in more generality later),
- individual or joint attribute retrieval and modification,
- navigation within structural objects to the next subobject of a given type,
- locating the next structured object in which a given object participates (remember that structured objects may overlap),

```
OBJECT TYPE program              OBJECT TYPE subprogram
    ATTRIBUTES                       ATTRIBUTES
        name   : STRING[30]              name   : STRING[30]
        author : STRING[20]              author : ...
        ...                              ...
    STRUCTURE IS subprogram          STRUCTURE IS subprogram
END program                      END subprogram


OBJECT TYPE library
    ATTRIBUTES
        name : STRING[30]
        ...
    STRUCTURE IS subprogram
END library
```

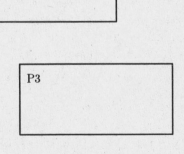

Fig. 1 An example DODM schema together with a database adhering to it

— copying object attributes or entire objects.

To illustrate the object concept introduced so far, consider the following rather simplified example of describing the source code of programs (figure 1). A program has a name, an author, and various other attributes. It may consist of a number of subprograms that may again contain subprograms. Moreover, subprograms of common interest are collected into a library. Figure 1 shows an excerpt of a database schema and a graphical representation using DODM concepts, together with a sample database adhering to this schema.

Object versions

Object versions allow to represent multiple instances of the (semantically) same object under the auspices of the DBMS; they offer a basic mechanism to deal with revisions, alternatives or whatever similar to them may be desired [Ditt85a]. The main characteristics of the DODM version concept are as follows:

- Versions are always associated with objects; more precisely, each version belongs to exactly one object, its *generic object*.

- Both, the generic object as a whole and its individual versions may have attributes and an internal structure. While the object attributes and internal structure are supposed to be common to all its versions, the version attributes and the composition from subobjects may differ.

- Generally, versions can be treated as objects in their own right. Linguistically, their type is denoted as <object type name>.VERSION with <object type name> being the type name of its generic object.

- Consequently, all versions of an object have the same kind of structure and the same attributes. They may even have versions themselves. Both, the entire object (with or without all its versions) or individual versions may be referenced.

- Among the versions of one object, an implicit predecessor-successor relationship is maintained which may optionally be linear, treelike, or acyclic; versions are numbered in creation sequence.

- Operators on versions allow to sequentially locate versions in the version graph for a given object where the order is determined by the graph structure or by version number, to locate the generic object of a given version, to insert and remove a version into/from the version graph of a generic object.

Figure 2 extends the example schema of figure 1 to include subprogram versions. Note that both, programs and libraries contain subprogram versions only and not generic subprogram objects. However, the data model alone (at least as far as discussed up to now) does not guarantee that exactly one version of a subprogram is part of a program or library object (in fact, this property is essential for programs but need not apply to libraries). Another version example may be found in figures 7 and 8.

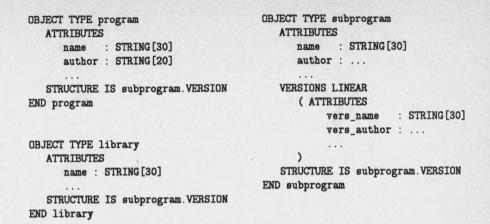

```
OBJECT TYPE program                OBJECT TYPE subprogram
    ATTRIBUTES                         ATTRIBUTES
        name   : STRING[30]                name   : STRING[30]
        author : STRING[20]                author : ...
        ...                                ...
    STRUCTURE IS subprogram.VERSION    VERSIONS LINEAR
END program                            ( ATTRIBUTES
                                             vers_name   : STRING[30]
                                             vers_author : ...
                                             ...
OBJECT TYPE library                    )
    ATTRIBUTES                         STRUCTURE IS subprogram.VERSION
        name : STRING[30]          END subprogram
        ...
    STRUCTURE IS subprogram.VERSION
END library
```

Fig. 2 An example DODM schema (cf fig. 1) involving versions

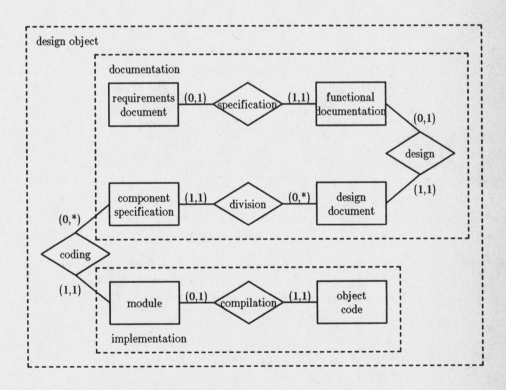

Fig. 3 A DODM schema for a software engineering database

Relationships

Relationships are n-place (n $\geq$ 1) bidirectional associations of objects. Each place is characterized by a *role attribute*, and relationships in their entirety may possess further attributes.

Similar to objects, the database schema describes relationship types with corresponding instances in the database. As an inherent consistency constraint, the user may specify for each role a minimum and maximum *cardinality* for each role. It defines how often an object at least must or at most may participate in a role of a given relationship type.

Relationships play a major part in defining structured objects: like subobjects, they may be included in them. Obviously, objects of any level, generic objects and individual versions may all be used to define relationships. Thus all kinds of inter-object or intra-object associations may be defined, and a powerful set of operators (similar to those for objects) allows to exploit them.

Examples

We are now in a position to discuss some more comprehensive examples. Figure 3 (omitting the dashed boxes for the moment) shows the diagramatic representation of a database schema using relationships (depicted by rhomboids) connecting various documents emerging from a typical software life cycle; cardinalities are related to each role (first number: minimum cardinality — 0 or 1; second number: maximum cardinality — 1 or * for "unlimited"). The object types represented by the dashed boxes are introduced to collect the results of the first phases into a structured object type "documentation", and those of the last two phases into an "implementation" object type. The overall "design object"-type represents a complete software system with all its phase-specific representations.

Figure 4 details the internal structure of "module" objects which is supposed to be a syntax tree consisting of "nodes" and their interrelationships ("fa_so"). As in the simple example of subprograms, modules may also be a part of "libraries" which also manage the import-export relationship (an inter-module relationship) necessary for languages supporting separate compilation like Modula 2 [Wirt82] or Ada [Ada83]. The "definition"-relationship connects defining and applied occurrences of module quantities (e. g. variables) and may be spread across module boundaries.

Figure 5 shows that on the instance level, a structured object may consist of an arbitrary number of — possibly unconnected if cardinalities permit — component instances (omitting the internal structure of the "module"-object of the schema of figure 4).

In figure 6, two possibilities to model a tree in DODM are given. They differ in that the recursive solution allows to operate on subtrees more conveniently, while the non-recursive one favors the treatment of the set of all nodes participating in the tree.

Finally, figures 7 and 8 show how to deal with configurations in DODM. Suppose that "design document" (treelike) and "component specification" objects (linear) of the schema shown in figure 3 come with versions (figure 7). The purpose of a configuration is to collect exactly one version of (in the example) each design document and all the component specifications related to it by the "division" relationships. Note that the "configuration" object type does not guarantee the "exactly one version"

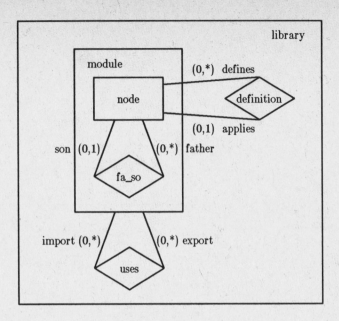

Fig. 4 A closer look at the internal structure of a "module"

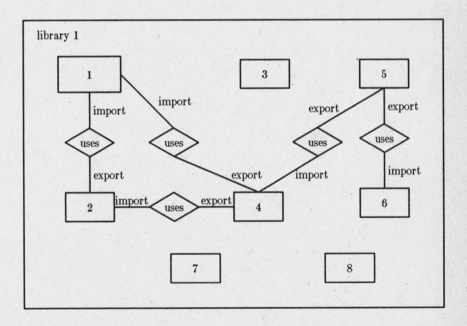

Fig. 5 Database instance of type "library" (of fig. 4). The numbers identify instances of type "module."

```
OBJECT TYPE node                      OBJECT TYPE node
   ...                                   ...
END node                              END node
RELSHIP TYPE f_s                      RELSHIP TYPE f_s
   RELATES father : node,                RELATES father : node,
           son    : node                         son    : tree
END f_s                               END f_s
OBJECT TYPE tree                      OBJECT TYPE tree
   ...                                   ...
   STRUCTURE IS node, f_s                STRUCTURE IS node, f_s, tree
END tree                              END tree
```

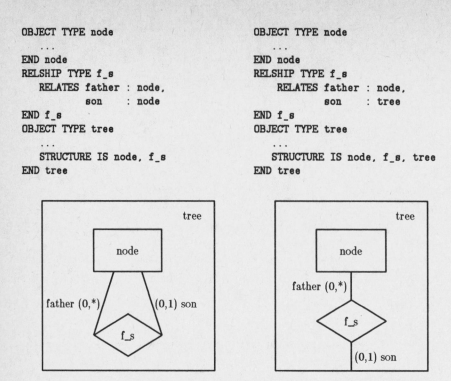

Fig. 6 Two solutions for representing a tree; left: set of related nodes,
right: recursion with subtrees

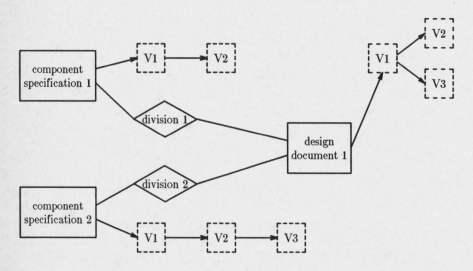

Fig. 7 Multiple versions of design documents and component specifications

conditions which is a typical consistency constraint in this area.

The generic "component specification" and "design document" objects are related by the "division" relationships. In figure 8, we introduced an additional "vers_div" relationship that has to be consistently derived from a "division" (e. g. "a vers_div relatioship may only exist between versions if a division relationship exists between their generic objects" — another typical consistency constraint to be dealt with by an appropriate additional mechanism). It allows to exploit the connections of the "configuration"-subobjects without referring to the generic objects. Note that obviously the selection of versions to be included into a configuration is completely the task of the designer; the database system can only help by maintaining or at least supporting the necessary consistency.

Attributes

As already implied by some of the examples, DODM provides several predefined value sets for object and relationship attributes (e.g. for integer, boolean, character and string values). Also, a number of value set constructors exists (subrange, enumeration, array and record type). A predefined value set deserving special attention is LONG_FIELD. Long fields [Hask81] are byte strings of arbitrary length that are used to represent document contents without making its internal structure known to the DBMS. Long field operators provide for their manipulation in a way similar to direct access methods for files.

Further concepts

DODM includes a number of additional features we cannot discuss here in detail for the lack of space. For example, it provides for *referential integrity* [Date81]: a relationship is automatically deleted if one of the participating objects is deleted. Another example are *cursors* that collect a number of otherwise distinct objects and/or relationships from the database and temporarily hold them as a unit for computation by an application program. The contents of a cursor is determined by a complex search expression that incorporates associative and structural criteria. Cursors can be introduced at will; they may be filled with a contents determined by a search expression; the contents may subsequently be ordered on the basis of a sort expression; the cursor may be emptied of its contents. Usually, cursors are lost after session termination. However, they may be saved across sessions and subsequently be restored; such permanent cursors must explicitly be removed.

The contents of cursors can be manipulated on an element-by-element or a set basis. Operators in the first class include those for inserting or removing an existing object or relationship into/from a cursor and for sequentially navigating through the cursor. Operators in the second class are the classical set operators of union, intersection and difference.

```
OBJECT TYPE configuration              RELSHIP TYPE vers_div
   ATTRIBUTE                              RELATES
     name : STRING[32]                       component_specification.VERSION
   STRUCTURE IS                             design_document.VERSION
     component_specification.VERSION,    END vers_div
     design_document.VERSION,
     vers_div
END configuration
```

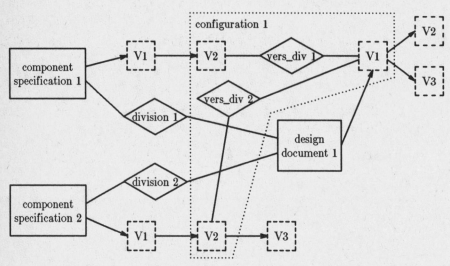

Fig. 8 A design document/component specification configuration (instance level); note that "vers_div" has to be consistently derived from "division". Above the DDL schema for the type "configuration" is given.

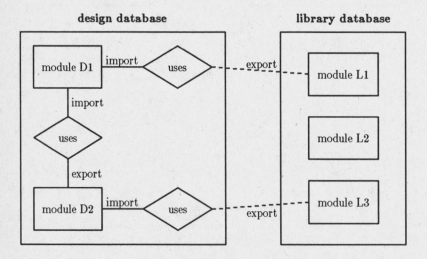

Fig. 9 Relationships extending across database boundaries

Discussion

Principally, the object-subobject structure of complex objects as well as object versions may be regarded as nothing but special cases of general relationships. There are at least two reasons that justify the dedicated concepts we chose for DODM:

- Since complex objects and object versions are standard requirements for the application area of interest, it is more convenient for the database designer to have appropriate data model counterparts. Also, as experience shows, the schema becomes much more comprehensible then a pure entity-relationship schema.
- As the DBMS knows about the special semantics, it can provide efficient implementations for complex objects and versions (e.g. delta storage [Dada84, Tich85] in the latter case).

3.2   Other system features

Of course, there are more concepts in a database system than just the data model. Most of them have to be reevaluated for DBMSs that are to be used in design environments because the classical solutions are not well-suited. We sketch just a few of the techniques we pursue in *DAMOKLES*.

Multiple databases

The classical concept of a single integrated database is inappropriate for design applications. For one, design processes involve a high degree of trial and error, return to earlier stages, test of hypotheses, and they may extend over days, weeks or even months. Consequently, design data often tend to be transient, volatile, tentative, and tied to individual designers. Such data — usually expressed by the notion of revision — should be kept in the private databases of designers. Only design data that have been released should be transferred to public databases which may themselves be organized on two or three levels such as team databases or a project database [Klah85]. Once designs have been completed and are not subject to further modification or even maintenance, they may be transferred to archives. Software objects that are suited for reuse in other projects or for separate marketing, or that have been acquired from outside sources, may be kept in separate libraries. Consequently, a SEE will usually deal with several databases.

DAMOKLES handles multiple databases, subject to the following rules:

- An object is a member of exactly one database; however, copies are allowed in other databases.
- Relationships may be established between objects in different databases. However, the relationship attributes are confined to one of the involved databases (figure 9).
- All databases satisfy the same (global) DODM schema; however, the schema of an individual database may be just a part of the global schema. We note in passing, that subschemas (views) may be defined similar to conventional systems.

Long transactions

Transactions in traditional DBMSs suppose that work units are of short duration and involve small quantities of data. Thus, the traditional mechanisms implement synchronization strategies on the basis of suspending transactions, complete rollback on transaction failure, and the like. By contrast, work units in design applications take considerable time and may involve complex data structures. Appropriate mechanisms for these *long transactions* [Hask81] are based on the check out/check in-paradigm: to start a long transaction, the user must check out the desired objects to his private database; after completion of his work, he checks them back in. In the meantime, others may still read the (previous state of) the objects in the source database, but cannot check out these objects themselves. However, they may always create new versions (which incidentally is what they do when working without database support; note, therefor, that versions should only be entered into the database in a well controlled way).

As for recovery, we provide a safepoint facility that allows to define application-specific database states a designer can reset his transaction to (instead of losing the results of a longer working period as would be the case with present-day transaction mechanisms).

Other features

To provide for the cooperation of software engineers in teams, we prefer to use an extended *object-oriented access control facility* (including individuals, groups, and "public" as subjects) instead of exploiting complexly nested transactions [Kim84]. A basic mechanism to be used, among others, for the enforcement of *complex consistency constraints* (outside the data model) is also included [Ditt85c]. It relies on arbitrarily definable events that trigger user-defined actions. This allows to check for consistency whenever appropriate, and to react to violations of constraints in a dedicated manner.

3.3 System environment

DAMOKLES is part of the UNIBASE project where a number of German software companies and research institutions cooperate to produce an integrated, yet open UNIX-based software engineering environment. The ultimate goal is to store all kinds of software development data in *DAMOKLES* databases (probably distributed in a network of database servers and workstations) and thus to integrate software tools of various sources by means of the common database interface.

The implementation of a comparatively complex data model like DODM is best achieved by devising a multilevel architecture [Ditt85b]. One of the key differences to the implementation of conventional data models is the requirement to provide efficient operation on (possibly large) complex objects.

Our approach, therefore, introduces a lower level interface below DODM, represented by a so-called *Internal Object Data Model (IODM)*. Like DODM, the IODM is object-oriented but breaks down the complexity of structured objects. This is achieved by the IODM-concept of *logical clusters*. The mapping from DODM to IODM then places all subobjects and relationships directly contained within a structured object into one logical cluster. In this way, the complexity of implementing arbitrary hierarchies of objects and relationships is reduced to the problem of implementing sets of simple objects and relationships.

In a further step, logical clusters (which obviously may overlap!) are split into disjoint physical clusters which in turn lead to variable-size records. Lower modules are responsible for storage management in a way similar to conventional DBMSs, but offer extensive physical clustering mechanisms. In summary, the information of which data should be clustered for efficient access is passed on from the top-most (semantic) level down to the (physical) storage management level.

The *DAMOKLES* implementation will also provide *object-oriented main memory databases* [Katz85, DeWi84] that allow users to identify or assemble the objects they plan to work with in order for the system to fix the necessary structures in main memory until they are explicitly released. This mechanism should provide much of the efficiency of file access without sacrificing all the advantages of database management.

A prototype system supporting the full DODM is scheduled for late 1986. The detailed specification of DODM has meanwhile been frozen and accepted by all cooperating partners. First experience has been gained by some companies who developed DODM schemas for various software tools. Not suprisingly, it took some effort to teach the concepts to people that were not used to think in terms of data models (incidentally, something that has also been observed for the pure entity-relationship concept!). However, the examples completed to date did not show any lack nor superfluity of DODM concepts, and after some training, engineers seem to do a good job in using the data model.

4. Conclusions

Up to now, there is little experience in using database technology in software engineering environments. With our experiments, we hope to be able to demonstrate that these systems and in turn their users can really benefit from incorporating an adequate DBMS.

While there are already advantages in integrating today's tools (even if they can hardly exploit the facilities for internally structuring the objects), we foresee major simplifications in the construction of future tools:

- Revision control tools and the like may become integral parts of the DBMS instead of being placed on top and thus render a really uniform object management interface for the builder of the "real" life cycle-supporting tools.

- Where appropriate, tools may conveniently use *common* database structures instead of redundant file contents that needs additional transformation. In addition, the definition of complex data structures can be shifted to the DBMS (where it is done once) instead of repeating it in numerous tools.

- When defining object structures in detail to the database, DBMS mechanisms may be used to collect useful statistics (software metrics, [Perl81]), enforce consistency constraints (e.g. "import quantities of a module have to be exported by some other module") and so on.

- Moreover, since a system like *DAMOKLES* also allows to define schemas resembling those of classical commercial DBMSs (namely by just not using complex objects, versions, etc.), the same DBMS may even be used as part of a software system built by using the software engineering environment.

Efficient operation is the main requirement for making DBMSs viable parts of complex systems. We are sure that the techniques currently developed by the database research community are promising steps towards this goal.

5. References

[Ada83]   American National Standards Institute, Inc.: The Programming Language Ada Reference Manual. ANSI/MIL-STD-1815A-1983. Lecture Notes in Computer Science, Vol. 155, Springer, 1983.

[Brod84]   Brodie, M. L., J. Mylopoulos and J. W. Schmidt (eds.): On Conceptual Modelling, Springer, 1984.

[Chen76]   Chen, P. P.-S.: The Entity-Relationship Model — Toward a Unified View of Data. ACM Transactions on Database Systems, Vol. 1, No. 1, March 1976, pp. 9-36.

[Dada84]   Dadam, P., V. Lum and H.-D. Werner: Integration of Time Versions into a Relational Database System. Proc. VLDB 10, 1984, pp. 509-522.

[Date81]   Date, C. J.: Introduction to Database Systems. 3rd edition. Addison-Wesley, 1981.

[DeWi84]   DeWitt, D. J. et al.: Implementation Techniques for Main Memory Database Systems. Technical Report, Electronic Research Laboratory, University of California, Berkeley, 1984.

[Ditt85a]   Dittrich, K. R. and R. A. Lorie: Version Support for Engineering Database Systems. Research Report RJ 4769 (50628) 7/18/85. IBM Research Laboratory, San Jose, CA 95193 (to appear in IEEE Trans. on Software Engineering).

[Ditt85b]   Dittrich, K. R., A. M. Kotz and J. A. Mülle: A Multilevel Approach to Design Database Systems and its Basic Mechanisms. Proc. IEEE COMPINT, Montreal, 1985, pp. 313-320.

[Ditt85c]   Dittrich, K. R., A. M. Kotz and J. A. Mülle: Complex Consistency Constraints in Design Databases. Technical Report No. 2, FZI Karlsruhe, 1985.

[Habe82]   Habermann, N. et al.: The Second Compendium of Gandalf Documentation. Department of Computer Science, Carnegie-Mellon University, Pittsburgh, May 1982.

[Härd86]   Härder, T. et al.: KUNICAD — Ein datenbankgestütztes geometrisches Modellierungssystem für Werkstücke. Universität Kaiserslautern, Bericht Nr. 22/86, Januar 1986.

[Hask81]   Haskin, R. L. and R. A. Lorie: On Extending the Functions of a Relational Database System. Proc. SIGMOD (ACM), June 1982, pp. 207-212.

[Hend84]   Henderson, P. (ed.): Proc. of the ACM SIGSOFT/SIGPLAN Software Engineering Symposium on Practical Software Engineering Environments. SIGPLAN Notices, Vol. 19, No. 5, May 1984.

[ISO82]   J. J. van Griethuysen (ed.): Concepts and Terminology for the Conceptual Schema and the Information Base. International Organization for Standardization, ISO/TC97/SC5/WG3, publication number ISO/TC97/SC5 - N 695, 1982.

[Katz85] Katz, R.: Information Management for Engineering Design. Springer, 1985.

[Lint84] Linton, M. A.: Implementing Relational Views of Programs. In: [Hend84], pp. 132-140.

[Klah85] Klahold, P., G. Schlageter, R. Unland and W. Wilkes: A Transaction Model Supporting Complex Applications in Integrated Information Systems. Proc. SIGMOD 1985, pp. 388-401.

[Kim84]   Kim, W., R. Lorie, D. McNabb and W. Plouffe: A Transaction Mechanism for Engineering Databases. Proc VLDB 10, 1984, pp. 355-362.

[Lock85] Lockemann, P. C. et al.: Database Requirements of Engineering Applications — An Analysis. Proc. GI-Fachtagung "Datenbanksysteme in Büro, Technik und Wissenschaft", Karlsruhe, März 1985 (in German). Also available in English: Universität Karlsruhe, Fakultät für Informatik, Technical Report 12/85.

[Nara85] Narayanaswamy, K., W. Scacchi and D. McLeod: Information Management Support for Evolving Software Systems. Technical Report USC TR 85-324, University of Southern California, Los Angeles, CA 90089-0782, March 1985.

[Perl81] Perlis, A., F. Sayward and M. Shaw: Software Metrics: An Analysis and Evaluation. MIT Press, 1981.

[Sidl80] Sidle, T. W.: Weaknesses of Commercial Database Management Systems in Engineering Applications. Proc. 17th Design Automation Conference, Minneapolis, June 1980, pp. 57-61.

[Tich85] Tichy, W. F.: RCS — A System for Version Control. Software Practice and Experience, Vol. 15, No. 7, 1985, pp. 637-654.

[Wirt82] Wirth, N.: Programming in Modula 2. Springer, 1982.

Acknowledgement

K. Abramowicz, C. Eick, R. Längle, T. Raupp and T. Wenner together with the authors have been involved in determining the requirements and designing the DODM. We are also grateful to our project partners in UNIBASE for their support and cooperation.

Toward a Persistent Object Base

John R. Nestor
Software Engineering Institute
Carnegie-Mellon University
Pittsburgh, Pa. 15213

Abstract

To better understand the needs of future programming environments, two current technologies that support persistant data in programming environments are considered: file systems and data base systems. This paper presents a set of weaknesses present in these current technologies. These weaknesses can be viewed as a checklist of issues to be considered when evaluating or designing programming environments.

1 Introduction

Every programming environment must support not only transient data that is used during computation but also support persistent data that is kept over some period of time. Two widely used current technologies support persistent data: file systems and database systems. There is increasing recognition that neither of these technologies alone will provide an adequate basis for the next generation of programming environments. Most new environment efforts are moving toward a more object oriented approach that is a synthesis of ideas from file systems and databases. Some examples are CAIS [DoD 85], the ESPRIT Portable Common Tool Environment [ESPRIT 85], the Common Lisp Framework [CLF 85], and Arcadia [Taylor 86]). This next generation of technology will be referred to as persistent object bases.

To better understand the nature of the technology needed by future programming environments, this paper considers the weaknesses that will have to be eliminated in traditional file systems and database systems to create a first class persistent object base. Section 2 sets the context for later sections by discussing the character and needs of future programming environments. Sections 3 and 4 cover, respectively, the weaknesses of traditional file systems and database technologies. Section 5 presents conclusions.

This work was sponsored by the Department of Defense. The views and conclusions contained in this paper are those of the author and should not be interpreted as representing official policies, either expressed or implied, of the Software Engineering Institute, Carnegie-Mellon University, the Department of Defense, or the U.S. Government.

2 Context

Modern software technologies allow software engineers to automate many of the processes that are often implemented by inefficient manual or semi-automatic procedures. Such improvements increase our expectations, leading to larger software projects. Larger projects, in turn, require improved communications among managers, users, designers, and maintainers of such projects.

As the software to be produced grows in size and complexity and the communication requirements increase in scope, the tools required to develop and support such software must become more powerful, and the computational system to support the software tools must grow proportionately in scope. In place of a single batch or time sharing machine, increasing emphasis is being placed on use of workstations, distributed computation, and networks to integrate previously separate computer systems into a single vast communication and computational system. Not only must the hardware evolve, but the environment itself must be developed, upgraded, and enhanced over a lifetime of many years.

Programming environments have become a focal point for much of the work directed toward improving the practice of software engineering. Such environments provide support for software development, management, and maintenance. The are some primitive programming environments already available; there are many next generation environments currently being designed; and work on environments will be a major technical thrust of software engineering for many years to come. There are two top level design goals that will make future environments successful: openness and integration.

Openness refers to the ability to incorporate tools, methodologies, and technologies into the environment as needs and opportunities arise. For an environment to be open, it must provide a set of interfaces that permit new features and tools to be easily inserted. The degree to which an environment can be extended to support a wide variety of new tools and methodologies is one measure of the degree to which that environment can be considered to be open. Openness can also be enhanced by the way in which the interfaces are made available; public availability (as opposed to proprietary control), quality documentation, ease of use, acceptable performance, stability, portability, and standardization can all contribute to the openness, in actual practice, of an environment.

Integration means that the components of the environment work together through a uniform interface, style of operation, and communication medium. The cooperation of the components allows for better use of information sharing, resulting in an intelligent environment.

Though openness and integration are important to software development environments, most systems to date have emphasized openness over integration, or vice versa: There are few existing examples of systems that achieve both. Nevertheless, this tension can be resolved in a way that will enable both goals to be achieved; the key lies largely in the design of the infrastructure of the environment, the kernel parts on which all other tools, features, and methodology support are built. If the infrastructure is not properly designed, increasing complexity of our environments and the systems they are used to construct will make quality increasingly difficult to achieve.

In earlier systems, the infrastructure was provided mainly by the operating system, in which the primary concern was resource allocation and scheduling. As a result of improved hardware technology, new software engineering tools, evolving views of the software development process, and ever increasing expectations, a shift of emphasis has occurred in our view of the role of the infrastructure.

Persistent object bases are a key part of the infrastructure of future programming environments. Providing a high-quality persistent object base is a necessary, although not sufficient, condition for achieving the full potential of future programming environments.

3 Weaknesses of Traditional File Systems

This section considers five areas where traditional file systems are inadequate for persistent object bases: organization, abstraction, history, attributes, and synchronization. Unix[1] [Ritchie 74] is used here as an example of a traditional file system. Other traditional file systems differ in their details from the Unix file system but display essentially similar weaknesses.

3.1 Organization

The Unix file system is organized as a tree of files, each of which is either a directory or an ordinary file.[2] Within the tree, directories appear as inner nodes and files appear as leaf nodes. The root of the tree is a unique directory from which all directories and files can be reached. Each directory is a mapping between file names and the files themselves. Each file has a unique path name given by the path from the root directory to the file. For example, the path name /usr/bin/man is for a file named man that is reached from the root directory via first the usr directory, then via the bin directory.

One problem with a tree structured file system is that the user is forced to represent a system in a way that does not reflect the structure of the data in the system. A related problem is that as a system evolves the user periodically must do major reorganizations of the data within the file system. These reorganizations are needed because the preexisting hierarchical structure increasingly deviates from the actual logical relationships.

Consider, for example, a system being built as part of some project called Q_Development. A directory is built for the project.

```
/projects/Q_Development
```

Initially, all files for the project are placed in that directory. Soon the number of files in that directory has grown to where more structure is needed. Suppose that both documentation files and program files exist. To provide more structure, two new directories are created.

```
/projects/Q_Development/documentation
/projects/Q_Development/program
```

All of the files are moved into one or the other of these two directories. Not only is there the extra work involved in moving the files into the two new subdirectories, but any shell scripts that

---

[1]Unix is a trademark of AT&T.

[2]There are also special files and links that for simplicity are not discussed here.

referred to `Q_Development` must now be changed to refer to one or the other or both of the two new subdirectories. For a persistent object base, no moves should be required and existing shell scripts should remain unchanged. Additional information would be added on top of the existing structure.

Consider next that it is time to release the Q system to users. Users should have the Q executable file and the Q user manual, but not the Q source code or the Q internal documentation. These files are a subset of the files in the two subdirectories. Since users should not have to know about the substructure of the Q project directories and be confused by all those other files that don't matter to them, a new directory is created to hold copies of the files that the users will need.[3]

```
/release/Q
```

Moving files was bad enough, but in this case there are now actually two copies of the same files.[4] For a persistent object base, information would be added, but files would not be moved or copied.

Finally, consider that it is time to produce a new version of the Q system while leaving the previous version of Q around. To do this, the directories must be split.

```
/projects/Q_Development/documentation/V1
/projects/Q_Development/documentation/V2
/projects/Q_Development/program/V1
/projects/Q_Development/program/V2
/release/Q/V1
/release/Q/V2
```

Here all the old files are moved into the `V1` directories. The `V2` directories will be used for the new version of the system. A simple way to do this is to start by copying all the `V1` files into `V2`. Work on the new version then can be done by changing the `V2` file while leaving the `V1` files intact.[5] Furthermore, when versions were introduced, why wasn't the directory tree split in one of the following ways?

```
/projects/Q_Development/V1/documentation
/projects/Q_Development/V1/program
/projects/Q_Development/V2/documentation
/projects/Q_Development/V2/program
/release/Q/V1
/release/Q/V2
```

---

[3]At least in some file systems symbolic links could be used to avoid the copy. In Unix, however, hard links can only be made between a directory and a file on the same physical volume. Symbolic links can cross volumes but result in an asymmetrical specification of a symmetrical situation.

[4]A well known software engineering "rule" states that when there are two identical copies of the same file at least one of them is different!

[5]Some file systems provide a search list mechanism where the `V2` directories are initially empty and a search list is set that searches first `V2` then `V1`. Any time a file not in `V2` must be changed it is first copied into `V2`. This is again sort of a solution but is tedious, confusing, and error prone.

```
/V1/projects/Q_Development/documentation
/V1/projects/Q_Development/program
/V1/release/Q
/V2/projects/Q_Development/documentation
/V2/projects/Q_Development/program
/V2/release/Q
```

The answer is that that there is no strong reason to prefer one of these structures over the others. In a persistent object base, all three of these forms should be indistinguishable.

3.2 Abstraction

Unix starts with the assumption that all files exist on the same physical volume (typically a disk). In order to deal with multiple physical volumes, Unix has a mount command. The mount command has two arguments: an existing directory and a new volume that itself holds a file system consisting of a tree of directories and ordinary files. A mount causes the file tree on the new volume to be "pasted" into the file tree in place of the specified existing directory. The net effect is that there is a strong coupling between the path name of a file and its physical location. As Unix has come to be used in distributed networks, several network file systems have been proposed, including Apollo DOMAIN [Leach 83], Sun NFS [Sandberg 85], and AT&T RFS [Hatch 85]. In all of these systems, the path name is coupled to the physical placement within the network.

Modern data abstraction [Shaw 84] shows that considerable benefits can be achieved by separating the logical structure of data from its representation. As can be seen above, the Unix file system blurs together the logical concept of path name with the representational concept of physical location. Representational properties frequently influence the logical structure of data. Since physical volumes have a finite maximum data size, the number of files within the subtree for a volume is constrained. When the data size exceeds the physical space, the user is forced into modifying the logical structure. In networks, data on a local disk is often faster to access than data on a remote node. By changing the physical placement of data within the network, and therefore its logical structure, a user can get faster file access. In both these cases, the user who wants to deal with the logical structure of the data frequently spends considerable time also dealing with the physical constraints of the file system.

The Unix file system does not support flexible physical representations. For example, there is no way in Unix to transparently store a file in a compressed format using text compression [Welch 84] or as a delta relative to some related file [Rochkind 75, Katz 84]. This kind of transparency would eliminate the user burden of explicitly invoking a decompressing program before each use of the compressed file.

Another kind of flexible representation is the use of multiple cached copies of the same file [Schroeder 85]. Within Unix, caching can be provided only by modifying the Unix kernel.

In a persistent object base, data abstraction should be practiced so that logical concepts are decoupled from physical representations; richer representations should be possible by providing the ability to program the implementation of file abstractions. The Apollo extensible streams mechanism [Apollo 86] is an example of such a data abstraction mechanism grafted on top of a Unix file system.

3.3 History

Two related history concepts are considered here: source versions and re-creation.

Every time a source file is edited, logically a new version is created, so that over time a linear sequence of versions is created. When alternatives occur, such as when a bug is fixed in an old release while work continues on the next release, the sequence can fork, and when alternatives come together separate sequences can join. Abstractly, a directed acyclic version graph is formed. Not all points in the version graph are equally important; in practice, users impose additional structure at one or more levels of granularity and do not preserve versions below some minimum level of granularity. The finest granularity corresponds to every edit. A coarse granularity would be at major release points. Intermediate granularities are frequently defined to aid the management of a development project. The concept of versions can be usefully extended to multiple related source files which may be considered to be progressing in parallel along a version graph.

One common way of handling source versions is through the use of naming conventions: either at the directory or the file level. Earlier in this paper, directory naming conventions were used as a way of representing versions of related sets of files. For example, the two directories below would hold all the Q system source files associated with each of the two versions.

```
projects/Q_Development/V1
projects/Q_Development/V2
```

A method for dealing with individual source files is use of a generation mechanism. Although Unix provides no special generation mechanism, the same effect can be realized by file naming conventions. For example, two versions of the same file could be named using a version extension.

```
/projects/Q_Development/Q_Control.ada.V1
/projects/Q_Development/Q_Control.ada.V2
```

One disadvantage of this approach is that all shell scripts need to be aware of the generation naming conventions, and any V1 shell script needs to be edited before it can be used for V2. [6] When using conventions for representing version relationships, the entire burden for ensuring consistency rests with the user. Although a convention for representing linear version relationships is obvious, conventions representing forks and joins in the version graph are less clear.

A more sophisticated source version system is provided by the Unix SCCS tool and by a similar but improved tool RCS [Tichy 82]. SCCS keeps track of all the versions of a single source file. It provides support for both forks and joins.[7] The SCCS implementation holds all versions of a source file in a single file called the s-file. Before any use of a particular version of that source can occur, it must be extracted explicitly from the s-file. Typically, shell scripts will contain calls to SCCS for this purpose. The big disadvantage of SCCS is that it is an *ad hoc* data encoding scheme implemented on top of the file system, rather than as part of it. In addition to its logical properties, SCCS also uses the representational method of source deltas to encode the ver-

---

[6]The edit could be avoided by passing the version as a string parameter which is then concatenated to all file names.

[7]The SCCS documentation suggests that forks be kept to a minimum to avoid structural complexity.

sions. This is yet another example of how logical properties and physical representation have been blurred together.

In a persistent object base, SCCS-like functionality would be provided in a transparently integrated manner. Versions and data compression would be handled by orthogonal mechanisms.[8] The DSEE system [Leblang 85] is one current example of how this could be done.

Re-creation is the ability to be able to go back to an old version of a system and repeat all of the steps that were involved in its creation. Re-creation implies that all information about system creation is captured. Traditionally, a lot of the system creation information was held only in the heads of the development team, making re-creation difficult. Re-creation is important for two major reasons. First, if a system is re-creatable, important structural relationships between the files of the system are captured. System maintainers can use the relationships directly and use support tools that depend upon having the relationships available. Second, if an old version of a system has a bug, re-creation means that a minor variation of it can be constructed in which the bug is fixed. To better understand re-creation, the concept of a derivation graph is used. Derivation graphs were used in Toolpack [Osterweil 83]. The definition used here is a somewhat simplified form of the model presented in [Borison 86].

Those files that make up a system can be divided into primitive and derived files. A primitive file is either a source file of the system or some file from outside the system that is used in its construction. A derivation step consists of an invocation that accesses a set of input files to produce a set of output files. The invocation includes a tool consisting of an "executable" file and a set of actual parameters to that tool, which could be either constants or files (or their names). It is assumed that the output files depend only upon the input files and the invocation involved in the derivation step.[9] Derived files are those that are output of some derivation step. The inputs of a derivation step and the file holding the tool being run in the derivation step must be either primitive files or output files of some earlier derivation step. The combination of all the derivation steps for a system is its directed acyclic derivation graph. A system is re-creatable if all of its derived files can be re-created identically. In terms of a derivation graph, re-creation is possible if each derivation step is known, the set of primitive files is known, and the primitive files have not been changed since the system was first created.

In Unix, creation is often accomplished using the Unix tool Make [Feldman 79]. Make applies a set of heuristics to a *makefile* that contains a list of explicit commands to determine and run a set of invocations.[10] Make is concerned with invocations, not with the more general concept of derivation steps. In general, it is not possible to tell the complete set of input files and output files of each derivation step of a system by looking only at the *makefile*; therefore, it is not pos-

---

[8]Version information, however, could be used to guide heuristics that identify candidates for delta compression.

[9]In practice, it is necessary to deal with things like steps that read the system clock or that interact with the user. For current purposes such problems are ignored.

[10]Although not discussed here, Make also uses heuristics to avoid reruning those derivation steps whose inputs have not changed since they were run last.

sible to determine the set of primitive files of a system. By convention, users normally include information about these file sets in their *makefiles*, but there is no check to be sure that this information is complete or even correct. The reason for this deficiency goes deeper than just the Make tool. In Unix, when a tool is invoked, there is no way to tell what files are opened for input and/or output. Such an inquiry is essential to guarantee re-creation but when arbitrary tools can be invoked during derivation[11], this inquiry can only be implemented by making modifications to the Unix kernel.

For re-creation, the set of primitive files must be determined, and each file in the set must be checked to ensure that it has not been changed since initial creation. Unix provides some assistance here in the form of a time stamp for each file that gives the time that each file was last modified. As long as the last modified time on a file is older than the creation time of the system, then it would seem that it is a correct file. The problem occurs when the Unix move command, `mv`, is used. This command moves a file between two directories and preserves its last modified time. So when `mv` is used, the primitive file may not be correct and re-creation can not be done.[12] Worse, there is a system call, `utimes`, that can be used to change arbitrarily the last modified time.[13]

The use of SCCS protects the user from changing old versions of a source file. This is a step forward, although the problem is still present at a deeper level because the s-file itself is subject to all the previous problems.

In a persistent object base, re-creation would be achieved by immutable objects and unique object identifiers, such as those provided by the Cedar System Modeller [Lampson 83]. All primitive files and the full derivation graph would be stored as immutable objects whose content can not be changed by any user. Each object is assigned a unique identifier at creation in a way such that no two objects ever will have the same unique identifier. The derivation graph would refer to primitive objects by their unique identifier, not by their file name; so move and copy operations would not confuse the identification of the primitive objects.

Keeping the information needed to re-create all the old versions of all systems on rotating magnetic media is generally considered too expensive. Write-once laser disks are just starting to become available [Fujitani 84]: They offer the ability to hold extensive historical information at acceptable costs. When write-once laser disks are combined with the use of compressed representations, there is no reason why all past versions of all source files can not be kept available on-line [Katz 84].

---

[11]Tools where the set of input and output files for an invocation can be determined easily present no problem. The C compiler, which can read arbitrary include files, involves moderate difficulty.

[12]In practice, it often looks as though re-creation happens correctly. Users frequently spend many confusing hours when the re-created system is subtly different from the original system.

[13]Tool designers have been known to use this call constructively to fake Make into doing "the right thing".

3.4 Attributes

Unix provides a fixed set of attributes for each file as part of its directory entry. These attributes include the name of the owner of the file, a set of file protection control bits, and times of file creation, modification and use. These attributes are mostly set and used by the system, although there are commands and system calls that permit the user to set and use them.

When additional attributes beyond those provided by Unix are needed, the user must find alternative ways of representing them, since there is no way to add new attributes to a directory. The set of additional attributes that could be of use in an environment is unlimited, being determined by the needs of a development effort and the tools it uses. A persistent object base must be able to support arbitrary attributes. Some examples of additional attributes include the unique identifier for the file, a string attribute that gives the reason why the file was created, and a boolean attribute that indicates whether the content of the file has been compressed.

Attributes can be used also to relate files. For example, the version graph can be represented by each file having as an attribute a set of the unique identifiers of the files that are its immediate version predecessors. Since the version graph is symmetrical, another attribute that is a set of version successors could be added also, but these two attributes contain redundant information. To avoid the redundancy and to preserve the symmetry, a better way of representing the version graph would be with a version relationship that relates predecessors with successors but that is not an attribute of either. So in addition to attributes, a persistent object base should support arbitrary relationships. Other examples of relationships include the derivation graph, and a relationship between C program files and the include files they reference.

In addition to files having attributes, a persistent object base should also permit relationships to have attributes.[14] For example, the version relationship could have an attribute that says why a successor version was produced from some predecessor version, and a derivation step within the derivation relationship might have an attribute for the time at which it was run.

Typically, when tools are built on top of Unix that depend upon attributes and/or relationships, then *ad hoc* encoding means are used. These means range from special purpose file encodings such as the s-files of SCCS, through special purpose database systems such as that used in Gandalf [Gandalf 85], to general purpose database system such as that used in DSEE. Not only is considerable effort wasted in building tools which each must do their own attribute and relationship support, but even greater problems occur when tools that use different *ad hoc* schemes must be integrated. Consider, for example, two systems, each of which uses its own special *ad hoc* scheme and where the information used partially overlaps so that redundant information must be synchronized between the two different schemes. The net result is that integration is very difficult, if not impossible.

---

[14]It even makes sense to have relationships between relationships.

3.5 Synchronization

When two or more users are working on the same system and therefore the same set of files, some means of synchronizing that use is needed. When two people are editing the same source file without synchronization, the changes made by one may overwrite the changes made be the other without either being aware of the problem. In the absence of automated support, users frequently do such synchronization by manual conventions. For example, a specific set of files are agreed to be "controlled" by some specified user who may change any of the files while other users may read but not modify the files. The weaknesses of this approach are that it is time consuming, error-prone, and often overly restrictive in limiting modifications.

Under Unix, the SCCS tool provides support for synchronization at the level of each source file. SCCS has two basic operations for synchronization: `get` a file for editing from the s-file; and `merge` the edited file back into the s-file. Only one user may have a given s-file in the editing state, between a `get` and a `merge`. This is overly restrictive because multiple edits could be proceeding safely on independently forked alternatives. The RCS tool solves this problem by permitting one edit to be occurring on each alternative fork. Both SCCS and RCS require explicit extra action by the user to `get` and `merge` a file when editing it. This is often enough of a burden to discourage users from using either SCCS or RCS. The DSEE system provides the synchronization in an integrated fashion that is less of a burden for the user and that is harder to subvert.

Another problem with SCCS and RCS is that the default mode of operation for `get` is to extract the most recent version on the main version line. At first this seems like a desirable feature, since most of the work on a system is with the most recent version. Problems can occur, however, when multiple people are producing new versions of the primitive files of a system. When a user changes some primitive files and then does a build based on most recent versions of all primitive files, the resulting system will incorporate not only the user's changes but also possibly arbitrary other changes made by other users to other primitive files. The net result is that the behavior of a most recently built system will often change over time in subtle ways that are not under the user's control. Normally, under Unix no derivation graph is recorded; thus it is difficult, if not impossible, to figure out which set of primitive files have changed since the previous system build. Time stamps are one clue to what has changed, but due to problems discussed earlier, they are not always reliable. Recall that primitive files include not only source files that belong to the system under development but also libraries and tools that are part of Unix. Normally, Unix libraries and tools are not version controlled; nevertheless, they are changed during periodic operating system releases and by Unix system software maintainers at arbitrary times to fix perceived "bugs". These changes cause not only unpredictable behavioral changes in the current system builds, but can also destroy the ability to re-create previous system versions.

A high quality programming environment must support synchronization that is simple for users, place no unnecessary restrictions on simultaneous access, support a version control system for both user and system files, record the full derivation graph, allow the user to control explicitly which versions of primitive files to use, and support inquiry so that users can determine easily which primitive files of a system have been changed. A persistent object base should provide the basic support layer on which such environments can be built.

4 Weaknesses of Database Systems

This section considers five areas where database systems are inadequate for persistent object bases: types, decentralization, time, distribution, and performance. Relational database systems [Codd 70] will be used as examples. Other database systems will differ in their details from relational systems but display essentially similar weaknesses.

Engineering databases, particularly those used for CAD/CAM, share many basic requirements with programming environments. Many of the weaknesses that have been identified in these applications [Hallmark 84, Hartzband 85] are similar to those discussed here.

Relational database systems are now just starting to be used within programming environments for applications including source program tree representation, dynamic execution behavior, and version and configuration control [Ceri 83, Snodgrass 84, Linton 84].

4.1 Types

Types in relational database systems are considered here from three perspectives: primitive types, structural types, and abstract types.

Relational database systems typically have a small predefined set of primitive types for attributes.[15] This set is often quite constraining when used for programming environments. For example, consider using a relation to represent the version graph.

```
Version : relation
        old:integer,      -- old version number
        new:integer,      -- new version number
        why:string        -- reason for change
     end
```

A value for this relation might be as follows.

Version		
old	new	why
1	2	"Added a new feature that permits inverted input"
2	3	"Fixed the bug introduced in v 2"

Here the **why** field is a string of arbitrary length. The only string type provided by many relational systems is a fixed length string. The effect of varying length strings can be achieved, but only by subverting the system.

```
Version1 : relation
        old:integer,       -- old version number
        new:integer,       -- new version number
        count:integer,     -- string index
        why:string(20)     -- reason for change
     end
```

---

[15]In database systems, the term domain is used to refer to a set of values for some attribute. The term type is used here instead of domain to emphasize analogies with the type mechanisms of programming languages.

Version1			
old	new	count	why
1	2	1	"Added a new feature "
1	2	2	"that permits inverte"
1	2	3	"d input "
2	3	1	"Fixed the bug introd"
2	3	2	"uced in v 2 "

Not only is the structure of the data obscured, but both space to store the data and time to access it are degraded. This kind of subversion only gets worse when trying to represent more complex programming environment data such as program source and relocatable, documentation, and graphics. Although all of these could be built up from the primitive types of a relational database system, the effort is large and the representation would be neither natural nor efficient.

Structurally, a relational database consists of a set of named relations. Consider, for example a database with two relations.

```
Version : relation
        old:integer,     -- old version number
        new:integer,     -- new version number
        why:string       -- reason for change
    end

Source : relation
        version:integer,-- version number
        day:integer,     -- day created
        month:integer,   -- month created
        year:integer     -- year created
    end
```

All of the relationships between relations are expressed implicitly. Typically, two relations are related by using the same type for some attribute in each so that they can be joined. For example, **Version.old** could be joined to **Source.version**. It is not the case, however, that if two relations have attributes with the same types that it always makes sense to join them. For example, joining **Version.old** to **Source.month** is not a sensible operation. One way to introduce more structure is by stronger typing such as that provided by the Modula-2 type declaration [Wirth 85].

```
type version_type = integer;
type day_type = integer;
type month_type = integer;
type year_type = integer;

Version : relation
        old:version_type,      -- old version number
        new:version_type,      -- new version number
        why:string             -- reason for change
    end

Source : relation
        version:version_type, -- version number
        day:day_type,          -- day created
        month:month_type,      -- month created
        year:year_type         -- year created
    end
```

Another structural approach is to use graphical entity-relationship diagrams [Chen 76].

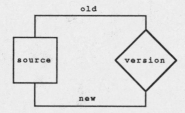

Extended relational models are another way of introducing more structure. One such system is RM/T [Codd 79]. In RM/T, system generated surrogate keys are attached to every tuple of every relation so that no two are ever identical.

```
Source : relation
        version:integer,-- version number
        day:integer,     -- day created
        month:integer,   -- month created
        year:integer     -- year created
    end

Version : relation
        old:key[Source],-- old version
        new:key[Source],-- new version
        why:string        -- reason for change
    end
```

Source

key	version	day	month	year
#003	1	10	5	85
#004	2	20	10	85
#005	3	4	3	86

Version

key	old	new	why
#001	#003	#004	"Added a new feature ..."
#002	#004	#005	"Fixed the bug ..."

The **key** attribute is automatically supplied and initialized by the system. Since joins now are based on unique surrogate keys, structural relationships are specified fully. Surrogate keys are closely related to the unique object identifiers discussed earlier and to the typed pointers of Modula-2.

If surrogate keys are placed not only on tuples but on entire relations, then relations can be used to relate other relations. For example, a directory tree like that of a file system can be represented. First, a relation type for directories is introduced.

```
Type Directory = relation
          name:string,
          file:key
      end
```

As an example, the following directory tree is used.

```
/Q_Development/V1/documentation
/Q_Development/V1/program
/Q_Development/V2/documentation
/Q_Development/V2/program
```

That tree is represented by the following instances of the **Directory** type.

#001 :Directory

key	name	file
#002	"Q_Development"	#003

#003 :Directory

key	name	file
#004	"V1"	#006
#005	"V2"	#009

#006 :Directory

key	name	file
#007	"documentation"	#012
#008	"program"	#013

#009 :Directory

key	name	file
#010	"documentation"	#014
#011	"program"	#015

The lack of abstract data types [Shaw 84] in relational database systems is perhaps the most significant type weakness. All data in a relational database exists at a structural level. There is no way to define a new abstract type in terms of its abstract properties and then define its implementation in terms of existing types. Reconsidering an earlier example, varying length strings could be defined as a new abstract type that used a variable number of fixed length strings as its representation. This kind of abstraction becomes even more important for complex objects such as those that represent graphic images.

Abstract data types gain much of their power from considering not just data in isolation, but data together with the set of operations. In relational database systems, the data specification written in some schema language is separated from the operations as expressed in some query language. Not only are the specifications physically separate, but often they are expressed in an incompatible language.

Another aspect of abstract data types is that the implementation can be changed without impacting the users of the specification. Database systems normally provide users with a limited level of control over the way in which the data is represented. For example, many database systems allow users to specify those places where redundant inverted indexes are to be created. When the user needs a representation that is not supported by the system, the only alternative is to modify the source code of the database system itself. Even in those rare cases where source code is available, the complexity of most database systems makes this a formidable task. A solution is to put more of the control for representations in the hands of the user via an abstract type mechanism.

A persistent object base system should provide a rich set of primitive types, enable expression of rich structural relationships such as those of the extended relational models, and provide a full abstract data type mechanism. There are obvious parallels between the needed future direction for database systems and the past evolution of type support within modern programming languages. Many of the same type features found in modern languages need to be brought into database systems; however, database systems face special problems brought about by the persistence of data that were not faced by the designers of programming languages.

4.2 Decentralization
Database systems typically have a single centralized schema that is maintained by a database administrator, DBA. For programming environments, it must be possible to define and control data locally. This need is demonstrated below by several examples.

As an initial example, consider the set of documentation files in a system including help files, user manuals, implementation descriptions, and even the source files of systems. These represent online versions of information that each user would previously have had in hardcopy. One advantage of hardcopy is that it is easy for each user to write in personal comments. The same approach could be used online by letting each user make a copy of the document and edit in personal comments, but it would be better to have a single copy of the document and let each user be able to have a separate "overlay" that contains personal comments. This kind of ability is becoming available though a class of environments called hypertext systems [Yankelovich 85]. Consider the following simplified relation types.

```
type Document = relation
        line_number:integer,
        line:string
    end;

type Comments = relation
        document:key[Document],
        line_number:integer,
        comment:string
    end;
```

Considerable progress toward decentralization is already implicit in the use of type definitions and surrogate keys. Type definitions permit multiple instances. Surrogate keys enable an object and its attributes to be stored separately. This separation is important not only for local control but also because it permits data, such as an instance of `Comments`, to be added to a preexisting data structure, such as an instance of `Document`, without modifying either the type definition or contents of that preexisting data structure. Not only must the database permit the right kind of definitions, it also must permit the needed operations. As basic operations, each user must be able to create locally an instance of `Comments` and to control the use of that instance. As a more general operation, users should be able to define their own relation types for their own local use. In many database systems, these abilities are centralized with the DBA. Making a user go through a DBA for these kinds of operations is not only bothersome but also logically unnecessary.[16]

As a second example, consider what happens when a new tool is added to a programming environment. This tool may need the ability to create and access new attributes and relationships of existing objects. The need for local definition, instantiation, and control are similar to those of the previous example. For tools, decentralization also can be an aid to integration. Since each tool can manage locally the attributes and relationships for that tool, independent tools will not place conflicting constraints on centralized data. Conflicts can be representational, such as multiple tools wanting to use word 23 of some control block, or naming, such as multiple tools wanting to use the attribute name `Next`. Particularly severe conflicts can arise when two versions of a single tool are being supported simultaneously. For example, both versions might have a `Next` attribute, but give it slightly different semantics. By giving each version its own instance of the `Next` attribute, multiple versions can coexist without interference.[17]

As a final example, consider integrating two previously independent databases. Such integration could occur when two isolated programming environment systems are connected via a network and a transparent network file system is installed. When centralized schema are used, integration will require merging these two schema into a single new schema. Conflicts are virtually certain to occur, forcing either massive recoding or a less transparent integration in which the two independent schema continue to exist.

---

[16]Analogies exist in the file system area when users are forced to go through a centralized system administrator to have structures created or modified that should be under user control.

[17]Local attribute instances of course do not solve all integration problems. Mechanisms, such as those in [Garlan 86], are needed for integrating tools that have logically related attributes where setting the attribute of one tool should modify the value of attributes of other tools.

For a persistent object base, decentralization of definition, instantiation, and control is essential. This implies that there will not be a database administrator doing all data definition. Another implication is that traditional kinds of normalization that are based on a single centralized schema can not be done. Since normalization is a method of removing redundancy and since controlled redundancy can be used to improve the engineering of software systems, full normalization may not only be limited but also undesirable.

4.3 Time

The basic relational data model views the database as having values that vary over time. Every attribute is considered to be variable and only its current value is available. As was previously discussed, programming environments must provide a history mechanism to record source versions and to support re-creation.

In many simple database systems that are used to support programming environment tools, the only way to preserve history is by making a complete copy of the entire database. In more powerful database systems, transaction journals are used to preserve history. A similar capability is provided in file systems by periodic backup of all the files on a system. All of these approaches have a common weakness: To go back in time, it is necessary to manually substitute a previous version of the data for the current version. This substitution can be either physical or logical. In a physical substitution, the current version is copied to a safe place and then the old version is brought back in the place of the new version. For logical substitution, the new version is left in place, but operations are logically changed to operate on the reconstituted old version.

For a persistent object base, the ability to record previous states and to change back easily and transparently to an arbitrary previous state is essential. To capture this ability cleanly and safely requires more than just the addition of attributes that can take on time values. A persistent object base must include time as an integral part of its underlying formal semantic model [Clifford 83].

Work on temporal database systems [Snodgrass 86] shows that time can be modeled with two dimensions whose axes are transaction time and real time. The transaction time axis measures the actual state of a system over time. By backing up along the transaction time axis to some previous time, the system state is logically returned to what it was at that previous time. By backing up along the real time axis, the system state is logically returned to the state of reality at that previous time (as determined by our best current knowledge). Transaction and real times will differ when either there is delay between the time at which an event occurs and the time at which it is first entered into the database or when some event is incorrectly entered and later corrected. Programming environments are unlike conventional database applications because the reality that is being modeled is data within the database itself. This implies that for programming environments transaction time is identical to real time. Suppose, however, that the concept of exact modeling of reality is replaced by the concept of exactly correct program behavior. Now forward progress of some program under development along the transaction axis represents increased (or modified) functionality, while forward progress along the correctness axis represents an increase in the number of bugs fixed.

4.4 Distribution

Most currently available database systems require that all data be kept within a single machine. Future programming environments will be based on multiple machines connected via many kinds of networks. Although considerable work is now being done on distributed database systems, current systems are still rather limited [Ceri 84]. Two aspects of distribution are considered: how data is distributed among multiple machines and how multiple users on different machines can share the same data.

The goal of data distribution is to place data physically so that it is available easily and quickly to its users while satisfying the hardware size constraints. The simplest way to distribute a relational database is to place different relation instances on different machines. The placement can be static, determined when the instance is created, or dynamic, changeable at any time. Independently, the placement can be manual, under the control of the user, or automatic, under the control of the system.

A more complex distribution would place different parts of the same relation on different machines. For example, consider the version graph relation. Accesses to that relation will tend to be to tuples for recent versions. Older tuples can be placed on remote, slower, and/or larger physical devices of the system.[18]

When two people are using the same data, then in general no one place is best for both. A solution is to permit separate copies of the data to exist at locations that are good for each user. When the users are reading the data and neither is modifying it, then permitting multiple copies is easier. A special case of read-only data is immutable objects. Many network file systems are now providing caching, a dynamic automatic mechanism for transparently creating and managing multiple copies of data [Schroeder 85, Morris 86].

Not all data in a programming environment can be immutable. At least some data must be mutable for progress to be made. A simple mechanism for dealing with mutable data in the presence of multiple users is to use a central server. A server is a specific machine that controls write access to data.[19] The server ensures that only one user is writing the same data at the same time. Before a user can modify data, a lock is set on the server so that other users can not modify that same data.

Servers limit effective distribution. The problem can be reduced by either minimizing the frequency with which a user interacts with the server or by modifying data in ways that do not require the use of a central server.

To understand how to minimize server interaction, it is instructive to consider how multiple users working on the same system interact when using a programming environment that provides no synchronization for data modification. In this case, the users often invent manual methods for synchronization. Other than failures that occur when someone forgets the state of the manually

---

[18]This includes migrating old tuples to magnetic tape.

[19]In practice, there can be multiple servers as long as each data item is handled by exactly one server.

set locks, such methods work just fine. An important distinguishing characteristic of these manual methods is the frequency of the synchronization operations. While common automated systems often operate with a frequency of many synchronization operations per second [Ousterhout 85], manual methods may have a frequency of only a few operations per day. By implementing analogues of these manual methods, server interaction rates can be lowered. As an example, consider the directory tree of a network file system. Every time a new file name is created, a synchronization operation is needed. Most users on Unix systems are creating and destroying files at a high rate. To lower the rate involves completely rethinking the role of global name spaces in programming environments.[20]

As an example of how data can be modified without involving a server, consider the version graph relation.

```
Version : relation
        old:key[Source],-- old version
        new:key[Source],-- new version
        why:string      -- reason for change
      end
```

Suppose that two users each want to create a successor of some existing version. Each will create a new source object and add a new tuple for it to the **Version** relation. There is no basic conflict between these additions. Since the tuples of a relation are an unordered set, the order of the additions will not affect the final value of the relation.

Since a network imposes finite delays[21], time within a network is relativistic [Lamport 78]. In relativistic time, there is no system-wide absolute clock. Each machine within the network is assumed to have its own clock that progresses at its own rate. In such a system, there is no total ordering of events. Consider again the two users, **A** and **B**, each of which has a machine within the same network, both trying to create a successor of the same existing version. To **A** it may seem as though the new **A** tuple appears before the new **B** tuple, while to **B** the order appears to be the **B** tuple followed by the **A** tuple.[22]

Now suppose that each new version is to be given the next new integer version number. This can only be done by having a single server that assigns those numbers. Many version management systems have a similar problem. When several alternative versions are present, one of them is designated as the "primary" version. A central server is needed to control which new version is to be the primary version.

For a persistent object base, automatic dynamic placement and caching of relations and parts

---

[20]Names in Unix serve two independent purposes, connecting uses to their definitions and communicating information between users. Uses can be connected to definitions by using unique identifiers instead of names. Each unique identifier may still have a name, but that name is used for local display purposes only; the connection is made via the unique identifier. A global name then is needed only in those relatively less frequent cases where information is passed between users. A single global name may be communicated for an entire system that internally contains thousands of local unique identifiers.

[21]These delays can be quite long when lots of data is transmitted over a dial-up phone line or when some link in the network is broken.

[22]A different approach that avoids a single central server for versions is given in [Ecklund 85].

of relations is needed. Various methods must be used to avoid high interaction rates with central servers.

4.5 Performance

The performance of database systems is tuned to access patterns that may be quite different from those expected in programming environments. Performance is considered here in terms of what is accessed and who is accessing it. A thorough understanding of the performance issues of using databases for programming environments can occur only after many more experiments are carried out and much more analysis is done. Based on what is still very limited experience, this discussion speculates on areas where performance problems seem most likely to occur.

Relational database systems typically are tuned to emphasize the performance of operations that deal with entire relations, such as join and projection. In a programming environment, operations that deal only with a single tuple from each of many relations may be more frequent. In programming environments, access patterns that traverse trees or directed graphs are common. Such traversals must extract a single tuple, from the relation that represents the tree or graph, at each step. Relational database systems typically assume that all tuples of a relation are equally likely to be accessed. In the version relation, for example, tuples for more recent versions are more likely to be accessed. Graph transitive closure operations are common in programming environments. For example, a query might be to determine all versions that are direct or indirect predecessors of some given version. Database systems are not normally tuned to make transitive closure efficient. Furthermore, relationally complete query languages can not in general even express transitive closure.

Many database systems are designed mainly to interact with people. In a programming environment, most of the use of the data will be by programs. Most database query languages are interpreted, not compiled. While users may accept small delays due to interpretation, the heavy use of data accessing programs may produce unacceptable performance degradation in programming environments. Of special performance significance is the use of surrogate keys. These keys serve exactly the same role as pointers do in most programs: They are used to build linked list structures such as trees and graphs. The efficiency of the pointer dereference operation is known to be a major factor in determining the execution speed of most system programs. Unless surrogate keys can be implemented with an efficiency approaching pointers, then relational databases may prove to be an unacceptable basis for programming environments.[23]

5 Conclusions

This paper has examined from several perspectives the weaknesses of file systems and database systems as a basis for persistent object bases of programming environments. Neither current file systems nor current data base systems are adequate to support a first class persistent object base. In many areas, however, current research and development is progressing toward systems that correct at least some of the weaknesses.

---

[23]A possible answer is to use memory addresses as the representation that programs see. Considerable engineering is obviously needed.

This paper provides designers and evaluators of persistent object bases with a checklist of issues to be considered and a list of problem areas where further work is needed. However, the real work of building a persistent object base may be less concerned with finding novel solutions to specific problems and more concerned with effectively integrating current technology.

6 Acknowledgements

Many of the ideas presented here originated in discussions with Joseph Newcomer and Ellen Borison. I would like to thank Haavard Eidnes, Purvis Jackson, Richard Snodgrass, Donald Stone, and Chuck Weinstock for providing many useful comments on earlier drafts of this paper.

7 References

[Apollo 86]   Apollo Computer. *Using the Open System Tool Kit to Extend the Streams Facility.* To appear April 1986.

[Borison 86]   Ellen Borison. A Model of Software Manufacture. *International Workshop on Advanced Programming Environments.* Trondheim, Norway. June 1986.

[Ceri 83]   S. Ceri and S. Crepi-Reghizzi. Relational Databases in the Design of Program Construction Systems. *SIGPLAN Notices,* Volume 18, Number 11, November 1983.

[Ceri 84]   S. Ceri and G. Pelagatti. *Distributed Databases Principles and Systems.* McGraw-Hill, 1984.

[Chen 76]   Peter Pin-Shan Chen. The Entity-Relationship Model - Toward a Unified View of Data. *ACM Transactions on Database Systems,* Volume 1, Number 1, March 1976.

[CLF 85]   CLF Project. *Introduction to the CLF Environment.* USC Information Sciences Institute, 1985.

[Clifford 83]   James Clifford and David S. Warren. Formal Semantics for Time in Databases. *ACM Transactions on Database Systems,* Volume 8, Number 2, June 1983.

[Codd 70]   E. F. Codd. A Relational Model of Data for Large Shared Data Banks. *Communications of the ACM,* Volume 13, Number 6, June 1970.

[Codd 79]   E. F. Codd. Extending the Database Relational Model to Capture More Meaning. *ACM Transactions on Database Systems,* Volume 4, Number 4, December 1979.

[DoD 85]   Draft Military Standard Common APSE Interface Set (CAIS). Proposed MIL-STD-CAIS. NTIS AD 157-587. January 31, 1985.

[Ecklund 85]   Earl F. Ecklund, Jr., Darryn M. Price, Rick Krull, and Denise J. Ecklund. *Federations: Scheme Management in Locally Distributed Databases.* Technical Report CR-85-39, Computer Research Laboratory, Tektronix Laboratories, November 1985.

[ESPRIT 85]   ESPRIT. *PCTE, A Basis for a Portable Common Tool Environment, Functional Specifications.* Third edition, Bull, The General Electric Company p.l.c., ICL International Computer Limited, Nixdorf Computer AG, Olivetti SPA, Siemens AG, 1985.

[Feldman 79]   S. I. Feldman. Make - A Program for Maintaining Computer Programs. *Software Practice and Experience,* April 1979.

[Fujitani 84]   Larry Fujitani. Laser Optical Disks: The Coming Revolution in On-Line Storage. *Communications of the ACM,* Volume 27, Number 6, June 1984.

[Gandalf 85]   Special Issue on the Gandalf Project. *The Journal of Systems and Software,* Volume 5, Number 2, May 1985.

[Garlan 86]   David Garlan. Views for Tools in Integrated Environments. *International Workshop on Advanced Programming Environments.* Trondheim, Norway. June 1986.

[Hallmark 84]   G. Hallmark and R. A. Lorie. Toward VLSI Design Systems Using Relational Databases. *IEEE Computer Conference.* Spring 1984.

[Hartzband 85]   David J. Hartzband and Fred J. Maryanski. Enhancing Knowledge Repesentation in Engineering Databases. *Computer,* Volume 18, Number 9, September 1985.

[Hatch 85]   Mark J. Hatch, Michael Katz, and Jim Rees. AT&T's RFS and Sun's NFS, A Comparison of Heterogeneous Distributed File Systems. *Unix/World,* Volume 2, Number 11, December 1985.

[Katz 84]   Randy H. Katz and Tobin J. Lehman. Database Support for Versions and Alternatives of Large Design Files. *IEEE Transactions on Software Engineering,* Volume 10, Number 2, March 1984.

[Lamport 78]   Leslie Lamport. Time, Clocks, and the Ordering of Events in a Distributed System. *Communications of the ACM,* Volume 21, Number 7, July 1978.

[Lampson 83]   Butler W. Lampson and Eric E. Schmidt. Organizing Software in a Distributed Environment. *Proceedings of the SIGPLAN '83 Symposium on Programming Language Issues in Software Systems.* SIGPLAN Notices, Volume 18, Number 6, June 1983.

[Leach 83]   P. Leach, P. Levine, B. Dorous, J. Hamilton, D. Nelson, and B. Stumpf. The Architecture of an Integrated Local Network. *IEEE Journal on Selected Areas in Communications,* November 1983.

[Leblang 85]   David B. Leblang, Robert P. Chase, Jr., and Gordon D. McLean, Jr. The DOMAIN Software Engineering Environment for Large Scale Software Development Efforts. *Proceedings of the 1st International Conference on Computer Workstations.* IEEE, November 1985.

[Linton 84]   Mark A. Linton. Implementing Relational Views of Programs. *Proceedings of the ACM SIGSOFT/SIGPLAN Software Engineering Symposium on Practical Software Development Environments.* SIGPLAN Notices, Volume 19, Number 5, May 1984. Software Engineering Notes, Volume 9, Number 3, May 1984.

[Morris 86]   James H. Morris, Mahadev Satyanarayanan, Michael H. Conner, John H. Howard, David S. H. Rosenthal, and F. Donelson Smith. Andrew: A Distributed Personal Computing Environment. *Communications of the ACM,* Volume 29, Number 3, March 1986.

[Osterweil 83]   Leon Osterweil and Geoffrey Clemm. The Toolpack/IST Approach to Extensibility in Software Environments. *Ada Software Tools Interfaces: Bath Workshop Proceedings.* Springer-Verlag, Lecture Notes in Computer Science, Number 180, 1983.

[Ousterhout 85]   John K. Ousterhout, Herve Da Costa, David Harrison, John A. Kunze, Mike Kupfer, and James G. Thompson. *A Trace-Driven Analysis of the UNIX 4.2BSD File System.* Technical Report UCB/CSD 85/230, University of California, Berkeley, April 1985.

[Ritchie 74]   D. M. Ritchie and K. Thompson. The Unix Time-Sharing System. *Communications of the ACM,* Volume 17, Number 7, July 1974.

[Rochkind 75]   M. J. Rochkind. The Source Code Control System. *IEEE Transactions on Software Engineering,* Volume 1, Number 4, December 1975.

[Sandberg 85]   R. Sandberg. The Design and Implementation of the Sun Network File System. *Proceedings Usenix,* June 1985.

[Schroeder 85]   Michael D. Schroeder, David K. Gifford, and Roger M. Needham. A Caching File System for a Programmer's Workstation. *Proceedings of the 10th ACM Symposium on Operating System Principles.* Operating System Review, Volume 19, Number 5, December 1985.

[Shaw 84]   Mary Shaw. Abstraction Techniques in Modern Programming Languages. *IEEE Software,* Volume 1, Number 4, October 1984.

[Snodgrass 84]   Richard Snodgrass. Monitoring in a Software Development Environment: A Relational Approach. *Proceedings of the ACM SIGSOFT/SIGPLAN Software Engineering Symposium on Practical Software Development Environments.* SIGPLAN Notices, Volume 19, Number 5, May 1984. Software Engineering Notes, Volume 9, Number 3, May 1984.

[Snodgrass 86]   Richard Snodgrass and Ilsoo Ahn. Temporal Databases. *Computer,* To appear 1986.

[Taylor 86]   Richard N. Taylor, Lori Clarke, Leon J. Osterweil, Richard W. Selby, Jack C. Wileden, Alex Wolf, and Michal Young. Arcadia: A Software Development Environment Research Project. *IEEE Transactions on Software Engineering,* To appear 1986.

[Tichy 82]   Walter F. Tichy. Design, Implementation, and Evaluation of a Revision Control System. *Proceedings of the 6th International Conference on Software Engineering.* IEEE, Tokyo. September 1982.

[Welch 84]   Terry A. Welch. A Technique for High-Performance Data Compression. *Computer,* Volume 17, Number 6, June 1984.

[Wirth 85]   Niklaus Wirth. *Programming in Modula-2.* Third Corrected Edition. Springer-Verlag, 1985.

[Yankelovich 85] Nicole Yankelovich, Norman Meyrowitz, and Andries van Dam. Reading and Writing the Electronic Book. *Computer,* Volume 18, Number 10, October 1985.

Choosing an Environment Data Model

Andres Rudmik

GTE Communication Systems
Phoenix, Arizona, 85027

Abstract

The semantic data model provides most of the capabilities needed to support software engineering projects. There are some aspects of supporting projects that are not adequately addressed by this model. This paper recommends several extensions to address these inadequacies. First, extensions are described to support the specification and enforcement of project data integrity. Second, extensions are described that support some of the behaviorial aspects of projects, such as methods. Third, extensions are described to control the scope of names and to control the visibility of operations and objects in a project. Software project examples are used to illustrate these extensions.

1. Introduction

The evolution of modern engineering databases is towards the use of higher level data models [KK, RL, ZW] with a number of researchers recommending the adoption of object oriented data models [MK, ZW]. An object oriented data model supports the use of data abstraction to define project data as objects that correspond to real world entities understood by people.

An abstract data type hides implementation details and presents a simplified view of the data object to users. A user sees an instance of an abstract type through the operations defined for that type. This simple concept has been used in modern programming languages to simplify the definition and manipulation of data within programs. These same simplifications apply also to the environment database.

Within an engineering environment, we observe that there are a large number of object types representing different kinds of data that can be created and manipulated. Associated with each object are properties (attributes) which in aggregation represent the value of the object. These properties may contain information for different disciplines and be used by different tools. For example, an object that represents a document may have properties that record the author, the data last modified, and the text of the document. In addition, the document may also have information to facilitate monitoring its development status, version information for use by configuration management, and relationships to other documents that described related issues.

As objects and relationships within an engineering environment database become more complex other problems are introduced that are not handled easily by existing data models. For example, if one modifies the text of a document then the object containing the formatted version of the document is no longer consistent with the text. In this case, the relationship relating the document text to the formatted document needs to be removed and the formatted document should be deleted. Some systems handle these kinds of consistency issues by using builtin knowledge about certain object types. A better strategy is to provide a facility in the data definition language to describe the integrity constraints and then have the system enforce these constraints.

Other issues include managing the name space of objects so that names used in one project do not constrain or interfere with names used in other projects. Furthermore, some object will be shared between projects, in which case they are visible in some outer scope or context. Programming languages handle these kinds of problems through scoping mechanisms that provide a unique interpretation of a name within a given scope. Similar mechanisms might be appropriate within environments that support multiple projects.

Some current data modeling techniques attempt to capture the behavioral aspects of data in the specification of transactions against the data items in the database. Within engineering projects there are many dimensions of dynamic behavior that need to be supported by the project database. For example, project objects will dynamically move between phases of the development life cycle as work is completed on these objects. In other situations, relationships will be created and destroyed dynamically as the values of objects change.

The driving factor for choosing a project database data model is the need to support engineering projects. This paper examines the semantic data model and recommends some extensions to the data model to provide better support for engineering projects.

Previous authors [KK,MK,ZW] have primarily focussed on the static properties of the environment data model. This paper presents extensions to these models to allow one to represent both the static structure of the objects and the dynamic interplay between the objects in a engineering project.

2. Environment Data Model

In the semantic data model the object type is defined as an abstract data type, where the object properties (attributes) specify the data values and the operations are the means by which these data values can be modified.

```
type <Object_Type_Name> is
    supertype <Object_Type_Name list>
    class <Class_Name>
    [operations <Operations>]
    [properties <Properties>]
end <Object_Type_Name>
```

Figure 1.   Object type definition

Figure 1 illustrates the main components of the object type definition in the semantic data model.   The semantic data model requires that new object types be defined in terms of existing object types, called supertypes.   Defining new types in terms of existing types captures the meaning that the new type exhibits characteristics of its supertypes.   The new type is called a derived type and typical has additional characteristics that distinguish it from its supertypes.   Type derivation also reduces the effort required to define new types by reusing existing type definitions.

A class is a named collection of all existing instances of objects of a given object type.   The class name is used in query expressions to compute subclasses of object instances that satisfy the query predicates.

```
type Text is
    supertype Null_Type;
    class Texts;
    operations
        function Create (in Name : String) return Text;
        procedure Edit (in out Pkg : Package);
    properties
        Name : String;
        Text_Store : file of Character;
end Text;


type Package is
    supertype Text;
    class Packages;
    operations
        procedure Browse (Pkg : Package);
        function Compile (in Pkg : Package) return Object;
    properties
        Review_Status : Status;
end package;
```

Figure 2.   Examples of object types

The operations are the only means by which the values of the object instances can be accessed and modified. These operations will typically be implemented as programs in the environment that operate on the objects specified as parameters to these programs.

The property types in the semantic data model are either basic types or subclasses. The basic types are integer, real, enumeration, string, and file, all equipped with the usual operations. Figure 2. illustrates the definition of the object type *package* which is derived from the object type *text*. In this example the operations that can be performed on instances of *package* are *Create, Edit, Browse,* and *Compile*. The operations *Create* and *Edit* were inherited from the object type *Text*.

A subclass is a subset of object instances of a given object type. A subclass represents relationships between the object containing the subclass property and the object instances in the subclass. In Figure 3, the *in_program* property is a subclass property that identifies the programs in which a given instance of a package is used. The fact that a Package is used in a program is expressed explicitly by adding that program instance to the subclass property *In_Program*.

```
type Program is
   class Programs;
   • • •
end Program;


type Package is
   • • •
   properties
      • • •
         In_Program : subclass Programs;
end Package;
```

Figure 3.   Subclass used to define relationships

In an engineering project the relationships that exist between objects are constrained. These constraints can limit the number of objects that can be related by constraining the relationships to depend on the values or the existence/nonexistence of objects. The following extensions to the semantic data model help to capture these constraints.

<Property Name> : **subclass** <Class name> [<Dynamic Constraint>] [<Cardinality>]

The presence of dynamic constraints indicate that the subclass is implicitly computed as state transitions occur within the project database. Dynamic constraints are represented as predicates on the existence or nonexistence of objects and the object property values. For example, consider an Ada[1] program that consists of a set of Ada packages. Initially, the program is empty of packages; but as new Ada packages are developed, they can be explicitly associated with the program. An implicit association between the program and its packages can be used to identify the packages that comprise the program. In our model an implicit subclass *Packages,* can be defined as part of a *Program* object type as shown in Figure 4.

type Program **is**
   • • •
  property
       Uses : **subclass** Packages **where** @ **in** Package.In_Program;
  end Program;

Figure 4. Dynamically constrained subclass

The property *Uses* is a subclass of the class *Packages* , whose members are instances of type *Package* , where the current instance of *Program* (denoted by @) is an member of the property *Package.In_Program* for each *Package* instance in *Uses*. The members of a implicit subclass are automatically computed from the information in the project database. Conceptually, every time a implicit subclass property is referenced, the subclass dynamic constraints are evaluated to identify the members of the subclass.

Cardinality constraints, on subclass properties, can be used to further constrain relationships to depend on the existence or nonexistence of objects. For example, if the subclass cardinality is "0 .. Many," then the subclass may have zero of more members representing a one to many relationship where the existence of the relationship is not dependent on the existence of other objects. On the other hand, if the cardinality constraint on a subclass property is "1 .. Many" then the creation of the object containing this subclass property must also specify at least one object as a member of that subclass.

3. Modeling Project Dynamic Behavior

One use of dynamic constraints is to model the dynamic behavior of projects. This section illustrates how the above extensions to the semantic data model can be used to represent the dynamic behavior of a development process (called a method).

A project, as shown in Figure 5, can be viewed as consisting of a set of input and output products, and a method by which those products are produced. At any given point in time there is associated with the project, a set of product instances which are created during the course of the project. As these

---

[1] Ada is a trademark of the DoD (Ada Joint Program Office).

products are created and modified they "move" between phases of the development method as illustrated by the labelled arcs in Figure 5. The High Level Design (HLD) document moves between the phases *Develop_HLD*, *Review_HLD*, and *Develop_DD*.

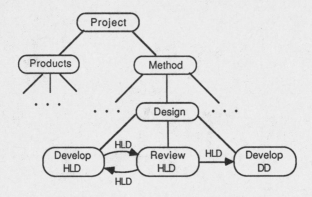

Figure 5. Project Structure

One can model a project method as follows. A method is represented as a hierarchy of steps, where each step represents an activity that creates or modifies some project products. The method specification includes rules about where a product can be created and the movement of products between steps of the method. For example, one might define the following rules for the method illustrated in Figure 5.

1. HLD in Develop_HLD if HLD.Status in [Not_Reviewed, Failed_Review];
2. HLD in Review_HLD if HLD.Status = Ready_For_Review;
3. HLD in Develop_DD if HLD.Status = Passed_Review;

Figure 6 illustrates the use of dynamic constraints to model the flow of the High Level Design (*HLD*) document between three steps of a method. For example, when the *HLD* document is created, its default status is *Not_Reviewed* and it is created within project P. Similarly, the step *Develop_HLD* is also instantiated within project P. The property, *HLD_Document*, within *Develop_HLD* can be read as follows. The set of *HLD* documents available within the *Develop_HLD* step are those instances that are in the same project as this step and the *Status* property of *HLD* is either *Not_Reviewed* or *Failed_Review*. The notation *@.In_Project* refers to the *In_Project* property of the current instance of the *Develop_HLD* step.

```
type Develop_HLD is
   . . .
   property
      In_Project      : subclass Project cardinality 1;
      HLD_Document : subclass HLD
                      where @.In_Project in HLD.In_Project
                      and HLD.Status in [Not_Reviewed, Failed_Review];
end Develop_HLD;


type Review_HLD is
   . . .
   property
      In_Project      : subclass Project cardinality 1;
      HLD_Document : subclass HLD
                      where @.In_Project in HLD.In_Project
                      and HLD.Status = Ready_For_Review;
end Review_HLD;


type Develop_DD is
   . . .
   property
      In_Project      : subclass Project cardinality 1;
      HLD_Document : subclass HLD
                      where @.In_Project in HLD.In_Project
                      and HLD.Status = Passed_Review;
end Develop_DD;
```

Figure 6. Modeling a software engineering method

This example has illustrated one use of dynamic constraints to model the dynamic behavior of software engineering projects. Other uses of dynamic constraints includes maintaining two-way relationships, where the relationship in one direction is dependent on the existence of the other relationship as illustrated in Figure 4. The advantage of using dynamic constraints in this manner is that the system will ensure the integrity of the relationships rather than having the user or tools maintain these relationships directly.

4.   Naming and Views

The issue of managing the name space of objects within large projects and between multiple projects needs to be addressed by the data model. The data model should provide facilities to specify contexts in which names must be unique and enforce these properties as objects are created and modified. Traditionally, this has been done by designating certain properties as keys, ensuring that all instances of a given object type can be uniquely identified by a value of the key properties.

The use of keys can be extended in the semantic data model to include the existence of objects as specified by subclasses. For example, the environment may require that the names of packages be unique within projects and unique within programs that use these packages (as required by the Ada Language Reference Manual). Packages can then be shared between projects and programs provided that their naming uniqueness criteria is satisfied. Figure 7 illustrates how this criteria can be defined.

```
type Package is
    . . .
    properties
        Name : String;
        In_Program : subclass Programs cardinality 0..Many;
        In_Project : subclass Projects cardinality 1..Many;
    key Name, In_Program, In_Project;
end Package;
```

Figure 7. Uniqueness criteria for package names

The properties listed as keys for the object type *Package* specify that the values (*Name* X pgm X proj) are unique for each instance of *Package*, where pgm is a member of *In_Program* and proj is a member of *In_Project*. For example, a package named List may occur exactly once in a program and exactly once in a project. Many programs and projects may share the List package provided that the name List is unique in each program and Project in which it is used.

In projects different kinds of users have different data needs and may be interested in different subsets of operations that have been defined for objects.

In the example in Figure 8, the view *Design_Library* can be used to constrain a user to a subset of the operations and properties defined in the *Library* object type. In addition the view also constrains the class of *Design_Libraries* to the set of *Library* instances where the *Library.Position* property is set to *Development*.

The use of keys allows one to state rules about how the values of objects can be formed relative to the structure in which the object is embedded. Views can be used to control the visibility of the operations and properties defined in the object type. These mechanisms are needed to support the definition of project data and to support the various uses of this data within a project.

```
type Library is
    supertype Null_Type;
    class Libraries;
    operations
        procedure Browse ....
        procedure Add_Pkg_Spec ....
        procedure Delete_Pkg_Spec ....
        procedure Add_Pkg_Body ....
        procedure Delete_Pkg_Body ....
    properties
        Ada_pkgs : subclass Package;
        Position : Development_Positions;
end Library;


view Design_Library : Library is
    subclass Design_Libraries where Library.Position = Development;
    Include Browse, Add_Pkg_Spec, Delete_Pkg_Spec, Ada_Pkgs;
end Design_library;
```

Figure 8. View example

5. Summary

This paper has proposed a number of extensions to the semantic data model to support engineering projects. These extensions provide better facilities for defining and controlling the integrity of project data. They also support the modeling of the dynamic behavior of projects. We feel that these kinds of extensions are necessary for engineering databases to address the problems encountered as the complexity of objects and relationships increase with higher levels of project data integration.

References

[EC] Ecklund D. J., "Robustness in Distributed Hypothetical Databases," Nineteenth Hawaii International Conference on System Sciences, 1986.

[HM] Hammer M. & McLeod D., "The Semantic Data Model: A Modeling Mechanism for Database Applications," International Conference on the Management of Data, 1978.

[KK] KIT/KITIA, "DoD Requirements and Design Criteria for the Common APSE Interface Set (CAIS), "October, 1984.

[MK] Moore, B. & Kou J. "Requirements for a Software Information Database," GTE Labs, TN No. 85-1552.01, 1985

[RL] Rudmik A., & Lubeck D., "Integrated Project Support in Third Generation Environments," Nineteenth Hawaii International Conference on System Sciences, January 1986.

[ST] Stars Joint Program Office, "Joint Services Software Engineering Environment (JSSEE) Operational Concept Document," November 1984.

[ZW] Zdonik, S., & Wegner, P., "Language and Methodology for Object Oriented Database Environments," Hawaii International Conference on System Sciences, January 1986.

Version Management
in an Object-Oriented Database

Stanley B. Zdonik
Brown University
Providence, RI 02912/USA
(401)-863-2364, sbz@brown

ABSTRACT

We describe a database system that includes a built-in version control mechanism that can be used in the definition of any new object types. This database system is object-oriented in the sense that it supports data abstraction, object types, and inheritance.

We show how this version control mechanism can be used to manage change in the definition of a system. In particular, we show how versions of type defining objects serve to maintain consistent behavior of objects as the system evolves over time. We also show how the system can use other information such as the *component-of* relationship to propagate changes to the appropriate places.

The version mechanism is also used to control consistency during the process of design. The notions of *consistency surface*, *design step*, and *slice* are introduced. The version mechanism also gives us a way of potentially tolerating more concurrency than in conventional systems.

1. Introduction

There has been much interest in the software engineering community in configuration mangement and version control. This interest has been fueled by the inherent complexities in the production of large software systems from separately created pieces. Keeping track of the dependencies that exist between these modules and the various working versions of a system (e.g., debugging version, released version) is a job that should be managed by the system.

This observation is not a new one, but current solutions tend to employ special-purpose systems that can be used to keep track of special kinds of objects (e.g., program modules). We shall argue that the problem arises in many settings in which people are engaged in the process of design. Programming is simply one such setting.

These techniques are applicable to any environment that can be characterized by its emphasis on the production of objects in an evolutionary manner. That is, we are particularly interested in environments that are characterized by change. This change can occur at the level of instances (i.e., individual objects) or at the level of types (i.e., system definitions).

This paper explores examples from the discipline of programming environments, but the ideas could equally well be applied to any other design-oriented environment. For example, we have already looked into the use of these concepts in the area of electronic computer-aided design (ECAD) and office information systems. An office system can, in part, be thought of as a design environment in which users are engaged in the task of designing documents, graphics, or presentations.

This paper introduces some facilities that are built on top of a general-purpose, object-oriented database system. These facilities are available for objects of any type that are managed by the database system. We will discuss how these techniques can be used to support the design process for several applications including the design of the database system itself.

We see the platform for a system such as this as being a high-performance, graphics workstation, possibly connected in a LAN to several other such workstations. Designers interact with this using any of several editors to create new designs or modify old ones. They will share information with co-workers or with other pre-existing designs.

2. The Object-Oriented Database

In order to adequately describe our version mechanism, we will briefly describe the object-oriented database system in which it is embedded. We will discuss its basic model of data since we believe that it is partially this powerful data model that make it possible for us to incorporate our mechanisms so easily into our overall scheme.

In our data model, a type is defined to have a set of explicitly-defined operations and properties and may inherit additional operations and properties from its supertypes. A type T is introduced in the data definition language by a specification of the following form:

> **Define Type** T
> **Supertypes:** <list of supertypes>
>   **Operations:**
>   <list of operations>
>   **Properties:**
>   <list of properties>

The basic idea of a type in our data model is similar to the notion of a class in Smalltalk [G81, GR83] or to the definition of a type in modern programming languages like CLU. We extend the basic object-oriented model in several dimensions to better cover the kind of expressive power that is need for complex design applications. For example, we have explicitly added the notion of a property object as way to express relationships between other entities. Properties are similar in concept to a property or relationship in many semantic database models [ADP83, Ch76, Co79, HM81, MBW80, S81]. We have also added the notion of constraints as a way of expressing the legal states of the database. By specifying that a type S is a supertype of T, an *is-a* relationship (i.e., property) is established between S and T.

Object-oriented databases [CM84, MSOP86, Z84, ZW86] differ from their programming language counterparts in the following fundamental ways.

1. persistence
2. unique naming
3. sharing
4. transactions

Objects that are created by a process persist beyond the lifetime of that process. The database system assigns all objects a unique identifier that is guaranteed to remain unique even across multiple processes. Any number of applications can share the objects that reside in this persistent memory space. In the process of using these objects a given process can define the boundaries of transactions that are guaranteed to be atomic and resilient and that preserve some set of correctness criteria. If we adopt a strong world view, these criteria might encompass serializability, however, they may also be defined to be weaker [SZR86].

2.1. Type Structure

All objects in the database must be an instance of one or more types. Objects of type T come into being by invoking the create operation that is associated with T. We say that T has been *instantiated*. The type is a specification or a template for all of its instances.

The most general object type is type *Entity*. All other types are either directly or indirectly subtypes of type *Entity*. All instances of Type *Entity* are by definition persistent. That is to say, any entity is automatically retained in a permanent store that is separate from the address space of the process that created it.

A database definition or "schema" is a textual device that contains all of the type definitions that are supported by the database. For each type, there is a well-defined block of text that specifies its behavior. When a schema is processed by the database system, the appropriate set of types is created and added to the database.

The following definition of the type *File* has a supertype "Entity", three operations, and one property.

> **Define Type** File
> **Supertypes**: Entity
>   **Operations**:
>   Create-file ( ) **returns** (F : File)
>   Open (F : File) **returns** (F : File)
>   Close (F : File) **returns** (F : File)
>   **Properties**:
>   Filename: String

The list of operations contains for each operation a specification of the types of its arguments and its return value. The list of properties follows, and for each property, its name followed by a colon and a description of the set of legal values for that property is given. The *Filename* property can have any instance of the type *string* as a legal value.

A type T determines the operations that can be performed on instances of T. An object is typically polymorphic in that it can be an instance of several types at the same time. It is an instance of a single *immediate type* T as well as an instance of every type that is on a path between T and Entity. The immediate type of an object x is the type that was specified in the operation that created x. It is, therefore, the lowest type in the type lattice of which x is an instance. The behavior of an object in the database is defined by this set of *types*. Each type of which it is an instance contributes some behavior by the system's inheritance mechanism.

Also, a type T specifies the *properties* that instances of T can have. A property is an object that relates two database objects. For example, a source program S is related to its object code O by means of a property that might be called *compiled-version-of*. A property can be thought of as a function that maps the object that possesses the property to the object or set of objects that are the values of the property. We, therefore, have compiled-version-of (S) = O.

When we write a type definition as above, we are implicitly defining several additional types. These types include one for each property and one for each operation. For example, the text given above as the definition of type *File* implicitly defines a type called *Filename* that corresponds to the property with that name. If it were made explicit it might have looked as follows:

> **Define Type** Filename
> **Supertypes**: Property
>   **Properties**:
>   **Operations**:
>   refines Get-value (FN: Filename) **returns** (S: String)
>   refines Set-value (FN: FIlename, S: String)

Notice that the operations *get-value* and *set-value* that would have been inherited from the supertype *Property* have been refined to further constrain the types of their arguments and return values as given above. (Type *property* defines these operations with the argument named S to be simply an Entity.)

Types also support data abstraction. That is, each instance has an internal state that is represented by an object of some other type. This representation object is not visible outside of the *type manager* code (i.e., the code that supports the operations of the type). For example, an object of type *set* might be represented by an array. At any point in time, a set S will be represented by an array containing all members of S. It is not appropriate to include this information in the schemas, since the schema specifies only the external behavior of the type and the representation should not be visible externally.

Types are objects, and as such, they can have the behavior of objects in general. This includes the ability to have properties. A type object has several properties including *properties-of* and *operations-of*. *Properties-of* has as a value the set of all the property types that can be associated with an object of the given type. Similarly, the property *operations-of* of a type T expresses the set of operations that can legally be applied to instances of T.

For example, in the definition of type *File* given above, the type *File* object has two properties *properties-of* and *operations-of* that it gets from being an instance of type *Type*. The *properties-of* property has as a value the set {Filename} and the *operations-of* property has as a value the set {create, open, close}. The schema definition that was given above is simply syntactic sugar for the proper operations to set up this structure.

Another important example of a property of a type is the *is-a* property. If we say that a type S is related to a type T by means of the *is-a* property (i.e., is-a (S) = T), then all instances of type S are also instances of type T. All of the semantics (i.e., all properties and operations) defined for type T must also pertain to type S. An instance of type S will have all operations and properties defined on T as well as any additional ones defined on S. We call this behavior *inheritance*. A file directory (similar to that used in UNIX) might be defined as follows:

> **Define Type** Directory
> **Supertypes**: File
>   **Operations**:

Enter-file (D : Directory, F : File)
        returns (D : Directory)
...

Here, the *Directory* type inherits all the properties and operations from the type *File* since *File* is defined to be a supertype. A type can have multiple supertypes and can, thereby, inherit properties and operations from several types. We call this *multiple inheritance*.

We treat properties as objects. It is, therefore, possible to have properties of properties. This is very useful for precise modeling of real world situations. Consider the property *compiles-into* that relates a source code module to its object code counterpart. If we wanted to express the fact that the compilation produced one warning message, we might very naturally wish to attach this fact to the property itself. It's not really a property of either the source module or the object module, but, rather, of the act of compiling. Perhaps, with a different compiler this message would not have occurred. We can define this as follows:

Define Type Source-Code-Module
...
  Properties:
    Compiles-into: Object-Code-Module

  Define Type Compiles-into
  Supertypes: Property
    Properties
      Warning-Messages: **Set of** String
    Operations
      Set-Property-Value (C : Compiles-into, O : Object-Code-Module)
      Get-Property-Value (C : Compiles-into)
               returns (O : Object-Code-Module)

We also view operations as objects. This leads to several interesting effects. First, much as with properties, it becomes possible to assert things about operations. Second, in an object-oriented approach to system building, a new application is constructed by building new higher level types out of previously defined types. All code is associated with the operations of some type. Since the operations are also objects, all new application programs are automatically subsumed by the database. The code (i.e., operation objects) persists by the general object storage mechanisms. Third, it is possible to use some of the more advanced features of the system like version control to manage the operations of an evolving application. Fourth, it is possible to create type definitions as objects that contain other objects (property types and operation types) that can be shared by means of the database facilities. Types are not shared simply by user-defined names as in many persistent environments that are supported by a bare file system. For example, a program might write an object of type T to a file along with the tag T indicating how it is to be interpreted. If another program reads this object there is no guarantee that it will interpret it using the same definition for T.

The structure of the basic data model is represented in Figure 1 using its own notion of type to describe the basic kernal of the system. The basic types in the system are related to each other by means of the *is-a* property type. All boxes in this picture are instances of the type *type* (including the type *type* itself). The root of the system is the type *entity* of which all objects in the system are instances. To say that an object is an entity, is to say that it is contained in our database. Applications are built by adding additional types to this structure.

Notice that the kernal types are broken down into four basic subtypes, *operations* which are the active elements in the system, *properties* which are used to relate objects, *types* which are those things that can be dynamically instantiated, and *aggregates* which are those things that group other entities together. Notice that the type *class* is a subtype of *aggregate* since classes are homogeneous collections of entities.

2.2. Associative Retrieval

Our database system supports a separate notion of *class*. This use of the term is borrowed from work in high-level database modeling [HM81]. It should not be confused with the Smalltalk use of the term which is more closely related to our notion of type. A class is a set of objects, as opposed to a type which is a description of the semantics of objects of that type. Every type T has an associated class C that holds all current instances of T (i.e., C = {x | type-of (x) = T}). For example, the header lines in the above file example indicates that the type *File* has an associated class named *Files*. Each time a new file object is created, it is automatically added to this class.

The class supports the ability to do associative retrievals of database object. The type *Class* supports the operation *Select* which has the following form:

Select (C : Class, P : Predicate) **returns** (S : Set)

Thus the function call *Select(C, P)* returns a set containing all members of C that satisfy P. For example, assume that the following type definition fragment has already occurred:

Define Type Program
Supertypes: Entity
Associated class: Programs
. . .

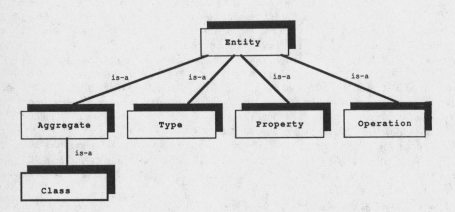

Figure 1. The Basic Type Hierarchy

Properties:
Body: Block
Date-last-modified: Date

In order to retrieve all programs that have been modified today, one would specify an appropriate predicate that would be applied to all members of the class *Programs* such as:

P = **lambda** (p)
      Get-property-value ("date-last-modified", p)
        = todays-date ())

This predicate can then be applied to select all programs whose property "date last modified" is "today's date" by the following **Select** instruction.

Select (Programs, P)

The ability to do arbitrary associative retrievals of objects of many different types from a programming environment database is one of the strengths of a pure database approach. It provides a step toward reusability by giving the user a way to index and retrieve previously created program pieces. Retrieval can be based on the relationships that objects have to each other. We will not describe the full power of the language for defining predicates here since it is beyond the scope of this paper.

3. Versions

A design environment is characterized by the evolution of objects over time. The artifacts that designers produce change throughout all phases of the design process. A version control system is a very important component of a database that will manage information in this type of environment. We have designed a version control mechanism and built it into our database management system at the level of the data model. Applications builders can make use of this facility for any new type that they design.

In this paper, we show how a general version control facility can be added to our object-oriented database system with a minimum of disruption to the system types. The version mechanism is contained in two new types. Version control can be selected an used on a type by type basis. Therefore, object types that do not need this capability do not have to incur the overhead.

3.1. The Basic Mechanism

Persistence is a property of the type *Entity* and therefore associated with all objects. Version control is associated with a subtype of *Entity* named *History-Bearing-Entity* which defines the operations and attributes needed for version control. A type T whose associated objects are to be subject to version control is simply defined to be a subtype of *History-Bearing-Entity*. An instance of T will then inherit some special properties that are used by the system to keep track of its version history. Each version is a version of some *conceptual object* that represents the object independently of time. A conceptual object is said to have versions. A B-tree access module is a conceptual object that might have several versions throughout its development as an engineer defines, debugs, and refines its structure. The type *Version-Set* is used to aggregate information about the conceptual object that is evolving. All versions of a conceptual object are members of some version set. Definitions of *History-Bearing-Entity* and *Version-Set* follow:

Define Type History-Bearing-Entity
Supertypes: Entity
  Operations:
    None
  Properties:
    Previous-version: **Set of** Entities
    Succeeding-version: **Set of** Entities
    Member-of-version-set: Version-Sets
    Timestamp: Integers
    Derived-by: Transactions

Define Type Version-Set
Supertypes: Aggregate
  Operations:
    Get-latest-version (VS: Version-Set) returns (E: Entity)
    Update (VS: Version-Set, E: Entity)
  Properties:
    None

If a type designer wanted a new type, for example the type *Module*, to record version histories, he need only make it a subtype of the type *History-Bearing-Entity*. Thus, version control need not be an inherent, built-in characteristic of all entities but rather a set of programmer-defined attributes transmitted to selected subtypes through the inheritance mechanism. Moreover several different forms of version control can easily coexist in the database by defining variants of HBE, although we provide one such mechanism in the base-level system.

A new object type T can be specified to be a subtype of the type *History-Bearing-Entity*. T then inherits the semantics of our version mechanism. All history-bearing-objects participate in version sets. That is, when a change is made to an object, it causes a new version to be added as the latest version of its version set. Version sets are partially ordered. Old versions cannot be changed; they can only have new versions inserted into their associated version set. If one adds a new version v2 to an object x that already has a new version v1, then v1 and v2 are said to be *alternatives*. Inserting an alternative into a version set has the effect of starting a new branch in the partial order.

As we stated earlier, a type T may be defined to be a subtype of several other types including the type *History-Bearing-Entity*. T inherits the properties *previous-version*, *succeeding-version*, *member-of-version-set*, *timestamp*, and *derived-by*. The first two of these properties express the partial order of version sequence, and the third relates each of the individual versions to its containing version set. The fourth records the time at which the new version was added to the version set, and the fifth records which transaction was responsible.

The version set accumulates all the versions of an object as it evolves over time. Often, this evolution can be represented by a linear ordering of versions; however, our model allows for version sets that can branch (i.e., are a partial ordering). The branching version set is useful when two versions of an object, Y and Z, compete to be the successor of an object X. We say that Y and Z are alternatives of X. This corresponds, for example, to the situation in which two coworkers independently produce new versions of the same object. Figure 2 shows a linearly evolving version set and a partially ordered version set (one that contains alternatives).

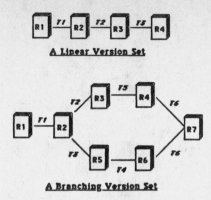

Figure 2 - Example version sets

When one changes an object, a new version of the object is created and it is related to its predecessor by the special property named *succeeding-verison*. The old object is also linked to the new object by means of the special property named *previous-version*. All the versions of this object are related to a version set object by means of another special property named *member-of-version-set* and the version set is related to its members by the inverse property *is-a-version-of*.

This model of object-oriented version support requires that the *create* operation for any type T that is a subtype of HBE be constructed specially. Whenever a create operation for an object x of type T is invoked, that code must not only create the instance of the type, but it must also create an instance V of the type *Version-Set* to contain x and all future versions. It must also insert x into V as a member. For example, if we have the type Module as a subtype of HBE, then an invocation of module$create (i.e., the create operation associated with the type Module) must create an instance of type Module and an instance of type version set. It must also connect these two objects properly with the member-of-version-set property.

3.2. Slices and Design steps

In a design environment, objects are often changed to account for shifting requirements and assumptions concerning a particular design. Keeping these changes consistent can be a major burden to the designer. One of the roles of a database in such an environment, is to assist in this process.

Database systems research has produced two major approaches to the problem of maintaining the consistency of data. The first involves a set of predicates (also known as *integrity constraints*) whose truth is maintained across all interactions with the database. The second assumes that all transactions are written such that they maintain integrity. In this approach, the problem arises from interleaving the steps of the otherwise correct transactions. The classical solution here is to insure that no interleaving is allowed that destroys the fiction of *serializability*. That is, the system insures that the result of executing a set of transactions makes these transactions appear to be *atomic*. We shall discuss how our version mechanism relates to both of these approaches.

We will now define some terms that make the management of these issues more tractable. A *transaction* is an interaction with the database which takes it to some new valid state. A transaction may be either a program or an interactive session with a user at a display terminal. A valid state is one that the creator of the transaction is willing to let the other users of the database see. Notice that there is no requirement here that a transaction be atomic, nor is there a requirement that all constraints must be enforced at the completion of a transaction. If these additional properties are desired, one can define subtypes of the type *Transaction* such as *Atomic-transaction* that refine our basic notion.

A *slice* is a set of versions that have been produced by a single transaction. It is the write-set of this transaction. Figure 3 shows a set of slices that were produced by four different transactions. Each enclosed region represents a slice.

A set of contiguous slices constitutes a *design step*. Intuitively, a design step corresponds to a set of transactions that are invoked by the user to achieve a common purpose. Usually, this purpose is the production of a new design. This new design is complete in that it responds to some intended global change, and in theory works as it is supposed to.

More precisely, if *Slices* is the class of all slices, a design step is a set of slices $D=\{S_1, \ldots, S_n\}$ such that:

$$[\forall S_i, S_j, S_k \in \text{Slices}]$$
$$S_i \text{ and } S_k \text{ can be in the same design step D iff}$$
$$[\forall r \in S_i] [\forall t \in S_k] \neg [\exists s \in S_j] [[S_j \notin D] \wedge [\text{precedes }(r,s) \vee \text{precedes }(s,t)]]$$

where precedes is a relation that expresses the fact that the first component of the tuple precedes the second in time.

A slice represents a set of changes to the database that occurred as an atomic unit. It is often useful to be able to make assertions about a group of changes. Since slices are object (i.e., instances of the type *Slice*), it is possible to assert things about them such as the time at which the changes were made. Also since a transaction makes these changes as a unit, it does not make sense to undo a single version of an object. The basic semantics for undoing in our system is the slice. One can only roll-back an entire slice which has the effect of denying the existence of some transaction. To undo a single version without considering the other versions that share its slice would result in a state of the database that could never have existed (given a world in which transactions are atomic).

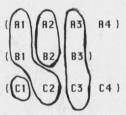

Figure 3 - Slices

4. The Use of Versions

Now that we have described the version model and some of its basic mechanisms, we will discuss several ways that it interacts with other aspects of the database.

4.1. Interaction with Component Hierarchy

The data structures that are used to record the version history of an object can be used to support the kind of semantics that we would like in an evolving environment. For example, when a new version is created for a component of a containing object, the system can automatically *percolate* the change to the containing levels by creating new versions of the objects at those levels as well.

Creating new versions of low-level components of an object can create new versions of each of the higher-level containing objects. This can best be seen by an example. Suppose that system S contains modules M_1 and M_2, module M_1 contains procedure P_1 and P_2, and module M_2 contains procedures P_3 and P_4. If a new version of procedure P_2 is created, its containing module M_1 is also changed since it now contains a different procedure. The effect, then, is to create a new version of M_1. Of course by a similar argument, this change could also be propagated to S, the containing system, by generating a new version of it.

It is not always desirable to propagate all changes at a lower level to all the higher containing levels. Conceptually, propagation of versions always makes sense. What is lost if we do not always force propagation? In the example above, we could simply collect all changes to procedures in their respective version sets and never propagate any of these new versions to the containing modules and systems. If we follow this course, information is lost. The intermediate states of the modules and the system are not recorded and could only be reconstructed if we stored some additional information (e.g., as an attribute) such as a timestamp that indicates when the version was written.

A simple example using the report structure outlined above will illustrate this. If P_1 and P_3 change as a result of one transaction, and paragraphs P_2 and P_4 change as a result of another transaction, each of the version sets for the four procedures will contain a new version. If these transactions do not cause their changes to be propagated, the information about the intermediate state created by the first transaction is lost. The procedures that it created can be seen, but the time sequencing of how these changes were made with respect to the second transaction has not been recorded. Propagation of the changes would solve this problem. The changes caused by the first transaction could cause a new version of the module and, likewise, the system to be created. This new system version is a snapshot of the intermediate state.

The decision of what changes should be propagated lies with the database schema designer. The definition of the containing object specifies which components should have their changes propagated. We say that a property type that supports pecolation is version sensitive if the percolation happens whenever a new version of one of the values of that property acquires a new version (i.e., has a new version added to its version set). Within the object schema for the *Module* type, one might find the following definition:

Procedures (**version-sensitive**): **Set of** Procedures

This would cause any change (by creating a new version) to any procedure in the *procedures* component of a chapter to cause a new version of that module to be created by propagating the changed procedures to the module level. Assume that p is a version sensitive property of y, and y.p has value x. If a new version of x is created, a new version of y will be created.

This behavior is accomplished by having two subtypes of the basic type *Property*. One is called *version-sensitive-property* and the other is called *identity-sensitive-property*. Adding the modifier in the declaration of a property (as in the above example) will cause the new property to become a subtype of the appropriate property type and the described behavior will be inherited.

It is also possible for a property type to be decalred to be *identity sensitive*. An identity sensitive property cause percolation to happen whenever the identity of a value of that property changes. Assume that p is an identity sensitive property of y, and y.p has value x. If the value of y.p changes to z, this will cause a new version of y to be created.

We have not described here the notion of a trigger, but suffice it to say that a trigger is a piece of code C and a predicate P that can be attached to any object O. Whenever O changes, if P is true of O then C is run. It is possible to attach a trigger to the version set for the system that is activated whenever a new version is added to it. This trigger would recompile the new system using the component modules that are attached to it via the *modules* property of the system.

A more complicated case arises when a version sensitive component of an object contains a particular component that is represented by a branching version set (i.e., an object that has alternatives). In this case, the system must be careful about how it propagates new versions. A new version along one alternative path must be propagated to the correct alternative at the parent level.

Assume that an object of type S contains a version sensitive component of type T. If an alternative exists for a T-object the creation of the alternative would have propagated a similar fork to the S-object level. If a new version of one of the S-object alternatives is created, to which T-object alternative is this change propagated? The system must insure that it is connected to the S-object alternative that has the same transaction as a value for *Derived-by* as the previous version on its alternative path.

If system S1 contains two modules M1 and M2 and two alternatives to M1 are created, M1x and M1y, then two alternatives to S1, S1x and S1y, will be created by version propagation. Further changes to S1x will propagate to the path that contains S1x since Derived-by (M1x) = Derived-by (S1x).

This is complicated still further if M2 also generates alternatives. Call these alternatives M2p and M2q. Since both S1x and S1y contain M2 as a version sensitive component, the change is propagated to both alternative reports. This creates two alternatives to S1x (i.e., S1xp and S1xq) and two alternatives to S1y (i.e., S1yp and S1yq).

4.2. Change in Type Definitions

We expect that the basic definitions in a system (i.e., its types) will change over time. Our database system will be dealing with persistent objects that might have been created under a definition for a type that is about to be superceded. Whenever this happens, we have to be careful not to make it impossible to access this old object. Traditionally, the system would have to perform some kind of conversion on all instances of a superceded type before installing the new definition.

We do not think that conversion of all such objects at the time of redefinition is desirable. It potentially requires a huge computational penalty and also requires treating everything in a uniform way, even when that is not required or desirable from the point of view of the application.

We use our version mechanism to allow the maintenance of multiple versions of type objects [SZ86]. In this way, it would be possible to have old objects and their old type definitions coexist with new objects and their new type definition. Conversion can be performed if and when an old object is to be treated as if it were a new object.

By allowing for multiple versions of a type, we also make it possible to control the amount of interference between different users who may be using the type-lattice concurrently. If one user is accessing type A via several of its instances, another user could change A to A' while the first user was still interested in the previous instances. This would cause unpredicatable results for the first user. The more correct approach is to make A' into a new version of A, thereby retaining the old semantics for the first user.

Since each database object always has access to the type defining object under which it was created, it is always possible to find the correct version of a type in order to get the code for its operations. For example, there could be several versions of the type *Report* each with a different set of operations. Maybe one has appendices and the other does not. Any report instance can access its corresponding type defining object; therefore, each instance preserves its proper behavior. All the variations of the *Report* type object are related by the fact that they belong to the same version set. It is possible to find all reports as all those objects that have been created as an instance of some *Report* type.

There also exists a mechanism that can be applied in some situations for making objects that were created under one version of a type appear as if they were created under a different version of that type (See Figure 4). In this scheme, the programmer supplies a set of *filter programs* (the box labeled *f* in Figure 4). A filter program makes use of the operations that have been defined on one version of a type to manifest the behavior of some operation on some other version of that type. The filter is defined in the context of some operation and links it to some other version of that type. Typically this is the previous version (as in the figure), however, it need not be. A filter that converts an operation of a newer version of a type from an older version of the type is called a *Backward filter*.

It is also possible to create filters that extend from an operation on an older version of a type to some newer version of that type. We will call this a *Forward filter*. The forward filter is useful for old programs that were written in terms of operations on older versions of a type and that need to work in the context of objects that are instances of newer versions

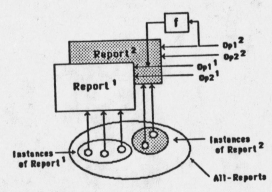

Figure 4 - Changing Types

of that type.

It is not always possible to create these filter programs. In those cases for which the appropriate filter is not defined, the system cannot iterate over the set of all instances of the conceptual type. The application can detect this and inform the user.

When a type in the type-lattice changes, it often requires that other related types change as well. This is accomplished by creating new version objects for these related types. For example, if A is a supertype of B, and A changes, (e.g., operations are added or deleted from its interface), then B implicitly changes as well. All future instances of B will have modified behavior since they will inherit operations and properties from the modified version of A. Therefore, creating a new version of the type object A should automatically create a new version of the type object B so that future instances of B will be related to a version of B that inherits the right behavior. A related approach to this problem that is based on exception handlers that can be added to type versions is described in [SZ86].

4.3. Concurrency control

The field of database management has produced a copious literature relating to the problems of concurrency control. Most of the solutions that have been posited are based on several assumptions. First, it is assumed that all transactions must be executed such that their results are equivalent to some serial execution of those transactions. This is required to preserve atomicity (and, therefore, consistency). Second, it is assumed that objects have a single value. In some concurrency control schemes, old versions are used for a short period of time to represent transient states, but when a transaction completes the values of old versions are not retained.

Contrary to the second assumption, our view is that all old versions of an object are made available through the version set mechanism. An element of a version set cannot be modified but can be read at any time by any transaction. Since versions are read-only, a transaction can safely use an old value and rely on the fact that it will not change. This makes it possible for readers and writers to work on the same object and never conflict. The effect of this is an increase in the level of concurrency in the system.

What happens when two writers try to modify the same object. This case occurs when two transactions, T1 and T2, both try to modify an object x. They might have both read the same old version of x, make some changes based on that value, and then try to install a new value. Consider the following schedule:

> T1: read x
> T2: read x
> T1: write x

In a timestamp-oriented concurrency control scheme, one would have to abort T1 when tried to perform the write operation that conflicts with T2.

In a design environment, transactions are likely to be performed by a user sitting at the workstation and to be of a very long duration. Aborting transactions is something that should be avoided at all costs. Given our version mechanism, we allow for these two transactions to proceed as they wish. At the time of T1's write, a new version of x is created. At this point, T2 is working with the old version x1 and T1 is working with the new version x2.

If the following operation follows the three operations given above,

T2: write x

then an alternative x3 of the old version of x1 is forked. T2 is now using one alternative x3 to the original x1, and T1 is using another called x2.

This situation leads to two different conceptual databases, T1's database with x2 visible and T2's database with x3 visible. All other objects in the two databases are the same. We call these alternative databases *surfaces of consistency*. Each database can be viewed as a surface containing a set of objects. Both surfaces intersect over much of their range, but they differ in the version of x that they support.

All objects in a surface of consistency (a.k.a. consistency surface) are defined to be consistent with each other. There are two definitions of consistency. One requires that all objects be consistent with respect to some set of constraints. That is to say, all constraints in some set must be satisfied when bound to any of the objects which are said to be consistent. Also, we say that objects are consistent if they are produced by a set of serializable transaction histories.

When a version set contains an alternative fork, we are, in effect, saying that the alternative objects do not need to be consistent. In this way, a consistency surface is a way of organizing all those objects that are guaranteed to remain consistent.

Any new transaction must run within one surface of consistency. Therefore, a specific surface of consistency is a parameter to the *create-transaction* operation. That transaction must make all of its changes within that surface or else it may fork additional surfaces (explicitly or by conflict). The system can keep track of the last surface of consistency in which each user operated and supply that user-id as a default parameter when that user next creates a transaction.

The process of reducing the number of surfaces that are active at one time is equivalent to the problem of resolving conflicts between two or more values that were created by transactions that violated serializability. For design transactions, this can often be done by having the custodians of the objects in question negotiate for how the versions will be merged. We call this process *conversational merging*. Conversational merging can be viewed as causing the alternative paths in a version set to coalesce.

5. Summary

We have briefly described an object oriented database system that is under development at Brown University. One of the first target applications for its use will be as substrate on which we build programming environments. The first example of this will be a fusion of this system with the GARDEN graphical programming environment.

We have shown how the basic features of such a database system can be easily extended to incorporate additional system-level concepts like version control. We have further shown how version control can be used in a generalized design environment.

We are working on the design of storage structures that allow for maximum efficiency. As we use our system in real applications (like GARDEN), we will instument it to discover where the bottlenecks are. We are already incorporating several obvious efficiency improvements such as clustering of related objects on secondary storage. We feel that efficiency can also be gained through the ability of type definers to customize the way in which the representation of an object maps to storage. This capability is largely missingfrom conventional database systems, but is essential in this environment.

6. Acknowledgements

The author wishes to thank Tom Atwood and Gordon Landis of OntoLogics, Inc. and Andrea Skarra of Brown University for many useful discussions about this material.

This research was supported in part by the Office of Naval Research and the Defense Advanced Research Projects Agency under contract N00014-83-K-0146 and ARPA Order No. 4786.

7. References

[ABBHS83] M. Ahlsen, A. Bjornerstedt, S. Britts, C. Hulten, and L. Suderland, "An Architecture for Object Management in OIS", ACM Transactions on Office Systems, Vol. 2, No. 3, July, 1983.

[ADP83] J.M. Smith, S. Fox, and T. Landers, "ADAPLEX: Rationale and Reference Manual", second edition, Computer Corporation of America, Cambridge, Mass., 1983.

[At84] M.P. Atkinson, P. Bailey, W.P. Cockshott, K.J. Chisholm, R. Morrison, "Progress with Persistent Programming" in P.M. Stoker, P.M.D. Gray, M.P. Atkinson (editors), "Databases - Role and Structure", Cambridge University Press, Cambridge, UK, 1984.

[BN78] H. Biller, E.J. Neuhold, "Semantics of Databases: The Semantics of Data Models", Inf. Syst. 3 (1978), 11-30.

[Bu84] P. Buneman, "Can We Reconcile Programming Languages and Databases?", in P.M. Stoker, P.M.D. Gray, M.P. Atkinson (editors), "Databases - Role and Structure", Cambridge University Press, Cambridge, UK, 1984.

[Ch76] P.P.S. Chen, "The Entity-Relationship Model: Towards a Unified View of Data", ACM TODS 1, 1, March 1976.

[CM84] G. Copeland and D. Maier, "Making Smalltalk a Database System", Proceedings of the ACM-SIGMOD International Conference on the Management of Data, Boston, Mass., June, 1984.

[Co79] E.F. Codd, "Extending the Database Relational Model to Capture More Meaning". ACM Transactions on Database Systems 4, 4 (December 1979), 397-434.

[DZ86] J. Davison and S. Zdonik, "A Visual Interface for a Database with Version Mangement", Proceedings of the Third International Conference on Office Informantion Systems, Providence, RI, October, 1986.

[DL85] K.R. Dittrich and R.A. Lorie, "Version Support for Engineering Database Systems", IBM Research Report, RJ 4769, IBM Research Laboratory, San Jose, California, July, 1985.

[E85] J. Estublier, "A Configuration Manager: The Adele Database of Programs", Proceedings of the GTE Workshop on Software Engineering Environments for Programming in the Large, Harwichport, Mass., June, 1985.

[EP84] E.F. Ecklund and D.M. Price, "Multiple Version Managment of Hypothetical Databases", Oregon State University, Computer Science Department, Tech. Report No. 84-40-1, July, 1984.

[GAL83] A. Albano, L. Cardelli, and R. Orsini, "Galileo: A Strongly Typed Interactive Conceptual Language", Technical Report 83-11271-2, Bell Laboratories, Murray Hill, New Jersey, July, 1983.

[Go83] J. Goguen, "LIL: A Library Interconnection Language for ADA", in "Report on ADA Program Libraries Workshop", SRI International, 1983.

[G81] A. Goldberg. Introducing the Smalltalk-80 System. *Byte* (August 1981), 14-26.

[GR83] A. Goldberg and David Robson. *Smalltalk-80: The Language and its Implementation.* Addison-Wesley, 1983.

[HM81] M. Hammer, D. McLeod, "Database Description with SDM: A Semantic Database Model", ACM TODS 6, 3, September 1981, 351-387.

[KL82] R.H. Katz and T.J. Lehman, "Storage Structures for Versions and Alternatives", Computer Sciences Department, University of Wisconsin - Madison, Technical Report No. 479, July, 1982.

[KL83] R.H. Katz and T.J. Lehman, "Database Support for Versions and Alternatives of Large Design Files", Computer Sciences Department, University of Wisconsin - Madison, Technical Report, 1983.

[KS85] P. Klahold, G. Schlageter, R. Unland, and W. Wilkes, "A Transaction Model Supporting Complex Applications in Integrated Information Systems", Proceedings of the ACM-SIGMOD International Conference on the Management of Data, Austin, Texas, May, 1985.

[LM85] D.B. Leblang and G.D. McLean, Jr., "Configuration Managment for Large-Scale Software Development Efforts", Proceedings of the GTE Workshop on Software Engineering Environments for Programming in the Large, Harwichport, Mass., June, 1985.

[LDEGPWWW84] V. Lum, P. Dadam, R. Erbe, J. Guenauer, P. Pistor, G. Walch, H. Werner, J. Woodfill, "Designing DBMS Support for the Temporal Dimension", Proceedings of the ACM-SIGMOD Conference on the Management of Data, June, 1984.

[MBW80] J. Mylopoulos, P.A. Bernstein, H.K.T. Wong, "A Language Facility for Designing Database-Intensive Applications", ACM Transactions on Database Systems, Vol 5, No. 2, June, 1980, pages 185-207.

[MSOP86] D. Maier, J. Stein, A. Otis, A. Purdy, "Development of an Object-Oriented DBMS", Oregon Graduate Center, Technical Report, CS/E-86-005, April, 1986.

[PL83] M.L. Powell and M.A. Linton, Database Support for Programming Environments, "Engineering Design Applications", SIGMOD Database Week, May, 1983.

[S81] D.W. Shipman, "The Functional Data Model and the Data Language DAPLEX", ACM TODS 6, 1 (1981), 140-173.

[Sc78] J.W. Schmidt, "Type Concepts for Database Definition", in Schneiderman, B. (editor), Databases: Improving Usability and Responsiveness, Academic Press, 1978.

[SS77] J.M. Smith, D.C.P. Smith, "Database Abstractions: Aggregation", CACM 20, 6 (1977).

[SZ86] A. Skarra and S. Zdonik, "The Management of Changing Types in an Object-Oriented Database", Proceedings of the Conference on Object-Oriented Programming, Systems, and Applications, Portland, Oregon, September, 1986.

[SZR86] A. Skarra, S. Zdonik, and S. Reiss, "An Object Server for an Object Oriented Database System", Brown University, Technical Report, April, 1986.

[TL85] I. Thomas and J. Loerscher, "MOSAIX - A Version Control and History Management System", Proceedings of the GTE Workshop on Software Engineering Environments for Programming in the Large, Harwichport, Mass., June, 1985.

[WMy77] H.K.T. Wong, J. Mylopoulos, "Two Views of Data Semantics: A Survey of Data Models in Artificial Intelligence and Database Management", INFOR 15, 3 (1977), 344-382.

[Z84] S.B. Zdonik, "Object Mangement System Concepts", Proceedings of the Second ACM-SIGOA Conference on Office Information Systems, Toronto, Canada, June, 1984.

[ZW86] S.B. Zdonik and P. Wegner, "Language and Methodology for Object-Oriented Database Environments", Proceedings of the Nineteenth Annual International Conference on System Sciences, Honolulu, Hawaii, January, 1986.

SOFTWARE ENGINEERING DATABASES

Chair   : Reidar Conradi (Norw. Inst. of Tech., NOR)
Assistant chair : Haavard Eidnes (Norw. Inst. of Tech., NOR)

Discussion

Reidar Conradi (Norw. Inst. of Tech., NOR):

I would like comments on the appropriateness of the underlying DBMS'es, on the
problems of external viewing (tool interfaces and formats), and on what data models
we should use. Also, highly structured databases are found both in PE, CAD/CAM,
VLSI, AI, etc.. And lastly, what I'd like to hear mostly is experience.

Bernard Lang (INRIA, FRA):

I am very interested in the possibility of object-oriented databases. A question to
Zdonik: Is this a methodology for implementing those objects in the persistent
object base? or, is there actually a language that is supporting it, so that you
can operate on the objects from a conventional programming language?

Stanley Zdonik (Brown Univ., USA):

There is hardly a suitable programming language to perform the operations which is
the active part. We now use C, because that's what we had available. We have a
project in the works that is going to try to build a programming language /
database symbiosis. When that exists, then you would write your application in that
programming language. We don't have that yet, but we do have the data definition
capabilities to allow you to define "operations" on object properties and so forth,
i.e., types. But the code that supports that is written in C.

Lynn Carter (GenRad, USA):

I have one concern about database-oriented programming environments. How do we
transmit a piece of information from your database to my system, when this piece is
a set of relationships of many components? Even if we use exactly the same
underlying software to implement our database system we have a problem, not to
speak of different computing and database systems. It really sounds like we're
going further into isolation.

Stanley Zdonik (Brown Univ., USA):

To some extent we have provoked some of those issues. I think that the answer has
to do with sophisticated mechanisms for importing types and behavior. Obviously you
can't get my objects unless you have an interpreter for my objects; and it's the
<u>types</u> that are the interpreters. So there has to be a way for me to say, "I want to
export this type to you". Then we can share the types, as well as share the
objects. Since types are just objects like anything else, how do I express the

exportation of those types?

Richard Snodgrass (Univ. North Carolina, USA):

I have a question on the aspect of _time_. Could both Klaus Dittrich and Stanley Zdonic comment on the use of _optical disks_ for persistent storage, e.g., to store multiple versions of objects?

Klaus Dittrich (FZI, FRG):

Our system does not have a built-in notion of absolute time (e.g., "object created at 16:11:13..."), we did not find a strong demand for that in our requirements analysis. However, by the automatic numbering of the versions of an object, there is to some extent a concept of _relative_ time: a version with number 3 has been created later than version 2 of the same object. If you need absolute times, you will have to use the standard data model facilities (with attributes) and do an appropriate database design.

Yes, optical disks might easily be incorporated into the system. I would do it by using our concept of multiple logical databases: mapping one or more of these to optical disks. Still, the tools and/or user have to decide which objects should go there (and transfer those to the appropriate logical database).

Stanley Zdonik (Brown Univ., USA):

My answer would just be "Yes": optical disks are the right thing. Versions are basically immutable objects, so optical disks are an obvious place to put them. One of the claims people make about version systems is that they're storage intensive, even if we can reduce the amount of space by delta storage. So cheap write-once memory is a great idea!

Robert Schwanke (Siemens, USA):

Suppose I want to use your relational software database for configuration management. You seem to be saying that a configuration instance can be easily represented as an aggregate. Can you easily and efficiently support versions of aggregates?

Klaus Dittrich (FZI, FRG):

The mechanisms are there, but we need some training and maybe even discipline to use them appropriately. We have to provide the methodology of how to use all these nice database concepts. From our own experience during the last six months with people from industry we can say that this is certainly not just hacking.

David Robinson (System Designers, GBR):

Versions are just one way to implement configurations, but there are other models of configuration. You might have to revise how you currently approach configuration control, and look at the new database models.

Lynn Carter asked a question about open systems. One of the problems for these new databases is to offer services to tools that are written and maintained under other systems. Obviously a view mechanism, which allows update through views to some common representation, can be a good help. Another solution is to allow existing tools to run on the underlying operating system as a kind of sub-process, communicating with the database through "filters".

We are speaking of two levels of integration: one is fairly strong in that the database governs and knows about a highly structured information flow. The other one is very loose, and the database only operates on "black-box" files with unknown contents, and can only give you basic configuration / version control. However, we can gradually move from loose to tighter integration.

Lynn Carter (GenRad, USA):

Some of what you say is true. But we need languages for describing the representations. I also think of the "MegaView", where you show all possible semantics associated with your objects. We then have a gigantic communication problem for just simple representation of this stuff. There's a lot of work before I can take a piece of program out of my SUN workstation and port it over to your workstation with your programming environment. We're talking about 10 times or 10 orders of magnitude more complex communication than normal ASCII text communication.

Stanley Zdonik (Brown Univ., USA):

Some canonical representation, maybe it's ASCII, is something that has to be decided on between the two communicators. There was a paper about "Remote Guardians" by Liskov and Herling at MIT that talked about how abstract types can communicate through a canonical representation given encode and decode operations on each side. I think it is possible to cast this technology into the terms of abstract datatypes (or types in general).

David Robinson (System Designers, GBR):

There are various levels of communication problems when importing and exporting between two systems that are the same, or that use the same model. Many people have presented object-oriented models, so your MegaView may indeed be possible. On the other hand, the worst case is between diverse models where you can achieve very little. And there are intermediate levels where a limited interchange is possible.

Arve Meisingset (Norwegian Telecom., NOR):

Sharing data from different databases with different data representations is possible in the ANSI/SPARC 3-schema architecture.

If you want insight into how to exchange conceptual schemas, it is described in the application layer protocol of the OSI-architecture.

Per Holager (ELAB-SINTEF, NOR):

Many speakers noted that we need much better efficiency if we want to store more detailed program data. If you use the Entity-Relation model or the pure relational model, then we are pulverizing the information into a lot af tiny items; the purpose is to have the full generality of combining these in every conceiveable or possible pattern. Then, related information gets spread out all over the disk. We should collect components that will probably be accessed together into one sort of contiguous mass of bits, and avoid references to indices and keys as much as possible. Therefore, the IDL system seems to be a promising starting point for an efficient database model. The typical relationship you have can often be modelled by containment. If a larger thing physically contains some component, then there's a relationship between them. There's no pointer; there's hardly any way to represent a relation more compact than that.

Bernard Lang (INRIA, FRA):

I have a similar question: How do you deal with granularity problems and efficiency when you have a large number of very small objects to be stored in the database?

Stanley Zdonik (Brown Univ., USA):

We are in the middle of a big study on general performance issues. There are a few obvious approaches. One technique mentioned by Klaus Dittrich is to cluster objects that are typically used together, physically together on secondary storage, i.e., creating "segments". This is a system-level view of objects that are transferred from secondary storage into main memory as a contiguous group. Obviously, if you store every character as a full-fledged object with the associated headers and pointers, that's going to be very expensive. So the solution to the small object problem is: don't do that. You essentially embed those objects in the containing object. Such an embedded object cannot be shared through pointers in the same way as other objects. But for most non-shared objects you can do indirect sharing to cut down space and overhead, and you can even let the contents define the object type.

Andy Rudmik (GTE Comm. Syst., USA):

We once prototyped a system for software engineering in the large. Our approach was somewhat different from systems where the granularity of information is much smaller. We did some benchmarks and used a relational database underneath a higher order, object-based data model (we actually bootstrapped the system with 100.000 lines of code from the prototype). We maintained all the relationships between the program components, the configuration information, etc.. For example, in ADA you have to recompile all the imported packages, before you compile a specific package.

Issuing a query to the relational database in identifying those components was done
<u>faster</u> than in conventional tools that used the compiler to search the regular file
system! I would emphasize that this approach cannot be easily extended outside its
domain unless you choose another strategy for managing the database.

We also have another in-house system in commercial use that manages very large
projects. It is based on a relational database with configuration management,
change control, etc., and it does a good job in the intended domain.

Reidar Conradi (Norw. Inst. of Tech., NOR):

First, a comment on the basic data model being object-oriented or not. Several
conferences are being held on semantic data modelling. I feel that the domain is
not mature yet.

Second, a comment on the interface to the particular tool, i.e., how to formalize
views and to get them as consistent as possible? I was not impressed by what I
heard today.

The third comment is on the support tools. Is IDL powerful enough (is it more or
less an add-on to some programming languages)? Do we need tighter integration?
There have been several attempts to fuse the database and the language more tightly
together: PS-Algol and 4-5 other languages, where you access the objects in the
database and in primary memory in a uniform way. Smalltalk does exactly that
(behind the curtain), and the Intel-432 processor attempted something similar, but
the performance was not encouraging.

So, are we speaking of a factor 10, or maybe even 50 or 100 in performance
problems? Fine-grained strategies, regardless of their semantic modelling, are all
more or less object-oriented. Is the basic problem that of efficiency?

Uwe Kastens (Univ.-GH Paderborn, W-G):

On the object-oriented approach and the other database-oriented approaches:

In the database approaches, I see at least two levels of disquieting things. They
have a very basic concept: the relation between objects. On the next level up you
can use relationships to specify certain semantics, like relationships between
representations, relationships between versions, etc.. However, you have relations
at different levels, and only one is the basic conceptual level.

In the object-oriented approach, you have all these semantics already in the
operations defined for the objects. To me, this will result in constructing
databases that are close to the outside world because the semantics are so deeply
incorporated in the specification that nobody else can go from there to the
outside. I'm lacking the basic concepts that are simple.

Steven Reiss (Brown Univ., USA):

Our Garden system is an object-oriented system sitting on top of an object-oriented
database. Even though we have all these objects floating around we have found an
efficiency that in interpreted form matches Lisp, and in compiled form matches
compiled Lisp.

We have done a lot of engineering to guarantee ourselves efficiency of in-core objects. This is why, for example, we have a dual database system - one for managing the in-core objects, and one for external database objects. The in-core system maintains knowledge for each object whether it is external or internal upon each object access. I think that with sufficient engineering, and with virtual and real memory becoming cheaper and cheaper, you can make such a system be quite efficient.

Mary Shaw (Carnegie Mellon Univ., USA):

Can you quantify "good enough"? We've heard remarks from both Dittrich and Nestor about the duty-cycles of automated PE systems being much heavier than the duty-cycles of normal database accesses. We've heard about your prototype system, and most of us have heard about Smalltalk systems kneeling down when there were lots of objects. So my provocative questions to all the speakers are: What rate of access are you expecting? what rate of access are you now seeing? how many objects are involved? and, how will this compare to the performance of full-scale systems?

Andy Rudmik (GTE Comm. Systems, USA):

There is a trade-off between performance and increased functionality. However, it surprised us in our prototype environment that because we maintained a lot of information (status information, change tracking, configuration management, relationships between various components), we could do high-level impact and traceability analysis just by relational queries. That's a considerable amount of functionality that the environment provided, at some expense to performance.

Bernard Lang (INRIA, FRA):

I would like to go back to Steve Reiss' remarks. I'm implementing an application in an object-oriented style towards a persistent database. The object-oriented view is both for central and persistent memory. My experience is that object-oriented programming is as run-time efficient as any other form of classical programming, and that the programs get more well-structured. However, I've not experienced thrashing of objects toward the persistent database, in spite of a fairly low bandwidth channel to the disk.

Mary Shaw (Carnegie Mellon Univ., USA):

The relational database systems were developed with a certain model of transaction processing in mind. That is, with a small number of types and a large number of uniformly-sized instances of the types, and with a duty-cycle of a few accesses per second. When you try to use such a database system for a software engineering development to represent programs and related information, most of those assumptions get violated. My question is, whether those relational systems are anywhere near matching the new, expected load? I have seen cases with absolutely disasterous performance. You simply have to say more than: "It seems be fast enough"!

David Robinson (System Designers, GBR):

In reply to that - we had a development environment that was an enitity-relationship system built on top of a CODASYL system. The exact problems that Mary Shaw talked about actually occurred because there was a mismatch in the expectancy of very short transactions. We used very long-lived transactions: minutes, half-hour, days.

I also think we have to incorporate a new versioning model into our system. A traditional DBMS has very short-lived transactions and locking is based on a pessimistic assumption that many people want to access the same information. In a software engineering environment, you don't have the same pessimistic approach. If you create <u>versions</u> of objects you have two sorts of concurrency on revision: because of on-going development, or through maintenance. Any version that is of public interest in the development environment is in a <u>read-only</u> state. You do not update in place, you create versions of it. Such a model could easily support development versions of objects and optimize in separate workspaces, although we have to formalize the incorporation of changes back into the central database. However, experience from our compiler people is that optimizing compilers come long after the introduction of the new language. So we must first come up with new concepts and then do the optimizing.

Reidar Conradi (Norw. Inst. of Tech., NOR):

We cannot wait 5-10 years for the database technology to mature. Remember that the first optimizing FORTRAN compiler was released 1-2 years after the completed language design, although it took us 10-15 years to formalize the optimization process properly.

Mary Shaw (Carnegie Mellon Univ., USA):

I'm not asking for optimizations now, I'm asking for back-of-the-envelope calculations that indicate whether it can possibly work before we go too far down this path.

David Robinson, (System Designers, GBR):

Sorry, my reply wasn't back-of-the-envelope calculations. For our prototype we had over 10.000 objects in a database; and, yes, we did have these problems.

Mary Shaw (Carnegie Mellon Univ., USA):

I have one positive data point now!

Steven Reiss (Brown Univ., USA):

I have some back-of-the-envelope calculations for you, Mary. We have put a lot of thought into the efficiency issue. We have Zdonik's database system that's split into two portions. The one I use contains the version control: I use it essentially as an object server. It offers a lot of efficiency mechanisms. For example, when you request an object that has been written out inside a segment, you get the whole segment back. In a single transaction you can get back very large sets of objects, so you get the whole "kernel" in effectively one transaction, or the whole "body" of a procedure. The Garden system also separates persistent from non-persistent objects, so that you only invoke the database system on the persistent ones. The object server maintains several classes of transactions to minimize their costs. We have, for example, "notifying triggers", where multiple people safely can have copies of objects in their memory areas and you get notified when somebody write-locks them. Our experience shows that start-up costs upon reading in objects from the database is the same as when we are creating all the initial objects from scratch. While we're running, everything turns up in memory once you've read it and you don't have any disturbing interferences.

Mary Shaw (Carnegie Mellon Univ., USA):

Does that constrain the objects that could be held in memory?

Steven Reiss (Brown Univ., USA):

In Garden, yes; but it doesn't matter since all objects are essentially small. For large objects you keep in memory a file pointer and fetch the object when you need it.

Lynn Carter (GenRad, USA):

I will elaborate on what Mary Shaw said. Bell Northern Research (BNR) reported to IFIP WG 2.4 group that they brought very large IBM computers to their knees just to do the inhale and exhale of typing information for doing separate compilations, which is probably one of the most trivial forms of databases imaginable. Therefore, importing more than you really need for programs in the mega-line area gives intolerable performance. Small program examples (less than 100.000 lines) may not generalize to a large number of applications. In my company we're talking about 300.000 lines of source and I'm only a company of 7 people.

Terrence Miller (Hewlett Packard, USA):

Some approaches to database access for larger programs:

- Lazy evaluation: pull in only what you need to show the user.

- Prediction: take advantage of user's thinking time to get next clump of information.

- Caching: keep in memory only recently used information.

Andy Rudmik (GTE Comm. Systems, USA):

We've got to look at evolution. A drastic transition to fine-grained use of databases is beyond today's technology. I see both GTE, TRW, and a few other companies seriously using database technology to support engineering environments for both hardware and software development. However, it's at a coarse level, and we're looking at the next generation toward more object-oriented paradigms. The problem is engineering and performance. But there is a lot of mileage to get out of software engineering environments today, and that should be a good starting point for the future.

Alfons Geser (Univ.Passou, FRG):

I'd like to come back to the versioning problem: the only interesting relationship between two versions is that they are ordered. For me, it's a bit astonishing to hear that this seems to be too much work.

Klaus Dittrich (FZI, FRG):

You have the generic objects and these generic objects may come with versions if you like. You can establish relationships between everything you want (like a normal chronological order), but normally it will be done between versions of different objects.

Let me give some indications to the questions Mary Shaw raised that might point into the correct direction.

First statement: Mary said, "what happens if we use traditional DBMS'es for the new kinds of applications?", and I agree that the answer would be "they would dim the light". But all the systems proposed this afternoon are not "systems like this". They try to meet the different requirements by using different internal techniques for access paths, storage management, etc..

Second statement: IBM research in San Jose, is experimenting with a system called XSQL which is a modification of their commercial SQL/DS and DB2 systems. It incorporates (among other features) complex objects that comprise sets of tuples spread across multiple relations. Appropriate operators, access paths and optimizations are also provided. They took a reasonably sized internal application and ran it both with and without the complex object mechanism. The speed-up factor in using the new concepts was up to 100 and brought the response time for queries back to acceptable levels.

Third statement: A German colleague used a conventional CODASYL type system to store CAD-data (which is comparable to what we are talking about). In one of his scenarios he stored data about cylinders and had to go 70 times to the database to get one cylinder out of it. With an object-oriented database you would have to go there only once.

Reidar Conradi (Norw. Inst. of Tech., NOR):

I'd like to follow up on this: Does that mean that there are some concrete and successful applications of object-oriented databases in this field? Are they available, are they reported properly, etc.?

Klaus Dittrich (FZI, FRG):

Maybe the only one is the XSQL system that is used internally at IBM research. There are some more that are just now getting into applications, and one is even said to be marketed in the near future. All of the other ones are still in the prototype phase.

Per Holager (ELAB-SINTEF, NOR):

A small comment on terminology: We are using "object-oriented" for two different things. One is the sort of SIMULA or SMALLTALK data structure, meaning data concatenated with access operations and a type/subclass hierarchy. On the other hand you have the idea of collecting all data pertaining to one object into one lump on the disk, and that's a different concept.

Reidar Conradi (Norw. Inst. of Tech., NOR):

As I understood, the point of lumping it together was to get both logical and physical locality. We may regard the segment both as a genuine high-level object and as a mere space optimization.

Per Holager (ELAB-SINTEF, NOR):

The "segmented" object-orientation involves more than just efficiency. I think we should see the typical relational model as the very extreme form of spreading out information. If you had your entire semantic tree represented in a relational system, you would have one table for the IF-statements, another table for the assignment statements, a third table for the arithmetic operators, etc.. In this case, Bell Northern Research probably would have one disk unit for the IF-statements and another disk unit for the assignment statements, and so on!

David Robinson (System Designers, GBR):

The ANSI/SPARC model does address the performance problem in its 3-level architecture. You do your modelling and logical operations at the conceptual level. At the internal level you can address the problems of performance tuning, access paths, and the like. You always maintain a logical and physical separation.

Klaus Dittrich (FZI, FRG):

I agree with you; but the conceptual data model must give you a handle to define the physical structures. If there is no such handle, you can hardly define a storage structure language (SSL) that does this job.

Abstract Data Types, Specialization, and Program Reuse

William L. Scherlis
Carnegie-Mellon University
Pittsburgh, PA 15213

Abstract. It is often asserted that our ability to reuse programs is limited primarily by the power of programming language abstraction mechanisms. We argue that, on the basis of performance considerations, this is just not the case in practice—these "generalization" mechanisms must be complemented by techniques to adapt the generalized structures to specific applications. Based on this argument, we consider a view of programming experience as a network of programs that are generalizations and specializations on one another and that are interconnected by appropriate program derivation fragments. We support this view with a number of examples. These examples illustrate the important role of abstract data type boundaries in program derivation.

1. Introduction

Developers of programming languages cite program reuse as a goal in the design of abstraction and structuring mechanisms. Powerful abstraction mechanisms permit ordinary code to be parameterized in such a way that it can be used, by direct incorporation, in contexts other than those that motivated the original development. Thus, by retaining genericity, leverage can be obtained from the original design effort.

Success in reuse, however, stems from more than just the power of the programming language abstraction mechanisms available. The potential for obtaining reusable material from a programming effort is also affected by the degree of conventionalization in the problem domain and by the performance requirements placed on the implementation. In the common model of programming activity, unfortunately, these various factors are usually in conflict, foiling efforts to develop code for reuse.

Just what do we mean by reuse? Reuse clearly entails the creation of some representation of the solution of a problem that can be applied to other similar problems. In programming, the most obvious representation of past experience is *code*, since code manifests the end result of the programming process. We (and others) have made the case that code is an insufficient representation of the results of a design process and that more generous representations, such as program derivations, significantly enhance our ability to represent and reuse the information and insights gained during the design process [Bauer85, Balzer83, Dietzen86, Green83, Scherlis83]. We illustrate in this paper several ways in which a program derivation approach is more compatible with the goals of reuse. Our focus, in particular, is on the role of specializations of abstract data types in the development of reusable material and in adapting existing models to new problems.

We start by considering the conflicting factors mentioned above and showing how the conflict is reduced when a program derivation paradigm is adopted. We then consider a number of examples to illustrate the dimensions of reuse that are supported in the paradigm. An advantage of the proposed paradigm is

*This research was supported in part by the Office of Naval Research under contract N00014-84-K-0415 and in part by the Defense Advanced Research Projects Agency (DOD), ARPA Order No. 5404, monitored by the Office of Naval Research under the same contract. The views and conclusions contained in this document are those of the authors and should not be interpreted as representing the official policies, either expressed or implied, of DARPA or the U.S. Government.

its diminished sensitivity (as compared with the conventional paradigm) to programming language design constraints. Programming language abstraction mechanisms take on a new role in this approach, as we illustrate. Our major example is a derivation of an efficient representation of queues as a specialization of the conventional data type of lists. The representation derived here is used in several derivations in [Jorring86b]. This derivation supports the view that successful reuse requires adaptation both of type interfaces and of type implementations.

2. The failure to achieve reuse.

Let us examine in some detail the factors affecting reuse in the conventional paradigm. Why has code development for reuse been more successful in certain application domains than in others? There are, of course, non-technical management factors that affect reuse; for example, a key factor is managerial willingness to invest resources at development time in order to anticipate change and future reuse, since reusability requires a robustness beyond immediate need. But even assuming favorable management disposition, why does it seem that the technical factors conspire together to inhibit useful large-scale reuse in most domains? (Several papers that examine issues in this area appear in a special issue of IEEE Transactions on Software Engineering [Boyle84, Cheatham84, Neighbors84].)

Abstraction mechanisms. Abstraction mechanisms permit implementors to define and enforce boundaries separating parts of a system. Richer abstraction mechanisms permit a greater variety of kinds of boundaries and more exacting placement of them. With respect to reuse, placement of boundaries translates into the creation of independently managable modules with well defined interfaces enabling them to be used in similar circumstances. More powerful abstraction techniques require fewer unnecessary commitments, so boundaries can be placed more naturally.

Object-oriented systems, for example, are a special kind of abstraction mechanism in which commitments can be postponed or avoided entirely both to the range of types supported by a given generic operator *and* to the range of operators that can apply to objects of a given type. That is, individual methods that apply a particular operator to objects of a given type can be defined without requiring commitment to the full range of possible types for the operator *or* operators for the type. The point is that reuse potential is enhanced by an ability to manage separately the components of a system.

Conventions in the problem domain. Abstraction mechanisms are necessary for boundaries to be delineated, but *conventions* are required in order to ensure a maximum agreement on where boundaries are to be placed, especially in cases where future needs cannot be fully anticipated. For example, in numerical software, while there is a rich variety of applications, the range of abstract notions manipulated is actually rather limited, embracing integers, reals, matrices, and other such conventional objects. But conventions concerning both abstract notions *and* implementations are required. Even if the abstractions are conventionalized, an absence of standards for implementing them limits sharing of code, since (often costly) explicit conversions must be carried out. In the case of numerical programming, hardware manufacturers essentially determine the conventions for representing integers and reals, while compiler writers generally determine those for vectors and matrices. Hence, in this domain there is genuine potential for reuse, and the potential has largely been realized.

In most non-numerical domains, however, convention is sorely lacking, both at the level of abstractions and at the level of implementations. But, of course, reuse has always been a strong argument for standardization. Large programming shops ("software factories") that can standardize interfaces realize an obvious internal reuse advantage.

A particularly vivid example of effective standardization is the Unix(tm) operating system and environment. By agreeing on text files as a common interchange medium, Unix tools (grep, awk, etc.) can easily be composed into aggregations suitable for specialized applications. The cost, of course, is that a Unix user who needs to organize and manipulate more highly structured objects, such as trees or graphs, cannot rely on standard tools and consequently must develop his or her own support [Kernighan84].

Concerning program specifications. In an environment in which we are developing *only* specifications we need concern ourselves only with abstractions and conventions for abstractions. As long as the meanings of the abstractions are understood, *implementations* or representations of abstract objects are not of concern. In such an environment, introduction and codification of conventions can often be successful even at high levels of abstraction.

In the world of specifications, there are two factors supporting reuse. First, use of abstraction mechanisms has only a conceptual cost, so additional abstraction and consequent introduction of convention is always possible. Second, expression of new concepts in terms of old ones is limited only by expressive and conceptual constraints, and such reductions become part of the accumulated base of abstractions. Therefore, it is possible to rely heavily on an accumulated base of abstractions, especially when the level of abstraction is high. This is illustrated in [Guttag85].

So it may seem that, given the richness of abstraction mechanisms in existing languages, reuse will become genuinely practical just when we can standardize on abstractions and suitable implementations for them. But it must be noted that standardization is a process of agreeing on commitments, while abstraction provides means to avoid them. Thus, while both abstraction and standardization promote reuse, they do so in often conflicting ways.

Performance requirements. In the real world of programming, where we must develop *implementations* as well as specifications, performance issues play a critical, almost dominant role. It is the need for efficiency that effectively eliminates most potential for reuse. Let us consider implementations for a moment. What distinguishes an implementation from a specification, in our view, is not simply level of concreteness, but also a complexity resulting from optimizations made for the sake of efficiency. We consider programming, *in the ideal*, to be a process of specialization, where interdependencies are introduced and general notions are replaced by more specific ones that are more efficient. The specialization is of *structure*, not functionality. The cost of this specialization, with its violation of the abstraction boundaries, is a loss of modularity, an introduction of dependency, and ultimately, a loss of clarity and adaptability. The sole benefit is improved performance. (A syntactic transformational approach that captures this idea, in part, is described in [Scherlis81 and 85]; the specific syntactic approach is not to be confused with the more general views presented here and in [Dietzen86].)

The point is this: Reuse in programming is undermined both by this specialization process, necessary for performance, and by the introduction of implementations for abstract notions, necessary for concreteness. If reuse is to be a possibility, then introduction of implementations requires conventionalization both of abstractions and representations. But specialization, however it may be accomplished, causes the abstraction boundaries to be violated, and, worse, it yields implementations tuned to externally imposed performance constraints. Implementations, that is, are generally organized into whatever specialized structures are appropriate for the problem.

Consider again the Unix example. Even if we can survive in the world of text strings, applications we develop by aggregating the Unix primitive operations eventually reach a threshold of unacceptable performance where programmers must consider developing more efficient special purpose tools.

3. Towards an alternative approach.

The analysis above is offered partly as an explanation of why large-scale reuse is an unlikely development in the current paradigm, no matter how powerful the abstraction mechanisms in a programming language. Convention, which is necessary for reusability and which is often attainable at the level of abstractions and, less so, at the level of representations, must bend in the face of performance needs.

But we do not offer the analysis simply to darken an already bleak picture. We argue, instead, that it points the way to an approach to programming that is more supportive of reuse. Perhaps it need not be said that reuse, properly managed, has a potentially huge effect on programming productivity. Ultimately, all representable programming knowledge is candidate for "reuse," at some level of consideration. By developing appropriate representations of programming knowledge, we capture notions appropriate not only for direct reuse of code, as might be the case in program modification or adaptation, but also more generalized representations suitable for program organizations, programming techniques, and so on. Some of these very general ideas are explored, particularly as they relate to analogical reasoning, in [Dietzen86]. The point is that the reuse issue is very closely linked with the broader issue of representing programming knowledge and the design of semantically based tools. We consider here a specific model of reuse that is based on adding a dimension of program transformation to the use of programming language abstraction mechanisms.

Our model of reuse is based on the specialization idea described above—and on the representation of sequences of such steps as *program derivations* [Scherlis83]. For our purposes, it suffices to say that a program derivation has two kinds of steps—steps that establish context for some (relatively) general-purpose part of a program and steps that exploit the context by means of simplification or transformation rules. Context is established, for example, by making a choice of representation or of computation order. These steps of establishing and exploiting context, taken together, manifest *commitment* steps in program development. Derivations are thus directional, in the sense that later steps manifest increasing degrees of computational commitment. In other words, more *'how'* information is present, increasingly obscuring the *'what'* information. It is important to understand that derivations are ideal structures and are not intended to represent the real process of program development. A derivation, instead, should be thought of as the end result of a programming process. (See the paper cited above for a more thorough development of these ideas.)

The program derivation framework permits a more flexible approach to abstraction mechanisms in programs. We illustrate that here, and show how this flexibility contributes to reusability. This view is also reflected, in part, in the presentation of [Jorring86b]. Indeed, the results of the major example derivation example presented here are applied to the examples in that paper.

We now move to the example derivations; while the examples are intended primarily to create a background for this discussion of reuse, they also provide illustrations of the sort of transformation techniques that could support our approach.

4. Lists and Specializations.

In this and later sections, we discuss a major example of adaptation of an abstract data type, the familiar type of lists, to various equally familiar contexts of use.

The methodology lurking behind the example is this: A general-purpose abstract type is used in a specialized way in a (relatively) high-frequency stage of a program. If the type operations have initial implementations, then the initial version of the program has the status of a prototype—it has the correct functionality, but perhaps unacceptable performance. In order to obtain adequate performance, we use transformation to exploit the specialized context of use of the type.

How is this done? First, the type signature is adapted to the context of use of the type. We can think of the type signature as describing the *boundary* of the type, and this adaptation process as a process of *moving* the type boundary. Boundary movement can involve *incorporating* new operations from outside the original type, *releasing* certain operation definitions from inside the type enclosure, and selectively *exposing* representational structure. (These operations are described in more detail in [Scherlis85].) In this example, we start with a use of the type of generic lists and specialize the boundary to the case where lists are used as first-in first-out accumulators.

Once the boundary is moved, then the implementation of the type can be optimized to exploit the new boundary. This is done by simplifying or eliminating computation that is not necessary to the specialized set of operations and by "shifting" computation along data paths to less frequent points or points where the computation can be carried out more efficiently due to context. In the case of our major example, these transformations are used to introduce a special destructive representation for the restricted variety of lists.

Once the type (signature and implementation) has been specialized, then the specialized form, together with intermediate results of interest, can be stored for use in similar circumstances. It could be considered that the ultimate specialization of a type is a complete unfolding, in which the type boundary is removed and the implementations of the type operations are incorporated into the surrounding context. Why, if performance is the main goal, is this not always done immediately at the outset? Why preserve type structure at all? The reason is that the type boundary is necessary for those transformations that move computation along data paths. Removal of the boundary results in the removal of any regulation of those data paths, so we can no longer use simple local syntactic transformations without global reasoning to support them. (Imagine, for example, trying to match in a Lisp program a given call to car with all possible calls to cons that could have created the cell.)

The point of our derivation example, then, is to show a number of stages of specialization along the way from the type of lists to the derived type of queues to the fully unfolded program integrating queues into surrounding code. The example is used as a framework within which our technical approach to reuse is presented. We discuss along the way several other lesser examples.

Although this paper is self contained, the actual techniques used in this derivation are presented in more detail elsewhere. The syntactic specialization rules of [Scherlis81] are used for ordinary structural operations; these rules are analogous to the unfold/fold rules, but are sound with respect to termination. The type manipulation rules described in [Scherlis85] are used for manipulating the abstract data types; a precursor to these rules is [Wile81]. Finally, the rules for manipulating destructive data operations are introduced in [Jorring86b]. As much as possible, we will follow the notation and conventions of that paper, which shows several examples that use the type derived in the derivation shown below.

A remark must be made concerning transformation rules. The purpose of most of the transformation rules we use, such as specialization rules, abstract type transformations, and so on, is to make structural changes in programs in order to facilitate local simplifications. The structural changes generally involve manipulation of abstraction boundaries for the purpose of syntactically juxtaposing computations that are computationally juxtaposed either along control paths or along data paths. The simplification rules are rules of a conventional sort for simplifying expressions in particular data domains.

The List type. We start with the type of generic lists, whose signature may be notated as follows.

adt *List*
   with
        nil : *List*
        hd : *List* → *A*
        tl : *List* → *List*
        cons : *A* × *List* → *List*
        null : *List* → *Bool*

This is a generic type, but for the sake of simplicity we omit the type parameter A. The type interface, together with axioms regulating the operations, provides enough information for manipulation of specifications using abstract lists. Some example axioms are:

$hd(cons(x, y)) = x$

$null(nil)$

not $null(cons(x, y))$

We should note that, strictly speaking, if we are to use equality it should be an explicit operator in the type. In the absence of such a declaration, we consider equality of abstract objects to be equality of representations. (This is the course we take in the examples below.)

In order to derive programs we must move toward a concrete representation, which requires us to make the first step of commitment. Every step of commitment is not only a step towards concreteness and efficiency, but also a step away from large-scale reuse. But, as we will see, the program derivation approach promotes reuse (1) by providing a representation of the connections between types and their specializations that includes all intermediate specializations, yielding a structured collection of more and less general types, and (2) by enabling use of derivation techniques to apply general and special purpose types from the collection to particular situations by adapting and specializing them.

Following [Jorring86b], we choose an initial representation which is the conventional one based on storage arrays, described using the equations,

$$Store = Ptr \rightarrow (A \times Ref)$$
$$Ref = Ptr + \mathbf{NIL} .$$

The *store* is a mapping of *pointers* to pairs consisting of elements of A and *references*, which are either pointers into storage or a special value nil (the only element of the set **NIL**). The set of pointers is a flat domain. An abstract list is represented as a element of Ref.

Since the type has internal state (the store), we must consider how to notate its implementation. Two choices are presented in [Jorring86b]. We choose here to adopt a conventional imperative notation, in which the state itself is implicit, operations on state are notated using assignment, and access to state is notated using selection (as in $\text{rep}(\ell)$.hd below). In this formulation, all lists are represented in a single store, permitting shared structure. Multiple instances of the list type (with distinct names) can be used to insulate one part of store from another as a consequence of type correctness of client code.

```
repn List
  with
        nil  ⇐ abs(nil)
        hd(ℓ)  ⇐  rep(ℓ).hd
        tl(ℓ)  ⇐  abs(rep(ℓ).tl)
        cons(a, ℓ)  ⇐  begin
                          new p;
                          p.hd ← a;
                          p.tl ← rep(ℓ);
                          return abs(p)
                       end
        null(ℓ)  ⇐  rep(ℓ) = nil
```

We use the functions abs and rep (mapping back and forth between Ref and $List$) to indicate type boundaries, as in ML. Clients thus manipulate lists without knowledge of the representation used. (We abuse our notation by using the symbol nil for both abstraction and representation.)

Observe that cons is the only operation that changes state. Because of this state change, expressions involving cons do *not* have a substitutivity property. Consider, for example, the expressions,

$$\text{let } x = \text{cons}(a, b) \text{ in } P(x, x)$$

and

$$P(\text{cons}(a, b), \text{cons}(a, b)) \quad ,$$

where P is, say, equality. Simplifications involving cons must be made with care because of this abuse of the functional notation.

Context of use. Scope mechanisms limit access to type definitions in programs. Within a scope, it is possible that a type is used only in certain restricted ways. For example, it is easy to imagine a context in which the type of lists is used to build at most one list, and with bounded length. In this context, clearly, a single vector of fixed length would suffice as the representation of the type.

In the context of reuse, there are two problems arising from this scenario: First, how do we describe the specialized contexts of use in a precise way, so program manipulation techniques can be applied to specialize the type implementations? We provide some examples below to illustrate some possiblities, but this is far from being a settled issue. Second, how can we effectively limit scopes of instances of types so greater specialization can be achieved? The approach we take here (elaborated upon below) is to keep scopes as narrow as possible and to partition different *uses* of a type into different type *instances*. By doing this, we increase the degree of specialization possible for individual instances. This is also illustrated below. (To avoid confusion, we use *context of use* to refer to the computational contexts in which individual instances of the type operations appear, and we use *scope of use* to refer to scope in which the type operations are accessible. We also often refer to type signatures as type *boundaries*.)

An example context. As an example of a specialized use of lists, consider the case of stacks. What distinguishes a list from a stack is that lists can have pointers to embedded suffix lists, while stacks grant access only to the top element. The resulting strictly linear structure yields a performance advantage to the implementor of stacks, especially when a strict size bound can be established.

In order to specify the context of stack-like use of lists, we make use of a special assertion on lists called exclusive-use (introduced in [Jorring86b]). Asserting exclusive-use(x), where x is a list, means that the variable x has exclusive access to the list structure it points to (*i.e.*, the internal structure of the list—not necessarily its elements). In an imperative program, this implies that this is the last use of x and that no other variables alias any part of the list x.

The exclusive-use assertion can also decorate an expression, as in '{exclusive-use} cons(a, x).' This asserts that at this point in execution, there are no other handles on the list cons(a, x) or any part of it, including x. Note that this implies that this is a last use of x.

A stack, then, is a list with no handles available to its internal top level structure. For example, the decorated expression cons$(a, \{\text{exclusive-use}\}\ x)$ denotes a stack with a as the top element. While a stack can have multiple variables and data structures referencing it, it is necessary that all but one of those references be dead when a push is evaluated, as indicated. Thus, stacks are a special case of lists, in which the list operations are used in a way that conforms to these exclusive use restrictions.

The first part of our technique, then, will involve the creation of specialized type signatures from existing types.

Scope and clone types. By narrowing the scopes of use of existing types, we have a greater chance that all uses of the type operations in a given scope are of a useful specialized form. There are two general approaches to this narrowing. One is to start with a program in which, say, all list variables are declared of type *List*, and then do global reasoning about the extent of objects in order to determine how the set of list variables can be partitioned into smaller "sub-scopes," in which lists may be used in specialized ways. This sort of global reasoning, unfortunately, becomes very difficult as programs grow in complexity.

One way to avoid the global reasoning is to proliferate abstract types at the earliest stages of program specification, when the greatest amount of structure exists. This is done by introducing a trivial type wrapper for each particular related collection of variables of a given type. Introduction of a type wrapper (*i.e.*, a new type name, but with the same type implementation and operations) effectively partitions all list variables (for example) in a given scope according to the new type names. The effect of this approach is to replace reasoning about extent by ordinary type checking.

What we have, essentially, is a set of *clones* of the list type—a set of types with different names, but with identical characteristics. The point of this simple technique is to isolate—from the outset—narrow scopes within which type operations might *possibly* be used in specialized contexts.

It is clearly unrealistic to hope that a perfect partitioning of variables in a scope can be achieved. In most cases, the new type boundaries will be imperfect; there will be cases where introduction of new boundaries requires introduction of explicit calls to conversion operations between objects of the various types, so the boundaries can be crossed. If the types are all unmodified clones of the same type, then the implementations of the conversion operators are all initially the identity function. As the type implementations are optimized to their specialized uses, the definitions of the conversion operations will be transformed as well. (This technique, and others, are specified in rigorous detail elsewhere, so we provide here only an informal description.)

The example, continued. Suppose that, after a narrowing of scope, every use of a list type operation is of one of the following forms:

> nil
>
> $cons(a, \{exclusive\text{-}use\} \ x)$
>
> $tl(\{exclusive\text{-}use\} \ x)$
>
> $null(x)$
>
> $hd(x)$

If this is the case, then all list operations in the local scope can be abstracted into one of the following function definitions:

> $emptystack \ \Leftarrow \ nil$
>
> $push(a, x) \ \Leftarrow \ cons(a, \{exclusive\text{-}use\} \ x)$
>
> $pop(x) \ \Leftarrow \ tl(\{exclusive\text{-}use\} \ x)$
>
> $nullstack(x) \ \Leftarrow \ null(x)$
>
> $top(x) \ \Leftarrow \ hd(x)$

If *all* operations in the scope are abstracted as such, then we can use the abstract type transformations to move the boundaries of the type (which may be a clone type) to conform to the boundaries suggested by the abstracted procedures. We could then optimize the implementation of the modified clone to adapt to the specialized signature (though we do not do that here).

A more specialized type. Once we have derived a specialized type for these stacks, we can consider more highly specialized types. Let MaxLength be a global constant.

> $emptystack$
>
> $\{length(x) < MaxLength\} \ push(a, x)$
>
> $\{x \neq nil\} \ pop(x)$
>
> $nullstack(x)$
>
> $\{x \neq nil\} \ top(x)$

In this more specialized case, all stacks have bounded size, and error checking has been moved out of the type and into the client context. That is, the type boundary can be moved to this set of operations only when it can be established, for example, that only nonempty stacks are popped or 'topped.' In the previous type, however, error checking must be done within the type, since pop and top can be called with any stack.

Let us do procedural abstraction *again* in order to incorporate the preconditions (or *qualifiers*) on push, pop, and top above into the operations. For convenience (and perhaps confusion), we used the same names again, but for the new, slightly more specialized operations. We can write the (still unoptimized) type implementation for these stacks as follows:

```
repn Stack
   with
         emptystack  ⇐  abs(nil)
         push(a, x)  ⇐  {length(rep(x)) < MaxLength} abs(cons(a, {exclusive-use} rep(x)))
         pop(x)  ⇐  {rep(x) ≠ nil} tl({exclusive-use} rep(x))
         nullstack(x)  ⇐  null(rep(x))
         top(x)  ⇐  {rep(x) ≠ nil} hd(rep(x))
```

It is important to bear in mind that because this type was derived from another type by boundary movement and abstraction, it can be used only in exactly the context from which it was abstracted. This is the only way that the (now hidden) qualifiers can be guaranteed to hold. The advantage, however, is that all unnecessary checking and case analysis has been omitted.

This approach seems to defy reuse, so let us look more closely. This specialization process actually has two major steps. First, the boundaries in a program are shifted to new, more specialized ones. Second, transformations are used to optimize the type implementation to new boundaries. The boundary shifting problem is unique to each context and application. But, the derivations of optimized type implementations can be reused (in whole or in part) in all similar cases. The point is that while the details of boundary shifting will be unique to each context, the optimized type implementations can be shared.

In this example, we omit the derivation of the specialized implementation of this type. But it is interesting to note that transformations can be used to propagate all storage allocation into what is initially the most trivial operation, emptystack. The derived version of the operation would allocate a vector of storage of length MaxLength + 1 for holding the stack and a stack pointer. The implementations of the other operations would then be the natural ones for stacks implemented in this fashion. We expect that this kind of representation change could be accomplished using the type transformation techniques described in [Scherlis85] combined with more conventional program transformation techniques. (We illustrate the process below, but using a more elaborate example.)

Collections of specialized types. Why are we considering type specializations? What, in particular, is the advantage of this approach over an approach of just developing *ad hoc* types and implementations when needed? Two advantages are immediately apparent. One obvious advantage is correctness. These new types are all derived from a type whose properties are known and for which there is a large body of miscellaneous code. By developing special purpose types by transformation, we automatically obtain a guarantee of correctness (relative to that of the initial type and, of course, the transformation rules). A second obvious advantage is that the peripheral routines can be transformed along with the type definition. For example, the list length function could be transformed along with the stack type above. In the latter implementation, this function simply looks in the length field of the derived stack representation—replacing a linear time operation by a constant time one while ensuring correctness and consistency of functionality with the original list version. Similarly, any *facts* we may know about the original type can be transformed as well, yielding an *a priori* base of knowledge about the new type.

But, as we noted earlier, there are two other key advantages for reuse that are obtained from this approach of deriving specialized types from existing well-understood types. First, a structured library of standard specializations is amassed, with obvious advantages. Second, the techniques are appropriate for deriving custom specializations, either from an initial general type or from some existing specialization.

An important methodological point, noted earlier, is that in a type transformation environment abstract types should be proliferated in the early stages of program derivation. Every menial array index subrange, every tuple for aggregating values, every simple list or tree—all of these should have their own declared layer of abstraction around their (trivial) implementations. Multiple instances of the same type used in conceptually different contexts should be separated by cloning.

How do we distinguish *useful* local scopes for type uses? Scopes are obviously distinguished by locality of use, but scope delineations are also suggested by staging (*i.e.*, frequency) boundaries in programs

[Jorring86a]. This is illustrated in the map example in [Jorring86b]. When scopes are distinguished in this manner, we must often introduce explicit conversion operations between scopes in order to maintain separation, as noted earlier. If specialized representations are developed for particular scopes, then the savings realized must be balanced, obviously, with the added cost of the derived conversion operations.

If, in the end, the proliferation of types was unwarranted in certain local segments of a program, then unnecessary type boundaries can simply be unfolded and eliminated. But there is a key point here, which is that it is easier to start with *too many* boundaries and to eliminate them than to start with *too few* and have to do global reasoning in order to introduce new ones.

The lesson is that type interfaces should be thought of as fluid—with a fluidity similar to the kind of fluidity of procedure boundaries obtained through the more conventional program transformations. Of course, this approach is only as good as the transformation rules that support it and, ultimately, the programming tools that embody those rules. In the remainder of this paper, we explore this question by means of a larger example involving destructive operations and a specialized use of lists. Rather than exhibiting only type interfaces and alluding to the implementations as we did above, in this example we carry out the manipulations on the type implementations. The techniques used are the specialization rules, the type transformations, and the destructiveness rules all cited above.

5. The Append Function.

Let us return to the simple type of lists and look at a well-known function defined in terms of the list operations.

$$\text{append}(x, y) \Leftarrow \text{ if } x = \text{nil then } y$$
$$\text{else cons}(\text{hd}(x), \text{append}(\text{tl}(x), y))$$

One of the advantages of writing specifications or prototypes using well known types is that they are generally supported by a large body of convention, which includes supporting functions such as this. Specialized uses of the type often involve auxiliary functions, and reuse at the specification level is supported by whatever convention exists among the functions.

Let us suppose that this list concatenation function is used in a certain specialized context in which the first argument, which is a list, is exclusively accessed at the function call site. That is, there are no other handles on the list or any part of its top level structure other than the actual parameter itself. In this case, it makes sense to recycle the storage space used for the input list to form the first part of the resulting list—in effect splicing the two lists together. Given the exclusivity property, this optimization (yielding a version of append usually called nconc by Lispers) is indistinguishable to callers. We are thus considering a transformation problem in which the initial definition is a version of append decorated with an exclusivity assertion.

$$\text{append}(\{\text{exclusive-use}\}\, x, y) \Leftarrow \text{ if } x = \text{nil then } y$$
$$\text{else cons}(\text{hd}(x), \text{append}(\text{tl}(x), y))$$

As a first preparatory step in our derivation, we render this program into an imperative form and, in the process, introduce new variables to aid in decomposing the computation into steps. This imperative form, we will see, renders the simplification process more comprehensible.

$$\text{append}(\{\text{exclusive-use}\}\, x, y) \Leftarrow \textbf{begin}$$
$$\text{if } x = \text{nil then return } y$$
$$u \leftarrow \text{append}(\text{tl}(x), y)$$
$$r \leftarrow \text{cons}(\text{hd}(x), u)$$
$$\textbf{return } r$$
$$\textbf{end}$$

(Both assignments are acting in the role of **let** constructs.)

At this point, we must commit ourselves somewhat to a representation of lists—at least to one that supports manipulations involving exclusive-use such as the rule set described in [Jorring86b]. Following those rules (and, in the absence of that paper, our intuition), we can infer that, once we have accessed the hd and tl of x and there are no more direct accesses, then the cell can be released. We introduce two new variables and a simultaneous assignment (also acting in the role of a **let** construct) to facilitate the transformation.

$$\text{append}(\{\text{exclusive-use}\}\ x, y) \Leftarrow \textbf{begin}$$
$$\textbf{if } x = \text{nil} \textbf{ then return } y$$
$$h, t \leftarrow \text{hd}(x), \text{tl}(x)$$
$$\textbf{release } x$$
$$u \leftarrow \text{append}(t, y)$$
$$r \leftarrow \text{cons}(h, u)$$
$$\textbf{return } r$$
$$\textbf{end}$$

We now seek to make this definition tail recursive, in order to reduce the need for implicit storage allocation. Our strategy for achieving this is to move computation forward of the recursive call as much as possible. Given that the last statement contains an reference to u, which is the result of the recursive call, this does not seem promising. But by making further commitment to a representation for lists, we become able to decompose the cons call into separate steps of allocation of the cell and assignment to the components. These commitments narrow the scope of accessability of the newly derived routines, but the price for performance is almost always specialization of some sort:

Following the example of the implementation of the *List* data type (in effect, unfolding the call to cons), we start by replacing the assignment '$r \leftarrow \text{cons}(h, u)$' by the three statements,

$$\textbf{new } r$$
$$r.\text{hd} \leftarrow h$$
$$r.\text{tl} \leftarrow u$$

Having done this, we can legally advance the first two of these statements before the recursive call (since they do not reference u) and simplify.

$$\text{append}(\{\text{exclusive-use}\}\ x, y) \Leftarrow \textbf{begin}$$
$$\textbf{if } x = \text{nil} \textbf{ then return } y$$
$$h, t \leftarrow \text{hd}(x), \text{tl}(x)$$
$$\textbf{release } x$$
$$\textbf{new } r$$
$$r.\text{hd} \leftarrow h$$
$$r.\text{tl} \leftarrow \text{append}(t, y)$$
$$\textbf{return } r$$
$$\textbf{end}$$

The juxtaposed **release** and **new** operations can be simplified to a single assignment of x to r. Since $h = \text{hd}(x)$ and $x = r$, the assignment of h to the hd of r is redundant. The program that results is now very simple.

$$\text{append}(\{\text{exclusive-use}\}\ x, y) \Leftarrow \textbf{begin}$$
$$\textbf{if } x = \text{nil} \textbf{ then return } y$$
$$x.\text{tl} \leftarrow \text{append}(\text{tl}(x), y)$$
$$\textbf{return } x$$
$$\textbf{end}$$

This is considerable progress, since there is now *no* explicit storage allocation. But we can do even better. Notice that the assignment to tl(x) is, in fact, redundant. (Notice, also, that we are still making implicit use of the storage allocated on the stack for recursive calls.) We prepare to carry out the simplification by composing to form an expression procedure for the assignment statement using the append definition above.

x.tl ← append({exclusive-use} tl(x), y) ⇐ begin
           if tl(x) = nil then begin x.tl ← y; exit end
           w ← tl(x)
           w.tl ← append(tl(w), y)
           x.tl ← w
       end

(We have simplified somewhat after making the substitution.) We can now eliminate the assignment to tl(x), since w already has the correct value. This illustrates a point made earlier—that, in large measure, the purpose of the structure manipulating transformation rules is simply to juxtapose program elements to enable low level simplifications.

x.tl ← append(tl(x), y) ⇐ begin
           if tl(x) = nil then begin x.tl ← y; exit end
           w ← tl(x)
           w.tl ← append(tl(w), y)
       end

The last line of this program is of the exact form as the program name, so this program is tail recursive. There are two bindings, one of y to y, which can clearly be omitted, and one of w to x. This iterative program can be rewritten as a simple **while** loop.

x.tl ← append(tl(x), y) ⇐ begin
           while tl(x) ≠ nil do x ← tl(x)
           x.tl ← y
       end

(We have eliminated the variable w by folding together the existing w assignment with the parameter assignment of w to x. Observe, by the way, that the assignment statements in the programs have had three kinds of origins: **let** binding, data structure modification, and parameter binding.)

As a final step, we incorporate this expression procedure into the main append program by unfolding the call. The expression procedure name and calls are replaced by the **while** loop and assignment.

append({exclusive-use} x, y) ⇐ begin
           if x = nil then return y
           u ← x
           while tl(x) ≠ nil do x ← tl(x)
           x.tl ← y
           return u
       end

This is the usual destructive list concatenation program called nconc in Lisp. At the cost of some minor commitments to the implementation of the list type, we have been able to derive an efficient special purpose function. This function, of course, can only be called in circumstances where exclusive use of the first argument has been established.

This illustrates the basic technique of procedure specialization. Specialization of procedures is, as we have noted, important for reuse and is an important element of the abstract data type specialization techniques illustrated below.

A slight embellishment. We will use the results of this derivation in the larger queue derivation to follow. Before plunging into that derivation, however, let us take one more preparatory step.

Suppose that in some context the first actual argument to append is in a less critical *stage* than the second. An example of such a situation is one in which there are repeated calls to append and the first argument changes less frequently than the second. In such a case, it is desirable to do as much computation as possible given only the first parameter. We illustrate here how, through procedure abstraction, we can arrange for this to be the case. (See [Jorring86a] for discussion of the technique behind this idea.)

Consider the final definition of append above. In the non-nil case, the second formal parameter y is accessed only just before the **return** is executed. We can use procedure abstraction to factor out much of the computation. (We omit the exclusive-use qualifier for brevity.)

```
append(x, y)  ⇐  begin
                    if x = nil then return y
                    B(x).tl ← y
                    return x
                  end

B(u)  ⇐  begin
            while tl(u) ≠ nil do u ← tl(u)
            return u
          end
```

The function B returns the last cell in the list u.

It is particularly interesting to introduce some minor case analysis on x. Let us suppose that $B(x)$ is already computed and available as the value of a variable w.

```
{x ≠ nil ∧ w = B(x)} append(x, y)  ⇐  begin
                                          w.tl ← y
                                          return x
                                        end

{x = nil} append(x, y)  ⇐  y
```

Observe that only a constant amount of computation remains after the x part of append has been computed.

A useful property. Suppose we are using the append operation to accumulate elements into a list. That is, the result of a call to append is supplied as an argument to another call to append. Now, every call involves a calculation of B; if the result is saved, it could be used to help calculate B for the append call at the next iteration. This motivates us to develop a specialized procedure for calculating $B(\text{append}(x, y))$ more efficiently than making the calls directly.

Since B is called only when its argument is nonempty, we assume here that at least one of the lists is nonempty. The result we obtain is:

$$\{x \neq \text{nil} \lor y \neq \text{nil}\}\ B(\text{append}(x, y))\ \Leftarrow\ \text{if } y = \text{nil then } B(x) \text{ else } B(y)$$

(The derivation is omitted.)

This derivation can, in fact, be accomplished in the domain of pure lists, with the result carrying directly over into the more committed representation of pointers and stores. Since there may be confusion on this point, we note explicitly that in the domain of pure lists it *cannot* be assumed that $\text{cons}(\text{hd}(x), \text{tl}(x)) = x$. As we interpret it, a domain in which this fact holds is a more specialized domain than the pure list domain, and, indeed, the more specialized domain is not consistent with the specialized domain in which we are operating in these examples.

If we assume that the second list is always nonempty, then specialize further to obtain the following expression procedure.

$$\{y \neq \text{nil}\}\ B(\text{append}(x, y))\ \Leftarrow\ B(y)$$

6. Lists and Accumulation.

We can now address the main problem, which involves the very common specialized use of lists for accumulating a list of values in first-in first-out order—in other words, in queue-like fashion. This specialization problem can be characterized by listing all allowable contexts of use of the list operations. Unlike the stack example, we do not want to *fully* commit ourselves to the specialized operations. That is, *once the list has been accumulated*, we do not want to make any promises concerning what will be done with it—it should just be treated as another list. We denote this operation of 'promoting to a first class list' by writing 'pass(x)'.

> nil
>
> append({exclusive-use} x, cons(a, nil)))
>
> pass({exclusive-use} x)

The three operations correspond to building an empty accumulator, accumulating a new element a to the end of an accumulator x, and returning a completed accumulator as a list. (With some exceptions, we henceforth omit the exclusive-use assertions.)

As in the stack example, we can create an abstract type boundary by abstracting all uses of the list operations in an appropriately narrowed scope, moving the list type boundary accordingly, and using the conversion operator pass at the scope boundaries to pass list values out. We call the new type *Qbuf*.

> **repn** *Qbuf*
> > **with**
> > > emptyq $\Leftarrow$ abs(nil)
> > >
> > > enq(x, a) $\Leftarrow$ abs(append(rep(x), cons(a, nil)))
> > >
> > > convQtoL(x) $\Leftarrow$ rep(x)

The type signature is as follows:

> **adt** *Qbuf*
> > **with**
> > > emptyq : *Qbuf*
> > >
> > > enq : *Qbuf* $\times$ *A* $\to$ *Qbuf*
> > >
> > > convQtoL : *Qbuf* $\to$ *List*

Let us now consider how we can transform the implementation of the list type and associated operations (such as append) to improve performance of the *Qbuf* operations. Clearly, the append derivation above suggests an approach.

A natural specialization strategy is to factor case analyses out of type operations and into the calling context whenever possible. While causing case tests to be distributed to all call sites, performance improvement can be obtained when the outcomes of the tests can be predicted. The principal case test in append is for an empty list x. This motivates us to consider a slightly simpler version of the *Qbuf* problem.

A more specialized queue problem. Suppose that in a more specialized context, we can always determine when empty accumulators are supplied to the operators enq and convQtoL.

> **repn** *Qbuf*
> > **with**
> > > emptyq $\Leftarrow$ abs(nil)
> > >
> > > enq(emptyq, a) $\Leftarrow$ abs(cons(a, nil))
> > >
> > > $\{x \neq$ emptyq$\}$ enq(x, a) $\Leftarrow$ abs(append((rep(x), cons(a, nil)))
> > >
> > > convQtoL(emptyq) $\Leftarrow$ nil
> > >
> > > $\{x \neq$ emptyq$\}$ convQtoL(x) $\Leftarrow$ rep(x)

Obvious simplifications exploiting the case analyses have already been made. It must be emphasized that this formulation of the implementation of the type is useful only when it is possible for *each* call to determine whether the accumulator is empty. But, perhaps surprisingly, this holds for a number of common examples. (See [Jorring86b] for a selection.)

The simplifications enable us to restrict our attention to a smaller number of operations, yielding a new type, on *nonempty* accumulators, which we also call *Qbuf* (since we will no longer refer to the older version immediately above).

> repn *Qbuf*
> with
> $\quad$ enqe$(a) \;\Leftarrow\; \text{abs}(\text{cons}(a, \text{nil}))$
> $\quad$ enq$(x, a) \;\Leftarrow\; \text{abs}(\text{append}((\text{rep}(x), \text{cons}(a, \text{nil}))))$
> $\quad$ convQtoL$(x) \;\Leftarrow\; \text{rep}(x)$

(Again, we are omitting exclusive-use assertions.) Since these operations constitute the entire type *Qbuf*, it should be clear that there is no way to supply enq or convQtoL with an empty accumulator.

Improving the type implementation. The type *signature* is now very highly specialized, but nonetheless useful. We are now ready to consider specializing the type *implementation* to obtain better performance. We undertake this specialization on the basis of an observation about the behavior of enq: Even if the destructive version of append is used by enq, the time it takes to insert a sequence of items into a *Qbuf* is quadratic in the length of the sequence. The source of the difficulty is in the repeated traversals of lists by the function B.

The inspiration for our improvements comes from the little fact about B stated earlier.

$$\{y \neq \text{nil}\}\; B(\text{append}(x, y)) \;\Leftarrow\; B(y)$$

The enq definition makes use of the specialized fact in an even more specialized way, namely:

$$\{y = \text{cons}(a, \text{nil})\}\; B(\text{append}(x, y)) \;\Leftarrow\; B(y)$$

We use a slightly awkward notation because of the lack of substitutivity of cons due to the imperative model.

What, exactly, is the inspiration derived from this fact? Observe that, in the current implementation of enq, append needs to compute B for its first argument, *which is itself* the result of a previous call to append (or a singleton from enqe). Given that it is so easy to compute B of the result of append, why not just *remember* that value when that result is supplied as a parameter the next time around?

We will use transformations to derive a new implementation for *Qbuf* that exploits this observation.

Further procedure abstraction. We saw earlier how easy it was to compute append given the value of B for its first argument.

$$\{x \neq \text{nil} \;\wedge\; w = B(x)\}\; \text{append}(x, y) \;\Leftarrow\; \begin{aligned} &\textbf{begin} \\ &\quad w.\text{tl} \leftarrow y \\ &\quad \textbf{return } x \\ &\textbf{end} \end{aligned}$$

$$\{x = \text{nil}\}\; \text{append}(x, y) \;\Leftarrow\; y$$

Let us work towards incorporating the B values into the $Qbuf$ objects. We do this by using procedure abstraction to further organize the destructive version of append we derived. A first step is to specialize that program to the case of nonempty lists, given our knowledge of the context of use of append in the $Qbuf$ implementation.

$$\{x \neq \text{nil}\}\ \text{append}(x, y)\ \Leftarrow\ \textbf{begin}$$
$$B(x).\text{tl}\ \leftarrow\ y$$
$$\textbf{return } x$$
$$\textbf{end}$$

$$B(u)\ \Leftarrow\ \textbf{begin}$$
$$\textbf{while } \text{tl}(u) \neq \text{nil } \textbf{do } u\ \leftarrow\ \text{tl}(u)$$
$$\textbf{return } u$$
$$\textbf{end}$$

The other specialized case is trivially obtained.

$$\text{append}(\text{nil}, y)\ \Leftarrow\ y$$

We now use procedure abstraction to obtain a pair representation for the first parameter. This packages together all information about the first parameter in a single object, which we will call a *queue pair*. The program below, while complicated, is just a reorganization of the program above.

$$\{x \neq \text{nil}\}\ \text{append}(x, y)\ \Leftarrow\ C(\text{Span}(x), y)$$
$$\text{Span}(x)\ \Leftarrow\ \langle x, B(x) \rangle$$
$$C(\langle x, w \rangle, y)\ \Leftarrow\ \textbf{begin}$$
$$w.\text{tl}\ \leftarrow\ y$$
$$\textbf{return } x$$
$$\textbf{end}$$
$$B(u)\ \Leftarrow\ \textbf{begin}$$
$$\textbf{while } \text{tl}(u) \neq \text{nil } \textbf{do } u\ \leftarrow\ \text{tl}(u)$$
$$\textbf{return } u$$
$$\textbf{end}$$

We note here that the new function Span has a trivial inverse, Unspan.

$$\text{Unspan}(\langle x, w \rangle)\ \Leftarrow\ x$$

Lisp programmers will notice that queue pairs are similar to tconc objects in InterLisp.

Towards a new representation. Our goal, now, is to carry out a shift of representations of $Qbuf$ objects such that they will all be of a form similar to the results of the Span function above—incorporating their own B values. A glance at the signature of the $Qbuf$ type reveals all such sites. They are (1) the first parameter to enq, (2) the result of enq, (3) the parameter to convQtoL, and (4) the result of enqe. Let us consider them in order. (We are carrying out preparatory steps for the *shift* transformation of [Scherlis85], but knowledge of that paper is not necessary to this exposition. For convenience, we omit calls to abs and rep for the time being.)

(1) The first parameter of enq. Let us suppose then that we are given a queue pair for the first argument to append. That is, suppose that we are given, along with x, the value of $\text{Span}(x)$. Obvious simplification yields:

$$\{x \neq \text{nil} \ \vee \ \langle x, w \rangle = \text{Span}(x)\} \ \text{append}(x, y) \ \Leftarrow \ C(\langle x, w \rangle, y)$$
$$C(\langle x, w \rangle, y) \ \Leftarrow \ \textbf{begin}$$
$$w.\text{tl} \leftarrow y$$
$$\textbf{return } x$$
$$\textbf{end}$$

Because of the assertion, we were able to eliminate the explicit calls to Span and hence B, and, as a consequence, our program now runs in constant time (assuming that $\text{Span}(x)$ is already computed). Note that, by unfolding append, we could write the definition of enq as:

$$\text{enq}(x, a) \ \Leftarrow \ C(\text{Span}(x), \text{cons}(a, \text{nil}))$$

(2) The result of enq. We must consider now how to transform enq so it can efficiently produce a queue object as output. The specialization problem we need to solve is the efficient computation of $\text{Span}(\text{enq}(x, a))$. Clearly, this derivation will interlock with the immediately proceeding one, since they will need to be consistent. But that does not keep us from retreating to an earlier (but equivalent) form of enq and append.

$$\text{Span}(\text{enq}(x, a)) \ \Leftarrow \ \textbf{let } s = \text{cons}(a, \text{nil}) \textbf{ in}$$
$$\langle \text{append}(x, s), B(\text{append}(x, s)) \rangle$$

We simplify the first component in the pair according to the immediately preceding derivation. The second component is simplified according to the "useful property" we obtained for B.

$$\text{Span}(\text{enq}(x, a)) \ \Leftarrow \ \textbf{let } s = \text{cons}(a, \text{nil}) \textbf{ in}$$
$$\langle C(\text{Span}(x), s), B(s) \rangle$$

In the case of singleton lists, B is the identity; we therefore unfold.

$$\text{Span}(\text{enq}(x, a)) \ \Leftarrow \ \textbf{let } s = \text{cons}(a, \text{nil}) \textbf{ in } \ \langle C(\text{Span}(x), s), s \rangle$$

(3) The parameter of convQtoL. The function convQtoL, recall, converts *Qbuf* objects into lists.

$$\text{convQtoL}(x) \ \Leftarrow \ x$$

If we are to change representation of *Qbuf* objects, then this function will have to do some work. In particular, we must consider the problem of supplying this function with the result of a call to Span. We make use of Unspan, derived earlier to accomplish the transformation. (More will be said to motivate this below.)

$$\text{convQtoL}(x) \ \Leftarrow \ \text{Unspan}(\text{Span}(x))$$

(4) The result of enqe. As in case (2) above, we seek to obtain an efficient way of computing Span(enqe(a)). Composing, we get the following program.

$$\text{Span(enqe}(a)) \;\Leftarrow\; \text{Span(cons}(a, \text{nil}))$$

Inserting a **let** abstraction as above and simplifying, we obtain a very concise program.

$$\text{Span(enqe}(a)) \;\Leftarrow\; \textbf{let } s = \text{cons}(a, \text{nil}) \textbf{ in } \langle s, s \rangle$$

Accomplishing the change. So far, all we have done is developed several specialized versions of the *Qbuf* functions. In order to accomplish the representation change safely, we make use of the *shift* transformation rule [Scherlis85].

For our purposes, this rule states that if *all* calls to rep in a given type are of the form Span ○ rep (where '○' is function composition), then a new type implementation can be obtained by *both* replacing all these calls by simply rep *and* replacing all abs calls by abs ○ Span.

This has the effect of shifting whatever work is represented by Span from object *access* time to object *creation* time. In our case, we will shift the work of finding the last cell in a list to a time where it is much more convenient to do so—the time when the list is created!

The preparations we made in the four steps above make this transformation easy to carry out. We start with the following type implementation (omitting the exclusive-use assertions):

> **repn** *Qbuf*
> **with**
>> $\text{enqe}(a) \;\Leftarrow\; \text{abs(cons}(a, \text{nil}))$
>> $\text{enq}(x, a) \;\Leftarrow\; \text{abs(append(rep}(x), \text{cons}(a, \text{nil})))$
>> $\text{convQtoL}(x) \;\Leftarrow\; \text{rep}(x)$

The simplifications we made in steps (1) and (3) above yield the following form:

> **repn** *Qbuf*
> **with**
>> $\text{enqe}(a) \;\Leftarrow\; \text{abs(cons}(a, \text{nil}))$
>> $\text{enq}(x, a) \;\Leftarrow\; \text{abs}(C(\text{Span(rep}(x)), \text{cons}(a, \text{nil})))$
>> $\text{convQtoL}(x) \;\Leftarrow\; \text{Unspan(Span(rep}(x)))$

Observe that all calls to rep are in the correct form.

We now make the *shift* transformation. The result is the following implementation of *Qbuf*:

> **repn** *Qbuf*
> **with**
>> $\text{enqe}(a) \;\Leftarrow\; \text{abs(Span(cons}(a, \text{nil})))$
>> $\text{enq}(x, a) \;\Leftarrow\; \text{abs(Span}(C(\text{rep}(x), \text{cons}(a, \text{nil}))))$
>> $\text{convQtoL}(x) \;\Leftarrow\; \text{Unspan(rep}(x))$

We are now ready to use the results of steps (2) and (4) to simplify.

> **repn** *Qbuf*
> **with**
>> $\text{enqe}(a) \;\Leftarrow\; \textbf{let } s = \text{cons}(a, \text{nil}) \textbf{ in abs}(\langle s, s \rangle)$
>> $\text{enq}(x, a) \;\Leftarrow\; \textbf{let } s = \text{cons}(a, \text{nil}) \textbf{ in abs}(\langle C(\text{rep}(x), s), s \rangle)$
>> $\text{convQtoL}(x) \;\Leftarrow\; \text{Unspan(rep}(x))$

Observe that there are no calls in the program to B! All the functions operate in constant time. As a final step, we unfold calls to Unspan and C. This unfolding is tricky, but completely mechanical.

> **repn** $Qbuf$
> **with**
> $\qquad$ enqe(a) $\Leftarrow$ **let** $s = \mathrm{cons}(a, \mathrm{nil})$ **in** $\mathrm{abs}(\langle s, s \rangle)$
> $\qquad$ enq(x, a) $\Leftarrow$ **let** $\langle x, w \rangle = \mathrm{rep}(x)$ **in**
> $\qquad\qquad\qquad$ **let** $s = \mathrm{cons}(a, \mathrm{nil})$ **in**
> $\qquad\qquad\qquad\qquad$ **begin**
> $\qquad\qquad\qquad\qquad\quad$ $w.\mathrm{tl} \leftarrow s$
> $\qquad\qquad\qquad\qquad\quad$ **return** $\mathrm{abs}(\langle x, s \rangle)$
> $\qquad\qquad\qquad\qquad$ **end**
> $\qquad$ convQtoL(x) $\Leftarrow$ **let** $\langle u, w \rangle = \mathrm{rep}(x)$ **in** u

7. Abstract Types and Implementations.

In the last several sections, we gave a number of illustrations relating to reuse, program derivations, and abstract types. We summarize the basic ideas here, and make several observations concerning process issues.

Types, derivations, and reuse. The basic problem we are addressing is this: How do we realize the benefits of reuse while obtaining acceptable performance? With respect to abstract types, the key to our approach is to separate the formulation of type signatures and abstract specifications from the derivation of implementations and the integration of the types into their contexts of use.

Consider: In Lisp, ML, and other languages, the type of lists is frequently used. From the point of view of reuse, it makes obvious sense to develop a rich library of list manipulating programs that can be applied in many contexts. In the case of Lisp, a typical implementation offers a large selection of such routines.

The problem is that, in many contexts of use, more specialized types would yield improved performance. In the usual paradigm, a programmer would be faced with a decision either (1) to carry on with lists, sacrificing performance for ease of development (and ability to take advantage of the heavy investment in supporting routines for lists), or (2) to develop a new specialized type, sacrificing access to the library of list routines for performance.

Our approach is a hybrid one, in which we start with the type of lists, with access to all the useful supporting routines, and then we specialize it to the context at hand, specializing, in addition, any of the auxiliary list routines that would be useful.

How, then, are we able to reuse this derived material? We do this by recording the *derivation*, along with others like it. We thus have a well understood starting point together with a set of specialized implementations derived from it. If we carry on with this kind of activity, specializing as new applications arise, we end up with a network of derived representations, linked by degree and kind of specialization. By keeping the derivation records, we can use previous derivations to obtain new ones that are either more or less specialized. And, further, any new routines from the starting type of lists can be propagated into the new representations simply by following the existing derivation steps.

Specifications and reuse. Suppose we encounter a new application, requiring, for example, an implementation of an editor buffer as a sequence of lines. At the specification level, we develop a Larch-like organization of data types, which could then can be used directly to direct the development of a suitable network of specialized implementations. We can therefore have the reuse advantages of specifications, together with the ability to carry over to implementations. Rather than keeping a large collection of unrelated data types and implementations, we have, instead, methods that take new data type specifications, expressed naturally in terms of other types, and derive from them efficient implementations, which we save in a (large) structured collection of derivations.

To summarize: There are two aspects to the method. First, we maintain a network of general and special purpose types and derivations of implementations linking them together. Second, we start by working at the specification level to establish that the types used correctly reflect the conceptualization of the problem—type structure and interdependency are chosen to be most natural for the problem. We *then* use derivation techniques to obtain the most efficient implementations. By working in this fashion, we realize the advantages that (1) modifications of a parent type can be propagated into specialized derivatives, (2) correctness is a consequence of technique, and (3) intermediate derivation steps can be used to guide intermediate specializations.

8. Conclusions.

We consider the problem of program reuse to extend beyond the level of simple reuse of code. We have demonstrated an approach to reuse based on the use of program derivations to separate and link specifications and implementations of programs. The examples indicate the value of abstract data type organization in providing a framework for representing reusable parts of programs and for organizing program derivations. Transformations that link program derivation steps can specialize types to context of use by explicitly shifting type boundaries, as illustrated in the stack and queue examples, and by specializing type implementations to improve performance, as illustrated in the queue example. By building a network of types and specializations of them, we can create a base of reusable material that does not demand *a priori* conventionalization of domains in order for reuse to be a real possibility. By weakening the need for conventionalization, we have a greater chance of obtaining a workable strategy for reuse and, hence, a more capital-intensive approach to software development.

9. Acknowledgement.

I thank Rod Nord for his comments on the paper.

Bibliography

[Balzer83]   Balzer, R., T.E. Cheatham, Jr., and C.C. Green, *Software Technology in the 1990's: Using a New Paradigm.* IEEE Computer, vol. 16, no. 11, pp. 39–45, November 1983.

[Bauer85]   Bauer, et al., **The Munich Project CIP**, Volume 1. Springer-Verlag, 1985.

[Boyle84]   Boyle, J.M. and M.N. Muralidharan, *Program Reusability through Program Transformation.* IEEE Transactions on Software Engineering SE-10, No. 5, September, 1984.

[Cheatham84]   Cheatham, T.E., *Reusability Through Program Transformations.* IEEE Transactions on Software Engineering SE-10, No. 5, September, 1984.

[Dietzen86]   Dietzen, S.R. and W.L. Scherlis, *Analogy in Program Development.* Second Conference on the Role of Language in Problem Solving. North-Holland, 1986. To appear.

[Green83]   Green, C.C. et al, *Report on a Knowledge Based Software Assistant.* Kestrel Institute Report, 1983.

[Guttag85]   Guttag, J.V., J.J. Horning, and J.M. Wing, *Larch in Five Easy Pieces.* DEC SRC Technical Report, 1985.

[Kernighan84]   Kernighan, B.W., *The Unix System and Software Reusability.* IEEE Transactions on Software Engineering SE-10, No. 5, September, 1984.

[Jorring86a]   Jorring, U. and W.L. Scherlis, *Compilers and Staging Transformations*. Thirteenth POPL Conference, 1986.

[Jorring86b]   Jorring, U. and W.L. Scherlis, *Deriving and Using Destructive Data Types*. IFIP TC2 Working Conference on Program Specification and Transformation, North-Holland, 1986.

[Neighbors84]   Neighbors, J.M., *The Draco Approach to Constructing Software from Reusable Components*. IEEE Transactions on Software Engineering SE-10, No. 5, September, 1984.

[Rich81]   Rich, C., *A Formal Representation for Plans in the Programmer's Apprentice*. Seventh IJCAI Proceedings, pp. 1044–1052, 1981.

[Scherlis81]   Scherlis, W.L., *Program Improvement by Internal Specialization*. Eighth POPL, pp. 41–49, 1981.

[Scherlis83a]   Scherlis, W.L. and D.S. Scott, *First Steps Towards Inferential Programming*. IFIP Congress 83, pp. 199-212, North-Holland, 1983.

[Scherlis83b]   Scherlis, W.L., *Software Development and Inferential Programming*. In **Program Transformation and Programming Environments**, edited by P. Pepper, Springer-Verlag, pp. 341-346, 1983.

[Scherlis85]   Scherlis, W.L., *Adapting Abstract Data Types*. Carnegie Mellon Technical Report, 1985.

[Wile81]   Wile, D.S., *Type Transformations*. IEEE Transactions on Software Engineering SE-7, pp. 32-39, January 1981.

Towards
Advanced Programming Environments
Based on Algebraic Concepts

Manfred Broy
Alfons Geser
Heinrich Hussmann

Universität Passau
Fakultät für Informatik
Postfach 2540
D-8390 Passau
F. R. of Germany

Abstract

As the formal basis for a methodology of software development an algebraic approach is proposed that can be supported by powerful programming environments. Algebraic specifications are formulated with equations, based on first order partial logic. The paper contains a short description of the Passau RAP system for prototyping algebraically specified abstract data types. It outlines the position of the RAP system within a future software environment and explains the environment concept that is currently studied within the ESPRIT project 432 METEOR at the University of Passau.

Introduction

Well-designed programming support environments can help to solve the difficult qualitative and quantitative problems of software design. However, the big advantage of such systems will be not so much the powerful hardware and a nice user interface. It will be their foundation within a tractable methodology that guides and supports the programmer and finally improves his confidence in the reliability of the produced piece of software.

Therefore research in programming environments always means research in programming methods, their formal foundation and, of course, the possibilities of their mechanical support, too.

The algebraic specification method has obtained broad interest during the last 10 years, since it closes a theoretical and methodological gap concerning questions of the design, specification and verification of data structures. By now well-developed theoretical foundations for algebraic specifications are available. First experimental support tools have been designed and some experience has already been gained.

It turned out that techniques of algebraic specifications can cover the whole process of software development. They may in particular serve as a formal support for the early phase of a software project, i.e. between requirements engineering and the definition of a proper formal specification. The algebraic framework provides formal criteria for the verification of development steps. Additionally, equational logic supplies powerful tools for machine-supported deduction "proofs". This has to a large extent been enabled by functional and logic programming techniques which allow to use algebraic specifications as prototypes.

At the University of Passau the experimental system RAP for the prototyping of algebraic specifications has been developed. For two years the system is in use and a number of examples have been carried out. Based on this experience the system is currently revised and will be integrated into a tool set prototype for the support of all phases of program development.

In this paper we describe the use of RAP and discuss how such a system can be extended to a programming support system based on algebraic concepts.

The RAP system

The RAP system is an experimental tool that supports the development of algebraic specifications. It is in use since the end of 1984 and has been installed at 10 external sites so far. More detailed information about the system and its use is given in [Geser, Hussmann 86].

The main components of the system in its present form are:

  - a syntax checker for hierarchical algebraic specifications

and, given a syntactically correct specification,

  - a symbolic term evaluator (by conditional term rewriting)

  - a theorem prover for solving systems of equations (by conditional narrowing).

In its most simple use the RAP system performs a syntax analysis for algebraically specified types. A syntax and (rigorous) context check is urgently needed for complex specifications even if these are written by very skilled people. In addition, RAP gives the specifications an operational semantics based on a deductive theory. This theory has been proven sound and complete w.r.t. the mathematical semantics associated with abstract types. RAP differs from other well-known support systems (such as e.g. OBJ2 [Futatsugi et al. 85]) mainly in its conditional narrowing feature. A theoretical treatment of the conditional narrowing algorithm including the proofs for soundness and completeness is given in [Hussmann 85].

Solving equations over a specification covers a lot of interesting questions, a specification designer may be interested in:

- "inverse" evaluation of specified functions: Given a function value, what are appropriate argument values to reach it?

- generation of fair sets of test data (cf. [Bouge et al. 85]),

- systematic test of specified functions for equality,

- proof or test of simple algebraic properties of the specified functions,

and so on.

As an example, consider the (toy) problem whether a sequence of natural numbers is sorted. The types NAT, BOOL are the built-in types of natural numbers, and truth values resp. We assume also a type ITEM to be given. The type SEQ of item sequences is then defined as usual:

type SEQ

    basedon NAT, BOOL, ITEM
    sort Seq
    cons empty : Seq,
           append : (Item, Seq) Seq
    func length : (Seq) Nat,
          isempty : (Seq) Bool

axioms all (s : Seq, x : Item)

    isempty(empty) -> true,
    isempty(append(x,s)) -> false,
    length(empty) -> 0,
    length(append(x,s)) -> succ(length(s))

endoftype

Legend: The basic specification unit is a hierarchical algebraic type enclosed in the keywords **type** and **endoftype**. SEQ is a type identifier. The keyword **basedon** is followed by a list of type names which are considered as primitive. With this clause, all objects defined in the primitive types are made available in SEQ. By the keyword **sort** a number of identifiers for data domains is introduced. **cons** and **func** announce a list of function names together with their functionalities ("arities"). The symbols in the **cons**-list are also called constructors. Sorts and function names together form a signature. The signature is followed by a list of **axioms**, i.e. logical formulae which describe the behaviour of the specified functions. In the framework of RAP, we restrict the axioms to equational Horn clauses. A Horn clause

$$p_1 = q_1 \& \ldots \& p_n = q_n \Rightarrow l \rightarrow r$$

is a formula of equational logic the meaning of which is that l may be replaced by r if the conditions $p_1 = q_1 \& \ldots \& p_n = q_n$ are fulfilled.

In the same way, the type of sequences can be enriched by the predicate issorted:

type ISSORTED

    basedon SEQ, ITEM, BOOL
    func issorted : (Seq) Bool

axioms all (x, y : Item, s : Seq)

    issorted(empty) -> true,
    issorted(append(x,empty)) -> true,
    $le_{Item}(x,y)$ = true =>
        issorted(append(x,append(y,s))) -> issorted(append(y,s)),
    $le_{Item}(x,y)$ = false =>
        issorted(append(x,append(y,s))) -> false

endoftype

A system of equations to be solved w.r.t. a given specification can be supplied via a task declaration. To speak in terms of data base systems, a type corresponds to a data base view, and a task is a query to the data base. The interpreter finally plays the role of the data base manager. For instance, a query asking for the evaluation of a term is given by the following denotation:

task ISS1

    basedon SEQ, ITEM, ISSORTED, BOOL
    unknown x : Bool

goals

    x = issorted(append(a,append(b,append(c,append(d,empty)))))

endoftask

The answer computed by RAP is [x = true].

The next example is typical for test data generation:

task GENSORT

   basedon SEQ, ITEM, BOOL, ISSORTED
   unknown s: Seq

goals

   issorted(s) = true

endoftask

Running this task, the RAP system starts to enumerate all ordered sequences:

```
[s = empty]
[s = append(*1,empty)]
[s = append(*1,append(*1,empty))]
[s = append(a,append(b,empty))]
[s = append(a,append(c,empty))]
[s = append(a,append(d,empty))]
[s = append(b,append(c,empty))]
[s = append(b,append(d,empty))]
[s = append(c,append(d,empty))]
[s = append(*1,append(*1,append(*1,empty)))]
...
```

Note that the solutions are most general, therefore some of them contain free variables (indicated by *<number>) for which any well-sorted term may be substituted to obtain a valid solution.

RAP is primarily intended to support the initial phase of program development, viz. the requirements engineering phase. But we regard RAP also as an important crystallization point of a development tool kit, still to be constructed. Currently at the University of Passau (and in collaboration with partners in the ESPRIT project METEOR), requirements for an extendible specification environment are investigated. Parts of such an environment will be realized extending RAP.

This prototype of a programming environment is a first step of a basic investigation for a software development method. The method will include requirements engineering, specification engineering, rapid prototyping, construction of design specifications, and the deduction and verification, resp. of each design step. The aim is to enable the user to treat and understand the whole program development process in a homogeneous framework.

An Algebraic View of Program Development

Algebraic techniques are based on the concept of equations. Equations are useful and important in many aspects of computer science and program development. Equational specifications turn out to be both expressive and easy to use. Therefore it may be interesting to analyse the program development task from an algebraic, i.e. equation-oriented viewpoint.

The algebraic viewpoint has a proper formal foundation (by a simple mathematical semantics) and therefore provides a rigorous approach to program development. However, rigor and formality are not the only objectives for software design methods; adequacy and tractability are at least as important. And the question how a method can be supported by interactive tools becomes more and more decisive. Here algebraic techniques clearly show a number of important advantages. The calculus of equational logic is the key to an operational semantics, for which machine support is offered by the techniques of term rewriting and logic programming.

The algebraic approach to software development we describe here is a continuation of the one developed in the Munich project CIP ([CIP 85]). CIP is a project in the field of programming methodology based on the idea of formal program specification and transformation. The algebraic approach followed with CIP is tuned especially towards the needs of software design. With respect to this, its particular characteristics are

- <u>hierarchical algebraic specifications</u>: Algebraic specifications are structured in hierarchies which allow a proper separation of concerns. Thus they introduce modularity in design and verification. In particular, the design of specifications is done along such hierarchies. In a hierarchical understanding of software systems we assume that we have a concrete understanding of certain "primitive" objects and functions. The interpretation of nonprimitive terms is generally understood in terms of the resp. primitive entities. The structure of algebraic specifications follows this view.

- <u>partial functions</u>: With computation the phenomena of divergence and undefinedness arise. For a design methodology it is vital that the programmer can concentrate during the initial design phase on the defined cases and does not have to care about undefinedness. Later, he may specify definedness separately. Currently, RAP uses total functions, but an extension to partial function semantics is in preparation.

- <u>loose semantics</u>: For an algebraic specification all term-generated models that fulfil the axioms are taken as the meaning (in RAP, even nonstandard models are included due to the absence of induction). No restrictions to initial or terminal (final) algebras are assumed. Not even the existence of such models is required. This increases the descriptive power of specifications and allows for instance that a development may procede by adding more and more specific axioms ("design decisions") to an algebraic specification and thus restricting the class of models step by step.

- <u>algebraic implementation:</u> Implementation is not done in one single step, but in several, possibly many, small steps. With each such step, a design decision takes place. As the correctness of the whole software product relies on each single step, the notion of implementation needs to be formalized. For abstract types, the algebraic implementation relation has been established that covers all relevant implementation aspects ([Broy et al. 86], see also [Ehrig et al. 82]).

Within the Munich project CIP algebraic specifications were restricted to systems of carrier sets and first-order partial functions on them. More elaborate concepts were included in a "nonalgebraic" way via the language constructs of a wide spectrum language. Currently the theory of algebraic specifications is further extended trying to include nonstrict and higher-order functions, infinite objects and nondeterminism. Then, system-specific programming styles such as communicating distributed systems can also be treated fully in an algebraic way; non-algebraic means can be left out.

We emphasize that also the production of a requirement specification must be understood as a dynamic design process which must be methodologically supported. It incorporates important design decisions which crucially influence all the further development. Therefore we speak about specification engineering.

In the following, we talk about the algebraic approach to programming on three levels: On the methodological level ("how to procede in a systematic way in program design"), on a conceptual level ("which steps and properties are relevant"), and on a technical level ("how to perform the steps, which logical and algebraic techniques can be offered").

An Algebraic Software Development Model (Methodological Level)

In software design after a requirement analysis the software construction process evolves through a number of levels of abstraction and detailization. According to an "algebraic" understanding the program construction procedes as follows:

(1) Reference to the Primitive Structures
The primitive algebraic structures are identified. This may just mean that a couple of built-in structures (such as booleans or the natural numbers) are taken. It can also mean the inclusion of structures that have already been designed in an earlier phase. This way an observability scenario is fixed.

(2) Introduction of the Nonprimitive Elements into the Signature
New (nonprimitive) sorts and function symbols (together with their functionalities) are introduced. Now the observability is syntactically fixed by the functions with nonprimitive sorts as domains and a primitive sort as their range.

(3) Specification by Introduction of Axioms
The semantics of the functions is specified by axioms in equation-based predicate logic (including, e.g., the special style of conditional equations).

(4) Analysis of the (Hierarchical) Types
The obtained (hierarchical) abstract type is analyzed. This comprises questions whether

e.g. the hierarchical type fulfils certain "hierarchy constraints" ([Wirsing et al. 83]).

(5) Validation of Types
During the requirements engineering phase, sessions take place to formulate requirements the final product shall meet. These requirements must now be satisfied by the specification. The sooner this can be checked, the sooner a possibly needed restart of the requirements engineering can take place. So the user is interested in the behaviour of the specification. For that, he may formulate queries, to be answered by rapid prototyping tools which provide him with certain insights on the proper modelling of the problem domain. This may also include proofs of further algebraic properties.

(6) Operational Enrichment
Additional function symbols are introduced. The meaning of the function symbols is given by defining equations. It has to be shown that the functions do not give rise to new elements ("junk", nonstandard elements).

(7) Change of the Axiomatization
The replacement of axioms by equivalent ones may lead to versions which are much more "efficient". Efficiency is always connected with certain restrictions. For instance, if the considered equations form a confluent term rewrite system, term rewriting can be used without loosing completeness.

(8) Implementation of Abstract Types by other Abstract Types
Important development steps are those that replace ("implement") a type hierarchy by another one. If certain implementation conditions hold, then such replacements can be done while maintaining the correctness of the program. Both the specification transformation and verification are valuable techniques for this, above all, when available within a support system. Today, the verification of programs over a fixed computation structure is rather well-understood. One of the key questions remains, however, how the design and the proof methodology can cope with changes of the computation structure.

(9) Transition to Classical Efficiency-Oriented Programs
A particular implementation step is to compile a specification of a certain form directly into efficient code. This point is discussed in more detail below.

To summarize, all the classical steps in software development can be modelled in the algebraic view. Thus the algebraic approach to software construction provides a comprehensive formal framework.

Design-relevant Structural Properties of Algebraic Specifications (Conceptual Level)

The development steps modelled in an algebraic approach are all of a rather similar nature. They consist of operational and axiomatic enrichments and hierarchical extensions as well as of the application of certain theorems and laws for the

462

transformation of algebraic specifications.

There are a number of significant properties of algebraic specifications involved in such steps, the knowledge of which allows to structure and to simplify the reasoning about algebraic specifications. Examples are

(1) Validity of additional algebraic theorems, e.g. commutativity for sets.

(2) The validity of hierarchy constraints (e.g. sufficient completeness and hierarchy consistency).

(3) Term rewriting properties (e.g. confluence, termination, and existence of normal forms).

(4) Existence of solutions to certain queries (rapid prototyping).

(5) The implementation relation between two types.

(6) Syntactic properties which are required to hold when the product shall be run at the target machine (e.g. integers may not overflow).

Note that many of these properties require for expressive means beyond the scope of algebra and first-order logic. They can, however, often be replaced by sufficient criteria.

The following diagram gives an impression how an analysis of an algebraic specification might work in the case of the type ISSORTED. Forked arrows denote the way of deduction:

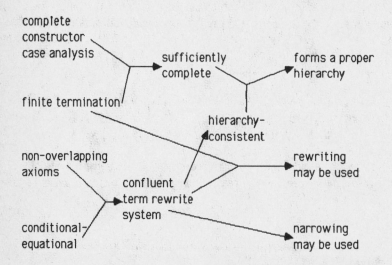

At the left hand side, we have purely syntactical properties which can easily be checked by automatic tools. Going to the right, propositions become more and more specific. Finally, we arrive at the genuine issues of interest, those issues which will be reported to the user. To get such a "criteria-driven" system work, a kind of "inference rule base on the meta level" must be established.

Verification Techniques on Algebraic Specifications
(Technical Level)

For proving properties of algebraic specifications we have basically two available techniques:

(1) Proofs in the deductive theory
Algebraic specifications lead to equational deductive theories which have well-known and easy-to-understand rules of inference.

(2) Induction Proofs
Based on the term generation principle, proofs by structural induction may be performed. Such proofs can become rather complicated such that system support is most important.

A very specific proof technique that may especially be relevant for consistency proofs is based on the existence of normal forms.

(3) Normal Form Proofs
If certain normal forms or even unique normal forms can be defined for the terms of algebraic specifications then usually other proofs can be simplified.

Term rewriting techniques can lead to powerful tools for supporting proofs such as

(4) Knuth-Bendix Completion
Some algebraic specifications can be (semi-)automatically transformed into a noetherian ("finitely terminating") confluent term rewrite system by the Knuth-Bendix completion algorithm. As term rewrite systems admit easy evaluation and proofs, such algorithms are of special interest. Furthermore, applications of the completion procedure include consistency checks and proofs by inductions (used e.g. in the system REVE, cf. [Kirchner 84]).

(5) Conditional Narrowing and Rewriting
Conditional rewriting is the important basis for the evaluation of terms. The conditional narrowing algorithm combines this functional evaluation with a resolution method in the spirit of logic programming. The resulting "equational logic programming" allows a flexible way of rapid prototyping, testing and test data generation on top of a specification.

(6) Further Tools
There is a large offer of automatic and user-guided tools, among others (syntax directed) editors, transformation systems, compilers, etc., which are tuned to service special areas of application. Provided with a carefully chosen set of such tools, a programming environment profits from the tool efficiency and the experience already gained in its application area.

The listed techniques will develop their full power in combination. Research in this area has to cover the power of the various techniques and combinations that can be formed.

Incorporation of Classical Efficiency-Oriented Programming Styles

Algebraic techniques are rather abstract and not primarily efficiency-oriented, a fact which we consider rather as an advantage at early stages of program development. Finally, of course, an efficient version for the designed system has to be established.

The algebraic approach to programming seems rather distinct to conventional programming languages and programming styles. So the question has to be faced whether (and if, how well) algebraic techniques can actually support conventional programming techniques such as program variables with selective updating and pointer structures with structure sharing. Other examples are concurrent programs communicating by message-passing via some shared memory.

Here the following remarks have to be made:

(1) The mentioned conventional techniques are very complicated such that none of the known design methods can deal with them in a satisfactory way. Therefore most of the design of such systems nowadays is done without effective formal support.

(2) In principle all the efficiency-oriented and control-flow oriented concepts can be modelled in an algebraic framework and therefore supported by algebraic techniques. In a recent case study, this has been investigated by means of a microprocessor specification ([Geser 86]). In a typical program notation, certain entities are referred just implicitly, such as local states, heaps where the references of pointers are stored, etc. With algebraic means, the user is forced to make those features explicit. This can, to our experience, always be done in a straightforward way, may however look rather technical and therefore desires support by better suited notational variants.

(3) Many of the classical efficiency-oriented implementation techniques are rather schematic and therefore may be mechanically supported, for instance within a direct compilation into code.

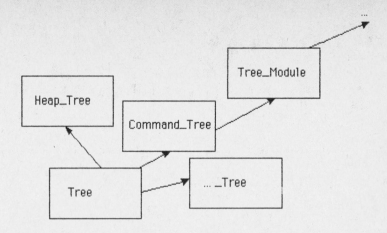

Certain steps in program design can be seen as very schematic, such as the transition from a tree to a pointer representation for trees or the transition from a tree to a module ("monitor") implementing a tree that can be used by several concurrent programs. Their application can be supported by rather mechanical rules. So the algebraic properties of such modules can be treated on a purely algebraic level, while the synchronisation properties are handled in a schematic way.

So far, the suitability of algebraic specifications for distributed programs has not yet been investigated in detail. The concept of tasks could be extended towards a concept of communicating agents. Notions such as nondeterminism and infinite objects will be needed. Here a lot of open questions remain as an area for future research.

Structure of the Support System

When the design process procedes, specifications are incorporated into the system and existing specifications are changed and/or completed and additional properties are derived.

Each of these properties is of significance in program development, since a verified property gives hints on design options, enables tools and allows to simplify the design or verification of programs. The power of verified properties becomes apparent when properties are reused. For this purpose, it must be possible to store verified properties in a design data base, such that they can be retrieved and combined with other information in the system and reused in later stages of the development. The system should take use of properties to guide and support the programmer in designing algebraic specifications and offer special procedures that rely upon those properties.

Here, for the sake of flexibility, it seems wise not to force the programmer to verify all his/her steps in detail from the very beginning. Often it might be more appropriate to support an experimental design where certain steps are performed unverified in order to do the verification later on. Such options need a very careful, sophisticated version control in the data base.

So, in a support system for program design based on algebraic concepts, we distinguish three classes of information:

Representations of
- objects: This includes specifications of data types and communicating agents.
- properties of objects
- design steps and proof steps.

This rather sophisticated kind of data base is used and updated by a number of interactive tools.

The system

- supplies information about its state

and offers tools for

- the constructive part: editing, transformation, refinement,etc. of specifications
- the analytic part: (semi-automatic) proofs of properties, condition generation, etc.

and compositions of these two. The system architecture might so roughly look as follows:

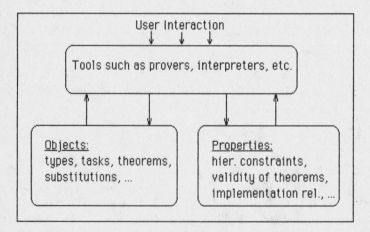

To represent the dynamic aspects of the design process, classical version-control and user-guiding facilities are needed.

An Example for Different Levels of Algebraic Specification

This section contains three different specifications of a sorting algorithm for sequences, proceeding from more abstract to more concrete formulations. The RAP system allows to perform experiments for prototyping of the specification.

We introduce a sort function on top of the types defined in the first chapter in the following style:

type SORT

    basedon ITEM, SEQ, ...
    func sort : (Seq) Seq

<< sort-axioms >>

endoftype

Now we give versions for the << sort-axioms >> on three levels. The three levels differ in their use of auxiliary functions and the form of the axioms.

Level 1: Full first order predicate logic

This is the most abstract level, describing a formal translation of the informal requirement associated with a "sorting algorithm". There is only one axiom for sort:

    sort(s) = r <=> issorted(r) = true & ispermut(s, r) = true.

Elsewhere we have to provide the auxiliary functions:

    issorted : (Seq) Bool,
    ispermut : (Seq , Seq) Bool

with the (non-algebraically represented) axioms:

    issorted(s) <=> [**all** (i, j : Nat) : i < j => le$_{\text{Item}}$(select(s,i), select(s,j))]
    ispermut(r,s) <=> [**all** (x : Item) : number(x, r) = number(x, s)].

We may assume that the functions select and number are predefined and made available within the resp. types. They are assumed to select an indexed element out of a sequence and the number of occurrences of an item in a sequence, respectively. Here we see that the specification of even a simple function can involve a lot of auxiliary functions. This does not mean a disadvantage at all as the auxiliary functions may be reused for the definition of other functions, and it makes the specification more transparent than a large, single definition.

Since specification interpreters like RAP cannot deal with quantified expressions in general, prototyping by RAP is impossible at this language level. To do prototyping, we must restrict the axioms to Horn clause specifications.

Level 2: Conditional Rewrite Rules

The type ISSORTED above provided us already with a specification of issorted using conditional equations. Similarly, we can specify ispermut:

    ispermut(empty, r) -> isempty(r),
    occurs(x,r) = true => ispermut(append(x,s),r) -> ispermut(s,remove(x,r)),
    occurs(x,r) = false => ispermut(append(x,s),r) -> false.

The auxiliary functions occurs (tests whether an item occurs in a sequence) and remove (removes exactly one occurrence of an item from a sequence) can be specified in the same style.

The axiom for sort has just to be slightly changed:

    issorted(r) = true & ispermut(r, s) = true => sort(s) -> r

Now we can use the RAP system to evaluate the sort function, e.g. for the sequence <c, b, c, a>. But this evaluation is extremely inefficient: The RAP system takes 600 CPU seconds (of a VAX 11/750) for this task.

Level 3 : "Fair" Conditional Rewrite Rules

The reason for the inefficiency above was the descriptive way of specifying sort: The evaluation has to search systematically for sequences which fulfil the precondition of the sort law. In order to reach a more concrete formulation we have to express the behaviour of sort by rewrite rules which can be applied in a depth first way and so do not give rise to a search. To do so, we have to specify some algorithm, e.g. sorting by insertion:

    sort(empty) -> empty,
    sort(append(x,s)) -> insert(x,sort(s)),

    insert(x,empty) -> append(x,empty),
    $le_{Item}(x,y)$ = true => insert(x,append(y,s)) -> append(x,append(y,s)),
    $le_{Item}(x,y)$ = false => insert(x,append(y,s)) -> append(y,insert(x,s)).

This formulation leads to a more efficient computation of the prototyping system: Sorting the previous sequence takes 2 seconds. Full efficiency can finally be achieved when the specification is compiled into machine code. This is possible since we have arrived at the level of functional programming.

Concluding Remarks

Algebraic specifications appear both easy and powerful to use. With algebraic specifications, the full range of programming styles beginning with abstract first order logic specifications and ending with hardware descriptions can be supported using a uniform notation and a homogeneous semantic framework.

As long as we stay within the framework of conditional equations, we are on proper theoretic grounds with a powerful deductive support. However, the use of general first order formulae for specifications is highly desirable, too. Here we might wish to prove the equivalence of a first order specification with a Horn clause specification.

In spite of many of the promising aspects of algebraic techniques, still a long way is to go until enough techniques, methods, and tools are available to make the algebraic approach to programming attractive also for industrial practice. It is not clear so far, how appropriate the derived framework finally will be. However, it is rather clear that the algebraic techniques have to be investigated in more detail and from a more application-oriented view to provide answers to those questions.

References

[Bouge et al. 85]
L. Bouge, N. Choquet, L. Fribourg, M. C. Gaudel: Test set generation from algebraic specifications using logic programming. Report No. 240, LRI, Orsay 1985. Preliminary version in: Proc. TAPSOFT 85 Conf., LNCS 186, pp. 262-265, 1985.

[Broy, Pepper 83]
M. Broy, P. Pepper: Program development as a formal activity. IEEE SE-7:1, 1981, pp. 14-22.

[Broy et al. 86]
M. Broy, B. Möller, P. Pepper, M. Wirsing: Algebraic implementation preserves program correctness. Science of Computer Programming 8, 1986.

[Futatsugi et al. 85]
K. Futatsugi, J. A. Goguen, J.-P. Jouannaud, J. Meseguer: Principles of OBJ2. Proc. 12th POPL Conf., 1985.

[Geser 86]
A. Geser: An algebraic specification of the intel 8085 microprocessor - A case study. Report MIP-8608, Universität Passau, May 1986.

[Geser, Hussmann 85]
A. Geser, H. Hussmann: Rapid prototyping for algebraic specifications - Examples for the use of the RAP system. Report MIP-8517, Universität Passau, Dec. 1985.

[Geser, Hussmann 86]
A. Geser, H. Hussmann: Experiences with the RAP system - a specification interpreter combining term rewriting and resolution techniques. Proc. ESOP 86 Conf., LNCS 213, pp.

339–350, 1986.

[CIP 85]
The CIP Language Group: The Munich project CIP, Vol. I: The wide spectrum language CIP-L. LNCS 183, 1985.

[Ehrig et al. 82]
H. Ehrig, H.-J. Kreowski, B. Mahr, P. Padawitz: Algebraic implementation of abstract data types. Theoretical Computer Science TCS 20, pp. 209-263, 1982.

[Hussmann 85]
H. Hussmann: Unification in conditional-equational theories. Proc. EUROCAL 85 Conf., LNCS 204, pp. 543-553, 1985.

[Kirchner 84]
H. Kirchner: A general inductive completion algorithm and application to abstract data types. Proc. 7th CADE, LNCS 170, pp. 282-302, 1984.

[Wirsing et al. 83]
M. Wirsing, P. Pepper, H. Partsch, W. Dosch, M. Broy: On hierarchies of abstract data types. Acta Informatica 20, pp. 1-33, 1983.

Program Development by Transformation and Refinement

Stefan Jähnichen
Fatima Ali Hussain
Matthias Weber

GMD Forschungsstelle an der Universität Karlsruhe
Haid-und-Neu-Str. 7
D-7500 Karlsruhe, West Germany

Abstract

The paper describes programming as a sequence of transitions. A specification is thus systematically transformed into an executable program. It is further argued that the transformational approach will only become widely accepted if the derivation process is formally described and can thus be partially automated. A calculus for the description is then introduced and demonstrated using the fold/unfold system as introduced by Darlington.

1 Introduction

The process of software construction can be viewed as consisting of a series of transformations starting from informal requirement documents and ending with an executable program which hopefully fulfills the initial requirement to the first. The validation or assertion of this equivalence condition as well as the problem to manage the process has lead to a separation of the construction process into steps of finer granularity. As these steps are defined by (more or less) precise input and output assertions, the management of the whole process is simpler and the proof of correctness of the separate parts is at least more reasonable than the proof of correctness for the whole process.

This aproach to software production became known as the software life cycle but it succeeded mainly to improve productivity and quality from management aspects. From a technical point of view only minor improvements were achieved because

- the proofs mentioned above and their constructive use are still not feasible,

- no specific support for technical activities is provided besides the definition of form and global contents of documents,

- the approach totally neglects the need for permanent maintenance of the product.

The latter is true even if maintenance is explicitly mentioned in the corresponding flow charts and diagrams, because any change of a program will never be approached on the specification level if the derivation of the program cannot be replayed (semi-automatically) and if the process of program derivation is not even recorded in a formal document.

The approach using wide spectrum languages improves the situation only locally. As the separation of the whole process is no longer visible at separate language levels, transformations can be applied in any order and only the input /output relation expressed in the same language is relevant. Thus the willingness of maintenance personal to start their work on the "specification" level may be higher, but still no support exists for the replay of the development. An internal recording may help, but fails in making the reasoning behind a development explicit and obvious.

Our [1] conclusion is that we need a means to describe software developments, a development language. The main requirement for such a language is the necessity to express all activities and objects relevant for software development in a uniform framework and to allow reasoning about them.

The ToolUse project aims at the development of such a language and an environment to support software designers in its use. The approach taken is rule based, activities are expressed as deduction rules, objects are methods, strategies, heuristics, programs, specifications etc. If we succeed in providing such a language, the main problem remains to build the corresponding knowledge base for software engineering. In [Sintzoff 86] this is called a handbook of mathematical algorithmics.

The following article is organized as follows. It starts with a discussion of transformational approach to software development and explains the meaning of transformations and refinements by some sketchy examples. It then briefly explains the ToolUse approach towards a development language and further uses this framework to describe in detail the well-known fold/unfold system of Burstall and Darlington and strategies for its use.

2   Transformations and Refinements

The transformational approach in programming can be interpreted in two ways:

- as a sequence of transitions which transform a program (or specification) into hopefully a better one. This approach presumes the existence of a well-defined goal which is precisely specified, and which is to be reached by the application of the transitions. This approach is called transformational. Its main characteristic is that a transformation does not add information to a program but merely transforms it into another, may be optimized, form.

- as a sequence of transitions replacing abstract parts of a program or specification by more detailed ones. An example is the efficient representation of data structures in the SETL language or the derivation of a loop from a postcondition expressed in predicate calculus by systematically constructing the invariant of the loop. Any such step is called a refinement.

Both approaches are often based on a uniform wide spectrum language (CIP, CHI, DRACO) being rich enough to express both specifications and programs, without precisely defining the borderline between the two of them.

Refinements are based on the creativity of the designer and his knowledge in the field of programming and in the application area. The full automation of such steps is thus unrealistic. Nevertheless is the formal description of such steps feasible and can definitely be used to stimulate the designers creativity and support him in the remaining clerical task.

Both, transformations and refinements, have to be supported by a development paradigm. The first because an understandable specification of a program has often to be transformed into a more efficient version. The second because they exhibit the main strategies and heuristics applied by experts which have to be caught for replay and partial automation.

---

[1]The participants of the ToolUse project [ESPRIT # 510]

2.1   Transformations

The application of transformations presume the existence of a program or a specification which is not suited for efficient execution but which is totally defined. The overall goal is to achieve a "better" version. The interpretation of better leads to the goal structure of the series of transformations. Key notions are heuristics and strategies which are well-defined in their effect and application conditions.

One example for the application of transformation rules is to improve the efficiency of logic programs. The goal of the transformations is e.g. to reduce the number of unification steps during the interpretation. Only by experience it is known that *unfolding* and *recursion elimination* are transformations which result in "better" code.

Another well-known example of a development system based on transformations is Darlington's HOPE language [Darlington 81]. It provides the user with a set of primitive transformations which are used to optimize a given program in the HOPE language.

In addition to these basic transformations, Darlington uses "second level tactics" to express the heuristics guiding the transformations. We will in the next chapter give a more precise definition of the system and its transformations.

The following examples from the area of imperative programming mainly serve to demonstrate the diverging aspects of transformations:

1. merging of loops

   multi pass algorithm → single pass algorithm

2. algorithmic improvement

   linear search → more efficient search

3. decomposition of structures

   large data structure → smaller units

4. recursion elimination

   recursive description → iterative description

5. "dumb" resolution (e.g. in backtracking)

   "dumb" backtracking → backtracking with strategy

2.2   Refinements

Refinement steps in program development serve to refine abstract entities by adding implementation details. The methodology of stepwise refinement is one example and demonstrates how algorithms can be derived in a nice top-down approach [Wirth 71]. The choice of adequate implementations for high-level data structures in SETL [Dewar 82] is another example and demonstrates limitations of automation in cases where complex considerations and creativity are needed.

The refinement paradigm is highly related to the problem of program decomposition and its formal derivation and descriptions. Strategies used depend on the context of a given problem as well as on the designers professional context and education. Previous experience and the availability of reusable components will influence the decomposition.

No formalised method is known to us how to derive a decomposition out of a formal specification, given e.g. in predicate calculus. Some heuristics are known as e.g.:

- to keep the decomposed parts on the same level of abstraction,

- to define the most general applicable function,

- to keep interfaces small.

Even the derivation of an algorithm out of its formal specification is hard to achieve if no additional information is supplied besides the pure functionality.

In contrast to the above mentioned transformations a refinement step adds, refines and even changes semantic properties. The intuition of this paradigm is to refine an abstract specification rather than to improve it. The paradigm can be extended and supported by the use of design schemata, deductive capabilities and the incorporation of constraints from the application area or target system. Interaction with the designers is a key issue if we want to achieve realistic results in an approach based on refinements.

3 The Design Calculus, an Informal Introduction

The Design Calculus (DC) as described in this chapter was introduced by M.Sintzoff in [Sintzoff 85]. As this paper is not intended to fully define or explain the calculus, we refer to [Sintzoff 86] and [Groote 86] for any further information. The rules given here are not at all intended to be complete but to give the reader an impression of its flavour and introduce the notation as it is used for the examples in the next chapter. Most of the illustrations are also taken from [Sintzoff 86].

A rule in the Design Calculus is written as:

$$P(x) \vdash Q(x,y) \quad \text{or} \quad \frac{P(x)}{Q(x,y)}$$

and can be interpreted as "if P is given then Q can be constructively produced". Examples for the interpretation of a rule may be

- program P is transformed into program Q

- program P can be verified against specification Q

x and y are the free variables of P and Q, x is universally and y is existentially quantified. The production symbol is purely syntactical, its interpretation depends on the level it is applied on (programs, specifications, or even developments). This freedom of interpretation gives us a means to reason about different objects in the software production process using a uniform calculus.

Rules can be nested and displayed in a two-dimensional style (they associate to the right).

$$\frac{a, \quad \dfrac{a}{b}}{b}$$

As an example we may describe that a development DEV guarantees that the resulting program P satisfies the specification S.

$$\frac{\text{DEV}}{P \vdash S}$$

Naming and binding of variables are further properties

$$\text{syllogism:}[a,b,c] \left|\frac{a \vdash b \,,\, b \vdash c}{a \vdash c}\right.$$

The example defines a context for the variables **a,b,c** in a rule identified as syllogism. An application of this rule can be interpreted as the predicate transformation for sequential composition of programs.

$$[a:=p,b:=q,c:=r] \text{ syllogism } <p \vdash q, q \vdash r> \Longrightarrow p \vdash r$$

This example implicitly demonstrates the instantiation of a rule by binding the free variables (e.g. **a:=p**) and the application to a specific term $(< .. >)$. The arrow $\Longrightarrow$ can be read as "evaluation".

Modus Ponens, which amounts to the application of a rule is written as:

$$\text{modus-ponens : } [a,b] \left|\frac{a \,, \quad \left|\frac{a}{b}\right.}{b}\right.$$

An interpretation of this rule reads: "Given **a** and a rule (**a** ⊢ **b**) we can construct **b**".

We may for the sake of clarity augment our variables with type informations. If e.g. **a** is a development and **b** the resulting program, we may describe this as:

$$[a:\text{development}; \atop b:\text{program}] \left|\frac{a \,, \quad \left|\frac{a}{b}\right.}{b}\right.$$

Another example for a rule is the 'divide and conquer strategy', described on a very high level of abstraction. It is divided into two cases: the elementary solution **'base'** and the solution **'induct'** by decomposing the problem into subproblems:

$$\text{base : } [P] \left|\frac{\text{is-elementary}(P)}{\text{direct-solve}(P)}\right.$$

$$\text{induct : } [P,P1,...,Pn] \left|\frac{\text{is-composed}(P,P1,..,Pn)}{\text{compose-sol}(\text{solve}(P1),..,\text{solve}(Pn))}\right.$$

This example makes explicit that the design calculus is not at all intended to mysteriously solve any kind of problem, but to provide a linguistic frame to describe methods and allows reasoning about them on a formal basis.

The next example will illustrate the interrelation between the application of development rules and additional user information. It demonstrates also the shortcomings of the approach. The example is to deduce a sorting algorithm by the 'divide and conquer' strategy. It is only a refinement of [Sintzoff 86].

The predicates occuring in 'divide and conquer' only suggest by their names that they really divide and conquer the given problem, any instantiation would need the proof that this is really fullfilled.

Applying divide and conquer to a sorting problem on sequences (s)

divide and conquer $[\mathbf{P} := \text{sort(s)}] <\text{sort(s)}>$

splits the problem into two parts:

$$\text{base}:[\mathbf{P}:=\text{sort(s)}]\ \left|\ \frac{\text{length-one(s)}}{s}\right.$$

$$\text{induct}:[\mathbf{P}:=\text{sort(s)}]\ \left|\ \frac{s=\text{ordcat(s1 , s2)}}{\text{cat(solve(sort(s1),solve(sort(s2))))}}\right.$$

The predicate "ordcat" is given as

$$\text{ordcat}:[\mathbf{s1,s2}]\ \left|\ \frac{\text{maxval(s1)}\leq\text{minval(s2)}}{\text{cat(s1,s2)}}\right.$$

quicksort is obtained by instantiation of the **divide and conquer** rules:

divide and conquer$[\mathbf{P} \rightarrow \text{sort(s)}$, is-elementary$(\mathbf{P}) \rightarrow$ length-one(s), direct-solve$(\mathbf{P}) \rightarrow \mathbf{s}$, $\mathbf{n} \rightarrow \mathbf{2}$, $\mathbf{P1} \rightarrow \text{sort(s1)}$, $\mathbf{P2} \rightarrow \text{sort(s2)}$, is-composed$(\mathbf{P,P1,P2})$ $\rightarrow \mathbf{s} = \text{ordcat(s1,s2)}$, compose-sol $\rightarrow$ cat$]$

Of course there is no relief from the correctness proof of the two rules for quicksort, nevertheless we were actually able to express the strategy for the development.

Obviously the selection of an appropriate algorithm for a given problem depends on 'non-functional' properties of the expected product. In our case these are constraints given as the number of elements and the complexity of the deduced algorithm. It is clear that these constraints have to be described, but their representation and relationship to the rules has not yet been tackled.

Current work on the definition of a Kernel Design Calculus (KDC) was started at UCL by P. de Groote [Groote 86]. This kernel will be the basis for the DC which, combined with Design Knowledge on particular methodologies, will lead to the language (called DEVA) to be used to express corresponding developments. A simple analogy by P. de Groote may make this process clearer:

KDC corresponds to propositional calculus

DC corresponds to predicate calculus (= propositional calculus + quantifiers)

DEVA corresponds to formal number theory (= predicate calculus + Peano-axioms)

4   An Example: the Fold/Unfold Method

Correct and efficient code is often hard to understand because the final program is the product of a long and complicated process in which the underlying algorithms are concealed. Starting from these well known problems of program development, J.Darlington has proposed a new approach of programming [Darlington 81], the transformation of a high level functional program into a more efficient one by a set of very simple transformation rules:

(a) definition

(b) instantiation

(c) unfolding

(d) folding

(e) abstraction

(f) application of rules

Darlington has used the transformational approach, such that the programmer first concentrates on producing a correct and understandable high-level version with no regard to efficiency. This version will than be transformed into a more efficient one. The fold/unfold-system is used to express these transformations and guarantees that partial correctness is maintained. Various clever strategies for automatic development have been proposed with this method [Burstall 77].

We understand the fold/unfold - method as a means for local-program improvement (programming in the small), and try to express it within the design calculus.

The presentation of the basics of the fold/unfold method is given in [Tooluse 86] . We focus our attention on the development strategies only.

4.1 Axioms of the Fold/Unfold - Methodology

The rules to be coded within DC which formalize the methodology are defined in [Darlington 81]. As they are the basis to describe development we will shortly characterize them in order to give the reader an intuitive understanding of the their nature and use. It should be remembered that we do not intend to reinvent the methodology but to express it in the design calculus.

The rules divide into three sets:

- rules for syntax-generation (how to write down functions, equations, ...)

- rules for transformation (the five basic rules of the method)

- rules about syntax-predicates and substitutions (various auxiliary syntactical checks and operations)

All these rules are defined in [ToolUse 86]. Because of the brevity needed for this paper we will not give them here, but use them for the following example.

4.2 Development - Strategies

We will now illustrate by an example how basic rules can be used to form developments. Consider a function g to sum up the squares of the elements of a list:

square(nil) = nil
square(cons(n,l)) = cons(n∗n,square(l))

sum(nil) = 0
sum(cons(n,l)) = n + sum(l)

g(l) = sum(square(l))

To execute g, we have to run over its argument-list 2-times, this is the price we have to pay for g's rather elegant formulation.

The definition of g can be improved by the following sequence of fold/ unfold-transformations:

$$
\begin{aligned}
g(\text{nil}) \quad &= \text{sum(square(nil))} &&\text{(Instantiation)}\\
&= \text{sum(nil)} &&\text{(Unfold)}\\
&= 0 &&\text{(Unfold)}\\
g(\text{cons(n,l)}) \quad &= \text{sum(square(cons(n,l)))} &&\text{(Instantiation)}\\
&= \text{sum(cons(n*n,square(l)))} &&\text{(Unfold)}\\
&= n*n + \text{sum(square(l))} &&\text{(Unfold)}\\
&= n*n + g(\text{l}) &&\text{(Fold)}
\end{aligned}
$$

A closer inspection of the transformation sequence reveals a certain rhythm within it.

- First, we instantiate with the type-constant and apply as much Unfolds as possible

- Second, we instantiate with the type-constructor, apply as many Unfolds as possible and then fold with the original definition.

Starting from these observations we will be able to formulate within the formal framework presented sofar a very simple strategy to improve the efficiency of evaluation of functions.

4.2.1 A Simple Strategy

Let us try to directly translate the structure of the above development:

A : B means syntax-generation rules ⊢ (**B** ⊢ **A**).

It can be read as : **A** is derivable from syntax-generation rules (a context free grammer) and **B** (a nonterminal).

$$
\textbf{simple-dev:}
$$

simple-dev:
[Eqs:setof(equation);
Eq: simple-rec-equation;
Eq0,Eq1:rec-equation]

$$
\text{define} \;\left|\dfrac{\textbf{Eqs}}{\textbf{Eq}}\right.
$$

$$
\text{base-dev} \;\left|\dfrac{\textbf{Eqs , Eq}}{\textbf{Eq0}}\right.
$$

$$
\text{induct-dev} \;\left|\dfrac{\textbf{Eqs , Eq}}{\textbf{Eq1}}\right.
$$

$$
\{\textbf{Eq0, Eq1}\}
$$

This rule can be applied on the previous example as follows : from now on we use '→' to denote the corresponding term

Eqs → { square(nil)=nil,
    square(cons(n,l))=cons(n*n,square(l)),
    sum(nil)=0, sum(cons(n,l))=n+sum(l) }

define rule: **Eq** → g(l)=sum(square(l))

base-dev rule :

instantiate : **Eq0** → g(nil)=sum(square(nil))

unfold : g(nil) = 0

inductive-dev rule :

instantiate : **Eq1** → g(cons(n,l)) = sum(square(cons(n,l)))

unfold : g(cons(n,l))=n∗n+sum(square(l))

fold : g(cons(n,l))=n∗n+g(l)

The rules for **base-dev, induct-dev** will of course be still given!
Two improvements of this rule are quite obvious:

- Select the argument position to be instantiated on explicitly (this is trivial in our example, since **g** has only one argument) and take care that it is equal in both subdevelopments.

- Explicitly represent the declaration of the function g (g: list(num) → num) to mechanize the correct instantiations of the subdevelopments.

Now consider **simple-dev** again:

If **define, base-dev** and **induct-dev** are valid, then the entire rule is trivially valid, if one interprets ⊢ as propositional implication. But **define** is valid since it is considered as an axiom.

So the justification of **simple-dev** can be established by a simple propositional reasoning. The price paid by the programmer for this fact is his burden to provide the proper instantiations, to produce a complete improved definition of the function he develops.

Thus the correctness of **simple-dev** is reduced to the correctness of **base-dev, induct-dev** .

Next, we will formulate these two subdevelopments.

Here is **base-dev** :

$$
\begin{array}{l}
\textbf{base-dev :} \\
[\textbf{Eqs:setof(rec-equation);} \\
\quad \textbf{Eq,Eq1,Eq2:rec-equation}]
\end{array}
\quad
\begin{array}{l}
\text{instantiate} \ \dfrac{\textbf{Eq}}{\textbf{Eq1}} \\[2ex]
\text{max-unfold} \ \dfrac{\textbf{Eqs , Eq1}}{\textbf{Eq2}} \\[2ex]
\hline
\qquad\qquad \textbf{Eq2}
\end{array}
$$

First we instantiate:

Eq → g(l)=sum(square(l)) to obtain:

Eq1 → g(nil)=sum(square(nil))

Second, we apply as many unfolds as possible to **Eq1**, obtaining:

Eq2 → g(nil)=0.

induct-dev is slightly more complex:

$$
\text{induct-dev :} \quad
\begin{array}{l}
\text{instantiate } \dfrac{\text{Eqs , Eq}}{\text{Eq1}} \\[1em]
\text{max-unfold } \dfrac{\text{Eqs , Eq1}}{\text{Eq2}} \\[1em]
\text{law-appl } \dfrac{\text{Laws , Eq2}}{\text{Eq3}} \\[1em]
\text{fold-strategies } \dfrac{\text{Eqs , Eq , Eq3}}{\text{Eq4}}
\end{array}
$$

induct-dev :
[Eqs:setof(rec-equation) ;
Laws:setof(equation);
Eq,Eq4:rec-equations]

$$\text{Eq4}$$

The first two premises are exactly the same as in **base-dev**.

law-appl allows us to apply laws (e.g. associativity or commutativity of involved functions) to an intermediate result of the development (not needed in our example). Naturally, the correctness of the rule now depends upon the correctness of the laws which must be established with extra proof-rules (not handled here). Note that laws cannot be defined since they are not in **rec-equation**.

The global variable **Laws** has to be additionally included in **simple-dev**.

An example for **fold-strategies** is a direct **fold** (as used in the previous example), more such strategies are given later.

Instantiations for **induct-dev** in our example:

$\text{Eq} \rightarrow \text{g(l)} = \text{sum(square(l))}$

$\text{Eq1} \rightarrow \text{g(cons(n,l))} = \text{sum(square(cons(n,l)))}$

$\text{Eq2} \rightarrow \text{g(cons(n,l))} = \text{n}*\text{n} + \text{sum(square(l))}$

$\text{Eq3} \rightarrow \text{Eq2}$ (since no laws were applied)

$\text{Eq4} \rightarrow \text{g(cons(n,l))} = \text{n}*\text{n} + \text{g(l)}$

4.2.2 Merge Separated Loops

This section will introduce a development strategy enabling us to merge two separated loops occurring within an expression and thereby improve its efficiency.

As a paradigmatical example we consider the fibonacci-numbers:

$\text{fib(0)} = 1$
$\text{fib(1)} = 1$
$\text{fib(n+2)} = \text{fib(n+1)} + \text{fib(n)}$

The cost of executing fib is obviously exponential, because the last expression contains two separated computations $(\text{fib(n+1)},\text{fib(n)})$ with a high-degree of redundancy.

In our framework we abstract the two loops

$\text{fib(n+2)} = \text{u+v where } <\text{u,v}> = <\text{fib(n+1)},\text{fib(n)}>$

and define a new function g, which merges both loops into one:

$$g(n) = <fib(n{+}1),fib(n)>$$

Next we try to derive a recursive definition of **g**.

The above **base-dev** runs perfectly yielding:

$$g(0) = <1,1>$$

In **induct-dev**, after **max-unfold**, we get stuck with the equation.

$$g(n{+}1) = <fib(n{+}1){+}fib(n),fib(n{+}1)>$$

To achieve a fold with definition of **g** we need an abstraction

$$g(n{+}1) = <u{+}v,u> \text{ where } <u,v>{=}<fib(n{+}1),fib(n)>$$

followed by a fold

$$g(n{+}1) = <u{+}v,u> \text{ where } <u,v>{=}g(n)$$

The combination of the last two steps is called a **forced-fold**, because we forcefully abstract all the necessary elements for a fold (fib(n+1), fib(n)) into one aggregate, so to make a fold possible. Let us now formalize the strategy outlined above.

We introduce a strategy-rule: **msl-dev** (**m**erge-**s**eparated-**l**oops)

$$
\text{msl-dev : [dEqs,Eqs: setof(rec-equation); Eq,Eq0,Eq1:equation]}
\quad
\begin{array}{l}
\text{define} \dfrac{\text{Eqs}}{\text{dEqs}} \\[2ex]
\text{ident-loops} \dfrac{\text{dEqs}}{\text{Eq , vlist , looplist}} \\[2ex]
\text{abstract} \dfrac{\text{Eq , looplist}}{\begin{array}{l}\text{e1 = e2}\\ \text{where <looplist > = <vl>}\end{array}} \\[3ex]
\text{base-dev} \dfrac{\begin{array}{l}\text{Eqs} \cup \text{dEqs ,}\\ \text{g(vlist) = <looplist>}\end{array}}{\text{Eq0}} \\[3ex]
\text{induct-dev} \dfrac{\begin{array}{l}\text{Eqs} \cup \text{dEqs ,}\\ \text{g(vlist) = <looplist>}\\ \text{forced-fold:fold-strategies}\end{array}}{\text{Eq1}} \\[4ex]
\hline
\begin{array}{l}\text{dEqs\\\{Eq\}} \cup \{ \text{Eq0,Eq1,e1 = e2} \}\\ \text{where <vl> = g(vlist)}\end{array}
\end{array}
$$

(looplist:elist, vlist,vl:varlist, e1,e2:exp, g:rec-functor)

Because of technical issues, this rule looks complicated. But in fact we only formalized what was explained above:

ident-loops selects the loops to be merged (**looplist**) and its variables (**vlist**) out of the set of definitional equations (the three equations for **fib**).

It requires the user to become active in the development and select the loops he wants to merge.

Then the rule abstracts on **looplist**, builds the necessary intermediate definition (g(vlist)=<looplist>) and finally applies **base-dev** and **induct-dev** as usual, except that an additional fold-strategy is included in **induct-dev**.

Here are the instantiations in our example:

Eqs $\to \emptyset$

dEqs $\to \{$ fib(0)=1, fib(1)=1, fib(n+2)=fib(n+1)+fib(n)$\}$

Eq $\to$ fib(n+2)=fib(n+1)+fib(n)

vlist $\to$ **n**

looplist $\to$ <fib(n+1),fib(n)>

e1 $\to$ g(n+1)

e2 $\to$ <u+v>

vl $\to$ <u,v>

Eq0 $\to$ g(0)=<1,1>

Eq1 $\to$ g(n+1)=<u+v,v> where <u,v>=g(n)

Now we give the strategy for forced-folding:

$$
\begin{array}{l|l}
& \textbf{Eq} :: \text{l=r} \ , \ \textbf{Eq}' :: \text{l'=r'} \ , \ \text{r'=} < f_1, ..., f_n >, \\
& \sigma : \text{substitution} , \\
\textbf{forced-fold} : & \text{occurs}(\sigma(f_i)) \text{ in (r)} \ , \ i = 1,...,n \ , \\
[\textbf{Eq,Eq',Eq''}: & \text{not(occurs}(f_i) \text{in}(f_j)) \ , \ \text{i,j} = 1,...,\text{n} \ (\text{i} \neq \text{j}) \\
\textbf{equation}] & \\
\hline
& \textbf{Eq''}:: \ \text{l=}[\sigma(f_1)/u_1,...,\sigma(f_n)/u_n]\text{r} \\
& \quad \text{where} < u_1,...,u_n > = \sigma \ (\text{l'})
\end{array}
$$

The first two lines of the premise divide the input-equations **Eq** , **Eq'** into their components l, r and l', r' respectively, and further divide r' into its components $< f_1, ..., f_n >$.

Instantiations from our example:

Eq $\to$ g(n+1) = < fib(n+1) + fib(n) , fib(n+1) >

Eq' $\to$ g(n) = < fib(n+1) , fib(n) >

n $\to$ **2**

$\sigma \to \epsilon$

Eq'' $\to$ g(n+1) = < u+v, u > where <u,v>=g(n)

occurs-in checks if all components of r' occur within r, but not within each other.

The verification of **msl-dev** and **forced-fold** is not easy anymore, since the use of elementary rules appears only implicitly in syntactical manipulations (e.g. definition of **g** in **msl-dev**).

Note the parametrisation of the rule sets: **induct-dev** in **msl-dev** has its default fold strategy **direct-fold** enlarged by **forced-fold**. Finally some words about **forced-fold**:

- The substitution σ is implicitly existentially quantified, which is not acceptable for a working system because of efficiency considerations. Therefore we need to define a set of rules **match**, which explicitly constructs the substitution σ or fails:

$$\forall\ i \in \{1,...,n\}: \text{match} \vdash (\ f_i, r \vdash \sigma\ )$$

- Sometimes the application of associativity and/or commutativity - laws is needed to make the **occurs-in** come true. This amounts to associative-commutative pattern-matching and, empirically, it is often used in transformation-sequences that manipulate the order of computation (from the original equation). More strategies (e.g. recursion-transformation and -removal) seem to be definable in this context.

4.2.3 Merge Nested Loops

Another development strategy concerns the merging of two nested loops into one.
Again we have a paradigmatical example:

flatten(nil) = nil
flatten(atom(a)) = cons(a,nil)
flatten(consb(x,y)) = append(flatten(x),flatten(y))

(**flatten** returns the list of elements of a given binary-tree)

sum (defined as in 4.2)

append(nil,l) = l
append(cons(a,l1),l2) = cons(a,append(l1,l2))

g(l) = sum(flatten(l))

The definition of **g** is very inefficient (because of the **append**)
Trying **simple-dev** on **g** we obtain

g(nil) = 0
g(atom(a))=a

for the base-case, and get stuck with

g(consb(l1,l2)) = sum(append(flatten(l1),flatten(l2)))

when trying to fold with **sum(flatten(l))**.

The problem is to note, that the part **sum** of the expression **sum(flatten(l))** matches with **sum** in the right hand side of the last equation, but the part **flatten** occurs in this equation after the term **append** (two times in our case).
So we introduce a lemma to "move" the missing subexpressions into the proper positions:

nf(sum(u1),sum(u2)) = sum(append(u1,u2))

(**nf** is a new recursive functor for a function that is implicitly defined by the above equation)
Now we rewrite with it:

g(consb(l1,l2)) = nf(sum(flatten(l1)),sum(flatten(l2)))

Finally we fold:

$$g(consb(l1,l2)) = nf(g(l1),g(l2))$$

An executable definition of nf can be developed in a quite simple way now, giving:

$$nf(0,u) = u$$
$$nf(1+v,u) = 1 + nf(v,u)$$

It seems in fact easy to formulate a simple strategy for development from implicit equations.

Let us again formalize the things explained so far, here is **mnl-dev**: (merge-nested-loops)

mnl-dev :
[Eqs:setof(rec-equation);
Eq:simple-rec-equation;
Eq0,Eq1:rec-equation]

$$\text{define } \frac{\text{Eqs}}{\text{Eq}}$$

$$\text{base-dev } \frac{\text{Eqs , Eq}}{\text{Eq0}}$$

$$\text{induct-dev } \frac{\text{Eqs, Eq, mismatch/}}{\text{lemma:fold- strategie}}$$
$$\text{Eq1}$$

$$\{ \text{ Eq0,Eq1 } \}$$

The only difference from **simple-dev** is the different parametrisation of **fold-strategies** by the **mismatch/lemma**-rule given next:

mismatch/lemma :
[Eqs:setof(rec-equation);
Eq,Eq',Eq":rec-equation]

$$Eq :: l = r ,$$
$$r :: f(h_1,...,h_n) ,$$
$$Eq' :: l' = f(h) ,$$

$$\text{match } \frac{(h , < h_1,...,h_n >)}{(\sigma_1,...,\sigma_k) , k \geq 2}$$

$$\text{implicit-dev } \frac{\begin{array}{l}\text{newfunc}(f(u_1),...,f(u_k))= \\ [\sigma_1(h)/u_1,...,\sigma_k(h)/u_k] \text{ r,Eqs}\end{array}}{Eq''}$$

$$l = \text{newfunc}(\sigma_1(l'),...,\sigma_k(l'))$$

in our example:

$f \rightarrow$ sum   (the partial matching)

$n \rightarrow 1$

$h1 \rightarrow$ append(flatten(l1),flatten(l2))

$h \rightarrow$ flatten(l)

$match(h,h1) \rightarrow (1 \rightarrow l1, 1 \rightarrow l2)$

newfunc $\rightarrow$ nf

match works as outlined earlier.

implicit-dev needs to be defined still (see above)

4.3 Technical Remarks, Further Strategies, Problems

We have not been alltogether rigid in our formulations given, especially the ordering of premises and arguments of the rules are not rigorous. Nevertheless it was our aim to present development rules so detailed (and not entirely as an suggestive notation), such that the level of technical syntactical problems (e.g. pattern-matching) is reached, because we think that some of the most important requirements of DC lie here. This is supported by the fact that one of the main problems in this presentation was the formulation of tricky syntactical constraints and the verification of rules containing them.

Of course, a lot of writing simplifications (e.g. for global-variables, by parametrisation of a **part**) should be introduced.

As the fold-unfold method is concerned, more strategies are suspected within the following areas

- computation-order change (recursion-removal,[Burstall,Darlington 80])

- implicit definitions (as already pointed out)

- abstract data type implementation [Darlington 80]

5 Acknowledgements

The work presented in this paper was done in the context of the ESPRIT project ToolUse funded partially by the EC. The basis of the work was provided by M.Sintzoff who presented first ideas on the Design Calculus and P. de Groote who works on its fomalization.

We would like to thank both of them for many fruitful discussions, but also all other colleagues from the ToolUse project.

6 References

[Arsac 79] Arsac, J., Syntactic Source to Source Program Transforms and Program Manipulations, CACM Vol. 22, No. 1, January 1979, pp. 43-53.

[Bauer 85] Bauer et al., The Muenchen Project CIP, Vol. I: The Wide Spectrum Language, CIP-L, LNCS 183, Springer-Verlag, 1985.

[Burstall 77] Burstall, R. M. and Darlington, J., A Transformation System for Developing Recursive Programs. Journal of the Association for Computing Machinery, Vol.24, No. 1, January 1977, pp. 44-67.

[Darlington 80] Darlington, J., Synthesis of Implementations for Abstract Data Types, Rep. 80/4, Dep. of Computing, Imperial College London, 1980 .

[Darlington 81] Darlington, J., The Structured Description of Algorithm Derivations, Algorithmic Languages, de Bakker/van Vliet(eds.) (c) , North- Holland Publishing Company, 1981,pp. 221-250.

[Dewar 82] Dewar, R. B. K. et al., Transformational Derivation of a Garbage Collection Algorithm, ACM TOPLAS, Vol.4, Oct. 82.

[Feather 85] Feather, Martin S., A Survey and Classification of some Program Transformation Approaches and Techniques, USC / Infomation Sciences Institute, September 1985.

[Gries 81] Gries, D., The Science of Programming, Springer-Verlag, 1981.

[Groote 86] Groote, P. de, Tentative Definition of a Subset of Sintzoff's Design Calculus, Universite' Catholique de Louvain Unite d'Informatique, T3.deva, 1986 .

[Horsch 85] Horsch, A., Moeller, B., Partsch, H., Paukner, O. and Pepper, P., The Munich Project CIP, Volume II: thr Program Transformation System CIP-S, Technische Universitaet Muenchen, Institut fuer Informatik Report TUM-I8509, June 1985.

[Martin-Löf 85] Martin-Löf, P., An Intuitionistic Theory of Types: Predicative Part, in: Logic Colloquium 1973, Rose and Shepherdson (Eds), North-Holland, 1975, pp. 73-118.

[Martin-Löf 85] Martin-Löf, P., Constructive Mathematics and Computer Programming, in: Mathematical Logic and Programming Languages, Hoare and Shepherdson (Eds), Prentice-Hall, 1985, pp.167-184.

[Mostow 85] Mostow, J., Towards Better Models Of The Design Process, The AI Magazine, Spring 1985.

[Partsch 83] Partsch, H. and Steinbrueggen, R., Program Transformation Systems, ACM Computing Surveys, Vol.15(3), Sep. 1983.

[Phillips 83] Phillips,J., Self-Described Programming Environments, Kestrel Institut, Palo Alto, [KES.U.83.1].

[Scherlis 86] Scherlis, William L., Abstract Data Types, Specialization and Program Reuse, IFIP WG2.4 International Workshop on Advanced Programming Environments, Trondheim, Norway, June 16-18 1986.

[Sintzoff 85] Sintzoff, M., Desiderata for a Design Calculus, UCL, T3.memo, Unite d' Informatique, June 85.

[Sintzoff 86] Sintzoff, M., Playing with a Recursive Design Calculus , UCL, T3.memo. Unite de informatique,1986.

[Smith 85] Smith, D.R., Top-down Synthesis of Divide-and-Conquer Algorithms, Artificial Intelligence, Vol. 27, No 1, September 1985.

[Sowa 84] Sowa, J.F., Conceptual Structures - Information Processing in Mind and Machine, Addison Wesley, 1984.

[ToolUse 86] ToolUse Task 3 Team, Requirements for the Definition of DEVA, Final Report Task 3.2, 1986.

[Wirth 71] Wirth, N., Program Development by Stepwise Refinement, CACM 14, April 1971,pp. 221-227.

PROGRAM REUSE AND TRANSFORMATIONS

Chair   : William Waite (Univ. Colorado, USA)
Assistant chair : Geir Skylstad (RUNIT, NOR)

Discussion

William Waite (Univ. Colorado, USA):

I would start off by posing a question to the first speaker, William Scherlis. He was not talking about incremental performance improvements, but gains of several orders of magnitude. This means that he really must be changing his algorithm, and how does he achieve that given the kinds of his transformations?

William Scherlis (Carnegie Mellon Univ., USA):

There is a whole literature of program derivations examples that have been concocted by a number of people. The point is that some fairly complicated, fast algorithms have been derived using these formal syntactic techniques. Some examples are: parsing algorithms such as Earley's algorithm, and the SUIK-algorithm??. In fact, Earley's algorithm was derived by at least three different people. I derived a linear time graph algorithm for strong and bi-connected components where the specifications can be interpreted as a program that runs in qubic time. The implementation, of course, runs in linear time. Why do we do these examples? Partly, we do them because they are fun and they provide dazzling examples of the power of seemingly benign transformation rules. Really, we do the examples because they show that it is possible to do significant algorithmic changes within a formal framework. Then, how can we manage large systems using these kinds of rules? Abstract-Tree transformations are a small step in that direction, but many more steps can be made.

Mary Shaw (Carnegie Mellon Univ., USA):

You have presented some transformation examples on how to derive algorithms that were presumably faster than the starting points. Have the transformations ever been used when the destination was not firmly in sight? It is, of course, interesting to go from ordinary parsing algorithms to Earley's algorithm. I would be much more convinced if the transformations could be used by non-experts to derive and improve unfamiliar algorithms.

William Scherlis (Carnegie Mellon Univ., USA):

There are people who actually have used derivation techniques to discover new algorithms. I would not claim that they are new and exciting algorithms, but they are original algorithms. On the other hand, I would say that our insight has not yet approached the level of insight that the algorithm designers have.

However, there are certain algorithms that I remember because I know how to derive them. For example, take a simple LISP or PASCAL program that takes a list and produces a reverse list. Another familiar program from introductory courses is to take a linear sequence of records with pointers connecting them, and turn all the pointers around without using extra storage. That's a tricky algorithm: you have to get the pointers maneuvering steps in the right order and to make sure all the boundary cases are right. I cannot remember the code because it's more than 7 lines, so I derive it instead which can be done in about 5 minutes. That's not true for all the other programs, but the derivation techniques are gradually improving.

Uwe Kastens (Univ. Paderborn, FRG):

I would strengthen the provoking question by the chairman. How far has program transformations progressed for daily life programming? I cannot remember the last time that I transformed programs operating on lists, except for preparing lectures. And by transformations, I mean more than preprocessors, editors, and the like.

David Wile (ISI, USA):

This afternoon I'll describe how conventional tools found in programming environments can be understood as compilations of sets of individual program transformations, such as compilers, code analyzers, etc.. In fact, much of the PQCC work was based on using transformations to explain the semantics of the compilation process. In effect, I am saying that transformations are not employed directly by programmers yet, but that the support environments are beginning to rely on them as specification devices.

Stefan Jähnichen (GMD, FRG):

We should not look for total automation of the development process for software. The creative process requires a lot of mental capabilities. We can perhaps achieve some support for the clerical tasks in program development. These may need the optimizations mentioned before so that changes of representations can be carried out automatically. Nevertheless, the process is a mental activity, and total automation seems not to be feasible.

William Scherlis (Carnegie Mellon Univ., USA):

Suppose you have a large program and you want to make a systematic change of representation in that program, e.g., by reordering some data bits. The easiest way to carry out a uniform change is to apply some formal syntactic operation, instead of a sequence of manual, ad hoc changes. An even better approach is to apply a formal derivation process where representational choices are localized instead of pervasive in code.

William Waite (Univ. Colorado, USA):

As you all know, OS-360 was based on a number of macros and this was an abstraction of basic operations. From time to time IBM had to change one or more of these basic macros. They found that when they made such a change, they were willing to except errors, obvious errors, by not recompiling the entire system because it was too expensive! This kind of systematic representational change may leave you in the same boat because it's a very similar situation.

Reidar Conradi (Norw. Inst. of Tech., NOR):

Systematic changes in a program can either be done manually by some transformation scheme, or automatically by a compiler. For example, you may change a module interface and the compiler can automatically update all the dependent modules. But sometimes these modules have to be systematically changed in some "manual" manner, due to name conflicts or changes in procedure parameters. Now, suppose I want to change the post- and pre-conditions of a SUM routine, concerning whwther it is the caller or the callee that should clear the sum? That is, how advanced semantic transformations can we entrust an automatic scheme to perform?

William Scherlis (Carnegie Mellon Univ., USA):

I showed variations of the stack examples. In the first one, you could always POP from the stack. In the second example, where you had a stack of bounded size, there was a qualifier saying that you couldn't pass an empty stack through the POP operation. Thus by moving that pre-condition into the formal interface, you are asserting that this property holds at every calling site. You can think of this transformation operation as really just syntactic techniques for moving abstraction boundaries in programs; although there is some ambiguity about where exactly that boundary is. So you can use transformation techniques to shift the boundary, and I think your SUM example can be handled.

Per Holager (ELAB-SINTEF, NOR):

Mary Shaw has asked a very interesting question and William Scherlis gave a very nice answer, but hardly to that question. So I will rephrase the question: So-called requirement specifications are usually very, very incomplete. We just stake out a claim of what we want the final system to do, giving an example here and there. Most of the later work will be filling out that partial function, and concerns of efficiency are rather minor. Coding usually represents 15% of the total and some part of the 15% is concerned with efficiency. What do we do to fill out our imprecise function? Are our transformation systems relevant for that? That's a question to all three speakers.

Alfons Geser (Univ. Passau, FRG):

First to Uwe Kastens' question on the use of transformations. Probably, you are using a compiler which is nothing but a large, automated transformation system. Then, is our transformation automatic enough to be performed by a compiler? I would say "probably" in most cases; otherwise, we have to use theorem provers.

Then, responding to Per Holager - By requirements engineering we always have to provide certain propositions that describe what the program should behave like. So we are beginning with examples, and then turn over to more general propositions. What we are basically doing is reasoning about those more specific and general questions on a very high level because we do not want to deal with implementation details here. Lastly, I would give you an example of a validated specification in our system concerning a macro-processor. The specification amounts to 30 pages of text and contains 39 abstract data types which have 250 laws. Several laws are 1/4 page large. The time needed was about 1 1/2 year. I found a lot of faults in the specification during the validation, so I believe that validation is both important and feasible.

Juha Heinanen (Tampere Univ., FIN):

William Scherlis seems to be considering transformations inside the modules. He was very concerned about consistency and wanted to do transformations on small algorithms in order to get them running faster and possibly reverse implementation choices. I got the impression that the upper levels are somehow irrelevant because the programs are trivial. I would like to really see that we have a formal requirements specification, and from that, derive an implementation by transformations, even a slow one. There are two approaches to this: 1) Top-down derivation of an implementation from a really high level specification and start improving that. Or, 2) Start bottom up as William Scherlis indicated, i.e., doing direct and fast implementation of small and trivial algorithms.

William Scherlis (Carnegie Mellon Univ., USA):

There are two main phases in software creation. One is a transition from informal to formal. That's usually called requirements engineering: formulating specification from requirements. The other phase is going from WHAT to HOW, i.e., going from specification to implementation. Now, by distinguishing those two phases, I am not insisting that they might be carried out sequentially. In fact, they are generally carried out concurrently, and often the specification is not formulated until a large part of the implementation is built. I am primarily addressing the latter of those transitions (from WHAT to HOW), and less the very hard one from informal to formal. However, the derivation approach allows for a fairly graceful transition from informal to formal because of the lack of insistence on a direct transition to a formal specification. You don't have to make a fixed choice, and you can build a partial prototype. In fact a prototype has various levels of abstraction, and anyone can make derivation steps in both directions from the specification and the implementation; and thereby, fill out the derivation. One might choose afterwards to fill out some derivation to carry on a validation process. There is nothing in this approach that forces a particular sort of methodology on the implementor.

Gerhard Goos (GMD, FRG):

William Scherlis mentioned case studies of how to do transformations which might improve the efficiency, but not increase the complexity. But we really need a methodology of systems integration: We should first do a modular design and later make it more efficient. It basically means that we try to remove some of the module interfaces.

Alfons Geser regarded the compiler as a powerful transformation tool. A much better approach would be to convert the compiler into an interactive expert system. When the compiler no longer is able to produce good code, it can go back to the user and say, "Look, I can make such and such transformations provided you can guarantee me the following pre-conditions." The idea is not to make it interactive all the time, but to be able to insert the assertions and user response into the source program so that later, the compiler can do the same transformations automatically.

William Scherlis (Carnegie Mellon Univ., USA):

I view the process of building derivations as a necessary interactive process. We are never going to be able to build fully automatic program synthesis machines until something about our perception of AI changes significantly. Furthermore, as you move closer toward the implementation and the derivation, the process becomes more and more automated. During compilation the entire derivation is constructed automatically by the compiler. As you move closer to specification it's likely that more human interaction, or at least more heuristicly based reasoning, is going to be involved.

Gerhard Goos (GMD, FRG):

That's because you do not know enough about the process.

William Scherlis (Carnegie Mellon Univ., USA):

That's right, but as we build derivations we should record and generalize these so we can broaden their range of application.

Then on verification - We can regard transformation as a syntactically <u>local</u> activity, while theorem proving is a syntactically <u>global</u> activity.

My third point concerns interface removal. In a separate paper in the Munich TC.2 working conference last April, we made use of "derived" implementations in a simple program with strange queues. You start with a program using a list of operations, with explicit reference to the list ADT. Then you observe that in the inner loop of that program the list operation is used in a specialized way. So you go up and separately derive the specialized implementation of the type with these fairly restricted operations. Lastly, you go back and integrate that implementation into the original program by simply unfolding the type and deleting the type in the interface. Then why do we ever have to introduce the type at all? Because the type boundary allows you to make those transformations in a syntactically global manner.

Robert Schwanke (Siemens, USA):

William Scherlis' Transformation methodology correctly treats requirements as informal, because they must be understood and agreed upon by non-technical people. Furthhermore, requirements frequently change. So, Scherlis' diagram should be redrawn to show iteration between the informal requirements and the transformation sequence.

Stefan Jähnichen (GMD, FRG):

First a reply to Per Holager: As we gain experience with program construction by transformation of specifications, we should be able to reuse, adopt, and expand previous specifications to solve the problem at hand.

An example that convinced me of the transformational approach: A student of mine was working for a German company analyzing electronic circuits which had been drawn by hand. He was to analyze them mathematically as a set of executable PROLOG rules. However, the implementation problem was too complex. So he started to simplify the rules by hand-optimization. This version did not work either, because of errors. So he had to go back to the first version and identify the errors because it was not possible to identify those errors in the optimized version. After several iterations, he finally succeded.

David Wile (ISI, USA):

Basically, William Scherlis mentioned formal development by recording the design process in the implementation phase. We are trying to use formal development to record the design of the specification. We claim that our high level editing commands are suited to characterize formally the changes we made to the specifications.

Jacky Estublier (L.G.I. C.N.R.S., FRA):

When you have a network of interconnected modules, it is not sufficient to transform the inside of a single module to improve performance.

William Scherlis (Carnegie Mellon Univ., USA):

There is a whole collection of type transformations. David Wile has come up with some, and I have come up with more. Among the latter, there are type transformations for merging and splitting types. You can use these to make significant changes to the organization of modules in a program. Let me give you an example: Suppose you have a type construct with two parameters, and those parameters arrive at different times, or with different frequencies (parameters at different stages of the program). You can then take whichever parameter is available and do as much computation only on that one. The effect from the transformation process is taking this type and splitting it into two: one for the low frequency stage, and the other for the high frequency stage. In effect, this will reorganize the modules based on performance considerations.

Reidar Conradi (Norw. Inst. of Tech., NOR):

I want the authors to comment on using expert systems to suggest and perform some of these transformations. It is not my original observation that 10% of a program is inspiration and 90% is detailed implementation work. You can often explain an algorithm or a program in one or two pages while the full thing expands to a hundred pages. All your elaborate transformations have vaporized when you look at the "rolled-out" code. I assert that we cannot improve our productivity unless we write less symbols!

The top-down approach of first writing a specification and then deriving the implementation (i.e., "automatic programming"), is generally not possible. The inverse bottom-up technique to prove that a given implementation conforms to its specification (i.e., "verification") is equally intractable. That is, we should develop hybrid transformation techniques over a wide area. But I have seen no evidence that this has been applied successfully to other than small toy examples.

The ISI effort has been going on for 10 years with meager practical results, so it's a long way.

Joseph Newcomer   (Carnegie Mellon Univ., USA):

William Scherlis' use of type boundaries to carry out refinements corresponds to what John Nestor and I did in the IDL implementation. We used various mechanisms of manual refinements including inline expansion of procedures. I would much rather have an automatic transformation system for that difficult piece of work; but at least we had a partial model.

Mary Shaw (Carnegie Mellon Univ., USA):

We have heard, and will later hear, descriptions of techniques for software development that use a very different kind of knowledge and apply to a very different period of the lifetime of the software. What kind of new design requirements will the new transformational techniques impose on existing systems for configuration control and software history reporting?

David Wile   (ISI, USA):

We have a prototype transformation system. It is being developed in itself, using parts of our specification techniques, an abstract database and a constraint base. Activities might be invoked based on changes in the database, and all that is used to model and develop the system in itself. We will use multiple versions of objects in the database to understand the transformational development of program objects.

William Scherlis   (Carnegie Mellon Univ., USA):

Responding to Shaw and Wile on configuration management tools: One of the ways to view configuration management is by doing algorithmic derivation-by-analogy in a particular framework. A configuration somehow describes a derivation. You keep derivations around so you can apply them later on by tweaking some earlier step. Hopefully, most of the derivation steps can be carried through, and once in a while you have to make a change. This is exactly what's going on in configuration management. Therefore, I think there is a certain compatibility here.

Wolfgang Polak   (Kestrel Institute, USA):

David Wile said some of what I should say. We also have a system that makes us feel reasonably hopeful that eventually these techniques will help solve the problem. I will also emphasize what William Scherlis just said. I believe that synthesis techniques and transformation techniques are applicable also to programming-in-the-large, such as building systems, releasing systems, etc.. I believe that the necessary deductions to make such derivations are fairly simple.

Creating
a
Software Engineering Knowledge Base

Andrew J. Symonds
IBM Corporation, Bldg. 920 Dept. B30
Data Systems Division
P.O. Box 390
Poughkeepsie, NY 12602
U.S.A.

1.0   INTRODUCTION

The Myers Corners Programming Laboratory in Poughkeepsie NY is the home of MVS/XA, IBM's most advanced operating system, which runs on large System/370 processors.

MVS/XA is the result of more than 20 years of continuous evolution of a system whose original ancestor was OS/360, developed in the early 1960's. Changes have been driven by users' needs for more computing power and the advances in processor, memory and storage hardware that these have necessitated. MVS/XA also supports the operation of major IBM subsystems for transaction control, data base control and network control, which are evolving independently in locations as far apart as Hursley in England and Santa Teresa in California.

Developing MVS/XA is thus a good example of programming in the large, where it is extremely critical to be able to manage to committed schedules (and costs) and produce a product that is defect free. More than 20 years of experience has led to a development process that has been quite successful at achieving these two objectives. The process embodies a waterfall model of software development whose features are:

- A design discipline that ensures stabilization of specifications, and their associated implementation and test plans, at a sufficiently early point in the cycle.

- An implementation discipline that uses formal inspection methods to ensure that programs are meeting their specifications and have no design or implementation defects.

- A build and test discipline that keeps track of program libraries comprising multiple product releases, controls the production of test environments, and controls the processes of testing systems, finding problems and fixing them.

The disciplines mentioned above rely heavily on computer automation, where the emphasis is on library and data base organizations designed to contribute towards administrative control over the process. The administrative controls have not noticeably improved the working environment for individual programmers and designers, which is what must happen before the next major productivity breakthroughs can occur. The next major challenge is therefore to improve the intellectual control over the processes concerned with designing, building, testing and maintaining releases of the system. The thesis of the paper is that it is practical to proceed directly towards a software engineering knowledge base as the solution approach. The reasons for this are:

1. A number of authors have already pointed out that the waterfall model, or paradigm, for software engineering has some deficiencies that have caused them to seek a different paradigm as a basis for achieving improved productivity. This they call the operational paradigm; it consists of continuous refinement of an operational model of the software under development, that culminates in the generation of optimized code.

2. The knowledge based systems, or expert systems, paradigm is a working example of the operational paradigm.

3. Commercially available knowledge engineering tools are available to support the knowledge based systems paradigm.

4. While construction of a persistent knowledge base management system remains as work to be done, the issues involved do not appear to be significantly different from those involved in constructing an object oriented data base management system. In both cases methods must be devised for staging data between a (relational) data base management system representation and a working memory representation, that provide adequate performance.

5. Relational data base management systems and knowledge based systems are now commercially available in the same computing environment, thus enabling them to be coupled together. This provides an environment for empirical investigation into the staging question.

The contents of the paper are:

1. A brief discussion of the waterfall model deficiencies and the notion of the operational model, or paradigm, for software engineering.

2. An overview of knowledge based systems technology.

3. A discussion of the issues involved in setting up a persistent knowledge base manager.

4. A brief description of how one would approach the task of setting up a software engineering knowledge base for a large programming activity such as the development of MVS/XA.

1.1 OPERATIONAL LIFE CYCLE MODEL

The waterfall model has a number of drawbacks that limit its value as a basis for complete automation of the software engineering life cycle. The discussion here draws heavily on observations made by Wegner (1).

Early stages of the life cycle specify an informal behavioral abstraction of WHAT is computed. This abstraction is progressively refined and eventually transformed into an operational specification of HOW the computation takes place. There is therfore a discontinuity in the process at the point where a behavioral specification of the software work product is turned into an operational specification from which source code is derived. This makes it difficult to verify that the source code matches the behavioral specification, let alone the more informal requirements description. The complexity of formal program specification and verification methods underscores this point.

Furthermore, maintenance is usually performed on low-level, optimized implementations. This is a problem because the software maintainer cannot relate the source code to the specification and design information from which it was derived, is thereby deprived of important knowledge, and consequently is more likely to make mistakes.

The conclusion has been reached that an alternative life cycle model, more susceptible to complete automation, needs to be found. The operational life cycle model is being proposed as the answer. From the earliest stages of the operational life cycle, the work product is an executable abstraction of HOW the software is supposed to work. This is as formal as a behavioral specification, but the behavior is specified implicitly via a set of executable specifications instead of explicitly in an implementation independent fashion. The operational software model is successively refined and transformed until the final optimized source code is produced. At the end of each refinement step there is a work product that can be automatically interpreted, either to verify consistency with previous steps or to emulate actual execution. Early feedback to designers and users is thus possible.

Transforming an executable specification into efficient source code is still a complex task. However it is more amenable to automation since the process does not have the built-in discontinuity of the waterfall life cycle model.

The electronic spreadsheet is a good example of an operational software model, since it demonstrates some important principles surrounding the translation of concepts into practical reality.

- The operational model used is one that is intuitively easy to understand, consisting as it does of a two-dimensional array of data elements that are related via formulas.

- The personal computer provides an interface that displays the model in a form easy for human interpretation, and allows direct manipulation of the model through instantaneous response to user actions. Direct manipulation is important because it reinforces the user's intuitive feel for what is represented in the model.

- The operational specification is immediately executable so that its behavior can continually be examined as changes are made.

Another example is the functional life cycle model devised by Hamilton and Zeldin (2), which is fully automated via an integrated family of tools called USE.IT. A consistent functional model is used for defining requirements through final specifications, and can be comprehensively analyzed for correctness at any point in the process. The final step is to generate source programs that are then compiled and executed.

1.2 KNOWLEDGE BASED SYSTEMS

Balzer et al (3) have also pointed out that the existing (i.e. waterfall) paradigm (model) does not lend itself to complete automation of the software engineering life cycle. They propose:

1. An operational life cycle paradigm.

2. Automated implementation support through a computerized software development assistant. The assistant is a KNOWLEDGE SYS-

TEM using a KNOWLEDGE BASE that evolves over time to provide more and more help to software developers.

The operational software specification is obviously an integral part of this software engineering knowledge base.

The software engineering knowledge base is the logical follow-on to the software engineering data base discussed in some of the accompanying papers. Creating a software engineering knowledge base requires the following:

1. A knowledge base representation model and associated storage mechanism must exist.

2. The knowledge base representation mechanism must be embedded in a knowledge system environment that allows it to be accessed, modified and executed.

3. The knowledge base must be primed with the initial version of an operational model of the software engineering life cycle.

The technology is available to get started on this work immediately, although invention will be required before the knowledge base can be extended to cover all the tasks outlined in reference (3).

The latest in durable knowledge base technology is epitomized by modern knowledge engineering tools (or expert system shells) that are used to build knowledge systems.

A knowledge base supported by these tools has the following components.

- A representation of the facts used to model information relevant to the problem domain under consideration.

- A set of production rules that allow conclusions to be drawn from facts.

- Reasoning strategies that specify how problems can be solved by successive application of production rules.

A knowledge base IS an operational specification since it describes how computations are performed. It can be continually verified since it can be "executed" to demonstrate its behavior. Techniques for knowledge base representation are an outgrowth of artificial intelligence (AI) research that has been going on for at least two decades. The evolution of practical approaches to knowledge representation and reasoning on computers has progressed through several stages, which are described in articles by Lenat (4) and Walker (5) and will not be summarized here. More recent emphasis in the commercial sector has been on the importance of a suitable representation of the factual component of a knowledge base and the availability of tools that make it easy to access, modify and manipulate (see Fikes and Kehler (6)). We will now describe the model for representing facts in a knowledge base, and it will be apparent that it looks like an entity-relationship model with structural and semantic extensions.

The main features of factual representation are described below - the discussion uses the terminology of reference (6).

- The basic object is a <u>FRAME OR UNIT.</u> There are two kinds of units - those that describe classes of objects and those that describe individual instances of objects. The former are known as "class" units and the latter are known as "member" units.

  Entity types, relationship types, entities and relationships are all units in a frame system. "source program" is an example of a class unit; "calls" is another example of a class unit; "X calls Y" is a corresponding member unit.

  A hierarchy of class units is allowed. "Cobol program" and "PLI program" are examples of subclasses of the "source program" unit. Units can be subclasses or members of more than one class.

- A unit can have attributes known as slots. Slots may have various values which describe different units. "source program" units have a "language" slot; "calls" units have slots for "calling program", "statement number", and "called program". Every unit has a "belongs to" slot describing all the classes or subclasses to which it belongs.

- A slot can have attributes known as facets. Facets may have various values which describe different slots. One of the facets is the slot's value. Examples of other facets are:

  - Value class, which specifies allowable values for the slot.

  - Cardinality, which specifies upper and lower bounds for the number of values the slot can have.

  - Inheritance role, which specifies how the slot will inherit attributes from units higher up in the class hierarchy. Inheritance is a notion that allows units to pass along their attributes to lower-level units. A member of the "PLI program" subclass of source programs could inherit its "language" attribute from the subclass.

Inheritance provides an economical way of storing data common to groups of objects and ensures consistency among objects in the knowledge base. This obviously makes it easier to modify and extend the knowledge base incrementally. Since units can be members and subclasses of more than one class, properties can be inherited from more than one path in the class hierarchy. This is called multiple inheritance.

- A slot can have a value that is actually a procedural program. This is called a procedural attachment, or method to use the parlance of object-oriented programming. Units can thus respond to messages and behave like active objects. Units with actions to perform can communicate with one another, executing actions in response to one another. Putting methods in slots makes it easier to visualize the operation of a complex system as part of the representational structure of the knowledge base.

- A slot can have a facet that specifies an active value for the slot. An active value is a unit containing methods that receive a message whenever the slot value is changed or referenced.

  Active values are useful for validation, monitoring and display of slot values.

The factual component of a knowledge base resembles a data base in that new facts can be asserted and its contents can be queried.

The other major component of a knowledge base is its reasoning capability, comprising a set of production rules and methods for applying them. Reasoning provides a means for a system to respond more intelligently to assertions and queries.

Suppose for example that we have managed to capture a knowledge rich frame structure that models a complex software system. By knowledge rich we mean that the frame structure "knows" a lot about the software system.

- It includes basic inventory information about each program.

- It includes basic inventory information about data structures, their scope and, if shared, which programs have access and update privileges.

- It includes connectivity information containing everything anyone would want to know about relationships between program and data structure modules.

- It includes a model of run-time objects such as queues, stacks and other types of storage structures. The run-time model also allows memory trace and dump information to be correlated with the frame structure.

In principle the frame structure enables the source of a problem to be discovered automatically, given a set of symptoms, by exhaustively searching for and evaluating all possibilities. This would typically take much too long and in any case it is unreasonable to assume that the structure contains ALL of the necessary information. What is needed is a way of narrowing the search, based on a more intuitive approach towards finding the likely source of a problem. This intuition is stored as production rules of the form

If   a set of values in the frame structure
        meets certain conditions

then   appropriate conclusions can be drawn

Reference (6) shows how rules can themselves be represented as units within a frame structure.

Automatic reasoning is the process whereby rules are successively selected and applied. Forward reasoning enables the system to respond to assertions by finding rules that draw conclusions from the new information. Backward reasoning derives answers to queries, when those answers are not available in the knowledge base, by finding rules that assert the desired answers and working backwards from there.

Knowledge bases are physically stored in main memory - virtual memory is viewed as being a form of main memory. Modern knowledge engineering tools provide a rich set of functions for accessing, modifying, debugging and executing knowledge bases. In many cases users are offered an advanced work station interface using graphics, windowing and direct manipulation techniques. This type of interface gives users a better intuitive feel for the knowledge base, or operational model, that they are working on.

Commercial products are available to support the creation of knowledge systems, and they are being used to solve real industrial problems. A comprehensive survey of the area has been written by Johnson (7).

Many software vendors are involved and their products run in a number of hardware environments. This paper will focus on IBM environments, of which there are two that are significant. One is the System/370 mainframe environment with its capacity to handle large quantities of data, both on disk and in main memory. An introduction to knowledge systems with an overview of IBM's System/370 software has been written by Symonds (8).

Another IBM environment is the RT (RISC Technology) PC, a recently announced engineering and scientific work station. A number of knowledge system products are announced or available on this machine.

- The Lucid Common Lisp product has recently been announced by IBM.

- Quintus Prolog has been announced by Quintus.

- The following vendors of expert system shells have announced that they will support the RT PC: IntelliCorp (KEE), Inference Corp. (ART) and Teknowledge (S1).

1.3 PERSISTENT KNOWLEDGE BASE MANAGER

A persistent knowledge base manager can be built by coupling together a knowledge system and a relational data base manager. The basic atom of knowledge in a frame structure can be viewed as a predicate of the form

  relation_name(unit_name,slot_name,facet_name,facet_value)

where "relation_name" differentiates between various logical collections of units.

A starting point would be to store predicates as corresponding tuples in a relational data base. Partitioning the tuples between different relations allows the data base manager to control knowledge base access, authorization and integrity. A mechanism would have to be devised for recognizing whether a particular unit name is local or a reference to a unit in another relation.

This tuple representation offers the most flexibility, but is clearly inefficient for representing a large number of "member" units in the same class, and with identical configurations of slot and facet values. The efficiency issue is obviously important, and alternative tuple representations should be provided. However we will not mention the issue further so that we can move on to discuss the synchronization of:

1. a user interacting with an active knowledge base in main memory, with

2. a backing store of tuples in a relational data base.

Synchronization is achieved via transactions that transfer information between the active knowledge base and the backing store. It is beyond the scope of this article to describe the transaction design. The key issue is knowing when to transfer an aggregate of one or more units. Some of the design considerations are:

- Transferring aggregates into main memory requires knowledge about the anticipated needs of the user.

- An exception handling mechanism, analogous to a paging exception, must exist to handle cases when units are required that were not preloaded.

- Transferring units out of main memory requires knowledge about: how to recognize that memory is being filled up; which units are least likely to be needed by the user; how to recognize which of these units have been changed.

A good design will be based very much on experience - what works well and what does not. To get this experience there needs to be a starter set of low-level primitives for transferring units between main memory and the backing store. Knowledge about when and how to invoke them can be included in the knowledge base. As more experience is gained, the knowledge base designer can gradually be relieved of this storage management burden.

There is no reason why the initial experience gathering phase cannot start immediately, since adequate knowledge system and relational data base implementations are available today. Again restricting ourselves to IBM environments, relational data base managers are available on System/370 mainframes and on the RT PC, which complement the knowledge systems discussed in the previous section.

We showed previously that a slot could have a value that is actually a procedural program, and all commercially available knowledge systems have this or an analogous capability. If we assume that these procedural programs can make calls to the relational data base manager, then we have our starter set of low-level primitives for transferring units between main memory and the backing store.

1.4 SOFTWARE ENGINEERING KNOWLEDGE BASE

Once we have a persistent knowledge base manager, we can start thinking about setting up the software engineering knowledge base to support an operational life cycle for a large software engineering project such as MVS/XA. This is obviously a formidable task that would have to be staged over a long period of time, and only after extensive study of the existing waterfall life cycle process. This type of study has not yet been done for MVS/XA and in any case its results would most certainly be IBM confidential information.

What can be presented here are some thoughts on how one would go about transforming a large project's process from the waterfall life cycle model to an operational model. First we identify the issues that initially need to be considered.

1. Modelling a large, complex operating system, at its highest level of abstraction, as a collection of cooperating objects, which include processors, channels and devices executing asynchronously.

2. Understanding, at least in principle, how successively lower levels of abstraction can be developed.

3. Using the results of the above to provide a frame of reference for objects dealt with by the current process, such as source programs, macros, test buckets and configuration definitions.

A frame structure can now be built by "reverse engineering" the software objects identified in 3. above. By analyzing them using tools built for the purpose, the following knowledge can be captured.

• Inventory information concerning programs and data structures

• Inter and intra module connectivity information

Analysis of load maps yields the information that allows memory trace and dump data to be correlated with the source module information.

Once this is done we are at a point where we can start thinking about how to automate problem determination. The knowledge base now has to be augmented manually, adding frames and rules based on how experts find the sources of problems given certain symptom information.

Problem determination experise would address areas such as:

• Given an initial set of problem data, how to recognize probable causes.

• How to pursue various hypotheses on probable causes, identifying what additional data is required to validate or disprove the hypotheses, and how it could be obtained.

The knowledge base is now at the point where it could materially assist the problem determination process. The next step would be to extend the knowledge base to assist with the processes of creating and testing the fixes required to solve the problems. These extensions would cover:

- Identification of <u>ALL</u> the objects to be changed to implement the fix.

- "Intelligent" static analysis of the modified objects.

- Selection of test buckets comprising a regression test plan that optimizes the trade-off between coverage and cost.

The knowledge base constructed so far contains considerable detail on implementation objects, together with their relationships to a high level abstraction of the conceptual system objects they are implementing. The major knowledge gap is the succession of continuous refinements that results in automatic generation of optimized implementation objects from the high level abstraction of the system.

All that can be said here is that capturing the expertise to close the gap completely will take a long time, and that critical components will always be crafted by hand. However there are definitely grounds for optimism as long as the task is viewed as a set of incremental steps, each with an identifiable pay-off associated with it.

1.5 REFERENCES

1. P. Wegner, Capital-Intensive Software Technology, IEEE Software, July 1984, pp 7 to 45

2. M. Hamilton and S. Zeldin, The Functional Life Cycle Model and its Automation: USE.IT, The Journal of Systems and Software, Vol. 3, 1983, pp 25 to 62

3. R. Balzer, T.E. Cheetham Jr. and C. Green, Software Technology in the 1990's: Using a New Paradigm, IEEE Computer, Nov. 1983, pp 39 to 45

4. D.B. Lenat, Computer Software for Intelligent Systems, Scientific American, Vol. 251 No. 3, Sept. 1984, pp 204 to 213

5. A. Walker, Knowledge systems: Principles and practice, IBM Journal of Research and Development, Vol. 30 No. 1, Jan. 1986, pp 2 to 13

6. R. Fikes and T. Kehler, The role of frame-based representation in reasoning, Communications of the ACM, Vol. 28 No. 9, 1985, pp 904 to 920

7. T. Johnson, Expert Systems, report published by Ovum Ltd., London, 1986

8. A.J. Symonds, An Introduction to IBM's Knowledge-Systems Products, IBM Systems Journal, Vol. 25 No. 2, 1986, to be published

The Unified Programming Environment: Unobtrusive Support

Terrence Miller
Jim Ambras
Martin Cagan
Nancy Kendzierski

Distributed Computing Center
Hewlett-Packard Laboratories
1501 Page Mill Road
Palo Alto, CA 94304
U.S.A.

Our organization has been charged with the task of significantly improving the productivity of professional programmers. We are doing so by designing a total environment that provides uniform access to all the information and services (programming and non-programming related) needed by a programmer. We call it the Unified Programming Environment (UPE).

At the center of the UPE is an object-oriented knowledge base storing information about the programming process and individual projects. This technology is being combined with that of *agents*, that mediate between the user and various tools and, when so instructed, carry out tasks on their own.

Because the success of a software project depends on the coordination and team-work of all the contributors, the UPE is being designed to support all team members. These include project management, documentation, marketing, quality assurance, and software distribution personnel. All parties are kept informed by the knowledge base and the agents software working together to infer and propagate the consequences of changes.

The UPE uses networks and servers to provide a single logical system to a programming team. However, the access to knowledge bases and the interaction with other programmers and servers is as unobtrusive as possible. The interactions are mediated by agents, giving each programmer the illusion (when desired) of working on a small problem, in the languages of his or her choice with minimal need to worry about coordination with others.

One of UPE's goals is to reduce the design and implementation cycle so that solutions may be prototyped rapidly. The model supports the notion of a programmer and customer working together to develop a mutually agreeable solution. Large libraries of reusable code, incremental interpreters and compilers, intelligent debugging, and unobtrusive system building tools help support this rapid prototyping.

Furthermore, many new applications are most appropriately implemented as a blend of symbolic and conventional languages. This is especially true for many expert system applications, such as instrument control, manufacturing, and data analysis applications. To this end, UPE has also been designed to help the programmer develop multi-lingual applications. Support is provided for language cross-calling and multi-lingual debugging. Our initial work involves Common Lisp, Objective-C[1], and the knowledge representation language HP-RL [Rosenberg83]. Others, including executable specification languages, are being considered.

1. Automation and Frustration

Many of the major advances in the process of creating software have come not from tools to help solve a problem but rather from tools which make the problem disappear. Many of the greatest frustrations faced by a programmer come from systems in which the attempt to hide a particular problem has not quite succeeded. An example which illustrates both sides is dynamic storage allocation. Pascal's heap management facility is a tool for controlling storage allocation. Lisp was designed to make storage management invisible. While storage allocation is in fact invisible, and has proved to be of great assistance to the programmer, in many systems, storage deallocation is far from invisible - one's whole world stops at inconvenient moments. Moreover, since allocation is transparent, it is difficult to recognize code which uses storage inefficiently. In planning our work on the UPE, we have tried to strike a balance making a real advance in the long-term and creating much short-term frustration.

A strong candidate for making radical gains in our ability to produce software is to apply AI techniques to make parts of the programming task disappear. Some areas we are looking at are:

- the production of code from specifications,
- the generation and modification of test cases, and
- propagation of changes.

We can envision the following scenario. A support programmer has just received a report of a problem. The UPE session goes as follows:

1. The defect report is visible in a window of a browser. The programmer

---

[1] TM - Productivity Products Inc

selects the version field from report and using a type-specific, pop-up menu establishes that version as the context for all future work.

2. The defect symptom is an error message describing the overflow of a queue. The programmer selects the error message and uses it to search the knowledge base for the abstract specification of the queue datatype.

3. She then enters a browser which shows that specification and its descendants. It shows an abstract specification, a concrete specification, and code.

4. Examination of the mapping between the abstract and concrete specification reveals that the original designer selected the "fixed-size" option for queues.

5. The programmer declares a new working context, the intent of which is to fix the bug. She then modifies the mapping to select the "variable-size" option. The necessary version checkout and locking is handled transparently and the new version is associated with the new context and the bug report.

6. When she then requests execution of the program, the concrete specification and code for queues are first automatically rebuilt and a new configuration rebuilt.

However, we do not believe that this dream is reachable in the 3-year interval planned for our initial efforts, and an imperfect attempt would be very frustrating. Thus we have considered a less ambitious system as an intermediate goal. In this version, the session for a programmer dealing with a bug report might be:

1. The defect report is visible in a window of a browser. The programmer selects the version field from report and using a type-specific, pop-up menu establishes that version as the context for all future work.

2. The defect symptom is an error message describing the overflow of a queue. The programmer selects the error message and uses it to search the knowledge base for the specification of the queue datatype.

3. She then sees that the queue implementation was selected from a library of reusable modules and that the variant which uses static storage had been selected.

4. The programmer declares a new working context, the intent of which is to fix the bug. She then specifies that within this context a different variant of the queue module should be used.

5. When she then requests execution of the program, the program is first rebuilt using the new queue variant.

The automatic generation of code from specifications has been replaced by use of existing modules from a library of reusable code.

2. Unobtrusive Support

For our first steps we will be trying to support not automate the programmer's primary creative activity - creating or modifying designs or code. That support comes in three areas which are:

- reducing the amount of such work needed (through libraries and tools that facilitate reuse of code),
- speeding up design and code entry (through tools such as language-knowledgeable editors), and
- increasing the amount of time the programmer can devote to the primary creative activities.

In the remainder of this paper we discuss only the last area, and further limit ourselves to the secondary activities of programming itself. These problem areas include:

- understanding and debugging code,
- generating effective documentation,
- reading and searching documentation,
- keeping track of the work of others, and
- keeping management informed.

At the center of the UPE is an object-oriented knowledge base that stores information about both the programming process and individual projects. The knowledge base serves as the primary communication medium for both tools and people.

We expect that information in the knowledge base will replace traditional documentation. The task of collecting information about a program will be largely automated using tools which record the history of a program's development, retain all levels of abstraction, and analyze the final code. Users can then obtain answers to specific questions without the overhead of reading large amounts of documentation.

By combining the agents technology with the knowledge base, the UPE helps the project members stay abreast of each other's activities by notifying them of relevant events. For example, if two programmers were viewing the same module, and a third programmer changed that module, the first two programmers would be notified of the changes. They would also be notified if the system inferred that the change affect the other modules they were working on. In addition, the documentation writers would be notified of any changes to the external specifications, and project management would be notified if there were any effects on the project schedule or dependencies.

3. Underlying Technologies

The UPE is implemented on the Hewlett-Packard AI Workstation [Cagan86] and is being constructed on a platform of other technologies. The maturing of some of these technologies is a major factor in the feasibility of our intermediate-range plans, while the expected advances in others over the next five years gives us a growth path into even more flexible and intelligent environments. The technologies are object-oriented programming, expert systems, a persistent object database, a persistent knowledge base, and agents.

3.1 Object-Oriented Programming

The UPE is implemented in CommonObjects - an object-oriented extension of Common Lisp [Snyder85]. It also uses the frame-based knowledge representation language HP-RL. As they both have evolved, the objects of CommonObjects and HP-RL frames have grown closer together. The goal is to have a unified object model that will serve both for abstract datatype implementation and knowledge representation.

Abstract datatype mechanisms and inheritance are also at the center of our work on code reuse. Both CommonObjects and Objective-C are being used as test cases.

3.2 Expert Systems

HP-RL provides a full set of tools for constructing expert systems. The system resides within Common Lisp. It implements an inferencing system over frames with both forward and backwards chaining rules controlled by a sophisticated agenda mechanism. The unification of CommonObjects objects and HP-RL frames will make all items in the knowledge base compatible with the rule system. HP-RL also provides a demon mechanism.

3.3 Persistent Object Database

Our Common Lisp and CommonObjects has been extended to work directly with persistent objects stored in a relational database. The information is stored in HP's ALLBASE[2] which provides shared, distributed storage. Objects may be retrieved using standard relational queries as well as by pointer reference.

ALLBASE allows us to work with large amounts of information. We expect that a reasonable-sized database would indeed accommodate the information describing

---

[2] TM - Hewlett-Packard Company

the mythical million lines of code, but the database would need to be replicated in order to service the corresponding army of programmers. Initial performance analysis work supports our plan to serve clusters of up to 15 or 20 programmers working together.

3.4 Persistent Knowledge base

Currently both the rule-based reasoning of HP-RL and the event detection controlled by agents occurs within a single UPE on the individual user's workstation. Information is retrieved from the database and then processed. Work has begun on an object-oriented data model [Derrett86], which is being implemented on ALLBASE. Our intent is to partially migrate the inference and event-detection mechanisms into the database, which then merits the name *knowledge base*.

The speed of access to the knowledge base will be a important factor in the success of UPE, and database and knowledge representation issues are receiving considerable attention. We are designing the UPE so that it can anticipate needs for particular information and maximize the granularity of knowledge base requests.

Software built using the UPE is represented by objects within the knowledge base (not files and directories). Both the traditional items (such as source text and derived binary information) and all the connections between them are represented by objects. Initially the raw text or binary information is being kept in files to permit access by conventional tools. Those files are reached only via the knowledge base.

Use of objects in a knowledge base allows arbitrary attributes to be associated with items. Representing connections between items as objects themselves allows the user to build up a network of connections of various types. Such a network better represents the programming process than a file and directory structure, which represents only one type of connection (directory linkage).

These objects (including those representing connections) are versioned objects. The versioning mechanism supports both a sequence of versions in time and multiple, simultaneously active variants.

3.5 Agents

In the future, the UPE will incorporate *intelligent agents* to act as mediators between the user and tools which have grown increasingly complex. Nils Nilsson has described intelligent agents as "artificial intelligence (AI) programs that can exhibit autonomous behavior in complex environments." In this particular instance, we want to put that autonomy to work directly for the user; the agent can be thought of as an expert consultant serving as an advisor or instructor in the use of the tools, or able to be instructed directly by a user to carry out various tasks.

The concept of agents is not new in AI [Bobrow75,Weyhrauch80]; more recent work has concentrated on what is required for distributed, communicating agents [Davis83,Rosenschein84,85]. In addition, the full realization of intelligent agents relies on supporting artificial intelligence technologies such as knowledge representation, planning, communication (including natural language), and methods for reasoning about beliefs, desires (goals, values), actions, and intentions.

Some programming tasks do not require much intelligence (artificial or otherwise), but rather depend on memory and watchfulness. For such tasks, the UPE can initially make use of what can be called dumb, but trainable, agents. Such agents have the ability to:

- be instructed in a nonprocedural way using simple rules, and
- operate autonomously.

The many programming tasks that can be handled by trained agents include version consistency checking, bug report tracking, and the automatic generation of mail messages describing changes. An example of the actions of a bug agent would be sending mail to the project manager if a bug report was not answered in two weeks.

For more complex tasks (e.g., project tracking), intelligent agents are required with access to specialized domain knowledge, as well as some general world knowledge and specific user knowledge.

The inclusion of agents in the design of the UPE is intended to provide a focus for the addition of intelligence and autonomy to the system. We believe that distributed AI systems are the key to future progress on real problems and intelligent agents is our way of moving towards that future. The process of gradual addition of intelligence may not be without its own attendant problems, however. Since we are intending to place these agents in direct communication with users, we must pay special attention to the user/agent interface. Such a human/computer interface may need to be qualitatively different from interfaces for other types of programs. On the one hand, the user needs to understand how to take advantage of the intelligence that is being made available; on the other, human-like intelligence (meaning that the agent interprets a request in the same way a "reasonable" human being would) will not be within our grasp for some time, and the user must be able to predict the agent's limitations.

4. Program Analysis

The UPE will contain a comprehensive set of intelligent, integrated tools to amplify a programmer's ability to understand the program's structure and behavior. Starting from MicroScope [Krohnfeldt85], we have developed a prototype of a package that analyzes a program both statically, by inspecting its source code, and dynamically, by monitoring its execution [Ambras86]. The current implementation handles 50,000 line Common Lisp programs using an in-memory knowledge base. It is being extended to handle Objective C.

Once a program has been analyzed, the prototype can answer complex questions about the program, graphically display the program's structure from different perspectives, and perform sophisticated monitoring of the program's execution.

Knowledge about the programming process itself will also be added to the UPE knowledge base. UPE will use this knowledge, coupled with its program analysis knowledge, to provide the framework for a number of knowledge-based assistants that help programmers in different phases of the software development process. The first such assistant, UPE's debugging assistant, will help to analyze the causes of anomalous program behavior and provide advice on the possible consequences of program modifications.

4.1 Static Analysis

The UPE analyzes the static properties of programs and stores the results of this analysis in the UPE knowledge base. There are two levels of static analysis: cross-reference analysis and source code analysis.

Cross-reference analysis captures program properties, such as which procedures are called by another procedure, or which procedures set a global variable. This component of the UPE is similar to the Interlisp Masterscope facility [Teitelman78].

After a program has been analyzed, programmers can use the query facility of the knowledge base to ask questions about the program's static properties. Both simple and complex questions (e.g., "Which procedures call the procedure foo?" and "Which global variables are not referenced anywhere in the program?") are handled.

The answers to many common classes of queries are available from a graphical cross-reference browser. The UPE also provides menus for query construction and access to the full power of HP-RL's knowledge base query language.

Source code analysis stores finer details about a program, such as lexical blocks, conditionals, and loops. Additionally, this level of analysis will provide data and control flow represented in a manner similar to the Programmer's Apprentice surface plans [Rich81] [Waters85] and the Designer's Algorithm Language [Steier85]. The data flow analysis will then be used to compute program slices [Wieser82]. Program slices define which parts of a program are capable of affecting the computation of a particular variable, and help focus the user's attention during debugging.

4.2 Dynamic Analysis

Programmers have traditionally used two methods for monitoring program execution - inserting debugging statements in the program's source code, and using the trace and break facilities found in most debuggers. But there is often too much information to analyze when viewing the tracing of all calls to a procedure, or all references to a variable. The UPE solves this problem by providing *event monitoring*.

Event monitors have been supported for both compiled languages and interpretive systems. They allow event descriptions and actions to be specified using source level constructs. Users may define new events in terms of primitive system events, such as a variable read/write or a function entry/exit, using the source language or some other description [Delisle84, Bates82].

The UPE provides a rich set of building blocks for defining events, and watches for any number of events at once. Examples of events are a loop reaching one of its exit conditions, or a variable being set to a particular type or range of values. When the UPE observes an event taking place during a program's execution, it create an *event frame* to describe the event. The UPE creates *call frames* to record procedure calls and method invocations, and keeps timing information on monitored procedures. These frames are added to the UPE knowledge base.

The UPE's *execution history browser* constructs from these event and call frames a display of the skeleton of the program's execution history. Commands to the execution history browser let users zoom in on interesting details, such as displaying monitored events or sorting procedures based on timing data.

5. Program Authoring

The programmer is an author creating or modifying a complex document. Different parts of that document are intended for different readers (both human and machine). During this authoring process the programmer develops small units of information, which are connected in an almost arbitrary pattern. Examples are:

- a statement in a program that is connected to a text annotation,
- two nodes in a structured analysis diagram that are connected by a dataflow arc, and
- two versions of a procedure that are connected by the description of the event which produced one from the other.

The UPE supports the creation of such networks. Parts of our work can be regarded as a generalization of NoteCards [Card86] for programming, extended to associate information with the arcs in the network.

5.1 Creation

As a software module is developed, all steps in the development of that module are recorded as arcs in the network. Each version of the module is maintained and can be retrieved on demand. Data on the changes to a module, the bugs found, the time spent, the module's documentation and test cases, and any annotations are saved in the knowledge base. Each UPE facility adds as much development history data as possible to the knowledge base so that the other UPE facilities, and other team members, can later use this information.

As the application evolves, and module dependencies are developed, the system records and maintains the relationships between modules, so it can help the programmer compile the application and run the test cases. Since each UPE tool accesses information via the knowledge base, agents can derive the actual dependencies between components.

5.2 Navigation

The programmer can use the UPE tools to navigate through the network of information stored in the knowledge base. However, as the program evolves over time and into multiple variants, the structure will become far too complex to be seen in its entirety. Thus UPE provides a context mechanism that selects particular versions of nodes and connecting arcs to display. Versioned connecting arcs allow different contexts to select independent alternatives for a given function. Thus they provide more flexibility than the layers of modifications defined by PIE [Goldstein80] and provide the functionality normally referred to as configuration control.

UPE tools also execute within the specified context. Thus the context mechanism guides system building. It provides the functionality of the DSEE configuration thread [Leblang85], but in a more unobtrusive style.

The current context is associated with the task the programmer is performing. This facility supports the user who switches between several tasks and needs to have a different context associated with each task.

When the programmer desires, he or she is able to navigate through the network of versions seeing change over time and/or parallel variants. For example, the programmer can view a module as it was a month ago, or the current version of a given module as it is defined for one of two different experimental implementations. Versions can be saved and retrieved without the programmer dealing with the idiosyncrasies of a particular version control system, again largely due to both the knowledge base and the agent-based interface.

517

6. Summary

A key to significantly improving the productivity of programmers is the construction of a unified environment that collects and manages all information needed by the programmer and automates many of the programming tasks, both creative and mundane. Much early progress can now be made working only on the mundane tasks while pursuing AI research to develop the technology needed to automate more creative tasks.

Creation of the UPE as we have described it requires a set of supporting technologies which are now becoming available. A strength of our effort is that we are collaborating with strong teams working in all of the supporting areas.

7. Acknowledgments

The work described here is being carried out by a team of people too numerous to list. All work described is going on within Hewlett-Packard's Distributed Computing Center directed by Ira Goldstein.

The UPE and database work is being carried out within the Software Technology Laboratory directed by Martin Griss. His assistance in preparing this document is gratefully acknowledged.

8. References

[Ambras86]   Ambras, J. *UPE: MicroScopic Analysis of Lisp Code*, Report STL-86-09, Software Technology Laboratory, Hewlett-Packard Laboratories, Palo Alto, California, June 1986

[Bates82]   Bates, P. and Wileden J. "EDL: A Basis for Distributed System Debugging Tools", *Proceedings of the 15th Hawaii International Conference on System Sciences*, 1982.

[Bobrow75]   Bobrow, R. and Brown, J. "Systematic Understanding: Synthesis, Analysis, and Contingent Knowledge in Specialized Understanding Systems," *Representation and Understanding*, edited by Daniel Bobrow/Allan Collins, Academic Press, Inc., 1975.

[Cagan86]   Cagan, M. "An Introduction to Hewlett-Packard's AI Workstation Technology", *Hewlett-Packard Journal*, 37(3), March 1986.

[Card86]   Card, S. and Moran, T. "User Technology: From Pointing to Pondering," *Proceedings of the ACM Conference on the History of Personal Workstations*, Palo Alto, California, January 1986.

[Davis83]   Davis, R. and Smith, R. "Negotiation as a Metaphor for Distributed Problem Solving," *Artificial Intelligence* 20(1), January 1983.

[Derrett86]   Derrett, N. P. et al. "An Object-Oriented Approach to Data Management," *Proceedings of Compcon Thirty-First IEEE Computer Society International Conference*, San Francisco, CA, March 1986.

[Desisle84]   Delisle, N. et al. "Viewing a Programming Environment as a Single Tool", *Proceedings of the ACM SIGSOFT/SIGPLAN Software*

Engineering Symposium on Practical Software Development Environments, SIGPLAN Notices 19(5), May 1984.

[Goldstein80] Goldstein, I. and Bobrow, D. *A Layered Approach to Software Design*, Report CSL-80-5, Xerox Palo Alto Research Center, 3333 Coyote Hill Road, Palo Alto, California, December 1980.

[Krohnfeldt85] Krohnfeldt, J. and Kessler, R., "MicroScope - Rule-Based Analysis of Programming Environments", *Proceedings of the Second Conference on Artificial Intelligence Applications*, IEEE Computer Society, December 1985.

[Leblang85] Leblang, D. and Mclean, G. "Configuration Management for Large-Scale Software Development Efforts," *Proceedings of the Workshop on Software Engineering Environments for Programming-in-the-Large*, Harwichport, Massachusetts, June 1985.

[Rich81] Rich, C. *Inspection Methods in Programming*, MIT Technical Report AI-TR 604, June 1981.

[Rosenberg83] Rosenberg, S. "HPRL: A Language for Building Expert Systems", *Proceeding of the Eighth International Joint Conference on Artificial Intelligence*, Karslruhe, West Germany, August 1983.

[Rosenschein84] Rosenschein, J, and Genesereth, M. *Communication and Cooperation* Technical Report 84-5, Heuristic Programming Project, Dept. of Computer Science, Stanford University, 1984.

[Rosenschein85] Rosenschein, J, and Genesereth, M. *Deals Among Rational Agents* Technical Report 84-44, Heuristic Programming Project, Dept. of Computer Science, Stanford University, March, 1985.

[Snyder85] Snyder, A. *Object-Oriented Programming for Common Lisp*, Report ATC-85-1, Software Technology Laboratory, Hewlett-Packard Laboratories, Palo Alto, California, 1985.

[Steir85] Steier, D. and Kant, E. "The Role of Symbolic Execution in a Model of Algorithm Design", *IEEE Transactions on Software Engineering*, SE-11(11), November 1985.

[Teitelman78] Teitelman, W. *INTERLISP Reference Manual*, Xerox Palo Alto Research Center, 3333 Coyote Hill Road, Palo Alto, California, October 1978.

[Waters85] Waters, R. *KBEmacs: A Step Toward the Programmer's Apprentice*, MIT Technical Report AI-TR 753, May 1985.

[Weiser82] Weiser, M. "Programmers Use Slices When Debugging", *Communications of the ACM*, 23(7), July 1982.

Beyond Programming-in-the-Large:
The Next Challenges for Software Engineering

Mary Shaw
Software Engineering Institute
Carnegie-Mellon University
Pittsburgh, PA 15213

Abstract. As society's dependence on computing broadens, software engineering is being called upon to address new problems that raise new technical and nontechnical concerns. Aspirations and expectations for the application of computers appear to be unbounded, but present software development and support techniques will not be adequate to build computational systems that satisfy our expectations, even at very high cost. Each order-of-magnitude increase in the scale of the problems being solved leads to a new set of critical problems that require essentially new solutions. The next challenges for software engineering will deal with software as one of many elements in complex systems, which we call *program-as-component*, and with the role of software as an active participant in the software development process, which we call *program-as-deputy*.

Software engineering is concerned with finding practical solutions to computational problems. Over the next few years, software engineering will be required to

- respond to society's needs for software in constantly widening application areas

- accommodate constantly increasing levels of expectation for software capability and performance

- gain intellectual control over software development and support

The major challenges that arise from these requirements will be to broaden substantially software engineering's traditional scope of attention and to increase by orders of magnitude the scale of systems that can be constructed successfully. This will require significant changes in the character of the problems that we work on and the methods that we use to solve these problems.

As software engineering has matured, the range of tasks for which computers are useful has widened dramatically. Constantly increasing numbers of people have become computer users. The unprecedented utility of computing has caused demand to escalate beyond our capacity to produce the software to satisfy that demand. Software engineering must expand both the scope of problems it can solve and the scale of the systems it can develop. To do this, software

This work was sponsored by the Department of Defense. The views and conclusions in this document are those of the author and should not be interpreted as representing official policies, either expressed or implied, of the Software Engineering Institute, Carnegie-Mellon University, the Department of Defense, or the U.S. Government.

engineers must become more aggressive about propagating new technology within the field and about adopting techniques from other fields.

This paper begins with a discussion of the effects of problem scale on software engineering. It defends this proposition with surveys of the kinds of issues now confronting software developers and of the events that are expanding the scope and scale of computing needs. It argues that software engineering must move from a labor-intensive basis to a technology-intensive basis rooted in sound models and theories. The paper concludes by proposing two new sets of issues that must be dealt with, program-as-component and program-as-deputy.

1 Effects of Scale on Software Engineering

Software engineering has progressed from solving small, simple problems to solving large, quite complex ones. Moreover, as the problem scale has increased, the essential character of the problems has changed. The tasks to be accomplished have become qualitatively more difficult, as seen for example in the progress from standalone computing, to multiprogramming, to timesharing, to distributed systems. At each stage in this history, the attention of the software engineering community has been directed toward some set of issues that can be understood as characteristic of the major issues of software development at that particular time. Each new generation of systems has been more ambitious than the previous, and new problems emerge as a consequence of this increase in scale. A significant increase in system scale and corresponding shift in the character of the critical problems seems to take place roughly every decade.

Each time there is an order-of-magnitude increase in the complexity of software systems, some different aspect of system development becomes the intellectual bottleneck. In the 1950's to mid-1960's the problem was writing understandable programs, and the solution was implemented through high-level languages. In the 1970's the problem was organizing large software system development, and the solution was implemented through tools for programming-in-the-large. When a shift of bottleneck takes place, the problems encountered with smaller systems remain, but the new bottleneck forces the field to attend to a new set of problems in a fashion that may be essentially different from the way we thought about previous problems. The earlier, smaller problems don't disappear, however; they usually remain as subproblems in the larger systems.

A number of different problems have held center stage in software engineering. In each period, however, the primary emphasis of the field has been shaped by a set of issues that arise in the most ambitious software that was ordinarily being developed at the time. Frequently, these issues had arisen in earlier systems; however, in systems that clearly press the limits of software engineering, the essentially different character of the resulting problems is often not recognized or dealt with, and the system developers cope with the problems on an *ad hoc* basis. It is when the problems begin to impede system development regularly that they are distinguished as arising from issues worthy of study in their own right.

A very early shift in the driving problems of software engineering took place before the term "software engineering" was coined. In the late 1950's and early 1960's, it was often a triumph simply to write a program that successfully computed the desired result. There was little widespread systematic understanding of program organization or of ways to reason about programs. In the mid-1960's, programming was influenced substantially by the recognition that programs could be the subject of precise, even formal reasoning. By establishing that algorithms and data structures could be designed and analyzed independent of their instantiation in any particular program and, indeed, independent of each other, Knuth established algorithms and data structures as fields of study [Knuth 68]. Dijkstra further refined our view of programming by arguing that we must simplify our programs in order to understand them [Dijkstra 68]. We might describe the resulting shift from *ad hoc* to systematic programming as a change from *programming-any-which-way* to *programming-in-the-small*.

The most familiar example of a mode shift driven by increases in scale is the shift from programming to software system management that took place in the mid-1970's. This involved the recognition that constructing large, complex systems is not at all the same task as writing small individual programs -- not even when the individual programs happen to require a large number of lines of code. Development of large systems requires the coordination of many people, maintenance and control of many versions, and remanufacture of old versions after the system has evolved. The problems associated with this shift had occurred in some systems many years earlier, and many of the problems were named in the conference that established the field of software engineering [Naur 68]. However, concrete prototypes of solutions did not become a significant focus of the field until a bit later. In the early 1970's, Parnas discussed techniques for modular decomposition [Parnas 72], and Baker investigated ways to organize teams of programmers [Baker 72]. DeRemer and Kron [DeRemer 76] addressed the task of describing large system structures and the essential differences between this task and the task of describing programs. They coined the terms *programming-in-the-small* and *programming-in-the-large* to identify the shift of attention from the problems encountered by a few people writing simple programs to the problems encountered by large groups of people constructing (and managing the construction of) large assemblies of modules. The significance of the distinction is that it is necessary to think about these two kinds of problems in essentially different ways, and DeRemer and Kron's contribution was to focus the attention of a significant fraction of the software engineering community on that new problem.

To explain the nature of this change, we can compare the shifts in several attributes of the problems and activities of programming-in-the-small and programming-in-the-large:

- *Characteristic problems:* The major focus shifted from emphasis on particular algorithms to emphasis on interfaces, system structures, and management of the people involved in system production.

- *Dominant data issues:* The chief concern about data shifted from data structures and data types to databases whose lifetimes transcend the execution of particular programs.

- *Dominant control issues:* The predominant view about flow of control shifted from the view that programs execute once and terminate to a view of an assembly of computational modules that are expected to execute continually.

- *Specification issues:* The shift in control issues led to a change in specification concerns. Whereas terminating programs can be specified as mathematical functions, the specification issue in a continually executing system deals with the sequence of states through which the system passes and the side effects of those states.

- *Character of state space:* The state space of a piece of software shifted from a small, easily comprehensible state space to a large state space with complex structure.

- *Management focus:* The management unit shifted from the individual effort to team efforts directed toward developing and maintaining large systems.

- *Tools and Methods:* Whereas the programmer-in-the-small uses data structures, compilers, linkers and loaders, the tools of the programmer-in-the-large are programming environments, integrated tools, version control, configuration management, document production, and report generation.

One way we deal with increases in problem size and complexity is by finding ways to reduce the apparent complexity of the problem. For example, higher-level languages reduce the number of lines of program text (the apparent complexity) required to achieve a given functional capability (the actual complexity). However, there are limits to our ability to deal with increased complexity by abstracting existing methods and extending existing solutions. On occasion, we must focus on a different set of issues.

An order-of-magnitude increase in problem size sometimes escalates a new aspect of the software development process to the status of a bottleneck. The phenomenon of issue shift with increased scale is generally one of emphasis -- of which issues are the critical ones -- rather than one of discovering essentially new issues in the software development process. However, the newly-important issues usually have not been explored thoroughly, and new solutions are required. In these cases, as well in the cases when familiar aspects grow complex, the fruitful approaches are the introduction of systematic methods, the automation of routine detail, and the reduction of apparent complexity.

When solutions to these issues are found, they often turn out to be useful for problems of smaller size as well. For example, many individuals make good use of version-control tools on one-person projects. Even if the new tools are not critical for solution of the smaller problems, they may nevertheless be extremely useful.

2 The Nature of the Software Problem

Concerns about problems in the software development and support process have increased over the past several years, perhaps because increases in the size and complexity of software systems have made those problems more apparent. Today, software is a dominant factor in fielding advanced technology systems, and software reliability is a crucial issue. As a result of those concerns, numerous studies have highlighted critical software problems. In general, the problems are related to cost, management, and performance. The problems can be attributed to some characteristics of the state of the practice: labor-intensiveness and inadequate use of available technology. They are further compounded by the sheer magnitude of the applications.

There is a real temptation to single out a single issue as "The Software Problem" and marshal resources to attack that problem. However, that view is too simplistic. The problems associated with software are economic, managerial, and technical; they involve production, maintenance, and use of systems. This section examines several facets of this complex of software problems.

Software can be a critical factor in large system development and operation. Simple software errors can cause expensive failures in large complex systems, and delegation of system control to software may lead to failure when unexpected conditions or interactions arise. An example of the first kind of failure caused Gemini V to splash down 100 miles off course [Fox 83]. In essence, the programmer confused sidereal time with solar time and assumed that any location on earth would return to the same position relative to the sun every 24 hours. Since this ignores orbital motion, the accumulated error led to an off-course landing. An example of the second kind of failure was the complete loss of power in a Boeing 767 in August 1983 [AP 83]. A computer-controlled descent to the landing airport was optimized for fuel efficiency, but the low power levels allowed ice to build up in the engine and block airflow necessary for engine cooling. As a result, the engines overheated and had to be shut down. (The engines were restarted safely for landing.) A second example of failure due to unexpected interactions took place at the Crystal River nuclear power plant in February 1980 [Marshall 80]. For unknown reasons, a short circuit led to erroneous indications of low temperature in the reactor. The automated controls responded by speeding up the reaction in the core. As a consequence, the reactor overheated, the pressure in the core increased to the danger level, and the reactor automatically shut down. To release the pressure, the computer opened a pressure relief valve, but pressure dropped so quickly that a high pressure injection system was automatically activated, which flooded the coolant loop. The operator prevented further damage by closing appropriate valves manually.

Software is an ever-increasing part of the computing problem. A growing percentage of computer-related costs is attributable to software, and both the total cost and the fraction attributable to software are expected to increase dramatically. For example, Figure 1 shows a projection of costs of computing involving software for mission-critical applications in the US Department of Defense [EIA 80].

Computing technology is only one dimension of the problem. As system complexity has increased, managerial and professional issues have assumed increasing importance. These are coming to be widely recognized and addressed, but they have not yet achieved the same stature as the technological issues. In addition, economic and legal considerations are playing an increasing role as the value of software as intellectual property grows.

Qualified personnel are scarce and productivity growth is low. Software costs for both development and maintenance are still largely labor-related, yet the supply of computer professionals is insufficient to meet the demand, and the supply and productivity of existing professionals are not increasing fast enough. Figure 2 compares the demand for software in one application area [Tomayko 85] with the overall productivity growth of programmers [Boehm 81]. Software maintenance activities are particularly understaffed, resulting in degraded operational support. Similarly, qualified personnel for management functions are scarce.

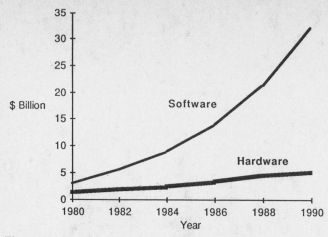

Figure 1: Projected Growth of Software and Hardware Costs

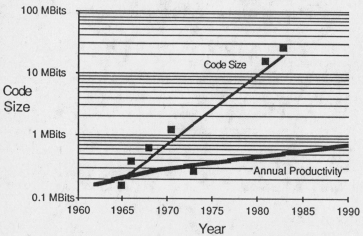

Figure 2: Onboard Code Size for Manned Spacecraft vs
Annual Programmer Productivity

Current technologies may not scale up to new problems. The major concern about a software system is often whether the system can be implemented at all, not the cost of implementation. Software engineering is continually developing tools to aid in the software development process. Some of the most important tools of current interest address the management of large and changing configurations of software. These tools are of some interest for systems of all sizes (programming-in-the-small), but they become critical only when system size reaches some critical threshold (programming-in-the-large). Large-scale systems already stretch our ability to achieve desired results. Since our aspirations grow faster than our productivity, we continually set out to build systems that are more complex than any we have built before; these can be heterogeneous real-time systems in which the software is a minor component interacting with electronic or electromechanical components. As a result, we can expect to need new tools for reducing the apparent complexity of very large systems; it is reasonable to expect that these tools will be useful but not critical for systems of sizes we can manage now.

Techniques for managing projects are inadequate. The software development process is not as well understood as other kinds of development efforts, and it is therefore more difficult to plan, schedule, and manage. A major problem is a lack of good quantitative information and models for interpreting it. In some cases, the management plans are not sufficiently detailed to account for the intricacies of the development process, do not provide a sound basis for management of the development effort, or are based on poorly defined requirements. Although considerable progress has been made in the last decade, techniques still in widespread use do not cope well with changes in requirements and specfications, which are the most significant drivers of cost and schedule growth. Figure 3 illustrates the kind of problem that frequently arose under these older management strategies. It compares the history of the estimates of total project cost (black diamonds) to the history of total cost to date (white circles) for a large software project; values are normalized to total project cost. This example suggests that initial estimates are unrealistic and that estimates are not updated until reality sets in, as apparently happened in months 9 and 24 of this example [Devenney 76].

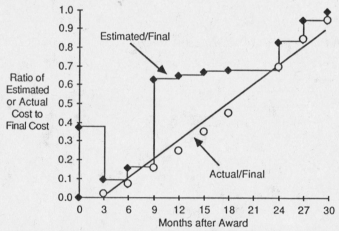

Figure 3: Growth of Estimated Total Project Cost and of Actual Accrued Costs
(as fractions of final cost)

Change is a fact of life. Because the underlying technology is evolving rapidly, software tools will change continually. So will the underlying paradigms for software development. The solutions of software engineering must make allowances for change, including the ability to upgrade systems regularly and to tolerate modest amounts of inconsistency as the upgrades take place. A more serious problem is that the rapidity of change means that we are always on the leading edge of the learning curve for the current technology. By the time we have assimilated the technology and found ways to exploit it, new technology has introduced new problems.

New technology is adopted slowly. Even though software engineering is evolving rapidly, technology transition still takes up to two decades from concept formation to widespread practical use [Redwine 84]. Reliability and integrity of systems are often limited by continued use of decade-old technology, and systems are often obsolete before they are released. In many organizations, development and support tools are insufficient, out-of-date, inefficient, and often mutually incompatible; reuse of existing code is not practiced sufficiently; and lack of standardization leads to unmanageable systems. Observed rates of technology transition in software engineering are rapid compared to some other fields, but there is considerable room for improvement. Figure 4 shows the rate at which some familiar software engineering techniques have moved toward practice [data from Redwine 84].

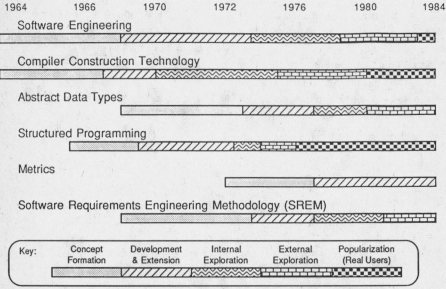

Figure 4: Progress of transition for some software technologies

Software is often the pacing component of an integrated system. Software is often embedded in a large heterogeneous system. It is frequently on the critical path of such systems, and software slippage translates directly into delays and compromises in release of the system. Moreover, major capital outlays may be required for the non-software components; in such cases, the direct cost of software delay is dwarfed by the cost of maintaining unusable hardware.

Intellectual control over software development is a central issue. Modern software is extremely complex, and its complexity rises as aspirations for system performance rise. Systems of the scale required over the next decade will be created successfully only if the software structure, the development process, and the maintenance process are understood in a precise and systematic fashion.

In summary, there is no single software problem; rather there are many problems that combine to form a large, complex set of issues. These issues span development and support tools, management techniques, strategies for buying and selling software, and availability of qualified software professionals.

3 Broadening Scope of Computing Systems

The nature of computing, and hence of software engineering, is changing rapidly. In order for software engineering to be prepared to address the problems of the 1990's, we must try to understand the forces that are shaping the field and to anticipate the roles that computers and software will play in the future. This section points out some of the trends that will affect the field over the next decade and describes some of the new phenomena and issues that may arise.

Computers are becoming smaller and cheaper, and they are being distributed across a wider and more varied population. Important current trends include:

- Decreasing hardware costs

- Increasing share of computing costs attributable to software

- Increasing expectations about the power and reliability of application systems

- Increasing range of applications, particularly those on which lives will depend

- Increasing use of software as component in integrated heterogeneous systems

- Increasing development of distributed computing and convenient network access

- Widening view of computers as an information utility and a basis for electronic publishing

- Increasing quality of interfaces to humans (voice, high-performance graphics)

- Increasing availability of computing power, especially in homes

- Increasing exposure of naive people to computers, both at home and at work

- Increasing general reliance on computers for routine day-to-day operations

- Continuing or increasing shortage of qualified professionals

- Increasing importance of "intelligent" systems requiring complex judgemental decisions

- Increasing legal and economic concerns about proper treatment of software

On the basis of these trends, we can extrapolate some future developments:

- *Pervasive Consumer Computing:* Computers will be extremely widespread, both as multiple-purpose machines in homes and offices and as dedicated machines for applications such as environment control and hazard monitoring. Most of the users of these machines will be naive--certainly the majority of them will not be programmers. As a result, most of the users of programs will not be creators of programs.

- *Information Utility:* We will come to think of computers primarily as tools for communicating and for accessing information, rather than primarily as calculating machines. Networks will provide a medium for making available numerous public databases, both passive (catalogs, library facilities, newspapers, bulletin boards) and active (newsletters, electronic mail, individualized entertainment). Real-time control applications will become more prevalent.

- *Broad Range of Applications:* The range of applications will continue to broaden, and an increasing number will be applications in which unreliable software could lead to risk of human life. As a result of this and widespread use by nonprogrammers, much of the software will provide packaged services that require little, if any, programming. There will be substantial economic incentives for producing general systems that can be tuned to individual, possibly idiosyncratic, requirements.

- *Changes in the Workplace:* Distributed systems and networks will facilitate a distributed workplace, but we doubt that the norm for office workers will be to work at home instead of in an office. Electronic communication will speed communication, but computers will not replace human interaction for decision-making. Electronic workstations will change the nature of work that now depends on paper flow, and robotics will change manufacturing substantially.

- *Massively More Complex Computers:* Some computer networks and large computers will be replaced by or evolve into massive computer systems whose capacity is orders of magnitude greater than that of any system now available. Such systems already are emerging: current systems include very large databases (nationwide banking records, interactive consumer catalogs, traffic information for ocean-going vessels, etc.). The first steps have already been taken by airline and hotel reservation systems. Eventually, these systems may be used by millions of people simultaneously.

- *Intelligent Systems:* Intelligent software systems will provide intellectual multipliers that substantially increase professional productivity in some areas. Intelligent robots will take over an increasing percentage of the industrial workload and perhaps even make a dent in the household chores. Increasingly sophisticated systems will lessen the need for programmers, and they may increase everyone's need for a basic understanding of computers. Further, today's expert systems may be tomorrow's oracles.

- *Effect on GNP:* The fraction of the GNP represented by computing and information handling--already large--will increase as our society becomes as dependent on information as on grain or metal.

Even if this projection is inaccurate in its details, there will nevertheless be a substantial qualitative shift in the role of computers in the world at large. This view of the future raises a number of issues:

- *Consumer Concerns:* The use of computers by large numbers of nontechnical people, together with the increasing number of sensitive applications that involve computers, will raise issues about the responsibilities of vendors towards their products. These will certainly include analogs of the familiar problems associated with product and professional liability, merchantability and warrantability (guarantees), usability and reliability, licensing, copyrights, and product safety (e.g., development of an analog to the certification that Underwriters Laboratories provides for electrical products). Other problems, such as security and privacy concerns, undoubtedly will arise from the special nature of computers.

- *Production and Distribution:* An expanding role for computers and computer-related products and services in the retail marketplace will introduce new problems in manufacturing, sales and service, equitable methods of charging for shared resources, and industry compatibility standards. Another class of problems will center on how to create software for a mass market, perhaps including some notion of mass production of software (e.g., by tailoring packages rather than by writing code and by using software to construct software).

- *Safety and Security:* In addition to the consumer-safety issues, we can expect questions concerning licensing, product and professional liability, and the trustworthiness of integrity of data provided via public databases. Existing concerns about security and privacy will increase. These concerns will be particularly acute when human life is at stake.

- *Economic Impact:* The economic impact of these major innovations will be widespread. Of particular concern for the computing industry will be the interplay between technological development and limiting factors, such as productivity, on the growth of the information sector. Accurate software cost estimates and well-considered marketing policies will be vital as the computer industry matures. Some of the most important economic changes will involve personnel, especially when unskilled positions are eliminated through automation or replaced by jobs requiring a high level of technical expertise.

- *Human Issues:* Currently, people deal directly with computers primarily by choice. As computers become pervasive, people will interact with them through necessity. There will be a variety of sociological consequences, including the necessity of systems designed for naive users, personnel dislocation caused by technical change, and major shifts in the content and style of education.

- *Social Issues:* The computer age could bring about a new underprivileged class of the computer illiterate. Women and minorities might make up the majority of this new class because of insufficient technical education. To prevent such a situation, computer scientists must be aware of the social implications of their work, and the society must be aware of the implications of this new technology.

The thrust of these examples is that software engineering must be able to respond to problems that involve naive users, highly heterogeneous systems, and increased requirements for product-level performance. We turn now to the software problems posed by these demands.

4 The Science of Software Engineering

Traditional methods of software development are *ad hoc* and labor-intensive. They will not be adequate to satisfy the increased demands on computing systems and the complexity of the resulting systems. Software engineering must move to a technology-intensive basis that draws on scientifically-based models and theories; it must be prepared to take advantage of advances in these areas as they become available. The education of software engineers is critical to this progress, for good ideas achieve practical utility only in the hands of people who use them wisely.

Over the past two decades this kind of shift in technology has taken place in many aspects of programming-in-the-small. Some of the earliest formal models supported the analysis of algorithms. Our understanding of algorithms for certain problem domains is now well structured, we can analyze the performance of specific algorithms, and we know theoretical limits on performance in many cases. Similarly, a theory to support abstract data types emerged during the 1970's. In the late 1960's computer scientists recognized the importance of good representations and their associated data structures. Refining this insight to derive a theory of abstract data types took about a decade; it required advances in formal specification, programming languages, verification, and programming methodology. Undergraduate computer science students should now routinely master algorithmic analysis and abstract data types; it is now reasonable but not entirely realistic to expect the material to be applied in routine practice.

Sound theories can also contribute significantly to our ability to construct software systems. For example, the compiler for a programming language is a medium-sized system with a structure that is now well understood. Whereas in the early 1960's the construction of a compiler was a significant achievement, compilers now often are constructed routinely. Good theoretical understanding of syntax led to effective techniques for constructing parsers, first manually and more recently automatically. Similarly, good theories for programming language semantics and type structures are leading to automation of other stages of compiler construction.

Although programming-in-the-large has a somewhat shorter history, formal models are beginning to emerge for the information management problems in that domain. For example, configuration management and version control began on an *ad hoc* basis with simple tools for organized (and often massive) recompilation, but at least a few models of system configuration and remanufacture are guiding the construction of software tools. The theoretical basis not only shows how to manage dependency information to reconstruct a system correctly, it also supports more efficient strategies of system reconstruction by avoiding unnecessary steps (e.g., recompilation of modules in which the only changes were comments or which depend only on unchanged portions of modules that were changed).

These examples give the flavor of the progress toward sound foundations for software engineering. There are clearly many areas in which the models, theories, and methodologies are still primitive. However, the power of soundly based theories in at least a few areas offers encouragement for developing and refining theories in other areas.

5 The Next Challenges

In the decade since software engineering recognized programming-in-the-large as a significant issue, the complexity of software systems has grown by another leap, and another shift is now taking place. Software engineers must now deal with complex systems in which software is one of many components in a large heterogeneous system and in which the software is expected to serve as a surrogate for a human programmer, taking an active role in the development and control of software systems. We will describe those new modes of operation as *program-as-component* and *program-as-deputy*, respectively. Their relation to programming-in-the-small and programming-in-the-large, as well as to the *ad hoc* programming of the 1960s, is suggested by Figure 5.

Identification of these new modes recognizes a change in the character of the problems that depend on computational solutions as well as a change in the character of the software development and support process:

- They are not necessarily amenable to algorithmic solution, and heuristic approaches may be important.
- They involve judgemental elements such as selecting among competing, non-absolute preferences.
- They depend on problem-specific knowledge that must be consulted dynamically.

Attribute	1960+5 years Programming-any-which-way	1970+5 years Programming-in-the-small	1980+5 years Programming-in-the-large	1990+5 years Program-as-component	1990+5 years Program-as-deputy
Characteristic Problems	Small programs	Algorithms and programming	Interfaces, management, system structures	Integration of heterogeneous components	Incorporation of judgement
Data Issues	Representing structure and symbolic information	Data structures and types	Long-lived data bases, symbolic as well as numeric	Integrated data bases, physical as well as symbolic	Knowledge representation
Control Issues	Elementary understanding of control flow	Programs execute once and terminate	Program assemblies execute continually	Control over complex physical systems	Programs learn from own behavior
Specification Issues	Mnemonics, precise use of prose	Simple input-output specifications	Systems with complex specifications	Software as component of heterogeneous system	Extensive reuse of design
State Space	State not well understood apart from control	Small, simple state space	Large structured state space	Very large state with dynamic structure and physical form	State includes development as well as application
Management Focus	None	Individual effort	Team efforts, system lifetime maintenance	Coordination of integration and interactions	Knowledge about application domain and development
Tools and Methods	Assemblers, core dumps	Programming languages, compilers, linkers, loaders	Environments, integrated tools, documents	Tools for real-time control, dynamic reconfiguration	Program generators, expert systems, learning systems

Figure 5: Emergence of Software Problems with Growth in System Complexity

- They are so complex that solutions cannot be specified a priori but must be evolved through experience.

- They involve integration of a heterogeneous set of system components including hardware as well as software.

- They require graceful accommodation of unreliable data and other vagaries of physical systems.

- They may involve external constraints that arise from the physical system being controlled rather than from the logical function of the system.

The role of *program-as-component* arises in large heterogeneous systems. Such systems include programs in multiple languages for significantly complex hardware systems; they may have mechanical constraints, produce noisy data, or impose real-time constraints on operation. To capture the nature of this shift of attention, we can consider the same attributes as before:

- *Characteristic problems:* The major focus of design is shifting from algorithms and interfaces to the integration of the system as a whole.

- *Dominant data issues:* We need integrated data bases that include not only symbolic and numeric information but also information about the physical status of the system that may in fact be a physically distributed system -- in which communication is a very significant issue.

- *Dominant control issues:* Software must now provide control over complex systems that may include data subject to physical or mechanical constraints as well as the usual purely symbolic data.

- *Specification issues:* Software specifications must address interfaces with non-software elements of the system as well as with other software elements.

- *Character of state space:* The state space of a large heterogeneous system may be very large. In addition, the structure may be dynamically reconfigured, and it may contain physical elements as well as symbolic elements.

- *Management focus:* The heterogeneous character of these systems increases demands on management to coordinate design, development, construction, and integration schedules which have very different characters.

- *Tools and Methods:* These systems require real-time control and interfaces for lay users; they must be capable of running complex control problems with very little human intervention.

The role of *program-as-deputy* arises when large, creative portions of the program development process are delegated to software. This shift has been taking place gradually ever since the first symbolic assembler assigned addresses to variables. As time has passed, more and more expertise about the software development process has been incorporated in programs that perform increasingly creative subtasks within the software development and management process. By delegating these subtasks to tools or program generators, we will raise the level of software reusability from code fragments to design elements. The attributes of this activity are:

- *Characteristic problems:* The major focus is on incorporating expertise and judgement in software tools. The shift that makes this an issue now is the attempt to incorporate into the automated tools judgements that may be partially subjective.

- *Dominant data issues:* Since software is now automatically carrying out some aspects of the software development process, we must represent not only the data of the application domain but also knowledge about that domain's specific expertise and the state of the software process. Further, we must choose representations that support learning -- retaining information about specific developments and using it to improve the overall performance of the tools.

- *Dominant control issues:* Programs must not only encode expertise but must also learn from their own prior use.

- *Specification issues:* Emphasis has shifted from reuse of code to reuse of design through automation.

- *Character of state space:* We must extend the state space to cover the development processes as well as the application domain.

- *Management focus:* Both qualitative and quantitative knowledge about the software development process and about the application domain must be acquired and managed.

- *Tools and Methods:* Program generators are significant early tools. As time passes, they are being joined by learning systems and knowledge representation systems.

These shifts reflect only the changes in the technology of software development and support. As system scale has increased, issues from several other areas also have become critical.

- *Professional Issues:* Software engineering will experience a significant personnel shortfall for at least the next 5-10 years. Attention to education, career paths, and professionalism will help to take up the slack.

- *Legal Issues:* Software is unlike either hard products or books. As a result, neither patent law nor copyright law is quite appropriate for software products and tools. Intellectual property law for software must deal with such issues as software protection, product liability, impediments to dissemination of new technology, and rights in technical data.

- *Economic Issues:* Costs of software development arise from many sources, and software consumes an increasing fraction of corporate resources. Software engineers often fail to appreciate cost components other than the ones directly associated with creating the software. The public marketplace rewards software contributions imperfectly, especially in cases where software must be modified for reuse. In addition, accounting rules for software influence corporate decisions about innovation.

- *Managerial Issues:* Management concerns have interacted with software technology ever since we recognized the issues of programming-in-the-large. As systems grow larger, managerial issues expand to include improved costing and estimating techniques, the visibility into software development necessary for effective control, adequate performance measures for human organizations, and incentives and risk reduction measures to encourage more productive software technology.

Although these areas generally have not been covered in software engineering education, their role now requires attention.

6 Conclusions

The issues and solutions discussed here cover an area somewhat larger than the one software engineering traditionally encompasses. They include many of the problems of end users, such as consumer-level product quality and systems in which software is an integral (and dedicated) component of a larger system. They also include material that usually is considered part of other parts of computer science, such as artificial intelligence. and computer architecture. For software engineering to respond to the problems it will confront over the next decade, it must cope with problems of

- *Scale:* Both the magnitude and the complexity of our systems will continue to increase, so we must seek ways to make the software a participant in managing its own development

- *Scope:* Computing will play an ever-broader role in specific domains, so we must learn to deal with software as a component of integrated heterogeneous systems

Software engineering should be broad enough to address the software design and integration issues and the software development and maintenance elements of those problems, including both technological and non-technological elements. It must be broad enough to shift focus to new issues, such as program-as-component and program-as-deputy, as the field grows and technical bottlenecks shift.

7 Acknowledgements

My understanding of software engineering has come from many discussions with other computer scientists, especially my colleagues at Carnegie-Mellon. Particular insights in this paper came from discussions with Bill Wulf, Allen Newell, Nico Habermann, and Jim Horning.

In addition to the direct citations, the following served as major sources: Some of the development of "The Software Problem" was prepared for [Barbacci 85]. The discussion of "Broadening Scope of Computer Systems" was originally presented in [Shaw 85]. The section on "The Science of Software Engineering" was prepared for [Shaw 86]. The author's view of the software problem was strongly influenced by the three-day retreat reported in [Musa85].

8 References

[AP 83] Associated Press story in Los Angeles Times, 24 August 1983, p. 1. Reported in *Software Engineering Notes* 8, 5, October 1983.

[Baker 72] F. T. Baker. "Chief Programmer Team Management of Production Programming." IBM Systems Journal, 11, 1, 1972, pp. 56-73.

[Barbacci 85] Mario Barbacci, A. Nico Habermann, Mary Shaw. "The Software Engineering Institute: Bridging Practice and Potential." *IEEE Software*, 2, 6, November 1985, pp. 4-21.

[Boehm 81] Barry W. Boehm. Software Engineering Economics. Prentice-Hall, 1981.

[DeRemer 76] Frank DeRemer and Hans H. Kron. "Programming-in-the-Large versus Programming-in-the-Small." *IEEE Transactions on Software Engineering*, 2, 2, June 1976, pp. 80-86.

[Devenney 76] Thomas J. Devenney. *An Exploratory Study of Software Cost Estimating at the Electronic Systems Division.* MS dissertation, Air Force Institute of Technology, July 1976 (approved for public release).

[Dijkstra 68] Edsger Dijkstra. "GOTO Statement Considered Harmful." Communications of the ACM, 11, 3, March 1968, pp. 147-148.

[Fox 83] Joseph M. Fox. *Software and Its Development.* Prentice-Hall, 1983, pp. 187-188. Reported in *Software Engineering Notes* 9, 1, January 1984.

[EIA 80] Electronic Industries Association, Government Division. *DoD Digital Data Processing Study -- a Ten Year Forecast.* 1980.

[Knuth 68] Donald E. Knuth. Fundamental Algorithms. The Art of Computer Programming, Vol. 1, Addison-Wesley 1968.

[Marshall 80] Elliott Marshall. "NRC Takes a Second Look at Reactor Design." Science, 207 (28 March 1980), pp. 1445-48. Reported in *Software Engineering Notes* 10, 3 (July 1985).

[Musa 85] John D. Musa. "Software Engineering: The Future of a Profession." *IEEE Software*, 2, 1, January 1985, pp. 55-62.

[Naur 68] Peter Naur and Brian Randell (eds). Software Engineering. Report on a conference sponsored by the NATO Science Committee, Garmisch, Germany, 7-11 October 1968.

[Parnas 72] David L. Parnas. "On the Criteria for Decomposing Systems into Modules." Communications of the ACM, 15, 12, December 1972, pp. 1053-1058.

[Redwine 84] Samuel T. Redwine, Louise Giovane Becker, Ann B. Marmor-Squires, R. J. Martin, Sarah H. Nash, William E. Riddle. *DoD Related Software Technology Requirements, Practice, and Prospects for the Future.* Institute for Defense Analysis, IDA Paper P-1788, June 1984.

[Shaw 85] Mary Shaw (ed). *The Carnegie-Mellon Curriculum for Undergraduate Computer Science.* Springer-Verlag, 1985.

[Shaw 86] Mary Shaw. "Education for the Future of Software Engineering." *Proc. of Software Engineering Institute Software Engineering Education Workshop*, Springer-Verlag 1986 (to appear).

[Tomayko 85] James Tomayko. Personal communication.

Reuse of Cliches in
The Knowledge-Based Editor

Richard C. Waters

MIT Artificial Intelligence Laboratory
Cambridge MA 02139/USA

The Knowledge-Based Editor in Emacs (KBEmacs) is the current demonstration system implemented as part of the Programmer's Apprentice project. The purpose of the system is to experiment with a number of AI-based programming support capabilities. It is expected that most of these capabilities will appear in one form or another in the programming environments of the future.

The most important of these capabilities is the reuse of cliches — i.e., the reuse of stereotyped algorithms and other pieces of programming knowledge. Using KBEmacs, a programmer can build up a program rapidly and reliably by selecting various standard algorithms and combining them together. Other key features of KBEmacs include a semantic, as opposed to syntactic, representation for programs and support for an assistant-like interaction between the system and the user.

The Programmer's Apprentice project uses the domain of programming as a vehicle for studying (and attempting to duplicate) human problem solving behavior. Recognizing that it will be a long time before it is possible to fully duplicate an expert programmer's abilities, the project is seeking to develop an intelligent assistant system, the Programmer's Apprentice (PA), which will help a programmer in various phases of the programming task. The Knowledge-Based Editor in Emacs (KBEmacs) is an initial step in the direction of the PA.

The programming environments of the future may or may not resemble KBEmacs in detail. However, there are a number of key features supported by KBEmacs which are quite likely to be a part of any advanced programming environment which attempts to apply AI ideas to software engineering.

An Example of Using KBEmacs

In order to give a feeling for the capabilities of KBEmacs, this section presents a condensed summary of the scenario in [Waters 85]. In that scenario, a programmer uses KBEmacs to construct an Ada program in the domain of business data processing. It is assumed that there is a data base which contains information about various machines (referred to as *units*) sold by a company and about the repairs performed on each of these units. In the scenario, the programmer

This work was supported in part by the Advanced Research Projects Agency of the Department of Defense under Office of Naval Research contract N00014-80-C-0505, in part by National Science Foundation grants MCS-7912179 and MCS-8117633, and in part by the International Business Machines Corporation.

constructs a program called UNIT_REPAIR_REPORT which prints out a report of all of the repairs performed on a given unit. The directions in Figure 1 might be given to a human assistant who was asked to write this program.

Define a simple report program UNIT_REPAIR_REPORT.
Enumerate the chain of repairs associated with a unit record, printing each one.
Query the user for the key (UNIT_KEY) of the unit record to start from.
Print the title ("Report of Repairs on Unit " & UNIT_KEY).
Do not print a summary.

Figure 1: Hypothetical directions for a human assistant.

A key feature of these directions is that they refer to a significant amount of knowledge that the assistant is assumed to possess. First, they refer to a number of standard programming algorithms — i.e., "simple report", "enumerating the records in a chain", "querying the user for a key". Second, they assume that the assistant understands the structure of the data base of units and repairs. Another feature of the directions is that, given that the assistant has a precise understanding of the algorithms to be used and of the data base, little is left to the assistant's imagination. Essentially every detail of the algorithm is spelled out, including the exact Ada code to use when printing the title.

The commands shown in Figure 2 can be used to construct the program UNIT_REPAIR_REPORT using KBEmacs. The Ada program which results from these commands is shown in Figure 3.

```
Define a simple_report procedure UNIT_REPAIR_REPORT.
Fill the enumerator with a chain_enumeration of UNITS and REPAIRS.
Fill the main_file_key with a query_user_for_key of UNITS.
Fill the title with ("Report of Repairs on Unit " & UNIT_KEY).
Remove the summary.
```

Figure 2: KBEmacs Commands for constructing UNIT_REPAIR_REPORT.

A key feature of the commands in Figure 2 is that they refer to a number of standard algorithms known to KBEmacs — i.e., "simple_report", "chain_enumeration", and "query_user_for_key". In addition, they assume an understanding of the structure of the data base. The "Fill" commands specify how to fill in the parts of the simple_report algorithm.

Without discussing either the commands or the program produced in any detail, two important observations can be made. First, the commands used are very similar to the hypothetical directions for a human assistant. Second, a set of 5 commands produces a 56 line program. (The program would be even longer if it did not make extensive use of data declarations and functions defined in the packages FUNCTIONS and MAINTENANCE_FILES.)

The KBEmacs commands and the hypothetical directions differ in grammatical form, but not in semantic content. This is not surprising in light of the fact that the hypothesized commands were in actuality created by restating the knowledge-based commands in more free flowing English.

The purpose of this translation was to demonstrate that although the KBEmacs commands

```
with CALENDAR, FUNCTIONS, MAINTENANCE_FILES, TEXT_IO;
use CALENDAR, FUNCTIONS, MAINTENANCE_FILES, TEXT_IO;
procedure UNIT_REPAIR_REPORT is
    use DEFECT_IO, REPAIR_IO, UNIT_IO, INT_IO;
    CURRENT_DATE: constant STRING := FORMAT_DATE(CLOCK);
    DEFECT: DEFECT_TYPE;
    REPAIR: REPAIR_TYPE;
    REPAIR_INDEX: REPAIR_INDEX_TYPE;
    REPORT: TEXT_IO.FILE_TYPE;
    TITLE: STRING(1..33);
    UNIT: UNIT_TYPE;
    UNIT_KEY: UNIT_KEY_TYPE;
    procedure CLEAN_UP is
        begin
            SET_OUTPUT(STANDARD_OUTPUT);
            CLOSE(DEFECTS); CLOSE(REPAIRS); CLOSE(UNITS); CLOSE(REPORT);
        exception
            when STATUS_ERROR => return;
        end CLEAN_UP;
begin
    OPEN(DEFECTS, IN_FILE, DEFECTS_NAME); OPEN(REPAIRS, IN_FILE, REPAIRS_NAME);
    OPEN(UNITS, IN_FILE, UNITS_NAME); CREATE(REPORT, OUT_FILE, "report.txt");
    loop
        begin
            NEW_LINE; PUT("Enter UNIT Key: "); GET(UNIT_KEY);
            READ(UNITS, UNIT, UNIT_KEY);
            exit;
        exception
            when END_ERROR => PUT("Invalid UNIT Key"); NEW_LINE;
        end;
    end loop;
    TITLE := "Report of Repairs on Unit " & UNIT_KEY;
    SET_OUTPUT(REPORT);
    NEW_LINE(4); SET_COL(20); PUT(CURRENT_DATE);
    NEW_LINE(2); SET_COL(13); PUT(TITLE); NEW_LINE(60);
    READ(UNITS, UNIT, UNIT_KEY);
    REPAIR_INDEX := UNIT.REPAIR;
    while not NULL_INDEX(REPAIR_INDEX) loop
        READ(REPAIRS, REPAIR, REPAIR_INDEX);
        if LINE > 64 then
            NEW_PAGE; NEW_LINE; PUT("Page: "); PUT(INTEGER(PAGE-1), 3);
            SET_COL(13); PUT(TITLE); SET_COL(61); PUT(CURRENT_DATE); NEW_LINE(2);
            PUT("   Date       Defect    Description/Comment"); NEW_LINE(2);
        end if;
        READ(DEFECTS, DEFECT, REPAIR.DEFECT);
        PUT(FORMAT_DATE(REPAIR.DATE)); SET_COL(13); PUT(REPAIR.DEFECT);
        SET_COL(20); PUT(DEFECT.NAME); NEW_LINE;
        SET_COL(22); PUT(REPAIR.COMMENT); NEW_LINE;
        REPAIR_INDEX := REPAIR.NEXT;
    end loop;
    CLEAN_UP;
exception
    when DEVICE_ERROR | END_ERROR | NAME_ERROR | STATUS_ERROR =>
        CLEAN_UP; PUT("Data Base Inconsistent");
    when others => CLEAN_UP; raise;
end UNIT_REPAIR_REPORT;
```

Figure 3: The Ada program UNIT_REPAIR_REPORT.

may be syntactically awkward, they are not semantically awkward. The commands are neither redundant nor overly detailed. They specify only the basic design decisions which underly the program. There is no reason to believe that any automatic system (or for that matter a person) could be told how to construct the program UNIT_REPAIR_REPORT without being told at least most of the information in the commands shown.

The leverage that KBEmacs applies to the program construction task is illustrated by the order of magnitude difference between the size of the set of commands and the size of the program. A given programmer seems to be able to produce more or less a constant number of lines of code per day independent of the programming language being used. As a result, there is reason to believe that the order of magnitude size reduction provided by the KBEmacs commands would translate into an order of magnitude reduction in the time required to construct the program. It should be noted that since program construction is only a small part (around 10%) of the programming life cycle, this does not translate into an order of magnitude savings in the life cycle as a whole.

Another important advantage of KBEmacs is that using standard algorithms (such as simple_report and chain_enumeration) enhances the reliability of the programs produced. Since the standard algorithms known to KBEmacs are intended to be used many times, it is economically justifiable to lavish a great deal of time on them in order to ensure that they are general purpose and bug free. This reliability is inherited by the programs which use the standard algorithms.

As an example of reliability enhancement, consider the loop in lines 23 through 41 of Figure 3. It contains all of the code necessary to handle the problem that the user may type in an invalid key causing an error when the UNITS file is read. Similarly, the program as a whole has exception handlers which insure that no matter what happens, all of the files opened by the program will be correctly closed. The key point here is that all of this error handling code was included in the program without the programmer making any explicit reference to this code in his commands (see Figure 2).

The Key Features of KBEmacs

KBEmacs supports three key AI ideas: cliches, the assistant approach, and plans. These ideas define the approach taken and are the basis for the capabilities of the system. In KBEmacs, these ideas are applied to the task of program construction. However, each of the ideas could be profitably applied to almost any programming task.

Cliches

In many ways the most important feature of KBEmacs is its use of cliches. The term *cliche* is used in this paper to refer to a standard method for dealing with a task — e.g., a lemma or partial solution. In normal usage, the word cliche has a pejorative sound which connotes overuse and lack of creativity. However, it is not practical to be creative all of the time. For example, when constructing a program, it is usually better to construct a reasonable program rapidly, than to construct a perfect program slowly.

A cliche consists of a set of *roles* embedded in an underlying *matrix*. The roles represent parts of the cliche which vary from one use of the cliche to the next but which have well defined purposes. The matrix specifies how the roles interact in order to achieve the goal of the cliche as a whole.

Cliches are a generalization of the same basic concept as a subroutine. In this light, roles are parameters, and the matrix corresponds to the code in the subroutine itself. Cliches differ from subroutines in two key ways. First, cliches are much more flexible in what they can represent. For example, the roles are not limited to being filled with data objects (as in the case of simple subroutines) or even limited to data types and functions (as in the case of generic subroutines). In addition to the above, roles can be filled with other algorithmic fragments, logical constraints, and design decisions stating preferences. Similarly, the matrix is not limited to merely containing program code and type constraints. In addition, it can specify arbitrary logical relationships between the roles.

A second key difference between cliches and subroutines is that cliches are intended to be modified when they are used. This makes it possible to make much wider use of a given cliche because it can be used in situations where it is almost right in addition to situations where it is exactly right. Although only a trivial instance of cliche modification (the deletion of the summary role) is shown in the example above, a modification-based approach to using cliches is one of the underlying themes of KBEmacs. More complex examples are discussed in [Waters 85].

As an example of a cliche, consider the cliched algorithm simple_report used in the example above. This cliche enumerates a sequence of items and prints them out.

The cliche simple_report has five main roles. The *title* is printed on a title page and, along with the page number, at the top of each succeeding page of the report. The *enumerator* enumerates some sequence of items. The *print_item* prints out information about each of the enumerated items. The *column-headings* are printed at the top of each page of the report in order to explain the output of the print_item. The *summary* prints out some summary information at the end of the report.

The matrix of the cliche specifies several different kinds of information. First, it specifies pieces of fixed computation which do not vary form one use of the cliche to the next. For example, how to print out a title page including the title, date, and time.

Second, the matrix specifies the control flow and data flow which connect the roles with each other and with the fixed computation. For example, data flow connects the output of the enumerator with the input of the print_item and control flow specifies that the summary will not be printed until all of the enumerated items have been printed.

Third, the matrix specifies various constraints on the roles. For example, the print_item is constrained to contain a computation which is appropriate for printing out the type of item which is enumerated by the enumerator. Similarly, the column_headings are constrained to correspond to the print_item.

When a cliche is used, it is *instantiated* by filling in the roles with computations which are appropriate to the task at hand. This creates an instance of the cliche which is specialized to the task. Figure 2 shows that in order to construct the program UNIT_REPAIR_REPORT, the enumerator of the cliche simple_report is filled in with a chain_enumeration, the title is filled in with the specified title, and the summary is removed. The constraints described above operate to fill in the print_item and column_headings with computation appropriate for printing out repair records. (The role main_file_key is part of the cliche chain_enumeration.)

Given a particular domain, cliches provide a vocabulary of relevant intermediate and high level concepts. Having such a vocabulary is essential for effective reasoning and communication in the context of the domain. It is important to note that this is just as important for human thought as it is for machine-based thought.

Both men and machines are limited in the complexity of the lines of reasoning they can develop and understand. In order to deal with more complex lines of reasoning, intermediate level vocabulary must be introduced which summarizes parts of the line of reasoning. Once this intermediate vocabulary is understood, it can be used to express the full line of reasoning in a sufficiently straightforward way.

Men and machines are similarly limited in the complexity of the descriptions they can communicate. Just as it is in general never practical to reason about something from first principles, it is in general never practical to describe something in full detail from first principles. Effective communication depends on the shared knowledge of an appropriate vocabulary between speaker and listener.

An essential part of the cliche concept is *reuse*. Once something has been thought out (or communicated) and given a name, then it can be reused as a component in future thinking (communication). There is an overhead in that something must be thought out very carefully in order for it to serve as a truly reusable component. However, if successful, this effort can be amortized over many instances of reuse.

A corollary of the cliche idea is that a library of cliches is often the most important part of an AI system. In KBEmacs, a large portion of the knowledge which is shared between man and machine is in the form of a library of algorithmic cliches. This library can be viewed as being a machine understandable definition of the vocabulary programmers use when talking about programs.

At the current time, the cliche library used by KBEmacs contains only a few dozen cliches. A full scale system would have to have a library of at least several hundred cliches. A comprehensive knowledge of programming would probably require several thousand cliches. Figure 4 illustrates the relationships between various cliches. At the bottom are very general low level cliches which are common to most areas of programming. They correspond to the kinds of things taught in introductory computer science courses. Rich has laid out a taxonomy of over two hundred cliches in this area (see [Rich 81]).

Moving higher in figure 4, the ellipses contain cliches which are more specific to particular kinds of programming tasks and which tend to be at higher and higher levels of abstraction. Each such area quite likely has several hundred of its own cliches. As mentioned above, significant effort would have to be applied in order to develop a good set of cliches for any given area. However, reusing these cliches would bring large benefits to any organization which intended to write many different programs in an area.

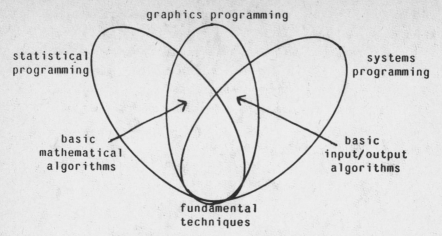

Figure 4: The structure of the cliche library.

Currently, a programmer using KBEmacs has to refer to cliches by name. If there were many hundreds of cliches this would clearly be unsatisfactory. KBEmacs should (and could) have a module which supports intelligent access to the cliche library. Such a module would make it possible to browse through the library and to reference cliches by means of their properties rather than by means of their exact names.

Plans

Selecting an appropriate knowledge representation is the key to applying AI to any task. As a practical matter, the only way to perform a complex (as opposed to merely large) operation is to find a knowledge representation in which the operation can be performed in a relatively straightforward way. To this end, many AI systems make use of the idea of a *plan* — a representation which is abstract in that it deliberately ignores some aspects of a problem in order to make it easier to reason about the remaining aspects of the problem.

To be useful, a knowledge representation must express all of the information relevant to the problem at hand. The plan formalism used by KBEmacs is designed to represent two basic kinds of information: the structure of particular programs and knowledge about cliches. The structure of a program is expressed essentially as a hierarchical flow chart where data flow as well as control flow is represented by explicit arcs.

While plans are hierarchical, KBEmacs does not assume that a program will necessarily be constructed in a top-down manner. Rather, it is assumed that a combination of top-down, bottom-up, and lateral modification will be used. Nevertheless, a hierarchical representation is chosen as a good way to summarize the current state of the program independent of the way it was created.

It is important to note that plans are used to represent both individual programs and the cliches in the cliche library. (In order to represent cliches, plans provide support for representing roles and constraints.) Expressing programs and cliches in the same representation greatly facilitates the use of cliches in program construction.

To be useful, a knowledge representation must also facilitate the operations to be performed. The two key operations performed by KBEmacs are simple reasoning about programs (e.g., determining the source of a data flow) and combining cliches together to create programs. The plan formalism is specifically designed to support these operations. For example, the fact that data flow is expressed by explicit arcs makes it easy to determine the source of a given data flow.

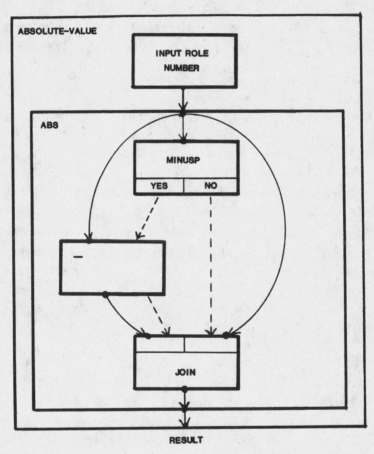

Figure 5: A plan for the cliche absolute-value.

Figure 5 shows a diagram of a simple example plan — the plan for the cliche absolute-value. The basic unit of a plan is a *segment* (drawn as a box in a plan diagram). A segment corresponds to a unit of computation. It has a number of *input ports* and *output ports* which specify the input values it receives and the output values it produces. It has a name which indicates the operation performed. A segment can either correspond to a primitive computation (e.g., the negation segment "-") or contain a subplan which describes the computation performed by the segment (e.g., the segment ABS). All of the computation corresponding to a single program or cliche is grouped together into one outermost segment. The roles of a cliche are represented as specially marked segments (e.g., the segment NUMBER).

As in a flow chart, control flow from one segment to another is represented by an explicit arc from the first segment to the second (drawn as a dashed arrow). Similarly, data flow is represented by an explicit arc from the appropriate output port of the source segment to the appropriate input port of the destination segment (drawn as a solid arrow). It should be noted that like a data flow diagram, and unlike an ordinary flowchart, data flow is the dominant concept in a plan. Control flow arcs are only used where they are absolutely necessary. In Figure 5, control flow arcs are necessary in order to specify that the operation "-" is performed only when the input number is less than zero.

A key feature of the plan formalism is that it abstracts away from the syntactic features of programming languages and represents the semantic features of a program directly. Whenever possible, it eliminates features which stem from the way things must be expressed in a particular programming language, keeping only those features which are essential to the actual algorithm. For example, a plan does not represent data flow in terms of the way it could be implemented in any particular programming language — e.g. with variables, or nesting of expressions, or parameter passing. Rather, it just records what the net data flow is. Similarly, no information is represented about how control flow is implemented.

Abstracting away from the syntactic features of a program has several advantages. One advantage is that it makes the internal operations of KBEmacs substantially programming language independent. Another advantage is that plans are much more canonical than program text. Programs (even in different languages) which differ only in the way their data flow and control flow is implemented correspond to the same plan.

A second important feature of the plan formalism is that it tries to make information as local as possible. For example, each data flow arc represents a specific communication of data from one place to another and, by the definition of what a data flow arc is, the other data flow arcs in the plan cannot have any effect on this. The same is true for control flow arcs. This locality makes it possible to determine what the data flow or control flow is in a particular situation by simply querying a small local portion of the plan.

The key benefit of the locality of data flow and control flow is that it gives plans the property of *additivity*. It is always permissible to put two plans side by side without their being any interference between them. This makes it easy for KBEmacs to create a program by combining the plans for cliches. All KBEmacs has to do is merely paste the pieces together. It does not have to worry about issues like variable name conflicts, because there are no variables.

A third important feature of plans is that the intermediate segmentation breaks a plan up into regions which can be manipulated separately. In order to ensure this separability, the plan formalism is designed so that nothing outside of a segment can depend on anything inside of that segment. For example, all of the data flow between segments outside of an intermediate segment and segments inside of an intermediate segment is channeled through input and output ports attached to the intermediate segment. As a result of this and other restrictions, when modifying the plan inside of a segment one can be secure in the knowledge that these changes cannot effect any of the plan outside of the segment.

One of the most powerful ideas underlying AI systems is the idea of a *representation shift* — shifting from a representation where a problem is easy to state but hard to solve to a representation which may be less obvious but in which the problem is easy to solve. Much of the power of KBEmacs is derived directly from a representation shift from program text to the plan formalism.

The Assistant Approach

When it is not possible to construct a fully automatic system for a task, it is nevertheless often possible to construct a system which can assist an expert in the task. In addition to being pragmatically useful, the assistant approach can lead to important insights into how to construct a fully automatic system.

Figure 6 shows a programmer and an assistant interacting with a programming environment. Though presumably less knowledgeable, the assistant interacts with the tools in the environment (e.g., editors, compilers, debuggers) in the same way as the programmer and is capable of helping the programmer do what needs to be done. It is assumed that the programmer will not be able to delegate all of the work which needs to be done to the assistant and therefore will have to interact with the programming environment directly from time to time in order to do things which the assistant is not capable of doing.

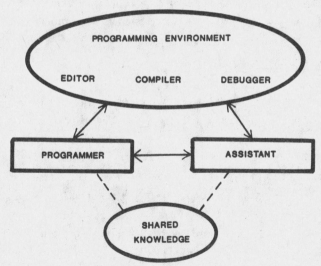

Figure 6: A programming assistant.

The key issue in using an assistant effectively is *division of labor*. Since the programmer is more capable, the programmer will have to make the hard decisions about what should be done and what algorithms should be used. However, much of programming is quite mundane and can easily be done by an assistant. The key to cooperation between the programmer and the assistant is effective two-way communication — whose key in turn is *shared knowledge*. It would be impossibly tedious for the programmer to explain each decision to the assistant from first principles. Rather, the programmer needs to be able to rely on a body of intermediate-level shared knowledge in order to communicate decisions easily.

The discussion in the last two paragraphs applies equally well to human assistants and automated assistants. KBEmacs is intended to interact with a programmer in the same way that a human assistant might. The long range goal of the PA is to create a "chief programmer team" wherein the programmer is the chief and the PA is the team.

An important benefit of the assistant approach is that it is non-intrusive in nature. The assistant is available for the programmer to use, but the programmer is not forced to use it. Note that this contrasts sharply, for example, with program generators which completely take over large parts of the programming task and do not allow the programmer to have any control over them. A key goal of KBEmacs is to provide assistance to the programmer without preventing the programmer from doing simple things in the ordinary way. The intent is for the programmer to use standard programming tools whenever that makes things easy and to use KBEmacs only when doing so delivers real benefits.

A key part of the assistant approach as described above is the assumption that the assistant is significantly less knowledgeable than the programmer. There are situations where one might want an assistant system which was more knowledgeable than the programmer (e.g., a system which assists end users or neophyte programmers). However, KBEmacs does not attack these kinds of problems. The goal of KBEmacs is to make expert programmers super-productive rather than to make bad programmers good.

The Current Status of KBEmacs

The KBEmacs system is the culmination of a multi-year effort which began with the Programmer's Apprentice proposal of Rich and Shrobe [1987]. The goal of this effort has been the production of a running system embodying the ideas discussed above. KBEmacs runs on the Symbolics Lisp Machine. It consists of 40,000 lines of Zetalisp [1984] code.

Figure 7 shows an architectural diagram for the system. KBEmacs maintains two representations for a program: program text and a plan. At any moment, the programmer can either directly modify the program text with a text editor or request that KBEmacs make a change to the plan by issuing a command to the knowledge-based editor phrased in terms of algorithmic cliches. An interface unifies these two modification modes so that they can both be conveniently accessed through a standard Emacs-style text editor. The analyzer is used to create a new plan whenever the program text is changed. The coder module is used to create new program text whenever the plan is changed.

The major value of KBEmacs stems from the fact that it has a knowledge base of algorithmic cliches and a significant amount of knowledge about how to combine them. The cliches

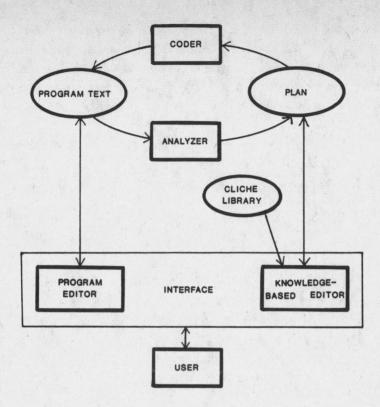

Figure 7: The Architecture of KBEmacs.

themselves are represented declaratively as plans in the cliche library. Much of the knowledge about how cliches should be combined is also represented declaratively in the form of constraints attached to the cliches in the library. A simple constraint propagation system in the knowledge-based editor module interprets these constraints. The knowledge-based editor module also contains special purpose procedures which perform the actual work of physically combining a cliche into the evolving plan for a program.

A user can build up a program rapidly and reliably by selecting various algorithms to use and delegating to the system the task of combining them together to construct a program. However, the system is non-intrusive because the user can fall back on ordinary text editing at any time.

KBEmacs is a research experiment. Rapid prototyping and rapid evolution have been the only goals of the current implementation. As a result, it is hardly surprising that KBEmacs is neither fast enough, robust enough, nor complete enough to be used as a practical tool. Due to these limitations, KBEmacs has not been used in actual programming situations, but rather only to illustrate that significant productivity gains are in fact possible.

General Purpose Automated Deduction

It has been decided that research in the Programmer's Apprentice group will focus on extending the fundamental power of KBEmacs rather than on remedying its pragmatic defects. The most important fundamental limitation of KBEmacs is that it does not contain a general purpose reasoning module. As a result, the system has very little ability to check that what the user is doing is reasonable. A second problem is that, other than support for simple constraints, KBEmacs can do little to reason about how additional design decisions follow from design decisions specified by the user.

Work has already begun on an extended system which will support all of the features of KBEmacs and which adds support for general purpose automated deduction (see [Rich 85]). This system will be able to check many aspects of a programmer's design. In addition it will be able to reason in a general way about what cliches should be used where. This will allow for a greater productivity enhancement while ameliorating the problem of selecting appropriate cliches from a large library.

Other Approaches To Improving Programmer Productivity

The greatest increase in programmer productivity to date has been brought about by the introduction of general purpose high level languages. A logical next step would be the introduction of a general purpose very high level language. The goal is to provide a further reduction in the size of program code by allowing a number of middle level details (e.g., data structure selection) to go unstated. Unfortunately, such languages have proven very difficult to compile.

The most important thing to say about the relationship between KBEmacs and general purpose very high level languages is that there is no competition between the approaches. Rather, they are mutually reinforcing. As soon as a general purpose very high level language is developed, it can be used as the target language of KBEmacs. The net productivity gain will be the product of the gains due to the language and due to KBEmacs. The basic claim here is that no matter how high level a language is, there will be cliches in the way it is used and therefore KBEmacs can be usefully applied to it.

Much of the work on innovative software tools can be looked as approaching the problem of supporting very high level languages from one direction or another. Of this work, two areas stand out: program generators and transformational implementation systems.

A program generator is, in essence, a compiler for a special purpose very high level language. When it is possible, using a program generator is more convenient than using KBEmacs. However, program generators are only applicable in certain narrow domains. Even a tiny bit outside of its scope, a typical program generator is nearly useless.

In contrast to a program generator, KBEmacs has a wide range of applicability. The prime domain of applicability of KBEmacs is defined by the contents of the cliche library. Within this prime domain, KBEmacs is somewhat similar to a program generator though its interface is very different. Beyond the edge of its prime domain of applicability, KBEmacs is very different from a program generator. It continues to be useful because the programmer can freely intermix cliched and non-cliched computation.

It should be noted that like KBEmacs, the heart of a program generator is knowledge of the cliched aspects of a class of programs. (Program generators are less flexible than KBEmacs in large part due to the fact that this knowledge is usually represented procedurally rather than declaratively.) Recent research on program generators (e.g., the work on PHI-nix [Barstow 84] and Draco [Neighbors 84]) is converging closer to the approach taken by KBEmacs in that it focuses on the idea that knowledge is the key and on ways to represent this knowledge more declaratively.

The predominant approach to supporting general purpose very high level languages is to use correctness preserving transformations to convert a program expressed in a very high level language into a low level executable form. See for example, the work on the languages Gist [Balzer 81] and V [Green & Westfold 82]. Neither of these systems is complete. However, they hold the promise of eventually supporting truly general purpose very high level languages.

As usually implemented, transformations have three parts. They have a pattern which matches against a section of program text (or parse tree) in order to determine where to apply the transformation. They have a set of applicability conditions which further restrict the places where the transformation can be applied. Finally, they have a (usually procedural) action which creates the new program section based on the old section.

The key difficulty in any transformational implementation system is deciding what transformation to use when. A key focus of much of the research on transformations has been attempting to automate the transformation selection process [Fickas 85]. However, in the interim, many transformational systems follow the assistant approach and rely on user guidance as to which transformations to use (see [Wile 83]).

In their essential knowledge content, transformations are quite similar to KBEmacs' cliches. However, cliches are used differently. Instead of applying correctness preserving transformations to a complete high level description of a program, the user of KBEmacs builds a program essentially from thin air by applying non-correctness preserving transformations. This supports an evolutionary model of programming wherein key decisions about what a program is going to do can be deferred to a later time as opposed to a model where only lower level implementation decisions can be deferred.

A more important difference between cliches and transformations is that cliches operate in the domain of plans rather than program text or parse trees. This raises the level at which knowledge is specified from the syntactic to the semantic. In addition, cliches are completely declarative whereas the action of a transformation is typically procedurally specified.

In conclusion, it can be seen that the basic idea of reusing cliched knowledge is at the heart of all the major approaches to software tools. There is considerable disagreement about how these cliches can best be represented and used to help a programmer. However, there is little disagreement that the knowledge they embody is essential to any advanced software tool.

Acknowledgments

KBEmacs is the result of a group effort which began with the original Programmer's Apprentice proposal of Charles Rich and Howard Shrobe. Over the years, many other people have contributed to that effort. Gerald Sussman has been an inspiration and mentor for us all. Kent Pitman implemented the user interface for KBEmacs and assisted with many other aspects of the system. Daniel Brotsky, David Chapman, David Cyphers Roger Duffey, Gregory Faust, Daniel Shapiro, Peter Sterpe, and Linda Zelinka contributed ideas to KBEmacs while working on related parts of the Programmer's Apprentice project. Special thanks are due Crisse Ciro for her assistance with the illustrations and Roger Racine (of the C.S. Draper Laboratory) for his assistance with regard to Ada.

References

R. Balzer, "Transformational Implementation: An Example", IEEE Transactions on Software Engineering V7 #1, 3-13, January 1981.

D. Barstow, "A Perspective on Automatic Programming", AI Magazine, V5 #1, 5-27, Spring 1984.

S. Fickas, "Automating the Transformational Development of Software", IEEE Transactions on Software Engineering V11 #11, 1268-1277, November 1985.

C. Green and S. Westfold, "Knowledge-Based Programming Self-Applied", Machine Intelligence 10, J. Hayes, D. Mitchie, and Y. Pao eds., Wiley, 339-359, 1982.

J. Neighbors, "The Draco Approach to Constructing Software from Reusable Components", IEEE Transactions on Software Engineering V10 #5, 564-573, September 1984.

C. Rich, "A Formal Representation for Plans in the Programmer's Apprentice", 7th IJCAI, 1044-1052, August 1981.

C. Rich, "The Layered Architecture of a System for Reasoning about Programs", 9th IJCAI, 540-546, August 1985.

C. Rich and H. Shrobe, "Initial Report on a Lisp Programmer's Apprentice", IEEE Transactions on Software Engineering V4 #6, 456-466, November 1978.

R. Waters, "The Programmers Apprentice: A Session with KBEmacs" IEEE Transactions on Software Engineering V11 #11, 1296-1320, November 1985.

D. Wile, "Program Developments: Formal Explanations of Implementations", Communications of the ACM V26 #11, 902-911, November 1983.

Zetalisp, Lisp Machine documentation (release 4), Cambridge MA, Symbolics Inc., 1984.

Organizing Programming Knowledge

into

Syntax-Directed Experts

David S. Wile

USC/Information Sciences Institute

4676 Admiralty Way

Marina del Rey, CA 90292

USA[1]

Programming environments of the future are certain to be "knowledge-based." Succinct statements of expertise, currently applied implicitly by programmers, will be available for explicit application by future programmers as well as opportunistic application by the environment itself. Considerable tension will exist between the desire to represent knowledge in a flat, decomposed form, and the desire for the efficiency available in compiled representations of this knowledge, as used in automatic processors, such as compilers, simplifiers, and code analyzers. I advocate specifying programming knowledge uniformly but organizing the knowledge into experts which solve "syntax-directed" problems, problems whose solution decomposition resembles the structure of the input data itself. This organization allows the efficiency of current ad hoc representations to be obtained and the resulting experts can coexist--in fact, cooperate--with more sophisticated problem solvers, including people.

1. Syntax-Directed Tasks in Program Synthesis and Optimization

For several years our group [Balzer 85] has been developing the technology necessary to support the design and implementation of program specifications through the use of correctness-preserving transformations. Such transformations constitute succinct encapsulations of programming knowledge. Our experience with transformational implementation has shown us that considerable automatic support will be necessary to make large program developments feasible.

The nature of this automatic support is problematical. On the one hand, we would like each bit of programming knowledge to be represented as a nice, pat, isolated encapsulation, so that the person guiding the transformation process can use it simply. On the other hand, we would like each bit of knowledge to be **integrated** into all of the automatic tools which could use it. Stated this way, it is clear that the transformations act as **specifications** of programming knowledge. Automatic tools such as compilers are **implementations** of some of that programming knowledge.

---

[1]The research reported herein was funded by the National Science Foundation, under contract number MCS-7918792, and by the Defense Advanced Research Projects Agency of the United States government, under contract number MDA903 81 C 0335.

Compartmentalizing knowledge into groups of rules constituting expertise has been proposed in the expert system literature [McDermott 83]. At an abstract level, one can treat program transformations as knowledge sources and seek organizing principles for compiled expertise. As in expert systems, program transformations should be organized into larger "experts" that are characterized by the goals they achieve in the programming environment, such as to produce a side-effect-free version of some procedural program or to produce an analysis of data flow structure. It is worth emphasizing that the original transformations must not be lost in this process of compilation and organization, for they indeed act as specifications for these experts. A single transformation could be incorporated into several experts.

Furthermore, to organize the knowledge within experts, the concept of a **syntax-directed** task is useful for partitioning the goals which must be achieved before a transformation can be applied. Generally, a transformation will be enabled by both semantic goals, e.g., "side-effect-free", and syntactic goals, e.g., "conditional-expression with no else clause". A syntax-directed task is one in which the abstract syntactic structure of an input directs the goal structure of the tool performing the task. By splitting out the syntactic goals, many existing tools used to support programming environments can be viewed as experts compiled from groups of transformations.

Both views of syntax-directed experts are enlightening: as codification and decompilation of existing syntax-directed tools, or as organization and compilation of transformations into larger chunks of expertise. A major goal here is to present a unified view of the manipulations in programming environments, from transformations to compilers.

1.1. Decompilation of Existing Syntax-Directed Experts

Generally, many tools needed in programming environments to support program specification, analysis, and transformation may be characterized as syntax-directed. The control structure of the tool follows the syntactic structure of the data. There is a wide spectrum of such tasks:

- Symbol table construction

- Type checking

- Program simplification

- Program translation

- Program conditioning[2]

- Transformation

- Optimization

Syntax-directed facilities to help produce such tools have been built into our (syntactic) programming environment generator Popart [Wile 81]. Our initial facility, called "tables," was an "action routine" mechanism [Kaiser 84] whereby users can specify tables of rules whose left-hand sides are (abstract syntactic) patterns in the language of interest. The right hand sides are simply Lisp code, but references to variables bound in the left hand side pattern are supported. The variables are bound to the abstract syntax tree representation that they match. In addition, macros are provided for use in the Lisp code to facilitate recursive mapping of the tables onto lists of arguments. The tables are explicitly called as functions, rather than invoked in a goal-directed manner.

A more sophisticated mechanism has been provided recently, in which different languages may be used on the left and right hand sides of rules. With this "translator" mechanism, one registers the set of nonterminals from which a translator can translate and the set of nonterminals into which it can translate. Each translator is available to a problem solver when particular expressions are to be translated. Implicit in this problem solver is a subgoaling mechanism which causes subexpressions of the left-hand side patterns to be translated to fit the slots of the right hand side patterns in which they occur. For example, to translate Algol's "$a+$b" into Lisp the mechanism must first translate "$a" and "$b" into Lisp arithmetic expressions, "&$a" and "&$b," respectively, before substituting in the right hand side, "(PLUS &$a &$b)." Such automatic translation has been termed "targeted homomorphisms" from the algebraic construct they resemble [Wile 86].

These represent two points in a spectrum of table-like problem solvers. If we consider the tables to be computing some result, F, on input tree, t, the spectrum can be characterized abstractly:

- Action routines (present tables):
  * simply compute F(t).

- Transformers (present tables with recursive pattern construction on right hand sides and present translators with same left and right languages):

---

[2]A term we use to mean transform a program into a form which matches a particular pattern; e.g., conditioning "(OR A B)" to match "(COND x y)" might produce "(COND (A) (T B))".

* computes $F(t)$ where $lang(t) = lang(F(t))$.

- Homomorphisms (single translator from L_1 into L_2):
  * computes $F(G(x,y)) = F(G) (F(x), F(y))$,
  * where $lang(G) = L_1$, $lang(F(G))=L_2$.

- Nested homomorphisms (heirarchy of translators from L_1 into L_2):
  * computes $F(G(x,y)) = F(G) (F'(x), F''(y))$,
  * where $lang(G) = L_1$, $lang(F(G))=L_2$,
  * and F', F'' are at most a restriction of F.

- Targeted homomorphisms (multiple translators, possibly multiple languages, L_i, related by problem solving engine):
  * computes $F(G(x,y))= F(G)(\&(x,F(G),1),\&(y,F(G),2))$,
  * where & computes the translation of x and y based on the
  * context of its use in $F(G)$.

Experience with the facilities above--the tables and translators--has led to a synthesis. A generalization of these mechanisms which supports the spectrum of solution strategies mentioned above is sketched below. Its most important features are:

- Syntax-directed knowledge can be represented uniformly despite considerable variation in the generality of the problem solving mechanism it is incorporated into; i.e., experts differ primarily in control flow (backtracking), not in their apparent structure.

- The constrained context represented by an expert's goals and input/output characterization allows more concise expression of expertise as well as opening up the potential for further compilation through automatic analysis of the experts themselves.

Before describing the mechanism, the abstract characterization of the problem begun above is continued, in which syntax-directed experts evolve from a flat, transformation-oriented knowledge base.

1.2. Aggregation of Transformations into Syntax-Directed Experts

At the opposite end of the spectrum from the highly specialized syntax-directed tools present in programming environments is the representation of programming knowledge as a large, monolithic set of program transformations, viz.,

$\{ L_i ==> R_i \}$.

In his Ph.D. dissertation Fickas [Fickas 85] used such a representation and treated program transformation as an expert-system task. A particularly useful feature of this representation was the explicit recognition and identification of the goals being achieved in the transformation task. For example[3], one rule might encapsulate the following knowledge:

- If the goal is to translate "a+b" from Algol into Lisp, first translate "a" and "b" from Algol to Lisp, then apply "PLUS" to those translations.

A little more formally,

$Algol\text{-}to\text{-}Lisp(In\text{-}Algol("\$a"),In\text{-}Lisp("\$AA"))$
and
$Algol\text{-}to\text{-}Lisp(In\text{-}Algol("\$b"),In\text{-}Lisp("\$BB"))$
$=>$
$Algol\text{-}to\text{-}Lisp(In\text{-}Algol("\$a+\$b"),In\text{-}Lisp("(PLUS \$AA \$BB"))$

Similarly, a bit of simplification knowledge, that "a+b" reduces to "$b" if "$a" reduces to 0:

$Reduces\text{-}To(In\text{-}Algol("\$a"),In\text{-}Algol("0"))$
$=>$
$Reduces\text{-}To(In\text{-}Algol("\$a+\$b"),In\text{-}Algol("\$b"))$

The clumsiness of the above leads us to group expertise by the common subgoals which they achieve. Here, groupings for Algol-to-Lisp and Reduces-To are suggested.

Grouping of knowledge sources has been recognized as an effective technique in expert systems [McDermott 83]. In those examined by McDermott, systems go through phases where one set of rules becomes active; it transforms the problem, then another set becomes active, etc. The knowledge there is referred to as "thin." Here, the control is quite different, for the groups (experts) will be activated in a recursive descent (depth first) fashion. The programming domain is a quite "thick" domain in terms of levels of representations of knowledge. Indeed, the syntax-directed experts are an attempt to compartmentalize the knowledge in the programming environment.

Another effort treating expert systems as **compilations** using knowledge-sources as specifications of expertise is Swartout's Explainable Expert Systems project [Neches, et. al 85]. He views the compilation process as an automatic process. Its record is later used to explain the compiled system's behavior. Because the goal of an expert system is so singular, his work does not relate very directly to compiling knowledge for several purposes, as needed in programming environments. In addition, the programming domain already identifies several target areas to compile toward, namely, the syntax-directed tasks identified above; expert system generators must discover such areas for each domain.

---

[3]Fickas' representation is not used here in its full generality.

The goals above--In-Algol and In-Lisp--are simple **syntactic** goals. There will be other more semantic goals, such as "side-effect-free", "contains-no-free-variables", "contains-no-bound-occurrences", "reduces-to", etc. We can take advantage of the grouping by allowing these syntactic goals to be separated out and made context sensitive to the expert in which the goals are achieved. Hence, we arrive at the following schema for characterizing a single, syntax-directed expert:

$F(tree,I,O,G)=$
$P_1(tree)=>$ *if exist* r_j *s.t.* $g_{1j}(d_{1,j}(tree),r_j)$
      then $C_1(r_1,...,r_{k_1})$;
$P_2(tree)=>$ *if exist* r_j *s.t.* $g_{2j}(d_{2,j}(tree),r_j)$
      then $C_2(r_2,...,r_{k_2})$;

...

$P_n(tree)=>$ *if exist* r_j *s.t.* $g_{nj}(d_{n,j}(tree),r_j)$
      then $C_n(r_n,...,r_{k_n})$;

An argument, tree, is passed to a generator, F, which dispatches to a subgoaling mechanism, if I(tree) holds. The input characterization predicate, I, was not distinguished in the examples above, but it could filter the applicability of the rule left hand sides or even heuristic information on when the expert's actions were desirable. The function is defined by a set of rules. Each rule's left-hand-side pattern, P_i, characterizes the syntactic situation in which the rule is applicable, binding components of the argument, tree, via decomposition functions, $d_{i,j}$. The right hand sides usually require subgoals be achieved on the components of the tree, g_{ij}. Then a composition function, C_i, constructs the result satisfying G(tree,result). The generator guarantees that its results will satisfy the output characterization predicate, O(result).

Notice that I and O can be used to establish the context for interpreting the patterns, P, and constructors, C. It is also important to mention that the subgoals, g_{ij}, need not be syntax-directed goals, but may be the semantic goals mentioned above.

For example, a portion of an Algol to Lisp expert:

```
Arith(tree,AlgolFactor,LispArithmetic,Algol-to-Lisp)=
  !a + !b => (PLUS &!a &!b);
  !c * !d => (TIMES &!c &!d);
  . . .
```

has the correpondences:

$$P_2 = \text{"!c * !d"} \qquad\qquad d_{2,1} = \text{"!c"} \qquad\qquad d_{2,2} = \text{"!d"}$$
$$r_1 = \text{"\&!c"} \qquad\qquad r_2 = \text{"\&!d"}$$

$$g_{2,1} = g_{2,2} = \text{Algol-to-Lisp}$$
$$C_2(r_1, r_2) = \text{"(TIMES \&!c \&!d)"}$$

A system providing syntax-directed facilities is described below wherein the generating functions, F, are registered with a centralized problem solving engine for choosing among those which can achieve the same goals, G. We presume, in general, that backtracking can proceed through the rule set itself, the patterns of the rules, and the search implied by the existential quantification. More restricted versions of these experts can be used for particular linguistic purposes (translation, simplification) and for less ambitious heuristic purposes (algorithms).

2. Declarations of Syntax-Directed Experts

The following general mechanism provides a way of registering these goals and functions, forcing the user to provide the backtracking and subgoal generation mechanisms. Further refinements of the experts which facilitate their concise expression are proposed in the next section. The definition mechanism is intended to work within Common Lisp.

defexpert(name,pattern-characterization, result-characterization,
      goal-achieved,
      match-generator, subgoal-generator,
      (left-hand-side, subgoal-bindings, right-hand-side),
      (left-hand-side, subgoal-bindings, right-hand-side) ...)

causes a table of rules to be defined. When **Solve** invokes this table on **tree** the following behavior is generated[4]:

```
choose rule || rules(name):
    choose match || match-generator(left-hand-side(rule),tree):
        choose subgoal-set ||
                subgoal-set-generator(subgoal-bindings(rule),
                                            match):
            choose solution || Solve(subgoal-set):
                    generate right-hand-side(rule)(solution)
```

The choices are made in a backtracking environment, as mentioned above. In addition, the **Solve** (backtracking) generator recursively invokes expert generators.

This mimics the abstraction above, with the index, **i**, corresponding to the rule generator; P_i

---

[4] I am using *choose* <name> || <generator> : <body> to mean establish a backtracking context around the choices generated by <generator>, bind <name> to the successive choices, and invoke <body> on it; <body> uses <name> freely.

corresponds to the pattern match generator for rule i; g_i are from the subgoal-set-generator, and the C_i are the right-hand-sides.

To understand further connections with the abstraction, it is necessary to describe the generator mechanism in some detail. Each generator is characterized by five functions:

- IS initial state: may be a function of several arguments.

- NS next state: function of current state only.

- TS terminated state predicate: function of current state only.

- DS decode state: function of current state, result is what is "generated."

- LS last state predicate: $\lambda s.LS(s) => TS(NS(s))$[5]; it is used for efficiency only. If it is identically true, only IS need be specified.).

One thinks of the generator as producing a sequence of elements, decoded from successive states by the DS function. Its internal workings are summarized by the first three functions: an initial state is formed, successive next states are pulsed until the terminal state predicate applies. It should be obvious that the product generator, ":," can be described as a generator function of its two input generators, exhausting the right hand side generator for each pulse of the left hand side.

The pattern match generator IS function must take the left hand side of a rule as its input and generate all matches with the table input parameter, **tree**. Its decoding function DS encodes the appropriate information for the subgoal set generator IS function; i.e., it provides the $d_{i,j}$. The subgoal set generator, in turn, generates as its DS function's result, a set of subgoals for solve; the $g_{i,j}$. Solve then returns a set of results satisfying the subgoals in a form suitable for combination by the right-hand-side of the rule.

Of course, the problem solving activity actually occurs in scheduling the appropriate experts to attack the syntactic unit. The pattern-characterization and goal-achieved predicates are used by the problem solving mechanism, **Solve**, for this purpose. Because the mechanism works across all experts, the results of these characterizing functions must produce inputs to guide the overall backtracking mechanism. The input to the Solve generator is a set of result requests for particular **subtrees** $(d_{i,j})$, characterized by some **input-characterization** predicates, to be turned into results satisfying **goal-to-achieve** predicates $(g_{i,j})$. Each pulse of the Solve generator will return a set of associations of results with inputs such that the subtree

---

[5]LS is optional (treated as identically false when ommitted

has been transformed into a value with the desired result characterization.

Experts are partial, in general. The expert merely promises that for **some** inputs characterized by its input-characterization function, it can produce a result which will always satisfy its result-characterization function, and which is in the goal-achieved relation with its input.

The current version of the Solve generator is described below. (It is likely to be refined over time as we gain more practical experience with the mechanisms.)

```
Solve(subgoal-set)=
  choose subgoal || subgoal-set:
    Solve'(subtrees(subgoal),
         input-characterization(subgoal),
         goal-to-achieve(subgoal))

Solve'(t,c,r)=
  choose expert || Experts:
    if c implies pattern-characterization(expert)
       and
         goal-achieved(expert) implies r
    then generate apply(expert,t)
```

Notice that Solve' finds experts whose goals are at least as refined as result, r, and whose inputs are characterized as at least as general as the characterization, c. It will be important to allow Solve' to choose experts which are not necessarily syntax-directed, to achieve the semantic subgoals mentioned above. This is the integration point where the semantic goals and syntactic goals are handled uniformly.

Although the attempted experts are generated in a random order above, the existing scheme actually generates experts by going from the most specific to the least specific. This is accomplished through the use of a classification scheme for results maintained in a type lattice, when the goals can be characterized syntactically in terms of the result-characterization predicate rather than the more general goal-achieved predicate. Furthermore, the finest input characterization would be generated first for the same output goal results. In general, theorem proving in the characterization space would be required for this optimization activity. It is not clear how far the mechanism must be extended in this direction to achieve practicality.

3. Refinement of Expertise

This is indeed, a general framework for syntax-directed problem solving. Less general versions may be obtained, in which specific contexts for pattern matching are established, and in which some backtracking is eliminated. This allows more concise expression of those experts, taking advantage of the additional context. More important, it allows more efficient application of expertise to syntax-directed problem solving.

3.1. Curtailing Backtracking

- An interesting case is when the generator for the rule set has as LS, the match of any lhs for the rule--i.e., whenever a rule matches, no subsequent rule could cause the expert to succeed. This type of expert needs no backtracking in the rule choices. We'll call such an expert *short-sighted*[6].

- Another interesting case involves patterns which must match uniquely or not at all. We'll call a rule with such a pattern, *simple*. An expert, all of whose rules are simple will also be called *simple*. Notice, it is not necessary for a simplistic expert to be short-sighted. (In fact, by building the rule sequence intelligently, simple non-short-sighted experts may be more efficient, i.e., expert.)

- A third curtailment of backtracking is possible in the acceptance and generation of subgoal sets. A rule that only generates a single subgoal set **for each match of its pattern** will be called *easy*. An expert whose rules are all easy will be called *easy*.

The net effect of specifying the above types of refinement is to eliminate each of the **choose** statements invoked by the **Solve** generator for an expert. Keywords can be added to the expert declaration function above to indicate the first three of these, curtailing backtracking appropriately.

None of the above refinements eliminates backtracking in the Solve generator. Curtailment of such backtracking must come from classification of the interactions between *groups* of experts. Perhaps whole groups should also be classified as short-sighted, simple and easy.

3.2. Linguistic Refinements

A different axis of refinement has to do with the languages used to express the rule left and right sides, and their relationships with the subgoal-variables.

- *Monolingual* experts are those whose left and right hand sides are simply patterns in a particular language.

- An interesting subclass of monolingual experts are *syntactic* experts: they require no subgoaling other than matching patterns and replacing them with their

---

[6]Perhaps it would be more accurate to accuse such an expert of "tunnel vision."

constituent variables in the right hand sides[7].

- Another interesting class of monolingual experts are *canonical* experts: they apply themselves to subtrees before substitution in right hand sides.

- *Translation* experts are characterized by distinct languages on the left and right sides of rules. Except when shared variables are in the same language these experts require subgoaling to transform their pattern variables into the language used to express the right hand sides[8]. Hence, they cannot be purely syntactic experts.

- Sets of these experts will be referred to as *targeted homomorphisms* for they behave as homomorphisms when sufficiently constrained as to the applicability of patterns.

Each of these can be supported syntactically. The Algol example described above, (a syntactic expert) is supported nearly as presented. Below a monolingual, non-syntactic, non-canonical expert is presented, with indications of what syntactic support for its expression would be desirable.

3.3. Sketch of a Real-World Example

The following example is derived from the simplifiers written for the Bliss compilers [Wulf 75]. They had a modicum of problem solving activity despite their non-AI nature. I believe the expert mechanism proposed herein generalizes their activity quite nicely.

The essential idea was to pass along a "target" with the expression being simplified. This target was used to indicate a preference for the format of the result desired from the simplification of the expression. Here, the targets become the $g_{i,j}$s--that is, they are generated by the subgoal-set-generators. A brief section on the logical expression simplifier should serve to illustrate the idea:

```
defmonolingual-expert(simplify-logical-expression,
                input-characterization=Boolean,
                result-characterization=Boolean,
                goal-achieved=SimplifiedBoolean,
                expert-qualifications={simple, easy},
[1]  not !Boolean
     if !Boolean = not !Boolean'
       => %!Boolean';
[2]  not !Boolean
       => not %!Boolean;
[3]  !Boolean and !Boolean2
```

---

[7]Intutitively, syntactic experts are similar to outside-in macro expanders, whereas monolingual experts in general may have a recursive subgoaling process applied before their right hand sides are constructed, as in an expression simplifier or canonicalizer.

[8]As in the Algol to Lisp example above.

if !Boolean = *not* !Boolean' *and* !Boolean2 = *not* !Boolean2'
   => *not* (%!Boolean' *or* %!Boolean2');
[4] !Boolean *or* !Boolean2
   if !Boolean = *not* !Boolean' *and* !Boolean2 = *not* !Boolean2'
   => *not* (%!Boolean' *and* %!Boolean2')
[5] *not* (!Boolean *and* !Boolean2)
   if !Boolean = *not* !Boolean' *and* !Boolean2 = *not* !Boolean2'
   => %!Boolean' *or* %!Boolean2';
[6] *not* (!Boolean *or* !Boolean2)
   if !Boolean = *not* !Boolean' *and* !Boolean2 = *not* !Boolean2'
   => %!Boolean' *and* %!Boolean2';
[7] !Boolean *and* !Boolean2
   => %!Boolean *and* %!Boolean2;
[8] !Boolean *or* !Boolean2
   => %!Boolean *or* %!Boolean2
[9] !Boolean *and* !Boolean2
   if %!Boolean = !Boolean3 *and* %!Boolean2 = !Boolean3
   => !Boolean3
   ...)

Extensive syntactic liberties have been taken here to communicate the essence of the expert. The notation here assumes a pattern is matched, the goals after the *if* are achieved, and then the right hand side is a valid simplification. The pattern variables are indicated with exclamation points. A percent sign indicates that the recursive simplification goal should be achieved. For example:

  not !Boolean
   if SimplifiedBoolean(!Boolean,!Boolean')
   => *not* !Boolean';

is represented simply as:

  not !Boolean
   => *not* %!Boolean

Notice how this works. If the expression

(*not* (*not* a *or* *not* b) *and* *not* (c *and* *not* d))

were input, the outermost "*and*" would cause the DeMorgan branch [3] to match, producing subgoals:

1. *not* !Boolean' = !Boolean = *not* (*not* a *or* *not* b)
2. *not* !Boolean2' = !Boolean2 = *not* (c *and* *not* d)

These are satisfied via:

1. !Boolean' = *not* a *or* *not* b
2. !Boolean2' = c *and* *not* d

Then the recursive simplification subgoal, SimplifiedBoolean, will be tried (via %), invoking:

3. simplify-logical-expression(*not* a *or not* b)
4. simplify-logical-expression(c *and not* d)

The first of these will simplify via [4] to

3. *not* (a *and* b)

While the second would reduce only if the rule:

!Boolean => *not not* !Boolean

were present. Assume no such constructive rules are present in this expert.

Hence, the back substitution will produce:

not (*not* (a *and* b) *or* (c *and not* d))

This may not be as simple as desired, but notice that another path--[7],[1],[4]--will generate

((a *and* b) *and not* (c *and not* d))

I am encouraged by the submission of this example to the mechanism. Several interesting issues arise which must be examined in the future:

- Should the expert actually be *easy* or would it be best to try all possible ways of achieving the target expression format?

- Is there any ordering mechanism which would produce the more reduced solution first? (Success at this would almost certainly allow the expert to be easy.)

- Can the efficiency of the mechanism approach that of the built in functions used in the original Bliss development?

4. Related Work

The present effort has been pursued in the context of automatic programming and program transformation. Many threads from programming environments support the current research, including action routines [Kaiser 84], attribute grammars [Reps 82], and compiler construction [Wulf 75]. Generally, these facilities are subcases of the general mechanism proposed, with the exception of optimizing compiler facilities, whose problem solving prowess is not succinctly expressed.

More directly related are the efforts in program transformation, particularly that of Fickas [Fickas 85]. His thesis reformulated the entire program transformation activity as an AI problem solving activity. Transformations became "methods" to solve goals. These goals were generated as enabling conditions of other transformations. Although this view of the transformation activity is important, it loses the syntax-directed nature of the transformation activity, and is hence, overly general for the normal case. It is certainly the case that understanding how syntax-directedness meshes with the user-directed transformation process is the major research issue now facing us [Wile 83].

5. Current Status and Future Directions

The "tables" and "translators" mentioned above have been implemented. Successful experimentation with them in producing a code analyzer, symbol table, type checker, and portions of two compilers, have led to the more generalized syntax-directed experts proposed here. The fully general experts have not been implemented, but the type lattice-directed translator invocation scheme has. Problems with the fully general scheme are predictable. In particular, the following open issues will require attention before all of our aspirations for these experts can be met:

- Organizing principles for groups of experts must be sought. How much interference can be eliminated by using the higher level concepts of easiness and simplicity for groups of experts?

- Hopefully, intelligent backtracking facilities can be developed in this context. There is considerably more context in these experts available to preanalysis of their interactions. Is the information available enough to curtail subsequent bad paths?

- Although attribute grammars are less general (since they are algorithmic rather than generative), they have the pleasing property that they are incrementally recomputable. The experts are not, but have the potential for analysis for incremental recomputability--much more so than the flat, transformation-rule-set knowledge-base has.

Of course, the interaction of syntax-directedness with user initiative and other more global problem solving schemes will be a major research issue in our study of the transformational implementation process.

Acknowledgements

Many of these ideas have evolved from discussions in our software specification group, headed by Bob Balzer, and including Don Cohen, Martin Feather, Neil Goldman, Lewis Johnson, Bill Swartout, and Kai Yue. The original syntax-directed facilities were invented by Neil Goldman and Phil London, and extended by Lewis Johnson and myself. Special thanks to Dennis Allard and Neil Goldman for critical reading of drafts of this paper.

References

[Balzer 85] Balzer, R., "A 15 Year Perspective on Automatic Programming," *IEEE Transactions on Software Engineering* SE-11, (11), November 1985, 1257-1268.

[Fickas 85] Fickas, S., "Automating the Transformational Development of Software," *IEEE Transactions on Software Engineering* SE-11, (11), November 1985, 1268-1277.

[Kaiser 84] Kaiser, G., *IE: An Implementor's Environment for Developing Language-Oriented Editors*, Ph.D. thesis, Carnegie-Mellon University, Computer Science Department, 1984.

[McDermott 83] McDermott, J., "Extracting Knowledge from Expert Systems," in *Proceedings of the Eighth International Joint Conference on Artificial Intelligence*, pp. 100-107, IJCAII, 1983.

[Neches, et. al 85] Neches, R., W. Swartout, J. Moore, "Enhanced Maintenance and Explanation of Expert Systems through Explicit Models of Their Development," *Transactions On Software Engineering*, November 1985. Revised version of article in Proceedings of the IEEE Workshop on Principles of Knowledge-Based Systems, December, 1984

[Reps 82] Reps, T., "Optimal-time incremental semantic analysis for syntax-directed editors," in *Conference Record of the Ninth Annual ACM Symposium on the Principles of Programming Languages*, pp. 169-176, ACM, 1982.

[Wile 81] Wile, D.S., *POPART: Producer of Parsers and Related Tools, System Builders' Manual*, ISI, 4676 Admiralty Way, Marina del Rey, CA, 90292, 1981.

[Wile 83] Wile, D.S., "Program developments: formal explanations of implementations," *CACM* 26, (11), November 1983, 902-911.

[Wile 86] Wile, D., "Local Formalisms: Widening the Spectrum of Wide-spectrum Languages," in *Conference on Program Specification and Transformation*, IFIP Working Group 2.1, April 1986.

[Wulf 75] Wulf, W., Johnsson, R., Weinstock, C., Hobbs, S., and Geschke, C., *The Design of an Optimizing Compiler*, American Elsevier, 1975.

Framework for a Knowledge–Based Programming Environment

Wolfgang Polak
Kestrel Institute
1801 Page Mill Road
Palo Alto, CA 94304

Abstract

We develop a formal model describing the basic objects and operations of the software development process. This model allows us to characterize functions performed by support environments and to formally define the semantics of environment tools. Representing information about available tools, administrative procedures, and constraints in a knowledge base allows automated support for many software development and life-cycle activities. Constraint maintenance within a knowledge base takes over many routine administrative tasks; program synthesis techniques can be used to generate complex plans.

1 Introduction

The term *environment* is used with different and conflicting meanings [3]. Many environments support program entry by providing syntactic and semantic assistance (e.g. [5,6,10,14,17,21]) Other environments and tools address specific facets of the software life–cycle such as requirements analysis, design, testing and debugging, version control, and system building (e.g. [13]).

In this paper we are not so much concerned with individual components and tools, rather we focus on their smooth integration and cooperation. By "environment" we mean a comprehensive system of integrated tools supporting all aspects of the software development and maintenance process. This view is similar in scope to [9]. Such a comprehensive environment must not only store source text but must also capture and deal with all objects and operations related to the software development and life–cycle; every operation performed outside environment control creates a potential source of error. Some authors have recognized the importance of database capture of all aspects of the program development cycle ([20]) and the importance of queries in aiding program understanding ([28]).

Rather than use traditional databases, we propose to utilitize such AI techniques as multiple inheritance, inference capability, and constraint maintenance. We refer to a database augmented with these capabilities as a *knowledge base*. These techniques allow us to build a truly intelligent agent which not only captures information, but also actively assists the software engineer during all phases of design, development, maintenance, and enhancement of software systems.

While AI techniques can significantly enhance the functionality of an environment, these techniques are no substitute for a thorough understanding of the problem domain. Before we can realize knowledge–based support of the programming process we need to develop a formal model or framework that describes the objects and operations of programming environments, their relations, constraints, and properties. Only after such a model has been developed can we begin to encode these concepts in a knowledge base.

In this paper we develop a formal model of domains of structured objects. This model can be used to describe the structure and interdependence of program modules, versions and development histories, requirements, specifications, program documentation, test cases, and so on. Based

The research presented in this paper was supported by the Naval Ocean Systems Center under contract N00039–86–C–0221. The views and conclusions contained in this paper are those of the author and should not be interpreted as representing the official policies, either expressed or implied of NOSC, the Department of the Navy, or the US Government.

on this formalism, we can define relations between these objects such as consistent compilation, satisfaction of requirements, and consistency with specifications. Further, operations within an environment including explicit user editing, compilation, documenting, debugging, testing, quality assurance, system releases, etc. can be described as programs that manipulate objects in the environment.

The definition of objects, their constraints and operations, and the description of higher level concepts such as versions, releases, etc. all constitute *knowledge* about the programming process in general as well as particular software systems. A knowledge–based programming environment will capture this knowledge and will be able to draw inferences based on this knowledge.

Certain aspects of programming environments have been investigated in detail and are well understood. Reps ([21]) presents a comprehensive treatment of concepts and techniques for creating syntax–directed editors. On the level of abstraction of this paper a syntax directed editor is considered a tool within the environment. Fritzson [7] presents a formal model which allows accurate description of incremental compilation in the DICE programming environment. Our approach is similar but broader in scope.

In the "Report on a Knowledge–Based Software Assistant" [8] the authors outline the architecture of a knowledge–based environment that addresses all aspects of the software life–cycle.

In his study of the software development process Sintzoff [25] uses metaprograms to describe the decision making process during program development. Programming methodologies, data and control structure selection, and introduction of parallelism can be described by metaprograms. In [26] Sintzoff proposes a calculus to describe development processes.

In contrast, our effort focuses on the semantics of these processes and the structure of the data being manipulated. Sintzoff's work is complementary; his design calculus may very well turn out to be a suitable language in which to reason about the operations performed in an environment.

The mathematical formalism used in our work is similar to that of [18], and [19]. A similar approach is taken in [2] where the authors are concerned with the description of complete systems down to the device level.

This paper presents ongoing research work that initially is aimed at developing of a formal environment model; we do not describe a particular environment. The following sections outline our basic approach. The final section presents some examples of the utility and functionality we expect to derive from a knowledge–based system built on these concepts.

2 A Formal Environment Model

The goal of our model is to provide rigorous mathematical foundations that can be used to describe the objects and operations performed in a programming environment. The model itself is independent of any particular programming language and programming methodology. The formalism provides a means for describing the semantics of tools used in a particular environment by defining the effect of a tool's application on the state of the environment. Module dependencies and recompilation requirements imposed by a particular language can be expressed as constraints. Rules and procedures of a particular methodology can be described concisely.

This model will enable integration of existing tools and automated support for their interaction. We believe that the model will guide us towards a more systematic design of more advanced environments, much in the same way that formal understanding of control and data structures guided us in developing better programming languages.

To cope with the variety of different objects in an environment, we partition these objects into disjoint domains, e.g. program modules, documentation objects etc. Each domain consists of hierarchically structured objects (e.g. modules, documents) and a set of dependencies between these objects. In addition, objects of any domain may exist in multiple versions. While some of the details will differ, we believe that all domains will have the same basic structure and can be described using the same technique.

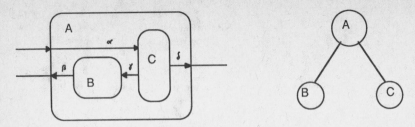

Figure 1: Two views of a structured object

The formalism used to model our domains is derived from Milner's Flowgraphs [19]. An object is modelled as a node in a graph. Each node has a number of labelled input ports (*references*) and output ports (*definitions*). Edges of the graph connect input to output ports with the same label.

The objects modelled represent *versions* (or instances) of software components, documents and so on. A component is given as an equivalence class of objects. The edges of the flowgraph represent the *"requires"*, *"references"*, or *"calls"* relationship; the nesting of modules represents the *"is built with"* relationship. Thus, the formalism captures the hierarchical structure of objects as well as details of their interconnection.

Objects are immutable and referentially transparent. As a consequence, (sub)objects can be shared among different composite objects and logical assertions about properties of objects can be stated without accounting for in–place changes.

Figure 1 shows two views of a structured object A composed from objects B and C. On the left we show how definitions and references of A, B, and C are interconnected (arrows indicating links from references to definitions). The right view abstracts from this interconnection detail and merely shows the containment relation.

Once we understand the structure of the domains, we can investigate relations and mappings between objects in different domains. The semantics of a compiler can be defined as a partial function from the domain of source objects to the domain of code objects. Preconditions on the applicability of the compiler can express compilation order constraints.

Relocatable binary code modules illustrate the structure of domains. Each module has a set of entry points and a number of external references. We can think of these as being typed, i.e. an entry point may refer to a function, a label, a constant etc. In typical implementations this type information may not be represented and type consistency may not be enforced. Objects of this domain can be composed to form new composite objects. A typical linker might combine multiple relocatable code modules. A loader maps relocatable modules into the different domain of absolute code modules.

A quite different example is the domain of documentation. Here the notion of definition and reference is less understood but still meaningful. We can think of a document as defining a set of concepts. In these definitions other concepts are used, which correspond to external references. Primitive documents can be grouped into sections, chapters, and manuals. The structure of a document could reflect the structure of the program being documented. If the program exists in different configurations then so does the associated documentation; multiple versions of a program object correspond to multiple versions of the documentation object. Differences between versions might be recorded explicitly; the print image of a document might represent differences to the previous version with *change bars*.

Other examples of domains are high–level programming languages, requirements, formal and informal specifications, design decisions, problem reports, test data, and so on.

The description of a complete environment involves a number of domains, all of which are structured and described uniformly. In addition, the environment will maintain relations between modules of different domains. For example, a document may "belong" to a program module, a relocatable object module may be "code for" this program module. Tools are viewed as functions on environment objects. In particular, user interaction, via a syntax directed editor, say, is viewed as a (non–deterministic) tool. Complex operations performed in the environment can be modelled as programs over tool applications.

Note, that while flowgraphs are useful in describing environments, they may not necessarily be the appropriate data structure for an implementation.

3 Structured Objects

Objects ($o \in O$) are instances (or versions) of components (e.g. modules, documents) and subcomponents. The granularity of components and subcomponents depends on the particular environment and domain. Objects have a number of attributes (e.g. the actual code, creation date, their sub–object structure). Two objects are considered equal only if all their attributes are equal.

L is a set of labels; we use greek letters (α, β, ...) to stand for elements of L. We do not make any further assumptions about labels; their interpretation will differ for different domains. Labels may correspond to names of functions, procedures, and other entities of a programming language. They could include signatures of functions and procedures. In other domains they may correspond to program labels.

We introduce the notion of a *structure* to describe how an object is composed of subobjects[1]. The set of structures (Σ) is defined as follows:

- Ω is a (empty) structure.

- $o \in O$ is a structure.

- For $\alpha \in L$ both α and $\overline{\alpha}$ are structures. An occurrence of α in a structure is called a *definition*; an occurrence of $\overline{\alpha}$ is called a *reference*.

- if A and B are structures then $A + B$ is a structure. Structure composition ($+$) is associative and commutative.

- If A is a structure then so is $A \setminus \alpha$ for $\alpha \in L$. The restriction operator "$A \setminus \alpha$" hides the definition of label α in A.

Each object has a structure attribute given by $Struct : O \rightarrow \Sigma$. For a structure A the function $Def : \Sigma \rightarrow 2^L$ returns the set of labels *defined* in A and $Ref : \Sigma \rightarrow 2^L$ denotes the set of labels *referenced* in A. In addition, we extend these definitions transitively to the structures of sub–objects of a structure; we call these functions Def^* and Ref^* (i.e. $Def^*(o) = Def^*(struct(o))$, and $Ref^*(o) = Ref^*(struct(o))$).

$$
\begin{aligned}
Def(\Omega) &= \{\} \\
Def(o) &= \{\} \\
Def(\alpha) &= \{\alpha\} \\
Def(\overline{\alpha}) &= \{\} \\
Def(A + B) &= Def(A) \cup Def(B) \\
Def(A \setminus \alpha) &= Def(A) - \{\alpha\}
\end{aligned}
$$

---

[1]To simplify the exposition we omit the relabelling operation of [19].

$$\begin{aligned}
Ref(\Omega) &= \{\} \\
Ref(o) &= \{\} \\
Ref(\alpha) &= \{\} \\
Ref(\overline{\alpha}) &= \{\alpha\} \\
Ref(A+B) &= Ref(A) \cup Ref(B) - Def^*(A+B) \\
Ref(A \setminus \alpha) &= Ref(A)
\end{aligned}$$

The meaning of a structure is as follows: in a composition $A + B$ the imports of A $(Ref^*(A))$ are satisfied by the exports of B $(Def^*(B))$ and vice versa. Any remaining imports become imports of the composition[2].

It is important to note, that the object containing the definition for a reference $\overline{\alpha}$ in o depends on the context, i.e. how o is composed with other objects. This property allows us to "share" objects.

We say an object o is *closed* if $Ref^*(o) = \emptyset$. Let o be a closed object and let $\{o_i\}$ be the set of all subobjects of o (including o). Then $Dep(o)$ is a binary relation on $\{o_i\}$ such that $(o_1, o_2) \in Dep(o)$ if and only if o_1 contains some reference $\overline{\alpha}$ which resolves to a definition α in o_2. A structure is *primitive* if it does not contain sub–terms $\in O$. To describe several different dependency relations in a domain a many–sorted set of labels can be introduced. Each sort describes one kind of dependency.

Consider source files pv.1, qv.1, qb.1, pb.1 containing the following Ada library units.

pv.1:   **package** p **is**
      function f **return** integer;
   end p;

qv.1:   **function** q **return** integer;

pb.1:   **with** q;
   package body p **is**
      function f **return** integer **is begin return** q; **end** f;
   end p;

qb.1:   **function** q **return** integer **is begin return** 1; **end** q;

We assume that source files are the smallest objects represented in our environment[3], that labels are identifiers of compilation units, and that dependencies being modelled are compilation order dependencies. We can describe the structure of the above Ada objects as follows:

$$\begin{aligned}
Struct(pv.1) &= p \\
Struct(qv.1) &= q \\
Struct(pb.1) &= \overline{p} + \overline{q} \\
Struct(qb.1) &= \overline{q}
\end{aligned}$$

Note, that this representation tells us which labels are imported and exported from objects. Only in the context of a larger system can this information be translated into dependencies between objects. For example, if we define a system c.1 as

$$struct(c.1) = pv.1 + pb.1 + qv.1 + qb.1$$

---

[2] We assume that there is at most one definition for every label. For certain domains this may not be appropriate. For example, when modelling Prolog programs, a definition might be given by several clauses in different "objects".

[3] Files are used as example to appeal to our intuition. This is not meant to suggest that files are the appropriate objects to model or represent. Any sophisticated environment should be centered around logical objects, not files.

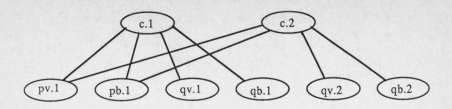

Figure 2: Multiple versions can share common subobjects.

the label $\overline{q}$ resolves to the definition of q in $qv.1$ and the reference $\overline{p}$ resolves to the definition p in $pv.1$. In this context then $pb.1$ depends on $pv.1$, $pb.1$ depends on $qv.1$, and $qb.1$ depends on $qv.1$, i.e. we have $Dep(c.1) = \{\langle pb.1, pv.1 \rangle, \langle pb.1, qv.1 \rangle, \langle qb.1, qv.1 \rangle\}$.

Note, Ada does not provide linguistic support for the composition of systems such as $c.1$, rather the structure of $c.1$ is determined "procedurally" by the order in which units are compiled into a library.

4 Multiple Versions

Let us now consider files qv.2 and qb.2, containing a new *"version"* of function q.

qv.2:   **function** q **return** natural;

qb.2:   **function** q **return** natural **is begin return** 3; **end** q;

with the structure

$$Struct(qv.2) \; = q$$
$$Struct(qb.2) \; = \overline{q}$$

Note, that introducing this new version of q does not change $c.1$ in any way. A system with the new version of q is denoted by a new object $c.2$ such that $Struct(c.2) = pv.1 + pb.1 + qv.2 + qb.2$ (see figure 2). It is significante that objects (e.g. $c.1$) are immutable; any assertion or property of $c.1$ will be unaffected by the creation of a new version of q.

For convenience we define an update operation $o[x/y]$ on objects which (transitively) replaces object x in o by y. New objects are created for the path from the root of $o[x/y]$ to y. Multiple parallel substitution $o[x_1, x_2, \ldots, x_n/y_1, \ldots, y_n]$ has the obvious meaning. For the above example we have $c.2 = c.1[qv.1, qb.1/qv.2, qb.2]$. We can also construct $c.1[qb.1/qb.2]$ (i.e. only change the body of q) but this leads to a compilation error later on.

Function q may go through many changes, i.e. there will be a series of objects representing q. These objects represent the *versions* of q; they are partially ordered. Merge operations between disjoint version threads are performed by an environment tool; we are not concerned with its detailed operation here. We call the equivalence class of all objects under the "version of" relation, a component. Thus, we might talk about the *parser* or the *code generator* as components of a *compiler*. While it seems natural to talk about the components of a compiler, this "subcomponent" relation may not be well defined in the presence of structure changes. Our view avoids these complications.

Users tend to think of their objects in terms of the functions they define and they view changes as in–place updates. This poses no problem; natural and convenient naming schemes can be built on top of our general representation. The name of a function f itself might denote the "latest" version; a particular version of this function can be selected by specifying version qualifiers as in $f.1.2.3$. In general users may have more complicated criteria when selecting a particular version of a component. It should be clear how general queries of the form "find a version of f such that $P(f)$" can be implemented.

In some terminology, a *configuration* selects one version for each component in a system. This notion of configuration is not meaningful in our model since each object completely defines all of its subobjects. In our view it may be more appropriate to have attributes of objects which indicate properties (such as intended target machines) relevant for configuring a system. Systems with special properties can then be specified, such as "latest released version x such that x runs on system y and uses the z algorithm".

If an environment captures the derivation history for each object then these histories inherit the object structure, i.e. they are naturally represented in their own domain of development histories.

5 Environment Operations

This section shows how the formal model presented above can serve as a framework for a knowledge–based environment. We will show how consistency within an environment can be expressed in our model and how the semantics of tools can be described.

The semantics of an environment tool is described as a function on environment objects. Properties of and relations between objects can be expressed as first order formulae. Referential transparency simplifies these definitions.

Clearly, the definition of tools and procedures depends on a particular environment; the examples given below assume some hypothetical Ada environment. It is described in terms of the following domains:

- Src, the domain of Ada source objects,

- Lib, the domain of Ada libraries. Libraries are assumed to be unstructured; there are no dependencies between libraries.

- Bin, the domain of binary code modules.

- Doc, documentation objects; we assume that documentation is structured but there are no dependencies.

- Tst, a domain of test cases. Tests are structured similar to the source domain. New source versions may or may not require new test cases. Dependencies between tests indicate testing order, e.g. perform all component tests before the system test. Each test has an attribute *subject* indicating the source object to which this test applies.

Next, our environment provides the following sparse set of tools, some of which are interactive and require user input.

- A compiler $comp : Src \times Lib \to (Bin \times Lib)$ is a partial function which compiles a source object into a library, updating the library (creating a new version) and generating a binary object.

- An editor $edit : Src \to Src$, $edit : Doc \to Doc$, $edit : Tst \to Tst$ for sources, documents, and tests.

- A debugger $test : Tst \times Bin \to \{true, false\}$ to perform testing of compiled systems against a set of test cases.

- A function $approve : Src \rightarrow \{true, false\}$ and $approve : Doc \rightarrow \{true, false\}$ implementing quality assurance procedures in source and documentation.

We can now define what it means for a source object s to be compiled into a binary object b, when a module is tested, and when a system can be released.

For a closed object s we can state that binary b is a consistent compilation of s; the predicate $compiled(s, b)$ describes this property. To define consistent compilation for arbitrary source objects we need to consider the compilation order dependencies derived from the context as well as a library in which a system is being built. The predicate $compiled(s, l, b, d)$ asserts that source object s is compiled into library l, that the binary object for s is b, and that the order of compilations into library l has been consistent with the dependency relation d.

$$compiled(s, b) \equiv closed(s) \wedge \exists l \in Lib : compiled(s, l, b, Dep(s))$$
$$compiled(s, l, b, d) \equiv \exists l' \in Lib : \langle b, l \rangle = comp(s, l') \wedge$$
$$\forall s' \in Srs : d(s, s') \rightarrow \exists b' \in Bin : compiled(s', l', b', d)$$

i.e., a source object s is consistently compiled into a binary b if s is closed and if there is a library into which s and all its components have been compiled in proper order (according to $Dep(s)$). Similarly we can define successful testing and documentation.

$$performed(t) \equiv closed(t) \wedge performed(t, Dep(t))$$
$$performed(t, d) \equiv (\forall t' \in Tst : d(t, t') \rightarrow performed(t', d)) \wedge$$
$$(\exists b \in Bin : compiled(subject(t), b) \wedge test(t, b))$$
$$tested(s) \equiv (\exists t \in Tst : subject(t) = s) \wedge$$
$$(\forall t \in Tst : subject(t) = s \rightarrow performed(t))$$
$$documented(s) \equiv (\exists d \in Doc : documentfor(s, d) \wedge approved(d)).$$

A hypothetical policy might state that system releases are subject to the constraint:

$$releasable(s) \equiv documented(s) \wedge approved(s) \wedge tested(s).$$

The user may now ask the system to perform all steps necessary to release the system $c.2$ (from section 4). The environment can deduce the required sequence of actions (tool invocations) from the current state and from the definition of $releasable$.

- Achieve $tested(c.2)$.

  - $t.2 \leftarrow edit(t.1)$ — ask the user to update the test suite for $c.1$ to apply to $c.2$, the test information for the subcomponents p and q may be reused.
  - Achieve $performed(t.2, Dep(t.2))$:
    * recursively achieve $performed(t', d)$ for all dependent tests $d(t, t')$.
    * achieve $compiled(c.2, b)$. This task in turn will set up subtasks $\langle b_j, l_j \rangle \leftarrow comp(s_k, l_k)$ to compile necessary subobjects of $c.2$ in proper order.
    * invoke the debugger to verify $test(t, b)$

- Achieve $documented(c.2)$

  - $d.2 \leftarrow edit(d.1)$ — ask the user to update the documentation for $c.1$.
  - Achieve $approved(d.2)$ — invokes management tool to obtain approval for $d.2$.

- Achieve $approved(c.2)$ — invokes management tool to obtain approval for $c.2$.

In the above way the system can set up an agenda of individual tasks which lead to the desired goal. Some of the tasks on the agenda are strictly mechanical while others require user interaction. These tasks are partially ordered. An intelligent system might reorder them to attempt those tasks first which will most likely cause an error, or to perform computational tasks in the background before the user requires the result.

At any time during the execution of this agenda the user might deviate, make additional changes, fix bugs, reword documentation, and so on. The system needs to recognize this situation and update the agenda appropriately.

6 Summary

We have presented an approach towards a model for describing and understanding the structure and dynamics of software development environments. We have alluded to some applications of this model towards the creation of intelligent tools; many other applications can be imagined.

It should be obvious that complete capture of the state of the environment allows for intelligent queries about the state. This knowledge can be used to build a better model of the status of a particular user's work, thus enabling the creation of intelligent user interfaces ([11]).

The granularity of the description of objects can be made finer. Incremental compilation can be integrated in this way if compilers with suitable interfaces become available.

Our approach is not limited to software development; CAD/CAM and VLSI design environments have similar requirements ([12]).

Components of an environment based on the ideas presented here and in [8] are being developed at Kestrel Institute.

References

[1] R. Balzer, D. Dyer, M. Fehling, S. Saunders, *Specification-Based Computing Environments*, Information Sciences Institute, April 1982

[2] J.A. Bergstra, J.W. Klopp, J.V. Tucker *Algebraic Tools for System Construction* in Proc. Logics of Programs, LNCS 164, Springer Verlag, 1983

[3] David R. Barstow, Howard E. Shrobe, Erik Sandewall, *Interactive Programming Environments*, McGraw-Hill, 1984

[4] Jan Chomicki, Naftaly H. Minsky, *Towards a Programming Environment for Large Prolog Programs*, Rutgers University, May 1985

[5] V. Donzeau-Gouge, G. Huet, G. Kahn, *Programming Environments Based on Structured Editors: The MENTOR Experience*, in [3]

[6] Peter H. Feiler, Raul Medina-Mora, *An Incremental Programming Environment*, Carnegie-Mellon University, April 1980

[7] Peter Fritzson, *Architecture of an Incremental Programming Environment and some Notions of Consistency*, Report LITH-IDA-R-84-02, Linköping University, 1984

[8] Cordell Green, David Luckham, Robert Balzer, Thomas Cheatham, Charles Rich, *Report on a Knowledge–Based Software Assistent*, KES.U.83.2, Kestrel Institute, Palo Alto, 1983

[9] Habermann, A., *The Gandalf Research Project*, Computer Science Research Review, Carnegie-Mellon University, 1978-79.

[10] Jean-Marie Hullot, *CEYX, A Multiformalism Programming Environment*, Institut National de Recherche en Informatique et en Automatique, May, 1983

[11] Karen E. Huff, Victor R. Lesser, *Knowledge-Based Command Understanding: An Example for the Software Development Environment*, University of Massachusetts, Amherst, June 1982

[12] R. H. Katz, T.J.Lehman, *Database Support for Versions and Alternatives of Large Design Files*, IEEE Transactions on Software Engineering, SE-10/2, March 1984

[13] Kernighan, B. and Mashey, J., *The Unix Programming Environment*, IEEE Computer, Vol 14 No 4:12-24, April 1981.

[14] **Paul Klint,** *Survey of Three Language-Independent Programming Environments*, INRIA, December 1983

[15] **H.C. Kuo, J. Ramanathan, D. Soni, M. Suni,** *System Architecture of an Adaptable Software Environment*, Ohio State University, 1983

[16] **H. J. Komorowski,** *Interactive and Incremental Programming Environments: Experience, Foundations and Future*, Report HARV-TR-09-83, Harvard University, 1983

[17] **Raul Medina–Mora,** *Syntax–Directed Editing: Towards Integrated Programming Environments*, Dept. of Computer Science, Carnegie–Mellon University, 1982

[18] **George Milne, Robin Milner,** *Concurrent Processes and their Syntax*, J.ACM 26/2, pp. 302–321, April 1979

[19] **Robin Milner,** *Flowgraphs and Flow Algebras*, J.ACM 26/4, pp. 794–818, October 1979

[20] **Matthew Morgenstern,** *Active Databases as a Paradigm for Enhanced Computing Environments*, Information Sciences Institute, USC, October, 1983

[21] **Thomas W. Reps,** *Generating Language-Based Environments*, MIT Press, 1984

[22] **Rich, C., Shrobe, H. and Waters, R.,** *Programmer's Apprentice Project*, MIT, Outline of Research, 1979-80.

[23] **Eric E. Schmidt,** *Controlling Large Software Development in a Distributed Environment*, XEROX Palo Alto Research Center, Ph.D Thesis, December 1982

[24] **Marshall I. Schor** *Declarative Knowledge Programming: Better than Procedural?*, IEEE Expert, Vol. 1/1, Spring 1986, pp 36–43

[25] **Sintzoff, M.,** *Understanding and Expressing Software Construction*, in NATO ASI Series, Vol. F8, Program Transformation and Programming Environments, P. Pepper (ed.), Springer Verlag, 1984

[26] **Sintzoff, M.,** *Exploratory Proposals for a Calculus of Software* Development, Rapport 84/2, Universite Catholique de Louvain, September, 1984

[27] **Sintzoff, M.,** *Desiderata for a design calculus*, RM 85-13, Universite Catholique de Louvain, June, 1985

[28] **Warren Teitelman, Larry Masinter,** *The Interlisp Programming Environment*, in [3]

[29] **Anthony Wasserman, Martin L. Kersten,** *Relational Database Environment for Software Development*, Vrije University, Amsterdam, October 1983

KNOWLEDGE-BASED AND FUTURE PROGRAMMING ENVIRONMENTS

Chair   : Gerhard Goos (GMD, FRG)
Assistant chair : Bernt M. Johnsen (URD, Trondheim, NOR)

Lead-in by chairman

Gerhard Goos (GMD, FRG):

Knowledge-based techniques is a programming paradigm which is best exhibited by rule-based systems where we separate the rules from the flow of control. Knowledge-based systems have the property that we deal with problem areas which we do not completely understand. However, expert systems are often advocated in a style which I would characterize as "over-sell" of a difficult subject. There is no substitution for first sitting down and analyzing a problem. So, knowledge-based systems is an ambivalent technology.

Questions to Andrew Symonds' presentation

Mary Shaw (Carnegie Mellon Univ., USA):

You said that there are expert systems available on the same systems on which databases are available. I didn't hear you say whether it is currently possible for those two to communicate with each other?

Andrew Symonds (IBM, USA):

The basic communications interfaces do exist. If you take the IBM RT PC as an example,

- there is a relational database manager as part of the system software.

- IBM has announced Lucid's CommonLisp, and Quintus has announced its PROLOG.

- a number of vendors have announced that their knowledge engineering tools will be available. They include IntelliCorp (KEE), Inference Corp (ART), and Technowledge (S1).

To pick one example, KEE allows procedural LISP code to be integrated into the knowledge base in a very natural way. Assuming a LISP foreign function call interface to the relational database manager, we have the communication mechanism.

The IBM mainframe environment also has knowledge systems and a relational database manager that can talk to each other.

Obviously other hardware environments can also be used.

Arve Meisingset (Norwegian Telecom., NOR):

You used the two words "semantics" and "knowledge". Can you give your formal definition of these?

Andrew Symonds (IBM, USA):

I don't think formal definitions of those two words can be really useful, but I can give an informal definition. "Knowledge" is the primary difference between this style of computing and the one that does not have this automatic reasoning capability. I think there's no essential difference between what the AI community calls "knowledge" and what your community calls "object-oriented databases" or "semantic modelling".

Questions to Terrence Miller's presentation

Robert Schwanke (Siemens, USA):

What is your model of versions that does not allow you to consider those two C compilers to be versions of each other?

Terrence Miller (Hewlett Packard, USA):

The two C compilers are perhaps versions of each other. I was saying connective objects were not necessarily versions of each other. It's a naming issue: certain entities are far enough apart not to be called versions of one another.

Robert Schwanke (Siemens, USA):

OK, where are those two considered far enough apart?

Terrence Miller (Hewlett Packard, USA):

By arbitrary choice in drawing up the example!

James Cordy (Queens Univ., CAN):

Your earlier comment about augmenting vs. replacing files leads me to this question: How do you propose to handle a knowledge base in your system? I haven't heard anyone talk about how to represent unreliable knowledge. In particular, it appears that management has unreliable knowledge on files augmentation, when you really meant to say file replacement. You gave another example of the priority of a bug report from a top manager. You might say with a certain kind of knowledge, that the likelihood of such a bug report to be correct is very high, and that it should rather get a low priority than high.

Terrence Miller (Hewlett Packard, USA):

I didn't say what the plan was. I merely said that the plan must be executed expeditiously in that case.

James Cordy (Queens Univ., CAN):

I'm not worried about that, I'm worried about representing information that is questionable, unreliable, and possibly changeable in the knowledge base.

Terrence Miller (Hewlett Packard, USA):

Some experts systems use probabilistic information to compute a confidence factor
in recommending a particular solution. The techniques are available. At the moment,
the expert system shell we're using does not have that facility. I don't think the
problem comes up that often in software projects.

Questions to Mary Shaw's presentation

Robert Schwanke (Siemens, USA):

I saw a similar slide in another talk on the widening gap in productivity. It struck me as a direct explanation for the proliferation of marginal software in the everyday world. The economic forces cause lots of people to become programmers that shouldn't be programmers! I am increasingly wary of establishing quality standards for our profession.

Mary Shaw (Carnegie Mellon Univ., USA):

How can I disagree?

Further, William Scherlis flinched when I said we were dependent on program termination for reasoning about PITS.

William Scherlis (Carnegie Mellon Univ., USA):

There are plenty of logics of programs that allow you to reason about non-terminating programs; temporal logic is one example.

Mary Shaw (Carnegie Mellon Univ., USA):

But that's not the classical tool for PITS. I think that was developed in response to other sets of issues.

William Scherlis (Carnegie Mellon Univ., USA):

True, but what's classically used is a historical phenomenon and not a technical phenomenon.

Anyway, you had this time scale slide of technology transfer and I can infer that software metrics has gotten out of the concept formation stage and into the concept hacking stage. I wanted to know: What were those concepts that have been formed?

Mary Shaw (Carnegie Mellon Univ., USA):

I took this data from a study by IDA in 1977. Halstead's metrics was published in 1972, and dates back to the late sixties.

In the area of cost estimation, there are many empirical models where you collect a lot of historical data and fit some curves to it. Those models can be effective in doing schedule prediction within the original domain. However, they require extensive recalibration if they're taken to another environment.

William Waite (Univ. Colorado, USA):

I always distrust these demand curves showing that a need is growing exponentially. After all, the demand for gold is probably growing exponentially too and nobody seems to worry too much about that.

Mary Shaw (Carnegie Mellon Univ., USA):

Or maybe it's rabbits or kangaroos. In the early 1900's there was a study on telephone operators. The conclusion was that by mid-century every man, woman and child had to be telephone operator to satisfy the demand. What happened was that we all became telephone operators!

William Waite (Univ. Colorado, USA):

That's clear, but suppose that this demand hadn't been met? Nothing would have happened; the world wouldn't have stopped. It just would have been harder to talk to other people. We have existed for thousands of years without computers. Where and what is this demand? It is completely artificial!

Mary Shaw (Carnegie Mellon Univ., USA):

If we're faced with demand like this we can try to meet it head on. But if you get a discrepancy like that, you've also got to ask whether that is appropriate. There are some kinds of software which we're coming to understand well enough to make the development of programs much more systematic, like 4'th generation languages in the database world. What will happen in the next 10-20 years is a substantial increase in systems that are created by systems software people, but operated by so-called non-programmers to produce particular pieces of software. And they will be "programmers" in the same sense that we are telephone operators.

Gerhard Goos (GMD, FRG):

If every American will be a programmer by say, 1997, what are the methods we have to develop for allowing that to happen?

Mary Shaw (Carnegie Mellon Univ., USA):

Consider the effects of spread-sheets in the last five years.

William Waite (Univ. Colorado, USA):

Also word processors.

Lynn Carter (GenRad, USA):

I realize that the Software Engineering Institute in Pittsburgh is given an important job, but SEI is not designed to continue forever. These programming environments are gargantuan systems - when and if they work. The technology transition you encourage is not going to come from very many universities, because the method of doing research and awarding researchers is exactly contrary to the system that we must produce. Many ideas I've heard today have been repeated the last 5-10 years, but very little seems to happen.

Mary Shaw (Carnegie Mellon Univ., USA):

Thank you, professor Carter! First, the Software Engineering Institute is intended as a continuing operation. The initial contract is for five years, which is a consequence of our government's spending cycles. The technology that will be required, I think, is not going to arise solely from the universities. The problems of getting it out to industry are at least as hard as to change the structure within the universities. I think that university and industry cooperation is a promising avenue.

Gerhard Goos (GMD, FRG):

Can you point to any knowledge-based systems that have gotten out of the hands of the designers and the knowledge engineers and are in daily use? And, what are the experiences?

Richard Waters (MIT AI Lab., USA):

I cannot think of one in software, but certainly in medicine. You can buy an electrocardiograph machine which at an extra 5% of the price, has a little expert system in it to do the standard interpretation of the signals recorded from the heart.

Terrence Miller (Hewlett Packard, USA):

I believe DEC is using an expert system for configuring orders as a practical tool.

Mary Shaw (Carnegie Mellon Univ., USA):

My understanding was that DEC's system got bigger and bigger, and finally they re-implemented it. But the development was certainly an expert system development. Whether you're still going to call it an expert system may hinge on whether an expert system is necessarily implemented as a set of rules in an inference engine, as distinguished from a piece of software that exhibits "expertise".

Terrence Miller (Hewlett Packard, USA):

Hewlett Packard has internally an expert system to assist maintenance engineers to do diagnosis.

Andrew Symonds (IBM, USA):

There are numerous examples of practical application of the technology within industry. To name one, AT&T has an application called ACE that can diagnose telephone cable faults based on analyzing the cable traffic records. This runs in production. There are also projects afoot within IBM for computer chip manufacturing, contract preparation, and even cafeteria layout.

The programming labs are looking at the technology along the lines I discussed in my talk, but this work is not so far along.

Lynn Carter (GenRad, USA):

The chairman asked whether some expert systems were available, or at least available to others. I don't think DEC will sell their system to me; and I've not seen cafeteria layout programs in any of IBM's price catalogs. Even though they might be available to others than the developers, they are not necessarily available to the outside.

Questions to Richard Waters' presentation

Robert Schwanke (Siemens, USA):

How does KBEmacs reconnect the parse tree to the "plan" after a substantial text edit?

Richard Waters (MIT AI Lab, USA):

KBEmacs does not reconnect the parse tree to the plan after a text edit. Rather, KBEmacs just makes a complete new plan. It would be beneficial if KBEmacs were more incremental.

Robert Schwanke (Siemens, USA):

I don't think you caught my question completely: You edit the text, and rebuild the parse tree as best you can. But what about the "plan" from which you used to generate the text in the first place? How do you salvage the parts of the plan that correspond to the new text?

Richard Waters (MIT AI Lab, USA):

Currently we don't salvage any of it. We throw it all away and reanalyze the whole thing.

James Cordy (Queens Univ., CAN):

From what we've been hearing about deriving programs and program transformations it seems backwards to derive a program plan from a program text. We ought to be going the other way around. So, Schwanke's question brings up the following - If you're going to reanalyze the text and come up with a new plan, presumably you would like to insure that there is some relation between the old plan and the new plan. And hopefully, it's a meaningful transformation of it.

Richard Waters (MIT AI Lab, USA):

There are two parts to your quuestion. First, why should anyone bother analyzing text in order to create a plan instead of simply always working down from a plan? Second, after textual editing, how can you insure that the new plan bears a reasonable relation to the old plan?

There are three reasons why analysis is important. First, if you want to allow the user to make arbitrary textual changes, then you must support analysis. It is important to support arbitrary modification so that you don't put the user in a strait jacket which requires him to always use system commands. Second, analysis allows the system to operate on old code which was not created with the system. Third, as shown in William Scherlis' paper, analysis is often necessary even when doing pure top down implementation. Often the key to a step is recognizing that a special case exists in the program. Analysis can be used to recognize an abstract plan that identifies the special case.

With regard to the second question - KBEmacs does not assume that the change made by the user is correctness preserving or that the new plan should be similar to the old one. KBEmacs is designed for expert users and it is assumed that they know what they are doing. Nevertheless, it would be good if KBEmacs could asses the same similarity between the old and new plans. Unfortunately, KBEmacs does not support this. The next demonstration system will.

James Cordy (Queens Univ., CAN):

What strikes me as wrong is that you are not asking the programmer what the plan is. Presumably he knows what the plan is before he starts to write his program. Why doesn't KBEmacs ask for this plan and then derive the program from it rather than analyzing program text to find out the plan?

Richard Waters (MIT AI Lab, USA):

With any system, there has to be some way for the user to say what he wants. With KBEmacs, this is done incrementally one command at a time. The user has to choose something to say first. Once this is said, KBEmacs gives immediate feedback by producing a partial program. The user then says someting else.

KBEmacs does not assume that the user necessarily has a complete picture of what he wants before he starts. Rather it assumes that the user might change his mind based on what he sees. KBEmacs expects that many of the user's statements will call for non-correctness preserving changes in the program.

This approach could also be used to create a specification rather than a program. In this context it may seem more reasonable that, with any program, there always has to be a time when the user has not yet decided exactly what he wants to do.

With regard to changes, note that if the user tells KBEmacs how to change the plan then it will change the plan directly keeping track of the correspondence with the old plan. If he uses textual editing then KBEmacs assumes that he could not think of any simple way to change the plan and that some complex change is being made. In this case it is expected that the new plan will be quite different from the old plan.

Questions to David Wile's presentation

Larry Morell (Coll. William & Mary, USA):

What do you mean by the control structure following the data structure?

David Wile (ISI, USA):

Basically, each rule has a pattern on the left which references an abstract syntax tree which it can handle. The result of the rule is some combination of results obtained by applying functions to the subcomponents of the pattern. For example, in converting an ALGOL "+" to a LISP "PLUS", the ALGOL terms are first converted to LISP S-expressions and then the results combined in an S-expression with the "PLUS".

Larry Morell (Coll. William & Mary, USA):

Would you say compilers fit that scheme?

David Wile (ISI, USA):

Absolutely! Most components can be described that way. What they are compiled into is usually less recognizable.

Final discussion

Reidar Conradi (Norw. Inst. of Tech., NOR):

Has the last speaker (Polak) some experience on the use of his system?

Wolfgang Polak (Kestrel Institute, USA):

I was looking at and trying to give support for the existing system building activities in our programming environment. But I didn't understand its version concept. So I set out to describe these objects within our system, and then derive properties and plans.

Johannes Grande (MCC, USA):

I have one observation: Terence Miller from HP talked about PE-support, and Mary Shaw talked about the future beyond PITL. With large systems there are a lot of people, but Mary Shaw did not bring up the team issue at all. I believe that teams work differently from individuals and PITS is only concerned about the individual programmer. When teams communicate, they don't just exchange information, they argue, disagree, sometimes compromise, but sometimes they also synergize. Work at MCC in Austin shows that teams imply much more exploration of alternatives than done by any individual designer.

Terrence Miller (Hewlett Packard, USA):

I envision that the database and query mechanism in the StageSys project is going to enhance the communication between people and make more effective, simple and creative interchanges. We also have to get rid of unproductive, "noisy" communication.

Mary Shaw (Carnegie Mellon Univ., USA):

The introduction of expert systems or learning systems will force us to redefine our roles as team members. Further, there is evidence that the software teams in constructing large embedded process systems are not communicating well with the overall system design teams.

Johannes Grande (MCC, USA):

I don't think that the current systems engineers can cope with the systems of tomorrow. It would have to be the software engineers that develop that technology as a discipline: a science for designing systems.

Mary Shaw (Carnegie Mellon Univ., USA):

I suggest that it will not be the software engineer as we know it either, but rather some synthesis of system and software engineers.

Alfons Geser (Univ. Passou, FRG):

There is always talk about executable specifications in knowledge-based systems. But after requirements analysis, we do not yet have the executable specification. We hardly have an initial high level specification. How can a knowledge based system treat such non-executable specifications?

Richard Waters (MIT AI Lab, USA):

A knowledge based system would not be able to execute a non-executable specification, but it could reason about it in other ways. Presumably, if you gave the specification to a human analyst he could help validate it. Whatever knowledge that person would use could, in principle, be captured in a knowledge based system.

Gerhard Goos (GMD, FRG): (showing slides)

First: To assist teaching and help classifying concepts, we should find _instructive_ _examples_ for PITL. David Gries' book on the "Science of Programming" contains about 20 examples to demonstrate PITS. That book is notable for its examples and for its verification attempts; and, for that its index does not contain the term: "abstract data types" (typical for PITL). So what typical examples could we identify for PITL? Maybe within a few years we could collect, say, 20 instructive examples? They should not deal with algorithm transformations and the like because large systems are mostly algorithm-free. Data structures are also absent in large systems.

Second: There are some missing issues in the workshop. One has already been mentioned: _programmer teams_. It involves more than communication between programmers: how do we really support teams? What are the technical problems in a given environment? What kinds of team management tools do we need?

Third: _Project management support_ is another issue. How can a programming environment ease the job of the project manager and also ease the formal managerial communication within a project? Terrence Miller showed a slide with data from TRW, saying that 32% of a programmer's time goes on _job communication_ and only 13% on writing programs. How can we cut that down by technical support?

Fourth: _Software quality._ Do we know what it means or how to control it?

Terrence Miller (Hewlett Packard, USA):

A good, succinct _example_ of PITL problems is almost a contradiction in terms. We can always talk about the disasters, and anecdotally describe situations where our grasp of a system has been lost. But to write it down as a simple example would be very difficult.

Further, the primary team support is in the database (knowledge base) and in an appropriate query mechanism.

It would help if the database is distributed and there is a parallell communications media. But certainly they should also be speaking to each other.

Mary Shaw (Carnegie Mellon Univ., USA):

It is indeed very difficult and laborsome to find small, comprehensible examples for PITL, but such examples would be an outstanding teaching device. They would rather look like case studies from business schools than the ones from Gries' book. SEI has an educational project where we are trying to develop such examples. Keep in touch!

William Scherlis (Carnegie Mellon Univ., USA):

Question for clarification to Goos: Do you really believe ADTs exist only in PITL, or was that provocation? In Gries' book, all the examples are using arrays. There aren't examples dealing with linked lists, for example.

Joseph Newcomer (Carnegie Mellon Univ., USA):

To Mary Shaw's point of case examples: Even if we could find them they're hard to carry out. They must not only be "understood", they must be "internalized". That is, the studies would not mean anything to students until they'd been down in the trenches and shot at by changing specifications, interfaces, and everything else. And after about 2-3 years of crossfire they finally realize what PITL is. Indeed, one of our major problems is to convey the practical experiences of the masters of this art.

Gerhard Goos (GMD, FRG):

I posed those questions because I am also unable to answer them; but I'm optimistic. It has taken ten years from the invention of ALGOL until we realized the methodology of structured programming. I hope that within the next ten years we will also develop a methodology to convey many of the PITL questions. That, of course, will also lead to positive and constructive case studies.

Ian Thomas (BULL, FRA):

I'd want to suggest some encouraging advice on how to help students internalize PITL. We could at the beginning of a four year degree course, give them a small example and insist that every month they add something to it. We then change the specifications periodically over the four year period. After four years they still have the same problem, and we could see how much of the original code is left.

Bernard Lang (INRIA, FRA):

First, it's very nice to have a database as a repository for information and pose questions to it. Second, how do we teach bridge building? We hardly keep a full-scale bridge for the students, but we can do simulations. Similarly, we could make a simulation of the management of a large software project on a computer in the same way as in business schools. Most engineering sciences have the same problem and they can benefit from each other's experiences and techniques.

Mary Shaw (Carnegie Mellon Univ., USA):

First, at our university the civil engineering students do build bridges: not big ones out of steel, but small ones out of balsa; but there is good extrapolation from the properties of the project bridges to the real ones. Second, we do have a computer simulation at the management school called management game. It currently consumes one person full-time to operate and maintain the system and it has a rather long development history.

Andrew Symonds (IBM, USA):

On quality requirements - Industry is spending a lot of recources to monitor, measure and maintain quality: and quality is really the ability to meet requirements. In the area of software, our very crude measure of quality is the number of defects discovered per shipped thousand lines of source code. At IBM, several other measures have been proposed, but no one generally accepted.

Kristen Rekdal (URD, NOR):

I'll propose the huge software-controlled telephone exchanges as the best examples for PITL. They are all very big systems in the mega-line area having required thousands of man-years of development effort. Most of the current systems started their developments in the seventies, and they are still developing or evolving, and will be maintained for several years to come. So test data will be, and are, available.

These systems comprise, for instance, the AXE system by Ericsson in Sweden, the EWSD system by Siemens in Germany, the No. 5 ESS system by AT&T in USA, the L10 system by NTT in LD Japan, and the System 12 by ITT. They are all performing a well understood, very much standardized service, but they have been developed by different methods, tools, languages, people, and cultures. So, you can expect a lot of information which will be challenging to collect and analyze.

William Waite (Univ. Colorado, USA):

On test cases - We've been teaching a course at the Univerity of Colorado in Boulder, called "Software System Development Practice", through assembly language programming. The point is to force the students through the experience of PITL by programming in assembly language, where something small is large. Not only is small large, but you have the ability to use any of the proposed mechanisms for solving PITL problems. You are not constrained by the language to one particular model solution. The feedback from students is that it _does_ simulate reality, and they find it the most valuable course that they've taken during their entire career. It is apparently the equivalent of the balsa bridge.

Andy Rudmik (GTE Comm. Systems, USA):

On PITL and project management - We should be looking more at project support environments. I really expected to hear presentations on that because Europeans are more notorious for having that focus. Some of the important issues are scoping in large projects. That is, how to provide scoping capabilities in our data and process models. How are we managing the large name spaces? How are we representing dynamic behavior: the movement of data between users and tasks? How do we define the relevant substructure of a large project? In traditional databases we have access control, but in the software engineering environment we have roles and associated activities.

Lastly, many aspects of large-scale projects have not been dealt with at this workshop, although versioning was really popular.

Kristen Rekdal (URD, NOR):

There was a conference a couple of years ago on software factories. After a presentation by a Japanese showing how they have set up a factory doing all the methods and so on, an American asked: "How do you get your people to accept using this or that method for performing specification and design?" After much silence, re-questioning and internal discussion, the final answer was: "This is not a problem in Japan, because people get together and agree on how to do it, and then they do it." So, some of our problems could be irrelevant in a different culture and therefore should not necessarily be addressed by developing yet another tool.

Arne Sølvberg (Norw. Inst. of Tech., NOR):

I won't try to give a definition of PITL - but it certainly involves many people. Therefore, programs must be understood fairly easy by different people. So a crucial point is: Is it possible to easily understand a program? If it is not easy to understand it with current programming technology, we are in trouble. Another way to phrase it: How should one abstract from a program text to infer the behavior of a piece of software in the context of the problem.

Lynn Carter (GenRad, USA):

My definition of PITL is that no single person can fully understand such programs! Further, we cannot tackle program maintenance unless we have a very high-level system description. Source programs are at too low a level, but our problems can be alleviated by tools that help us look at and understand pieces of that source in a structured manner.

Also, the telephone switching systems are probably too big to serve as test cases.

Joseph Newcomer (Carnegie Mellon Univ., USA):

Many people are building project management software. Most of them have come out of the culture of business schools and they generally apply to any big project, testing scheduling, cost overruns, etc.. We're simply talking about managing complicated human activities, whether that is construction and maintenance of source code or whatever.

Johannes Grande (MCC, USA):

I both agree and disagree about giving students an example of PITL. We really need to look beyond programming and development software and study how we design in an environment where the requirements change every week.

David Levine (Intermetrics, USA):

There was some work on chief programmer teams and ego-less programming some years ago. My sense is that software is produced by putting people in a group who meet periodically for too much time and then go off and program. So we really need automated support tools. However, design is fantastically difficult and computer-assisted education is not more successful than our attempts of increasing our software productivity.

Perhaps a good paradigm for learning programming is to take a senior programmer and have a junior apprentice sit next to that person for some weeks. The same learning system seems to work for doctors and other skilled workers.

Terrence Miller (Hewlwtt Packard, USA):

The junior person is particularly the person that is easiest to automate. That is exactly the goal of our research project. You can try to get them all up to the senior level with automated help.

David Levine (Intermetrics, USA):

A perpetual problem is how to train new people; so learning systems are important. An apprentice system will also dissipate knowledge for future maintenance.

Richard Waters (MIT AI Lab, USA):

The system must supply immediate short term benefits to the user by using the information he provides to his advantage. If the benefits are large enough, the user will be eager to provide the information.

Reidar Conradi (Norw. Inst. of Tech., NOR):

Why is it that we always change specifications? First, the software medium is so malleable that it is possible to do that. Second, hardware people are constantly coming up with new devices that change our way of applying computers. So we are always on the wrong end of the learning curve.

Further, there is a schism between theorists and practitioners, and that goes for students, teachers, and industry. If you don't get practical experience through project work during your studies, you are reluctant to end up in a software engineering job. At our university we teach the students PITL by practice in four years, and it has a profound effect on them.

Lastly, what about the future? We can certainly gain a lot by developing new techniques and gluing all kinds of tools together. But will that give us a productivity boost to meet the expected increase in demand? If the demand increases 30-40% a year, i.e., a doubling every second year, we can never cope. The effect is, of course, we will not have that increase! We can never manage, even if the streets get covered by PCs and everybody becomes a programmer. There is no economic benefit for everybody to be a programmer; the very purpose of using computers is to give new and better functionality at a reduced cost. Then, what kind of techniques will we have to rely upon? A lot of papers from conferences have introduced their own paradigms, but many hardly are used by their creators. My own contribution is to develop an integrated programming environment (EPOS) to fuse certain tools together through a database. But I don't think it will give you a productivity factor of ten. Maybe a factor two or three, and combined with powerful workstations, a factor two on top of that. Where are you going to get a factor of 5-10 on top of that? Maybe AI and non-algorithmic paradigms for problem solving can contribute?

Richard Waters (MIT AI Lab, USA):

I believe that everybody indeed will have to program. Everybody learns to read, but reading was a rather weird skill in the middle ages and had no relevance to most people's lives. So everybody will somehow learn to program!

Per Holager (ELAB-SINTEF, NOR):

A comment on the missing issues in Goos' list. Many of these were indirectly addressed by most presentations, e.g., PITL techniques can alleviate programming management and improve software quality, and tools for configuration and version control can help support distributed program development and will generally assist management.

Robert Schwanke (Siemens, USA):

I think that project management software, as it exists today, should be taken with a great many grains of salt. The software project management course and tools literature that I see typically ignores two very important issues: learning curves, and risk. Learning curves are important for entering new application areas, for bringing new team members up to speed, and for allocating persons to tasks. Programmers seem to bo most productive when given long-term responsibility for a particular subject area in the system. Programmers are not interchangeable!

Risk management is even touchier. Most software projects are riskier than the average project in other fields, because we are such a young field and because we are frequently breaking ground in new application areas. To manage this risk, we must deliberately schedule regular risk assessment sessions, in which we re-evaluate the time and resources needed to complete the project and adjust scope and schedule accordingly. Fortunately, Barry Boehm is working on a model of software project management that includes risk, but I don't yet have a good citation.

Nonetheless, a good management information system interfaced to, for example, a knowledge-based software engineering environment, would help software managers apply whatever ad-hoc techniques they posess.

Joseph Newcomer (Carnegie Mellon Univ., USA):

I am very suspicious of attitudes like "Gee, we don't know how to do this, but if we automate it, it will be right". I get some of the same circulars Robert Schwanke gets, and I see a lot of snake oil being sold.

Lynn Carter (GenRad, USA):

On the telephone operator example - We solved the problem by creating a new mechanism for placing phone calls. Conradi questions how programming environments is going to result in a dramatic increase of productivity. The answer is probably that the "programmers" of tomorrow will do different tasks. Men will do what men are good at, and similarly for programs and machines. So everybody is not going to program in PASCAL, BASIC or ADA like the spread-sheet people who are writing "computer programs" their way. Essentially, we should develop new man-machine systems for solving the problem of problem-solving.

Reidar Conradi (Norw. Inst. of Tech., NOR):

Even if you get a 10 times increase, it will only last for 6-7 years with a 30-40% annual increase in demand.

Lynn Carter (GenRad, USA):

The capacity of our telephone system has probably increased by a factor 1000 in the last 50-60 years. It is always hard to anticipate future technology and its impact on man-machine and human relation. I assert our goal is to recognize new goals and to recognize new roles for the human and for the machine.

Jean-Pierre Keller (Thomson CSF/DSE, FRA):

Responding to Goos on problems of management and communication: I was once involved in cost-predicting a large software project with a budget of several million francs. I thought that the importantsocial factors were personal egos, office politics, and so on. Modelling these social activities turned out to produce very good results.

Mary Shaw (Carnegie Mellon Univ., USA):
(Showing slide of 12-15 proposals for the most important PE factors)

Monday I asked about the most important factors to improve software productivity. Twelve or fifteen people replied and in these slides I am acting as a reporter rather than an advocate. There were suggestions that the big problem lies not in some particulars; that we should be more concervative about what we can and cannot do; and about not overselling what we produce. There were some pleas to establish better relations between the research and development communities and the actual users, i.e., better technology transfer.

This is the list of proposals for technologies that might make a difference with counts of the number of people who proposed each of the points:

Number of times mentioned	Improvement factor	
5	Specifications:	- high level - executable - rigorous/formal - matching domain
3	Reusability :	- transformations - program generators - saving specs with code
2	Measurement :	DO & REPORT
3	Interfaces :	- formal hardware/software - user views & models

Various proposals:

1	Requirements formulations
1	Models for user domain
1	Project management
1	Processor speed
1	Macro-discoverer (post fact.)

The most popular suggestion was for specifications of appropriate types. Reusability was also very popular, and there were some requests for measurement, both doing it and reporting it. There were a number of requests for miscellaneous interfaces. I report this list and I leave it to you to contemplate.

Joseph Newcomer (Carnegie Mellon Univ., USA):

If we can get a factor of 2.15 out of any three pieces of technology up there, we're looking at a factor 10 totally. (2.15 ** 3 = 10)

Mary Shaw (Carnegie Mellon Univ., USA):

A factor of 2.15 is a big one. I personally do not believe that there is any one thing that will produce a factor of 10 through the whole process. I think there are a number of places where we could get a factor of 2-5 and conceivably 10 in some particular aspects of the process, but I don't really believe I see any routes that will lead us to a factor of 100 in the whole process, even after combining individual pieces.

Richard Waters (MIT AI Lab, USA):

We cannot possibly get an improvement of more than a factor five, since implementation is not even half the process. However, if the technology of "automatic programming" advances to the point of implementation having almost zero costs, we're left with design and maintenance. But the very reason we're doing maintenance is that it is cheaper than re-implementation! Thus, maintenance in the classic form may also disappear, and we're left with design and re-design. This may lead to very unstable systems since we may have the technology to carry out massive structural changes at little cost. Total software costs will not go down in such a super-malleable environment, even if the programming productivity increases by 100-1000 times.

Stefan Jähnichen (GMD, FRG):

Short proposal: We collect together all the knowledge we already have, communicate it and use it.

William Waite (Univ. Colorado, USA): (summing up)

This is a difficult task. I decided finally to emulate the chief executive of the state of Colorado, Richard Lamb, who is known to puncture the balloons put up by politicians. I'd like to address four questions.

First question: What _is_ a programming environment?

There is a tight analogy between the definition of programming environments and the definition of pornography: It is very hard to define, but it's easy to recognize. Moreover, whether something is pornography - oh, sorry, a programming environment or not - is purely a matter of taste. In my opinion, the precise definition is rather uninteresting.

Second question: How can we make progress?

Programming environments seem to be the classic example of the failure of the normal life cycle model. We can't write a set of specifications, proceed to a design, implementation and so on, because we haven't any idea of what we want. We need experience with prototypes, but they are not without problems either. That is, a lot of the practicioners are academics; they need to publish. Therefore they will tackle easy problems. Unfortunately, getting experience with prototypes is not an easy problem. We need measurements, experience, and some hard numbers. Moreover, and perhaps most important, we need to be our own _users_.

Third question: What has this workshop accomplished?

I was tempted to say "nothing", but I think it is not true. We've shared some ideas, we've met the players in the game and people have told us something about their experiences - perhaps not enough, but at least it is better than nothing.

The fourth question is a philosophical one, not closely related to programming environments: Why are we so impatient?

We have a lot of grandiose ideas and there's a lot of evangelism: "My syntax-directed editor will get you out of all your problems; all you have to do is to convert!" I've talked to practitioners in this area, and they tell me: "Well, sure, you can use my system, but you'll have to write all your programs in LISP." Unfortunately, I already have a lot of knowledge-bases and I understand that encoding knowledge is the most difficult process. These _knowledge-bases_ are called _programs_. They are written in PASCAL or C. If I want to know something, I can invoke the program. There's hundreds of thousands of lines of embodied knowledge in those programs. I'm not going to write them all over in Lisp again! Another analogy to the telephone system: When we replaced the operators, we didn't replace all the operators world-wide by No. 5 ESS's by AT&T; it was done one office at the time. We need to follow an evolutionary, rather than a revolutionary path. The same happened in the machine tool industry. The numerically controlled machine tools of today didn't appear full-blown on the scene.

Having left you with these questions, the last thing that I need to do is to once again thank our host Reidar Conradi, and all of his people, for the marvellous job that they've done in arrangements and for putting up with all of us. Thank you very much!

Index of Discussion Participants

List of attendants at the PE Workshop, Trondheim, Norway, June 16-18 1986

Ambriola, Vincenzo
Universita' Di Pisa
Dipartimento Di Informatica
Corso Italia 40
56100 PISA
Italy
Phone:+39 050 40862
Email:mcvax!delphi!dipisa!ambriola

Aschim, Frode
Sysdeco A.S
Chr. Michelsens gt. 65
0474 OSLO 4
Norway
Phone:+47 2 383090

Bahlke, Rolf
Technische Hochschule Darmstadt
Magdalenstr. 11c
6100 DARMSTADT
West-Germany
Phone:+49 6151 163414

Belkhatir, Noureddine
L.G.I. C.N.R.S
L.G.I.
BP 68
38402 St. Martin D'Heres
France
Phone:+33 76 514600
Email:belkhatir@imsy.uucp

Borison, Ellen
Carnegie Mellon University
Dept. of Computer Science
Pittsburgh, PA 15213
USA
Phone:+1 412 2683043
Email:borison@a.cs.cmu.edu.arpa

Botella, Pere
Facultat D'Informatica U.P.C.
Dept. Programacio
c/ Pau Gargallo 5
08028 Barcelona
Spain
Phone:+34 3 3338308/3330311

Bovey, John David
The University of Kent at Canterbury
The Computing Laboratory
The University, Canterbury, Kent
England
Phone:+44 224 66822 ext 4688
Email:uk.ac.vkc!jdb

Brenna, Vegard
IDA A.S
P.O.Box 1163
Sentrum
0107 OSLO 1
Norway
Phone:+47 2 158690

Campbell, Roy H.
University of Illinois
1304 Springfield
240 Digital Computer Lab.,
Urbana, IL 61801
USA
Phone:+1 217 3330215
Email:campbell@uiuc.uucp or uiucdcs!campbell

Carter, Lynn Robert
Gen Rad Designs
1158 E.Missouri Ave.
Phoenix, A2 85014
USA
Phone:+1 602 2662032
Email:carter%asu@csnet-relay.arpa

Conradi, Reidar
Norwegian Inst. of Technology
Division of Computer Science
7034 Trondheim-NTH
Norway
Phone:+47 7 593444
Email:conradi%vax.runit.unit.uninett@tor.arpa

Cordy, James R.
Queens University at Kingston
Dept. of Computing & Information Science
Kingston
Canada K7L 3N6
Phone:+1 613 5476616
Email:cordy@gucis.bitnet

Didriksen, Tor
The Norwegian Inst. of Technology
Dept. of Computer Science
7034 Trondheim-NTH
Norway
Phone:+47 7 593441
Email:didriksen%vax.runit.unit.uninett@tor.arpa

Dittrich, Klaus
FZI
Haid-und-Neu-Strasse 10-14
7500 Karlsruhe 1
W. Germany
Phone:+49 721 690640
Email:dittrich@germany.csnet
     dittrich@uka.uucp

Ellison, Robert
Carnegie Mellon University
Pittsburgh, PA 15213
USA
Phone:+1 412 2687705
Email:ellison@sei.cmu.edu.arpa

Estublier, Jacky
L.G.I. C.N.R.S.
L.G.I. BP 68
38402 s' Martin D'Heres
France
Phone:+33 76 514600
Email:estublie@imag.uucp

Evans, Arthur
Tartan Laboratories, Inc.
477 Melwood Avenue
Pittsburgh, PA 15213
USA
Phone:+1 412 6212210
Email:evans@tl-20b.arpa

Garlan, David
Carnegie-Mellon University
Dept. of Computer Science
Pittsburgh, PA 15213
USA
Phone:+1 412 2687698
Email:garlan@gandalf.cs.cmu.edu

List of attendants at the PE Workshop, Trondheim, Norway, June 16-18 1986

Geser, Alfons
Fakultat fur Mathematik und Informatik
Postfach 2540
D - 8390 Passau
W-Germany
Phone:+49 851 509353

Goos, Gerhard
GMD Forschungsstelle and der Univ. Karlsruhe
Haid-und-Neu-Strasse 7
7500 Karlsruhe
W-Germany
Phone:+49 721 662211
Email:goos@germany.arpa

Grande, Johannes
MCC
9430 Research Blvd
Austin
Texas 78759
USA
Phone:+1 512 3359
Email:grande@mcc.arpa

Guyard, Jacques
Centre de Recherches en Informatique de Nancy
BP 239
54506 Vandœuvre les Nancy Cedex
France
Phone:+33 83 289393
Email:mcvax!vmucnam!crin!guyard

Hallsteinsen, Svein O.
RUNIT/SINTEF
7034 Trondheim-NTH
Norge
Phone:+47 7 593010
Email:hallsteinsen%vax.runit.unit.uninett@tor.arpa

Hansen, Hans-Ludwig
GMD
Schloss Birlinghoven
5205 St. Augustin
W-Germany
Phone:+49 2241 142440

Hedin, Gørel
Lund Institute of Technology
Dept. of Computer Science
Box 118
22100 Lund
Sweden
Phone:+46 109644
Email:!enea!agaton!pandor!gorel

Heensåsen, Ola
RUNIT/SINTEF
Strindv. 2
7034 Trondheim-NTH
Norway
Phone:+47 7 593006
Email:heensaasen%vax.runit.unit.uninett@tor.arpa

Heinanen, Juha
Tampere University of Technology
Computer Systems Lab.
P.O.Box 527
33101 Tampere
Finland
Phone:+358 31 162578
Email:jh@tut.uucp or enea!tut!jh@seismo.arpa

Hjelle, Birger Olaf
Norsk Data
Boks 25, Bogerud
0621 Oslo 6
Norway
Phone:+47 2 627000

Holager, Per
ELAB-SINTEF
7034 Trondheim-NTH
Norway
Phone:+47 7 592695

Horspool, Nigel
University of Victoria
Dept. of Computer Science
P.O.Box 1700
Victoria B.C.
V8W 2Y2
Canada
Phone:+1 604 7217227
Email:uvicctr!nigelh@washington.arpa

Hoyer, Wolfgang
Siemens AG
ZTI SOF2
Otto-Hahn-Ring 6
8000 Munich 83
W-Germany
Phone:+49 89 63644234

Jaehnichen, Stefan
GMD Forschungsstelle an der Univ. Karlsruhe
Haid-und-Neu-Strasse 7
7500 Karlsruhe
W-Germany
Phone:+49 721 662215
Email:jaehn@germany.arpa

Jaray, Jacques
Centre de Recherche en Informatique de Nancy
Boite Postale 239
54506 Vandouvre Les-Nancy Cedex
France
Phone:+33 8 3289393

Johansen, Harald
Norwegian Telecom. Admin.
Res. Dep.
P.O.Box 83
2007 Kjeller
Norway
Phone:+47 2 739100
Email:paal@tor.arpa

Juul-Wedde, Kari
RUNIT/SINTEF
Strindvn. 2
7034 Trondheim-NTH
Norway
Phone:+47 7 593009
Email:juul-wedde%vax.runit.unit.uninett@tor.arpa

Kakehi, Katsuhiko
Waseda University
Centre for Informatics
Okubo 3
Tokyo 160
Japan
Phone:+81 3 2001681

Kamel, Ragui
Bell Northern Research
P.O.Box 3511
Station C
Ottawa K1Y 4H7
Canada
Phone:+1 613 7263609
Email:kamel@toronto.csnet

List of attendants at the PE Workshop, Trondheim, Norway, June 16-18 1986

Kamkar, Mariam
Linkøping University
Dept. of Computer and Information Science
581 83 Linkøping
Sweden
Phone:+46 13 282168

Kastens, Uwe
Universitat-GH Paderborn
Matematik/Informatik
Fachbereich 17, Warburgerstr. 17
D-4790 Paderborn
W-Germany
Phone:+49 5251 602653

Keller, Jean-Pierre
Thomson CSF/DSE
2 Rue de Mathurins
92223 Bagneux
France
Phone:+33 1 46571365

Kneuper, Ralf
University of Manchester
Dept. of Computer Science
Manchester M13 9PL
England
Email:ralf@uk.ac.man.cs.ux.arpa

Kristensson, Eva
Ericsson Radio Systems AB
Box 1001
431 26 Mølndal
Sweden
Phone:+46 31 671000

Krogdahl, Stein
University of Oslo
Inst. of Informatics
P.O.Box 1080, Blindern
0316 Oslo 3
Norway
Phone:+47 2 454364
Email:steink@oslo-vax.arpa

Kuo, Jeremy
GTE Laboratories, Inc.
40 Sylvan Road
Waltham, MA 02254
USA
Phone:+1 617 4662934
Email:j.kuo@gtel.csnet

Lang, Bernard
INRIA
Domaine de Voluceau - Rocquencourt
BP 105
78153 Le Chesnay Cedex
France
Phone:+33 39 635644
Email:...!mcvax!inria!lang

Lemoine, Michel
Onera-Cert-Deri
2, Ave E. Belin
31 055 Tolilouje Cedex
France
Phone:+33 61 557073
Email:vmucnam!rls-cs!lemoine

Lennartsson, Bengt
Linkøping University
Dept. of Computer and Information Science
581 83 Linkøping
Sweden
Phone:+46 13 281427

Levine, David
Intermetrics, Inc.
733 Concord Ave.
Cambridge, Mass. 02138
USA
Phone:+1 617 6611840

Lie, Anund
The Norwegian Inst. of Technology
Dept. of Computer Science
7034 Trondheim-NTH
Norway
Phone:+47 7 593443

Mac Gregor, K.J.
University of Cape Town
Dept. of Computer Science
Private Bag
Rondebosch 7700
South Africa

Martinsen, Hjalmar
Norwegian Telecom. Admin.
Res. Dep.
P.O.Box 83
2007 Kjeller
Norway
Phone:+47 2 739100
Email:paal@tor.arpa

Meiling, Erik
Dansk Datamatik Center
Lundtoftevej 1c
2800 Lyngby
Denmark
Phone:+45 2 872622

Meisingset, Arve
Norw. Telecom. Admin.
Res. Dep.
P.O.Box 83
2007 Kjeller
Norway
Phone:+47 2 739100
Email:paal@tor.arpa

Menicosy, David E.
Elektrisk Bureau A.S
EB Communications
P.O.Box 98
1360 Nesbru
Norway
Phone:+47 2 843060
Email:menicosy@oslo-vax.arpa

Miller, Terrence C.
Hewlett-Packard
1501 Page Mill Road
Mail Stop Bldg. 3U
Palo Alto, California 94304
USA
Phone:+1 415 8578476
Email:goldstein@hplabs.arpa

Morell, Larry
College of William & Mary
Dept. of Computer Science
Williamsburg
Virginia, 23185
USA
Phone:+1 804 2534748

List of attendants at the PE Workshop, Trondheim, Norway, June 16-18 1986

Morgan, Charles Robert
Massachusetts Computer Associates
26 Princess Street
Wakefield, MA 01880
USA
Phone:+1 617 2459540
Email:morgan@radc-20.arpa

Moriconi, Mark
SRI International,
BN 176
333 Ravenswood Ave.
Menlo Park, CA 94025
USA
Phone:+1 415 8595364
Email:moriconi@sri-csl.arpa

Muchnick, Steven
Sun Microsystems, Inc.
MS 5-40
2550 Garcia Avenue
Mountain View, CA 94043
USA
Phone:+1 415 9607233
Email:ucbvax!sun!muchnick

Mughal, Khalid Azim
University of Bergen
Dept. of Informatics
Allegt. 55
5000 Bergen
Norway
Phone:+47 5 212879
Email:mughul%vax.runit.unit.uninett@tor.arpa

Møller-Pedersen, Birger
Norwegian Computing Center
P.O.Box 335, Blindern
0314 Oslo 3
Norway
Phone:+47 2 466930
Email:birger@vax.ur.uninett

Neal, Lisa
Harvard University
Aiken Computation Laboratory
Cambridge, MA 02138
USA
Phone:+1 617 4959516
Email:lisa@harvard.harvard.edu.arpa

Nestor, John
Carnegie Mellon University
Software Engineering Institute
Pittsburgh, PA 15213
USA
Phone:+1 412 2687722
Email:nestor@sei.cmu.edu.arpa

Newcomer, Joseph M.
Carnegie Mellon University
Software Engineering Institute
Pittsburgh, PA 15213
USA
Phone:+1 412 2687721
Email:newcomer@sei.cmu.edu.arpa

O'Mahony, Donal
Trinity College
Dept. of Computer Science
200 Pearse S.
Dublin 2
Ireland
Phone:+353 1 772941
Email:heagate%iruccvax.bitnet@wiscvm.arpa

Olsen, Kai A.
Møre and Romsdal DH
6400 Molde
Norway
Phone:+47 72 51077

Paakki, Jukka
University of Helsinki
Dept. of Computer Science
Tukholmankatu 2
00250 Helsinki 25
Finland
Phone:+358 90 410566

Pfreundschuh, Mary
University of Iowa
Dept. of Computer Science
101 Mac Lean Hall
Iowa City, IA 52242
USA
Phone:+1 319 3536885
Email:pfreund@uiowa.csnet

Polak, Wolfgang
Kestrel Institute
1801 Page Mill Road
Palo Alto, CA 94304
USA
Phone:+1 415 4936871
Email:wp@kestrel.arpa

Poole, Peter C.
UNI of Melbourne
Dept. of Computer Science
Parkville
Australia 3052
Email:pcp@mulga.oz

Reiss, Steven
Brown University
Dept. of Computer Science
Box 1910
Providence, RI 02912
USA
Phone:+1 401 8631835
Email:spr@brown.csnet

Rekdal, Kristen
URD Information Technology A.S
Dybdahls vei 3
7000 Trondheim
Norway
Phone:+47 7 937020
Email:rekdal%vax.runit.unit.uninett@tor.arpa

Robinson, David
Systems Designers
Pembroke House
Pembroite Broadway,
Camberley, Surrey, GU15 3XD
England
Phone:+44 276 686200
Email:uucp: ukc!sysdes.co.uk!dsr

Rudmik, Andy
GTE Communication Systems
2500 W. Utopia Rd.
Phoenix, AZ 85027
USA
Phone:+1 602 9961234

Ræder, Georg
Norsk Regnesentral
P.O.Box 335, Blindern
0314 Oslo 3
Norway
Phone:+47 2 466930
Email:raeder@vax.ur.uninett